Islamic Accounting and Finance

A Handbook

Transformations in Banking, Finance and Regulation

Print ISSN: 2752-5821
Online ISSN: 2752-583X

Presently, the banking and finance sectors evolve within a globalized and highly uncertain environment. Each business and financial decision requires careful consideration of country-specific and international factors due to high levels of shock transmission and volatility spillovers. Furthermore, it would be remiss to omit the COVID-19 health crisis, which caused harmful effects to all areas of the real economy and made profound changes in the way our firms, economies, and markets used to function.

Many other already well-known aspects, including the repercussions of quantitative easing policies, disruptive technologies in finance (e.g., FinTech, Big Data, Data Analytics, Artificial Intelligence, and Blockchains), as well as innovative financing instruments for startups (e.g., ICOs and crowdfunding) are currently revolutionizing banking and finance and posing numerous challenges to regulatory bodies and policymakers. Climate change emergencies also put pressure on governments and firms worldwide to improve policy on governance, corporate social responsibility, and sustainability practices.

This book series "Transformations in Banking, Finance, and Regulation" attempts to address these issues by focusing on transformative perspectives in banking and finance. Accordingly, it provides evidence-based guidance, recommendations, and pathways to assist businesses and policy decision-makers through an interdisciplinary and in-depth understanding of ongoing changes in the behavior of economic agents.

Published

Vol. 6 *Islamic Accounting and Finance: A Handbook*
edited by Khaled Hussainey and Hidaya Al Lawati

Vol. 5 *FinTech Research and Applications: Challenges and Opportunities*
edited by Daisy Chou, Conall O'Sullivan and Vassilios G Papavassiliou

Vol. 4 *Modern Finance and Risk Management: Festschrift in Honour of Hermann Locarek-Junge*
edited by Tony Klein, Sven Loßagk, Mario Straßberger and Thomas Walther

For the complete list of volumes in this series, please visit
www.worldscientific.com/series/tbfr

Transformations in Banking, Finance and Regulation
Volume 6

Islamic Accounting and Finance
A Handbook

Editors
Khaled Hussainey
University of Portsmouth, UK
Hidaya Al Lawati
Sultan Qaboos University, Oman

World Scientific

NEW JERSEY • LONDON • SINGAPORE • BEIJING • SHANGHAI • HONG KONG • TAIPEI • CHENNAI • TOKYO

Published by

World Scientific Publishing Europe Ltd.

57 Shelton Street, Covent Garden, London WC2H 9HE

Head office: 5 Toh Tuck Link, Singapore 596224

USA office: 27 Warren Street, Suite 401-402, Hackensack, NJ 07601

Library of Congress Cataloging-in-Publication Data
Names: Hussainey, Khaled, 1972– editor. | Lawati, Hidaya Al, editor.
Title: Islamic accounting and finance : a handbook / editors Khaled Hussainey, University of Portsmouth, UK, Hidaya Al Lawati, Sultan Qaboos University, Oman.
Description: New Jersey : World Scientific, 2023. | Series: Transformations in banking, finance and regulation, 2752-5821 ; volume 6 | Includes bibliographical references and index.
Identifiers: LCCN 2022001511 | ISBN 9781800612419 (hardcover) | ISBN 9781800612426 (ebook) | ISBN 9781800612433 (ebook other)
Subjects: LCSH: Banks and banking--Islamic countries. | Finance--Islamic countries.
Classification: LCC HG3368.A6 I84 2023 | DDC 332.10917/67--dc23/eng/20220307
LC record available at https://lccn.loc.gov/2022001511

British Library Cataloguing-in-Publication Data
A catalogue record for this book is available from the British Library.

For any available supplementary material, please visit
https://www.worldscientific.com/worldscibooks/10.1142/Q0366#t=suppl

Desk Editors: Jayanthi Muthuswamy/Adam Binnie/Shi Ying Koe

Typeset by Stallion Press
Email: enquiries@stallionpress.com

It is with genuine gratitude and warm regard that Khaled Hussainey dedicates this book to his family.

Hidaya Al Lawati dedicates the book to her parents, her husband Ahmed, and her lovely children, Zahra'a, Hadeel, and Mohammed.

https://doi.org/10.1142/9781800612426_fmatter

Foreword

It is my privilege and honor to write the foreword for this book on Islamic Finance and Accounting. I found that this book includes comprehensive analysis, intellectual discussions, and empirical solutions and to be among the pioneer guides and references for academia, professionals, decision-makers, students, and policymakers alike.

The Islamic banking and finance sector has witnessed significant growth over the past couple of years, especially in the MENA region. According to the Islamic Finance Development Report (2020), the Islamic banking and finance industry was worth about USD 2.88 trillion at the end of December 2019, representing an annual growth rate of about 14%. This is driven by growing consumer demand for Sharia-compliant products and services. Moreover, Islamic finance seeks to contribute toward global well-being through its fundamental socially conscious philosophy that existed even before the Environmental, Social and Governance (ESG) term was ever invented. Issuance of the so-called "green sukuk" has risen sharply in the past decade — and the Islamic Development Bank issued an innovative USD 1.5 billion sustainability sukuk in 2020 to tackle the aftermath of the COVID-19 pandemic. Likewise, green and socially responsible investment sukuk flourished in many countries, such as Saudi Arabia, the UAE, and those in Southeast Asia. This is crucial as the social role of Islamic finance could unravel new growth prospects as core markets implement the UN Sustainable Development Goals. Interestingly, this book covers several fascinating topics, making it a must-read book on the subject of Islamic finance and accounting.

Given the importance of Islamic banking and finance, it is extremely useful to have a dedicated handbook on Islamic accounting and finance. This handbook edited by Professor Khaled Hussainey and Dr. Hidaya Al Lawati is an outstanding source on the topic. This book includes 26 chapters across four parts that present theoretical and empirical research on Islamic accounting and finance. The Islamic accounting parts cover interesting topics such as application of Islamic accounting in Islamic finance transaction, the ontological and epistemological construct of Islamic accounting, literature reviews of prior research on Islamic accounting and on zakat, CSR, forensic accounting, *Accounting and Auditing Organization for Islamic Financial Institutions* (AAOFIF), sukuk disclosure, risk disclosure, sustainability reporting, CSR reporting, Islamic ethics and governance, value-based intermediation (VBI), and cryptocurrency investment. The Islamic finance parts cover concepts, forms of Islamic finance, investments and portfolio management, blockchain and crowdfunding, capital adequacy, capital structure, bank performance and COVID-19, liquidity, blended Islamic finance for poverty reduction, liquidity risk, Basel Accords and COVID-19, and the interest of Indonesian Muslim millennials in performing waqf.

I feel the content coverage, selected issues, and subtopics reflect well the intensity of the authors' knowledge and exposure as well as their insights. As everyone has been searching for a master key for this most timely knowledge, I am confident this book will prove to be useful and fitting.

I wish to congratulate the editors and all the contributors for their scholarly work and wish the readers a stimulating read.

Ahmed Elamer
Brunel Business School
Brunel University London
London, UK
October 31, 2021

https://doi.org/10.1142/9781800612426_fmatter

Preface

Part I: Islamic Accounting: Theoretical Perspectives

Chapter 1 (Aleraig and Asutay)

Islamic banks and financial institutions have demonstrated unprecedented success since their emergence in commercial form in the 1970s. The expansion of the asset base of the industry and its diffusion into the main financial centers in the world is a clear indication of its success. While Islamic finance is constituted through Islamic normativeness as expressed through Sharia compliance processes coupled with the standards developed by the Accounting and Auditing Organization for Islamic Financial Institutions and the Islamic Financial Services Board within the dual banking system, the accounting system follows the conventional system of accounting, which is based on the fictitious claim that accounting is value free. However, this chapter is developed through the assumptions that neither economics and finance nor accounting and management are value free as value systems and ontologies determine their nature and operations. In expanding this assumption, this chapter aims to identify the Islamic accounting implication for Islamic finance with the hope that Islamic banks and financial institutions, in particular, and Muslim societies, in general, can move onto an authentic accounting system and philosophy shaped by Islamic ontology and epistemology. This chapter hence aims to develop and identify the way Islamic accounting can apply to Islamic finance transactions and contracts as well as institutions such as *zakat*. It also presents some critical reflections on the practice of Islamic accounting and accounting standards.

Chapter 2 (Aleraig and Asutay)

The emergence of the Islamic economics movement in the post-colonial period is aimed at developing a system of Islamic economy with the normative worldview of Islam and *Sharia* rules. This is rationalized on the grounds that economics, finance, management, and accounting are not value free as assumed by conventional thinking, which is imposed on the rest of the world as the truth, by the West. In this authentic search, Islamic finance proved to be a successful proposition, and therefore, the trajectory of development has been unprecedented, which is constituted through the *Sharia* compliance process. However, in order to develop a system understanding, the governance, management, and accounting of the Islamic financing institutions should reflect the same worldview and the value system. As the literature indicates, research, practice, and institutional formation have been scarce in these areas. This is due to the subaltern assumption that these areas are value free. Accepting such an operating assumption has resulted in asymmetry in the knowledge base and operation of Islamic banks and financial institutions. While their financing operations are constituted in a *Sharia*-compliant manner, their management and accounting are left to the conventional system. However, Islam, through its value system and worldview (*tawhid*), has implications for accounting too. This chapter, therefore, aims to identify the ontological and epistemological construct of Islamic accounting through its value system and worldview to overcome the observed asymmetry through social constructivism. In doing so, historical contributions of Muslim scholars and practice within the Islamic realm are used to bring historical evidence for the proposition developed in this study. Thus, this study argues that Islamic accounting is a subdiscipline of the system of Islamic economics or Islamic moral economy and essentializes it through Islamic normativeness, which urges the use of Islamic accounting, beyond the standards of Accounting and Auditing Organization for Islamic Financial Institutions, to establish consistency within the Islamic finance sector.

Chapter 3 (Alaqrabawi et al.)

With the increased number of Islamic institutions, the necessity for a standardized Islamic accounting framework has emerged.

The origin of Islamic accounting can be traced back further than conventional accounting. Many studies show that Islamic accounting was the primary source of the basic accounting fundamentals. Besides, the critical role of Islamic accounting is to provide financial reports which adopt the Islamic objectives and laws. The Islamic beliefs hold ethics and morals that drive and influence accounting, auditing, and reporting procedures of the Islamic financial institutions. Accordingly, many studies have emphasized the morality and characteristics of Islamic accounting and economics disciplines required in different institutions and banks. This chapter has adopted the systematic literature review technique to explore the overall available articles and studies on Islamic accounting and the growth of these studies over the years. The researchers have addressed 30 papers retrieved from a variety of online databases according to a set of inclusive and exclusive criteria. The systematic literature review methodology results synthesize different aspects of the topic, methods, and theories used in Islamic accounting studies. This chapter indicates broad concepts and objectives of Islamic accounting retrieved from various online databases with a set of recommendations for further research to fill the gap in this field.

Chapter 4 (Neifar and Aissa)

Due to the growing role of zakat in reducing poverty, a trend of research has been calling attention to the necessity of this Islamic duty on the individual and social levels. A common debate in Islamic taxation relates to the question of difference between zakat and taxation and about what drives zakat compliance. Few are the studies that have examined zakat, and most have generally tried to understand the individual tax compliance behavior. Thus, the area of corporate zakat is a challenging area and needs to be analyzed more. This chapter presents the basic settings that review the definition of zakat and its different perspectives and provides a comparison between zakat and conventional taxes. It also describes the legal form of zakat in the different MENA countries. Moreover, this chapter reviews major papers that have examined zakat. This study can help the non-specialist reader understand the Islamic taxation (zakat) and the specificity of each of the MENA countries regarding zakat.

Chapter 5 (Aryani and Zuchroh)

The implementation of corporate social responsibility (CSR) will be examined in various perspectives along with the distinction of some theories. CSR is a kind of action for communicating with stakeholders to show that companies have already paid attention to the environment, nature, and society. The theories relating to CSR implementation can be discussed from different perspectives. Agency theory focuses on the relationship between agent and principal and may give rise to a conflict of interest. Legitimacy theory places the public as its responsibility. Disclosing information about social and environmental performance is a path for companies to maintain or regain their legitimacy from society's point of view. Meanwhile, entity theory focuses only on satisfying the shareholders, hence the company activities are only directed to meet the welfare of the owners. Enterprise theory recognizes the responsibility toward the owners and broader stakeholder groups. However, Sharia enterprise theory pays attention in two directions consisting of vertical accountability to God and horizontal accountability to direct and indirect stakeholders, that is, people, environment, and society.

Chapter 6 (Alshurafat et al.)

Forensic accounting is a modern occupation that covers many services, including fraud investigation, IT forensics, litigation support, and business valuation. Few, if any, have come across forensic accounting based on an Islamic perspective. The religion of Islam ascribes to a wide spectrum of the highest morals and virtues. Our research involved a review of the previous research on forensic accounting and we benchmarked it to the Islamic Sharia and law within the Jordanian context. The findings show that Islamic perspectives would lend robust foundations to forensic accounting in its endeavors to detect and prevent fraud and assist the trier of fact. This chapter contributes to the previous literature on forensic accounting by providing an optimal set of Islamic concepts that might be of benefit to forensic accounting practitioners, academics, and regulators.

Part II: Islamic Accounting: Empirical Perspectives

Chapter 7 (El-Halaby et al.)

The Accounting and Auditing Organization for Islamic Financial Institutions (AAOIFI) began to issue standards long ago and by 2021 will mark its 31st anniversary. The present literature on AAOIFI, which has had its share of supporters and critics, may be categorized into the following three parts: (1) literature evaluating compliance levels, (2) literature examine the AAOIFI determinants, and (3) literature assessing the economic consequences of AAOIFI. Thus far, the third strand in the first research phase has no practical study evaluating the impact of AAOIFI adoption at a national level. Therefore, this report adds a study by measuring the macroeconomic effect of AAOIFI on economic size and growth rate based on foreign direct investment (FDI), economic development (ED), corruption, and stock market development (SMD). Data for 150 Islamic banks (IBs) in 22 countries for 10 years (2010–2019) are collected, using an ordinary least squares (OLS) approach. Our results indicate that IBs across countries that adopt AAOIFI are further getting an advantage by growing in FDI and GDP than non-adopters. Our results further support the role of AAOIFI adoption by countries rather than adoption by banks on reducing the level of corruption. After applying several robustness checks, our results remain the same, with slight variations. Our results provide value for central banks, regulators, setters of an accounting standard such as AAOIFI and IASB, investors, and all categories of Islamic Financial Institution (IFI), whether adopters or not, by identifying the contributions of AAOIFI adoption. The contemporary international literature is deficient in practical confirmation on the consequence of AAOIFI adoption on the macro level on FDI and corruption. To the authors' knowledge, we are one of the original papers that provide confirmation about the significance and influences of AAOIFI adoption from the countrywide angle.

Chapter 8 (Tawfik and Elmaasrawy)

The study aims to propose a framework for disclosing sukuk risks, shows the types of risks to which sukuks are exposed in various studies, and shows how to disclose sukuk risks in international standards such as IFRS, IFSB, and AAOIFI. The chapter deals with the disclosure of the risks of sukuk in the accounting standards divided among the following. First is IFRS, which focuses on the various risks to which conventional Islamic financial instruments are exposed in general, such as market risk, credit risk, liquidity risk, and other risks. Second is AAOIFI Standards that focus on the risks of Islamic financing formulas in general on the basis of which sukuk are issued. Third is IFSB Standards, which focus on the risks of non-compliance with Islamic law and legal risks to which sukuk are exposed. In addition, the chapter deals with a case study of Qatar Islamic Bank and an attempt to obtain field evidence about the level of the bank's disclosure of sukuk risks through the annual reports of the bank. The researchers found that the disclosure of sukuk risks on Qatar Islamic Bank was very limited, and the focus in the disclosure of sukuk risks was on quantitative disclosure, while the descriptive disclosure of sukuk risks was very limited. The researchers proposed a framework for disclosing the risks of sukuk, which are divided into quantitative risks and descriptive risks.

Chapter 9 (Radwan and Ali)

This study explores the status of the online risk disclosure practices on the listed Islamic banks in the Egyptian exchange market. Manual content analysis was employed as a research approach to examine the practices of the online risk disclosure for the three listed Islamic banks in Egypt, and based on a prior study, the authors developed a risk index composed of 10 main categories and a total of 61 sub-items as a research tool. The empirical analysis presents that all listed Islamic banks in the Egyptian exchange market have websites and all these banks report risk information in their published online reports (full annual report and full financial report). Furthermore, the results provide confirmatory evidence that there is a high adherence by all listed Islamic banks in Egypt to the mandatory risk disclosure requirements on their websites, while there is a low level of voluntary risk disclosure on the websites of these banks as well; in addition, the study pointed out that Al Baraka Bank has the highest average (67.2%) online risk disclosure level among all Islamic banks, followed by Faisal Islamic Bank with an average of 65.5%, and finally, Abu Dhabi Islamic Bank with an average of 60.6%. What's more, the yielded data show that the total average level of online risk disclosure of the Islamic listed banks in Egypt is 64.5%. Finally, the results of this study outline that there are no significant differences between the levels of online risk disclosure at the level of the common categories for all Islamic listed banks in Egypt. The limitations of this study are as follows: the way the content analysis was conducted; in its reliance on the websites and the published online reports for examining risk disclosure information; due to its focus on the financial and non-financial risks; due to its focus on Islamic listed banks in Egypt; and due to its focus on the context of the Egyptian environment.

Chapter 10 (Selim)

Through a case study of three Egyptian Islamic banks, this study examines the concept of corporate social responsibility from an Islamic perspective, the role of Egyptian Islamic banks in social and environmental responsibility, and the extent to which they participate in sustainable development activities. The chapter provides a brief overview of the concept and dimensions of corporate social responsibility; the Islamic perspective of social responsibility and its fields and dimensions toward stakeholders; and the definition of Islamic banks, their nature, and how they support social activities and sustainability, and the differences between them and traditional banks. According to the report, Islamic banks in Egypt play an effective and pioneering role in sustainable development and social and environmental responsibility, as evidenced by the programs that these banks have established to participate in a variety of social projects and activities such as health care, education, charity institution assistance, social housing, persons with special needs, qard hasan, the environment, and sustainability.

Chapter 11 (Kolsi and Al-Hiyari)

Islamic banks are presumed to behave ethically toward numerous stakeholders including investors, customers, governmental authorities, and the public in general within the Islamic jurisprudence (Sharia) prescriptions. One of the most important pillars of Sharia prescriptions is the protection of all parties' interests rather than the conventional notion of financial performance maximization of shareholders. This principle is the core value of the stakeholder's theory and the derived corporate social responsibility (CSR) notion. In this chapter, we compare CSR practices as proxied by the reported ESG performance score for a sample of both Islamic and conventional banks in the GCC region for the period 2009–2019. Our results show that conventional banks and Islamic banks display different outcomes in ESG performance score, especially in the reporting of individual pillars (environmental, social, and governance). In that, Islamic banks perform *on average* better than conventional banks in most of the ESG performance pillars. Most importantly, our findings show that Islamic banks' and conventional banks' sustainability practices differ when the individual pillars are disaggregated into their main components: emission score, environmental innovation, and resources use for the environmental pillar; human rights, workforce, community, and product responsibility scores for the social pillar; management, CSR strategy, and shareholders scores for the governance pillar. Our findings can be helpful for Islamic banks' managers looking for more compliance with sustainability standards, and for markets and standardization authorities when issuing new sustainability guidelines.

Chapter 12 (Harahap)

The purpose of this study is to explore the implementation of Islamic ethics and identify *corporate governance.* This study is a qualitative case study using a phenomenological approach and paradigm interpretive in which the paradigm focuses on social understanding. The data collection method in this study used secondary data, namely, data obtained from the documentation and annual report of PT. Pertamina (Persero). The data analysis technique uses explorative qualitative methods, namely, research that aims to map an object in depth. This study uses a content analysis approach. The results of this research consist of the following: (1) PT. Pertamina (Persero) has implemented Islamic ethics in running its business to improve the company performance; (2) Islamic ethics have been in accordance with the principles of *corporate governance*, which include transparency, accountability, responsibility, independent, and fairness at PT. Pertamina (Persero); (3) honesty, the value of truth (fairness), justice, transparency, accountability, and integrity have been applied at PT. Pertamina (Persero).

Chapter 13 (Hamad et al.)

Value-based intermediation (VBI) has been recently announced by the Central Bank of Malaysia (Bank Negara) as a vital driver in expanding the responsibilities and influence of Islamic finance in the future. It aims to reinforce the foundations of Islamic finance in social justice and advocate a value-based economy via increased integrity, inclusivity, and sustainable growth. This chapter analyses the current practices of VBI information for Islamic banks operating in Malaysia. Also, it proposes a guideline to communicate VBI information to stakeholders through the bank's business model as the core of integrating reporting (IR). Using a sample of all the 16 Islamic banks operating in Malaysia, content analysis was employed to collect data over a four-year period from 2017 to 2020. The results revealed that the adoption of IR and VBI has seen considerable interest among the research sample. Approximately 82% of all banks in our selection have embedded the VBI information in the annual reports of 2020. More than half (7 out of 13) of VBI adopter banks have applied IR to draw and communicate the VBI information to stakeholders. Additionally, the IR framework and business models represent the best strategic tools banks could utilize to provide the VBI progress in a holistic, concise, and useful manner compared to traditional reporting practices. This chapter contributes to the Islamic finance literature by offering vital perceptions to banks' management, analysts, shareholders, and policymakers on the importance of the VBI information disclosures and how to deliver it using the business models.

Chapter 14 (Alfafa and Mukhlisin)

The purpose of this chapter is to evaluate how a company should report cryptocurrency investment on their financial statements. In dealing with it, the research problems address the status of positive law and Islamic law in cryptocurrency, and how the current economy responds to cryptocurrency. A qualitative descriptive approach and literature review with content analysis method using NVivo 12 plus software are used. The data for this study were obtained from interviews and a review of documents. The finding shows that investments in cryptocurrency held by the companies can be treated as investments in equity with minor adjustments. The content analysis conducted shows that stakeholders are neutral toward this issue. This chapter proposes a standard on how cryptocurrency should be treated in financial reports under Indonesian Sharia-based Statement of Financial Reporting Standards/PSAK Syariah since the transaction of cryptocurrency investment has not been accommodated in financial reporting standard in Indonesia.

Part III: Islamic Finance: Theoretical Perspectives

Chapter 15 (Khalfi and Saâdaoui)

Islamic finance or Qur'anic finance is ethical finance based on Sharia, prohibition of riba, prohibition of gharar and maysir, and sharing of losses and profits (3P) because it promotes investment in licit sectors, and it prohibits investment in illicit sectors. These principles are the main pillars of Islamic banking governance. In this context and given the subject of Quranic finance in this chapter, we sought to highlight the theoretical foundations relating to the notion of efficiency in general and more particularly of its specificity on Islamic finance since the latter has occupied more and more a rather important place in scientific research. We then presented the different forms of banking efficiency. Finally, we presented Islamic banking governance, risk management within Islamic banks, and governance of these banks.

Chapter 16 (Elmoghany)

Investment in Islamic portfolios and funds must be subject to the provisions of Islamic Sharia standards in all their activities. The main objective of the Islamic investors and Islamic portfolio managers is not only achieving the conventional investment goal but rather achieving this goal in accordance with Sharia standards. In the absence of Islamic financial markets with Islamic financial instruments, Islamic investors and portfolio managers need to know the

Islamic criteria for forming and managing different types of Islamic portfolios and funds. This study provides them useful insights and a practical framework for the Sharia standards and Islamic contracts' terms, which are agreed upon by most scholars and Sharia boards, to invest in various types of financial instruments.

Chapter 17 (Bayomi)

In this study, we discussed several aspects, including the definition of the general concept of traditional crowdfunding, which aims to finance emerging small projects and innovative ideas, as well as financing medium-sized projects that cannot provide sufficient guarantees for banks to obtain the necessary liquidity for their projects. Companies use crowdfunding to obtain this required liquidity for new projects through electronic platforms. In the same context, some of the challenges facing these companies when obtaining crowdfunding from these electronic platforms were discussed, with the presentation of the regulatory framework for crowdfunding in light of Islamic funding standards, which differ from traditional funding in that Islamic funding is essentially non-profit as much as it targets charitable and social work, as well as regulating the collection of funds and the distribution of profits to the principles of Islamic finance. On the other hand, the general concept of blockchain, its general characteristics, and working mechanisms were discussed. Then the reasons that may lead to the shift from traditional models in Islamic crowdfunding to the use of blockchain in enhancing Islamic crowdfunding mechanisms were discussed through exposure to the Ventera project model of crowdfunding using blockchain technology, as well as exposure to other models of Islamic crowdfunding, where the study suggests that it can improve their performance through the use of blockchain technology as it may bring them a number of benefits and help them overcome a number of challenges. This chapter aims to explore the impact of the application of blockchain technology in Islamic crowdfunding operations and also bridge the gap between the academic side and the applied professional side in the field of using modern technologies, such as blockchain as a safer, faster, and lower-cost alternative in Islamic finance projects, as there are only few studies that have dealt with this area despite its importance. This chapter discusses the benefits of blockchain in Islamic crowdfunding with an illustration of some projects as an applied model, after identifying the challenges facing traditional Islamic crowdfunding and the advantages of developing it using blockchain applications; this study ends by presenting models of Islamic crowdfunding projects that can be developed using blockchain technology.

Part IV: Islamic Finance: Empirical Perspectives

Chapter 18 (Ibrahim et al.)

This study aims to compare capital adequacy and financial stability in Islamic and conventional Saudi banks and investigate the impact of capital adequacy on the financial stability of a bank. Our study uses the annual data of five conventional banks and four Islamic banks listed on the Saudi Stock Exchange for the period 2016–2020. The Z-score has been computed and used as the measure of the stability of listed Saudi Islamic and conventional banks for the period 2016–2020. This study uses ordinary least square regression to investigate the impact of capital adequacy on the financial stability of banks. The researchers adopt the development of research hypotheses in light of the theory of stakeholders, and the foundations of Islamic law. The findings indicated that, first there are significant differences in the capital adequacy ratio between conventional and Islamic banks. This difference is due to the increase in the mean capital adequacy ratio of Islamic banks over conventional banks. Second, our result found significant differences in financial stability between conventional and Islamic banks. This difference is due to the increase in the mean of the Z-score for Islamic banks over conventional banks. Third, our result refers to significant negative impacts of capital adequacy ratio on financial stability. Our study applied to listed Saudi banks from 2016 to 2020. The empirical results of our study are very useful for supervisors, bank management, investors, bank customers, and policymakers. The results contribute to knowing the unexpected negative effects of increased capital adequacy and its negative impact on the bank's profits and the threat to financial stability, in addition to knowing the main indicators of capital adequacy and financial stability for Islamic and conventional banks in a way that helps bank supervisors, policymakers, and investors in rationalizing. Their decisions are specific to both Islamic and conventional banks, in addition to identifying the factors that help to enhance the financial stability process. This study is among a few studies that provide empirical evidence for the claim that the increase in capital adequacy rates is always one of the positive indicators to achieve financial stability, in addition to the great role of Islamic banks in achieving this. The study found a rejection of the validity of this claim and reached unexpected results.

Chapter 19 (Toumi)

The research aims to empirically investigate the banks' capital structure determinants by considering 386 listed and unlisted banks categorized into 74 Islamic banks, 256 conventional banks, and 56 hybrid banks from 20 countries for 2008–2016 based on corporate and regulatory approaches. The main findings are interesting. From a corporate approach, we find differences between IBs, CBs, and HBs regarding the determinants of their capital structure which offer an empirical confirmation of the reduced information asymmetry in an Islamic finance context. From a regulatory approach, the findings show similarities regarding the negative impact of deposit insurance schemes on the regulatory capital for all types of banks. When focusing on IBs, we evidence that banks subject to Sharia-compliant deposit insurance schemes hold lower capital than those subject to conventional deposit insurance schemes.

Chapter 20 (Sghaier and Guizani)

This study aimed to analyze the profitability in Islamic banks and conventional ones in the Middle East and North Africa (MENA) region. After restatement, our sample consisted of 184 banks (132 conventional banks and 52 Islamic banks) in 11 countries in the MENA region. For our analysis period of 11 years (from 2009 to 2019), we collected 2024 observations. We noticed that the profitability of Islamic banks was significantly different from that of conventional ones. After examining bank risk, asset quality, environmental influences such as the level of interest rate, and country effect, we found that the cost and profit efficiencies of Islamic banks are similar to those of conventional banks. Our results suggest that the country-specific variables have a significant impact on the cost and profit efficiencies of banks operating in the MENA region, and we have confirmed that Islamic banks are more profitable than conventional ones, whereas the total loan to total assets for Islamic banks is higher than that of conventional banks. Based on the regression test, return on asset (ROA) is a factor of profitability for conventional banks and Islamic banks. ROA has an important relationship with the independent variable, total equity to total asset. The deterioration of the bank's profitability poses a threat not only to the interests of consumers and internal staff but also affects investors who may equally suffer from significant financial losses. It is important to establish an effective system that assists investors in their investment choices. In prior literature, traditional models were developed but achieved short-term performances. This chapter applies a data analysis method to distinguish between conventional and Islamic banks in the MENA region. This method can successfully identify nonlinearity and correlations between the financial indicators used. The results demonstrate the superior performance of the proposed method.

Chapter 21 (El Shaarani)

The first objective of this research is to explain and analyze the financial indicators of the Islamic banking sector in the Middle East and North Africa (MENA) countries before and over the COVID-19 pandemic period, and the second objective is to explore the key determinant that might affect Islamic banks' performance before and during the COVID-19 pandemic period. Orbis Bank Focus database and annual financial reports are used to collect financial information of Islamic banks in MENA countries over two years: 2019 and 2020. Descriptive statistics, t-test, and multiple regression are employed to analyze the financial structure and performance of Islamic banks before and during the COVID-19 pandemic period. The results of this study reveal that there is a sharp drop in financial indicators in Islamic banks during the pandemic period with liquidity risk, bank size, managerial efficiency ratio, and oil price shocks being the determinants of Islamic banks' profitability before the appearance of COVID-19. Credit risk, bank size, liquidity risk, managerial efficiency, inflation, and oil price shocks are the determinants of Islamic banks' profitability during the pandemic period. Finally, there is no significant impact of GDP and capital structure on Islamic banks' profitability before and during the COVID-19 pandemic period.

Chapter 22 (Tahir et al.)

Today, not only financial but also non-financial attributes are considered vital for the financial health of banks. To validate this argument, the current study investigates factors affecting the liquidity position of banks and examines its impact along with the moderation of the Sharia board on the liquidity of Islamic banks in Pakistan. Collecting panel data, this study applied a fixed-effect model on Pakistani Islamic banks for the post-financial crises period 2009–2020. Empirical findings revealed that total assets and profitability are positively and significantly linked to the liquidity position of Islamic banks. However, the deposits and capital adequacy ratios were found to have a negative influence on the Islamic banks' liquidity. Among the macroeconomic factors, none has established significant nexus with the liquidity of Islamic banks in Pakistan. Interestingly, the insignificant relationship between funding cost and liquidity of Islamic banks became significant with the moderating factor of Sharia board size. The study provides important insights for the shareholders, customers, investors, and policy-makers of Islamic banks. The empirical findings offer practical guidance for the regulators of Islamic banks to strengthen their Sharia boards to manage the liquidity position by regulating the funding costs. The Islamic banks' liquidity position can also be managed by generating high profits, maintaining capital adequacy ratio, and increasing deposits. To the best of the authors' knowledge, this is the first empirical study that investigates the moderating role of Sharia governance in managing the liquidity of Islamic banks in Pakistan. This research offers a new and most important direction for future studies to investigate the role of non-financial attributes along with the financial indicators in evaluating the financial soundness of Islamic banks.

Chapter 23 (Munir et al.)

The objective of this research is to answer the main question of how to integrate Islamic redistribution instruments with other developmental aids in addressing the persistent poverty issues in Pakistan. Data were collected from both government and private organizations. Thematic analysis was done on the data. The results indicate that in Pakistan, zakat is the most important driving tool, whereas Islamic microfinance, mainly interest-free loans, is making a place in the market. However, waqf still needs to make a place in private ownership. Moreover, no major role is being played by waqf properties for poverty elimination. Being a new and emerging topic in Islamic finance, no proper definition is available for blended Islamic finance. However, it can be said to be the utilization of Islamic social finance funds, such as waqf, sadaqah, qard hasan, and zakat, and government development aids in mobilizing resources from the private sector, including institutional impactful investors, in financing sustainable development initiatives in developing countries. Moreover, BIF can be used to attain the ultimate maqasid Sharia, which is the well-being of the people, with a focus on the poor and needy.

Chapter 24 (Hunjra et al.)

We analyze the systematic (macroeconomic) and unsystematic (bank specific) determinants of liquidity risk in Islamic banks. We extract the data from DataStream of Islamic banks in Pakistan, Qatar, Malaysia, UAE, Bangladesh, Bahrain, and Saudi Arabia from 2011 to 2020. We collect macroeconomic variable data from the World Development Indicator (WDI). We apply generalized method of moment (GMM) to analyze data. We find that non-performing loans, capital adequacy ratio, leverage ratio, bank size, return on equity, gross domestic product, and inflation have a significant impact on liquidity risk. We recommend that Islamic banks should be strong enough to face the liquidity risk coming from systematic and unsystematic ways.

Chapter 25 (Salami et al.)

The purpose of this chapter is to evaluate the relationship between the capital adequacy ratio (CAR) and explanatory variables as well as the possibility that any of the three Basel Capital Accords adopted in Islamic banks is appropriate to combat the effect of the COVID-19 pandemic. This study employed reverse regression estimation techniques, using random effect estimator and interaction modeling. Data were obtained from the IFSB database. The findings of this study indicate that bank asset quality and ROE exhibit a conditional negative relationship with CAR, while ROA and bank liquidity exhibit a conditional positive relationship. Therefore, the relationship between CAR and bank asset quality, bank profitability, and bank liquidity fulfilled the conditional hypothesis, that is, the relationship varies according to the Basel Capital Accords approach adopted by the Islamic banks. Among the three Basel Capital Accords, the capital requirement by Basel III could not be met, thereby making it inappropriate for adoption during the period of the COVID-19 pandemic, while the capital requirement of Basel I exposes Islamic banks to serious challenges which support a non-risk sensitivity framework in developing Basel I. This finding is novel, as previous studies on Basel Capital Accord neither simultaneously examined all the three Basel to make inferences nor explored the possibility of a conditional relationship in their CAR studies. This is the first empirical study that establishes the existence of a conditional hypothesis relationship between CAR and the explanatory variables using reverse regression.

Chapter 26 (Akbar and Al Ihsan)

This chapter aims to identify factors that may influence the interest of Indonesian Muslim millennials in performing waqf. Five variables, namely, waqf literacy, religiosity, trust in waqf institutions, income, and social influence, were tested using the SEM-PLS method. Data are obtained through online questionnaires with the number of sample being 321 Muslim millennials from the five major islands in Indonesia. The finding shows that four variables, literacy, religiosity, trust in waqf institutions, and social influence, have a significant impact on their interest in waqf donation. As a result, waqf institutions must nurture trust of the prospective wakif through massive socialization such as social media which is widely accessed by millennials. This may attract their attention, leave a good impression, and create a supporting environment. In addition, waqf institutions need to instill trust by being more open, honest, and transparent about the programs they created through campaigns by bringing social and religious issues packed with excellent and exciting delivery that can help increase the interest of Muslim millennials in performing waqf. Furthermore, the quality of nazhir should be improved, collaboration should be promoted, and the utilization of digital technology is highly recommended.

https://doi.org/10.1142/9781800612426_fmatter

About the Editors

Khaled Hussainey is a Professor and Research Lead of Accounting and Financial Management at the Faculty of Business and Law, University of Portsmouth, UK. He has over two and a half decades of teaching and research experience at both undergraduate and postgraduate levels. He has a growing research reputation in the field of accounting and finance. He has featured in the "World Ranking of Top 2% Researchers" in the 2021 database (Published: October 19, 2021) created by experts at Stanford University, USA. He has published about 150 articles in peer-reviewed journals and has written a number of book chapters and edited a textbook on corporate governance in emerging economies. He also won the best paper award from the *British Accounting Review* in 2007 and the *Journal of Risk Finance* in 2012. He has supervised more than 60 PhD scholars and has examined more than 120 PhD theses. He has received research grants from the Economic and Social Research Council (ESRC), the British Academy, Qatar National Research Foundation (QNRF), Financial Reporting Council (FRC), Plymouth University, the University of Portsmouth, and Abu Dhabi University. His research papers are published in top-ranked journals such as *Accounting and Business Research*, *British Accounting Review*, *Journal of Accounting and Public Policy*, *International Review of Financial Analysis*, *Journal of International*

Accounting, Auditing and Taxation, *Review of Quantitative Finance and Accounting*, and *International Journal of Finance and Economics*. He is Co-Editor of the *Journal of Financial Reporting and Accounting*, and *Journal of Contemporary Issues in Accounting*. He is Associate Editor of the *Journal of Applied Accounting Research*, *International Journal of Accounting, Auditing and Performance Evaluation*, and *International Journal of Emerging Markets*, and a Guest Editor for *Journal of Risk and Financial Management and Green Finance*.

Hidaya Al Lawati is an Assistant Professor and the Assistant Dean for Undergraduate Studies at the College of Economics and Political Science, Sultan Qaboos University, Oman. She started her university education in 2007. In 2010, she completed her master's degree in Accounting at the University of New South Wales, Australia. She received her PhD degree in January 2021 from the University of Portsmouth, UK, under the supervision of Professor Khaled Hussainey. The PhD thesis was titled, *Audit Committee Characteristics, Financial Reporting Quality and Corporate Performance: The Case of Oman*. She has published a number of articles in various fields, such as corporate governance, financial and narrative reporting, and tax avoidance.

https://doi.org/10.1142/9781800612426_fmatter

About the Contributors

Amal Aissa is a Researcher at the Faculty of Economics and Management of Sfax Tunisia. She obtained her master's degree in Islamic finance from the Faculty of Economics and Management of Sfax Tunisia in March 2021. Her research interests include zakat, corporate social responsibility, and corporate governance. Email: amalaissa@yahoo.fr.

Nashr Akbar is a Lecturer and head of the Islamic economics department at Tazkia Islamic University College, Indonesia. He holds a master's degree in economics from International Islamic University Malaysia. He has authored two books. One of the books, *Tafsir Ayat Ekonomi Kontemporer*, was awarded the best book in the Islamic Book Fair, Indonesia, 2018. Several of his articles in the field of Islamic economics and finance have been presented in international conferences and published in reputable journals. He has also been Managing Editor of *Tazkia Islamic Finance and Business Review* since 2016. Email: n.akbar@tazkia.ac.id.

Alamir Nasser Salim Al-Alawi is presently the Assistant Dean for Academic Affairs at the University of Technology and Applied Sciences (UTAS), Salalah, Sultanate of Oman. After acquiring a BSc from Sultan Qaboos University and MBA from Hull University, Dr. Alamir earned his PhD from the Plymouth University, UK, in 2017. Starting his career at the Salalah College of Applied Science under the Ministry of Higher Education, Sultanate of Oman, in 2000, Dr. Alamir became the Director of the Administration & Finance Department in 2006. As a member of the main committee of Quality Assurance, he headed the Governance and Management Committee. He has also served two terms as the Dean in Delegations at the College of Applied Sciences before taking up his present position. Actively involved in scientific research, Dr. Alamir has acquired USD 28,000 and USD 31,000 as research grants in two consecutive years from the TRC, Sultanate of Oman. Besides publishing articles in Scopus-indexed academic journals, he has attended and presented papers in several international conferences and workshops. A passionate entrepreneur, Dr. Alamir, along with two co-founders from France and Tunisia, is presently involved in the development of two mobile applications for social media as a business venture. Email: alamir.sal@cas.edu.om.

Merwiey Alaqrabawi is a master's student in Accounting and Finance at the Hashemite University, Jordan. She got her bachelor's degree with a double major in Business and Accounting at Arab Open University, Kingdom of Saudi Arabia, with an excellent GPA of 3.78/4. She currently works as a Teaching Assistant at the Hashemite University. She is particularly interested in accounting and accounting education, digital accounting transformation, intelligent accounting systems acceptance and adoption, Islamic accounting & audit standards, and corporate social responsibility. She has published several articles in peer-reviewed journals and international conferences. Merwiey Alaqrabawi is keenly seeking an excellent opportunity to complete her PhD in Accounting. Email: 2070005@std.hu.edu.jo.

Mahmoud Ali Aleraig completed his PhD in Islamic finance at the Durham Centre for Islamic Economics and Finance, Durham University Business School, UK. His research is focused on construction of Islamic accounting through Islamic ontology and epistemology along with classical knowledge and practice. He has also researched the differences between Islamic accounting and conventional accounting systems and standards by conducting empirical studies in Islamic accounting and finance. While he currently practices accounting professionally, he is also attached to the Durham Centre for Islamic Economics and Finance as a Visiting Academic Researcher to develop his research portfolio. Email: aleraig@yahoo.co.uk.

Qisthi Wajanatin Alfafa earned her undergraduate degree from Tazkia Islamic University College, Indonesia, majoring in Islamic Accounting. She is currently continuing her postgraduate studies in

Islamic Accounting at the same university and works part time at a co-op and learning hub that focuses to provide best practices on farming with a co-operative system. Besides cryptocurrency study, Qisthi is passionate about integrating Islamic values in accounting, finance, and agriculture. Email: qisthi.alfafa@gmail.com.

Ahmad Al-Hiyari has been an Assistant Professor of Accounting at Liwa College of Technology (LCT) since 2019. He received his PhD in accounting from the College of Business (COB) at the University Utara Malaysia in 2016. He graduated in 2010 with a master's degree in accounting from the University of Jordan. His teaching interests include financial accounting, managerial accounting, auditing, and financial management. He published several papers in reputable international journals such as *Journal of African Business*, *Social Responsibility Journal*, and *Journal of General Management*. Email: ahmed.alhiyari@ect.ac.ae.

Nur Fikriani Fiqih Al Ihsan earned her bachelor's degree in Islamic Economics at Institut Agama Islam Tazkia. She was very active in student organizations and involved in other social activities. She worked in the Indonesian Waqf Board for an internship program. Currently, she is working in one of the e-commerce entities in Indonesia. Email: nurfikriani639@gmail.com.

Nada Omar Hassan Ali is a Teaching Assistant at the Accounting and Auditing Department, Faculty of Commerce, Assuit University, Assuit, Egypt. She is a PhD student at the Faculty of Finance and Accountancy, Budapest Business School, Budapest, Hungary. She was a Teaching Assistant at Szeged University, Hungary, in 2017. She received a master's degree from the Faculty of Economic and Business Administration at Szeged University, Hungary. Email: nada.omar@aun.edu.eg.

Khaled Omair Alotaibi is an Assistant Professor of Accounting. He got his PhD in accounting from Plymouth University, UK, and master's degree in financial accounting from DMU (De Montfort University, UK), as well as bachelor's degree from King Abdulaziz University, KSA. He is interested in researching CSR, governance codes, and policy. He is a Commissioner of the Dean of the Community college and a member of the committee for development of university strategies. Email: kalotaibi@su.edu.sa.

Ahmad Alqatan is Assistant Professor at Arab Open University in Kuwait. He was formerly a Visiting Scholar in the Accounting & Finance Department at Bangor University, Business School, UK. Ahmad Alqatan has published 19 refereed papers in academic journals, three chapters, and one book. He has organized, and been a member of committees, discussant, and presenter in more than 55 international conferences. His principal research area is concerned with corporate governance, diversity earnings management, and firm performance. He has received several awards such as the prestigious 2019 Best Paper Award of the honor issuer Financial Economics Meeting: Post-crisis Challenge conference and the prestigious 2019 Best poster Award of the 15th Research and Innovation Conference, Most viewed paper award (2019). Dr. Ahmad got the title of "The Pride of Kuwait" from the Youth Public Authority in 2019. Alqatan is a Co-Editor-in-Chief of eight international journals. Recently, he ranked fifth in Accounting research (Kuwait) according to VHB, ABDC, CABS, and the Scimago index Researcher Ranking (2021). Email: drahmadalqatan@gmail.com.

Hashem Alshurafat is an Assistant Professor in Accounting at the Hashemite University. He obtained his PhD in Accounting from the University of Southern Queensland, Australia. His research is currently focused on forensic accounting, accounting education, and technology adoption in accounting. He is an editor and reviewer for many scholarly journals and conferences and has research papers published in academic journals and conferences indexed under data source Scopus and ISI. Email: hashema@hu.edu.jo.

Abdallah Bader Mahmoud Alzoubi is an Assistant Professor at the accounting department of the Hashemite University. He obtained his PhD in 2015 from Queensland University of Technology, Australia. Before his PhD studies, he worked for the Income and Sales Tax Department in Jordan for four years. His research interests include forensic accounting, financial reporting, and corporate governance. Email: abdallahb@hu.edu.jo.

Murugesh Arunachalam holds a PhD from the University of Waikato and a master's degree in accounting and finance from the University of Stirling in Scotland. He is also a Chartered Accountant.

Prior to his academic career, he had 20 years of industrial experience in accounting and financial management as a senior accountant and financial manager. Murugesh has taught in universities in Malaysia and New Zealand, specializing in financial and management accounting as well as corporate finance. He is working in the domain of CSR, financial and management accounting, and methodological issues, and he has published a number of articles in top-tier journals. Email: murugesh@waikato.ac.nz.

Dwi Nita Aryani received a PhD in Business and Management from the University of Gloucestershire, UK, in 2016. She has been a lecturer at STIE Malangkucecwara, Malang, Indonesia, since 1997; she was also the head of an International Office and trainer for Banking Risk Management Certification. She used to work at banks for almost 10 years. She has published more than 20 papers in academic journals and international conference proceedings. She is currently an Editor of *International Journal of Accounting & Finance in Asia Pacific*, and reviewer of *Journal of Accounting, Business, and Management*, *International Journal of Applied Business and International Management*, and *Estudios de Economía Aplicada*. Email: dwinita@stie-mce.ac.id.

Mehmet Asutay is a Professor of Middle Eastern and Islamic Political Economy & Finance at the Durham University Business School, and the Director of the Durham Centre in Islamic Economics and Finance as well as Programme Director of Islamic finance master's programs. Mehmet's teaching, research, publication, and supervision of research are all related to the topics of Islamic moral economy/Islamic economics, Islamic finance and banking, Islamic political economy, Islamic governance, and management and the Middle Eastern political economies. His articles have appeared in various international academic journals and professional magazines. He has also published manuscripts and edited books on aspects of Islamic moral economy and Islamic finance, the latest of which are as follows: *A Model for Islamic Development: An Approach in Islamic Moral Economy* (with S. Jan, 2019) and *Mapping the Risks and Risk Management Practices in Islamic Banking* (with W. Eid, 2019). Mehmet's recent research includes the construction of Islamic moral economy and Islamic political economy, and their articulation in economic and sustainable development. In addition, his research focused on locating Islamic banking and finance within the expressed ideals of Islamic moral economy by essentializing the sharing and collaborative economy nature of Islamic finance. Mehmet is also involved in empirical research on various aspects and dynamics of Islamic banking and finance as well as examining the political economy determinants and consequences of various Islamic finance industry development models. Mehmet is the Editor-in-Chief of the *American Journal of Islamic and Society*, the *International Journal of Islamic Economics and Finance Studies*, and the *Review of Islamic Economics*. Mehmet is also a Board Member of the International Association for Islamic Economics. Email: mehmet.asutay@durham.ac.uk.

Bassam Said Mohamed Bayomi is a Teaching Assistant as well as PhD Researcher in the field of blockchain in Auditing at the Faculty of Business, Ein Shams University, Egypt. Being interested in accounting information systems, he obtained a master's degree in 2018 on XBRL in accounting and worked as ERP Consultant, and obtained Certificates in Big Data, blockchain, robotics, IOT, and cybersecurity in accounting and auditing. He also participated in a Tanta University conference in Egypt, conducted research on robotics in auditing, and presented a number of international lectures in Libya, Iraq, Palestine, Jordan, and Kuwait on the uses of blockchain in accounting and auditing. Email: bassam.mohamed2619@std.bus.asu.edu.eg.

Hani El Shaarani is a Professor of Financial Management and a financial consultant in many public institutions. He is a member of many boards of directors in many family firms in the MENA region. He is the Director of Business School at Beirut Arab University (Lebanon) and manager of IBERA (International Business and Economic Research Academy). He is a Visiting Professor at various universities, research centers, and international organizations. His research interest includes finance, family business, corporate governance, entrepreneurship, and SMEs. Email: h.shaarani@bau.edu.lb.

Sherif El-Halaby is an Assistant Professor in the Arab Open University, Kuwait Branch, Kuwait. He obtained a PhD in Accounting from Plymouth University, MSc in Accounting from the Bradford University, and MBA from Arab Academy in Financial and Banking

Sciences. He has published 20 papers in different journals, including *Journal of Risk and Financial Management*, *Journal of Islamic Accounting and Business Research*, *Journal of Financial Reporting and Accounting*, *Accounting Research Journal*, *International Journal of Emerging Markets*, and *Journal of Accounting and Applied Business Research*. He has authored five chapters in different books published by World Science Publishing and Springer. He has participated in more than 20 global conferences such as BAFA and AAA. He has more than 20 years of experience in teaching accounting for under- and postgrads in many universities in Egypt, Kuwait, and the UK. Email: shielhalaby@msa.edu.eg.

Hamada Elsaid Elmaasrawy Elsayed Ghazi is an Assistant Professor, Department of Accounting, Tanta University, Egypt. He has published many articles in the fields of accounting, finance, auditing, and corporate governance and is a reviewer for a number of journals listed in the Scopus database. He is also a co-author of a book about presentation skills and writing reports in the field of accounting and auditing. Email: hamada.ghazi@commerce.tanta.edu.eg.

Hanaa Abdelaziz Elmoghany received her BSc degree with honors in Business Administration, Faculty of Commerce, from Alexandria University in Egypt in 1990. After her graduation, she joined the same university as a Teaching Assistant where she obtained her MSc degree in Business Administration (Finance and Investment) in 2001. In 2012, she obtained her PhD in Business Administration (Finance, Investment, and Islamic Finance) from Alexandria University. She is currently working in Alexandria University as an Assistant Professor. She also worked as an Assistant Professor at Taiba University in Saudi Arabia during the period 2018–2019. Her research interests include corporate finance, investment, Islamic finance, international finance, and financial markets and institutions. Email: hanaa.abdelazez@alexu.edu.eg.

Asma Guizani is a member of "Groupe de Recherche Angevin en Économie et Management" (GRANEM Laboratory), University of Angers. She has works on several research topics such as machine learning, artificial intelligence, governance, bankruptcy, and finance. She has published many papers, chapters, and articles. She has participated in several international conferences in France, Tunisia, and London. The following are some of her published work "Sovereign

Wealth Funds and Equity Pricing: Evidence from the Implied Cost of Equity of Publicly Traded Targets", *Journal of Corporate Finance* in 2018, "Tourism Development, Energy Consumption and Environmental in Tunisia, Egypt and Morocco: A Trivariate Analysis" article published in *Geo Journal*, in 2018, and "Effects of Corruption on Human Capital and Economic Growth in Developing Countries", Chapter 3, *Part I: Theme for Understanding Corruption, Handbook on Geographies of Corruption*, Barney Warf editor. Email: asmaguizani@gmail.com.

Haitham A. Haloush received an LLB, LLM, and PhD in Law, Leeds University, England, Aberdeen University, Scotland, and is currently working at Al-Ahliyya Amman University, Faculty of Law, Jordan, on a sabbatical leave from the Hashemite University, Jordan. Email: haloush@hu.edu.jo.

Salaheldin Hamad is currently a Graduate Assistant and PhD scholar at the Management and Humanities Department, Universiti Teknologi PETRONAS (UTP), Malaysia. He serves as an Assistant Lecturer at Faculty of Commerce, Kafrelsheikh University, Egypt. He has been teaching at Kafrelsheikh University since 2009. He completed his bachelor's degree in Commerce and master's degree in Accounting from the same university in Egypt. His research interests are in the areas of financial accounting, integrated reporting, sustainability, and corporate governance. Salah published several papers in indexed journals and presented in local and international conferences. Email: salaheldin17008482@utp.edu.my; salahhamad8@gmail.com.

Mahnoor Hanif holds a Master of Business Administration (MBA) in Finance from University Institute of Management Sciences PMAS-Arid Agriculture University, Rawalpindi, Pakistan. She worked on the corporate finance and corporate governance domains during her master's thesis. She is an early career researcher and has published her work in refereed journals. Email: mahnoorhanif289@gmail.com.

Lili Wardani Harahap is a Lecturer at the Universitas Negeri Medan (2008–present). She completed her bachelor's degree at the University of North Sumatra majoring in Accounting in 2003 and completed her master's degree in on Accounting at the University of North Sumatra in 2006. She is now a doctoral candidate (2021) at the University of Sebelas Maret. Email: liliwardani7808@gmail.com.

Ahmed Imran Hunjra is an Associate Professor at Rabat Business School, International University of Rabat, Morocco, and in the Department of Business Administration, Ghazi University, Dera Ghazi Khan, Pakistan. He has more than a decade of teaching and research experience at both graduate and post-graduate levels. His research interests are corporate finance, corporate governance, and sustainability. Ahmed has published in well-reputed journals such as *Finance Research Letters*, *Technological Forecasting and Social Change*, *Journal of Environmental Management*, *Quarterly Review of Economics and Finance*, and *International Journal of Emerging Markets, Risks, and Sustainability.* He participates as a chair/discussant in conferences/seminars, and is a reviewer of top international journals. At times, he has acted as a resource person for workshops on quantitative techniques. Email: ahmedhunjra@gmail.com.

Mahmoud Mohamed Elsayed Ibrahim completed his PhD in Economics from Ain Shams University in 2021; his master's degree in economics from Ain Shams University on "Risk Management & Governance" in 2015 and another master's degree in International Arbitration from the Faculty of Law, Ain Shams University, in 2010; and his bachelor's degree in accounting from the Faculty of Business, Ain Shams University, in 2005. He participated in many conferences on the topics of economics and accounting. He published his research through Ain Shams University, Egypt, and Alahlia University, Bahrain. He worked as Corporate Banking Relationship Manager, 2013–2021, Feasibility Studies Credit Analyst, 2006–2008, NBE initial Trainer, 2017–2019 and in The Arab Academy for Management, Banking and Financial Sciences, 2019–2021. Email: almamoood@gmail.com.

Nahla Mohamad El Sayed Ibrahim is Assistant Professor of Accounting and a Member of the Sustainability Committee and the Academic Guidance Committee at King Faisal University, Business School, Saudi Arabia. He did his PhD, master's, and bachelor's degrees in Accounting, Faculty of Business, Ain Shams University, and did his master's degree in International Arbitration, Faculty of law, Ain Shams University, Egypt. His research interests are in the fields of financial accounting, corporate governance, environmental sustainability, accounting administration, creative accounting, and

Islamic accounting. He has participated in many conferences relating to contemporary accounting and economic issues. He has several published research studies in the field of financial accounting and supervised many theses. He seeks out everything new in accounting. Email: netman@kfu.edu.sa.

Ahmad Ali Jan is pursuing his PhD in Management from Universiti Teknologi PETRONAS, Malaysia. His areas of interest are, but not limited to, Islamic banking and finance, Islamic corporate governance, bankruptcy forecasting, corporate sustainability, economic growth, and sustainable development. Mr. Jan's work has also been published in reputable journals such as the *Journal of Cleaner Production*, *Quality and Quantity*, and *Journal of Chinese Economic and Foreign Trade Studies*. Moreover, his research papers in the areas of Sharia governance and integrated reporting have also been presented at International Conferences. Email: ahmad.alijan91@gmail.com.

Monjia Khalfi currently works at the Higher Institute of Technological Studies of Kasserine (ISETK). She is also a member of the laboratory of Algebra, Number Theory, and Nonlinear Analysis at the Department of Mathematics of University of Monastir. Monjia conducts research on Islamic finance, governance, banking efficiency, and financial data mining. Email: monjiakhalfi@hotmail.fr.

Mohamed Chakib Kolsi has been an Associate Professor of accounting at Liwa College of Technology (LCT) since 2012 at the University of Sfax, Tunisia. He has more than 19 years of teaching experience and 10 years of experience as head of the accounting department. He received his PhD in accounting sciences from the University of Manouba, Tunisia, in 2010. He has published many research papers in specialized/indexed journals and served as reviewer/referee for many submitted papers/dissertations. Dr. Kolsi has supervised many research projects at the levels of bachelor's, master's, and PhD degrees. His research interests include CSR, Islamic finance, auditing, earnings management, and corporate governance. Email: Mohamed.Kolsi@ect.ac.ae.

Muhammad Imran Majeed is a Fellow Chartered Manager CMI UK (CMgr FCMI), Associate Member of Project Management (APM) UK, and Experienced Lecturer with a demonstrated history of working in the higher education industry. He has experience in analytics, IT & HR consulting, team building, leadership & management, and project management with a background of working in diverse multinational companies. He is an education professional, with a PhD in Management via the HEC as a Pakistan Scholar from PBS-UPM Malaysia with a Master of Science (MS) degree focused on Project Management, Leadership, and Management from COMSATS Institute of Information and Technology. He is also an active Member of the Chartered Management Institute UK. Email: muhammadimran.phdmgt18@grad.putrabs.edu.my.

Rashid Mehmood holds his PhD in Finance from PMAS-Arid Agriculture University Rawalpindi, Pakistan. Currently, he is working as an Assistant Professor of Finance at UE Business School, Division of Management and Administrative Science University of Education, Lahore, Pakistan. His research interests include corporate governance, corporate finance, and risk management. He has published in well-recognized journals and has refereed articles in well-reputed journals. Email: rashidm1005@gmail.com.

Murniati Mukhlisin earned her degrees in Islamic accounting from International Islamic University of Malaysia (undergraduate), Universitas Indonesia (postgraduate), and University of Glasgow (doctoral). She previously worked in banking and IT services both in Indonesia and Malaysia, then started her career as a lecturer in Islamic Accounting in 2002. She was an affiliate staff at University of Glasgow and lecturer/researcher at University of Essex, UK, from 2015 to 2017. Her work involves a critical perspective on Islamic accounting and finance. Murniati is currently a Rector, Tazkia Islamic University College, Indonesia. She sits as a board member in several institutions and serves as consultant and Sharia expert. Email: murniati@tazkia.ac.id.

Sahar Munir is an Assistant Professor at the University of Agriculture, Faisalabad. She received her PhD in Finance from the University of Gloucestershire, UK. Her research interest is related to Islamic Derivatives and Sharia Compliance in the context of the Pakistani market. Moreover, she has a vast undergraduate and postgraduate teaching experience of 11 years. Recently, she completed her Postdoctorate from Putra Business School, University of Putra Malaysia with a focus on Blended Islamic Finance. Additionally, she is a CFM-UK certified with distinction. She is the author of various publications and a reviewer of various journals. Furthermore, she has the experience of working as a Finance and Grants Manager for a USAID-funded project for food security. Email: sahar.munir@uaf.edu.pk.

Souhir Neifar is an Assistant Professor in accounting and taxation at the faculty of Economics and management of Sfax Tunisia. Dr. Neifar received her doctorate degree in accounting from the Faculty of economics and management of Sfax Tunisia in June 2016. She received her Habilitation in Management Sciences in May 2021. Her research interests include tax management, earnings management and game theory, and zakat. She has several publications in many indexed journals such as the following: *The International Journal of Finance and Accounting*, *International Journal of Accounting and Economics Studies*, *Journal of Applied Accounting Research*, and *Review of Accounting and Finance*. She is also a reviewer for many prestigious journals such as *Journal of Applied Accounting Research and INFOR: Information Systems and Operational Research*. She has participated in several research stays at the department of Business Taxation and Auditing in the Faculty of Economics and Business administration at TU Chemnitz Germany. She has conducted several seminars on tax advantages in Tunisia under the DAAD projects. She was the coordinator of a DAAD project between TU Chemnitz Germany and FSEG of Sfax in 2020. Email: souhir.neifar@fsegs.usf.tn.

Qutaiba Adeeb Odat recently graduated in Accounting and Finance from the Hashemite University, Jordan, in 2022; he got his master's degree with an excellent GPA of 3.68/4. He earned his bachelor's degree in Accounting at Hashemite University in 2020 with a very good GPA of 3.03/4. He works as a Teaching Assistant at Hashemite University and works in the department of laboratories and quality control in the Jordan Petroleum Refinery Company. He is particularly interested in accounting and accounting technology, FinTech, intelligent systems acceptance and adoption, Islamic accounting, finance and audit standards, taxation, and corporate social responsibility. He has published several articles in peer-reviewed journals and international conferences. Qutaiba Adeeb Odat is interested in finding an outstanding opportunity to complete his PhD in Accounting and finance. Email: 2070014@std.hu.edu.jo.

Elhassan Kotb Abdelrahman Radwan is a Teaching Assistant at the Accounting and Auditing Department, Faculty of Commerce, Assuit University, Assuit, Egypt. He is a PhD student at the Department of Business Studies and Economics, University of Naples, Napoli, Italy. Also, he was a Teaching Assistant at Szeged University, Hungary. He has more than eight years' experience in teaching accounting and related courses in Egypt and Hungary. He received his master's degree from Szeged University, Hungary, with an excellent grade in accounting specialization. Email: elhassan.kotb@aun.edu.eg.

Foued Saâdaoui works at the Department of Statistics of the Faculty of Sciences at King Abdulaziz University (KAU). He is also a Professor at IHEC, University of Sousse. Foued is a Statistician/Mathematician, with expertise spanning various fields in mathematical education, theoretical and applied statistics, as pertaining to applications in the areas of business, engineering, and physical sciences. Email:fsadawi@kau.edu.sa; foued.saadaoui@gmail.com; foued.saadaoui@isgs.rnu.tn.

Monsurat Ayojimi Salami is an Assistant Professor in the Department of Real Estate Development and Management, Ankara University, Turkey. She received all her degrees from International Islamic University Malaysia (in the field of finance and business administration). She was a postdoctoral research fellow at IIUM Institute of Islamic Banking and Finance (IIiBF) between September 2018 and August 2019, and received an Honorable Mention in CIFE from Eithica Institute of Islamic Finance, the USA, in October, 2019. She also earned professional certification from the certified quantitative risk management (CQRM) program in March, 2018, from the International Institute of Professional Education and Research (IIPER), Washington, D.C., USA. Email: masalami@ankara.edu.tr; ayojimi123@gmail.com.

Resul Sapar, Dr., holds a PhD from INCEIF and is currently working with Putra Business School, University of Putra Malaysia. He possesses experience in Islamic finance subjects, specifically Islamic financial products and services, Islamic capital market, and waqf, and has been teaching since January 2012. Moreover, he has vast experience in civil construction, ICT, proton car dealership, petrol kiosk operation, consultancy, and project management businesses, along with exposure to the banking sector. Email: resul@putrabs.edu.my.

Adel M. Sarea is the winner of the Emerald Literati Award 2014 (UK). He has published his work in over 100 publications. He has been bestowed with many awards and summoned as the keynote speaker on several occasions. He serves on the editorial team of several international journals published by Elsevier, Emerald, and Taylor & Francis. He is a member of the Accounting and Finance Association of Australia and New Zealand (AFAANZ). In 2015, he was appointed as a recognized PhD supervisor by Brunel University London. In 2021, he was entitled as the Senior Editor of the *International Journal of Emerging Markets* (Emerald). Email: sarea@ahlia.edu.bh.

Nada Said Awad Allah Selim has a bachelor's degree in Accounting with a very good degree from the faculty of commerce Zagazig university. She got a master's degree in accounting on a subject entitled *The Impact of Financial Performance on the Relationship between Corporate Social Responsibility and Dividends*. She is carrying out preparatory study for her PhD in accounting. Her research interest is in the field of financial accounting and accounting for sustainability and social responsibility. Email: nadas8173@gmail.com.

Asma Sghaier is a Researcher at the IHEC School, University of Sousse Tunisia. She is a member at "Laboratoire Management de l'Innovation et Développement Durable" (LaMIDED Laboratory), University of Sousse (Tunisia), and LEAD, University of Toulon France. Dr. Asma Sghaier's research interests focus on Big Data, entrepreneurship, governance, innovation, finance, digital disruptions in accounting and finance (FinTech, blockchain, cryptocurrencies), Islamic finance, and sustainable development. She is an editor of several books: *Islamic Finance, Critical Aspects of Conventional Finance*, L'Harmattan, Collection: *The Economic Spirit — The World in Question*; Series: *Economy Finances Religions Islam.* She has published 30 papers as chapters and articles. She is an invited speaker in international universities and an academic member of the committees of several international conferences in France, Tunisia, and Turkey. She is an editorial board member of more than 10 indexed journals (Scopus). Dr. Sghaier is a member of the scientific broad of the *Global Journal of Economics and Business*, a reviewer in the *Journal of the Knowledge Economy, Economics Bulletin, International Journal of Management and Enterprise Development*

Inderscience Enterprises, International Journal of Social Ecology and Sustainable Development, Journal of Global Information Management, Journal of Global Entrepreneurship Research, Journal of Finance and Market, the International Journal of Public and Private Perspectives on Healthcare, South Asian Journal of Business Studies, International Journal of Digital Innovation in the Built Environment, African Development Review, Business and Management Research Journal, and *the Net Journal of Business Management*. Dr. Sghaier had presented her research findings in many international conferences. Email: asmasghaier1983@yahoo.fr.

Muhammad Kashif Shad is a Lecturer at the Management and Humanities Department, Universiti Teknologi PETRONAS (UTP) Malaysia. He earned his PhD in Management and M.Phil. in Management degree with concentration on Enterprise Risk Management from the Management and Humanities Department, UTP Malaysia. Previously, he obtained his Bachelor of Business Administration (BBA) degree with concentration in Finance from Hazara University Mansehra, Pakistan, in 2012. Dr. Kashif has published more than 25 articles in indexed journals and presented in local and international conferences. His research interests are in the areas of enterprise risk management (ERM), economic value-added analysis (EVA), and corporate sustainability. Email: kashif.shad@utp.edu.my.

Syed Quaid Ali Shah is currently pursuing a Doctor of Philosophy (PhD) in Management at the Department of Management and Humanities, Universiti Teknologi PETRONAS (UTP) Malaysia. Syed Quaid Ali Shah has also worked as an Accountant in Clear Image Technology, Dubai, UAE. His research interests include intellectual capital, enterprise risk management, corporate governance, and sustainability reporting. He has presented a paper in an International Conference, *Eurasia Business and Economics Society*, in Istanbul, and published papers in journals such as *Journal of Chinese Economic and Foreign Trade Studies, Sustainability, Colombo Business Journal*, and *the Dialogue Journal*. Email: syedquaidalishah@gmail.com.

Muhammad Tahir is working in COMSATS University Islamabad, Abbottabad Campus, as an assistant professor of economics. His area of specialization is international trade, economic issues of developing countries, econometric modeling, and terrorism. Dr. Tahir has published in refereed international journals such *as Asia Business Studies, Journal of Chinese Economic and Foreign Trade Studies, Contemporary Economics, Quality and Quantity, International Journal of Disaster Risk Reduction, Economic Systems, Applied Economics Letters, Applied Research in Quality of Life, African Development Review, Borsa Istanbul Review, China Economic Journal, International Journal of Social Economics, Journal of Economic Studies*, and *International Journal of Emerging Markets* recently. Email: mtahir0086@gmail.com.

Harun Tanrıvermiş is a Professor at the Department of Real Estate Development and Management, Faculty of Applied Sciences at Ankara University, Turkey. He received his MSc and PhD degrees from the Department of Agricultural Economics (in the field of land and real estate economics, land, and real estate valuation) at Ankara University. He has also obtained another MSc degree in environmental management under the European MED-CAMPUS Programme. His research interests include real estate and asset valuation, real estate project development and project appraisal, land acquisition and expropriation, facility and real estate economics and management, real estate investment analysis and finance, and environmental economics. He has been a staff member at Ankara University since 1991 and has been working as a research specialist and consultant in the fields of research interests. He has many academic publications such as articles, books, and proceedings. He has 30 international and 25 national peer-reviewed articles in variety of high impact factor journals. He has published 58 international and 45 national full or abstract proceedings in different kinds of conferences. He is the author of 39 books and 15 book chapters. He is the Head of the Department of Real Estate Development and Management and the Dean of the Faculty of Applied Sciences at Ankara University. He has been acting as coordinator of university real estate development and construction works. He has coordinated all graduate students' research studies and theses as well as postdoctoral research at the department. He is a member of the Royal Institution of Chartered Surveyors (MRICS), other international occupational institutions (Urban Land Institute (ULI), International Facility Management Association (IFMA), International Real Estate

Federation (FIABCI)), and national organizations. Email: tanrivermis@ankara.edu.tr.

Yeşim Tanrıvermiş is an Associate Professor at the Department of Real Estate Development and Management, Faculty of Applied Sciences at Ankara University, Turkey. She received her MSc degree from the Department of Agricultural Economics (in the field of land and real estate economics, land, and real estate valuation), Ankara University, and her PhD degree from the Department of Real Estate Development and Management, Ankara University. Her research interests include management and conservation of land resources, land resources economics, real estate analysis and economics, real estate, and asset valuation studies. She has been giving lectures for six years. She has been publishing academic papers since 2006. She has 15 international and 16 national peer-reviewed articles. She has published 42 international and three national full or abstract proceedings in a variety of conferences/congresses. She has also published 30 books and 6 book chapters. She also works as the deputy head of the Department of Real Estate Development and Management at Ankara University. She has worked as a researcher and consultant in many public and private sectors in the field of real estate asset analysis, real estate finance and valuation, land and building conservation practices, and real estate economics and management. In addition to these, she also actively works to improve cooperation with domestic and foreign institutions and on the mobilization of financial resources for research projects. She is a board member of the Turkish Appraisers Association (TDUB) and she manages practical training and certificate programs. Email: aliefendioglu@ankara.edu.tr.

Omar Ikbal Tawfik earned a PhD in Accounting in 2004, with experience in teaching both bachelor and master levels in Accounting & Management. He evaluated several research papers published in Sage Open and *Journal of Islamic Accounting and Business Research.* He has also, He has also published several research papers in Scopus and five books on different topics of accounting. He is interested in cloud accounting, corporate governance, and auditing. Currently, he works in the Accounting Department of Dhofar University in the Sultanate of Oman with the rank of Associate Professor. Email: otawfik@du.edu.om.

Kaouther Toumi is an Associate Professor of finance at Paul Sabatier Toulouse 3 University in France. Kaouther's teaching interests spanned the areas of Islamic banking and finance, market, and corporate finance. Kaouther's research activities are related to Islamic finance and banking. She was a visiting academic/researcher at Durham university (UK) and Zitouna university (Tunisia). She is a member of diverse academic and professional networks interested in Islamic finance. She acted as a chair, co-chair, and member of several scientific and organizing committees of international conferences and professional meetings on Islamic finance and economics. She is a referee for diverse scientific reviews. Email: kaouther.toumi@iut-tlse3.fr.

Fong-Woon Lai is an Associate Professor at Management and Humanities Department, Universiti Teknologi PETRONAS (UTP) Malaysia. He holds a Bachelor of Science degree in Business Administration and a Master of Business Administration from the University of Nebraska-Lincoln, USA. He obtained his PhD from University of Malaya. Dr. Lai has been teaching in higher education institutions since 1998. Prior to joining academia, he worked in two stock broking companies in Malaysia. Dr. Lai has co-authored management books, published papers in indexed journals, and presented in local and international conferences. His research interests are in the areas of corporate finance, strategy, risk management, and socio-economic analysis. Email: laifongwoon@utp.edu.my.

Mohamed Abd Elmoneim Abou ElSoud Zaied is a PhD Researcher at the Faculty of Commerce, Sadat City University, Egypt. He has a Master of Business Science degree, with a major in Accounting, from Menoufia University in 2017 and has research interests in financial accounting, specifically corporate governance, environmental sustainability, quality of financial reports, accounting disclosure, and Islamic accounting. He has participated in many conferences in Egypt with interest in contemporary accounting issues, and has several published studies in the field of financial accounting. He seeks to look up and research everything new in accounting, especially financial and Islamic accounting. Email: mohamed.zaied@egypttechnology-eg.com.

Imama Zuchroh, the Co-Author of "CSR in Sharia Theory Perspective", has been a Lecturer in STIE Malangkucecwara, Malang, Indonesia, for more than 20 years. In recent years, she majored in Sharia-based Economic, Financial, and Business studies. She graduated from the University of Wollongong, Australia, with a Commerce postgraduate degree. She founded a Sharia-based Financial Service in Malang and was also involved in the Sharia insurance industry as a Financial Planner. She is often invited as a speaker in financial and business seminars and training, and has also joined several international conferences as speaker and published a number of proceedings in journals. Email: imamazuchroh@yahoo.com.

https://doi.org/10.1142/9781800612426_fmatter

Acknowledgments

First of all, we would like to express our gratitude to Almighty Allah for enabling us to complete this book.

We would like to thank Professor Sabri Boubaker and Professor Duc Khuong Nguyen (Series Editors) for giving us the opportunity to edit this book. We also would like to thank Natalie Watson and Michael Beale (World Scientific Publishing, Europe) for their helpful comments and editorial assistance. We are grateful to Dr. Ahmed Elamer who kindly agreed to write the foreword to this edited book. Our sincere thanks also go to all the contributing authors. Their contributions to *Islamic Accounting and Finance* are greatly appreciated.

Hidaya Al Lawati conveys her sincere gratitude to her supervisor Professor Hussainey. Without his continuous and infinite support and help, this book would have been a minor success. His considerable experience and expertise have guided this project to a great success with the completion of this book. May Allah shower him with his blessings and rewards.

All expressed views in the chapters remain the sole responsibility of the authors.

https://doi.org/10.1142/9781800612426_fmatter

Contents

https://doi.org/10.1142/9781800612426_fmatter

List of Figures

https://doi.org/10.1142/9781800612426_fmatter

List of Tables

https://doi.org/10.1142/9781800612426_fmatter

Introduction

Islamic finance is one of the fastest-growing sectors. The growth of Islamic finance has massively increased, driven by its importance and ease of accessing Islamic services. Across the world, and in particular the Middle East and North Africa (MENA) and Gulf Cooperation Council (GCC) regions, the dual finance system, where Islamic finance coexists along with conventional finance, is allowed to be implemented. The growth of Islamic finance is motivated by the huge demand for Sharia-compliant products, and it is expanding not only in the Muslim's countries but also worldwide, thereby making it a global industry.

This book is a collection of high-quality scrupulously gathered chapters that examine the role of Islamic finance in companies' economies and prospects. We are delighted to invite researchers from all around the world to enrich the Islamic finance literature from both theoretical and empirical perspectives. The theoretical section of the book will be a compilation of chapters, theoretical and conceptual, that enable readers to critically evaluate and expand the broader areas of accounting and finance knowledge. The empirical section of the book will be dedicated to empirical studies, which consist of chapters that offer empirical evidence that discusses and interprets the findings and how they contribute to society and regulators by providing appropriate practical implications.

This handbook provides readers insights on Islamic accounting and finance. This handbook comprises 26 chapters on theoretical and empirical research on Islamic accounting and finance. There are a total of 57 co-authors representing 18 countries (Bahrain, Egypt, France, Hungary, Indonesia, Italy, Jordan, Kuwait, Lebanon, Malaysia, New Zealand, Oman, Pakistan, Saudi Arabia, Tunisia, Turkey, United Arab Emirate, and United Kingdom).

There are four parts to this handbook. Part I, entitled Islamic Accounting: Theoretical Perspectives, addresses issues related to the applications of Islamic accounting in Islamic finance transactions (Chapter 1); the ontological and epistemological construct of Islamic accounting; the methods (Chapter 2); a systematic literature review on topics and theories used in Islamic accounting research (Chapter 3); a systematic literature review on zakat research (Chapter 4); corporate social responsibility (CSR) in a Sharia theory perspective (Chapter 5); and forensic accounting from an Islamic perspective (Chapter 6).

Part II, entitled Islamic Accounting: Empirical Perspectives, covers empirical research on Islamic accounting that addresses the consequences of *Accounting and Auditing Organization for Islamic Financial Institutions* (AAOFIF) adoption (Chapter 7); disclosure practice of the risk of Islamic financial instruments (sukuk) (Chapter 8); risk disclosure practice on Islamic banks, websites (Chapter 9); CSR and sustainable reporting in Islamic banks (Chapter 10); sustainability performance disclosure practice in Islamic and non-Islamic banks (Chapter 11); Islamic ethics and corporate governance (Chapter 12); value-based intermediation (VBI) (Chapter 13); and accounting issue in cryptocurrency investment (Chapter 14).

Part III, entitled Islamic Finance: Theoretical Perspectives, covers theoretical research on Islamic finance that addresses the basic concepts, forms, and specifications of Islamic finance (Chapter 15); Islamic investments and portfolio management (Chapter 16); and the role of blockchain in enhancing Islamic crowdfunding mechanisms (Chapter 17).

Part IV, entitled Islamic Finance: Empirical Perspectives, covers empirical research on Islamic finance that addresses capital adequacy in Islamic and non-Islamic banks in Saudi Arabia (Chapter 18); the determinants of capital structure in Islamic and non-Islamic banks (Chapter 19); the performance of Islamic and non-Islamic banks in the Middle East and North Africa (MENA) region (Chapter 20); the determinants of Islamic banks' profitability during the COVID-19 pandemic period (Chapter 21); determinants of liquidity in Islamic banks in Pakistan (Chapter 22); blended Islamic finance for poverty reduction (Chapter 23); determinants of liquidity risk in Islamic banks (Chapter 24); Basel Capital Accords and COVID-19 in Islamic banking (Chapter 25); and factors influencing interest of Indonesian Muslim millennials in waqf (Chapter 26).

Part I

Islamic Accounting: Theoretical Perspectives

https://doi.org/10.1142/9781800612426_0001

Chapter 1

Islamic Accounting Applications of Islamic Finance

Mahmoud Ali Aleraig and Mehmet Asutay

Abstract

Islamic banks and financial institutions have demonstrated an unprecedented success since their emergence in commercial form in 1970s. The expansion of the asset base of the industry and its diffusion into main financial centers in the world is a clear indication of its success. While Islamic finance is constituted through Islamic normativeness as expressed through *Sharia* compliance process coupled with the standards developed by the Accounting and Auditing Organization for Islamic Financial Institutions and the Islamic Financial Services Board within dual banking system, their accounting system follows conventional system of accounting which is based on the fictitious claim that accounting is value free. However, this chapter is developed through the assumptions that neither economics and finance, nor accounting and management is value free as value system and ontologies determine their nature and operations. In expanding this assumption, this chapter aims to identify the Islamic accounting implication for Islamic finance with the hope that Islamic banks and financial institutions, in particular, and Muslim societies, in general, can move onto authentic accounting system and philosophy shaped by Islamic ontology and epistemology. This chapter hence aims to develop and identify the way Islamic accounting can apply to Islamic finance transactions and contracts as well as institutions such as *zakat*. It also presents some critical reflections on the practice of Islamic accounting and accounting standards.

Keywords: Islamic Accounting, Islamic Finance, Accounting and Auditing Organization for Islamic Financial Institutions (AAOIFI), Islamic Financial Services Board (IFSB).

1.1 Introduction

There is no doubt that Islamic Banking and Finance (IBF) has become an alternative and innovative financial tool and institution since it emerged in 1975, which is also considered an ethical financial proposition. IBF Institutions (IFBIs) provide "*Sharia*-compliant" financial products and undertake many transactions that are, at least in theory, different from conventional accounting transactions and which are subject to Islamic principles, such as *riba*, profit–loss sharing, risk sharing, asset-based financing, as well as the compulsory alms giving *zakat* and special Islamic financial instrument such as *mudharabah*, *musharakah*, *ijarah*, and *istisna*.

Despite the mentioned success trajectory of IBFIs, the industry is not without its challenges. One of the reasons as part of the observed challenges is that IBFIs are trying to operate and invest in markets where the regulations and financial reporting frameworks are disparate, which means these types of accounting standards might not meet the requirements of IBFIs.

Literature on accounting from an Islamic perspective and accounting in Islamic banks has increased over the last three decades with the development of the IBF industry to establish accounting standards that meet the requirement of these institutions, as the alternative financial transactions are considered as an important factor that can affect accounting and can lead to the development of particular accounting treatment and standards. The aim of constructing an Islamic accounting system is a relatively new approach in the modern world while historical experience rationalizes its existence.

Therefore, this work attempts and aims to understand how the religious or Islamic principles affect the choice of accounting and reporting policies made by these banks, and it also presents the mechanisms and instruments of Islamic finance, such as *mudarabah, musharakah, murabahah*, in addition to *zakat* and *qard-ul-hassan*, to identify their treatment as an accounting issue. Thus, this chapter aims to develop and identify the way Islamic accounting can apply to Islamic finance transactions and contracts as well as institutions such as *zakat*. In other words, this chapter aims to identify the Islamic accounting implication for Islamic finance with the hope that Islamic banks and financial institutions, in particular, and Muslim societies, in general, can move onto authentic accounting system and philosophy shaped by Islamic ontology and epistemology. It also presents some critical reflections on the practice of Islamic accounting and accounting standards.

1.2 Islamic Finance: Principles

The discussion so far has focused on rationalizing Islamic accounting through ontology, epistemology, and historical practice. An important aspect of this rationalization relates to the contemporary needs and practices, thus bringing us to Islamic finance. Due to the rise and expansion of Islamic finance, the debate on whether there should be Islamic accounting to correspond to the needs of Islamic finance has risen. Therefore, this section focuses on Islamic finance to particularly emphasize Islamic accounting-related implications.

As the discussion so far indicates, Islamic accounting is based on a particular ontological worldview, which historically was also shaped by the anthropological realities of Muslim life and the way Muslims articulated Islamic principles in their everyday life, e.g., in accounting practices. Significantly, given that Islamic accounting is a tool to register transactions, there must also be a "subject" to which Islamic accounting principles should be applied. This brings us to the *Sharia*-compliant economy and financial practices shaped by Islamic principles. In other words, existing Islamic accounting practices also have peculiar Islamic financing methods being different from conventional practice, financial modes, and instruments.

While Islamic finance came to prominence in the late 20th century, the *Qur'an* directly relates to certain principles pertaining to economics and financing, and therefore, because of the original Muslim societies in Makkah and Madinah, various financial instruments, institutions, and financial practices developed through the norms, principles, and values of Islam.

Thus, in order to provide further rationale for Islamic accounting, this section presents the distinguishing principles of Islamic finance, which by definition requires a different accounting treatment to justify why Islamic accounting is a necessity beyond ontological reasoning, as debated earlier. Therefore, the following section discusses the salient features of Islamic finance, which have accounting implications.

1.2.1 *Riba (Interest, usury)*

Prohibition of *riba* is the most prominent feature in Islamic economics and finance, which the *Qur'an* and *Sunnah* clearly prohibits, as explicitly identified by Islamic law (Ayub, 2007; Asutay, 2015; Billah, 2019). Hence, the presence of *riba* in financial transactions is contrary to many commercial practices in modern economics. For example, the conventional banking system is systematized based on a fixed payment named interest, which in turn makes the activities and performance of the conventional banking system incompatible with the philosophies of Islam that rigorously forbid *riba* (Asutay, 2010). Literally, there are too many detailed interpretations of *riba* (Thomas, 2005). The following sections aim to provide a conceptual understanding of the term *riba* and its implications for accounting.

1.2.1.1 *Definition of riba*

Riba is derived from the Arabic word root $r - b - a'$, which is the past tense of the word *riba,* meaning to increase (El-Gamal, 2006). However, in the economic context, the word *riba* is often translated as "interest". The concept of interest in Islam implies profit without effort, such as profit obtained free from indemnification, etc. More precisely, *riba* is a pure return (or rent) on money *per se*, where neither business risk is borne nor other goods or services provided (Thomas, 2005; Billah, 2019). In this respect, the majority of modern *fuqaha'* (Islamic scholars) interpret *riba* as being equivalent to "interest" (Karim, 1999). Chapra (1992) also argues that all Muslim scholars agree that interest is synonymous with *riba.*

Nevertheless, in the broader context, *Sharia* has suggested a precise meaning for *riba,* including "increase", "addition", "expansion", "gain" or "growth" (Sulaiman, 2003). Moreover, in the context of *Sharia*, Saleh (1992: 16) defines *riba* "as generally agreed, as an unlawful gain derived from the quantitative inequality of the counter-values in any transaction purporting to effect the exchange of two or more species (*anwa'*, singular *naw'*), which belong to the same genus (*jins*) and are governed by the same efficient cause (*'illa, pl. 'illa*)".

Furthermore, Saleh (1992: 16) argues that "deferred completion of the exchange of such species, or even of species that belong to different genera but are governed by the same *illa* is also *riba*, whether or not the deferment is accompanied by an increase in any one of the exchanged counter-values". In short, *riba* contains any unjust or excessive business activities (Gambling & Karim, 1991).

1.2.1.2 *Prohibition of riba in Islam*

Islam prohibits *riba,* as evidently revealed in the *Qur'an* and the *Sunnah.* Similarly, all practices that use prediction of the future are also forbidden. According to *Sharia*, *riba* is strictly prohibited since it leads to unearned income and wealth. Islam considers financial activity an embedded economy, implying that finance is directly connected to productive economic activity (Ayub, 2007; Asutay, 2010). Since "interest" does not provide a return to the capital owner due to their direct participation in the economic activity, as a partner, interest is considered to be "unlawful" in terms of bringing a fixed return. Therefore, the prohibition of *riba* has been completely agreed upon by all Islamic schools of thought. For the reason that Muslims take all their guidance from sources that they do not doubt, the *Qur'an* and the *Sunnah*, there is general unanimity among all Muslims on the fact that the practice of *riba* is prohibited in Islam (Ariff & Iqbal, 2011).

The word *riba* and its prohibition are mentioned in numerous verses of the *Qur'an*, the primary source of Islamic worldview. The *Qur'anic* verses that instruct the prohibition of usury are clear and reflect the severity of the admonition administered on those who do not abide by it. The verses that strongly condemn *riba* are those in *surat Al-Baqarah* verses 275, 276, 278, and 279 and verse 130 in *surat' Ali Imran.*

Since *riba* is defined as one of the major sins in Islam, this provides the necessary motivation for eliminating the practice *of riba* from society. Thus, Muslims are asked, when dealing in financial transactions involving further obligation (debt), to write down faithfully and precisely this obligation (*Qur'an*, 2: 282), because as Muslims, we have to consider avoiding any forms of *riba* whenever we undertake any financial transactions. Therefore, the requirement of accounting practice in Islam helps prevent *riba* by recording the rights and dues of all parties (Ahmed, 1994).

Prohibition of *riba* is not only limited to the *Qur'an* but in the *Sunnah* as well. Several *ahadith* of the Prophet Muhammad (*pbuh*) illustrate that he clearly convicted *riba* in money and commodity transactions. For example, in the saying "[avoid the seven great destructive sins]. The people inquired, O Allah's Messenger! What are they? He said, to associate others in worship along with Allah..., to eat up *riba* (usury)...". (Sahih al-Bukhari: 840; Sahih Muslim: 161). The Prophet equates the person who earns *riba* to the one who believes in partnership with God, which is the biggest sin in Islam.

Prophet Muhammad placed his wrath (cursed) on the earner of *riba* and its payer and the writer and the two witnesses. Jabir said that "the Prophet Muhammad cursed the receiver of usury and its payer, and one who records it, and the two witnesses, and he said: They are all equal" (Sahih Muslim: 3881).

Due to the importance of *riba*, the Prophet Muhammad did not forget, among other things, to enforce the prohibition of *riba* in the Farewell Pilgrimage given on the 9th of *Dul-hijjah*, 10 *Hijri*. He said, "God has forbidden you to take *riba*; therefore, all *riba* obligations shall henceforth be waived. Your capital, however, is yours to keep. You will neither inflict nor suffer inequity. God has judged that there shall be no *riba* and that all the *riba* due to Abbas ibn Abd al Muttalib shall henceforth be waived" (Sahih Muslim: 2803).

1.2.1.3 *Types of riba (usury) in Islamic law*

From the earlier discussion, it is apparent that the *Qur'an* did not identify any specific type of *riba*, although the word *al-riba* in the *Qur'an* generally explains the type of dealing that people used to practice before Islam (*riba al-jahiliya*) (Ahmed, 1992). However, according to *ahadith*, when Islam first emerged, the Prophet Muhammad defined two *riba* types: *riba-al-fadl* and *riba-an-nasia* (Chaudhry, 1999).

Riba al-nasia, or the "usury of deference" is the worst form of *riba*, also known as *riba al-jahiliya* practiced in pre-Islamic Arabia (El-Ashker, 1987; El-Gamal, 2006, Billah, 2019). The term *nasia* means to postpone or to wait. In other words, it means extending the period of a loan by charging more than the principal value. Therefore, it refers to the time permitted for the debtor to pay back the loan in profit with the accumulation of the premium. Consequently, it denotes the interest on loans (Chapra, 1984; El-Ashker,

1987; Thomas, 2005). The prevention of *riba al nasi'ah* signifies that the agreement in advance of a positive return on loan as a reward for waiting is not permitted in Islam (Chapra, 2006).

Riba al-fadhl, or "usury of increase" is the type of *riba* associated with exchanging an entity for the same kind of entity for an increase in quantity (El-Ashker, 1987). *Riba al-fadl* is defined as "an unlawful excess in the exchange of two counter-values, where the excess is measurable through weight or measure" (Usmani, 2002: 253). Therefore, it forbids the exchange of commodities with similar categories and types with different quantities (El-Gamal, 2006). The following tradition (*hadith*) of the Prophet Muhammad is an authority on the prohibition of *riba al-fadl*. The Prophet Muhammad said that, "Gold for gold, silver for silver, wheat for wheat, barley for barley, dates for dates, and salt for salt, like for like, equal for equal, and hand-to-hand; if the commodities differ, then you may sell as you wish, provided that the exchange is hand-to-hand" (Sahih Muslim: 3853–3854; Sahih Al-Bukhari: 382).

1.2.1.4 *Impact of riba on accounting and reporting policies*

For the reason that accounting is a part of an environment that reflects the business practices of society, the prohibition of *riba* does have a direct influence on accounting practices that comply with the requirements of Islamic *Sharia*. According to Sulaiman (2003), at first, it will affect the capital structure of a business, which in turn will impact the disclosure practices of financial reporting. This is because the balance sheet of an Islamic firm is likely to exclude loans with interest and debentures, and all practices use prediction of the future because the future is in the hands of *Allah*. Thus, the following section discusses the potential impact of Islamic financial principles on accounting principles.

1.2.1.4.1 Capital structure

The capital structure of Islamic companies is not the same as conventional companies because Islamic enterprises are not permitted to include any type of *riba* in their operations and transactions. In addition, Islamic finance, in its aspirational sense, does not encourage debt transactions, although interest-free debts are not prohibited in Islam (*Qur'an*, 2: 282). Thus, it could be argued that Islam does not permit debentures because those debentures have a fixed ratio of interest (Sulaiman, 2003). Furthermore, preference shares are not an exception since they have fixed dividends, which are prohibited in Islam (Hamid *et al.*, 1993). However, if the fixed dividend rate attached to preference shares is to be eliminated as a form of capital, these preference shares would not disturb any precepts of the *Sharia*. In effect, it would be comparable to the role played by a partner in a *musharakah* or a *mudarabah* (El-Ashker, 1987; Mohsin, 1992).

In addition, the structure of long-term loans that usually comes with a period of more than 10 years, such as infrastructure financing which are also reported as non-current liabilities, can take the form of a *mudarabah* partnership in IBF's framework. In this form, the bank and the company are sharing the profit and the loss made. In the case of making a profit, the bank and the company divide the profit in accordance with a prearranged ratio. However, if there was a loss, then the bank loses the capital, and the company loses the provision of labor (Sulaiman, 2003). This would encourage banks to make an additional effort by working more carefully with enterprises to ensure that their assets are managed efficiently. This means, Islamic banks will interfere in any work and decisions made by their clients, which is not always the case in conventional banks (Sulaiman, 1997).

Consequently, from the earlier discussion, it could be argued that the capital structure of *Sharia*-compliant business will contain any preference shares with a fixed rate of dividend or debentures that have a fixed rate of interest, which is different from the one employed in the West. This implies that different accounting practices are essential to endogenize their practices based on Islamic principles.

1.2.1.4.2 Disclosure

Financial reporting in an Islamic society shaped by an Islamic moral economy should be more detailed than the one which exists in Western societies. More relevantly, perhaps, there would be more emphasis on transparency and disclosure. This would include disclosure of transactions that are particularly prohibited in the Islamic code, such as *riba* (interest). However, IFIs should not participate in any businesses relating to interest, even at the lower levels of direct measurement (Sulaiman, 2003). Moreover, according to the Islamic system, firms are not just required to illustrate the amount of interest paid, but additionally, a detailed account is likely to be provided to explain the reasons of how this interest occurred and the steps which they have taken to avoid the payment of interest (such as taking a loan from Islamic banks) (Sulaiman, 2003). Hence, different accounting principles are essential to respond to such distinguishable business practice, specifically the necessity of Islamic accounting.

1.2.2 *Gharar and maysir (Uncertainty and gambling)*

Gharar is an Arabic word, which literally means "deception" (Cornell, 2007; Ayub, 2007). In *fiqh*, it is defined as the ambiguity that carries the risk of reduction, uncertainty, and hazard in any commercial trade, or fraud, deceit, or excessive benefit (Al-Dareer, 1997; Obaidullah, 2005). Moreover, scholars have defined the concept of *gharar* as "a trade which is known not to exist or not, whose measure is not known to be large or small, and that is undeliverable" (Al-Dareer, 1997: 10; Zuhayli *et al.*, 2007: 84). Gambling is an example of which the result is hidden. Such a transaction is highly risky and may lead to undesirable consequences and enmity; besides, obtaining something for less or nothing is a type of injustice (Al-Suwailem, 2000: 65).

The *Qur'an* and the *Sunnah* have evidently prohibited all transactions that lead to unfairness in any form to any parties. Unlike *riba*, *gharar* is not strictly prohibited in the *Qur'an*, and there is no such explicit prohibition of *gharar*. However, many verses in the *Qur'an* warn believers to be aware of the ambiguous character of worldly pleasures and not to be deceived by such temptations (e.g., *Qur'an*, 4: 29) (Obaidullah, 2005). The *Sunnah* uses the word more obviously than the *Qur'an*, and there are several *hadiths* of the Prophet prohibiting commercial transactions involving *gharar* (uncertainly), including any type of transaction which is not known to occur, e.g., "birds in the sky" and "fish in the water" or "the catch of the diver", as well as any object that may not yet exist, such as purchasing an "unborn calf in its mother's womb". The rationale for prohibiting such transactions is that the buyer does not know what they are paying for (El-Gamal, 2001, 2006; Obaidullah, 2005).

Al-Dareer (1997: 10) argues that *gharar* could occur in essence or in the terms of a contract, which includes:

> 'two sales in one', 'down-payment (*'arboon)* sale', 'the pebble', 'touch', and 'toss' sales, 'suspended (*mu'allaq*) sale', 'future (*mudhaf*) sale', or it could arise *gharar* in the object of contract which also includes; 'ignorance of the genus', 'ignorance of the species', 'ignorance of the attributes', 'ignorance of the quantity of the object', 'ignorance of the specific identity of the object', 'ignorance of the time of payment in deferred sales', 'inability to deliver the object', 'contracting on a non-existent object', 'not seeing the object'.

Apart from the earlier discussion, contracts involving a risk factor are not always void from an Islamic point of view. For example, profit-and-loss modes of finance, such as *mudarabah* (discussed in the next section), in which one party provides funds and the other invests these funds, including a risk factor, are acceptable and indeed preferable in the Islamic framework. However, it is forbidden to accept unnecessary risk on unpredictable results. Moreover, financial transactions such as options and forward sales are not permitted (except for *salam* sales, discussed later in this chapter). The rationale for the prohibition of *gharar* stems from causing harm to the transaction. For example, consider forward contracts such as currency forward contracts: if the agreed price upon currency rises to the extent that it exceeds the exercise price, the seller will lose, and vice versa, which includes trading of risks and harm. Thus, *gharar* has also been linked to the possible occurrence of asymmetric information between the seller and the buyer, making trade implications unclear to the counterparty (Ali, 2015).

In addition to the ban on (excessive) *gharar*, commercial activities and financial transactions are also subject to additional restraint: the prohibition on *maysir*. *Maysir* is an Arabic word, which means gambling and speculation. Islam does not accept any agreement where financial achievement arises from speculation or chance (Visser, 2009). Muslim scholars see gambling as a zero-sum game. If one party gains, it does so at the expense of the other party, and thus, it does not contribute to a rise in overall welfare (Tag El-Din *et al.*, 2007). Islamic jurists claim that gambling (*maysir*) and uncertainty (*gharar*) are related to each other, as wherever features of *gharar* are presented, the elements of *maysir* are commonly found (IIBI, 2009). Similarly, with regard to *riba* and *gharar*, the *Qur'an* clearly bans *maysir* in several verses (2: 219, 5: 90, 91).

Sharia scholars argued that the contracts of conventional insurance are fundamentally gambling contracts. For instance, when the policyholder aims and hopes to gain more than the amount of premium s/he pays if the incident that has been insured against does not occur, s/he will lose the amount of money paid for the premium. By contrast, if the incident occurs in an earlier stage of the premium and the claim is far higher than the amount paid by the policyholders, the company will be in deficit (IIBI, 1999). The objection is not against the concept of insurance but due to the involvement of *riba* (usury), *maysir* (gambling), and *gharar* (uncertainty). The same applies to financial markets where numerous contracts do not specify the exact nature, date, or value of what is received in exchange (Visser, 2009).

Therefore, it could be argued that in contrast to conventional law, Islamic law prohibits selling commodities that a person does not own at the time of contract, but also these sales are not valid under *Sharia* even if the seller actually has the product in ownership and delivers it to the buyer, given that most of the sales end on liquidating the transaction by the payment of the price differential (Al-Dareer, 1997). It is also worth mentioning that contrary to *mudarabah* and *murabahah*, contracts involving a risk factor, such as insurance, are avoidable from the Islamic point of view.

1.3 Profit–Loss Sharing (PLS) and Risk Sharing and Debt-Based Islamic Finance Instruments and Their Accounting

As previously discussed earlier, receiving a fixed rate or floating payment in addition to accepting specific interest or fees *riba* for loans of money is prohibited by *Sharia*. Thus, taking part in risky economic activity and sharing profit and loss among stakeholders is the fundamental technique to avoid such prohibitions (Hasan, 1985). In other words, profit and loss sharing (PLS) was considered as the Islamic solution and response to principal interest-based banking so as to comply with the prohibition of interest (Tahir, 2007).

In this context, Ayub (2007) argues that to avoid interest, IFIs have to use one of the key instruments as the basis of their intermediary activities. Profit or loss sharing (PLS) arising on investments, earning a return on their trading and leasing activities, is the important axis around which economic and business activities take place (Asutay, 2010; Abdul-Rahman *et al.*, 2014). The Islamic solution of PLS suggests sharing risks and loss/profits equally between the parties participating in a financial transaction (Abdul-Rahman *et al.*, 2014; Asutay, 2015). Furthermore, Siddiqi (1978) argues that the profit and gains on a transaction will be characterized as *riba* (interest) unless there was a risk involved while the transactions were made. Therefore, bankers and investors have to make sure that the profits and returns on the original amount are directly associated with the risk undertaken on the investment.

The majority of Islamic economists state that PLS relies on two primary forms of financing, known as commends (*mudarabah*), when only one partner — the bank — provides the capital, and partnerships (*musharakah*), when both partners contribute the capital (Udovitch, 1970; Ayub, 2007). These were the original equity-based instruments suggested in the Islamic economics literature in order to avoid lending on interest (Chapra, 1992). Ibrahim (2000) and Asutay (2015) also state that *murabahah* (or cost-plus pricing technique) financing is extensively used in the Muslim world, including Islamic banks. Although it is a debt-based instrument, *murabahah* has been widely used by Islamic banks, while the use of *mudarabah* and *musharakah* is limited (Abdul-Rahman *et al.*, 2014; Asutay, 2012; Mergaliev *et al.*, 2021).

The following sections aim to briefly discuss financial instruments.

1.3.1 *Mudarabah (Sharing the profit and losing with venture capital)*

The concept of *mudarabah* has been used broadly as one of the operating principles in Islamic finance for joint business ventures. It is an Arabic term derived from the root verb *darb*, which means to "walk or travel in the land", in the language of Iraq, as in the medieval period, the *darib* had to travel to a land far from his home to undertake risky trading to make profits (Chaudhry, 1999). The word *darb* is used for the same meaning in verses of the *Qur'an*, for instance (4: 101). In addition, the word *almudarabah* (in the language of Iraq) is synonymous with other Arabic terms which are used to designate this contract: *almuqaradah* is derived from the root verb *qirad* (in the language of Hijaz), which means a loan that indicates the surrender of rights over the capital by the owner to the user (Abu Saud, 1976). Al-Zuhaily (2007) claims that while the first name emphasizes that both the capital owner (*rabb ul mal*) and the entrepreneur share profits, the second name highlights that the capitalist provides part of his capital and part of his profit to the entrepreneur. Moreover, the word *mudarabah* has been translated in different ways by various scholars, who have defined it as "trust financing", while others have described it as "'trustee profit sharing', 'equity sharing', a 'sleeping partnership' and 'profit sharing"'(Ahmed, 2010: 115).

In the language of law and business organization, *mudarabah* means a partnership contract, where one partner is the owner (*rabb-ul-mal*) and is eligible to profit on account of his stock (*ras al-mal*). By contrast, the other partner is suitable for a profit on account of his labor because he is given to managing the property (*mudarib*) (Hamid *et al.*, 1993; Bacha, 1997; Kamal *et al.*, 2009; Abdul Rahman, 2010). In other words, it is "cooperation between an investor who gives funds or capital to a party who will manage the fund or capital for trading" (Arshad & Ismail, 2011: 157).

The practice of *mudarabah* is not a new phenomenon; the Prophet Muhammad worked as a *darib* for Khadijah before the message (Chaudhury, 1999). Nevertheless, this type of practice is not mentioned in any verse of the *Qur'an* or the tradition of the Prophet (Chaudhury, 1999). Therefore, it is assumed and more likely that the rules and regulations of this practice were established and developed by his companies and Muslims, in addition to the duties and rights of the *darib* and the *mudarib*, duration of the contract, etc. (Ayub, 2007). Several jurists call *mudarabah* a partnership contract, as both the *mudarib* and *darib* divide the profits; nevertheless, some others call it an agency contract between the principal *mudarib* and the agent *darib* because the entire loss is borne by the principal (Chaudhury, 1999).

A *mudarabah* contract can be conducted between the Islamic banks as a *mudarib* and investment account holders as providers of funds and the Islamic banks. It could also "be determined between the Islamic bank as a provider of funds, on behalf of itself or behalf of investment account holders, and business owners and other craftsmen, including farmers, traders, etc." (AAOIFI, 2003: 87).

There are two types of *mudarabah* contracts, namely, restricted *mudarabah* (*mudarabah muqayyadah*) and unrestricted *mudarabah* (*mudarabah mutlaqah*) (Hamid *et al.*, 1993; Abdul Rahman, 2010). In the restricted contract, the investor specifies a particular business for the manager, who may then invest in that specific business only. Restricted *mudarabah* financing could be used for financing a particular project given to the client. In the unrestricted contract, however, the investor allows the manager to invest in any type of business. For instance, a *mudarabah* contract could be used toward financing a client's working capital requests (Abdul Rahman, 2010; Arshad & Ismail, 2011). "Based on these two types of *mudarabah* contracts, Islamic banks have two types of investment accounts, unrestricted and restricted investment accounts" (AAOIFI, 2003, Para. 11: 27).

In *mudarabah* financing, the bank cannot request a guarantee from the *mudarib* for the repayment of capital because the bank accepts the financial risks. However, some Islamic scholars permit banks to ask for guarantees against the *mudarib's* omission (AAOIFI, 1999: 173). Hence, the capital provider (*rabb-ul-mal*) shares the risks and the profits with the worker (*mudarib*). Profits are shared by the two parties at an agreed ratio. In the *mudarabah* contract, the *mudarib* cannot ask for any monthly salary or payment for the work he has undertaken. In case of loss, *rabb-ul-mal* will be borne and pay all the losses, and the *mudarib* obtains no profit on their work. This means the liability of the *mudarib* is limited to his effort unless because of misbehavior or carelessness concerning the terms and conditions agreed upon by the Islamic bank. In those cases, *mudarib* will be borne and pay the loss (Karim, 1995; AAOIFI, 2003, Para. 9a: 27; Abdul Rahman, 2010).

1.3.1.1 *Accounting treatment of mudarabah investment account*

Financial Accounting Standard No. 6 (FAS 6) published by the Accounting and Auditing Organization for Islamic Financial Institutions (AAOIFI) states that "equity of unrestricted investment account holders shall be presented as an independent category in the statement of financial position of the Islamic bank between liabilities and owners' equity" (AAOIFI, 2003: 206, Para 16).

In line with the above standard, Ibrahim (2007) states that unrestricted investment accounts (URIA) in the form of *mudarabah* should not be determined to be liabilities but a special class of equity in the form of quasi-capital. Whereas, restricted investment accounts are not the assets or liabilities of the bank, although they should be reported off the balance sheet in the funds are collected under *wakala* or restricted *mudarabah*. Karim (2001) defends this by claiming that investment accounts are not a bank liability, which is different from debt instruments since they earn their returns by sharing the profits produced from their funds and tolerate their share when they experience any losses.

Furthermore, Islamic banks do not guarantee the value of these investment accounts. The fact that the *mudarabah* contract is neither debt nor an equity instrument means that it is not an amalgam instrument consisting of debt and equity (Karim, 2001). It has been added that investment account holders should not be observed as a liability, as by the nature of the *mudarabah* contract, they stand to bear all losses, nor are they shareholders because they stand to bear all losses, nor are they shareholders because they would contribute to the profit-sharing of their investment before dividend distributions and are not able to vote. Therefore, leaving out these customers' exposure or reporting them as liabilities would acutely misrepresent the status of these account holders (Sultan, 2006).

1.3.2 *Murabahah (Set profit sale)*

Murabahah is a type of sale that is considered lawful or *Sharia* compliant from the Islamic point of view for the benefit of contractors and the community at large (Thani *et al.*, 2003). Islamic banks extensively use this type of financing for house and motor vehicle financing (Abdul Rahman, 2010).

Linguistically, *murabahah* means "profitable action", in which the Arabic root *r.b.h* is the source of the term *ribah*, which has the literal meaning of profit (Thomas *et al.*, 2005). It is known as "cost-plus financing" or "financing resale of goods", which means it is the sale of goods at cost plus an agreed mark-up (Haniffa & Hudaib, 2002; Dar & Presely, 2000). In the form of *murabahah*, the buyer agrees with the seller on a commodity whose price includes a stated profit known to both seller and purchaser (Thani *et al.*, 2003; Chong & Liu, 2009; Abdul Rahman, 2010).

Murabahah financing is not deliberated either as interest *riba* nor a conventional loan. In a *murabahah* transaction, the intermediary purchases the commodity and sells them to the customer in instalments at a mark-up. This means profit is made in the exchange of money for goods and not money for money (Thani *et al.*, 2003). To be *Sharia* compliant, the sale entity must exist at the time of the sale and the buyer should know the cost (which also includes any other costs incurred by the seller). In addition, the seller should already possess the goods or purchase them (Abdul Rahman, 2010). Furthermore, one of the conditions for the contract's legitimacy is that it should not include any kind of *riba* (Hassanien, 1996: 20).

Murabahah financing has other forms, specifically *bai' muajjal* (credit sale) and *bai' bithaman Ajil* (deferred payment sale) (Abdul Rahman, 2010). *Bai' muajjal* is a shortened form of *bai bithaman ajil* (Obaidullah, 2005: 68; Visser, 2009: 57). The term is a composite of two words, *bai* and *muajjal*, which are derived from the Arabic words *bai* (purchase and sale) and *ajal* (fixed time or fixed period) (Khan & Bhatti, 2008). Thus, *bai' muajjal* can be defined as a financing method used by Islamic banks, which takes the mode of *murabahah muajjal*. Additionally, it is a term that refers to the sale of commodities requested by the client on a postponed payment basis at a price, which includes the bank's mark-up (profit) agreed by both parties in a lump sum or fixed instalments. However, the price cannot be increased in case of default (Sarker, 1995; Ibrahim, 1997; Abdul Rahman, 2010).

The permissibility and legitimacy of a deferred payment financing sale is mentioned in the *Qur'an* (2: 275), "but *Allah* has permitted trade and has forbidden interest". This verse is understood as the price increase in the deferred payment sale is lawful, given that the rise in the deferred sale is part of the price of the product can be esteemed at any price. The increase in loans, however, is prohibited because money can only be evaluated by similarity (Abdul Rahman, 2010). Many Islamic scholars (Mullhem, 1989; Hassanien, 1996) agree with this point of view, arguing that mark-up charged over the original cost is not interest. In contrast, some Islamic scholars (such as Al-Abadi, 1988; Abdullah, 1996; Ahmed & Dzuljastri, 2005) claim that profit degree which is calculated by Islamic banking, have some elements of *riba* and *gharar* similar to that being practiced in conventional banks; therefore, *murabahah* is *non-Shar'ia* compliant (Pisol *et al.*, 2012).

This raises a persuasive argument that if this financing as practiced by Islamic banks is similar in some aspect to a loan provided by a conventional bank, the conventional accounting standards, such as IAS18/IFRS15 and IAS39/IFRS9, which require that the financing charges separated from the profit margin are suitable to account for *murabahah* transactions. However, mark-up charged over the actual cost is not dividable into transaction profits and separate charges from recognition because this could be to treat the recognition capability as a loan and part of the mark-up as interest on this loan. Therefore, IFRS accounting standards require the identification of profit margins and, moreover, that the interest charges are not appropriate from the Islamic point of view (Archer & Karim, 2001).

As a result, the AAOIFI provides FAS 2 for the treatment of *murabahah* and *murabahah* to the purchase orders. To be *Sharia* compliant, AAOIFI adopted the method and recognized the profits at the time of contracting if the sale is cash or on credit not exceeding the current financial period (AAOIFI, 2003: 122, FAS 2, Para. 8). However, profits of credit sale whose payment is due after the recent financial period shall be recognized using one of the following methods:

(i) Proportionate allocation of profits, whether or not cash is received: The AAOIFI preferred and adopted this method for the profits over the period of the credit as the basic treatment (AAOIFI, 2003: 122).
(ii) Cash basis when the instalments are received is allowed as an alternative to recognized profit: Accrued amount of profit which is not yet received is disclosed. The costs of goods sold shall be recognized at the time of concluding the contract (AAOIFI, 2003: 122).

Furthermore, AAOIFI prefers to value assets available for deferred payment sale at the end of the financial period, at their fair value, because these assets are treated as an investment rather than fixed assets. This would assist the institution in recognizing and measuring any unrealized gains and losses arising from the investment (Abdul Rahman, 2010). On the contrary, conventional accounting (IFRS) generally employs historical cost (or lower) to calculate and value assets and liabilities. While the idea of presenting fair value measurements is evident and real, its working is relatively complicated due to its difficulty and as it is hard to verify (Hameed, 2009).

From the earlier discussion, it could be argued that deferment of profit is permissible as long as it is recorded separately as a deferred profit and not as interest. Moreover, IAS18/IFRS15 issued by IFRS is not an appropriate standard to treat this type of financing, given that it recognizes the difference between fair value and the nominal amount of consideration in a sale of goods as interest revenue.

1.3.3 *Musharakah (Partnership)*

The term *musharakah* means sharing. In the context of *Sharia*-compliant financing, Usmani (2002: 1) defines it "as an investment-based technique to joint enterprise in which all the partners share the profit or loss of the joint venture". As in *musharakah*, the company and the client contribute to the capital of the business in variable amounts and agree to share the net profit in proportion to the amounts invested by each (Thani *et al.*, 2003). In Islamic jurisprudence, the term *shirkah* is more common than *musharakah. Shirkah* (partnership) can be translated to mean the "participation of two or more persons in a certain business for sharing profit and loss in a specified proportion" (Siddiqi, 1985: 15).

According to the *Sharia, musharakah* is divided into two broad types. *Shirkat al mulk* (property partnership) is the combined possession by two or more people of a particular asset or assets without its joint mistreatment. For instance, the joint ownership of a house left to the inheritors of a dead person. *Shirkat al aqd* (contractual partnership) is a partnership where the partners share the profit or loss that is an outcome of their endeavor (Usmani, 2002; Thani *et al.*, 2003). *Shrikah al aqd* has three different categories. The first is *shirkat al mal* (finance partnership), where money is the foremost principle of creating the partnership. In Islamic banks, this type of *musharakah* is the obvious method of partnership (Thani *et al.*, 2003). The other two categories are *shirkat al a'mal* and *shirkat al wujooh* (credit partnership); while the partnership in the former is based on the experience or skills of a partner, the latter uses credit alone for the partnership investment (Usmani, 2002; Thani *et al.*, 2003).

The contract of *musharakah* can be discontinued at any time, provided that the partner gives his associate notice to this effect. Concerning this, if the assets of the *musharakah* are in cash, this has to be allocated *pro rata* among all the partners. Otherwise, the partners may find another solution, such as liquidating the assets or allocating them between the partners (Usmani, 2002). The *musharakah* contract can also be terminated in this case if one of the partners dies, becomes insane, or otherwise becomes unable to perform commercial transactions (Usmani, 2002; Abdul Rahman, 2010). According to this discussion, it could be argued that there are at least two types of *musharakah* financing: constant *musharakah* and diminishing *musharakah* (*musharakah mutanaqisah*). The partner's share in the first type remains throughout its period, whereas in the second type, one party has the right to buy a part of the other party's share, which decreases until one becomes the only owner of all the capital (Abdul Rahman, 2010).

Similar to *mudarabah* and *murabahah* financing, *musharakah* is a replacement for interest-based financing with extensive effects on both production and distribution. In *musharakah*, the financier will face losses if the joint venture fails to make a profit, whereas the interest-based loan cannot suffer losses, whether or not they make a profit. The amount of profit to be distributed between the partners has to be arranged at the time of affecting the contract. Otherwise, the contract is not valid from a *Sharia* point of view (Usmani, 2002).

Consequently, the accounting treatments for *musharakah* financing in connection with the measurement of capital in kind and profit recognition is very similar to *mudarabah* financing.

According to the AAOIFI FAS 4:

> The Islamic bank's share in *musharakah* capital (cash or kind) shall be recognized when it is paid to the partner or made available to him on account of *musharakah*. This share shall be presented in the Islamic bank's books under a *musharakah* financing account with (name of client), and it shall be included in the financing statements under the heading "*Musharakah* financing" (AAOIFI, 2003: 168, Para. 3).

The share of the Islamic bank in *musharakah* capital is measured at the end of the financial period at a historical cost (the amount which was paid or at which the asset was valued at the time of contracting) (Abdul Rahman, 2010). In the case of diminishing *musharakah* financing, however, the Islamic bank's share at the end of a financial period is determined at historical cost less the portion transferred to the partner at fair value. Therefore, the variation is recognized as profit (loss) in the income statement (Karim, 1996). Moreover, if the diminishing *musharakah* financing is settled before the bank's share is reassigned to the partner, the recovered amount (by liquidation) from the Islamic bank's share must subsequently be credited to the Islamic bank's *musharakah* financing account. Hence, the profit (loss) from the difference between the book value and the recovered amount must be identified in the Islamic bank's income statement (Abdul Rahman, 2010).

Consequently, it has been argued that FAS 4 (the form of equity or profit-and-loss financial instrument) is comparable to IAS 31 (IFRS11). IAS 31 does not allow the cost method in such cases; however, it allows the equity method. Furthermore, to be *Sharia* compliant, FAS 4 requires that the Islamic bank's share is recognized as receivable, due from the partner and not presented in the partner's capital in the *musharakah* in the case of liquidation or settlement of account the Islamic banks' due share of profit remains unpaid (AAOIFI, 2003: 170, Paras. 14 and 16).

The equity method requires the share of undistributed profits to be integrated into the carrying amount of the investment, which can be split into two components on the balance sheet: the cost element (partner's capital for FAS 4 requirements) and the share of undistributed profits (a *musharakah* account receivable for FAS 4 requirements). Thus, FAS 4 is compatible with IAS31 (Mustafa, 2003: 23). This means harmonizing the IFRS and AAOIFI might be able to be employed in Islamic institutions.

1.3.4 *Ijarah and ijarah wa iqtina (Leasing)*

Ijarah is the Arabic word for leasing contract as well as hiring contract. It is the terminology that denotes the sale or agreement of *manfaah* (usufruct), whereby the lessor (owner) leases out an asset or object to its customer (not the ownership of the equipment itself, that have to remain with the lessor) at an agreed rental fee and predetermined lease period upon the *aqad* (contract) (Thani *et al.*, 2003; Tag El-Din & Abdullah, 2007). Abdul Rahman (2010: 139) has defined *ijarah* "as a process by which the usufruct of a particular property is transferred to another person in exchange for rent claimed from him/her".

Leasing might take the form of an operating lease, where the bank usually owns the asset for renting purposes, and the client asks the bank to rent the asset for a specific period. It may also take the form of a capital lease, which is referred to as *ijarah wa iqtina* or *ijarah muntahia bittamleek*. Under the *Sharia* concept of *ijarah wa iqtina*, the client might ask the bank to purchase a fixed asset, e.g., a machine or building, and then lease the asset for a long-term contract, or the contract can contain a promise of transfer of ownership from the lessor to the lessee (Thani *et al.*, 2003).

Ijarah wa iqtina (*ijarah muntahia bittamleek*) in an Islamic context is different from the leasing concept in conventional finance. The main difference between the two versions is that under *Sharia* compliance, the lessor (*mu'ajir*) undertakes full ownership risks and the maintenance of the corpus of the leased asset unless the damage is caused by the carelessness or the misbehavior of the lessee (*musta'jir*), whereas in a conventional lease, these costs are passed on to the lessee (Kettell, 2011). Furthermore, the IAS 17 classifies the lease "as finance lease if it transfers substantially all the risks and rewards incident to ownership of the asset; otherwise, it would be classified as an operating lease". By contrast, the FAS 8 classifies the lease as operating *ijarah; if* there was no promise, it confirms that a legal title will pass to the lessee. If there is a promise, however, it is *ijarah muntahia bittamleek*, which is still not the same as the element over form regulation as in the IAS 17 (Abdul Rahman, 2010). The FRS 8 also states that the benefits must be *Sharia* compliant since *Sharia* does not authorize *ijarah* to be used in an asset where the interest (*riba*) is involved (Abdul Rahman, 2010; Kettell, 2011).

Accordingly, the FAS 8 issued by the AAOIFI to treat *ijarah* (leasing) differs from the international accounting standard (IAS 17 issued by the IFRS. For example, due to differences in the substance of the contracts between conventional lease and *ijarah*, the returns recognition and the influence of remaining value are different. Therefore, the IAS 17 is a reminder to the lessor to record the uncertainty over the collectability of lease charges income and the future level of interest rates. However, the FRS8 for *ijarah* does not mention the provision of doubtful debt or require any records on interest rate uncertainty.

In *Sharia* law, the rental fee is fixed throughout the ijarah contract and the lessor cannot increase the rent individually (Abdul Rahman, 2010).

From the earlier discussion, it can be understood that leases with *Sharia* compliance operate leases. This is different than the finance lease found in conventional finance; therefore, these differences affect accounting treatments. In the case of *ijarah*, leased assets are presented in the lessor's statement of financial position under investments in *ijarah* assets (AAOIFI, FRS8, Para. 8: 244). In the case of a finance lease, however, the lessee treats the leased asset as its own property (fixed assets) and recognizes the equivalent liability for lease payment, whereas the lessor recognizes an account receivable for the lease payments. Thus, according to this criterion, there is no harmonious existence between IAS 17 and FAS 8. This means all the Islamic institutions applying the IFRS system to treat Islamic financial products may not be *Sharia* compliant.

1.3.5 *Salam financing (Advance purchase)*

A *salam* contract is an alternative method of debt used by Islamic businesses. It is also known as *bai' salaf* or borrowing (Thani *et al.*, 2003). It has been defined as "a contract involving the purchase of a commodity for deferred delivering in exchange for immediate payment according to specified condition" (AAOIFI, 2003: 229; Khaldi & Hamdouni, 2011: 153). The contract, in overall terms, permits an early payment (the price) for the sale of a defined product (the sale object) to be delivered later at a specified time (Al Zaabi, 2010). In Arabic, the term *al-musallim* alludes to the owner of capital or the buyer, the seller or the party who takes on the obligation to deliver the object or goods at a future date called *al-musallam ilayhi*. The term *ras ul mal* refers to the price paid in advance, while the term *musllam fihi* alludes to the purchased commodity or the sale object (Al Zaabi, 2010).

Similar to many other methods of sales, *salam* sale is permitted by the Prophet Muhammad for poor farmers who required money to procure seeds and feed their family until the time of the next harvest by selling their agriculture commodities in advance since Islam has prohibited *riba* (usury) that could occur due to the loans on products or assets which have not yet been produced or manufactured.

This type of sale is also permitted for small entrepreneurs (Taqi Usmani, 2009, cited in Karim, 2010). However, the permission was subjected to some strict conditions. For example, the buyer has to pay the full price to the seller at the time of completing the contract. In addition, the *salam* sale can be only applied to goods that can precisely specify their quantity and quality. Therefore, this type of sale also cannot be particularized to a specific product or on a specific product on the farm. Besides, the buyer and the seller have to clearly agree on the amount of the product as well as the exact place and date of delivery (Taqi Usmani, 2009).

The Islamic bank can use parallel *salam* that permits the bank to purchase a product through a *salam* contract with one client for deferred delivery on one side and as a seller on another side by selling the same product for future delivery on another contract to another customer. This is allowed as long as the two contracts are not legally related or binding; hence, mutual exclusivity is essential. Furthermore, the seller in the first contract cannot be made buyer in the parallel *salam* contract, for the reason that it will be a buy-back contract and therefore not acceptable in the *Sharia* (Kettell, 2011). This discussion came at the same time as a *fatwa* issued by the Sharia Supervisory Board of the *Rajhi* Bank, which permits parallel *salam* as long as the two contracts are not made dependent on each other (AAOIFI, 2003). By contrast, several modern *fuqaha* or scholars have forbidden this type of finance, especially if such business becomes regular for the purpose of trading, which might involve *riba* (AAOIFI, 2003).

As the relationship between depositors and borrowers in conventional finance (interest based) is different from *salam* finance offered by Islamic banks, the accounting treatment in return is different. Therefore, AAOIFI issued the FRS 7 standard, which addresses accounting rules relating to *salam* financing and parallel *salam*. FRS 7 requires Islamic banks to recognize *salam* financing when the capital (cash, kind, or benefit) is paid or when it is made ready to the client (*al-musallam ilayhi*) at the time of contracting the capital measured by the amount paid if it was cash. Otherwise, it will be measured at the fair value agreed between the parties. In the case of receiving a different quality of a commodity or with different market value, the differences shall be recognized as profit or loss. However, if the *salam* contract is partly or completely canceled and the client could not repay the capital of *salam*, the amount is recognized as a receivable due from the client. All these transactions must be recorded in the financial statement under the heading of *salam* financing (AAOIFI, 2003: 223–224).

In the case of parallel *salam*, the Islamic back recognizes the transactions after they receive the capital of *salam* (in cash, kind, or benefit). Therefore, these transactions must appear in the Islamic bank's statement as a liability under the heading parallel *salam* (AAOIFI, 2003: 223).

As discussed above, *bai' salam* is an alternative technique to loan with interest or borrowing in conventional finance. The IASB has issued IAS 23 for borrowing costs, such as interest on short- and long-term borrowings and other costs sustained for borrowing funds. Borrowing costs shall be identified as an expense in the period in which they are sustained; while concerning the benchmark treatment, borrowing costs are recognized as an expense in the period in which they are acquired, irrespective of how the borrowings are utilized (Mirza & Holt, 2011). In the case of FRS 7 issued by the AAOIFI (2003), when the client fails to deliver the products on time and the delivery date is extended, the book value of *al-musalam fihi* shall remain -135- as it is. However, in the case of borrowing costs, there will be an increase in the interest. Because this standard treats borrowing costs with interest, it is not appropriate for treating *salam* financing, which means that the AAOIFI standards are required in Islamic institutions to treat such business.

1.3.6 *Istisna'a (Contract of manufacture)*

Istisna'a means a sale on order, a type of *bai' muajjal* used to finance work-in-progress inventories in manufacturing or construction. It is defined as "a contract to purchase now, for a definite price, something that may be manufactured or constructed later according to agreed specifications. The object of *istisna'a* is not often available nowadays, although it will be made later by the manufacturer or contractor" (Zarqa, 1997: 68). In other words, the purchaser asks the seller to supply a specific product for an agreed price and payment method. The conditions of validity for the *istisna'a* are that the price and future delivery date are fixed with the parties' consent and that the necessary specification of type, quality, and quantity of the commodity (intended to be manufactured) is fully settled between them (Usmani, 2002).

Istisna'a or commissioned manufacturing is quite similar to *salam* (discussed above) in the method of selling something that is not owned or under the seller's control at the time of the sale and thus make it a lawful sale according to *Sharia* compliance. Moreover, both *istisna'a* and *salam* can be used in a parallel method. This means the bank (financier) might involve a forward contract, such as selling the goods to a third party on the spot payment, to avoid the risk emerging from the price of the goods. Similar to *salam,* the contract must be legally independent of the original contract (AAOIFI, 2003).

Conversely, there are several differences between them. While *istisna'a* is a contract of sale of a commodity, which always needs manufacturing, *salam* is the deferred sale of goods that do not involve manufacturing. In the case of *salam,* the contract cannot be canceled individually, whereas, in *istisna'a,* the contract can be canceled as long as the manufacturer has not started the work. Furthermore, in the case of *salam,* the contract has more restrictions on the payment, which must be paid in full, and the time of delivery has to be identified at the time of the contract. However, in the case of *istisna'a,* the payment and delivery time can be delayed as it is not necessary for it to be fixed (Usmani, 2002; Thani *et al.*, 2003).

It is believed that *istisna'a* used by Islamic banks is different from the investment finance form, which is used in conventional institutions; thus, the AAOIFI issued FAS 10 to address the accounting rules of *istisna'a* and parallel *istisna'a.* Islamic banks as sellers would measure and recognize the costs revenues from *istisna'a* and parallel *istisna'a.* Costs experienced during a financial period and the pre-contract costs in an *istisna'a* working-in-progress account or *istisna'a* cost account in the case of parallel *istisna'a* and reported under assets in the statement of financial position of Islamic banks (AAOIFI, 2003). Under the IAS 39, assets categorized as loans or receivables are determined at their remunerated costs using an efficient interest rate to consider the time value of the money. On the contrary, an *istisna'a* finance receivable would be valued at a historical cost under FAS 10 of the AAOIFI (Tayyebi & Hijazi, 2010).

1.3.7 *Zakat*

The fundamental principles of *zakat* and how they can affect the structure and mechanisms of accounting are discussed above. This section, however, focuses on the significant differences between *zakat* and conventional taxation and their accounting treatment.

Zakat is financial worship and is one of the pillars of Islam; hence, payment of *zakat* is indispensable in fulfilling this obligation. Furthermore, it is considered to be a significant solution to the social and economic problems in the world, primarily poverty, as the social aim of *zakat* is to act as a mechanism for the distribution of wealth among the poor or to be spent by the state for the welfare of the needy and helpless, to reduce the economic gap between the poor and the rich (Yusoff, 2006; Adnan & Abu Bakar, 2009; Abdul Rahman, 2010). This philosophy is different from the conventional taxation system imposed by the government according to the tax law that might be subjected to modifications due to changes in government or the economic climate.

Furthermore, conventional taxation is based on economic factors and ignores religious and ethical values, such as submission to God, seeking the pleasure of God and accountability to Him, and believing in the hereafter (Abdul Rahman, 2010). As a result, Muslims would be more unlikely to cheat on *zakat*, seeing as it is a spiritual duty they have to account for in the hereafter, although a Muslim might still cheat on tax (Adnan & Gaffikin, 1997). Tax and *zakat* are different in their rules and in the causes for which they are spent. Thus, payment of tax does not rule out the obligation of *zakat*, while tax is not deducted from the amount of *zakat* due, where as if tax is due before the time of determining *zakat*, it is deducted prior to arriving at the *zakat* base, as it represents a liability (account payable) (AAOIFI, 2003: 288).

The importance of *zakat* in Islam could be judged from the fact that it is considered an essential part of financial responsibility and an instrument of fiscal policy for an Islamic state. This gives *zakat* an indispensable role in the Islamic macroeconomic system if there is a robust foundational system for collecting *zakat* (Chaudhry, 1999; Quraishi, 1999). In this context, Tahir (1998) studies the relationship between *zakat* through an Islamic macroeconomic model by concentrating on determining aggregate output and the degree of variations in an Islamic economy. He concludes that the aggregate output is influenced by autonomous expenditures, income distribution, and *zakat* flows (Yusoff, 2006).

Zakat payment can be individual, which means the owners who are accountable for defining the amount that has to be paid out as *zakat* or in relation to a business is judged to be a separate legal entity, it would be required to gratify the obligation to pay *zakat* itself, either as an entity or on behalf of its owners (Sulaiman, 2003). Hence, it has been claimed that one of the main aims of accounting in an Islamic society is to provide information to enable individuals and legal companies to determine their *zakat* liability to achieve socio-economic justice. This information will also allow customers to guarantee that their Islamic organizations operate within Islamic restrictions (Gambling & Karim, 1991). For example, FRS 9.3 requires the Islamic bank to disclose all the information related to the *zakat,* as a holding company pays its *zakat* from its subsidiaries, and whether or not it accumulates and pays *zakat* on behalf of holders of investment accounts and other accounts (AAOIFI, 2007, FRS9; Paras. 13, 18). The standard also requires the Islamic bank to treat *zakat* in the financial statement as a non-operating expense and be included as a deduction from net income. In the case of unpaid *zakat,* it should be treated as a liability of the Islamic bank and presented in the liabilities section (AAOIFI, 2007, FRS9; Para. 9). Moreover, (FAS9; Para. 15, 18) required the banks to state in their financial statement to have full disclosure in the following cases:

(i) "Whether or not the Islamic bank as a holding company pays its share of zakat obligations in its subsidiaries" (Para. 15).
(ii) "Whether or not the Islamic bank collects and pays zakat on behalf of holders of investment accounts and other accounts" (Para. 18).

According to the earlier discussion, it could be argued that Islamic accounting is required to report or disclose any *zakat* collection and distribution activities as well as *zakat* calculation and measurement. Fairness of values is required in Islamic accounting to ensure that no group is disadvantaged by its rightful share of wealth. Thus, the valuation of *zakat* needs to be based on current market value, although Adnan and Gaffikin (1997) state that historical cost and periodicity concepts are likely to be used for calculating zakat. Their justification for this was that Islamic accounting might have a strong realization principle with assets being carried at historical cost until used or sold (Napier & Haniffa, 2011). However, the valuation of stocks at the lower end of cost (IAS 2) and net achievable value is definitely not acceptable from an Islamic point of view, given that it leads to lower profits (in times of rising prices) and, therefore, *zakat* being undervalued. This leads to a reduction of the rights of *zakat* beneficiaries. Furthermore, in some cases, current valuations of items, such as goodwill and brands are not predictable, which may, in turn, lead to over-valuation of shares in the past and end up defrauding outsiders. Hence, the continued use of a historical cost model may result in negative wealth transfer effects (Hameed, 2000).

The FRS 9 on the valuation of trading assets makes it clear that "trading assets should be valued for *zakat* purposes at their market selling price (cash equivalent value), and not at a historical cost. This is for the *zakat* base to include the historical cost and any holding gains (losses)" (AAOIFI, 2003: 289). This rule is irrelevant to the IFRS rules and practices. Consequently, most of the asset information contained in traditional Western balance sheets valued at a lower cost is inconsistent with Islamic law (Abdul Rahman, 2010). In addition, Islamic analysis emphasizes productive assets, while the traditional Western balance sheet incorporates provisions for deferred tax assets, capitalized expenses, goodwill on consolidation, etc. The compulsory information for appropriate determination of the amount of *zakat* places exceptional demands on accounting information systems, demands that cannot be ascertained in Western accounting reporting standards (IFRS) (Gambling & Karim, 1986).

According to the earlier discussion, it can be concluded that the continued use of IFRS alone in the Islamic institution may result in a negative impact on Islamic compliance because it seems very likely indeed that IFRS may fail to cover all the accounting needs for Islamic banks, such as *zakat* determination and calculation. Thus, due to *Sharia* compliance issues, IFRS cannot be followed in full. This means a capable accounting system for appropriately calculating and disclosing the amount of *zakat* payable is imperative (Hameed, 2000; Taheri, 2000).

1.4 Practice of Islamic Accounting and Accounting Standards

Despite discussion on the rationale of Islamic accounting through Islamic ontology and historical knowledge and practice, nowadays, the majority of countries in the world, including Muslim countries where most IFIs operate, are increasingly moving toward adoption of or convergence with IFRS developed by the IASB, with Western culture in mind, to report on financial performance and position by both public and private companies. For the reason that IFRS remain the only globally recognized set of financial reporting standards and is the responsibility of all publicly listed companies in Europe. The approval of Islamic accounting standards by IFIs may affect their ability to register in major capital markets, such as in the European Union, in addition to being queried by investors if financial statements are arranged using accounting standards other than IFRS. Thus, to remain part of the global financial system and be competitive, they feel obliged by definition to follow IFRS.

Consequently, most of the IFIs demonstrate their financial statements by employing a framework and certain globally acceptable standards, which are trustworthy, which therefore means that the performance of entities can be more easily compared. However, as previously discussed in this chapter, several Islamic financial instruments and religio-financial instruments, such as *zakat*, *murabahah*, *mudarabah*, and *musharakah*, need special treatments that are not adequately covered by IFRS. Thus, it is necessary that they account and present their financial statements in accordance with the form of *Sharia* rules by adopting the AAOIFI standards. This section presents some examples on the subject of accounting practices in different Islamic banks operating in different countries.

Numerous studies have compared the differences between the practice of Islamic banks in some Islamic countries and the standards recommended by the AAOIFI in accounting treatment for Islamic instruments. For example, Karim (2001) and Sarea (2012) argue that majority of Islamic banks treat investment accounts as *mudarabah* contract in terms of liabilities and report them on balance sheets. Karim (2001) states that the justification for Islamic banks to treat investment accounts as a liability item is that investment accounts are similar to deposits in a commercial bank. However, "[s]uch a justification is not entirely unfounded" (Karim, 2001: 184). Other banks, accordingly, have treated investment accounts on the balance sheet, as they reported them as part of equity and classified these accounts as participating shares or what is known as class "B" shares. (Karim, 2001). He added that this treatment is similar to deposits in commercial banks, as the laws that govern some of these banks were adopted from commercial banking perspectives that operate in these countries (Karim, 2001). Conversely, some banks have treated investment accounts as "fiduciary" investments and, accordingly, they report them as off-balance sheet items. The reason behind treating investment accounts as an off-balance sheet item is because the nature of these accounts is similar to funds under management (Karim, 2001; Sarea, 2012). This accounting treatment is in line with IAS 30, which argues that banks perform as trustees and in other fiduciary capacities, which result in the holding or placing of assets on behalf of individuals, trusts, retirement benefit plans, and other institutions; subsequently, these assets are not the assets of the bank and, therefore, are not included in its balance sheets (IAS 30, Para. 55).

Karim (2001) provides an example from the Faysal Islamic Bank of Bahrain (FIBB). He argues that during 1995, 1996, and 1997, the PWC auditing agency used IAS to issue financial statements for FIBB, and they treated URIAs to the off-balance sheet. However, this was rejected by the Capital Intelligence rating agency that rates and ranks several Islamic banks worldwide when it was rating and qualifying the FIBB in December 1996. The agent required the FIBB to transfer URIAs that treated off-balance sheet to the balance sheet. This is in line with the recommendation of AAOIFI's Islamic Financial Accounting Standard (IFAS) No. 1 that treats URIAs on the balance sheet) on the bank's liquidity and capital adequacy ratios (Karim, 2001).

Capital Intelligence (1998, cited in Karim, 2001: 178) argues that using the AAOIFI standards by FIBB to present the supplementary information allows a client to produce a more accurate picture of the financial health of FIBB. For example

> ... under the new accounting treatment (including unrestricted investment accounts on balance sheet), profitability ratios such as return on average assets become more meaningful (2.06% as opposed to 6.4% using IAS). Thus in analysing the composition

> of FIBB's asset structure, we have assumed unrestricted investments to be part of the Bank's balance sheet since they have a direct effect on the Bank's liquidity and profitability and give a more accurate reflection of the magnitude of business operations (Capital Intelligence, 1998; cited in Karim, 2001: 178).

Moreover, according to Tag El-Din and Abdullah (2007), the current accounting treatment of *ijarah wa iqtina* or *ijarah muntahia bittamleek* (Islamic hire purchase) in Malaysia is based on IAS hire-purchase standards. Nevertheless, it is different from the hire-purchase method employed by conventional financial institutions. This is because there is no *Sharia* law evident that regulates the process of Islamic hire purchase exactly; therefore, in Malaysia, any institution offering this facility tends to impose its own rules based on the *Sharia* principle and in the spirit of the Hire Purchase Act 1967 and Contract Act 1950 (Tag El-Din and Abdullah, 2007). Conversely, in a double banking system, it is evident that Islamic hire purchase is confronted by similar challenges in adjusting to the conventional system which has been in place for a lengthy period of time, as several conventional practices are in conflict with the principles *of Sharia*, which means that these aspects are unacceptable. As a result, promoting harmonization between conventional and Islamic regulations might be the most appropriate solution to avoid the redundancy of laws in the Islamic banking system.

On critically reflecting, it should be stated that it is essential to have industry standards as developed by AAOIFI and IFSB, which aim to develop a robust Islamic finance industry. These institutions have *Sharia* boards, and their standards are the product of a robust *Sharia* compliance process. However, at the end of the day, these standards aim to locate Islamic financial institutions and their operation in the market system and logic (Rundnyckyj, 2014). In other words, the standards have endogenized market logic into Islamic finance by instrumentalizing Islamic ethics (Sencal & Asutay, 2019). Thus, with the language of Portes (2010), Islamic logic is grafted by market logic to produce a hybrid identity rather than sustaining authentic Islamic identity or Islamic logic (Asutay, 2012, 2013, 2018a). Portes (2010) explains the emergence of institutions and practices through organic emergence, where they are the product of the value system and normative articulation of the value system of a respective society. However, with the imposition of neoliberal values in the world, every society was faced with the reality of market logic and its institutions in an imposed manner, as happened in the Muslim societies on top of colonialization and Westernization processes (Asutay, 2018b). Thus, economic, financial, accounting, and management institutions and practices in the Muslim countries have been developed by Western and hence market logic.

The emergence of the Islamic economic movement led to a search for authenticity in the Muslim world *vis-à-vis* economy and finance (Warde, 2000; Asutay, 2007), which represents to develop a counter-hegemony in an aspirational sense. However, in its current practice, the operational nature of Islamic finance demonstrates a convergence to conventional economy and finance by mimicking its theories and practices (*see*: El-Gamal, 2006; Asutay, 2007, 2012, 2018a, 2018b; Khan, 2010). The result has been a grafting process as Islamic ethics and morality is instrumentalized for market outcomes as expected by market logic, while Islamic logic is relegated to interest-free nature by ignoring Islamic consequences or substantive morality as identified by *maqasid al-Sharia* (Asutay & Yilmaz, 2018). Consequently, while the imagination was organic emergence, the outcome has been hybridity through the grafting of market logic into Islamic logic through essentializing form at the expense of substance (Zaman & Asutay, 2009; Asutay, 2012, 2013, 2018a, 2018b). Islamic accounting, hence, can be instrumental in overcoming the observed convergence by identifying the authentic process toward organic emergence, which can also help AAOIFI and IFSB to move beyond form-oriented standards into substance and authenticity through Islamic logic.

1.5 Conclusion

This chapter has explored the Islamic financial principles and how these principles are different from conventional practices and financial modes and instruments affecting the existence of Islamic accounting practices. For example, it is argued that PLS-type instruments, namely *mudarabah and musharakah*, as well as debt-based products, such as *murababah*, would affect accounting practice in Islamic banks as they need special treatment to be *Sharia* compliant; otherwise, it is sensible to assume the adoption of IAS. Nevertheless, as discussed in this chapter, Islamic principles influence the view of transactions in Islamic banks, which in turn can reflect on the form of accounting practice and regulation. This can be seen clearly from the comparison between AAOIFI's accounting standards to treat Islamic financial instruments and IAS that some Islamic banks are applying to treat those instruments.

It is interesting to note that there has been disagreement between Islamic banks on whether to treat investment accounts on the balance sheet and report them as part of equity (according to IFS 1) or to treat investment accounts as "fiduciary" investments and report them as off-balance sheet items (according to IAS 30). The example of the FIBB bank changing the accounting treatment from IAS to the AAOIFI standards made profitability ratios, such as the return on average assets, more meaningful. In addition, treating URIAs on balance sheets would provide a more precise image of the degree of business operations.

References

AAOIFI (2007). *Accounting Auditing and Governance Standards for Islamic Financial Institutions.* Manama Bahrain: AAOIFI.

Abdul Rahman, A. R. (2010). *Introduction to Islamic Accounting Theory and Practice.* Kuala Lumpur: Cert Publication.

Abdul-Rahman, A., Radziah, A. L., Muda, R., & Abdullah, A. (2014). Failure and potential of profit-loss sharing contracts: A perspective of New Institutional, Economic (NIE) Theory. *Pacific-Basin Finance Journal, 28*, 136–151.

Abdullah, S. (1996). *Islamic Banking and Interest.* New York: E.J. Brill.

Abu Saud, M. (1976). Money, interest and qard, studies in Islamic economics. In Ahmad K. (Ed.), *Studies in Islamic Economics.* Leicester: The Islamic Foundation UK.

Adnan, M. & Abu Bakar, N. (2009). Accounting treatment for corporate zakat: A critical review. *International Journal of Islamic and Middle Eastern Finance and Management, 2*(1), 32–45.

Adnan, M. & Gaffikin, M. (1997). *The Shari'ah, Islamic Banks and Accounting Concepts and Practices: The Accounting, Commerce and Finance. The Islamic Perspective International Conference.* Macarthur: University of Western Sydney.

Ahamed, K. M. & Dzuljastri, A. R. (2005). Islamic home financing through Musharakah Mutanaqisah and al-Bai Bithaman Ajil contracts: Comparative analysis. *Journal of The International Association for Islamic Economics, 9*(2), 7–14.

Ahmed, A. U. F. (2010). *Developments in Islamic Banking Practice: The Experience of Bangladesh.* Florida: Boca Raton.

Ahmed, E. A. (1994). Accounting postulates and principles from an Islamic perspective. *Review of Islamic Economics, 3*(2).

Ahmed, Z. (1992). The theory of Riba. In*An Introduction to Islamic Finance.* Sheikh Ghazali, Syed Omar, Adit Ghazali (Eds.), Kuala Lumpur: Quill Publishers.

Al-Abadi, A. (1988). A comprehensive view of murabaha to purchase. *Paper presented at the Fifth Islamic Fiqh Academy Conference*, Jeddah.

Al-Dhareer, S. (1997). Al-Gharar in contracts and its effects on contemporary transactions. Eminent scholars' lecture series No.16, Islamic Research and Training Institute. Islamic Development Bank. Jeddah. Accessed 5 May 2013. http://www.irtipms.org/PubAllE.asp.

Al-Suwailem, S. (2000). Towards an objectives measure of Gharar in exchange. *Islamic Economic Studies, 7*(1), 61–102.

Al Zaabi, O. S. (2010). Salam contract in Islamic law: A survey, *Review of Islamic Economics, 14*(2).

Ali, A. J. (2015). *Handbook of Research on Islamic Business Ethics.* Cheltenham: Edward Elgar Publishing Limited.

Archer, S. & Karim, R. (2001). Presuppositions behind accounting standards and the issue of economic reality: The case of islamic financial instruments. *Paper Prepared for the EIASM Workshop on Accounting and Regulation*, Siena.

Ariff, M. & Iqbal, M. (2011). Introduction to Islamic financial institutions. In M. Ariff & M. Iqbal (Eds.), *The Foundations of Islamic Banking: Theory, Practice and Education.* Cheltenham, UK: Edward Elgar.

Arshad, N. & Ismail, A. (2011). Regulation on the paramaterized of mudharabah contract: A critical analysis. *Islamic Economics and Finance Research Centre, School of Economics Universiti Kebangsaan Malaysia, 2*(3), 157–189.

Asutay, M. (2007). Conceptualisation of the second best solution in overcoming the social failure of Islamic banking and finance: Examining the overpowering of homoislamicus by homoeconomicus. *IIUM Journal of Economics and Management, 15*(2), 167–195.

Asutay, M. (2010). Islamic banking and finance and its role in the GCC-EU relationship: Principles, developments and the bridge role of Islamic finance. In C. Koch & L. Stenberg (Eds.), *The EU and the GCC: Challenges and Prospects under the Swedish EU Presidency.* Dubai: Gulf Research Centre.

Asutay, M. (2012). Conceptualising and locating the social failure of Islamic finance: Aspirations of Islamic moral economy vs. the realities of Islamic finance. *Journal of Asian and African Area Studies, 11*(2), 93–113.

Asutay, M. (2013). Islamic moral economy as the foundation of Islamic finance. In V. Cattelan. (Ed.), *Islamic Finance in Europe: Towards a Plural Financial System*. Cheltenham: Edward Elgar.

Asutay, M. (2015). Islamic finance: Principles, institutions and development. *Trade and Finance*, Winter, 4–26.

Asutay, M. (2018a). *An Introduction to Moral Economy and Rationalizing Islamic Moral Economy*. Working Paper, Durham Centre for Islamic Economics and Finance.

Asutay, M. (2018b). *Islamic Political Economy/Moral Economy: Rationale, Foundations and Philosophy*. Working Paper, Durham Centre for Islamic Economics and Finance.

Asutay, M. & Yilmaz, I. (2018). Re-embedding Maqasid al-Shari'ah in the essential methodology of Islamic economics. In Mohamed El-Tahir El-Mesawi (Ed.). *Maqasid Al-Shari'ah: Explorations and Implications*. Kuala Lumpur: Islamic Book Trust.

Ayub, M. (2007). *Understanding Islamic Finance*. Hoboken, New Jersey: John Wiley and Sons.

Bacha, O. I. (1997). Adapting *Mudarabah* (profit sharing) financing to contemporary realities: A proposed financing structure. Accessed 10 September, 2012. https://mpra.ub.uni-muenchen.de/12732/1/Adapting_Mudarabah2.pdf.

Billah, M. M. (2019). *Islamic Financial Products Principles, Instruments*. New York: Palgrave.

Capital Intelligence, (1998). *Rating Report*. Faysal Islamic Bank of Bahrain EC.

Chapra, M. U. (1984). The nature of riba in Islam. *Hamdard Islamicus 7*(1), 3–24.

Chapra, M. U. (1992). *Islam and the Economic Challenge*. Leicester: The Islamic Foundation.

Chapra, M. U. (2006). The Nature of *Riba* in Islam. *The Journal of Islamic Economics and Finance, Bangladesh, 2*(1).

Chaudhry, M. (1999). *Fundamentals of Islamic Economic System*. 1st edn. Pakistan: Burhan Education and Welfare Trust.

Chong, B. S. & Liu, M. H (2009). Islamic banking: Interest-free or interest based? *Pacific-Basin Finance Journal, 17*(1), 125–144.

Cornell, V. J. (2007). *Voice of Islam*. USA: Praeger Publishers.

Dar, H. A. & J. R. Presley (2000). Lack of profit loss sharing in Islamic finance: Management and control imbalances. *International Journal of Islamic Financial Services, 2*(2), 1–16.

El-Ashker, A. (1987). *The Islamic Business Enterprise*. London: Croom Helm Ltd.

El-Gamal, M. A. (2001). *An Economic Explication of the Prohibition of Gharar in Classical Islamic Jurisprudence*, First Version.

El-Gamal, M. A. (2006). *Islamic Finance: Law, Economics and Practice.* Cambridge: Cambridge University Press.

Gambling, T. E. & Abdel-Karim, R. A. (1986). Islam and social accounting. *Journal of Business Finance and Accounting, 13*(1), 39–50.

Gambling, T. E. & Abdel-Karim, R. A. (1991). *Business and Accounting Ethics in Islam.* London: Mansell Publishing Limited.

Hameed, S. (2000). *The Need for Islamic Accounting: Perception of its Objectives and Characteristics by Malaysia Accountants and Academics.* Ph.D. Thesis, University of Dundee.

Hameed, S. (2009). *IFRS vs AAOIFI: The Clash of Standards?* https://core.ac.uk/download/pdf/7296862.pdf.

Hamid, S., Craig, R., & Clarke, F. (1993). Religion: A confounding cultural element in the international harmonization of accounting? *ABACUS, 29*(2), 131–148.

Haniffa, R. M. & Hudaib, M. A. (2002). A theoretical framework for the development of the Islamic perspective of accounting. *Accounting, Commerce and Finance: The Islamic Perspective Journal, 6*(1/2), 1–47.

Hasan, Z. (1985). Determination of profit and loss sharing ratios in interest-free business finance. *Journal of Research in Islamic Economics, 3*(1), 13–29.

Hassanien, F. (1996). *Murabaha Sale in Islamic Banks.* Cairo: The International Institute of Islamic Thoughts.

Ibrahim, A. (1997). Legal framework of Islamic banking. *Undang: IKIM Law Journal, 1*(1), 1–29.

Ibrahim, S. H. (2007). IFRS Vs AAOIFI: The clash of standards? Accessed 11 August, 2012. http://mpra.ub.unimuenchen.de/12539/1/The_Clash_of_Standards_international_accountant_article.pdf.

Ibrahim, W. (2000). *Islamic Finance in the Global Economy.* Edinburgh: Edinburg University Press.

IIBI (1999). Islamic Insurance (Takaful), *Institution of Islamic Banking and Insurance.* Accessed 9 July, 2013. Islamic Insurance (Takaful) — islamic-banking.com.

IIBI (2009). Islamic economics order. *Institution of Islamic Banking and Insurance.* Accessed 9 July, 2013. http://www.islamicbanking.com/prohibition_of_gharar_masir_riba.aspx.

Kamal, A. A., Fahmy, E. Y., & Kashoogie, J. (2009). Islamic finance: Debt versus equity financing in the light of *Maqasid al-Shariah.* Accessed 15 July, 2013. http://mpra.ub.uni-muenchen.de/20722.

Karim, R. A. A (1995). The nature and rationale of a conceptual framework for financial reporting by Islamic banks. *Accounting and Business Research, 25*(100), 285–300.

Karim, R. A. A. (1996). The impact of the Basle capital adequacy ratio regulation on the financial and marketing strategies of Islamic banks. *International Journal of Bank Marketing*, *14*(7), 32–44.

Karim, R. A. A. (1999). Islamic finance and standardisation of accounting for Islamic financial institutions. *New Horizon*, (93), 5–7.

Karim, R. A. A. (2001). International accounting harmonization, banking regulation, and Islamic banks. *International Journal of Accounting*, *36*(2), 169–193.

Karim, W. J. (2010). The economic crisis, capitalism and Islam: The making of a new economic order? *Globalization*, *7*(1–2), 105–125.

Kettell, B. (2011). *The Islamic Banking and Finance Workbook: Step-by-Step Exercises to Help you Master the Fundamentals of Islamic Banking*. UK: John Wiley and Sons.

Khaldi, K. & Hamdouni, A. (2011). Islamic financial intermediation: Equity, efficiency and risk. *International Research Journal of Finance and Economics*, *65*, 145–160.

Khan, F. (2010). How 'Islamic' is Islamic banking? *Journal of Economic Behavior & Organization*, *76*, 805–820.

Khan, M. M. & Bahtti M. I. (2008). Development in Islamic banking: A financial risk-allocation approach. *The Journal of Risk Finance*, *9*(1), 40–51.

Mergaliev, A., Asutay, M., Avdukic, A., & Karbhari, Y. (2021). Higher ethical objective (*Maqasid al-Shari'ah*) augmented framework for Islamic banks: Assessing the ethical performance and exploring its determinants. *Journal of Business Ethics*, *170*(4), 797–834.

Mirza, A. A. & Holt, G. H. (2011). *Practical Implementation Guide and Workbook for IFRS*. (3rd edn.) Hoboken: John Wiley and Sons Inc.

Mohsin, M. (1992). Assessment of corporate securities in terms of Islamic investment requirements. In S. G. S, Abod, S. O. S, Agil, & A. Ghazali (Eds.), *An Introduction to Islamic Finance*. Kuala Lumpur: Quill Publishers.

Mullhem, A. (1989). *Murabaha Sale and its Applications in Islamic Banks*. Amman: Al-Risalah Al-Haditha.

Mustafa, B. G. (2003). *The Implementation of Accounting Standards for Islamic Banks: A Study of Preparer's and Auditor's Opinions in Sudan*. Guildford: University of Surrey.

Napier, C. & Haniffa, J. R. (2011). *Islamic Accounting: Elgar Miniseries*. Cheltenham, UK: Edward Elgar.

Obaidullah, M. (2005).*Islamic Financial Services*. Saudi Arabia: Scientific Publishing Centre, King Abdulaziz University.

Pisol, M. I., Asmak, A. R., Hezlina. M. H., & Abd Mutalib, B. E. (2012). Shariah views on the components of profit rate in Al-Murabahah asset financing in Malaysian Islamic bank. *International Journal of Social, Education, Economics and Management Engineering, 6*(7), 290–295.

Portes, A. (2010). *Economic Sociology: A Systemic Inquiry.* Princeton: Princeton University Press.

Quraishi, M. A. (1999). *The Institution of Zakat and its Impact on Society, Islamic Finance.* Accessed 12 January 2013. http://ifp.law.harvard.edu/login/contact.

Rundnyckyj, D. (2014). Economy in practice: Islamic finance and the problem of market reason. *American Ethnologist, 41*, 110–127.

Sahih Al-Bukhari. *Sale and Trade* Vol. 3, Book 34, Number 382.

Sahih Al-Bukhari. *Punishment of Disbelievers at War with Allah and His Apostle*, Vol. 8, Book 82, Number 840.

Sahih Muslim. *Pilgrimage* (*Kitab Al–Hajj*). Book 7, Number 2803.

Sahih Muslim. *The Book of Faith Book, Emaan Ka Bayan* Book 1(1). 161.

Sahih Muslim. *The Book of Transactions* (*Kitab Al-Buyu'*). Number 3853–3854.

Sahih Muslim. He (The holy prophet) cursed the one who accepts interest and the one who pays It, Vol. 10, Book 24, Number 3881.

Saleh, N. A. (1992). *Unlawful Gain and Legitimate Profit in Islamic Law.* (2nd edn.) London: Graham and Trotman.

Sarea, A. M. (2012). The level of compliance with AAOIFI accounting standards: Evidence from bahrain. *International Management Review, 8*(2), 27–32.

Sarker, A. A. (1995). Islamic financial instruments: Definitions and types. *Review of Islamic Economics, 4*(1), 1–16.

Sencal, H. & Asutay, M. (2019). The emergence of new Islamic economic and business moralities. *Thunderbird International Business Review, 61*(5), 765–775.

Siddiqi, M. N. (1978). *Some Aspects of the Islamic Economy.* (2nd edn.) Pakistan: Islamic Publications, Ltd.

Siddiqi, M. N. (1985). *Partnership and Profit-sharing in Islamic Law.* Leicester: The Islamic Foundation.

Sulaiman, M. (1997). *Testing a Theory of Islamic Corporate Reporting: The Case of Malaysia*, PhD Thesis, University of Otago, Dunedin, New Zealand.

Sulaiman, M. (2003). The influence of *riba* and *zakat* on Islamic accounting. *Indonesian Management and Accounting Review, 2*(2), 149–167.

Sultan, M. S. A. (2006). An overview of accounting standards for Islamic financial institutions. *Finance Bulletin.*

Tag El-Din, S. & Abdullah, I. N. (2007). Issues of implementing Islamic hire-purchase in dual banking system: Malaysian experience. *Thunderbird International Business Review, 49*(2), 225–249.

Tag El-Din, S. & Irwani, A. N. (2007). Issues of implementing Islamic hire-purchase in dual banking system: Malaysian experience. *Thunderbird International Business Review*, *49*(2), 225–249.

Taheri, M. R. (2000). The basic principles of Islamic economy and their effects on accounting standard-setting. Accessed 18 November, 2013.

Tahir, S. (1998). Macroeconomic theorizing from Islamic perspective. In Kahf, (Ed.), *Lessons in Islamic Economics*, Vol. 1, pp. 301–310.

Tahir, S. (2007). Unresolved issues in Islamic banking and finance: Deposit mobilization. Fundamentals and contemporary issues. *Islamic Research and Training Institute of Islamic Development Bank*, *47*.

Taqi Usmani, M. (2009). Forward sales and manufacturing contracts: Salam and istisna. Accessed 18 November, 2015. http://www.albalagh.net/Islamic_economics/salam_istisna.shtml.

Tayyebi, A. & Hijazi, S. (2010). Harmonising financial reporting of Islamic finance. *ACCA and KPMG*, 1–24.

Thani, N. N. Abdullah, M. R. M., & Hassan, M. H. (2003). *Law and Practice of Islamic Banking and Finance*. Petaling Jaya: Thomson Sweet and Maxwell Asia.

Thomas, A. S. (2005). *Interest in Islamic Economics: Understanding Riba*. London: Routledge.

Thomas, A. S. Cox. S., & Kraty, B. (2005). *Structuring Islamic Finance Transactions*. London: Euo-money Books.

Udovitch, A. L. (1970). *Partnership and Profit in Medieval Islam*. New Jersey: Princeton University Press.

Usmani, M. T. (2002). *An Introduction to Islamic Finance*. Netherlands: Kluwer Law International.

Visser, H. (2009). *Islamic Finance: Principles and Practice*. UK: Edward Elgar Publishing Limited.

Warde, I. (2000). *Islamic Finance in the Global Economy*. Edinburgh: Edinburgh University Press.

Yusoff, M. B. (2006). Fiscal policy in an Islamic economy and the role of zakat. *IIUM Journal of Economics and Management*, *14*(2), 117–145.

Zaman, N. & Asutay, M. (2009). Divergence between aspirations and realities of Islamic economics: A political economy approach to bridging the divide. *IIUM Journal of Economics and Management*, *17*(1), 73–96.

Zarqa, M. (1997). Istisna financing of infrastructure projects. *Islamic Economic Studies*, *4*, 67–74.

Zuhayli, W., El-Gamal, M. A., & Eissa, M. S. (2007). *Financial Transactions in Islamic Jurisprudence*. Syria: Dar al-Fikr, pp. 353–366.

https://doi.org/10.1142/9781800612426_0002

Chapter 2

The Impact of Islamic Worldview on Shaping the Accounting System: An Islamic Moral Economy and Historical Exploration in Rationalizing Islamic Accounting

Mahmoud Ali Aleraig and Mehmet Asutay

Abstract

The emergence of the Islamic economics movement in the post-colonial period aimed at developing a system of Islamic economy with the normative worldview of Islam and *Sharia* rules. This is rationalized on the grounds that economics, finance, management, and accounting are not value free as assumed by conventional thinking, which is imposed on the rest of the world as the truth by the West. In this authentic search, Islamic finance proved to be a successful proposition, and therefore, the trajectory of development has been unprecedented, which is constituted through the *Sharia* compliance process. However, in order to develop a system understanding, the governance, management, and accounting of the Islamic financing institutions should reflect the same worldview and the value system. As the literature indicates, research, practice, and institutional formation have been scarce in these areas. This is due to the subaltern assumption that these areas are value free. Accepting such an operating assumption has resulted in asymmetry in the knowledge base and operation of Islamic banks and financial institutions. While their financing operations are constituted in *Sharia*-compliant manner, their management and accounting are left to the conventional system.

However, Islam, through its value system and worldview (*tawhid*), has implications for accounting too. This chapter, therefore, aims to identify the ontological and epistemological construct of Islamic accounting through its value system and worldview to overcome the observed asymmetry through social constructivism. In doing so, historical contribution of Muslim scholars and practice within the Islamic realm is used to bring historical evidence for the proposition developed in this study. Thus, this study argues that Islamic accounting is a subdiscipline of the system of Islamic economics or Islamic moral economy and essentializes it through Islamic normativeness, which urges the use of Islamic accounting, beyond the standards of Accounting and Auditing Organization for Islamic Financial Institutions, to establish consistency within the Islamic finance sector.

Keywords: Islamic Moral Economy, Islamic Accounting, Accounting and Auditing Organization for Islamic Financial Institutions.

2.1 Introduction

Cultural environment is a system that combines several factors such as language, law, morals, attitudes, values, and religion. Thus, there is a growing tendency in the international accounting literature that one of the most effective factors that influence the practices of accounting systems worldwide is cultural environments. Consequently, the influence of culture on accounting systems has been explored within the field of international accounting in recent years, which has recognized that the disparate cultural values found worldwide can impact the application of uniform and universal accounting practices.

Religion as one of the cultural environment factors has also been noted to have had a profound influence on accounting values across the world. This means Islam, as a religion, with its emphasis on non-separation between sacred and secular aspects of life, is not an exception. Therefore, it can also have a powerful and effective impact upon national accounting systems, which needs to be taken into account by organizations concerning national accounting practices, as the discussion on the effect of religion on accounting practices evidences.

Reflecting on the emergence of accounting issues in Islamic financial institutions (IFIs), several scholars of Islamic accounting have suggested that the primary objectives of IFRS no longer satisfy the requirements of IFIs. Therefore, an alternative "Islamic accounting system" that assists Muslims is required to evaluate their own accountabilities to God by providing stakeholders with applicable information on an institution, by which they would be able to make sure that the institution is constantly operating within the frame of Islamic rules (*Sharia*) and moral norms. Suchan's argument rationalizes the need for specialized and perhaps culturally defined institutions. In the case of IBF, this led to the creation of AAOIFI (2017).

The literature on accounting from an Islamic perspective and accounting in Islamic banks has increased over the last three decades with the development of the IBF industry. However, their accounting system is based on conventional system alongside the standards developed by AAOIFI and IFSB. This results in an asymmetry as the financing operations of IBFI is *Sharia* compliant, while their accounting system, management, and governance are based on conventional system. This asymmetry should be overcome and this is the aim of constructing an Islamic accounting system by means of the Islamic moral economy through essentializing the axiomatic foundation of Islam, which can generate an authentic accounting philosophy and practice.

This chapter, hence, addresses and reviews the literature concerning the religious reasons behind existing Islamic accounting in the form of Islamic moral economy and therefore will rationalize the necessity of Islamic accounting through Islamic normative principles by referring to the ontology and epistemological construct of Islamic accounting through Islamic value system and worldview. In doing so, historical contribution of Muslim scholars and practice within the Islamic realm is used to bring historical evidence for the proposition developed in this study. Thus, this study argues that Islamic accounting is a subdiscipline of the system of Islamic economics or Islamic moral economy and essentializes it through Islamic normativeness, which urges the use of Islamic accounting, beyond AAIOFI standards, to establish consistency within the Islamic finance sector. Finally, the objectives and characteristics of Islamic accounting are discussed. The conclusion and a summary are provided in the last section.

2.2 Religion as a Deterministic Factor of Accounting with Special Reference to Islam

Religion is considered an essential factor determining individual behavioral norms and impacts organizational and institutional goals and behaviors, transcending national borders. It is argued that religion, which is defined by a set of beliefs, is recognized to be an essential factor influencing all social institutions and influences the way also, for example, how business is conducted and recorded. Thus, religion can also influence and determine accounting systems (Belkaoui, 1990; Gambling, 1987; Tomas, 1989; Briston & El-Ashker, 1986).

While some argue that religion is part and parcel of culture, reflecting on Muslim perceptions, others state that religion is the very spirit and core of culture (Faruqi, 1989). In terms of their consequences for culture, there are three different general groups of world religions, with a concept that is related to cross cultures, international faiths, and moreover, local religions which are related to a particular culture or particular national religious groups and new religious activities that are related to recently improved faiths (Graham, 2000).

Numerous definitions have been proposed by theoreticians; however, in general, religion is a complex term to define (Acquaviva, 1979). This is because the terms of religion and culture can be similar in the way they are articulated and embedded in everyday life. They are easy to employ in normal discourse though complex to provide an exact definition for (Dow, 2006).

It has been argued that the term "religion" is derived from a similar root as the term "ligament" that links muscles to bones. Thus, the meaning of the root term is "to link, to relate to each other, altogether". As a result, it can be argued that the exact meaning of "religion" is "continuously tying it all together" (Aleyomi, 2012: 130). If we use this idea, then "religion" can be defined as Gibran (1952) did in *The Prophet*. In the book, the main character, a sage, was asked for his final advice on some issues such as love, marriage, giving, pleasure, and sorrow, and some other matters before his departure. Responding to the definition of religion, the sage in *The Prophet* says, "Have I spoken this day of aught else? Is not religion all deeds and all reflection...? Or to phrase it less poetically, all actions and all thought" (Gibran, 2004: 43). This implies an encompassing definition of religion through embeddedness.

Swenson (2009: 8) defined religion in concepts of the sacred by arguing that "religion is the individual and social experience of the sacred that is manifested in mythologies, ritual, ethos, and integrated into a collective or organization". Additionally, in the concept of the spiritual and the scared, another definition of religion is provided by Jaja and Badey (2011: 4), arguing that "religion originates in an attempt to represent and order beliefs, feelings, imaginings and actions that arise in response to direct experience of the sacred and the spiritual". Furthermore, Geertz (1973) states that the term religion is occasionally used as an alternative together with "belief system" or "faith"; however, religion is unlike faith in that it has a public characteristic. He defines religion as a cultural system by claiming that (Geertz, 1973: 90) "a religion is a system of symbols which acts to establish powerful, pervasive, and long lasting moods and motivations in men by formulating conceptions of a general order of existence and clothing these conceptions with such an aura of factuality that the moods and motivations seem uniquely realistic".

It should be noted that since the 1970s, culture and hence religious values have been recognized to impact everyday business and commerce. The emergence of cross-cultural management and later Islamic finance and management clearly vindicates the role played by religion in finance, business, and management alongside culture. Accounting, indeed, could not be kept away from such a transformation in our understanding of religious impact. After years of holding the opinion that culture has a direct impact on accounting environments, in recent years, the investigation moved toward understanding the relationship between accounting and religion and the possible impact of the latter on the former (Gambling, 1987; Hamid *et al.*, 1993; Clarke *et al.*, 1996; Gambling & Abdel-Karim, 1986; Gambling & Abdel-Karim, 1993). However, Jaggi (1975) was at least one of the first to acknowledge and suggest this relationship by claiming that religion, considered as one of the main cultural elements, could influence accounting practices and, in turn, financial disclosure systems (Askary, 2001).

Violet (1983a) also discusses the influence of culture and religion in the process of developing IAS from a different angle. He states that accounting is a product "of its culture". He added this idea or statement is true with religion by claiming that "... the religion of a society incorporates the philosophical beliefs and very often the legal statues of the society... " (Violet, 1983a: 3). Due to the positive relationship between culture, accounting, and religion, Violet (1983a: 9) argues that "since accounting is culturally determined, other cultural customs, beliefs and institution influences it".

Accordingly, religion could be wisely considered one of the general frameworks of the cultural ethics of a society. According to this statement, it has been argued that using Hofstede and Gray's model is a significant approach to investigating the relationship between religion and accounting. Furthermore, following the discussion in the previous section that referred to the models proposed by Hofstede and Gray, religion was seen as one of the cultural factors that have a possible influence on accounting practices in societies (Askary, 2001). Therefore, it is not a surprise to argue that Islamic finance, which is based on *Sharia*, influences the implication of IFRS in the IFIs and makes it invalid for reporting Islamic finance transactions.

Hofstede (1980) and Gray (1988) presented religion as an organizational factor with equivalent standards with other fundamental general social substructures. They argue that as long as social morals and organizational factors, including religion, directly influence the management, and legal, political, and education systems, etc., those social values will, in turn, impact the accounting practices and morals driving it.

Gray (1988) has linked his conceptualization of accounting values to Hofstede's cultural hypothesis by a model seen in Figure 2.1 to explain the link between social and accounting morals and accounting systems. Subsequently, he splits the authority and implementation of accounting systems from the disclosure and measurement matters of accounting practices (Gray, 1988). It is stated by Baydoun and Willett (1995) that Gray associates the two former factors to the accounting's cultural morals of uniformity and professionalism. Accordingly, it could be argued that, depending on Hofstede's approach to cultural morals, religion will influence accounting practices through the techniques organizations have designed and the procedures that they apply. For instance, the value of conservatism will affect assets' measurement and profits. In contrast, the nature

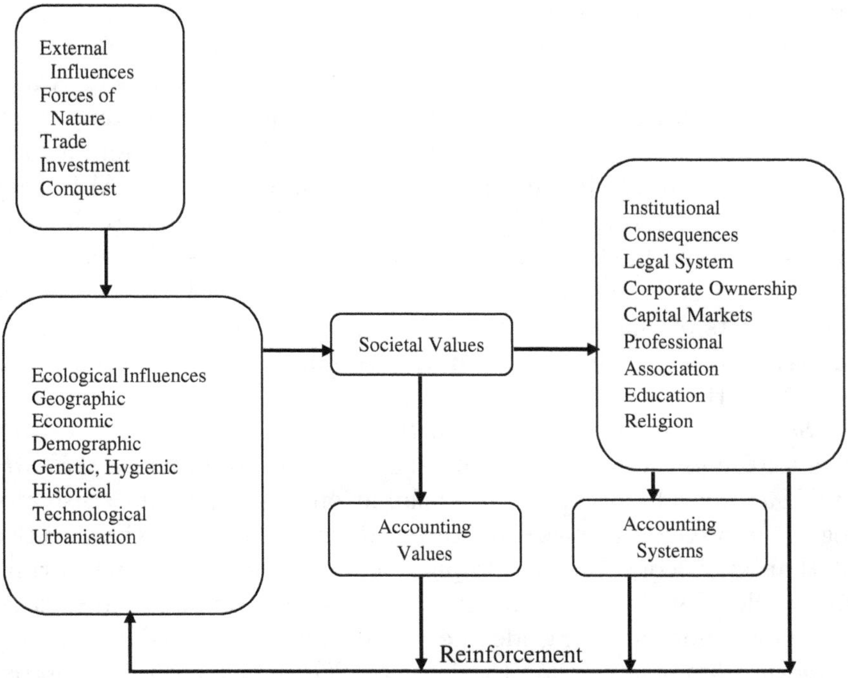

Figure 2.1. Culture, societal values, and the accounting subculture reinforcement.
Source: Gray (1988: 7).

and extent of disclosure practices would be affected by the value of secrecy (Sulaiman & Willett, 2003).

In the debate related to the impact of religion, Islam is a particular case in point. According to the Islamic perspective, religion is defined as "a system of beliefs and worships which includes a code of ethics and a philosophy of life with the worship of One God as its central theme" (Ahmed, 1995: Section 1). Thus, it is simply defined as a way of life (Hamid, 2004). It should be noted that semantically, Islam means "peace" and "submission". It is a strongly monotheistic religion that emerged through the divine revelations sent to the Prophet Muhammad approximately 1,500 years ago (Hamid *et al.*, 1993; Abdul Rahman, 2010). Having implications on everyday practices of life, Islam also aims to shape and structure the behavioral and contractual norms between the faithful and between Muslims and non-Muslims through the principles of *Sharia* (Islamic regulation), which originated from the *Qur'an* and other sources, depending upon one's Muslim sect, and the community and the environment. Karim (1995) and Baydoun and Willett (2000) argue that in comparison to accounting practices in Western societies, Islam suggests a form of social accountability instead of private accountability. Al-Buraey (1990) argues that as a religion, Islam is considered a comprehensive social code for life, emphasizing the responsibilities of people in a society but not the individual's rights. In addition, in Islam, *Sharia* law consists of Islam's central expression (Esposito, 1991). Williams (1994) claims that Islam is mainly a moral religion concerned with doing the right things.

Sharia is a code of law taken from the *Qur'an* as well as from the teachings and examples of the Prophet Mohammed (*Hadith* and *Sunnah*). In other words, Islamic ontology and its epistemological expression is based on revealed knowledge and the practice of that knowledge by the Prophet of Islam, which as the normative worldview aims to shape individual, organizational, and societal behavioral norms. Alongside the moral dimension of Islam, namely *maqasid al-Sharia* or the objectives of *Sharia* (which is interpreted as the well-being of humans and other stakeholders), *Sharia* is a set of divine values, commands, advice, and general principles, including the rules of all aspects of a Muslim's life as well as being foundations for all Islamic institutions (Sulaiman & Willett, 2003). This differs from the existing conventional system-based Enlightenment ontology in which fundamental business ethics flow from codes established and required by specialized governments (Baydoun & Willett, 2000).

Gambling and Karim (1986) explain that beyond the ontological differences, in terms of the operational side, three *Sharia* instructions set Islamic financial transactions apart from the conventional system. First is a strict ban on interest or *riba* or interest along to avoid *gharar* that fundamentally means extreme risk-taking and uncertainty (Asutay, 2015). Second, prohibition of involvement in immoral trades or sin industries such as alcohol, gambling, pork trading, and other economic activities considered harmful to humans (Ayub, 2007; Asutay, 2015; Billah, 2019), as *Sharia* is interpreted as "well-being of humans and other stakeholders" (Asutay, 2018). In addition, Islamic principles encourage profit–loss-sharing financing and risk-sharing over debt-based financing (Asutay, 2007b, 2012, 2015).

It should be noted that considerable attention has been devoted to the *Qur'an* and the *Hadith* (sayings) and *Sunnah* (actions) of Prophet Mohammed for the prohibition of interest and debt (*riba*). For example, the *Qur'anic* verse (3: 130) states that "O you, who have believed, do not consume usury, doubled and multiplied, but fear *Allah* that you may be successful". Furthermore, it was mentioned in another verse that "*Allah* has permitted trade and has forbidden interest" (*Qur'an,* 2: 275). In actualizing this, the Prophet Muhammad said in his farewell sermon in 10 Dul-hajj, 10 Hijra or 523 AD:

> God has forbidden you to take *riba* therefore all *riba* obligations shall henceforth be waived. Your capital, however, is yours to keep. You will neither inflict nor suffer inequity. God has judged that there shall be no *riba* and that all the *riba* due to "Abbas ibn" Abd al Muttalib shall henceforth be waived (Islamica, 2009: 2).

Ribawi or interest-based transactions are unlawful transactions in Islamic financing law. The literal meaning of *al-riba* is interest and linguistically has the meaning "to rise" and "to add-on" (Ayub, 2007; Billah, 2019). In *Sharia*, however, *riba* is a concept of a transaction between two parties exchanging the same kind of commodity, and in paying back, the creditor receives extra from the debtor of what the former gave without involving any investment risk for the lending party (Razi, 2008). Islamic normativeness suggests that it is immoral for the creditor to have a fixed and certain return while the creditor experiences unguaranteed and changing returns. In general, *Sharia* prohibits all detrimental or harmful products that are prohibited in Islamic law, which means the preferred stock is also unlawful (Baydoun & Willett, 2000).

As argued before, the Islamic ethical system aims to regulate every aspect of life and finance and accounting. To understand and contextualize the Islamic accounting position, Table 2.1 summarizes some significant variances between financial accounting systems in the West and Islamic systems.

Another aspect of Islamic accounting objectives that needs to be dealt with in the context of its effect on the accounting system is mandatory social responsibility, such as the case with *zakat.*

Table 2.1. Key differences between Western financial accounting systems and the Islamic system.

Characteristics	Western financial accounting system	Islamic corporate reports
Philosophical viewpoint	Economic rationalism	Unity of God or *tawhid*
Principles	Secular; individualistic; profit maximization; survival of fittest process	Religious; communal; reasonable profit; equity; environment
Criteria	Based upon modern commercial law; limited disclosure; personal accountability	Based upon ethical law originating in the *Qur'an*; full disclosure; public accountability

Source: Baydoun and Willett (2000: 82).

According to Haqiqi and Pomeranz (1987) and Abdul Rahman (2010), *zakat* is the fourth essential pillar of Islam for those obliged to pay *zakat*. In the literal sense, *zakat* has the meaning of "purifying", which means the purification of a Muslim's wealth and soul to return the right of society to society in the form of wealth distribution. "Wealth purification implies the enlistment of assets for the determination of financial growth and justified distribution, whilst purification of the soul means freedom from hatred, jealousy, selfishness, nervousness and greed" (Siddiqi, 1982: 8). Thus, it has more significant effects than just paying a tax (Haqiqi & Pomeranz, 1987).

Zakat is a legitimate religious alms that all adult Muslims have to pay as long as their wealth exceeds a particular threshold (*nisab*) (Qardawi, 1999; El-Ashker, 1987; Kuanova *et al.*, 2021). Clarke *et al.* (1996) argue that in the West, tax is considered as an evil that all people attempt to avoid by asking their accountants to find a way to reduce tax without cheating the system or breaking the law, whereas paying *zakat* is an act of worshipping *Allah* and an essential religious duty that devout people compete to pay.

It should be noted that *zakat* is paid on gold, silver, livestock, the net balance that is not used for a whole lunar year, business inventories, and profits at 2.5%; although in the case of the agricultural output of staple food crops, it is 5% or 10% depending on whether the land is watered naturally or otherwise (Qardawi, 1999; Mohamad

Ibrahim, 2000). However, it is not always easy to calculate the correct amount of *zakat* since there are some obligations that have to be considered before paying. For example, *zakat* is only required for those of legal age and have the wealth that exceeds the *nisab* for one year or more. The mentioned obligations are characterized into two comprehensive groups: *zakat* performer and *zakat* asset (Gambling & Karim, 1986; Clarke *et al.*, 1996).

According to Clarke *et al.* (1996), the majority of the asset information enclosed in a conventional balance sheet does not comply with Islamic law. For example, they use the current market value as an estimate for calculating *zakat,* whereas IFRS value the inventories at the lowest cost or market value, which is normally net achievable value. In practice, this law often has consequences in "cost" being the valuation of the balance sheet. This cannot be applicable to calculate *zakat* as the evaluation should be the selling price only. Thus, this means the evaluation that IFRS is using does not comply with *Sharia*; therefore, it cannot be followed by devout Muslims.

According to the discussion earlier, it could be argued that Islam's prohibition of interest and its own authentic Islamic financial instruments and *zakat* might possibly have an impact on the system and the structure of accounting in the Islamic world and therefore obstruct the international harmonization and the use of the IFRS in the IFIs because interest calculations are an essential element of the accounting standards in the West (Shaari *et al.*, 1993).

2.3 Defining Islamic Accounting

Prior to delving further, it may be necessary to provide a brief definition of "Islamic accounting". The term accounting in Islam has many implications according to the situation it is used in. Arabic dictionaries refer to "counting and recording financial actions and transactions" while also referring to the accountability and responsibility of the individual or by others. The term account (*hisab* in Arabic) is used in the *Qur'an* in its general meaning, in relation to somebody's responsibility to account to *Allah* on all matters relating to human effort (Lewis, 2001). The word *hisab* is derived from the root $h - s - b$. With regard to this, 9 forms occur 109 times in the *Qur'an* (Badawi & Abdelhaleem, 2008), and moreover, the term *hisab* is repeated over 80 times in various verses of the *Qur'an* (Askary & Clarke, 1997). The basic meaning of *hisab* is reckoning, accounting, calculation, and judgment, which is clearly indicated in the *Qur'an* (e.g., 4:86; 14: 41). As can be perceived, these are mainly spiritually orientated definitions.

The term *hisab* can also mean reward and retribution or adjectively according to several *Qur'anic* verses (3: 27; 78: 27, and 78: 35), it can also mean sufficient, fitting, and occasionally plenty.

Hasib (accountant) is another form derived from the root $h-s-b$, which is mentioned twice in the *Qur'an* (21: 47). *Hasib* basically means "one who reckons" or "one who works out an account" (Badawi & Abdelhaleem, 2008). The *Qur'an* required Muslims to keep records of their debt and to confirm just and fair financial transactions between people (2: 282). It should be understood that this specific verse explained the following accountancy terms: "'debt', 'debt quantity', 'debt', 'debt writer', 'fair in writing', 'dictator', 'special cases', 'witnesses', 'writing aim', 'exceptions' and 'neutrality'" (Kantakji, 2003: 3). Therefore, it is substantiated that Islam has provided the main principles and guidelines for how people can record and report their transactions (Lewis, 2001). Therefore, it could be argued that the Islamic *Sharia* was the first to create financial systems not only to record transactions but also to make it a religiously prescribed duty similar to *ibadah* or "worshipping". Hence, such systems with material and spiritual methods are different from conventional ones (Kantakji, 2003).

According to Napier (2006, 2009), the concept of "Islamic accounting" could have historical and geographical implications. In other words, it may be considered as Islamic accounting due to the fact that a particular accounting system prevails in one specific part of the Muslim world (Napier, 2009). However, beyond such a pragmatist understanding, Islamic accounting "can also be understood in a religious sense and used as a tool, which enables Muslims to evaluate their own accountabilities to God" (Napier, 2009: 123). Thus, Islamic accounting in a field of practice and study is related to such a definition, as Islamic principles and moral economy help socially construct such an accounting system as in the case of Islamic banking and finance.

In this context, Triyuwono (2004) defines Islamic accounting (*Sharia* accounting) as a science or a process of accounting that functions as a medium for providing information and fulfilling accountability to awaken users' consciousness regarding God. However, in a financial context, accounting was defined as a practice that provides applicable information to shareholders regarding an institution that would allow them to make sure that the organization always operates in accordance with Islamic *Sharia* rules (Hameed, 2000). He also defined it as a significant language, and to be specific, it is used as a tool by IFIs and banks to monitor and achieve their objectives, which are considered to be different to the objectives of conventional entities and will make decisions in a manner consistent with Islamic morals to achieve *maqasid al-Sharia* (Hameed *et al.*, 2005).

2.4 The Rationale for Islamic Accounting: An Islamic Moral Economy Approach

A number of scholars of Islamic accounting have provided arguments regarding the effect of the Islamic religion on accounting practices (e.g., Hamid *et al.*, 1993; Baydoun & Willett, 1997, 2000; Sulaiman, 2000; Lewis, 2001). Such arguments took place in both normative and practical Islamic banking transactions through which they argued for a significant relationship between Islam and accounting. In line with this argument, Hofstede (1980) also ascertained that religion in Islamic societies considerably affects the way accounting is practiced. Therefore, a different set of standards may efficiently serve institutions and organizations, such as Islamic banks.

The rationale for distinguishing Islamic accounting practices and values from conventional ones is the same ontological rationale that resulted in the emergence of IFIs in the first place (Tag El-Din, 2004). Thus, the growing industry in IFIs is considered an important element that necessitates an alternative Islamic accounting system. In other words, due to the unique needs of the IFIs, the IFRS do not satisfy these needs in their financial reporting (Tag El-Din, 2004). In line with this argument, Ibrahim (2007: 2) claims that "the Islamic financial industry needs a corresponding alternative set of accounting standards which can at best be harmonized, not standardized due to the different nature and activities of the Islamic banks and financial institutions".

The main issue of his statement is that the Islamic economic system and the operations and mechanisms of IFIs differ from the mechanisms and the system of capitalism and socialism that underlies current IFRS. In addition to the ontological and ideological difference, the objectives of conventional accounting differ from the objectives of Islamic accounting; while the former is based on a "decision usefulness framework", the latter is based on accountability within a *Sharia* compliance framework (Ibrahim, 2007). In other words, Islamic accounting complies with the objectives of financial accounting by providing "useful information to users of these reports" to "enable them to make "legitimate decisions" in their dealings with Islamic banks, as opposed to buying, selling or holding decisions to increase their wealth" (AAOIFI, 2010: SFA 1). In addition, according to Sarea and Hanefah (2013: 70), one of the main objectives of financial accounting for IFIs with regard to accountability with the *Sharia* compliance framework is to "determine the rights and obligations of all interested parties, including those rights and obligations resulting from incomplete transactions and other events, in accordance with the principles of Islamic *Sharia* and its concepts of fairness, charity and compliance with Islamic business values". Ibrahim (2007) has related the variations in and gaps between the two accounting systems to the difference in nature and structural objectives of the IFIs economic system and the capitalist system.

Besides the differences and changes in the business environments, the prohibition of interest in Islam, and the use of alternative financial transactions, is another factor that has an effect on accounting, as these alternative transactions undertaken by Islamic entities are not covered in conventional accounting standards. Moreover, the functions and contracts applied by IFIs are not the same as those applied by ordinary banks taking an interest in loans. In order to avoid receiving or paying interest, Islamic banks across the world use different contracts, for instance, a *mudarabah* contract or an agency contract, which is allowed to earn profit in Islam. In the case of a *mudarabah* contract, the bank would manage the investment of others (as a *mudarib*) and receive a percentage of the returns as long as there is a profit. Nevertheless, the bank receives no reward for its effort if there is a loss, and these losses are allocated by the provider of funds or *rabb al-mal.* On the other hand, in the case of an agency contract, the bank receives a reward concerning either profit or loss. The reward could be a lump sum or a percentage of the invested amount (Ibrahim, 2007). Such a transactional nature is considered to be best served with a particular accounting system.

According to the earlier discussion, the prohibition of interest in financial transactions is one of the main reasons that require establishing an accounting system, which might efficiently serve the Islamic environment. In addition, there are several other factors and exceptional details that rationalize the formation of an Islamic accounting system. However, to develop a particular accounting system that significantly satisfies the specific requirements of the Islamic environment, it is crucial to understand the Islamic worldview.

Muslims undoubtedly believe that Islam provides a comprehensive way of life that is beyond a belief system. They also think that the Islamic worldview and its articulations, such as Islamic jurisprudence, is universal for all humankind, perfect and comprehensive for all things and affairs, permanent for all times, and indivisible and inseparable, as supported by one *Qur'anic* verse, which states, "We have neglected nothing in the book" (*Qur'an*, 6: 38).

In terms of the ontological position and defining and shaping humans' relationship with God in a profound manner, Islam regulates economic, social, and political affairs in mundane spaces. The *Qur'an* (the holy words of God) and *Hadith* and *Sunnah* (the Prophet Mohammed's sayings and deeds) are the primary sources of Islamic *Sharia* or the Islamic worldview and its articulations. These two sources are the only ontological and epistemological sources of Islam, which aim to provide meaning to social reality in everyday life, regardless of the profane or mundane. In the hierarchical order of knowledge, these two sources are also supplemented by the *ijma'*, precisely the third source of *Sharia* or the consensus of Islamic scholars on issues not discussed explicitly in the *Qur'an* and *Sunnah* (Abdul Rahman, 2010). This characterizes the Islamic law of social behavior that controls all matters concerned with Muslims' lives. Islam as a whole system thus consists of a set of sub-systems which integrate and act together to achieve individuals' spiritual and secular satisfaction.

The Islamic economic system is a subsystem of the Islamic order (As-Sadr, 1984; Sadr *et al.*, 2020; Al Jarhi, 2021). Islam encourages commerce and trade but requires that any transaction should be conducted in accordance with *Sharia*, or Islamic law, which prohibits — among other things — transactions involving *riba* (interest), unlawful and speculative trade, *gharar* (uncertainty), and *maysir* (gambling) and also requires Muslims to pay *zakat* or give alms (Billah, 2019). Thus, several positive and negative measures relating to the economy are directly mentioned in the *Qur'an* (Asutay, 2013), such as the prohibition of *riba*, "*Allah* has permitted trading and forbidden *riba* (usury)" (*Qur'an*, 2: 275–276).

Compared to individualistic behavioral norms, the Islamic worldview also essentializes social responsibility, as the "rights of society should be returned to society" as in the case of *zakat* payments from one's own wealth (Asutay, 2007a). The Islamic worldview essentializes that everything belongs to *Allah* and that people are trustees and temporary users of what has been given to them, as *amanah* or trust by *Allah* (Sadr *et al.*, 2020; Abdul Rahman, 2010). If, therefore, business activities are performed with obedience to the commands of *Allah* and the Islamic code of behavior, then these activities can also be considered as part of *ibadah* (Ahmad, 1988). Therefore, Islamic economics is defined as "the knowledge and application of injunctions and the rules of *Sharia* that prevent injustice in the acquisition and disposal of material resources, in order to provide satisfaction to human beings and enable them to perform their obligations to Allah and society" (Hasanuzzaman, 1984: 52).

The question of how the Islamic worldview would affect the choice of particular accounting and reporting policies in everyday life is an important one, although the effect of religion has rarely been investigated at an organizational level. The Islamic worldview incorporates both *al-dunya* (the worldly aspects) and *al-akhirah* (the religious aspects), in which the former aspect has to be connected in a profound and devoted manner to the latter aspect, with the *al-akhirah* having the final and ultimate importance (Abdul Rahman, 2010) in terms of human salvation. Specifically, it means that while we are performing our *ibadah*, including *muamalat* (transactions), we also must do the best in our work in this world without indicating any intention of ignoring or being forgetful of the *dunya* aspect (Abdul Rahman, 2010). The fourth *Khalifah* Ali Ibn Abi Talib (600–661) (the Son-in-law of the Prophet Muhammad *pbuh*) highlights this by stating, "Do for this life as if you live forever, do for the afterlife as if you die tomorrow". As stated by this quotation as well, Islam does not prohibit human beings from pursuing happiness in this world, but it is not determined on material wealth only or only in connection with happiness in this world. In fact, Islam calls for a balance between life in this world and the hereafter, as *falah* or the welfare concept in Islam (Kuran, 1995; Asutay, 2012). Chapra (1992) argues that economic and indeed accounting practices are considerably affected by the holistic approach to life, which encourage Muslims to have a balance in satisfying both the material and spiritual needs of all human beings, *as falah* is defined as a tangible quality to seek and achieve the pleasure of God (Siddiqi, 1972).

In the Islamic worldview, the objective function of individuals in whatever they are undertaking is expressed as *falah*, precisely salvation in this world and the hereafter. Thus, accounting is immediately part and parcel of individual objective function through *falah*, as the consequences of this life are received in the hereafter through an evolutionary process by God. However, individual-level *falah* or accounting-cum-salvation is not enough for *falah* to be actualized, which has to be substantiated with *ihsan* as a social capital; to be precise, "beneficence" (Asutay, 2012; Zaman & Asutay, 2009). In other words, to reach *falah*, each individual is expected to conduct *ihsan* in the sense of contributing to the *falah* of the fellow individuals (Asutay, 2007b, 2018; Zaman & Asutay, 2009). Thus, *ihsan* becomes an important "constituent" and "substance" of the *falah* process at an individual and social level (Asutay, 2018). The *Qur'an* mentions the term *falah* or its derivatives in 40 distinctive places. A perusal of these verses guides us to define the forms of *falah* at different levels, such as the spiritual, cultural, economic, and political levels (Khan, 1984).

In the context of the economy, to achieve *falah*, all economic activities in Islam, such as trade, business, buying, and selling, are part of religious services called *ibadah-muamalah*, which aims to assist individuals in reaching *falah* (Nasution, 2009). It has also been argued that if any economic decisions, including financial reporting regarding economic activities in any society, are made especially in Islamic society, then Islam should have a direct influence upon the accounting system (Abdul Rahman, 2010).

Having the hereafter as a reality endogenized in Islamic thinking and everyday life has accounting implications. As explained, this provides spiritual accountability from an individual's sense in a state of mind to assess their gains and losses not only for this world but also for the hereafter. This defines the foundation of accounting in

Islamic tradition, as the famous proverb states: "What have you done for Allah today?" This is a simple definition of personal accounting in everyday life in line with Islamic teaching. However, the heavy emphasis on *haqq* (right) and *adalah* (justice) by definition requires a form of accounting to be implemented so that the *haqq* and *adalah* can be served for all the stakeholders.

The primary purpose of accounting is to release the accountability of enterprise as a result of the separation of ownership and management. Stockholders, creditors, possible investors, and the community are the primary users of accounting information. The term accountability, in Muslim society, holds a profound meaning of vice regency or *khalifah*, implying that individuals are created to represent God on earth (this will be discussed in more detail later in the chapter) (Naqvi, 1994). Within such responsibility, Islamic teaching perceives that the duty of an individual in this world is to achieve the function of its being in the universe, who was consequently created as trustee and accountable for all their personal actions during their lives on the day of resurrection (Napier, 2007), as stated in the *Qur'an* (4: 86): "certainly, *Allah* is ever a careful account taker of all things".

It should be noted that the *Qur'an* uses the word *hisab* (account, calculation) and its derivative more than 80 times in different verses (Askary & Clarke, 1997: 42 cited in Napier, 2007: 4). *Muhasabah* is an Arabic word that means "accounting", which as a term is derived from the verb *hisab* can also be pronounced as "reckoning" (Napier, 2007). As a concept, this brings about feelings of responsibility toward God, His created beings, and the soul which is accountable for adhering to the commands and prohibitions of the *Sharia*. By means of *muhasabah*, human being comes to understand that he is created with a purpose, that God gave him responsibility on this Earth and that man will be responsible to God for his actions and the trust placed in him, and that he must return to *Allah* (Chaudhry, 1999).

In Islam, providing financial information to the public and users is not the only function of accounting, rather the accountants should discharge their accountability by providing information to enable society to follow the commandments of God as prescribed by the concepts of *tawhid*, *adalah*, *ihsan*, *rububiyah*, and *tazkiyah* in the process of facilitating *falah* (Abdul Rahman, 2010). Hence, from this perspective, Gambling and Karim (1991) argue that accountants as ethical governors have to ensure the accountability and transparency of the internal procedures of the institution so that policy and governance issues are discussed and recorded correctly at the point where ethical difficulties arise in the first place.

It is, therefore, the aim of the Islamic economic system, from the point of view of ambition, to obtain the economic well-being and improvement of people through the establishment of social justice, equal distribution of material resources, and the provision of human needs, as well as achievements of moral and material development, given that development is defined as "human centred" and for "human well-being".

As the discussion so far indicates, Islam has a different worldview that also impacts its believers' social and economic actions. This, in turn, affects the accounting system, as accounting is a public action and organization that has to reflect the values of its society and helps to reach its social and economic objectives (Hameed & Yaya, 2005).

Consequently, Islamic ontology and epistemology are also articulated in nature and the everyday accounting practice, resulting in "Islamic accounting". Hameed (2000) argues that the differences in worldviews and morals lead to differences in economic systems and therefore require different accounting systems that meet their needs. Even though several religious scholars recognize the worldview of Islam as a monotheistic religion following the five pillars of faith, the axiomatic framework of Islamic moral economy shaping the nature of Islamic accounting is discussed as follows.

Tawhid (the unity of God and sovereignty as Islam is a code/system of life given by *Allah*) is the foundation of the Islamic faith which indicates the vertical dimension of the ethical system (Asutay, 2007a, 2007b). According to Naqvi (1994: 26), *tawhid* particularly denotes the vertical dimension of Islam-linking the imperfect and finite social institutions with a Perfect and Infinite Being". The concept of *tawhid* refers to the unity of God and faith and that the creation did not come into existence accidentally but was created by God (Sulaiman, 2005; Abul Hassan, 2005). As the central pillar of Islam, *tawhid* ensures the integrative manner of life, indicating through complementarity that methodologically in life, everything is integrated and interacted in a complementarity sense to reach unity (Asutay, 2018). Therefore, any analysis has to consider such integrated understanding and interactiveness. Thus, *tawhid* suggests that every stakeholder is considered an essential part of the whole (Asutay, 2007a, 2007b, 2018; Ather, 2009). It should also be added that Islam encompasses both *Hablum-min'Allah wa Hablum-min'annas* (the relationship between human beings and *Allah* and the relationship between human and human) (Abdul Rahman, 2010). Hence, in Islam, practical accounting covers social actions in everyday life in terms of a horizontal relationship (with other human beings/*Hablun-mia'annas*), reflecting on the social nature of accounting, although it also relates to a vertical relationship (with *Allah/Hablun-mia'Allah*) as a path to individual development and accountability (Murtiyani, 2009).

Consequently, accountants in Islam should maintain a good and proper relationship with God by satisfying the religious requirements, which in turn the human and public relations would be enthused by the significance of honesty, justice, tolerance, and respectability since the basic principle of the accountants, who comply with the worldview of *tawhid* (oneness of God) is to regard life in the hereafter as their essential point because it is eternal life (Abdul Rahman, 2010). However, he added that this does not mean that individuals should forget their share and aims of this world as long as they are within limits provided by religion (Abdul Rahman, 2010).

It should be observed that to increase the level of beauty in life (*hayat al-tayyebah*), both person and group, human beings should also follow the law of equilibrium, specifically *Al-'adl wa Al-'ihsan* or justice and beneficence, the "horizontal" dimension of Islam, which entails promoting social harmony and preserving just balance in the basic construction of society together with unity (*tawhid*), in which individual actions must follow an integrated whole (Naqvi, 1997; Ahmad, 2003). In other words, all humankind is accountable for human and material growth, for their own thoughts and actions and for their relations with the "other" and with nature around them (Osman, 1998). Therefore, it could be argued that although this axiom provides freedom in which individuals have to act, they must do so while bearing the general well-being of present and future generations (Asutay, 2007a, 2007b, 2018).

Al-'adl (justice) is the second essential axiom, meaning justice, fairness, and equitableness, which fundamentally encompasses two features: first, the basis of equilibrium has to be sustained between individuals with respect and appreciation to their rights; second, every individual should obtain things that are due to him and give things that are due from him (Naqvi, 1994; Khan, 2003), as what *Allah* has intended is percentage and balance in the fairness of rights (Khan, 2003; Siddiqi, 2004). For that reason, it could be claimed that *al-'adl* requires that everyone should be provided with all of their ethical, social, financial, political, legal, and public rights (Khan, 2003).

Al-'adl in Islamic culture is a moral principle. Therefore, each person in society should look for justice in all their actions and transactions, including accounting. Kamali (2010) states that justice is fundamentally a social concept because it includes social relations (*muamalat*) based on the concept of *ukhuwwah* (Islamic brotherhood). He added that economic justice is a prerequisite of social justice. Therefore, as a technical term, "social justice" is often associated with economic justice, although it does not equalize it (Kamali, 2010). This can be understood clearly form the statement by Qutb (1953), cited in Gambling and Karim (1991: 32), the "Islamic economic system should be viewed from a holistic perspective, which involves an understanding of the concept of God, the universe, life, and the human being. This holistic approach provides an appreciation of the nature of social justice in Islam".

According to Ahmad (1979), the social and economic morals of Islamic finance include beneficence or *al-'ihsan*. *Ihsan,* or "doing what is beautiful", is to accept with pleasure less than what is due to receive readily and payback a larger share than what is due (Murata & Chittick, 1994; Zaman & Asutay, 2009). Therefore, *al-'ihsan* is a significant value of Muslim society. It is beyond and greater than the legal fairness of justice (*al-'adl*), and it is practiced voluntarily as it aims to establish equilibrium in the society between different stakeholders (Asutay, 2013, 2018). Thus, it is argued that *ihsan* is "a cluster of various values such as *amanah*, (honesty), *ithar* (sacrifice) *ta'awun* (cooperation), *sabr* (patience), *shukr* (thanksgiving), *tawakkul* (trust), *infaq* (spending), and *silatur rahm* (joining of kinship ties), etc.". (Uddin *et al.*, 2013: 15).

The importance of *al'adl wa al'ihsan* can be noticed from the number of times it is mentioned in the *Qur'an*. For example, in *Surah Al-Nahil*, the *Qur'an* states that "*Allah* commands *al'adl* (justice) and *al'ihsan* (beneficence)..." (16: 90). Justice and kindness is a wide-ranging term and possibly consists of all the qualities of cold philosophy. Conversely, religion invites people to perform good acts, which are exceedingly generous and more human, although they are not necessarily required by justice. In other words, it means generosity in giving and taking for people (Amer & Bin Yahya, 2014). For example, the hadith of the Prophet of Islam states that "paying the agreed amount of money for someone who works for you before his sweat dries is due to *adl*". However, if this person is paid more money than what is due, it is out of *ihsan* (Ansari, 2011). The *Qur'an* (e.g., 10: 26; 55: 60) indicates that the reward of the righteous will be far more than in proportion to their merits in this life and the hereafter (*hayat al-tayyebah*).

The prophet stated that *ihsan* is "to worship God as if you see Him since if you do not see Him he sees you" (Chittick, 1998: 350). Given that *Allah* knows everything, whether visible or hidden, including most secret thoughts, as the *Qur'an* (33: 51) has indicated, thus "*ihsan* demands that people be aware of God's presence and act appropriately, but also demands that they think, feel and intend appropriately" (Murata & Chittick, 1994: 278). Therefore, it could be argued that the Prophet's definition of *ihsan* presents us with profound meaning and perception into the quality's inner dimension and its psychology, and it clarifies human attitudes and inspirations that go hand in hand with *ihsan* (Murata & Chittick, 1994).

In Islamic finance, the implementation and encouragement of *ihsan* is significantly required by *Sharia* to make the economic cycle run smoother and provide a humanistic dimension by emphasizing the moral aspect of human transactions (Kamali, 2010).

In reflecting upon *ihsan* and its articulation for accounting, accounting standards for IFIs have to be improved reliably by taking the unique objectives of financial accounting for IFBIs into consideration (Tag El-Din, 2004). Consequently, Islamic auditors can arrange their financial reports on an organizational level, which follow these particular concepts and allocate them over and above its main practices (Khan, 1985). Thus, consistent information has to be presented in the correct form and full disclosure, as it is required according to the concept of social accountability in Islam. Related and truthful disclosure of the information is essential in various features of Islamic life (Lewis, 2001). For example, "... be maintainers of justice ..." (4: 135) is one of the *Qur'anic* references referring to the meaning of "relevance" and the other one (2: 71) "... now you have brought the truth..."; therefore, it is argued that financial information is related to an Islamic view as long as it contains the quality of "truth-fair" and perfect disclosure of the materials at hand (Lewis, 2001).

Al-adl wa al-ihsan, according to Islamic conception, is also referred to as the fair and equitable distribution of wealth. In this context, to distribute the recourses of the economy with fairness and justice, the Islamic economic system has implemented a highly structured system of *sadaqah* and *zakat* in addition to other Islamic morals, e.g., kindness and sympathy (*ihsan*), which "encourage people to contribute more than they are ordained and take less than they are authorised", between Muslims in the community, as the *Qur'an* occasionally indicates (e.g., 9: 13) (Chaudhry, 2003; Kamla *et al.*, 2006; Amer & Bin Yahya, 2014), such as the case with pious foundations or the *awqaf* system.

In order to protect and sustain the harmony of Islamic society as a unit and ensure the accountability of business and trade, several institutions were established during the seventh and eighth centuries, which is the time of the Abbasids State, including the institution of *al-hisba* that regulates the market and protects society from fraud and corruption (Wilson, 1997; Kamla, 2009). One of its main objectives was to emphasize the fundamental components of Islam, including the fairness of all Muslims and the prohibiting of unfairness because of race, sexual orientation, or class since *ihsan* is relevant to every aspect of human behavior. According to Gambling and Karim (1991) and Kamla (2009), the *muhasib* (accountant) was selected to certify whether the marketplace and dealers in the region accorded with the *Sharia* as well as to maintain public values and the health of government capitals and to prevent market controls, such as control of prices. As a result, the central role of the *muhasib* was to certify fairness (*adl*) and beneficence (*ihsan*) in society, including both religious and material dimensions (Murtuza, 2000).

Formally, the Islamic economic system is presented as an optimum system, as it revises the discipline of the economy to suit the needs of changing times. To achieve this, freedom has turned out to be the *sine qua non* of serving as a guide for additional legislation or rule-making by Muslims. Therefore, freedom is considered as one of the objectives of *Sharia* (Ibn Ashur, 2006). Siddiqi (2010) argues that the laws of Islam (*Sharia*) identified as blessed and representing the *Qur'an* and Prophet Muhammad's *Sunnah* (way of his life and action) and found in the *hadith* and *sirah* are above human.

However, their understanding, interpretation, and implementation are entrusted to the community of believers of the former by Islamic jurists, specifically Islamic jurisprudence (*fiqh*). This in itself requires freedom of thought and expression, the right to assemble, to converse, and to take part in the dialogue because Muslims, as mentioned in the *Qur'an,* have been directed "to conduct their affairs by mutual consultation among themselves" (42: 38). Sen (2000: 53) claims that "enhancement of human freedom in both is the main objective and the primary means of development".

Freedom should provide and ensure both aspects, the procedure of free decision-making and real opportunity of choice because there will be no meaning of freedom if there is no real opportunity to make a choice and vice versa, the choice being undertaken by someone else (Sen, 2003; Siddiqi, 2010). Nevertheless, the concept of freedom in Islam has a different meaning to the ordinary concept of the absolute autonomy of the individual, which is not secured in the Islamic attitude that relates freedom to *Allah's* will (Naqvi, 1997).

Freedom in Islam is linked to accountability; as humans are given free will (*irada-i juzziya*) to determine their own destiny, they are accountable for every decision or choice they are taking. It is a known fact that accountability cannot be established without free will, and justice or *adalah* cannot be determined. Therefore, the Islamic moral economy considers freedom as an essential axiom in constructing the Islamic accounting system. In other words, Islamic accounting is also the consequence of the freedom that individuals are given by God. Hence, this axiom also rationalizes Islamic accounting as a social construct through revealed knowledge and its implications to humans (Asutay, 2007a, 2007b).

Similar to all other rights, the right to freedom is accompanied by responsibilities (Siddiqi, 2010). Responsibility (*fard*) is essential in Islam's all-encompassing and primary belief system, moral value, social norms, and judicial principles (Abdul Rahman, 2010). Hence, Islam requires every individual to consider full responsibility for society as a whole. For example, Islam emphasizes the social responsibilities of paying *zakat,* and the individual cannot enjoy life or earn profit unfairly, while others cannot (Sirageldin, 2000; Lewis, 2001). This is obvious in the *Qur'an* (9:71): "the believers, men and women are *Auliya'* supporters and protectors of one another; they enjoin Islamic monotheism and all that Islam orders Muslims to do, and forbids all that Islam has forbidden; they perform prayers and offer obligatory charity (*zakat*) and obey *Allah* and His Messenger".

Muslims have no doubt that *Allah* gave man responsibility in this life, and he will be accountable to Him for his actions and the trust placed in him. Responsibility (*fard*) in Islam does not honor but commissions (*taklef*), which means Muslims are responsible for their actions or inaction in this life and the hereafter. Each person has a book kept about them, which confirms all their small and great actions (deeds) that they will be responsible and accountable for on the Day of Resurrection (Al Safi, 1992), which once again relates to accounting.

Both the *Qur'an* and *Hadith* emphasize the accountability and responsibility of human beings toward the rest of creation. The *Qur'an* (18:49) states, therefore, that "... therein they will say, 'ah woe to us! What sort of book is this, it leaves neither a small thing nor a big thing but has recorded it with numbers', and they will find all that they did place before them: And your Lord treats one with injustice". This has also been emphasized by numerous other verses in the *Qur'an* (99: 7–8). Therefore, accountability in Islam entails everyone in society to ensure that their actions and conduct in this life are performed according to Islamic regulations (Afifuddin & Siti-Nabiha, 2010).

Furthermore, Prophet Muhammad also explained individual and collective responsibility. He said, "Surely every one of you is a guardian and is responsible for his charges: The Imam (ruler) of the people is a guardian and is responsible for his subjects; a man is the guardian of his family (household) and is responsible for his subjects; a woman is the guardian of her husband's home and his children and is responsible for them" (Sahih Bukhari, 3.46.730).

In general, the discussion above demonstrates a strong relationship similar to a hand and a tight-fitting glove between responsibility and accountability. For example, Afifuddin and Siti-Nabiha (2010) argue that accountability is used to explain the responsibility of those who direct or manage the resources of others. Similarly, Kearns (1994: 186) states that "accountability is holding individuals and organizations responsible for performance measured, as objectively as possible". Consequently, in this context, accountability signifies accountability to society (*ummah*) or the community as a whole (Lewis, 2001). Lewis (2001) also argues that there is a fundamental similarity and relationship between accounting and *hesab* in Islam in the way that everyone in Islamic society is responsible for performing duties, as explained in the *Qur'an.*

Providing the correct information to the *ummah* is the most significant aim of Islamic accounting, seeing as this information will assist users in understanding the results and the transactions of an institution on its interests and in being guided with the requests of *Sharia* as to how this has been achieved. In the context of calculating *zakat,* as one of the responsibilities (*fard*), which entails disclosure of the value of resources, it identifies the capability of a Muslim to do so. Reporting with full disclosure is essential concerning expecting the requirements in the future and evaluating investment risk in Islamic corporations (Lewis, 2001). Considerable suspicion has to be raised whether reporting with IFRS regarding asset assessment and the measurement of income would comply with *Sharia* (Lewis, 2001). Those requirements are not available in the IFRS, which are more appropriate to the model of private accountability. As a result, "an accounting system based on the accountability (rather than decision-usefulness) framework, which stresses the responsibility of the accountee to God and community in addition to investors, may be more suitable for Muslim users" (Hameed, 2000: 15).

Khilafah "indicates an individual's role as God's vicegerent on earth" (Asutay, 2007b: 170). The conceptions of *khalifa* (vicegerent) and *amanah* (trust) develop from the principle of *tawhid* (Naqvi, 1994; Asutay, 2018) According to the *Qur'an, the* human being is chosen as a *khalifa* (vicegerent), and each individual is given this duty and honor in the form of God's trust (Abul Hassan, 2005). *Qur'anic* verse (2: 30) states, "Behold, thy Lord said to the angels: 'I will create a vicegerent on earth'". They said, "Will you place therein those who will make mischief therein and shed blood? While we glorify You with praises and thanks and sanctify You". He said, "I know that which you do not know".

The concept of *khilafah* has been defined by several authors. For example, Sulaiman (2003: 152) defines it as "a person's status and role, specifying the individual's responsibilities to himself and his responsibility to the *ummah* (community of believers)". The duty of human beings as God's *khalifah* "is to fulfil God's will on earth, promoting what is good, forbidding what is wrong, establishing justice (*'adl*) and promoting beneficence (*ihsan*), resulting in attaining high levels of a good life (*hayat al-tyyebah*), both individually and collectively" (Ahmad, 2003: 193 cited in Asutay, 2007a: 8). For this, man is given freedom, that is, freedom of choice and action "also within limits" (Kamla *et al.*, 2006). Many verses in the Holy *Qur'an* (such as 45: 15) strongly emphasize this concept.

The concept of *khilafah,* the right of the vicegerent of man on the earth, is closely linked with justice in the *Qur'an,* and they both partake in *amanah* (Sulaiman, 2003; Kamali, 2010; As-Sar, 1984; Sadr *et al.*, 2020). With regard to the *Qur'an,* utterances can be noted pointing to vicegerent (*khilafah*) and justice (*adalah*). For example, the famous verse with this meaning is when the prophet David is summoned to judge with truth (*haqq*) among his subjects because he is the vicegerent of God (*khalifa*) (38: 26). From this verse, it can be argued that there is accountability whenever it locates a link between one axiom and another. It also emphasizes human accountability before God as it reminds the vicegerent not to forget the Day of Judgment as "man is accountable to God and his success in the hereafter depends on his performance in this life on earth, as he is only a trustee of God"(Afifuddin & Siti-Nabiha, 2010: 1136).

Individuals as trustees of *Allah's* resources are not only accountable for spiritual aspects but also for social, business, and contractual dealings (Ibrahim & Yaya, 2005). The *Qur'an* states that God commands you to return trusts (*amanah*) to their owners (4: 58). Therefore, an accountant in Islam as a trustee of God and holder of *amanah* on Earth, is encouraged to provide work and excellent service to the *ummah* with *Sharia* compliance (whom they are due). It has been suggested that it is possible to use this kind of accountability as the most essential aim of Islamic accounting; thus, it is subsequently called Islamic accountability (Hameed, 2000). Khir (1992) supported this idea by stating that this thought is strongly believed in Islamic society, which, in turn, would provide the ultimate enthusiasm for improving Islamic accounting practices.

Arif (1989) states that *rububiyyah* is one of the fundamental philosophies of the Islamic economic system, which refers to "divine arrangements that relate to nourishment, sustenance, and the power of directing all things towards their perfection" (Ahmed, 1979: 12). Asutay (2013) argues that it is the fundamental law of the universe that focuses on the divine form of the stakeholders' development and contributes to the support and sharing of resources. In other words, as an axiom, it suggests that everything has been created with a developmental path (*fitrah*). Accordingly, characterized by the development process in accordance with this approach, sustainability is derived from the continuity of rights in the worship of God.

As another axiom, *tazkiyah* or purification (and development) was the task of all the messengers of God in all human relationships, God, man, the natural environment, society, and state (Asutay, 2013). Therefore, the Islamic concept of development has to be derived from the concept of Islam in the testimonial because it is directed at the problem of human growth in all its dimensions, and as it is interested in developmental expansion in the direction of perfection, through the purification of attitudes and relationships, the consequence of testimonial is *falah*, in this world and the next (Asutay, 2007a, 2007b).

Tazkiyah is the purification of a human being in the sense of purifying their "self" from anything (physical and non-physical) that is not required, purifying the relationship between creature and creature, between creatures and the Universe, and between the creature and God (Mulawarmanet *et al.*, 2006). Thus, Islam aims to purify all actions of individuals whether they are visible or invisible, including souls, while Islamic law emphasizes purification and "sanctifying" which are mentioned in the *Qur'an* (9: 103): "Take, [O, Muhammad] alms from their wealth to purify them and sanctify them with it. And invoke *Allah* for them. Verily, your invocations are a source of security for them; and *Allah* is the All-Hearing, All-Knower".

One of the aspects of self-testimonial is to keep away from the repudiation of passion and selfishness, in addition to purifying the human self (*nafs*) from all evil, vices, and acts and coping with desires and evil inclinations. To achieve this, there are several factors, such as self-accountability and sincerity, whose principal aim is to worship *Allah* alone, which is the condition of the acceptance of good deeds. The *Qur'an* (98: 5) states that "And they recommended not but that they should worship *Allah*, [being] sincere to Him in religion, inclining to truth, and perform prayers and to give *zakat*, and that it is the right religion".

An accountant in Islam is expected to have a high level of moral standards, which are discussed earlier, because accounting practices could be considered as a part of *ibadah* to *Allah* (worshipping) as long as these practices are implemented to comply with the guidelines of

Allah conducted in accordance with *Sharia* (Ahmad, 1988; Ibrahim & Yaya, 2005). In line with this argument, Sulaiman (2003) states that the key concept of accounting is based on the honesty and personal accountability of the accountant. It has also been claimed that the direction and rules of accounting should be taken from its values instead of its concepts. In other words, accounting should attend to the behavior of accountants rather than the book of accounting. With regards to the devout accountant, since the Islamic code of conduct has particular personal accountabilities and duties to society, the accountant with testimonial soul (*nafs*) cannot simply cheat or deceive others, cannot betray, and should command good and forbid what is evil (Gerboth, 1987). Suliaman (2003) implies that the devout accountant in a perfect Muslim community will be directed by the following verse in the *Qur'an* (8: 27) in purifying his accountability: "O you, who believe Betray not *Allah* and His Messenger, nor betray knowingly your things entrusted to you and all the duties which *Allah* has ordained for you".

This axiomatic foundation is completed with a methodology that is *maqasid al-Sharia,* which is the foundation or the directing principle of Islamic economics and Islamic finance (Asutay & Yilmaz, 2018). It relates to everything: laws, behavior, attitudes, products, transactions, activities, and services. The meaning of *maqasid* includes the understanding and knowledge behind rulings, the purposes of specific actions, while the meaning of the term *Sharia* is to follow the commands of Allah or the way of Islam (din) (Dusuki & Abdullah, 2007). Therefore, *maqasid al-Sharia* signifies the purposes and the justification of the *Sharia* (Dusuki & Bouheraoua, 2011). Furthermore, it reflects the holistic view of Islam since Islam is an absolute and combined pattern of life and its objective includes the personal and the public as a whole, in this life and on the Day of Judgment (Kamali, 1998; Ibn-Ashur, 2006; Asutay, 2007a, 2007b; Dusuki, 2009a).

Muslims believe that the main objective of *Sharia* decisions is to protect and conserve the community's benefits (*maslahah*) in all aspects of life, including the Islamic economy, Islamic finance, and in turn, Islamic accounting, especially as it permits more flexibility, vitality, and originality in social strategy (Mumisa, 2002; Hallaq, 2004; Sencal & Asutay, 2019). According to Imam Al-Ghazāli (d.1111) cited in Dusuki (2009a: 4) and Asutay

(2007a: 9), "The objective of the *Sharia* is to promote the well-being of all humankind, which lies in safeguarding their faith (*din*), their human self (*nafs*), their intellect (*aql*), their posterity (*nasl*) and their wealth (*mal*). Whatever ensures the safeguard of these five serves the public interest and is desirable". However, as further explored and argued by Asutay and Yilmaz (2018), Asutay and Harningtyas (2015), and Mergaliyev *et al.* (2021), Najjar's extended *maqasid* framework suits better concerning the contemporary realities as it includes the development or invigoration (rather than safeguarding) of the following categories: the value of human life (faith, rights, and stakeholding governance), the human self (self and intellect), the society (posterity and social entity), and the physical environment (wealth and ecology).

Accordingly, it could be argued that each decision in *Sharia* (*maqasid al-Sharia*) is ruled with a specific aim, which benefits the individual and society at large, and its regulations are designed to protect a human's benefits and to develop perfection and the conditions of human lives in this life if this perfection relates to the purpose of the hereafter (Dusuki, 2009a). According to Abdul Rahman (2010), the primary objectives of *Sharia* (*maqasid al-Sharia*) are established upon three areas, which are to "educate individuals", "constitute justice", and "realize benefit" (*maslahah*) to the public. There is a general agreement from the Islamic jurist that all laws in *Sharia* seek to secure *maslahah.* Furthermore, the protection of interest is another aspect in the meaning of *maslahah,* which can be classified under three types: the necessities (*darurriyat*), the supplements or complimentary (*hajiyah*), and the ameliorations or embellishment (*tahsiniyat*) (Abdul Rahman, 2010; Hassan & Asutay, 2017). The theory of *maslahah* can contribute to the development of Ansari Abdul Rahman (2003, 2010) argues that according to the principles of *maslahah,* there are three levels that accountants can use as guidelines when they determine moral conflicts, which are as follows.

First, no matter what the decisions are in financial and accounting disclosures of business actions and transactions, protecting the subsistence of human life, property, and intellect is a priority. Therefore, any business activities, which have an effect on these fundamental elements, have to be revealed and discussed in relation to their financial effects as well as in relationship to their vital social effects. This includes all business activities that could destroy in addition to endanger people's lives, the environment, and natural surroundings, such as air and water pollution; also activities that might damage nature, property and lives because of environmental degradation; and damage an individual's brain because of the production and trading of unlawful drugs for public consumption (Abdul Rahman, 2003, 2010).

Second, accountants must account for and protect all complementary public interests, even though any negligence or action would not lead to difficulties or disruption to the public. Involvement in trading with the manufacture of or selling tobacco, drugs, and alcohol that will affect the public's health is one of the examples that might fall under this type of protection. Moreover, participating in fur trading, animal abuse, and animal research that destroys animals' lives, and selling or issuing and publishing magazines and producing videos that inspire bad moral behavior in society are other examples of the activities which the public must be protected from. Consequently, accountants have to reveal the consequences of such business activities regarding their financial effects and the social effects. Therefore, rather than being attached to the process, consequentialism is essential in considering the nature of an action, including accounting practice (Abdul Rahman, 2003, 2010; Asutay, 2013).

Third, the accountants' reports have to reflect achievements and all the necessary actions that are taken to improve things that are necessary to the public. Hence, those reports have to reflect all the relevant information and attributes such as reliability, inclusiveness, objectivity, suitability, and comparability. Accountants usually are aware of such attributes, although sometimes they have been a foregone conclusion. The major criticism of accountants' reports is that they use complex technical terms and jargon, which are inappropriate for the general public to understand. Thus, reports must be simple so that the public can understand them (Beattie & Jones, 1992). In addition, over-portraying to the client on the status of the financial reporting might reflect the bias of accountants, which raises questions concerning the independence of accountants and therefore means that confidence is lost in financial reporting (Moizer, 1985).

According to the earlier discussion, Islamic accounting is the outcome of Islamic ontology and epistemology as articulated in the axiomatic approach, which rationalizes Islamic accounting. While the historical rationale and legitimacy are presented in the following section, the ontological position should motivate individuals to construct Islamic accounting while taking complete account of the working mechanism of IFIs. Therefore, it is better for Muslims to use an accounting system based on an accountability framework, which emphasizes the accountability of the accountee to *Allah* and the public. Hence, applying the conventional accounting system in an organization operating under the Islamic worldview might cause incompatibility between the aims of the organizations and the standards they use to report their activities and performance (Hameed, 2000).

2.5 History of Islamic Accounting

After presenting the ontological and epistemological rationale for Islamic accounting, it should be noted that history has evidenced Islamic accounting practices in various forms and institutions.

Historically, Islamic accounting emerged from the Islamic ontology and socio-economic development and economic and financial developments around trade during the various stages of the Muslim Empires of the past. Ibn Khaldun's *Al-Muqaddimah*, which was written in 1337, archives an early view of general history, including the history of Islamic accounting. He discusses how the *diwan* was established during the time of the second Caliph, Umar bin Al-Khatab (Napier, 2009). The *diwan*, being the main administrative center, was a system used to record all the transactions of the state, including *zakat*, *sadaqah*, and people's annual salaries paid from the public treasury. Ibn-Khaldun (2005: 199, cited in Napier, 2009: 131) states that:

> [The *diwan*] constitutes a large part of royal authority. In fact, it is the third of its basic pillars. Royal authority requires soldiers, money, and the means to communicate with those who are absent. The ruler, therefore, needs persons to help him in the matters concerned with "the sword", "the pen", and finances. Thus, the person who holds the office (of tax collections) has (a good) part of the royal authority for himself.

Lasheen (1973) argues that the word *diwan* is originally a Persian phrase used by Arabic people, whereas Al-Qalqashandy (1913) claims that it is an Arabic term. He argues that the word *diwan* is a noun derived from the Arabic verb *Dawwana* or "writing down". This view is supported by several Muslim scholars, such as Sybaw' weh (the Arabic grammarian), An-Nahhas, and Ibn Abbas. Initially, the term *diwan* was used as a name for a book that records all the incomes and outcomes and was a place where they record and maintain accounting books. After that, it was only used to mean an office.

Napier (2009) and Trokic (2015) argue that Islamic accounting history recently developed in the shadow of Western accounting history. Similarly, in a recent study, Mulawarman and Kamayanti (2018) discuss the way secular anthropology has shaped accounting theory and practice in Indonesia, which is a common thread throughout the Muslim world due to colonialization and Westernization processes. Therefore, authors of accounting history do not have that much to say about accounting in Islam. It is also important to state that an important reason for the limited material on Islamic accounting history and data on accounting issues in the Muslim world is due to the destruction of archives in the national library in Baghdad by Mongol invaders in 1258.

In recent years, the history of Islamic accounting has received great attention and numerous researchers, many originating from Muslim countries, who have attempted to review the field. According to Napier (2009), several contenders, such as Yayla (2007a), Orbay (2005), Cizakca (1995), and Toraman *et al.* (2007), were able to study the record of *waqfs* (pious foundations) that managed to survive given that these articles were established with continuous donations, which then were available in different countries that were under the control of the Ottoman Empire. Moreover, using the Ottoman archives, Toraman *et al.* (2006a) were able to consider the financial records of the Eregli Coal Enterprise, which in the 1840s was considered to be one of the largest Ottoman businesses. Its accounting system was relatively different from the modern accounting system employed in the West regarding single-entry and double-entry systems. Furthermore, Scorgie (1994a) discovered accounting systems from various ventures in Cairo from the 11th and 12th centuries, especially after relevant material was discovered in the storeroom *geniza* of a synagogue, which had survived because of a dislike of destroying any material which had writing that included the name of God (Napier, 2009: 129).

2.5.1 *Development of accounting systems in the early Islamic administrations*

Teachings of Islam directly impacted the development of knowledge in Muslim societies, including the development of accounting. For example, establishing the organization of *zakat* in the year 2 H (AD 624) was one of the Islamic teachings that led to the need for accounting to calculate and pay *zakat due to* conducting business and making a profit (Zaid, 2004). However, there was no real formulation for this in the form of accounting book systems, models and recording processes until the period of the Second Caliph, Umar bin Al-Khattab, who governed the Islamic State between 13 and 23 *Hijri* (AD 634–644). However, during his reign, the *diwans* (accountants' council) were established to record the incomes and costs of *Baitul Mal* (public treasury), and as a result, Islamic accounting emerged as a distinct way of accounting (Zaid, 2000a). During that time, "the terms of accounting and accountant were not used", although the people in charge of accounting matters, specifically the *kateb al-mal* (accountant or bookkeeper), which became the dominant title in different regions of the Islamic State (Zaid, 2000b: 330). The first time the words *muhasabah* and *muhaseb* were used was by Al-Khwarizmi in his book *Mafatieh Al-Uloom* (*Keys of Sciences*) in 365 H (AD 976). He used the former term for the function of (accounting) and the latter for the person responsible for this function (accountant).

In his book, Al-Khwarizmi described the types of records kept by *diwans* and that the books were used to record accounts (Zaid, 2004). Since recording and documenting accounting systems has become important in Muslim society, many Muslim scholars, such as Al-Qalqashandi, Al-Nowayri, Al-Mazenderany, Al-Gazali, Qudamahibn Ja'afar Demashki, and Al-Marodi, engaged in formulating the theoretical and practical base of accountancy (Kantakji, 2004).

Al-Nowayri in 733 H (AD 1355) cited the first professional accountancy when he wrote the first essential accounting reference in human history. He explained the reason for having the accountants' council (*diwan*) and described the things that accountants might need concerning accountancy and its belongings. In addition, he discussed what accountants should record and report with regards to one's income and the tax to pay and, moreover, the method the accountant should employ for calculating together with the difficulties that may arise (Kantakji, 2004 cited in Djeffal, 2014).

As an important contributor, Al-Qalqashandi (1356–1418), a medieval Egyptian author and mathematician during the Mamluk rulers, was the author of *Subh al-a 'sha fi sina'at al-insha* (*Blind's Morning in Making Compositions*), a 14-volume encyclopedia in Arabic. This vast book included a section discussing requests for the person of the book (*al-katib*) who "would be technically experienced, well-versed in Islamic *Sharia* law (particularly the law of commercial transactions — *fiqh mu'amalat*)" (Napier, 2009: 132).

Qudamah ibn Ja'far (AD 337/948), from the Abbasid State, was the author of *Kitab al-Kharaj wa Sina'at al-Kitabah* (*The Book of the Land-Tax and the Methods of Recordkeeping*), a work on Islamic administration composed in Baghdad in the early 14th century, which contained eight chapters; however, only Chapters 5–8 have survived (Heck, 2002). Moreover, out of the eight chapters, only chapter seven deals with taxation, while the others deal with administration, geography, and history (Ben Shemesh *et al.*, 1958). Heck (2002) examined Qudamah's book and argues that section "vii" is devoted to taxation laws or, more accurately, the jurisprudence of revenue (*wujah al-amwal*). Heck (2002), therefore, concluded that Qudamah's book provides an explanation and examination of a fourth-century administrative manual and is a significant contribution to our understanding of and approach to the history of knowledge in Islamic civilization.

Al-Mazenderany was also among Muslim scholars who contributed to the Islamic accounting field by authoring *Risalah Falakiyyah Kitabus Siyakat* (*The Message Astronomical Book Contexts*) in 765 H (AD 1363). In the 14th century, several historians in the political and economic sectors extensively used his study in the Middle East as a foundation of data on government, tax, prices, and other aspects (Napier, 2009). Using *Mafatieh Al-Uloom's* book (*Key of Knowledge*) as a reference, he explained the accounting system used in the Islamic State in more detail than Al-Khwarizmi (Zaid, 2004). According to Zaid (2004), both books documented seven particular accounting practices established and used in the Islamic State, as follows.

Accounting for livestock: This was considered as stable accounting supervised by stable management. This type of system required all related transactions and procedures to be documented as they occurred. The system reported the transactions for all kinds of animals used as transport for commercial, military, and civil purposes;

animal food, in addition to purchasing animals, selling, donated, slaughtered, or dead; and wages of the people who took care of the animals. This system was also used by the private sector to record their transactions and measure annual profit and to calculate payment of *zakat* for the reason that the public was involved in livestock as well. Macve (1994) argues that this system is similar to today's practices that account for the overall "profit" or "loss", local income, and loaning bankers of modern society.

Construction accounting: This was a procedure of project accounting applied to construction projects undertaken by the government. This system uses many terms not used in other methods of accounting, such as progress project; therefore, it requires all the related dealings, activities, and transactions to be recorded in a separate journal for each construction site, while the person responsible for the project supervised all the records from the beginning of the project to its completion. Construction costs are recorded in the *jaridah* (journals), including materials received and wages paid to different construction workers. In addition, it required accounting for and disclosing the extras or shortages when the project was completed and that any discrepancies should be explained. Similarly, the current-day practices of construction accounting systems involve charging construction costs to the applicable contract. This is obvious from the IAS 11, which states "contract costs included costs related directly to the specific contract, plus costs that are attributable to the contractor's general contracting activity to the extent that they can be reasonably allocated to the contract, plus such other costs that can be specifically charged to the customer under the terms of the contract" (Deloitte, 2011: 8).

Agricultural accounting (*Rice farm accounting*): This was a system that specialized in recording the quantities of rice received and distributed. It should be noted that this model was structured for financial reporting rather than for regions that had rice farms to record the harvest of rice and accounting for the quantities received and distributed for *zakat*. This system described by Al-Mazendarany and Al-Khwarizmi did not specify a separation of responsibilities between recordings and managing the account, which meant the bookkeeper was the only one who had the duty of recording and keeping all the records at the same time. This accounting system differs from others that combine exact internal and general or overall control processes.

Therefore, Macve (1994: 59) states that "the rice farm accounting system was alike to the grain accounts of Zenon's or Appianus Egyptian estates, which also required recording receipts and issues of grain in physical terms and without reference to the measurement of money".

Warehouse accounting system: This system appears to have been established and structured to account for the state's procurements of materials. The types of goods received were recorded in detail into specified books immediately. However, the system did not determine whether these records were in financial terms only or in both financial and physical terms, which seems most likely in practice. Instead, the stock count and stocks recorded in the books were compared at the end of the financial period. If there were any differences, the storeman was questioned about them because he was the only person accountable for any shortage between the records in the book and the tangible records. This means that a system of internal control existed since the bookkeeper and the storeman are not the same person. Macve (1996: 6) claims that "the warehouse accounting system differed from that of the ancient world, where the inventories of items were maintained solely in quantitative, physical terms".

Mint accounting (*Currency accounting*): It is believed that this accounting system was established and practiced in the Islamic State in late 13th century AD. Accordingly, to prevent the theft of the bullion and coins, it was required to convert the gold and silver immediately after they were received by the mint authority and delivered back to the person in charge. Thus, each modern public treasury received an equal amount of bullion and coins. Three specific journals (*jaridah*) were required to be used by the mint accounting system: one for recording inventory, one for income records, and one for expenses. It was also obligatory to record the purchases and salaries on top of the costs of the services provided by the mint authority in the expenses journal. The mint authority's income was paid either in accordance with a fixed amount or in accordance with the method of paying 5% of the cost of gold or silver.

Sheep grazing accounting: This method was one of the most crucial accounting systems during the Islamic era. It was also known as farm accounting, which was used by the particular department in the government and private business to measure "profits" or "losses", which was helpful in calculating the amount of *zakat* that was to be paid at the end of the year. Macve (1994: 78) argues that this system was different from the farm accounting system applied in Roman and Greek States, "where the accounts did not purport to show any more than movements of cash and kind, any dependence or fixation on the accounting figures in forming ideas about profitability seems much less likely". However, this system used a special book designed to record all important transactions, such as the animals provided to a shepherd, incomes received, either in kind or in cash, and all losses, including those due to natural disasters. The book used to record the expenses was different from the one used to record assets and the animals provided. This meant that more than one book was required for recording and documenting the accounting processes. However, it did not demonstrate whether the received animals were treated as profits or added to the capital and recorded in the book of assets. Similar to any type of accounting, there were disclosures pertaining to farm accounting. Thus, it was required to have a separate document to classify each type of animal, whether it was male or female, sheep or goats and their offspring, etc., and to classify and record sheep slaughtered and meat products distributed.

Treasury accounting: This type of accounting system concentrates on transactions involving the inflow and outflow of cash. It is usually used in the public sector at all levels, from small to national branches. For example, this system was used in the state administration a long time ago. The administrations required a daily record of all cash flow activities, such as treasury revenues and expenses, whether financial or non-financial, cash or kind, including inventory required by the government, for example, silver and gold. Under this system, cash transactions were recorded on a separate column from the non-cash transaction, which was categorized with regards to their nature, color, and other conditions and subsequently recorded in detail.

Unlike other accounting systems, the treasury accounting system comprised two methods of recording. The method used by Arabs to record the cash and goods inflows on the right side and outflows on the left side of the journal, whereas the method used by Persians used two separate books to record the inflows and outflows of cash and goods. In the former method, the journal (*jaridah*) was formed to work as a journal and a book; thus, there was no need to have a separate book as in the latter's case. Second, analyzing the inflow and outflow activities was required in the Arabian methods, whereas it was not required under the Persian process; thus, the Arabian method was considered a superior system.

2.5.2 *Accounting recording in the early Islamic administrations*

The general meaning of accounting in Islam refers to the operations of recording, which are clearly explained in the *Qur'an* (2: 282). This verse has provided the main guidelines and accounting principles, such as the importance of achieving rights and obligations (Napier, 2009; Afifuddin & Siti-Nabiha, 2010). However, the development of business and *zakat* accountability in the Islamic State created the importance of having accounting records and the measurement of business results. Hence, the accountability of accountants expanded further than just recording transactions for disclosing monthly (*al-khitmah*) and annual reports (*al-khitmah al-jame'ah*) to release the religious, financial accountability of paying *zakat* as requested by *Sharia* (Islamic law) (Zaid, 2000b). As *zakat* should be paid on wealth, which has been kept for at least a year, it is difficult to calculate the completion of one year (*Al-Haol*, or 12 calendar months) on each item of wealth because purchase dates may vary. To overcome this difficulty, accounting records and reports could assist the government as well as people to take the correct decision while they calculate *zakat* (Zaid, 2000b). Imam Ash-Shafi'ie stated that "... who learnt accounting will make an appropriate decision.... This means that the trader or any other person cannot express an appropriate opinion or make the right decision without the assistance of the information recorded in the books" (Shahata, 1993, 45).

When the *diwan* was established in the period of Caliph Umar ben Al-Kattab, accounting records were in the Roman, Persian, Coptic, and Arabic languages. However, the Caliph of Umayyad State, Abdul-Malek, who ruled between 73 and 86 H (693–705 CE), mandated his assistant *Surjoor* and Saleh bin Abdur-Rahman the assistant of Al-Hajjaj, to change the *diwan* of Al-sham, Iraq and Egypt, into Arabic (Zaid, 2000). Whereas, his son Al-Waleed, who ruled between 86 and 96 H (750–847 CE), was the first to introduce bound records and registers (Lasheen, 1973).

The awareness of the importance of having records with a high classification and relevant reports directly impacted the development and improvement of accounting practices in the Islamic State. The establishment of the accounting books achieved its most significant level of growth between 132–232 H (750–715 CE) during the *Addawlah Al-Abbasiyah* (the third of the Islamic caliphates), which also improved *diwan al-Jund* (Department of Army Personnel) and *diwan al-Kharaj* (Department of Land *Zakat*) under the supervision of Kahlid Ibn Barmak (Zaid, 2000).

During that time, auditing or the "review of books" played a significant role in the Islamic State. The reviewer's primary function was to "check what was written in the books" (Al-Qalqashandy, 1913: 130). Al-Gazaly (1980) states that self-control is the vital principle of the religion and *Sharia Islami'ah*, which is influenced by the belief of Muslims that *Allah* is acquainted with all humankind's thoughts and actions. As a result, Muslims should watch their actions and judge themselves in this life before *Allah* judges them in the hereafter, which as a normative principle, provides the grounds for the notion of "accounting" in a spiritual sense with implications for this world. It could be argued, as previously mentioned, that accountability and having the hereafter as a reality endogenized in Islamic thinking and everyday life has profound implications for accounting.

2.5.2.1 *Types of accounting records*

While accounting as a philosophy and normative understanding is well established in Islamic teaching, the practice of accounting as an articulation of such an understanding had also been developed historically. During the early periods of Muslim history, loose leaves were used for accounting records. Later, other books were used for recording, primarily *jaridah* (Bin Jafar, 1981: 23), which was an individual journal and one of the accounting books that was established and implemented by the Islamic administrations (Murtiyani, 2009). Al-Mazendarany 767 H (1363) mentioned the term *jaridah* in his book and observed that the special bookkeeping in the form of *jaridah* started with the expression *Basmallah* (in the name of Allah) and that it had to be registered before it could be used. Registration occurred by numbering all the pages and stamping the *jaridah* with the sultan's seal before it was used (Ziad, 2000a; Murtiyani, 2009).

Accounting books and *jaridah* were established and improved during *Ad Dawlah Al Adawiyah* (Umayyad Caliphate). For example, Ibn Saad (1957) states that Umar bin Abd-Alaziz, who ruled from 99 to 101 H (717–720 CE), was the first person who established an independent department for each category of income. However, early Islamic history only referred to books established during *Ad Dawlah Al Abbasiyah,* who ruled during 132–232 H (749–846 CE) because they had developed the accounting system and accounting books (Murtiyani, 2009). Accounting *jaridah* commonly used during that time are described as follows.

***Jaridah Al-Kharaj*:** It was used to record the *zakat* imposed on earnings from agricultural products, livestock, and debt repayments, whose design was similar to the modern subsidiary ledger and based on the alphabet, in order to simplify referencing the book, which contained a significant number of pages and accounts. Each page included two columns in the form of debit and credit, where the debit was in the form of accountability and credit as the payment (Lasheen, 1973). This book recorded all the harvests of land crops and animals due for *zakat* (*Kanoon al-Kharaj*), which was also demonstrated as *al-Kharaj* obligations that people had to pay, in addition to instalments paid until the whole obligation was completed (al-Khawarizimi, 1984). The index of *Jaridah Al-Kharaj* was quoted geographically in order to show that the classification of total tax had been collected and to recognize the outstanding regional amounts of *zakat al-Kharaj* easier (Zaid, 2000a).

***Jaridah Annafakat (Expenditures journal)*:** It was used to record all the State's expenditures, including the expenses of the Caliph. Similar to *Jaridah Al-Kharaj*, the indexing of this *jaridah* was quoted in alphabetical order according to the type of expenditures that the *diwan* had incurred (Zaid, 2004).

***Jaridah Al-Mal (Funds journal)*:** *Diwan Al-Mal* or the Department of Treasury was using this *jaridah* to record all types of *zakat*, the receiving of it and its payment, as required in the *Qur'an* (Zaid, 2004).

***Jaridah Al-Musadareen (Confiscated funds journal)*:** The name of this *jaridah* was derived from the *Diwan Al-Musadareen,* which had used it to record funds impounded from people acting against the requirements of *Sharia,* including officials working for the government who abused the system (Zaid, 2004).

In addition to these journals or *jaridah*, there are other books or *daftar* (in Arabic) used for accounting records. Several of these books are discussed by Al-Khwarizmi and Ibn Khaldoon and are described as follows.

***Daftar Al-Yawmi'iah (Daily book)*:** It was defined by Al-Khwarizmi (1984: 81) as "the daily book used to record expenses and other financial transactions associated with *zakat al-Kharaj*. According to this definition, it could be argued that the specialization of books was essential; *Jaridah Al-Kharaj* was used for recording *al-Kharaj* revenues, whereas *Daftar Al-Yawmi'iah* was employed for recording *al-Kharaj* expenses.

This type of book and all associated documents were expected to be kept and indexed in a straightforward manner, which would allow them to be located whenever they were required, once the recording and filing were completed (Zaid, 2004). Therefore, the Sultan's stamp was used as a copy that would be kept as proof of recording in the central records. This recording illustrates the significance of *Daftar Al-Yawmi'iah* as the foremost reference and the source for posting subordinate books (Lasheen, 1973).

***Daftar Attawjihat (Book of directions)*:** This was one of the most significant books used by the Islamic administration, which has a similarity in nature to the current general book. This book was used for recording budget expenditures classified concerning the kind of action and budget classification to dominate regional expenditures and to guarantee sultanate/provincial fulfilment with budget distributions and conditions. Historically, the Muslim empires used two types of budgets, specifically *itlakiyyah* (discretionary budget) and *mukarrariyah* (operational/recurrent budget). While the former budget was flexible, which meant that it could be changed and modified by either the sultan or any authorized administrators, the latter budget was strictly adhered to (Zaid, 2000a, 2004).

***Daftar Attahwilat (Book of transfers)*:** Historically, each *Wilayah* (State) within the Islamic State maintained this type of book in order to record the funds transferred from a *Wilayah* to the central government. According to the system developed, the budget of each *Wilayah* had to be approved by the federal government. It should be noted that various elements were taken into account when ratifying the budget, such as the *Wilayah zakat* collections, payments, population, and geographical size (Zaid, 2000a, 2004).

This type of book contained information on all incomes collected by the *Wilayah* and transfers from and to the *Wilayah*. Hence, to control the budgetary process, two books were kept: *daftar Attawjihat* and *daftar Attahwilat*. While the former was designed to control the expenditure, the latter was designed to control incomes and modifications for shortages or excesses. At the end of the financial year, they extracted the difference between the two books, specifically the incomes and expenditures books. Subsequently, any surplus or deficits were transferred from or to the federal government and recorded in the *daftar Attahwilat* (Zaid, 2000a, 2004).

2.6 Contribution of Islamic Accounting to the Development of Modern Accounting

As the preceding sections indicate, Muslim history evidences the contribution made in developing the principles of accounting and also of accounting practice. There is a growing argument nowadays that accounting used during the Muslim empires of the past might positively impact the modern-day accounting system. Have (1976: 11) claims that "the Italians borrowed the concept of double entry from the Arabs". Concerning this argument, Zaid (2000a) states that there is historical confirmation maintained in Turkey and Egypt, which signifies that accounting records and statements created in the early Muslim empires were equivalent to those used in the Italian Republics outlined by Pacioli in 1494. Furthermore, a number of the records and reports used at various times in the old Muslim empires are very similar to modern books and reports. Furthermore, Zaid (2000a) relates the influence of accounting records in the Italian Republics and the commercial link between Muslim and Italian traders. The main point with respect to this association is that the Italian primary book *Zournal* is the exact translation of the Arabic word *Jaridah* (Zaid, 2000a: 89). In addition, Zaid (2000a) claims that the design of several books, chiefly the accounts receivable subsidiary ledger and the classification of debts into three core groups as collectable, doubtful, and uncollectible could be seen as an indication of the influence.

Nobes (2001: 207) argues that "there are clear influences from the Muslim world on some antecedents to Western accounting developments and some features of pre-double-entry accounting in the West". However, no verification is provided in that literature or by Zaid (2000) to argue about the double-entry method originating in Italy. The main point of this rebuttal is that no evidence can sustain Zaid's argument that records concerned with double entry and reports were used in the Islamic State, which influenced the model used in the Italian Republics. Conversely, Kam (1990) believed that historically, double-entry bookkeeping was used in Italy in approximately the 13th century. In support of the Islamic influence, Shehata (1998) added that the term accounting was formerly mentioned in Muslim documents, which occurred before the double-entry method was established by Pacioli in Italy in 1494.

In addition, Nobes (2001) claims that Zaid (2000: 81) suggested that the word *journal* or *zornal* used in the Italian Republics' accounting system "may be based on the translation of the Arabic word Jaridah". Nevertheless, the word *journal* has the same meaning as the English word *diurnal*; obtained from the French *journal* and related to the Italian *giornale*, which was taken from (like the English word "diurnal") the Latin adjective *diurnalis* and the ancient Latin adjective *diurnus* (both meaning diurnal or daily). It should be noted that this is visible in modern English dictionaries (e.g., OED, 1970: 1069) (Nobes, 2001).

Have (1976: 130), in contrast, argues that "the adoption of the expression "journal" and possibly the phrase "in the name of God" could be a suggestion that the Italians adopted knowledge from other cultures". Thus, it seems that Pacioli had translated what existed in other cultures (possibly Islamic culture, as they used the phrase "in the name of God" *Basmallah* in the beginning of their writing) (Chatfield, 1968: 45).

It might be true that there is no strong evidence demonstrating that the double-entry process used in Italy was directly influenced by the Islamic double-entry system. However, whether or not there is enough evidence, it is clear that numerous elements of pre-double-entry accounting were applied in the Islamic world prior to being applied in the West (Nobes, 2001). Moreover, considering that there have always been trade relations between both shores of the Mediterranean, it is inevitable that there should be some exchanges of practices related to accounting. In particular, considering that the knowledge created by Muslim scholars in the medieval period contributed to the development of the Reformation period in Europe, it is inevitable that accounting-related knowledge would have been exchanged.

2.7 Conclusion

This chapter has sought to raise several important issues surrounding the impact of the Islamic worldview on shaping the accounting system. It began by discussing the rationale for Islamic accounting and explaining the reason for the need to develop a specific accounting model that may serve Islamic societies better. It also attempted to answer the question of how the Islamic worldview would affect the choice of particular accounting and reporting policies in everyday life by including a literature review of writing on Islamic axioms, such as *falah, tawhid, al-'adl wa al-'ihsan, khilafah, tazkiyah,* and *maqasid al-Sharia*, although the effect of religion has rarely been investigated at the organizational level. This chapter further discussed the history of Islamic accounting, defining the term Islamic accounting and explaining the development of the accounting system in the early Islamic State and how it has contributed to the development of the modern accounting system.

References

AAOIFI (2010). *Accounting Auditing and Governance Standards for Islamic Financial Institutions.* Manama, Bahrain: AAOIFI.

AAOIFI (2017). *Shari'ah Standards.* Manama, Bahrain: AAOIFI.

Abdul Rahman, A. R. (2003). Ethics in accounting education: Contribution of the Islamic principle of Mashlahah. *IIUM Journal of Economics Journal of Economics and Management*, *11*(1), 31–49.

Abdul Rahman, A. R. (2010). *Introduction to Islamic Accounting Theory and Practice.* Kuala Lumpur: Cert Publication.

Abdul-Rahman, Y. (2010). *The Art of Islamic Banking and Finance. Tools and Techniques for Community-Based Banking.* New Jersey: John Wiley & Sons.

Abul Hassan (2005). Islamic economics and the environment: Material flow analysis in society-nature interrelationships. *Journal of King Abdulaziz University: Islamic Economics, 18*(1), 15–31.

Acquaviva, S. S. (1979). *The Decline of the Sacred in Industrial Society.* New York: Harper and Row.

Adnan, M. K. (1996). *An Investigation of Accounting Concepts and Practices in Islamic Banks: The Cases of Bank Islam Malaysia Berhad and Bank Muamalat Indonesia.* PhD Thesis, University of Wollongong, Australia.

Afifuddin, H. & Siti-Nabiha, A. (2010a). Towards good accountability: The role of accounting in Islamic religious organisations. *World Academy of Science, Engineering and Technology, 66*, 1132–1144.

Afifuddin, H. & Siti-Nabiha, A. (2010b). Towards good accountability: The role of accounting in Islamic religious organizations. *World Academy of Science, Engineering and Technology, 42*, 1119–1125.

Ahmad, K. (1979). *Economic Development in an Islamic Framework.* Leicester: Islamic Foundation.

Ahmad, K. (2003). The challenge of global capitalism: An Islamic perspective. In John H. Dunning (Ed.), *Making Globalization Good: The Moral Challenges of Global Capitalism.* Oxford: Oxford University Press.

Ahmad, S. F. (1988). The ethical responsibility of business: Islamic principles and implications. Paper of the Seminar on Islamic Principles of Organizational Behaviour held at Herndon, Virginia USA.

Ahmed, W. (1995). *A Book of Religious Knowledge.* (2nd edn.) USA Fazl: Omar Press.

Al-Buraey, M. (1990). *Management and Administration in Islam.* Saudi Arabia: Al-Dhahran.

Al-Gazali, A. H. (1980). *Ihya' Uloomud Dien.* Beirut: Darul Fikr.

Al-Ghazali, A. H. M. (1356/1937). *Al-Mustasfā min Ilm al-Usūl.* Cairo: Al-Maktabah al-Tijariyyah.

Al-Jarhi, M. A. (2021). *Economic Analysis: An Islamic Perspective.* Istanbul: TKBB and ASBU.

Al-Khawarizmy, M. A. Y. (1984). *Mafatieh Al-Uloom.* The House of the Arabic Book, Beirut.

Al-Qalqashandi, A. (1913) *Subh al-A'Asha fi-Sinaat al-Insha.* Cairo.

Al-Safi, A. K. (1992). *Accountability: Islam versus the Man-made Doctrines.* Kuala Lumpur: Darulfikr.

Aleyomi, M. B. (2012). Ethno-religious crisis as a threat to the stability of nigeria's federalism. *Journal of Sustainable Development in Africa, 14*(3), 127–140.

Amer, S. H. & Bin Yahya, S. (2014). Development of accounting theory based on Islamic teachings: A glance over principle of Al-Adl and Al-Ihsan. *Research Journal of Finance and Accounting*, *5*(4), 13–20.

Ansari, A. H. (2011). Distributive justice in Islam: An expository study of zakah for achieving a sustainable society. *Australian Journal of Basic and Applied Sciences*, *5*(8), 383–393.

Arif, M. (1989). Towards establishing the microfoundations of Islamic economics: The basis of the basics. In A. Ghazali & S. Omar (Eds.), *Readings in the Concept and Methodology of Islamic Economics.* Selangor Darul Ehsan: Pelanduk Publications.

As-Sadr, M. B. (1984). *Iqtisaduna (Our Economics).* Tehran: Wofis.

Askary, S. (2001). *The Influence of Islamic Culture on the Accounting Values and Practices of Muslim Countries.* Ph.D. Thesis. The University of Newcastle, Newcastle, Australia.

Askary, S. & Clark, F. (1997). Accounting in the quranic Verses. Proceedings of international conference accounting, commerce and finance. *The Islamic Perspective Journal*, 139–152.

Asutay, M. (2007a). A political economy approach to Islamic economics: Systemic understanding for an alternative economic system. *Kyoto Bulletin of Islamic Area Studies*, *1*(2), 3–18.

Asutay, M. (2007b). Conceptualisation of the second best solution in overcoming the social failure of Islamic banking and finance: Examining the overpowering of homoislamicus by homoeconomicus. *IIUM Journal of Economics and Management*, *15*(2), 167–195.

Asutay, M. (2012). Conceptualising and locating the social failure of Islamic finance: Aspirations of Islamic moral economy vs. the realities of Islamic finance. *Journal of Asian and African Area Studies*, *11*(2), 93–113.

Asutay, M. (2013). Islamic moral economy as the foundation of Islamic finance. In Valentino, C. (Ed.), *Islamic Finance in Europe: Towards a Plural Financial System.* Cheltenham: Edward Elgar.

Asutay, M. (2015). Islamic finance: Principles, institutions and development. *Trade and Finance*, Winter, 4–26.

Asutay, M. (2018). *An Introduction to Moral Economy and Rationalizing Islamic Moral Economy.* Working Paper, Durham Centre for Islamic Economics and Finance.

Asutay, M. & Yilmaz, I. (2018). Re-embedding Maqasid al-Shari'ah in the essential methodology of Islamic economics. In Mohamed El-Tahir

El-Mesawi (Eds.), *Maqasid Al-Shari'ah: Explorations and Implications*. Kuala Lumpur: Islamic Book Trust.

Ather, S. M. (2009). Islamic accounting system and practices. *The Cost and Management*, *37*(6), 9–16.

Ayub, M. (2007). *Understanding Islamic Finance*. Singapore: Wiley.

Badawi, E. S. M. & Abdel Haleem, M. A. (2008). *Arabic-English Dictionary of Qur'anic Usage*. Boston: Leiden. Brill.

Baydoun, N. & Willett, R. (1995). Cultural relevance of Western accounting systems to developing countries. *Abacus*, *31*(1), 67–92.

Baydoun, N. & Willett, R. (1997). Islam and accounting: Ethical issues in the presentation of financial information: Accounting, commerce and finance. *The Islamic Perspective Journal*, *1*(1), 1–25.

Baydoun, N. & Willett, R. (2000). Islamic corporate reports. *Abacus*, *36*(1), 71–90.

Beattie, V. & Jones, M. (1992). The use and abuse of financial graphs in annual reports. *Accounting and Business Research*, *22*(88), 291–303.

Belkaoui, A. (1990). *Judgment in International Accounting: A Theory of Cognition, Cultures, Language, and Contracts*. New York: Quorum Books.

Ben Shemesh, A., Goitein, S. D., & Yahya, B. A (1958). *Taxation in Islam. Kitāb al Kharaāj*. Leiden: Brill.

Billah, M. M. (2019). *Islamic Financial Products Principles, Instruments*. New York: Palgrave.

Bin Jafar, K. (1981). Al-*Kharaj Wa Sina'at Al-Kitabah, Commentary By Dr. Mohammad Hussain Al-Zibet*. Baghdad. Dar Ar: Rasheed Publishing.

Briston, R. & El-Ashker, A. (1986). Religious audit: Could it happen here? *Accountancy*, *98*(1118), 120–121.

Chapra, U. (1992). *Islamic and the Economic Challenge*. UK: The Islamic Foundation.

Chatfield, M. S. (1968). *Contemporary Studies in the Evolution of Accounting Thought*. Belmont: Dickenson Publishing Company.

Chaudhry, M. S. (1999). *Fundamentals of Islamic Economic System*. (1st edn.) Pakistan: Burhan Education and Welfare Trust.

Chaudhry, M. S. (2003). Fundamentals of Islamic economic system. Accessed 17 March, 2013. http://www.muslimtents.com/shaufi/b16/b16_13.htm.

Chittick, W. C. (1998). *The Self-Disclosure of God Principles of Ibn Al-'Arabī's Cosmology*. Albany State: University of New York Press.

Çizakça, M. (1995). Cash Waqfs of Bursa, 1555–1823. *Journal of the Economic and Social History of the Orient*, *38*(30), 313–354.

Clarke, F., Craig, R., & Hamid, S. H. (1996). Physical asset valuation and Zakat: Insights and implications, advances in international accounting. *JAI Press Inc.*, *9*, 195–208.

Deloitte. (2011). IASB issues revised exposure draft on revenue recognition. Accessed 17 June, 2013. File:///E:/My%20Research/Important%20 articals/deloitte%20IAS11.pdf.

Djeffal, K. (2014). The effect of economic knowledge in Islamic civilization on accounting evolution. *International Journal of Arts and Commerce*, *3*(7), 103–116.

Dow, J. W. (2006). The evolution of religion: Three anthropological approaches. *Method and Theory in the Study of Religion*, *18*(1), 67–91.

Dusuki, A. W. (2009). *Challenges of Realizing Maqasid Al-Shari'ah (Objectives of Shari'ah) in the Islamic Capital Market: Special Focus on Equity-based Sukuk Structures.* ISRA Research Paper No. 5. Kuala Lumpur: ISRA.

Dusuki, A. W. & Abdullah, N. I. (2007). Maqasid al-Shariah, Maslahah, and corporate social responsibility. *The American Journal of Islamic Social Sciences*, *24*(1), 25–45.

Dusuki, A. W. & Bouheraoua, S. (2011). *The Framework of Maqasid al-Shariah (Objectives of the Shari'ah) and Its Implications for Islamic finance.* ISRA Research Paper No. 22. Kuala Lumpur: ISRA.

El-Ashker, A. (1987). *The Islamic Business Enterprise.* London: Croom Helm Ltd.

Esposito, J. L. (1991). *Islam and Politics.* (3rd edn.) New York: Syracuse University Press.

Faruqi, I. (1989). *Toward a Critical World Theology. Toward Islamization of Knowledge.* (6th edn.) Herndon, Virginia, USA: International Institute of Islamic Thought.

Gambling, T. E. (1987). Accounting for rituals. *Accounting, Organizations & Society*, *12*(4), 319–329.

Gambling, T. E. & Abdel-Karim, R. A. (1986). Islam and social accounting. *Journal of Business Finance and Accounting*, *13*(1), 39–50.

Gambling, T. E. & Abdel-Karim, R. A. (1991).*Business and Accounting Ethics in Islam.* London: Mansell Publishing Limited.

Gambling, T. E. & Abdel-Karim, R. A. (1993). *Business and Accounting Ethics in Islam.* London: New York Mansell.

Geertz, C. (1973). *Religion as a Cultural System.* New York: Basic Books.

Gerboth, D. L. (1987). The conceptual framework: Not definitions but professional values. *Accounting Horizons*, September, pp. 1–8.

Gibran, K. (1952). *The Prophet.* New York: Knopf.

Gibran, K. (2004). *Classic Poetry Series.* New York: The World's Poetry Archive.

Graham, H. (2000). *Indigenous Religions: A Companion.* London: Cassell.

Gray, S. J. (1988). Towards a theory of culture influence on the developing of accounting systems internationally. *Abacus, 24*(1), 1–15.

Hallaq, W. B. (2004). *A History of Islamic Legal Theories: An Introduction to Sunni Usul Al-Fiqh.* Cambridge: Cambridge University Press.

Hameed, S. (2000). *The Need for Islamic Accounting: Perception of its Objectives and Characteristics by Malaysia Accountants and Academics.* Ph.D. Thesis, University of Dundee.

Hameed, S. & Yaya, R. (2005). The emerging issues on the objectives and characteristics of Islamic accounting for Islamic business organizations. *Malaysian Accounting Review, 4*(1), 75–92.

Hamid, A. W. (2004). *Islam the Natural Way.* London: Mels.

Hamid, S., Craig, R., & Clarke, F. (1993). Religion: A confounding cultural element in the international harmonization of accounting? *Abacus, 29*(2), 131–148.

Haqiqi, A. & Pomeranz, F. (1987). Accounting needs of Islamic banking. Advances in international accounting. *Accounting Organizations and Society, 12*(2), 153–168.

Hasan, Z. & Asutay, M. (2017). Maslahah in stakeholder management for Islamic financial institutions. *The Islamic Quarterly, 61*(4), 505–537.

Hasanuzzaman, S. M. (1984). Definition of Islamic economics. *Journal for Research in Islamic Economics, 1*(2), 51–53.

Have, O. T. (1976). *The History of Accounting.* Bay Books: California.

Heck, P. L. (2002). *The Construction of Knowledge in Islamic Civilization: Qudama b. Ja'far and his Kitab Al-Kharaj Wa-Sina'at Al-Kitaba.* Leiden. E. J. Brill.

Hofstede, G. H. (1980). *Culture's Consequences: International Differences in Work-Related Values.* Beverly Hills, Calif: Sage Publications.

Ibn Ashur, M. A. T. (2006). *Treatise on Maqasid Al-Shari'ah.* (M. E.-T. El-Mesawi, Trans). Washington: The International Institute of Islamic Thought.

Ibn Saad, M. (1957). *At-Tabakat Al-Kubra.* Beirut: Beirut House for Printing and Publishing.

Ibn-Khaldun. (2005). *The Muqaddimah: An Introduction to History.* Trans. F. Rosenthal. (Abridged edition). Princeton: Princeton University Press.

Ibrahim, S. H. (2007). IFRS Vs AAOIFI: The clash of standards? Accessed 11 August, 2012. http://mpra.ub.unimuenchen.de/12539/1/The_Clash_of_Standards_internationalaccountant_article.pdf.

Ibrahim. S. H. & Yaya, R. (2005). *Objectives and Characteristics of Islamic Accounting: Perceptions of Muslim Accounting Academicians.* Yogyakarta, Indonesia: International Islamic University Malaysia.

Jaggi, B. L. (1975). The impact of the cultural environment on financial disclosures. *International Journal of Accounting, 10*(2), 75–84.

Jaja, J. M. & Badey. P. B. (2011). Impact of Christian religion on African cultural values. Langlit. *International Journal, 1*(2), 1–16.

Kam, V. (1990). *Accounting Theory.* New York: John Wiley and Sons.

Kamali, M. H. (1998). Al-Maqasid al-Shari'ah: The objectives of Islamic law. *The Muslim Lawyer, 3*(1), 1–7.

Kamali, M. H. (2010). Environment care in Islam: A *Qur'anic* perspective. *Conference Proceeding of the 15th General Conference on the Environment in Islam.* Amman.

Kamla, R. (2009). Critical insights into contemporary Islamic accounting. *Critical Perspectives on Accounting, 20*, 921–932.

Kamla, R., Gallhofer, S., & Haslam, J. (2006). Islam, nature and accounting: Islamic principles and the notion of accounting for the environment. *Accounting Forum, 30*(3), 245–265.

Kantakji, S. M. (2003). The role of Islamic civilization in developing accounting thought. Accessed 14 July, 2013. http://www.kantakji.org.

Kantakji, S. M. (2004). *Islamic Accounting Fiqh.* Published Ph.D. Thesis, Al-Risalah foundation, Damascus, Syria.

Karim, R. A. A. (1995). The nature and rationale of a conceptual framework for financial reporting by Islamic banks. *Accounting and Business Research, 25*(100), 285–300.

Kearns, K. (1994). The strategic management of accountability in nonprofit organizations an analytical framework. *Public Administration Review, 54*(2), 185–192.

Khan, A. M. (1984). Islamic economics: Nature and need. *Journal of Research in Islamic Economics, 1*(2), 51–55.

Khan, A. M. (1985). Role of the auditor in an Islamic economy. *Journal of Research in Islamic Economics, 3*(1), 31–41.

Khan, M. A. (2003). *Accounting Issues and Concepts for Islamic Banks: Accounting Issues in Islamic Banking.* London: The Institute of Islamic Banking and Insurance.

Khir, M. (1992). *Accounting in a Changing Society: Islam Accounting, Auditing and Management from an Islamic Perspective.* Jakarta: Trisakti University.

Kuanova, L. A., Sagiyeva, R., & Shirazi, N. S. (2021). Islamic social finance: A literature review and future research directions. *Journal of Islamic Accounting and Business Research, 12*(5), 707–728.

Kuran, T. (1995). Further reflections the behavioral norms of Islamic economics. *Journal of Economic Behavior and Organization, 27*(1), 159–163.

Lasheen, M. A. (1973). *At-Tandheem Al-Muhasaby Lil-Amwal AlAmmah Fil-Islam*, M.A. Thesis, Faculty of Commerce, Al-Azhar University.

Lewis, M. K. (2001a). Islam and accounting. *Accounting Forum, 25*(2), 103–127.

Lewis, M. K. (2001b). *Islam and Accounting.* Oxford: Wiley-Blackwell.

Macve, R. H. (1994). Some glosses on "greek and roman accounting", Reprinted in B. S. Yamey & R. H. Parker (Eds.), *Accounting History: Some British Contributions.* Oxford: Oxford University Press.

Macve, R. H. (1996). Pacioli's legacy. In Lee T. A., Bishop A., & Parker R. H (Eds.), *Accounting History from the Renaissance to the Present.* New York: Garland Publishing Inc.

Mergaliev, A., Asutay, M., Avdukic, A., & Karbhari, Y. (2021). Higher ethical objective (*Maqasid al-Shari'ah*) augmented framework for Islamic banks: Assessing the ethical performance and exploring its determinants. *Journal of Business Ethics, 170*(4), 797–834.

Mohamad Ibrahim, S. H. (2000). *The Need for Islamic Accounting: Perceptions of its Objectives and Characteristics of Islamic Accounting.* PhD Dissertation, UK, University of Dundee.

Moizer, P. (1985). *Independence in Current Issue in Auditing.* (D. Kent, M. Sherer & S. Turly, Eds.). London: Harper and Row.

Mulawarman, A. D. & Kamayanti, A. (2018). Towards Islamic accounting anthropology: How secular anthropology reshaped accounting in Indonesia. *Journal of Islamic Accounting and Business Research, 9*(4), 629–647.

Mulawarman, I. Triyuwono, D., & Ludigdo, U. (2006). *Reconstruction of Intergalactic Technology in Shari'ah Accounting: Shari'ate Value Added Statement.* 9th National Accounting Symposium (SNA).

Mumisa, M. (2002). *Islamic Law: Theory and Interpretation.* Maryland: Amana Publications.

Murata, S. & Chittick, W. C. (1994). *The Vision of Islam.* London and New York: I.B. Tauris.

Murtiyani, S. (2009). The historical facts and development concept of Shari'ah accounting. *Indonesian Scientific Journal, 15*(26), 43–58.

Murtuza A. (2000). Hisba: The Islamic variation for the regulation of marketplace and commerce. *Paper Presented at the Sixth Interdisciplinary Perspective on Accounting Conference.*

Napier, C. J. (2006). Accounts of change: 30 years of historical accounting research. *Accounting, Organizations and Society, 31*(4/5), 445–507.

Napier, C. J. (2007). Other cultures, other accountings? Islamic accounting from past to present. *Paper Presented at the 5th Accounting History International Conference,* Banff, Canada.

Napier, C. J. (2009). Defining Islamic accounting: Current issues, past roots. *Accounting History, 14*(1–2), 121–144.

Naqvi, S. N. H. (1994). *Islam, Economics and Society.* London: Kegan Paul International.

Naqvi, S. N. H. (1997). The dimensions of an Islamic economic model. *Islamic Economic Studies, 8*(2), 1–24.

Nasution, M. (2009). Islamic spirit and moral in economics. *Journal of International Development and Cooperation, 15*(1–2), 113–124.

Nobes, C. W. (2001). Were Islamic records precursors to accounting books based on the Italian method? A comment. *Accounting Historians Journal, 28*(2) 207–214.

Orbay, K. (2005). On the Mukata'a revenues and the revenue collection of Bayezid II's Waqf in amasya. *Wiener Zeitschrift für die Kunde des Morgenlandes, 95*, 139–162.

Osman, F. (1998). Monotheists and the 'other': An Islamic perspective in an era of religious pluralism. *The Muslim World, 49*(3/4), 2–8.

Qardawi, Y. A. (1999). *Fiqh Al Zakah: A Comparative Study of Zakah, Regulations and Philosophy in the Light of Qur'an and Sunnah.* Jeddah: Scientific Publishing Centre King Abdulaziz University.

Qutb, S. (1953). *Social Justice in Islam.* New York: Islamic Publications International.

Razi, M. (2008). Riba in Islam: Fiqh of contemporary issues. Accessed 18 June, 2013. http://www.kantakji.com/riba/riba-in-islam.aspx?download.

Sadr, K., Mirakhor, A., & Iqbal, Z. (2020). *Handbook of Ethics of Islamic Economics and Finance.* Berlin Boston: De Gruyter.

Sahih Al-Bukhari. *Manumission of Slaves.* Vol. 46. Book 3. Hadith Number 730, Lahore: Kazi Publication.

Sarea, A., M. & Hanefah, M. M. (2013). The need of accounting standards for Islamic financial institutions: Evidence from AAOIFI. *Journal of Islamic Accounting and Business Research, 4*, 64–76.

Scorgie, M. E. (1994a). Medieval traders as international change agents: A comment. *Accounting Historians Journal, 21*(1), 137–143.

Sen, A. (2000). *Development as Freedom.* (1st edn.) New York: Anchor Books.

Sen, A. (2003). *There is a Better Way: An Introduction to the Development as Freedom Approach.* Nairobi: International Institute for Sustainable Development.

Sencal, H. & Asutay, M. (2019). The emergence of new Islamic economic and business moralities. *Thunderbird International Business Review, 61*(5), 765–775.

Shaari, H., Russell, C., & Frank, C. (1993). Religion: A confounding cultural element in the international harmonization of accounting? *Abacus, 29*(2), 131–148.

Shahata, H. (1993). *Usoolul Fikr AlMuhasabi AlIslami.* Cairo.

Shehata, S. I. (1998). The theoretical framework for accounting in Islamic banks: Analysis and diagnosis. Available at HAL Open Science, 1–2.

Siddiqi, M. (2004). *Riba, Bank Interest and the Rationale of its Prohibition. Islamic Research and Training Institute.* Jeddah: Islamic Development Bank.

Siddiqi, M. N. (1972). *The Economic Enterprise in Islam.* Delhi: Markazi Maktaba Islami.

Siddiqi, S. A. (1982). *Public Finance in Islam.* Delhi: Adam Publishers.

Siddiqi, S. A. (2010). Establishing the need and suggesting a strategy to develop Profit and Loss Sharing Islamic Banking (PALSIB). *Journal of Islamic Economics, Banking and Finance, 6*(4), 29–52.

Sirageldin, I. (2000). Elimination of poverty: Challenges and Islamic strategies. *Islamic Economic Strategies, 8*(1), 1–16.

Sulaiman, M. (2000). Corporate reporting from an Islamic perspective. *Akauntan Nasional,* October, 18–22.

Sulaiman, M. (2003). The influence of Riba and Zakat on Islamic accounting. *Indonesian Management and Accounting Review, 2*(2), 149–167.

Sulaiman, M. (2005). *Islamic Corporate Reporting: Between the Desirable and the Desired.* Research Centre, Kuala Lumpur: IIUM.

Sulaiman, M. & Willett, R. (2003). Using the hofstede-gray framework to argue normatively for an extension of Islamic corporate reports. *Malaysian Accounting Review, 2*(1), 1–35.

Swenson, D. (2009). *Society Spirituality, and the Sacred: A Social Scientific Introduction.* Toronto: University of Toronto Press.

Tag El Din, S. I. (2004). Issues in accounting standards for Islamic financial institutions. Accessed 15 May, 2013. http://www.sbp.org.pk/departments/ibd/.

Thomas, A. P. (1989). The effects of organizational cultural on choices of accounting methods. *Accounting and Business Research, 19*(76), 363–378.

Toraman, C., Ogreten, A., & Yilmaz, S. (2006a). From the first corporate accounting practices in the Ottoman empire: Eregli coal company and accounting book records 19th century. Paper Presented at the 11th World Congress of Accounting Historians, Nantes.

Toraman, C., Tuncsiper, B., & Yilmaz, S. (2007). Cash Awqaf in the Ottomans as philanthropic foundations and their accounting practices. Paper Presented at the 5th Accounting History International Conference, Banff, Canada.

Triyuwono, I. (2004). *Trust (Amanah): The Divine Symbol: Interpretations in the Context of Islamic Banking and Accounting Practices.* Fourth Asia Pacific Interdisciplinary Research in Accounting Conference, Singapore.

Trokic, A. (2015). Islamic accounting: History, development and prospects. *European Journal of Islamic Finance, 3*, 1–5. Doi: 10.13135/2421-2172/1043.

Uddin, H., Ullah, H., & Hossain, M. (2013). An overview on the basics of Islamic audit. *European Journal of Business and Management, 5*(28), 9–17.

Violet, W. (1983). The development of international accounting standards: An anthropological perspective. *The International Journal of Accounting Education and Research, 18*(2), 1–12.

Williams, David R. (1994). The measurement of religion in epidemiologic studies: Problems and prospects. *Religion in Aging and Health, 67*(1), 25–48.

Wilson, R. (1997). *Economics Ethics and Religion Jewish Christian and Muslim Economic Thought.* New York: New York University Press.

Yayla, H. E. (2007a). "Operating regimes of truth: Accounting and accountability change in sultan suleyman waqf of the ottoman Empire (the 1826 Experience)". Paper Presented at: The 5th Accounting History International Conference, Banff, Canada.

Zaid, O. A. (2000a). Were Islamic records precursors to accounting books based on the Italian method? *Accounting Historians Journal, 27*(1), 73–90.

Zaid, O. A. (2000b). The appointment qualification of Muslim accountants in the middle ages. *Accounting Education, 9*(4), 329–342.

Zaid, O. A. (2004). Accounting systems and recording procedures in the early Islamic state. *Accounting Historians Journal, 31*(2), 149–170.

Zaman, N. & Asutay, M. (2009). Divergence between aspirations and realities of Islamic economics: A political economy approach to bridging the divide. *IIUM Journal of Economics and Management, 17*(1), 73–96.

https://doi.org/10.1142/9781800612426_0003

Chapter 3

Methods, Topics, and Theories in Islamic Accounting Research: A Systematic Literature Review

Merwiey Alaqrabawi, Qutaiba Adeeb Odat, and Hashem Alshurafat

Abstract

With the increased number of Islamic institutions, the necessity for a standardized Islamic accounting framework has emerged. The origin of Islamic accounting can be traced back further than conventional accounting. Many studies show that Islamic accounting was the primary source of the basic accounting fundamentals. Besides, the critical role of Islamic accounting is to provide financial reports which adopt the Islamic objectives and laws. The Islamic beliefs hold ethics and morals that drive and influence accounting, auditing, and reporting procedures of the Islamic financial institutions. Accordingly, many studies have emphasized the morality and characteristics of Islamic accounting and economic disciplines required in different institutions and banks. This chapter has adopted the systematic literature review technique to explore the overall available articles and studies on Islamic accounting and the growth of these studies over the years. The researchers have addressed 30 papers retrieved from a variety of online databases according to a set of inclusive and exclusive criteria. The systematic literature review methodology results synthesize different aspects of the topic, methods, and theories used in Islamic accounting studies. This chapter indicates broad concepts and objectives of Islamic accounting retrieved from various online databases with a set of recommendations for further research to fill the gap in this field.

Keywords: Islamic Accounting, *Sharia* Accounting, Islamic Banking, Islamic Accounting Research, Systematic Literature Review.

3.1 Introduction

When the concept of "Islamic Accounting" is heard by a regular reader for the first time, their thought is directed to the idea that it is a religious aspect specified only for few countries or nations. However, the extent of Islamic accounting is demonstrated way further in history, including a deep focus on many fields of accounting as much as conventional accounting. Many authors have embarked on Islamic accounting as the main topic in many fields of accounting. There have been many definitions introduced for Islamic accounting closely, such as providing sufficient and appropriate information to the potential stakeholders of the firms to sustain the continuous operations with the Islamic boundaries and Sharia standards (Halim, 2017; Baydoun *et al.*, 2018). Moreover, Islamic accounting is defined in detail by Napier (2009), who defined Islamic accounting as a general concept, where the accountability of accounting practices is extracted from the Qur'an and Sunnah. Accordingly, the main aim of Islamic accounting is clearly recognized for the need of Islamic intuitions for a source of knowledge that provides a theoretical, conceptual framework that sustains the development of Islamic accounting aspects (Majid & Haliding, 2014; Siswantoro, 2015). Nowadays, articles are way ahead of comparing conventional accounting and Islamic accounting. There are more important objectives for authors to include in the Islamic accounting body of knowledge, such as introducing the determines of corporate social responsibilities linked to Islamic institutions (Farook *et al.*, 2011; Abdullah, Percy, & Stewart, 2015) and other topics such as the compliance with the Accounting and Auditing Organization for Islamic Financial Institutions Standards (AAOIFIS) (Vinnicombe, 2010; El-Halaby, Aboul-Dahab, & Bin Qoud, 2021).

Islamic accounting standards compliance and authority are influenced by high morality and ethics due to strict rules of Sharia laws (Nawaz, Haniffa, & Hudaib, 2021). These laws have introduced new concepts in the accounting basics in both accounting and finance conceptual framework such as riba (interests), i.e., eschewing of usury, sukuk (a form of Islamic finance), and murabahah (finance with a mark-up) (Hesse, Jobst, & Sole, 2008; Razak, Saiti, & Dinç, 2019). As the bottom line of Islamic finance and accounting laws expands from religious beliefs, they contribute to enriching the social and economic welfare. In addition, the core feature in Islamic accounting and finance that writers focus on are whether Islamic contracts and transactions are complying with Sharia law, debt trading with profit (*riba*), and corporate governance policies with their determinants (Hesse *et al.*, 2008; Almutairi & Quttainah, 2019).

In this context, some Islamic firms may face certain challenges in deciding to adopt accounting standards and Islamic values, where some studies showed a positive impact in using Islamic accounting in illustrating some models to catch up with the modern accounting and finance fields (Restuningdiah, Wafaretta, & Furqorina, 2020). A reasonable number of Islamic accounting studies have been conducted by authors seeking different objectives, concluding that Islamic accounting is still a growing area (Hassan, Aliyu, & Hussain, 2019). Therefore, to fuel this growth, authors have to follow as many trends as in articles, such as theories, topics, and concepts for Islamic accounting and overcoming any potential challenges while researching this field. (Hesse *et al.*, 2008; Sacarcelik, 2010).

This is where the chapter will gather all of the previous works of literature to present all trends of theories, topics, and new concepts included in scholarly articles related to Islamic accounting. Upon the widespread and range of Islamic accounting studies, this chapter will systematically review the available articles to answer two crucial questions provided in the research questions. This chapter will be organized into five sections that will accordingly discuss the availability of Islamic accounting articles adopting theories. Although there is a reasonable number of adopted Islamic accounting topics, there is a lack of systematic or meta-analysis studies. Systematic mapping study is required within the vast and different types of research. All fields, such as the Islamic accounting field, address various models, theories, and different topics (Salama, Bahsoon, & Bencomo, 2017). Therefore, this chapter will provide a reference base for researchers in the Islamic accounting area. This chapter can be considered as a first step in examining available studies to help literature in the future. The main contribution of this chapter is to expand the literature adoption in the Islamic accounting context and validate the proper focusing by using theories and new topics available in the field. In addition, this chapter will provide gaps that have been located while exploring concerning studies to give a list of possible future research. We hope that this chapter will provide practical methodological guidance that will systematically expand the existing literature knowledge.

This chapter is structured as follows: In the next section, the researchers have provided a research methodology of this chapter. Then, the data and data collection method used to contribute to the study are discussed. After that, Section 3.4 presents the data synthesis, which outlines the main characteristics attributed to the included papers. Section 3.5 elaborates the recommendations for future works. Finally, Section 3.6 presents the conclusions, implications, and the overall limitations.

3.2 Research Method

The systematic review method has been used in this chapter. According to Petticrew and Roberts (2008), systematic review studies rely on evidence-based approaches presented by different literature reviews in the common field. Systemic review studies effectively scheming out the overall points of uncertainty and indicate only the relevant studies available in the standard search area, suggesting where the best fit for new studies is required (Salama *et al.*, 2017). By contrast, the systemic review finalizes the last results with descriptive-qualitative procedures analysis (Crowther, Lim, & Crowther, 2010).

Many studies showed that methodologies such as systematic and meta-analysis help prevent bias and develop the legitimacy and reliability of studies (Walker, 2010; Ahmad & Omar, 2016).

Systemic review methodology helps researchers dive into all the existing empirical evidence, especially in Islamic accounting, to structure a new source of knowledge over prior knowledge (Mukhlisin & Antonio, 2018). Hence, this chapter will discover in-depth literature reviews that synthesized Islamic accounting areas in general theories and different topics. Therefore, this chapter will conduct a systematic evidence-based review in Islamic accounting. Findings will contribute to helping potential researchers answer questions such as: On what did previous literature focus? What is the range that has been applied and by whom was it done?

Hence, what is supposed to be added to the Islamic accounting area is far from new models and accounting theories. Therefore, the

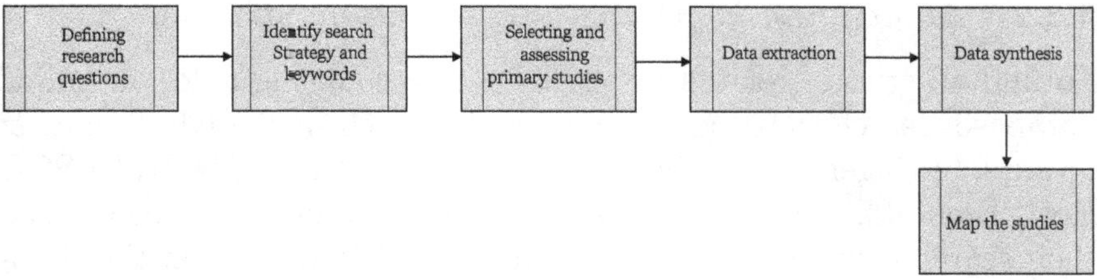

Figure 3.1. Systematic literature review protocol.

researchers have embraced the main guidelines of systematic analysis from Ahmad and Omar (2016)'s study, conducting a systematic review in corporate governance models. This chapter is customized according to the six steps shown in Figure 3.1.

3.2.1 *Defining research questions*

As this chapter aims to obtain a comprehensive overview of the current research work in the Islamic accounting area, we have defined the following questions to elaborate on the main objectives. Many types of research hold different methods to contribute articles that dovetail with the Islamic accounting elements. Therefore, we suggest the following question that will structure the paper as follows:

RQ1. What are the different methods of research that have been presented in the literature over the years?

RQ2. What are the most common topics in accounting literature mainly used?

The expected answer for this question will be defined through the gaps among the various methods and types of research used. The main goal for this question is to summarize the primary types of research the existing studies used to get a broad overview of all forums. In addition, the topics introduced are the field of accounting that authors relied on to contribute their studies.

RQ3. What theories are often used to publish research on the Islamic accounting aspect?

Literature works presented a vast type of theories that are not limited to the accounting field only. This question aims to explore the contribution of different theories from non-accounting theories.

3.2.2 *Identifying keywords and searching strategy*

To find all studies related to the Islamic accounting field, an online database search has been conducted, which included Taylor & Francis, Springer Link, Wiley, Sage, Science Direct, JSTOR, EBSCO Host, Emerald, as seen in Table 3.1. The researchers have conducted their search using chains of words, including keywords that the chapter seeks, finding possible articles and studies. As shown in Table 3.2, the researchers have identified the search chain, including the Boolean operators (AND, OR, and NOT). Therefore, the required research focus can be pointed out as follows: Islamic accounting methods, Islamic accounting theories, and Islamic accounting topics. In the next step, the researchers define the search strategy for related papers from the selected database. This strategy will facilitate searching in an advanced way to collect all possible and proper articles. Furthermore, three search strings have been used in some

Table 3.1. Distribution of publications over the online database.

Database	Retrieved studies	Selected studies
EBSCO host	12	4
Emerald	12	9
Taylor & Francis	13	4
Springer link	2	0
Wiley	7	3
Sage	2	2
Science direct	9	6
JSTOR	2	2
Total	**59**	**30**

Table 3.2. Search strings used for searching.

Concept	Keywords and strings	Boolean operators
Islamic accounting methods	[Islamic AND Accounting] [method OR methods]	AND
Islamic accounting theories	[Islamic AND Accounting] [theory OR theories]	AND

databases and some minor changes in others since not all databases can search for the chains of keywords used seen in Table 3.2.

3.2.3 *Selecting and assessing the quality of the selected studies*

After selecting the proper searching chains, they have been used in the selected eight databases. All findings from articles, chapters, journals, and thesis have been stored. In the next step, all results have been screened; titles, abstracts, keywords, and skim-read all the papers to decide if to include the findings or not. Since the chapter's key focus is methods, topics, and theories, the search has been emphasized in each paper, ensuring that each is using a clear concept of what is desired. The researchers have found 1260 papers from 1995 to 2020 retrieved from the online databases. Then, they have screened all papers to retrieve 59 relevant papers. Next, 53 papers were recovered and selected after excluding the duplicates. All studies' reputations have been checked using the SJR and Scopus indexes, and 44 relevant papers got through. In the following stage, we have implemented the inclusion and the exclusion criteria to all articles individually; 30 papers were relevant to this systematic review. Figure 3.2 is the Prisma flow diagram for our searching process to include and exclude based on the procedure of searching.

The researchers have developed three categories to divide each study into accounting topics and theories. These categories will classify each study according to the methodology used by the literature to answer the second research question.

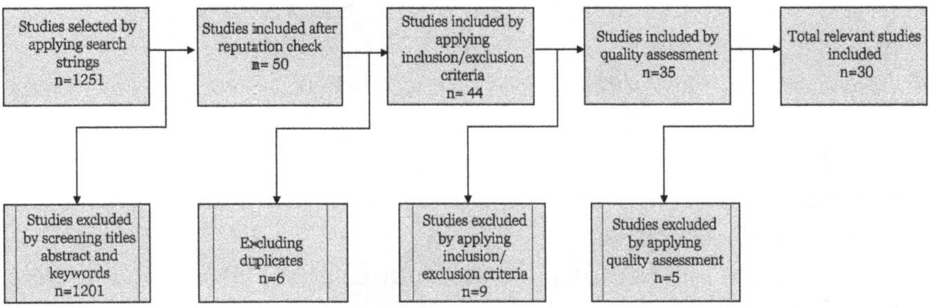

Figure 3.2. Replacement for Prisma flow diagram.

3.2.4 *Inclusion criteria*

- *Papers that explicitly discussed Islamic accounting*: The researchers have included all papers that focused on elaborating any field of Islamic accounting as a central idea of the research.
- *Studies that explore Islamic accounting methods, theories, and topics*: As the researchers continue searching and collecting papers, they have aimed to choose papers that adopted specific methods, theories, and topics that explored Islamic accounting concepts.
- *Studies discovered either all or some of the following elements*: Islamic accounting standards, Sharia accounting laws, Islamic corporate governance, and Islamic corporate social responsibilities.
- *Studies that represented a contrast of strengths and weaknesses between conventional accounting and Islamic accounting*: Although most papers have mentioned at least a line or two about the differences between conventional and Islamic accounting, researchers have concentrated on the papers which presented Islamic accounting aspects' strengths and weaknesses.

3.2.5 *Exclusion criteria*

- *Duplicate studies which have been found in a different database*: During the collection process, the researchers have faced duplicate papers that have been published in multiple databases.
- *Papers mentioned Islamic accounting in the abstract only*: Some studies have used Islamic accounting as an example for interpreting one concept or two as a subhead, not as the main head.
- *Editorial paper, books or book reviews, conference proceedings, and workshops*: All papers are checked by scientific journal rankings (SJR) and Scopus websites to ensure the validity of the study, non-trusted journals and sites have been excluded.
- *Presentations, keynotes, dissertations, thesis, annals, panel discussions, books, technical reports, and non-per-reviewed journal articles*: Books and book reviews have been excluded since they do not present novel results or primary literature but sums up a gather up of previous articles.
- *Non-English publications*: Some non-English papers have been found discussing the main idea of this research. However, they were excluded.

3.2.6 *Quality assessment*

The researchers used SJR and Scopus to check the paper's ranks and journal reputation. They have adapted Tranfield, Denyer, and Smart's (2003) guidelines in literature review procedures which rate the quality of journals according to SJR and Scopus. Apart from the inclusion and exclusion criteria set, this process provides the extraction of only high-quality and reliable studies to include in this chapter. Therefore, all studies selected in this chapter are indexed with a rating in SJR or Scopus or both.

3.2.7 *Data extraction procedure*

Researchers used NVivo 12 software to extract qualitative metadata of research. The software works to convert the results into Excel sheet tables with chosen studies with data characteristics. NVivo 12 software manage data collected to store them, then add codes for inclusion and exclusion criteria, which are crucial in the meta-analysis and systematic review studies. In addition, a plan for the data process of extraction has been structured, as shown in Figure 3.3. The figure shows the steps followed for the protocol of final data collected and then extracted. Planning is the first step discussed in part two of the chapter. Step two is to collect all relevant studies, scan all primary studies, apply quality assessment, and finally synthesize data for the chosen studies. The third step is reporting the final results via systemic review guidelines retrieved from Tranfield *et al.* (2003), ending the process with proofreading.

3.2.8 *Data synthesis*

To answer the chapter questions, the researchers have concluded the following two data synthesis perspectives according to the chosen studies:

(1) General studies characteristics.
(2) Primary classification scheme.

The general study characteristics are discussed in the next section, interpreting the overall features of the selected studies. These characteristics are extracted from NVivo 12 software and Microsoft Excel sheets creating an organized panel for all included

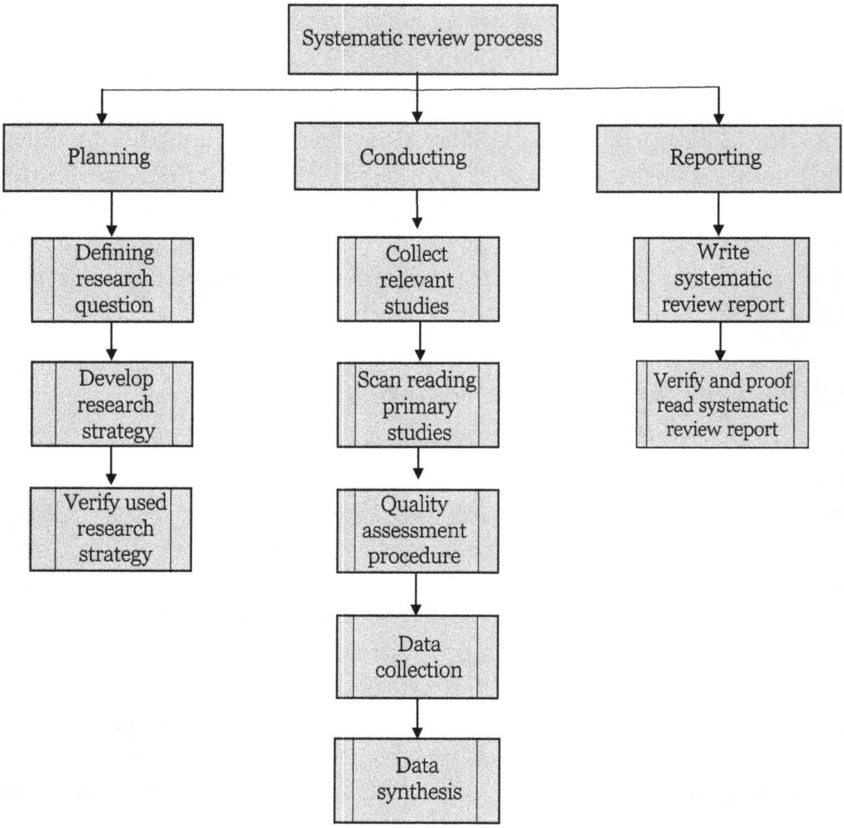

Figure 3.3. Systematic analysis protocol.

studies. Besides, the primary classification scheme is the answer to the chapter's questions. In order to answer them, researchers have developed a system in screening all studies via Nodes in NVivo 12 to extract the scheme of classification for each adopted study.

3.3 Data Collection

This part of the chapter intends to discuss all studies collected into two different sections as discussed before:

(1) General studies characteristics.
(2) Primary classification scheme.

3.3.1 *General data included characteristics*

This part aims to state some of the general characteristics of the general chosen studies. Researchers have developed a system to analyze some of the possible studies' characteristics, such as identifying years' distribution of studies, country-based distributions, number of publications on each online database, and distribution of journals for studies selected. Therefore, the developed system was created on NVivo 12 then extracted to Microsoft Excel sheet to facilitate tracking the nature of general characteristics, including author name, reference type, year, journals, place published, and keywords. Each of the study's characters has its analysis qualitatively in Section 3.4.

3.3.2 *Classification scheme*

Using the qualitative analysis software NVivo 12, we have quickly developed a set of classifications for all papers as discussed previously. The papers were categorized in Excel sheets under research contribution, research types, and its area of focus.

3.3.2.1 *Contribution type*

The contribution type is where the papers have added a new lead or impact over the Islamic accounting field. Many authors have used multiple tools from different accounting areas to interpret new trends or modern papers to publish. Each study selected was classified into the availability of using one or more of the following categories:

- Topics in different accounting fields guided by Islamic perspective.
- The theoretical framework of the study.

3.3.2.2 *Research focus*

According to this chapter, topics have been addressed in each selected study as a lens of focus. Therefore, the following categories have been created:

(1) *Theory adoption in this group*: The researchers have identified all available theories which studies are primarily focused on mapping out the theoretical part of their papers. Many theories were discussed multiple times, which were classic and highly

known among authors, and others were new papers in the Islamic accounting area. Therefore, theories have been classified concerning the accounting field or others, such as business, social, economics, and education.

(2) *Topics adopted by authors*: Authors used many domains in accounting to interpret their objectives, such as financial accounting, managerial accounting, audit, and finance.

3.4 Data Synthesis

3.4.1 *General characteristics*

The overall character of each study included in this chapter's objectives and questions have been examined. This section discusses the publications distribution based on years, countries, databases, journals, and methods. Researchers have found a total of 30 publications scattered from 1995 to 2020. Figure 3.4 shows a timeline for the period. Results show that from 1995 to 2006, the line was steady as one paper was published per year. However, from 2013 to 2019, authors introduced the concept into their studies, indicating a new interest rate among authors. In addition, the findings reveal the increasing trend among authors at the higher peak in 2020, assigning five studies at that year. The growth is attributed to the development of Islamic institutions in the last decades. (Haniffa & Hudaib, 2010; Rusydiana *et al.*, 2020).

Islamic accounting research was not limited to Islamic countries only; authors from different countries worldwide have conducted a study on Islamic accounting. Table 3.3 shows the distribution of countries and authors around the world. We have found 14 different countries that published Islamic accounting studies. The United Kingdom is ranked first for the highest publications assigning seven papers, while Malaysia has contributed five papers. The least ranked

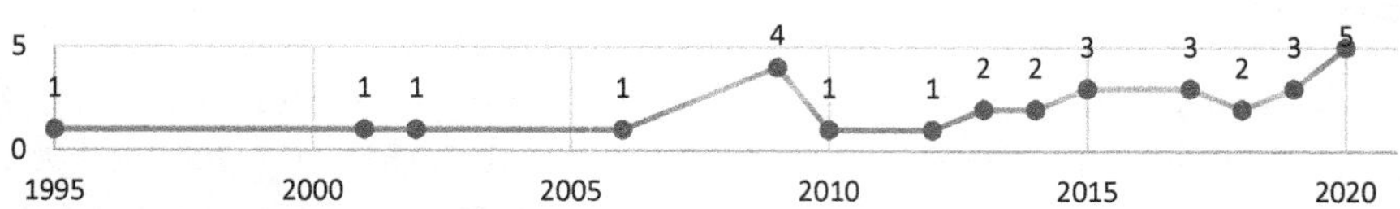

Figure 3.4. Distribution of publications based on years.

Table 3.3. Countries distribution.

Country of research	**No. of publications**	**(%)**	**Selected references**
United Kingdom	7	23	(Nobes, 2001; Kamla, Gallhofer, & Haslam, 2006; Kamla, 2009; Napier, 2009; Kamla & Alsoufi, 2015; Kamla & Haque, 2019; Nawaz *et al.*, 2021)
Malaysia	5	17	(Amin, Rahman, & Ramayah, 2009; Salihin, Fatima, & Anam Ousama, 2014; Velayutham, 2014; Abdullah *et al.*, 2015; Kabir, Masih, & Bacha, 2017)
Indonesia	3	10	(Mulawarman & Kamayanti, 2018b; Baehaqi, Birton, & Hudaefi, 2020; Ridwan & Mayapada, 2020)
Jordan	2	7	(Abu-Tapanjeh, 2009; Altarawneh & Lucas, 2012)
Tunisia	2	7	(Abd El Afou, 2017; Mnif, Jarboui, Hassan, & Mouakhar, 2020)
Nigeria	2	7	(Abdul-Baki, Uthman, Olanrewaju, & Ibrahim, 2013; Umar & Kurawa, 2019)
Australia	2	7	(Rammal & Parker, 2013; Mihret, Alshareef, & Bazhair, 2017)
United States	2	7	(Maurer, 2002; Hassan, Rashid, Wei, Adedokun, & Ramachandran, 2019)
Sweden	1	3	(Saidani, Taktak, & Hussainey, 2020)
Brazil	1	3	(El Khatib, 2018)
China	1	3	(Siswantoro, 2015)
Russia	1	3	(Abdel Karim, 1995)
Germany	1	3	(Vinnicombe, 2010)
Total	**30**	**100**	

countries were Russia, Sweden, Germany, and China, providing one paper only, see Figure 3.5.

In reference to RQ1, most of the research methods of the included studies were qualitative methods. The qualitative method has been

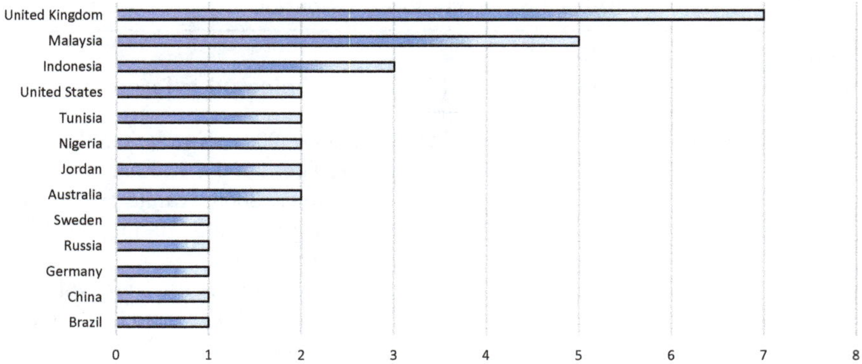

Figure 3.5. Distribution of publications based on countries.

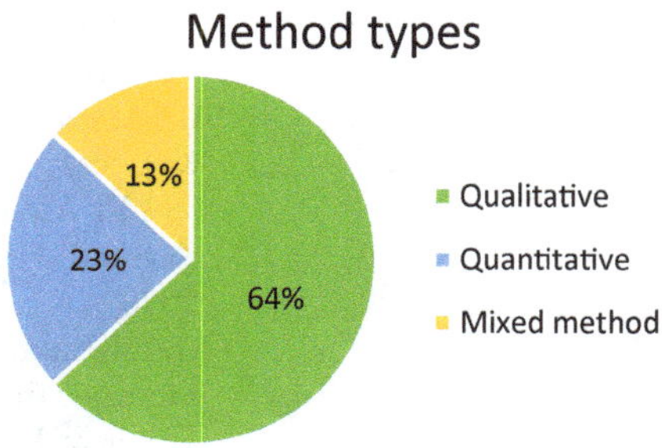

Figure 3.6. Studies method types.

used in 64% of the studies, as shown in Figure 3.6. It is assumed that most studies used the qualitative method for its theoretical nature depending on theories and descriptive conceptual framework. For example, some studies have used various theories lenses to frame their studies introducing a qualitative study to look at Islamic accounting from a managerial perspective. Accordingly, such qualitative studies will provide a comprehensive understanding of decision-making techniques that the Islamic conceptual frame-work provided. This study has explored four different theories in the literature review presentation and discussion: stakeholder theory, wealth maximization theory, decision usefulness theory, and Islamic accounting theory.

However, studies used quantitative methods to explore empirical evidence using quantitative tools. For example, a study examined conventional accounting instead of Islamic accounting in Islamic countries. This paper used the quantitative method by using a questionnaire distributed to accounting members in Jordan, examining the factors and reasons that influence the use of Islamic accounting in their firms (Altarawneh & Lucas, 2012).

As mentioned in Section 3.2, researchers have searched eight different online databases. The findings of each database were vast since the Islamic accounting concept can be used in different fields of business, economics, law, and politics. However, we have used other databases that are not mentioned because they did not contain any publication about Islamic accounting. Therefore, researchers have screened and analyzed all database platforms carefully to sift high-quality papers with new contributions in this field. Emerald database has held the most significant proportion of studies by (30%). Then, ScienceDirect is ranked in the second place by 20%, retrieving six papers, as shown in Figure 3.7. EBSCO Host and Taylor & Francis are potent platforms; four papers were found relevant, with 13% of the total findings. SAGE, JSTOR, and Willy signed 7%, and 10%, respectively, for consisting relevant studies for this chapter. To proceed in the underlining sifting process, all journals in SJR ranks and Scopus indexed journals have been checked in order to assure the good reputations for the founded journals. In addition, as shown in Table 3.4, several journals have published Islamic accounting related studies. A total of six articles were ranked in the *Journal of Islamic Accounting and Business Research*, while *Critical Perspectives on Accounting* published four articles. *Journal of Sustainable Finance and Investments* as of the least published by one article.

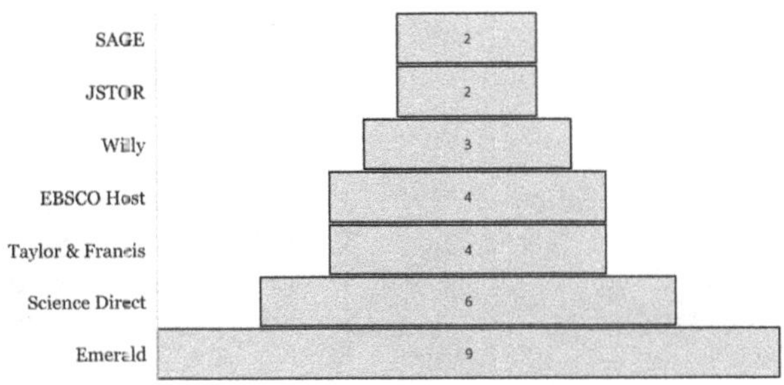

Figure 3.7. Publications selected database.

Table 3.4. Distribution of the publications-based journal.

Journals	#	(%)	References
Journal of Islamic Accounting and Business Research	6	20	(Altarawneh & Lucas, 2012; Abdul-Baki *et al.*, 2013; Salihin *et al.*, 2014; Velayutham, 2014; Ben Abd El Afou, 2017; Baehaqi *et al.*, 2020)
Critical Perspectives on Accounting	4	13	(Kamla & Haque, 2019; Mihret *et al.*, 2017; Kamla, 2009; Abu-Tapanjeh, 2009)
Accounting Forum	2	7	(Kamla *et al.*, 2006; Kamla & Alsoufi, 2015)
Accounting History	2	7	(Napier, 2009; Rammal & Parker, 2013)
Accounting and Business Research	1	3	(Abdel Karim, 1995)
Accounting Historians Journal	1	3	(Nobes, 2001)
Advances in Accounting	1	3	(Vinnicombe, 2010)
Emerging Markets Finance and Trade	1	3	(Kabir *et al.*, 2017)
Intelligent Systems in Accounting, Finance, and Management	1	3	(Mnif *et al.*, 2020)
International Journal of Business and Society	1	3	(Mulawarman & Kamayanti, 2018b)
International Journal of Finance & Economics	1	3	(Nawaz *et al.*, 2021)
International Journal of Islamic and Middle Eastern Finance and Management	1	3	(Amin *et al.*, 2009)
ISRA International Journal of Islamic Finance	1	3	(Umar & Kurawa, 2019)
Journal of Contemporary Accounting & Economics	1	3	(Abdullah *et al.*, 2015)
Journal of the Royal Anthropological Institute	1	3	(Maurer, 2002)
Quality Assurance in Education	1	3	(Siswantoro, 2015)
Revista de Negócios	1	3	(El Khatib, 2018)
Singapore Economic Review	1	3	(Saidani *et al.*, 2020)
Thunderbird International Business Review	1	3	(Hassan, Rashid *et al.*, 2019)
Journal of Sustainable Finance & Investment	1	3	(Ridwan & Mayapada, 2020)
Total	**30**	**100**	

3.4.2 *Results of the classification scheme and research question*

According to the classifications defined in the previous sections, we have created two focus points: the domains authors introduced and the theories that authors have adopted to outline the theoretical parts of their papers.

3.4.3 *Classifications analysis*

3.4.3.1 *Topics adopted by authors*

In reference to RQ2, in this part, researchers have discovered that there are flexible possibilities to introduce Islamic accounting into all fields of accounting with no barriers since Islamic accounting is comprehensive with the conceptual framework as much as conventional accounting. Some works in the literature clarified which area of accounting they have focused on. At the same time, some of them decided to write their paper with integrated fields, which has made an excellent synergy for the literature. Researchers have generally found four topics in accounting. Most of the selected papers have studied: financial accounting, managerial accounting, audit, and corporate finance. Then, they have added an extra field for studies that used two or more topics. Figure 3.8 shows the number of publications that propose their studies.

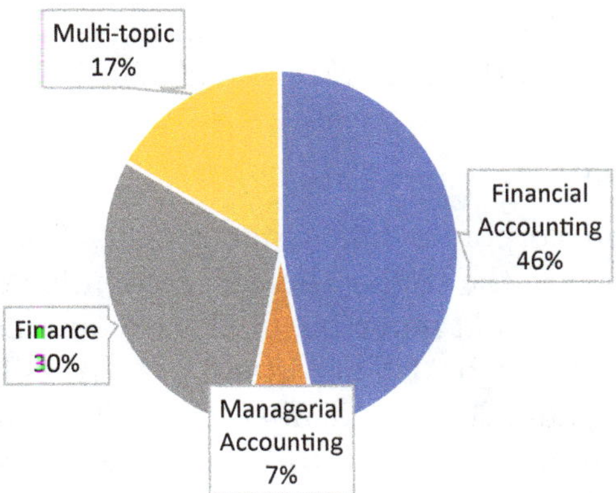

Figure 3.8. Topics contributions.

3.4.3.1.1 Financial accounting

In this field, most of the topics introduce the financial firms' operations and transactions, financial statements, financial standards, and conceptual accounting framework. Researchers have found 14 papers out of 30 that have introduced financial accounting as the main topic (46%). Some papers have introduced Islamic accounting knowledge to professionals as a new system in Islamic and non-Islamic institutions (Nobes, 2001; Vinnicombe, 2010; Abd El Afou, 2017; El Khatib, 2018). These papers have explored the accountants' preferability in prepositions using the Islamic Accounting Auditing Organization for Islamic Financial Institution (AAOIFI) for different countries. While Kamla *et al.* (2006), Salihin *et al.* (2014), Siswantoro (2015), and Kamla and Haque (2019) have presented the Islamic accounting principles with awareness of the nature of this type of accounting in Islamic institutions. Hence, according to Abdel Karim (1995), the study compared the conceptual framework of conventional accounting with the Islamic conceptual framework. This paper found that Financial Accounting Organization for Islamic Banks and Financial Institutions (FAOIBFI) has supported the Islamic accounting systems to frame the objectives and policies of Islamic accounting. In addition, some studies have stated the issues that Islamic accounting can struggle in the application for firms. Altarawneh and Lucas (2012) have interpreted the reasons for neglecting Islamic accounting in Islamic countries. The findings of this study refer to economic dependency as a significant factor in determining the accounting system such as Islamic accounting. Thus, some authors introduced modern studies to the Islamic financial accounting topics, discussing the big data tool used in this field (Mnif *et al.*, 2020).

3.4.3.1.2 Finance

The finance and corporate finance area held 30% of the selected papers. According to the studies, Islamic accounting corporate social responsibility (CSR) and reporting disclosures are major topics presented and integrated by Islamic standards (Abu-Tapanjeh, 2009; Ridwan & Mayapada, 2020; Saidani *et al.*, 2020; Nawaz *et al.*, 2021). According to Abdullah *et al.* (2015), institutions that adopted the Islamic accounting framework have a crucial part in the corporate governance mechanisms that enhanced CSR disclosure. In addition,

Kamla and Alsoufi (2015) and Kabir *et al.* (2017) contribute to show the finance tools that are used to avoid riba (interests) in the Islamic institution for investments and finance.

3.4.3.1.3 Managerial accounting

Managerial accounting is an essential field for works of literature; this field holds 7% of the total selected paper. This field discusses the management and internal need of Islamic accounting versus conventional accounting for the firms. Based on Abdul-Baki *et al.* (2013), the Islamic accounting perspectives have added new ideas and techniques in management accounting decisions aligned with the Islamic views, including cost–benefit comparison and contribution margin. In addition, Hassan *et al.* (2019) used the balanced scorecard techniques to examine firms that use Islamic accounting systems worldwide.

3.4.3.1.4 Multi topics

This classification holds all studies that discussed multi-topic Islamic accounting. Here, 17% of selected papers interpreted two or more topics in accounting. Amin *et al.* (2009) discussed accounting education and elective courses in accounting, including Islamic accounting. The results indicate that student's attitudes and the amount of information affect the student's intention to enroll in an Islamic accounting course. Another study has compared and debated the overall concepts in accounting with Islamic accounting in many fields. Such studies seek to find the natural history of Islamic accounting and where it started (Velayutham, 2014; Mulawarman & Kamayanti, 2018a). In addition, Mihret *et al.* (2017) have examined the Saudi Organization of Certified Public Accountants (SOCPA) regulations guided by Islamic accounting norms and principles.

3.4.3.2 *Theory adoption*

Regarding RQ3, researchers have addressed 13 different theories that the selected papers have adopted. These theories were divided into five types: accounting, management, economics, social, and education.

In the accounting theories group, AAOIFI Conceptual Framework theory is the most selected; the theory consists of the basics in accounting, including the Islamic accounting and auditing regulations. This theory illustrates Sharia laws in accounting identification, measurements, and recognitions (Siswantoro, 2015; Umar & Kurawa, 2019). At the same time, Velayutham (2014) compared the two theories, normative and positive accounting, to examine the assumption around the conventional accounting competitivity with Islamic accounting principles and regulations. This paper has found a misconception about the assumption of the incompatible Islamic accounting with conventional accounting and is attributed to culture and economic dependency (Velayutham, 2014).

On the other hand, the managerial theories have discovered one of the most popular theories in accounting and business, namely stakeholder theory, that has been ranked in the second place among authors. This theory argued the need for firms to strive to do the right thing for stakeholders' benefit (Sarea & Hanefah, 2013; Ridwan & Mayapada, 2020). According to Sarea and Hanefah (2013), they integrated the stakeholder theory to discuss the acceptability of Islamic accounting standards such as the AAOIFI. They found that Islamic institutions find some obstacles to applying Islamic standards. Furthermore, the agency theory rendered on the corporate governance issue in Islamic firms. This theory discusses two parties which are agent and principal. Abu-Tapanjeh (2009) examined the association between the Islamic corporate and its agents through disclosures transparency and its implications.

Moreover, the legitimacy theory interprets the contract between the Islamic institution in this context and the society. According to Abdullah *et al.* (2015), the paper stated the determinants of Islamic institution to public voluntary disclosure. They found that some factors are related to the firm's characters such as size of Islamic institution, political and civil authoritarianism, and the legal system, where these characters can influence the level of disclosures.

While the economic theory presents that both investors and consumers are pretty rational, this theory has been discussed by Rammal and Parker (2013); the economics of states theory plays a significant role in governing society, which leads to a development in accounting regulation and accountability. In addition, this theory aids studies to analyze the decision made for applying Islamic accounting in Islamic institutions (Kamla, 2009; Baehaqi *et al.*, 2020).

Authors who have adopted theories from outside accounting and business areas are the most who contribute to this field. For example, Mihret *et al.* (2017) presented the actor-network theory to explore accounting professionalization in the Saudi case in Islamic institutions. This paper found that the accounting profession in Saudi Arabia is secured by SOCPA aligned with Islamic standards and regulations. In addition, other social theories, such as the functionalist theory stated by Maurer (2002), present a framework for how society sees the complex system of Islamic accounting anthropology. Ibn Ashur's (Maqasid al-Sharia) theory, according to Baehaqi *et al.* (2020), defined it as controlling and implementing the law or orders according to Islamic laws from prevention of harm received and benefits gained from well-being actions.

Lastly, educational theories are also a new brand contribution for the Islamic accounting field. Kamla and Haque (2019) involved their study in the new appearance of Islamic accounting based on the AAOIFS. They used the collaborative theory, which states that the relational model between two parties engaged in real time with no boundaries and a peer-to-peer learning. In this context, the author used the theory to discuss the association between the Islamic standards and the world's global politics with economics.

3.5 Recommendations for Future Research

This section emphasizes the primary goal of the systematic and literature reviews studies by identifying the significant gaps among reviewed papers. There were various paper types and results critiqued in this chapter. Therefore, the researchers offered a set of recommendations and guidelines for future researchers to address the gaps and recommendations. They have recognized three gaps that we believe faced absence among writers.

3.5.1 *Islamic corporates social responsibility*

As we proceed in reviewing the papers, we found that CSR and corporate governance mechanisms in developing countries lack sufficient empirical evidence, most of which apply the Islamic accounting model

(Bhuiyan, Darda, & Hossain, 2021). This area is critical due to the importance of applying CSR disclosures and mechanisms along with Islamic ethical and philanthropic regulations and policies such as Zakat policies (Al-Malkawi & Javaid, 2018). Moreover, CSR disclosures have many dimensions that can be adopted and comprehended with Islamic accounting procedures, such as the company's environment and culture (see for example, Platonova *et al.*, 2018). It is recommended for future literature to corporate the new concepts of CSR disclosures discussing the determinants that influence the presence of web-based disclosure for firms that use the Islamic model. In addition, researchers believe that the CSR area for Islamic countries that apply Islamic accounting has less pressure for the perseverance in this area; therefore, these suggestions are a call for more papers to enrich this vital field.

3.5.2 *Islamic accounting adopting blockchain and cryptocurrencies*

Accounting information systems is one of the most critical domains that have been required in the Islamic business environment to align with modern developments. Researchers believe that the Islamic accounting model can quickly adapt to the modern facilities in this area. However, they found a lack of literature in this area. Perhaps Islamic accounting and finance can propose a new cryptocurrency that aggregates all Muslim countries' currencies, making transactions and finance procedures easier. It is suggested to offer a new perception for the future Islamic accounting blockchain and cryptocurrency field. The integration between Islamic accounting and information systems allows expansion of the literature in this field, resulting in a new synergy. The researchers believe that the information technology domain is a tremendous domain that needs to be deeply explored, accompanied by Islamic accounting topics such as finance tools for Islamic institutions.

3.5.3 *Further theories, methodology, and topics suggestions*

Researchers have considered the following suggestions for further research using those theories, methodology, and topics that defiantly solve the narrow scope issue for Islamic accounting articles. We suggest the following to enrich this part:

- As in any field in social studies, accounting can adopt some educational and pedagogical theories that interpret the perspective of a student, tutor, and curricula designer (Alaqrabawi & Alshurafat, 2020). According to the previous literature defined in Table 3.5 classified by the theory, it has been observed that educational theories were barely considered. Some theories, such as

Table 3.5. Theory contributions.

Theory	**Type of theory**	**Reference**
AAOIFI conceptual framework	Accounting	(Siswantoro, 2015; Saidani *et al.*, 2020; Abd El Afou, 2017; Abdul-Baki *et al.*, 2013; Umar & Kurawa, 2019; Velayutham, 2014; Kamla & Alsoufi, 2015; Abdel Karim, 1995)
Stakeholder theory	Management	(Abdul-Baki *et al.*, 2013; Ridwan & Mayapada, 2020; Hassan & Rashid, *et al.*, 2019; Abdullah *et al.*, 2015)
Agency theory	Management	(Abu-Tapanjeh, 2009; Abdullah *et al.*, 2015; Nawaz *et al.*, 2021; Ridwan & Mayapada, 2020)
Economic of states theory	Economics	(Rammal & Parker, 2013; Baehaqi *et al.*, 2020; Kamla, 2009)
Legitimacy theory	Management	(Abdullah *et al.*, 2015)
Actor-Network theory	Social	(Mihret *et al.*, 2017)
Collaborative theory	Education	(Kamla & Haque, 2019)
Dependency theory	Economics	(Altarawneh & Lucas, 2012)
Contingency theory	Management	(El Khatib, 2018)
Functionalist theory	Social	(Maurer, 2002)
Ibn Ashur Maqasid al-Sharia theory	Social	(Baehaqi *et al.*, 2020)
Positive and Normative theory	Accounting	(Velayutham, 2014)
Stewardship theory	Management	(Ridwan & Mayapada, 2020)

the neo-correspondence theory, can develop Islamic accounting as standalone courses for students to exploit in the work environment. Such studies are an exciting factor for curricula designers and teaching notes for educators.

- Meta-analysis and literature reviews offer critical insight for overall papers published concerned by Islamic accounting and related topics. According to El-Halaby *et al.* (2021), they have applied a systematic literature review for papers that involves AAOIFI standards. This paper has located and systematically analyzed all papers that discussed AAOIFI standards carried in different research tracks. Such papers are recommended to widen the trend and interests about the Islamic accounting different tracks.
- Trends and new events that have been worldwide stories must be included for further research. For example, the COVID-19 pandemic and how it influenced the Islamic institution's sectors. Moreover, some economic events that happened in the Islamic community or internationally must be addressed to guarantee the involvement as a new contribution, for instance, the IPOs of Islamic institutions.

3.6 Conclusion

In conclusion, this chapter has served two objectives by answering stated questions and offering recommendations to fill the literature gaps. This chapter identified the type of research used, theories, and domains in accordance with the Islamic accounting perspective. Moreover, this chapter has explored all selected papers to introduce two types of Islamic studies' contributions. These contributions help to extend the Islamic accounting field by bringing more intention to it. The two classification schemes for the contributions were concerned with the theories constructed by the authors and the possible topics defined in different domains in accounting. The general characteristics for papers are based on the following: online database, years of publication, country of publications, and journals.

Moreover, the researcher's investigation among literature reviews was systemic based on a set of exclusion and inclusion criteria which has limited the results along with 30 selected papers. Researchers have discussed three types of research, qualitative, quantitative, and mixed methods. Hence, they have discussed four domains in accounting fields: finance, financial accounting, managerial accounting, and multi-topics. In addition, they have found 13 different theories in five different categories of theories. Finally, the researchers have suggested some possible ideas that can benefit future literature to introduce new work in the Islamic accounting area. Moreover, some trends which are convenient to be employed in this field to expand the presence of Islamic accounting field.

Furthermore, the contribution of this chapter lies in offering new ideas for scholars and literature to expand the research in Islamic accounting domains. Beyond this board purpose, researchers believe that this chapter will outline a framework for readers, future researchers, and students in Islamic accounting courses. The main limitation for this chapter is the selected scope of theories selected by authors and the domain the authors choose to discuss, i.e., the results of online databases. In addition, we have used only studies that have been retrieved after the inclusion and exclusion criteria to serve the overall purpose of this chapter. Researchers believe that it is needed to have more in-depth research with a quantitative test. It is recommended for future literature to widen the scope into models or perspectives that are used to illustrate any issue concerning the Islamic accounting field.

References

Abd El Afou, R. B. (2017). Knowledge of Islamic accounting among professionals: Evidence from the Tunisian context. *Journal of Islamic Accounting and Business Research*, *8*(3), 304–325.

Abdel Karim, R. A. (1995). The nature and rationale of a conceptual framework for financial reporting by Islamic banks. *Accounting and Business Research*, *25*(100), 285–300.

Abdul-Baki, Z., Uthman, A. B., Olanrewaju, A. A., & Ibrahim, S. A. (2013). Islamic perspective of management accounting decision making techniques. *Journal of Islamic Accounting and Business Research*, *4*(2), 203–219.

Abdullah, W. A. W., Percy, M., & Stewart, J. (2015). Determinants of voluntary corporate governance disclosure: Evidence from Islamic banks in the Southeast Asian and the Gulf Cooperation Council regions. *Journal of Contemporary Accounting & Economics*, *11*(3), 262–279.

Abu-Tapanjeh, A. M. (2009). Corporate governance from the Islamic perspective: A comparative analysis with OECD principles. *Critical Perspectives on Accounting*, *20*(5), 556–567.

Ahmad, S. & Omar, R. (2016). Basic corporate governance models: A systematic review. *International. Journal of Law and Management*, *58*(1), 73–107.

Al-Malkawi, H.-A. N. & Javaid, S. (2018). Corporate social responsibility and financial performance in Saudi Arabia: Evidence from Zakat contribution. *Managerial Finance*, *44*(6), 648–664.

Alaqrabawi, M. & Alshurafat, H. (2020). Alignment between accounting graduates' competencies and workplace needs: Neo-correspondence perspective and meta-analysis. 8th International conference on new ideas in management, economic, and accounting, Budapest, Hungary.

Almutairi, A. R. & Quttainah, M. A. (2019). Corporate governance and accounting conservatism in Islamic banks. *Thunderbird International Business Review*, *61*(5), 745–764.

Altarawneh, G. & Lucas, M. (2012). Understanding the dominance of Western accounting and neglect of Islamic accounting in Islamic countries. *Journal of Islamic Accounting and Business Research*, *3*(2), 99–120. Doi: 10.1108/17590811211265920.

Amin, H., Rahman, A. R. A., & Ramayah, T. (2009). What makes undergraduate students enroll into an elective course? The case of Islamic accounting. *International Journal of Islamic and Middle Eastern Finance and Management*, *2*(4), 289–304. Doi: 10.1108/17538390911006359.

Baehaqi, A., Birton, M. N. A., & Hudaefi, F. A. (2020). Time value of money in Islamic accounting practice: A critical analysis from maqāsid al-Sharī'ah. *Journal of Islamic Accounting and Business Research*, *11*(9), 2035–2052.

Baydoun, N., Sulaiman, M., Willett, R. J., & Ibrahim, S. (2018). *Principles of Islamic Accounting*. Singapore: John Wiley & Sons.

Ben Abd El Afou, R. (2017). Knowledge of Islamic accounting among professionals: Evidence from the Tunisian context. *Journal of Islamic Accounting and Business Research*, *8*(3), 304–325. Doi: 10.1108/JIABR-03-2015-0008.

Bhuiyan, M. A. H., Darda, M. A., & Hossain, M. B. (2021). Corporate social responsibility (CSR) practices in Islamic banks of Bangladesh. *Social Responsibility Journal*, (ahead-of-print). Doi: 10.1108/SRJ-07-2020-0280.

Crowther, M., Lim, W., & Crowther, M. A. (2010). Systematic review and meta-analysis methodology. *Blood*, *116*(17), 3140–3146.

El-Halaby, S., Aboul-Dahab, S., & Bin Qoud, N. (2021). A systematic literature review on AAOIFI standards. *Journal of Financial Reporting and Accounting*, *19*(2), 133–183. Doi: 10.1108/JFRA-06-2020-0170.

El Khatib, A. S. (2018). Accounting standards for islamic financial institutions in United Kingdom and Indonesia. *Revista de Negócios*, *21*(2), 7–24.

Farook, S., Kabir Hassan, M., & Lanis, R. (2011). Determinants of corporate social responsibility disclosure: The case of Islamic banks. *Journal of Islamic Accounting and Business Research*, *2*(2), 114–141. Doi: 10.1108/17590811111170539.

Halim, H. A. (2017). Understanding and awareness of Islamic accounting: The Case of Malaysian accounting undergraduates. *International Journal of Academic Research in Accounting, Finance and Management Sciences*. *7*(4), 33–39.

Haniffa, R. & Hudaib, M. (2010). The two Ws of Islamic accounting research. *Journal of Islamic Accounting and Business Research*, *1*(1), 5–9. Doi: 10.1108/17590811011033370.

Hassan, M. K., Aliyu, S., & Hussain, M. (2019). A contemporary review of Islamic finance and accounting literature. *The Singapore Economic Review*, *67*(01), 7–44. Doi: 10.1142/S0217590819420013.

Hassan, M. K., Rashid, M., Wei, A. S., Adedokun, B. O., & Ramachandran, J. (2019). Islamic business scorecard and the screening of Islamic businesses in a cross-country setting. *Thunderbird International Business Review*, *61*(5), 807–819.

Hesse, H., Jobst, A., & Sole, J. (2008). Trends and challenges in Islamic finance. *World Economics -Henley on Thames*, *9*(2), 175–194.

Kabir, S. H., Masih, A. M. M., & Bacha, O. I. (2017). Risk–return profiles of Islamic equities and commodity portfolios in different market conditions. *Emerging Markets Finance and Trade*, *53*(7), 1477–1500.

Kamla, R. (2009). Critical insights into contemporary Islamic accounting. *Critical Perspectives on Accounting*, *20*(8), 921–932.

Kamla, R. & Alsoufi, R. (2015). Critical Muslim intellectuals' discourse and the issue of "interest" (ribā): Implications for Islamic accounting and banking. *Accounting Forum*, *39*(2), 140–154. Doi: 10.1016/j.accfor.2015.02.002.

Kamla, R., Gallhofer, S., & Haslam, J. (2006). *Islam, Nature and Accounting: Islamic Principles and the Notion of Accounting for the Environment.* Paper presented at the Accounting forum.

Kamla, R. & Haque, F. (2019). Islamic accounting, neo-imperialism and identity staging: The accounting and auditing organization for Islamic financial institutions. *Critical Perspectives on Accounting*, *63*, 102000.

Majid, J. & Haliding, S. (2014). The need for the Islamization of knowledge in accounting. *Al-Iqtishad: Jurnal Ilmu Ekonomi Syariah, 6*(1), 11–22.

Maurer, B. (2002). Anthropological and accounting knowledge in Islamic banking and finance: Rethinking critical accounts. *Journal of the Royal Anthropological Institute, 8*(4), 645–667.

Mihret, D. G., Alshareef, M. N., & Bazhair, A. (2017). Accounting professionalization and the state: The case of Saudi Arabia. *Critical Perspectives on Accounting, 45*, 29–47.

Mnif, E., Jarboui, A., Hassan, M. K., & Mouakhar, K. (2020). Big data tools for Islamic financial analysis. *Intelligent Systems in Accounting, Finance and Management, 27*(1), 10–21.

Mukhlisin, M. & Antonio, M. S. (2018). Meta analysis on direction of accounting standards for Islamic financial institution: Case studies in United Kingdom and Indonesia. *Al-Iqtishad Journal of Islamic Economics, 10*(1), 231–254.

Mulawarman, A. D. & Kamayanti, A. (2018a). Islamic accounting anthropology: A constructivist methodological alternative. *International Journal of Business and Society, 19*(2), 302–311.

Mulawarman, A. D. & Kamayanti, A. (2018b). Towards Islamic accounting anthropology. *Journal of Islamic Accounting and Business Research. 9*(4), 629–647. https://doi.org/10.1108/JIABR-02-2015-0004.

Napier, C. (2009). Defining Islamic accounting: Current issues past roots. *Accounting History, 14*(1–2), 121–144.

Nawaz, T., Haniffa, R., & Hudaib, M. (2021). On intellectual capital efficiency and Shariah governance in Islamic banking business model. *International Journal of Finance & Economics, 26*(3), 3770–3787. Doi: 10.1002/ijfe.1986.

Nobes, C. W. (2001). Were Islamic records precursors to accounting books based on the Italian method? A comment. *Accounting Historians Journal, 28*(2), 207–214.

Petticrew, M. & Roberts, H. (2008). *Systematic Reviews in the Social Sciences: A Practical Guide*. New Jersey, USA: John Wiley & Sons.

Platonova, E., Asutay, M., Dixon, R., & Mohammad, S. (2018). The impact of corporate social responsibility disclosure on financial performance: Evidence from the GCC Islamic banking sector. *Journal of Business Ethics, 151*(2), 451–471.

Rammal, H. G. & Parker, L. D. (2013). Islamic banking in Pakistan: A history of emergent accountability and regulation. *Accounting History, 18*(1), 5–29.

Razak, S. S., Saiti, B., & Dinç, Y. (2019). The contracts, structures and pricing mechanisms of sukuk: A critical assessment. *Borsa Istanbul Review, 19*, S21–S33.

Restuningdiah, N., Wafaretta, V., & Furqorina, R. (2020). A mapping of Islamization of accounting. *KnE Social Sciences*, *4*(9), 420–436.

Ridwan, R. & Mayapada, A. G. (2020). Does sharia governance influence corporate social responsibility disclosure in Indonesia Islamic banks? *Journal of Sustainable Finance & Investment*, 1–20. Doi: 10.1080/20430795.2020.1749819.

Rusydiana, A., Taqi, M., Firmansyah, I., Assalafiyah, A., & Kustiningsih, N. (2020). A bibliometric analysis of Islamic accounting research indexed by dimensions. ai. *Library Philosophy and Practice (e-journal)*, *4803*.

Sacarcelik, O. (2010). Trends and challenges in Islamic finance: A case study of Switzerland. *Swiss Review of Business and Financial Market Law/Schweizerische Zeitschrift für Wirtschafts-und Finanzmarktrecht, Forthcoming*, *82*(1), 10–21.

Saidani, R., Taktak, N. B., & Hussainey, K. (2020). The investment account holders disclosure level in the annual reports of Islamic banks: Construction of IAHs disclosure index. *The Singapore Economic Review*, *67*(01), 87–111.

Salama, M., Bahsoon, R., & Bencomo, N. (2017). Managing tradeoffs in self-adaptive software architectures: A systematic mapping study. *Managing Trade-offs in Adaptable Software Architectures*, *11*(01), 249–297.

Salihin, A., Fatima, A. H., & Anam Ousama, A. (2014). An Islamic perspective on the true and fair view override principle. *Journal of Islamic Accounting and Business Research*, *5*(2), 142–157. Doi: 10.1108/JIABR-12-2011-0005.

Sarea, A. M. & Hanefah, M. M. (2013). The need of accounting standards for Islamic financial institutions: Evidence from AAOIFI. *Journal of Islamic Accounting and Business Research*, *4*(1), 64–76. Doi: 10.1108/17590811311314294.

Siswantoro, D. (2015). Perception and awareness of Islamic accounting: Student perspectives. *Quality Assurance in Education*, *23*(3), 306–320. Doi: 10.1108/QAE-08-2012-0031.

Tranfield, D., Denyer, D., & Smart, P. (2003). Towards a methodology for developing evidence-informed management knowledge by means of systematic review. *British Journal of Management*, *14*(3), 207–222.

Umar, U. H. & Kurawa, J. M. (2019). Business succession from an Islamic accounting perspective. *ISRA International Journal of Islamic Finance*, *11*(2), 267–281. Doi: 10.1108/IJIF-06-2018-0059.

Velayutham, S. (2014). "Conventional" accounting vs. "Islamic" accounting: The debate revisited. *Journal of Islamic Accounting and Business Research*, *5*(2), 126–141. Doi: 10.1108/JIABR-05-2012-0026.

Vinnicombe, T. (2010). AAOIFI reporting standards: Measuring compliance. *Advances in Accounting, 26*(1), 55–65.

Walker, K. (2010). A systematic review of the corporate reputation literature: Definition, measurement, and theory. *Corporate Reputation Review, 12*(4), 357–387.

https://doi.org/10.1142/9781800612426_0004

Chapter 4

Review on the Conceptual and Empirical Studies on Zakat

Souhir Neifar and Amal Aissa

Abstract

Due to the growing role of zakat in reducing poverty, a trend of research has been directed toward calling attention to the necessity of this Islamic duty to individual, cooperation, and the society in general. A common debate in Islamic taxation relates to the question of difference between zakat and taxation and about what drives zakat compliance. Few are the studies that have examined zakat, and most have generally tried to understand the individual tax compliance behavior. Thus, the area of corporate zakat is a challenging area and needs to be further analyzed. This chapter presents the basic settings that review the definition of zakat and its different perspectives and a comparison between zakat and conventional taxes. It also describes the legal form of zakat in the different MENA countries. Moreover, this chapter reviews major papers that have examined zakat. This study can help the non-specialist reader understand the Islamic taxation (zakat) and the specificity of each of the MENA countries regarding zakat.

Keywords: Zakat, Tax, Corporate Governance, Corporate Social Responsibility.

4.1 Introduction

Zakat is an Islamic concept and an obligation for every Muslim whose wealth exceeds the tax threshold and has been immobilized for a year. Recently, zakat has become an interesting issue around the world since the high level of importance it has in the Islamic financial system and the crucial role it plays in stimulating the circulation of money by reinjecting a social surplus into economic life. As a result, zakat has become a key element in the global economy. A considerable body of research has highlighted the importance of zakat, especially during the period of spread of the COVID-19 pandemic. For example, the study by Al Anshory *et al.* (2020) demonstrated the vital role played by zakat in preventing the impact of COVID-19 and mitigating issues impacted by the virus.

Apart from this obligation, there exists another legal form of taxation, which is the tax. Zakat and taxation are two notions that have some similarities and dissimilarities. Taxation and zakat are distinguishable in their theoretical foundation, respective legislative sources, rates, objectives, exemptions, and expenditures (Barizah, 2007). However, taxation is adopted and applied while zakat remains abstract.

Note that Zakat is not restricted to individual responsibility, but it is also of all corporations and organizations toward the society that complies with Islamic law. The zakat rate on a company is about 2.5%. Hence, all Islamic financial institutions are liable for the payment of zakat, but the problem is that there are differences toward zakat obligation among countries, which vary from obligatory to voluntary, and despite its importance, there are some institutions that ignore it definitively. The problem of irresponsibility of companies to pay zakat motivates some researchers to provide a solution to the problem of not yet optimizing the capability of zakat by examining the impact of zakat on firm performance and to focus on the factors that can play a growing role in stimulating the payment of zakat in order to encourage and sensibilize them.

Several papers have examined the importance of zakat. However, limited are the studies that have investigated the implementation of zakat practice to enhance the performance of Islamic financial institutions and the determinants of zakat compliance, especially for Islamic companies.

Due to the importance of the role of zakat, researchers will benefit from a report of existing research in zakat to investigate new research ideas on the issue. Thus, the objective of this chapter is first to overcome the ambiguities associated with zakat to know more about the role of this concept from a different perspective. Second, this chapter aims to compare the notion of conventional taxation and zakat on the different aspects (economic, legal, ethical, social, and spiritual). Third, this chapter aims to summarize the different studies that focus on the relation between zakat compliance, firm performance, and corporate governance.

In addition, in this chapter, we seek to answer the following questions:

- How is zakat an important concept?
- What is the relation between zakat, corporate governance, and Islamic firm performance?

This chapter contributes to the literature by providing a comprehensive and global explanation and understanding attached to zakat using previous theoretical and empirical studies. So, this chapter can be used as a reference that includes and resembles the main theoretical and empirical studies on zakat.

This chapter is divided into two main parts. The first is dedicated to explaining the concept of zakat: the definition of zakat and the differences between zakat and tax. The second part reviews the different empirical studies on zakat.

4.2 Concept of Zakat

4.2.1 *Definition of zakat*

4.2.1.1 *Traditional definition of zakat*

Zakat is one of five pillars of Islam. In Arabic, and according to Qardhawi (1969), "zakat" is derived from the verb zakat, which means "to purify, grow, and increase" wealth. Most Islamic jurists have defined zakat as "a duty that was tasked by God for economic and social efficiency". Thus, the definition above expresses the belief that zakat is mandated by God and that it has effective functions for the economy and society.

In the technical Sharia meaning, zakat is defined as a part of wealth whose payment was made obligatory by Allah and his prophet. The zakat is one of the five pillars of Islam. So, it is for Muslims an act of worship. Moreover, it is a wealth tax in the economic sense, including a tax on hoarded wealth, agricultural products, livestock, and commercial goods on condition that their value exceeds a certain limit called Nissab. It is actually a mandatory payment for the benefit of the poor and needy, as explained in detail in the Qur'an. Zakat is thus a moral obligation based on a levy on the surplus of the rich, which acts as an income redistribution instrument, often playing a decisive role in the reintegration of the poor into the economic and social circuit of a country (Abdullah & Suhaib, 2018). In the historical context, Zakat was considered one of the efficient mechanisms of redistribution of income from the rich to the poor and hence a means to mitigate social exclusion and therefore the well-being of countries' economies that adopted zakat charity.

These definitions are considered as the traditional definition of zakat because they present zakat only as a religious duty that lacks legal elements, which is why it must be neglected when zakat is considered as a tax.

4.2.1.2 *Zakat as tax*

The definition of zakat as a tax should be extrapolated from the definition of tax and connected to features not only related to religiosity. Hence, it is necessary to mention the definition of tax, defined technically in Oxford Advanced Learner's Dictionary of current English (1989), as "a sum of money to be paid to a government by people or business for public purposes". It takes, also, the meaning of an obligation imposed by the state on the citizens. Authors such as Zaim (1998) defined tax as a mandatory levy by taking a surplus from the money or wealth of the Muslims members who are comparatively well-to-do and give it to the destitute and needy.

According to Morse and Williams (2008), tax is defined as "a mandatory levy imposed for public purposes by the government". Tiley and Loutzenhiser (2012) state that "the authority of the legislature obliged by a public body is the organ responsible for the imposition of taxes and that they are intended for public objectives". So, zakat is a levy obliged by Allah and stated in the Qur'an that shall be collected from individuals, which clearly indicates its obligation: "take *zakat from their wealth...*" (Qur'an 9: 103).

Allami (2009, p. 85) mentions that zakat is *a mandatory, flat levy, that is obliged by the Quran, and its fund must be distributed to the eligible beneficiaries.* This definition allows three basic elements related to zakat, which are as follows: first, the obligation of zakat by the Qur'an; second, the flat rates feature; third, the fund of zakat must be oriented to specific beneficiaries. In addition, this definition makes clear the originality of imposition of zakat, which is mentioned in the Qur'an. *The alms are only for the poor and the needy, and those who collect them, and those whose hearts are to be reconciled, and to free the captives and the debtors, and for the cause of Allah, and for the wayfarer; a duty imposed by Allah* (Qur'an, *Surat Al Tawbah,* 9: 60).

4.2.2 *Origin of zakat*

Initially and at the start of Islam, the notion of zakat was only a religious duty, like alms in Christianity, which was a voluntary duty. Then, it had transformed to become an economic duty. After few years, the Qur'an imposed zakat on Muslims as a compulsory tax: "take zakat take from their wealth a charitable offering to cleanse them and purify them thereby ... (Al-Quran, Tawbah, 9: 103). In fact, it has been considered the third pillar of Islam. The applicability of zakat is demonstrated by the above verse and its statement. Furthermore, this highlights that zakat ought to be an imposed levy and not only a solely voluntary activity. According to Salim (2008), the zakat has been transformed from a voluntary act to a compulsory one, which justifies the act of penalizing those who are negligent in paying it. So, the evasion of this entails punishment.

4.2.3 *Zakat in different perspectives*

4.2.3.1 *Zakat in economic perspective*

The transfer of wealth from the rich in society to the poor represents not only a form of redistribution but also an operation with a direct impact on macro- and microeconomic aggregates. From a macroeconomic point of view, zakat stimulates the circulation of money by reinjecting a social surplus into economic life. Indeed, the rich looking to disposes of surplus wealth is facing two alternatives: to consume the surplus, by which one avoids paying the zakat and, in this case, demand and investment increase, or accept to pay this surplus and therefore allow the other low-income groups to spend to consume. Boudjelal (2013, p. 7) and Alaoui (2014) define zakat as an instrument of social investment according to the following mechanism: The redistribution of income through zakat will increase the level of consumption by individuals with low incomes, which will increase demand for primary goods and services and therefore the incentive of enterprises to mass production, and in turn, the demand for jobs will increase (Lakhyar *et al.*, 2019).

From a microeconomic point of view and according to Lahjouji (2020), zakat can contribute to different issues. First, zakat can ensure the satisfaction of the basic needs of the poor, such as clothing, food, and education. Second, it can ensure the development of human capital through the financing of students without financial means or the provision of vocational training to facilitate the integration of beneficiaries into the labor market. Third, Zakat acts as savings because savings in the form of money or gold becomes taxable in zakat after a certain period of time, which increasingly pushes investment.

Adding to that, the appearance of COVID-19 across the world that led to economic crises (health, economic, social, and lifestyle problems) has demonstrated that zakat has an important role in facing this crisis, as an Islamic social fund, by helping those who are affected by the crisis. Al Anshory *et al.* (2020) said that zakat is one of the efficient mechanisms that help the government in mitigating COVID-19. This can be carried out in various fields, including health, economy, social, Islamic preaching, and education. In the health sector, the institution of zakat supports studies that entail the vaccine for COVID-19 to prevent the spread of the virus infection. According to Fabeil *et al.* (2020), zakat institutions have a big role in helping small businesses that are more impacted by this crisis.

4.2.3.2 *Zakat in sociological perspective*

In a sociological perspective, the objective of zakat should be essentially to help poor people ameliorate their lives (Fathonih, 2019). Therefore, zakat collection has an important role in improving the lifestyle of the needy. To explain in detail, zakat income recipients can use these resources to create commercial projects that are likely to improve their standard of living and will even became contributors to zakat. Moreover, institutions like public social banks or the Islamic banks are responsible for collecting zakat since they provide social solidarity service, which is represented in collecting and redistributing zakat to achieve development projects, such as hospital construction, equipment of universities and schools, or to offer services to the poor. Among these banks, we can mention the Nasser Social Bank in Egypt and Fayçal Islamic Bank. In addition, Hafidhuddin (2004) explained that zakat can be distributed to victims of natural disasters. COVID-19 has been considered a disaster; therefore, it is very possible to use zakat funds to help people affected by COVID-19.

4.2.3.3 *Zakat in a political perspective*

Zakat is collected either formally or informally. The formal management of zakat is that it is collected by institutions recognized by the state (Lahjouji, 2020). While informal management consists of the payment of zakat to trusted persons in charge of redistributing it. One of the important informal zakat management is zakat funds. Several Muslim countries have established zakat funds, such as Qatar, United Arab Emirates, Algeria, Saudi Arabia, and Jordan, to identify the total zakat allocated to poor families through a quarterly, semi-annual, or annual allocation. Then, in a political perspective, zakat management in different institutions must be controlled by the government. According to Fathonih (2019), government plays a crucial role in taking strategic policies related to zakat management. The management of zakat must be regulated and legalized under a government law to conserve the efficiency of zakat distribution to the poor people and to prevent any person or institution from collecting zakat without government approval. In this situation, the government must maximize its roles and duties to optimize zakat management.

4.2.4 *Similarities and dissimilarities between zakat and tax*

4.2.4.1 *Similarities between tax and zakat*

There exist many similarities between tax and zakat. First, in the state where zakat is compulsory, zakat is susceptible to be collected by force from evaders, similar to tax (Tanzi & Shome, 1993). The Qur'an and Sunnah clearly explain the obligation of an Islamic state which follows Islam to collect zakat. The main evidence for this is the punishment given to those who refused to pay zakat to the state. Second, the state treasury is the place reserved for the zakat collected in an Islamic state, in a separate account, like a tax (Hannan, 1998). The state collects taxes through zakat. Therefore, when non-government organizations or communities collect zakat, these should be kept securely like in the case of any public fund. Third, the Qur'an describes clearly that zakat is similar to tax on the return of this act, which means that the zakat payer waits for the return in the life hereafter: *if you lend a goodly loan he will double it for you, and will forgive you, and Allah is most ready to appreciate and to reward, most forbearing* (Al-Quran 64:17), and the taxpayer may receive some service from the state in return (Barizah *et al.*, 2007).

4.2.4.2 *Dissimilarities between tax and zakat*

As there exist some similarities between zakat and tax, there are also differences between them. First, and according to Al-Ghazali (1983, pp. 53–73), Zakat is an act of worship that has been made obligatory by Allah in Muslims' lives to indicate thanks and to gain nearness of Allah. Tax is distinct to zakat since it is a social duty that has no relation to Allah. Hence, zakat is essentially a thing between Allah and his servants, but tax has been a matter between citizens and the state authorities. Second, the main basis of zakat is Nisaab. Zakat exempts any wealth below a limit. This is different with taxes; therefore, the concept of exemption exists just when and where the government or tax authorities specifically prescribe. Third, zakat is different also from tax in the system. Zakat is a permanent and regular system since it uses fixed rates based on Islamic law (Qur'an, 70, pp. 24–25). So, no one can change it. On the contrary, taxes change from time to time because the tax rate can be changed by governments in progressive rates.

These are the important conceptual differences between zakat and tax. There is, also, the difference in the objective and intent between zakat and tax. The main objective of zakat is to ameliorate the moral sense by making wealth pure and cleansing the heart of Muslims: *Take from their wealth Charity (Zakat) so that thereby you make them clean and pure and pray for them. Your Prayer (for them) is a source of comfort for them. Allah is all hearing, all-knowing* (*Al-Quran*, 9: 103). Thus, the intent of zakat is spiritual, while the objective of tax is worldly (Hossain, 2012).

Table 4.1. Differences between zakat and tax.

Differences	Zakat	Tax
Payers	Imposed on Muslim states	Imposed on all citizens
Type of duty	Religious duty	Economic responsibility
Methods of distribution	The methods of distribution are clearly definite in Quran	No definite methods of distribution
Beneficiary	A tax taken from rich to the needy or poor	Not necessary
Rate	Fixed rate	Changeable rate
Levy on	The productive wealth	Consumption of expenditure
Exemptions	Realistic exemptions	Accountable exemptions
Obligation	Act of worship	Possibility of evasion
Cheaper or higher rate	Cheaper than conventional tax	Higher than zakat
Divine guarantee	Divinely guaranteed	Non-divine right to collect money
Sanction	Never be waived	Can be forgiven

In Table 4.1, we present differences that exist between zakat and tax according to a comparative study conducted by Barizah (2007).

4.2.5 *Reglementary framework of zakat in MENA countries*

4.2.5.1 *Differences between MENA countries in practice of zakat*

The practice and management of zakat vary significantly from country to country from being obligatory to voluntary contributions. So, the way zakat is administered differs from one country to another. There exist states which consider zakat as an obligation or a tax, such as Yemen, Saudi Arabia, Libya, Sudan, Pakistan, and Malaysia; others consider it as a charitable activity, such as Egypt, Jordan, Kuwait, Iran, Bangladesh, Bahrain, and Iraq. Thus, the contemporary zakat practice can be divided into three types: states that do not oblige zakat, others that have an official institution to collect zakat as a charitable endeavor, and states that enforce zakat as a tax. In this chapter, we focus on MENA countries, and we identify the differences and similarities between those countries regarding the zakat system.

In some MENA countries, such as Yemen, Saudi Arabia, Libya, Sudan, Pakistan, and Malaysia, the government has opted compulsory zakat management. Other countries, such as Jordan, Iran, Egypt, Bahrain, Kuwait, Bangladesh, and Iraq, opted for institutions specialized in the state but in which public contribution is voluntary (Hassan, 2010). For other countries (the case of Tunisia and Morocco), there is absence of a legal framework. Therefore, charities collect zakat in mosques and by individuals and recently by some municipalities (Machado *et al.*, 2018).

4.2.5.2 *Types of zakat system*

4.2.5.2.1 Zakat as a voluntary system

Table 4.2 shows the first class of states that do not have a governmental system to collect zakat such as Syria, Morocco, Algeria, Mauritania, Tunisia, Qatar, Oman, and Iraq. In those countries, zakat is only a voluntary activity that's practiced in Islamic communities by imams in mosques or by giving the money informally to the poor or needy. Hence, zakat is not obligatory but charitable, and it is not a tax or an imposed levy.

The second class of states devotes an official institution to the collection of zakat as an act of charity. These states intend to implement zakat for charitable purposes but through official institutions. This is like charitable practices, except that they are collected by official institutions. Zakat funds in Bahrain, United Arab of Emirates, Egypt, Iran, Jordan, Kuwait, and Lebanon are examples of this second class of zakat collection. Note that, in this class, zakat is not obligatory, but it is collected by an official institution.

4.2.5.2.2 Zakat as an obligatory duty

The third class of zakat practice includes states that enforce zakat as an imposed levy in the form of taxation. In Asia, Pakistan imposes zakat as tax. In Africa, Sudan enforces zakat as an imposed levy. In the Arab Gulf, Saudi Arabia and Yemen consider zakat as tax. These countries have enacted zakat laws, and their governments have the authority to collect zakat and sanction evaders (Salim, 2008).

Table 4.2. Zakat status in MENA countries.

Country	States
Algeria	No government system
Bahrain	Voluntary
Egypt	Voluntary
Iran	Voluntary
Iraq	No government system
Jordan	Voluntary
Kuwait	Voluntary
Lebanon	Voluntary
Libya	Mandatory
Mauritania	No government system
Morocco	No government system
Oman	No government system
Pakistan	Mandatory
Qatar	No government system
Saudi Arabia	Mandatory
Sudan	Mandatory
Syria	No government system
Tunisia	No government system
United Arab Emirates	Voluntary
Yemen	Mandatory
Malaysia	Voluntary

Source: Adapted from Hasan (2015). Human security and philanthropy: Islamic perspectives and muslim majority country practices. New York: Springer.

4.3 Empirical Studies on Zakat

Previous studies argued that zakat plays a crucial role in growing Islamic economics. Thus, analyzing the potential and the practice of zakat and finding way to increase this practice seem a challenging research area. Much of the literature and empirical studies have focused on analyzing the determinants of zakat compliance. Others were interested in the relation between zakat and corporations by examining the impact of zakat on Islamic firm performance. However, few studies have investigated the relation between the corporate governance of Islamic financial institutions and their financial performance. Hence, in this section, we summarize papers that have examined zakat in corporations. Note that previous studies have used several proxies to measure zakat (see Table 4.3).

Table 4.3. Measures of zakat.

Zakat variables	Measures of zakat	Studies
Zakat compliance	Individual factors of theory of planned behavior (items–survey)	Abdullah and Sapiei (2018) Othman and Fisol (2017)
Intention to pay zakat	Theory of planned behavior and zakat literacy (items–survey)	Aligarah *et al.* (2020) Yusfiarto *et al.* (2020)
Zakat performance	Ratio of zakat/net assets	Mkadmi (2020)
Zakat	Personal income transfer = zakat/net income	Paranata and Laela (2020)

4.3.1 *Zakat and corporate social responsibility*

Zakat is not restricted only to individual responsibility, but it is also a responsibility of all companies. Zakat is an ethical activity in an Islamic corporation and one of the important components of CSR depending on AAOIFI. For this reason, some studies, such as that by Malkawi and Javaid (2018), that are interested on the issue of zakat use it as a proxy of corporate social responsibility (CSR). Moreover, according to Faisol *et al.* (2020), corporations with a higher practice of ethical activities serve to guarantee trust and ensure the satisfaction of stakeholders, which will affect positively the financial performance of the company. Hence, the application of ethical activities in the center of a company will lead to a better firm performance. From this perspective, previous research has investigated the association between zakat, CSR, and firm performance. Al Malkawi and Javaid (2018) have tested the impact of zakat, as a measure of CSR, on financial performance by investigating a sample of 107 non-financial firms in the Saudi Arabia stock market from 2004 to 2013. The results indicated that there is a strong and positive nexus between zakat and financial performance. Moreover, they found that companies that are more socially responsible by way of paying zakat will contribute to enhancing the economy, reducing inequality, and leading to a successful firm considering it as a win–win strategy. Seddiki and Reskino (2016) have investigated the influence of zakat on the reputation and performance of 10 Indonesian Islamic banks in the period from 2011 to 2014. The results show that zakat has a

Table 4.4. Zakat and CSR.

Studies	**Country**	**Period**	**Type of analysis**	**Dependent variable**	**Variables having a significant effect and sign found**
Malkawi and Javaid (2018)	Saudi Arabia	2004–2013	Multiple linear regression	Corporate financial performance	Zakat/Price to book ratio PB (+) Zakat/Return on equity (+)
Sidik and Reskino (2016)	Indonesia	2011–2014	Logistic regression	Company performance	Zakat (+) Islamic corporate social responsibility ICSR (+)

positive and significant impact on firm performance. As a conclusion, the paper indicates the importance of zakat and CSR as a business strategy for the Islamic banking market. Muhammad (2020) examines the presence of zakat information disclosure in the annual report of Islamic banks in Bursa of Malaysia for the year of 2011. The main outcome is that the extent of zakat information was zero, which is an indicator of the absence of transparency in the disclosure. Table 4.4 presents the main results of empirical studies that have investigated the relation between zakat, CSR, and firm performance.

Studying the effect of zakat on firm performance is still an active research area. Abbas (2020) presented the relation between zakat and firm value and profitability. The author indicates that *zakat contribution can be considered as a reputation strategy* as it ensures an important role in providing a good business image with stakeholders that can help a firm to possess a highly positive trust in the market. According to the author, in order to earn the confidence of firm value on profitability or marketability, companies must engage in zakat payment. In addition, Auliyah (2020) has examined the effect of the practice of ethical value (zakat) of financial performance using a sample of eight Sharia banks listed on the Indonesian stock exchange in the period of 2014–2018. The main outcome of this research is that zakat disclosure affects significantly the financial performance measured by ROA.

As a summary, the main findings of these studies indicate that zakat contribution affects positively and significantly company financial performance (see Table 4.5).

4.3.2 *Zakat and corporate governance*

Corporate governance is essential for the success of any activity in financial institutions. For this reason, previous researchers have examined the relation between corporate governance and zakat as an ethical activity in Islamic financial institutions. Scholars such as Muhammad and Saad (2018), Mubtadi and Susilowati (2018), and Ghani *et al.* (2018) demonstrated that good corporate governance has a great role in stimulating zakat compliance and thus in enhancing firm performance and strengthening trust toward zakat stakeholders. Note that there is a little regard from zakat researchers concerning the relation between corporate governance mechanisms and zakat. The existing studies have examined the effect of personal and demographic individuals' factors (subjective norms, attitude, gender, education, etc.) on individual zakat compliance using the qualitative method of research questionnaire (Aligarah *et al.*, 2021; Abdullah & Sapiei, 2018; Yusfiarto *et al.*, 2020; Othman *et al.*, 2017). These papers showed mixed results, as indicated in Table 4.4. Other studies such as those by Mkadmi (2020), Pranata and Laela (2020), Harun *et al.* (2020), and Budiyono *et al.* (2018) have examined the effect of board characteristics on zakat performance using a quantitative regression. These papers reveal that certain corporate governance mechanisms have a great role in stimulating zakat compliance. Table 4.6 summarizes the empirical findings on the relationship between zakat and corporate governance.

Finally, and to summarize the review of empirical studies that have examined zakat compliance, we can note the existence of a gap on zakat compliance research. In addition, the samples used by previous papers are limited to a single enterprise sector and a single country analysis, which may restrict the generalizability of the results found. Second, limited are the variables that have been used to serve as determinants of zakat compliance. So, for more efficient results, future research can investigate the relation between zakat, firm performance, and corporate governance using a sample that includes

Table 4.5. Zakat and firm value.

Studies	Country	Period	Type of analysis	Dependent variable	Variables having a significant effect and sign found	Variables that do not have a significant effect and sign found
Auliyah and Basuki (2021)	Eight sharia banks listed on IDEX	2014–2018	Multiple linear regression	Financial performance (Return on assets/Return on equity)	Zakat/Return on assets (–)	Zakat/Return on assets (–) CSR/Return on assets (–) CSR/Return on equity (+)
Abbas (2020)	114 mining and manufacturing companies Of Indonesia stock exchange	2018	Linear regression	Firm value (Return on assets/Return on equity, tobin Q)	Zakat/Return on equity (+) Zakat/Return on assets (+) Zakat/Tobin Q: (+)	

Table 4.6. Zakat and corporate governance.

Studies	Country	Period	Type of analysis	Dependent variable	Variables having a significant effect and sign found	Variables that do not have a significant effect and sign found
Mkadmi (2020)	17 Malaysian Islamic banks	2005 to 2011	Panel regression	Zakat performance ratio	The visibility of the Sharia Supervisory Board VSSB(+)	The size of Sharia committee SSSB(−) Competence of Sharia Supervisory Board CSSB(+) Board of director size SBD(+) Independence of the board of director INDEP(−) The duality of the board of director DUAL(+) Size of bank SB(+) Age of bank AB(−) Leverage of bank LB(−)
Pranataand Laela (2020)	Islamic bank in Indonesia	2009–2017	Quantitative research with panel data regression PLS	Jalb Al Maslahah measured by zakat	Commissioner dual position BOC_CRM;(+) Commissioner independence BOC_IND;(+) Sharia supervisor dual position DPS_CRM; (−) Firm size SIZE_CMP; (+)	Commissioner stock ownership BOC_OWN;(+) Director stock ownership BOD_OWN;(−) Director tenure BOD_TEN; (+) Commissioner expertise BOC_EXP;(+) Sharia supervisor expertise DPS_EXP;(+) Commissioner tenure or term of office BOC_TEN;(+) Profit growth GROWTH(+)

other financial institutions. Also, the use of other variables related to Sharia committee (the number of meetings, presence of women in the Sharia committee) can present new insights in zakat compliance research.

4.4 Conclusion

This chapter presents an insight into the zakat concept by providing a review of the different theoretical and empirical literature. It seeks to understand more fully the notion of zakat and presents multiple empirical studies that investigate the relation between zakat, firm performance, and corporate governance. As theoretical implications, this chapter highlighted the importance of zakat in the provision of economic and social well-being, thereby mitigating the issues relating to people and society. Also, by reviewing the existing literature on the topic, this chapter demonstrated that zakat is beginning to gain more and more importance and interest in the Islamic financial system, in commercial companies in general, and in Islamic banks. Moreover, this study argues that zakat greatly differs from conventional taxes and that the practices of zakat in MENA countries vary between mandatory and voluntary. As practical implication, this chapter provides evidence for the importance of implementing zakat on companies for better financial performance and the need for good corporate governance mechanisms to increase zakat compliance in Islamic institutions. So, this chapter contributes to the literature by focusing on the importance of zakat, differences between tax and zakat, and analyzing the practice of zakat in different MENA countries. Also, this chapter helps in growing the knowledge about the nexus between zakat, corporate governance, and firm performance.

However, this work is limited to the review of the theoretical and empirical studies that focus on the notion of zakat.

Future research can investigate on the role of zakat during the period of COVID-19 in the different sectors and its importance at the center of different Islamic financial institutions.

In conclusion, this work is seen as a step toward encouraging experts to increase efforts to do additional research and thinking about ambiguities associated with zakat in the different dimensions.

References

Abbas, A. (2020). Does zakat signal the firm value? *International Journal Of Zakat*, *5*(1), 55–66.

Abdullah, M. & Sapiei, N. S. (2018). Do religiosity, gender and educational background influence zakat compliance? the case of Malaysia. *International Journal of Social Economics*, *45*(8), 1250–1264.

Abdullah, M. & Suhaib, A. Q. (2011). The impact of zakat on social life of muslim society. *Pakistan Journal of Islamic Research*, *8*(1), 85–91.

Ahmad, S., Nor, N. G. M., & Daud, Z. (2011). Tax based modeling of zakat compliance. *Jurnal Ekonmi Malaysia*, *45*(1), 101–108.

Al Anshory, A. C., Hudaefi, F. A., Junari, U. L., Zaenal, M. H., & Ramdhoni, R. (2020). The role of zakat institution in preventing COVID-19. *Policy Brief*, 1–11.

Alaoui, M. (2014). "*La Zakat Un Réajustement É thique Pour Le Monde Des Affaires*", *Colloque* "*Ethique Et Religions Pour Une Economie Juste*". Paris: Fondation Singer-Polignac.

Al-Ghazali, M. (1983). *Inner Dimensions of Islamic Worship, the Islamic Foundation*. London (Translated by Muhtar Holland), Kube publishing Ltd (version 2012).

Aligarh, F., Nugroho, A., Raharja, B. S., Pratama, B. C., & Wirayuda, A. W. (2020). Do individual factors, religiosity factors, and demographic factors predict intention to pay zakat? *Al-Uqud: Journal of Islamic Economics*, *5*(1), 151–165.

Allami, A. (2009). Zakat as Islamic taxation and its application in the contemporary Saudi legal system. *Journal of Islamic State Practices in International Law*, *5*(83), 1–13.

Auliyah, R. & Basuki, B. (2021). Ethical values reflected on zakat and csr: Indonesian sharia banking financial performance. *The Journal of Asian Finance, Economics, and Business*, *8*(1), 225–235.

Barizah, N., Rahim, A., & Rahman, A. (2007). A comparative study of zakah and modern taxation. *Journal of King Abdulaziz University: Islamic Economics*, *20*(1), 32.

Bilo, C. & Machado, A. C. (2020). The role of zakat in the provision of social protection: A comparison between Jordan and Sudan. *International Journal of Sociology and Social Policy*. Available at https://www.emerald.com/insight/content/doi/10.1108/IJSSP-11-2018-0218/full/html.

Boudjelal, M. (2013). La Zakat et le Waqf: Un segment de la finance islamique au service du développement économique et social. *Centre de Recherche en Développement économiques*, N1, 42–43.

Fabeil, N. F., Pazim, K. H., & Langgat, J. (2020). The impact of COVID-19 pandemic crisis on micro-enterprises: Entrepreneurs' perspective on business continuity and recovery strategy. *Journal of Economics and Business, 3*(2), 837–844.

Farah, A., Rashidah, A. & Normah, O. (2012). Zakat and poverty alleviation: Roles of zakat institutions in Malaysia. *International Journal of Arts and Commerce, 1*(7), 61–72.

Fathonih, A. (2019). Zakat as an alternative revenue and financing resources for the state. *AL-'ADALAH, 16*(1), 115–134.

Ghani, E. K., Aziz, A., Tajularifin, S., & Samargansi, N. (2018). Effect of board management and governmental model on zakat payers' trust on zakat institutions. *Global Journal Al Thaqafah, Special Issue*, 73–86.

Hafidhuddin, D. (2004). *Zakat Dalam Perekonomian Modern.* Jakarta: GemaInsani Press.

Hannan, S. A. (1998). Zakah and the tax system. In Hannan *et al.* (Eds.), *Zakah and Poverty Alleviation.* Dhaka, Bangladesh: Islamic Economics Research Bureau.

Hasan, S. (Ed.). (2015). *Human Security and Philanthropy: Islamic Perspectives and Muslim Majority Country Practices.* New York: Springer. https://scholar.google.com/citations?user=Fz2ixiAAAAAJ&hl=fr&oi=sra.

Hassan, K. (2010). An integrated poverty alleviation model combining zakat, awqaf and micro-finance, *Seventh International Conference — The Tawhidi Epistemology: Zakat and Waqf Economy, Bangi — Malaysia* 2010, 261–281.

Hossain, M. Z. (2012). Zakatin Islam: A powerful poverty alleviating instrument for Islamic countries. *International Journal of Economic Development Research and Investment, 3*(1), 1–11.

Kasri, R. A. & Yuniar, A. M. (2021). Determinants of digital zakat payments: Lessons from Indonesian experience. *Journal of Islamic Accounting and Business Research, 12*(3), 362–379.

Lahjouji, H. (2020). L'institutionnalisation de la zakat: Un chantier de lutte contre la pauvreté. *Journal d'Economie de Management, d'Environnement et de Droit, 3*(1), 114–124.

Lakhyar, Z. & Hamdi, F. (2019). L'impact socio-économique de la zakat. *Recherches et Applications en Finance Islamique (RAFI), 3*(2), 181–188.

Machado, A. C., Bilo, C. & Helmy, I. (2018). *The Role of Zakat in the Provision of Social Protection: A Comparison Between Jordan, Palestine and Sudan.* Working Paper.

Malkawi, H. A. & Javaid, S. (2018). Corporate social responsibility and financial performance in Saudi Arabia. *Managerial Finance*, *44*(6), 684–664.

Mkadmi, J. E. (2020). Impact of Islamic and conventional corporate governance mechanisms on ethical performance of Islamic banks: Evidence from Malaysia. *National Accounting Review*, *2*(2), 174–187.

Morse, G. & Williams, D. (2008). *Principles of Tax Law*. (6th edn.). London: Sweet & Maxwell. 2008.

Mubtadi, N. A. & Susilowati, D. (2018). Analysis of governance and efficiency on zakat distribution: Evidence from Indonesia. *International Journal of Zakat*, *3*(2), 1–15.

Muhammad, F. B. (2020). Zakat disclosure by Malaysian *Shariah*-compliant companies. *International of Zakat and Islamic Philanthropy*, *2*(1), 210–217.

Muhammad, S. A. & Saad, R. A. J. (2016). The impact of public governance quality, accountability and effectiveness on intention to pay zakat: Moderating effect of trust on zakat institution. *International Journal of Management Research and Review*, *6*(1), 1–8.

Mursal, M., Ritonga, M., Sartika, F., Lahmi, A., Nurdianto, T., & Alam, L. (2021). The contribution of amil zakat, infaq and shadaqah Muhammadiyah (LAZISMU) institutions in handling the impact of COVID-19. *Journal of Sustainable Finance & Investment*, 1–7.

Othman, Y. & Fisol, W. (2017). Islamic religiosity, attitude and moral obligation on intention of income zakat compliance: Evidence from public educators in Kedah. *Journal of Academic Research in Business*, *7*(2), 726–737.

Pranata, M. W. & Laela, S. F. (2020). Board characteristics good corporate governance and maqâshid performance in Islamic banking. *Journal of Islamic Monetary Economics and Finance*, *6*(2), 463–486.

Qardhawi, Y. (1969). *Fiqh Al-Zakah: A Comparative Study of Zakah Regulations and Philosophy in the Light of Quran and Sunnah*. Translated by Monzer Kahf. Saudi Arabia: Scientific Publishing Centre.

Salim, A. (2008). The shift in the zakat practice in Indonesia: From piety to an Islamic socio-political-economic system. http://handle.uws.edu.au:8081/1959.7/532868.

Sidik, I. & Reskino, R. (2016). Zakat and Islamic corporate social responsibility: Does it take effect to the performance of Shari'a banking? *Shirkah: Journal of Economics and Business*, *1*(2), 161–184.

Tanzi, V. & Shome, P. (1993). A primer on tax evasion. *Staff Papers*, *40*(4), 807–828.

Tiley, J. & Loutzenhiser, G. (2012). *Revenue Law*. 7th edn. Oxford: Hart Publishing.

Yusfiarto, R., Setiawan, A., & Nugraha, S. S. (2020). Literacy and intention to pay zakat. *International Journal of Zakat*, *5*(1), 15–27.

Zaim, S. (1989). Recent interpretations on economic aspect of Zakah. In Imtiazi, I. A. *et al.* (Eds.), *Management of Zakah in Modern Muslim Society*. Jeddah: IRTI/IDB, p. 101.

https://doi.org/10.1142/9781800612426_0005

Chapter 5

CSR in Sharia Theory Perspective

Dwi Nita Aryani and Imama Zuchroh

Abstract

The implementation of corporate social responsibility (CSR) is examined from various perspectives, as well as the distinctive features of some theories. CSR is a kind of action for communicating with stakeholders to show that companies pay attention to the environment, nature, and society. The theories relating to CSR implementation can be discussed from different perspectives. Agency theory focuses on the relationship between agent and principal and may give rise to conflict of interest. Legitimacy theory places the public as its responsibility. Disclosing information about social and environmental performance is a path for companies to maintain or regain their legitimacy in the society's point of view. Meanwhile, entity theory focuses only on the satisfaction of the shareholders, hence the company activities are only directed to meet the welfare of the owners. Enterprise theory recognizes the responsibility to the owners and broader stakeholder groups. However, Sharia enterprise theory pays attention in two directions, consisting of vertical accountability to God and the horizontal accountability in direct and indirect stakeholders for humans, the environment, and society.

Keywords: CSR, Sharia Enterprise Theory, Legitimacy, Stakeholder, Environment.

5.1 Introduction

Today, corporate responsibility toward stakeholders has become a very interesting topic and increasingly being discussed in the world. This relates to the awareness of a company or organization about not only to on how to generate profit but also how the profit can benefit the community and how to improve their lives further. This phenomenon changed when the public became aware of the importance of corporate social responsibility (CSR) implementation.

Business activities or businesses when not based on ethics actually end with problems that afflict the company and even become a scandal inevitably. Scandals in modern business, such as the Enron and WorldCom scandals in 2001 and 2002, the Volkswagen emissions scandal in 2015 (Rhodes, 2016), and the construction company scandals in Britain Mabey and Johnson (M&J), are a few examples of business activities that deviate from ethics and religious values and increase concern for the role and responsibility of a business company (Khurshid *et al.*, 2014).

In the past, the business goal was more profit oriented, without regarding the environment, and even increasingly exploited the environment. The rapidity of economic growth and industrial sector are rapidly in line with the decline of environmental quality. However, since the 19th century, the company has changed its image by paying attention to and taking sides with the community, the environment, the economy, and social affairs by carrying out CSR activities. Social responsibility is not only a corporate obligation, but it has become a responsibility of all parties, private companies and government agencies, individuals and entities, profit-oriented organizations, or non-profit organizations.

Several theories have explained the importance of addressing the needs of stakeholders and pay attention to the environment because they think that stakeholders will increase company profits and support the company's sustainability. However, there is an assumption that doing CSR activities will actually burden the company, increase costs, and reduce company profits. Therefore, the question is whether companies do CSR activities for moral or social reasons or only for marketing orientation.

Companies have different goals when doing CSR activities. Companies might be forced to do it because of regulations that push them to hold CSR activities. In general, CSR activities provide many benefits for companies, society, and the environment. Indeed, the impact of CSR activities cannot be felt instantly in the short term, but it will have long-term impact and even support the organization's sustainability in the long term.

Before understanding further the concept of CSR, we need to explore Islamic values in life. Islam is a complete way of life because it is based on aqidah, worship, and morality. Aqidah means a belief or faith and never doubt what Allah created, as stated in the Qur'an. Some examples of aqidah in everyday life include acknowledging the oneness of Allah SWT, carrying out Allah's commands, staying away from all His prohibitions, and holding firmly to the Qur'an and the hadith of the Prophet SAW; the second Islamic value is worship, which means to devote oneself to Allah SWT.

This can be interpreted that what we do is solely for the purpose of getting the approval of Allah SWT. Worship in its implementation can be classified into three forms, namely:

(1) physical and spiritual worship, namely praying and fasting;
(2) spiritual and maliyah worship, namely paying zakat;
(3) physical worship, spiritual, and maliyah exemplified by performing the pilgrimage.

The concept of worship in general can be grouped into two, namely worship *mahdhah* and *ghairu mahdah. Mahdah* worship is activities that connects humans with God or can be referred to as a vertical relationship. The vertical relationship between a human and his god can be applied through prayer, zakat, fasting, and pilgrimage. While *ghairu mahdah* worship is worship related to the reciprocal interaction of fellow human beings, it can be called *muamalah. Muamalah* worship is a horizontal relationship between human beings that is carried out for good. In daily life, *muamalah* worship can be in the form of giving alms, building a place of worship/mosque, and mutual relationship. The third value is morality, namely the inherent nature of a person, which can be in the form of actions that have good or bad values. If it is associated with CSR, then CSR activities can certainly be realized through *mahdah* and *ghairu mahdah* worship and are also classified as *spiritual* and *maliyah* worship.

What is interesting is that the CSR concept is not new to the teachings of Islam, as written in Sharia. Islam, through the concept of caliphate (caliph), calls for business activities or companies to not only focus on securing financial resources for shareholders, but also these activities must have benefits for the community so that the owners of the company and shareholders by implementing CSR ultimately get blessings from God (Dusuki, 2008). This implies an inevitable need for companies to embed good CSR practices in their business behavior, covering issues such as: environmental practices, work safety, philanthropic contributions, and beneficial and harmless social initiatives. In other words, the god consciousness paradigm inspires companies to always operate in a good and socially responsible way.

5.2 Definition of CSR

The concept of CSR is discussed in various forums very dynamically. The meaning, approach, and even terminology used are always debated. There are various terms that are used interchangeably to describe CSR, such as corporate citizenship, sustainable entrepreneurship, triple bottom line, business ethics and sustainability, corporate environmental management, business and society, business and governance, business and globalization, and stakeholder management (Panwar *et al.*, 2006).

CSR has many definitions but has the same essence and now has been applied by companies to many kind activities. Council for Sustainable Development (WBCSD) mentions that CSR is the commitment of business to contribute to sustainable economic development, working with employees, their families and the local communities (WBCSD, 2001). In addition, CSR can be defined as an organization's dedication to act in an ethical manner and enhance economic development while improving the quality of life of employees, community, and society (Turcsanyi & Sisaye, 2013). Spitzeck (2009, p. 497) defines CSR as "a set of policies, practices, and programs that are integrated throughout business operations and decision making process, and intended to ensure the company maximizes the positive impacts of it operations on society".

Some writers such as Gray, Owen, and Maunders (1987, p. IX) wrote that the definition of social accounting, which is now known by CSR reporting, is "the process of communicating the social and environmental effects of organisations' economic actions to particular interest groups within society and to society at large. As such, it involves extending the accountability of organizations (particularly) companies; beyond the traditional role of providing a financial account to the owners of capital, in particular shareholders. Such an extension is predicated upon the assumption that companies do have wider responsibilities than simply to make money for their shareholders".

Overall, there seems to be some evidence to indicate that CSR is an obligatory social responsibility of an organization through a commitment to carry out activities that can provide benefits for stakeholders and society; however, not all the definitions consider sustainability of nature or environment.

5.3 The Importance of CSR

Basically, CSR is a form of attention from a company that is directed to three specific pillars that are popular called triple bottom line by Elkington (1998). The three pillars are Profit, People, and Planet. **Profit** — Profit is the most important purpose in a business. All activities should be able to support the means of achieving profit, such as by increasing productivity in all the business processes, and cost efficiency so that the company can reach the competitive advantage that may lead to increasing the company's value addition. **People** — It is a must that a company should be taking care of people's wealth. People in the company are part of the company's important stakeholder. The supports from surroundings are crucial for business process sustainability and business growth. **Planet** — Everyone with all the activities always connects to the environment. Everyone also needs the benefits of natural resources; therefore, we have to maintain the natural environment. However, sometimes, natural damages in some places are caused by companies' irresponsible business process. Some environmental issues that come from business process are water quality, water supply, waste disposal, and climate change.

As mentioned earlier, CSR rises because a company run ethically and sustainably coping with social and environmental impacts. CSR is not going to answer the problems of the world. However, CSR is a way for companies to profit while also assisting the society. In brief, some of the important aspects of CSR are: driving the business process in a company in terms of innovation, cost saving, brand differentiation, long-term thinking, customer engagement, and employee engagement (https://www.forbes.com). Furthermore, CSR can increase the company's public image that leads to increasing brand awareness and recognition. **Innovation** — As known widely, innovation contributes a lot to the sustainability of the business and also contributes to society and the environment. It is argued that CSR initiatives can **lead to innovation** through the use of "social, environmental or sustainability drivers to create new ways of working, new products, services, processes and new market space" (Little, 2006), which has led many companies to redefine their business models. An example: General Electric (GE) had Healthy Imagination Programme that involved associates with CSR. GE made a decision to help reduce the problem of mortality of infants in India because of a lack of incubators for premature infants. GE and its research and development tried hard to develop cheaper incubators. However, the price was still around USD 2,000. R&D then tried to make product innovations. At last, GE could produce an incubator for USD 200 that could keep a baby warm for about six hours by combining a sleeping bag with pads that could be heated in water. **Cost Saving** — CSR brings about sustainability by cost saving. An example for this case is General Mills, which could reduce its energy saving around 20% by 2015. From the CSR report 2015, General Mills could save USD 600,000. **Brand Differentiation** — Brand differentiation is one of the brand strategies where CSR goes hand in hand with brand strategy. CSR creates a specific position in the mind of the customers. By having specific positioning, customers will be easier to differentiate the brand amongst the brands' competitors. In general, customers will support companies that show concern for employees' wealth, community development, environment sustainability, and human rights. Directly or indirectly, these thoughts will increase brand differentiation.

Khatun and Alautiyat (2012) stated that the most important thing about CSR is involvement in social issues. They said that these included poverty, illiteracy, new diseases, income and wealth inequality, worker exploitation, resource wasting, and environmental risks. Companies that do CSR help the government's task to overcome those problems because the government is no longer able to handle, control, and solve all these problems, which are very interrelated. In the era of globalization, it is believed that the most effective players to help solve the problems are large companies, where they are able to control the flow of people, finance, and natural resources. From this belief, the idea of CSR arises with the aim to involve corporations in social growth and environmental issues to achieve sustainable community development, environment, and the economy of a nation (Khatun & Alautiyat, 2012).

Furthermore, Januarti and Apriyanti (2005) mentioned that there are three perspectives that arise related to CSR. First is a business perspective which considers the importance of reputation. Second is eco-social perspective, which means that CSR is a strategy to ensure the sustainability of a company. Finally, right-based perspective emphasizes that consumers, workers, public, and shareholders have a right to know the company's business activities.

In terms of relationships, CSR activities can be carried out in the interests of horizontal and vertical stakeholders. The horizontal part can be addressed to three parties, namely direct stakeholders, indirect stakeholders, and nature. Included in direct stakeholders are those who are directly related to the company or reap the benefits and use the services, such as customers and employees, while those who are indirect stakeholders are regulators. Whereas, vertical CSR activities relate to God. Referring to Sharia enterprise theory, CSR needs to be supported by the opinion of the Sharia Supervisory Board and the disclosure of fatwas and operational, aspects which are obeyed and not obeyed with reasons (Novarela & Sari, 2015).

Humans might have the tendency to cause damage on Earth, nevertheless Islamic education makes corrections to the behavior of the business through social activities. Along with that, CSR becomes mandatory to encourage humans to be more actively involved in growth and economic development. Hence, companies must also have a social commitment to make an impact to ensure a better life for humans. It is also explained that Islam is very concerned about the preservation of nature. It can be concluded that all business and non-business must guarantee natural preservation. In addition, the activities in any organization should consider economics development, environment protection, and social welfare.

5.4 Perspective of CSR

CSR is conventionally explained in agency theory, stakeholder theory, legitimacy theory, entity theory, and enterprise theory. These theories merely pay more attention to the horizontal side, such as stakeholder, shareholders, the environment, and nature, but they do not consider the vertical side, namely accountability to God — Allah SWT. Meanwhile, Sharia CSR adds a vertical side, placing God as the highest stakeholder. God is the highest and the sole purpose of human life. According to the Sharia enterprise theory (SET), stakeholders include God, humans, and nature.

This part discusses theories regarding the relationship between companies, humans, and nature, in addition to the God in CSR perspective.

5.4.1 *Agency theory*

Agency theory is widely used in economics for the underlying relationship between the parties within an organization or company. Jensen and Meckling (1976) asserted that agency theory is an association between shareholders as the owner or principals and managers as the agent. A manager receives mandates from shareholders in order to manage the company and hand over their authority in making decisions. This indicates that the manager has to pay attention to how to increase shareholders' welfare. However, this contractual relationship could create an agency problem because of conflict of interest between manager and shareholders. The manager has their own interest to maximize their wealth; meanwhile, the shareholders want to achieve high dividend. This theory assumes that individuals act toward their own interests. This theory emphasizes the relationship between two parties, namely between managers and shareholders. The relationship is limited to how managers are required to provide welfare for their shareholders so that the company becomes only profit-oriented without considering the welfare of the community. Thus, it can be concluded that the relationship between manager and shareholder is kind of a horizontal relationship, nevertheless both parties have different interests. This theory also does not pay attention to the sustainability of nature and vertical relationship.

5.4.2 *Stakeholder theory*

Post, Preston, and Sachs (2002, p. 8) stated "stakeholders in a firm are individuals and constituencies that contribute, either voluntarily or involuntarily, to its wealth-creating capacity and activities, and who are therefore its potential beneficiaries and/or risk bearers".

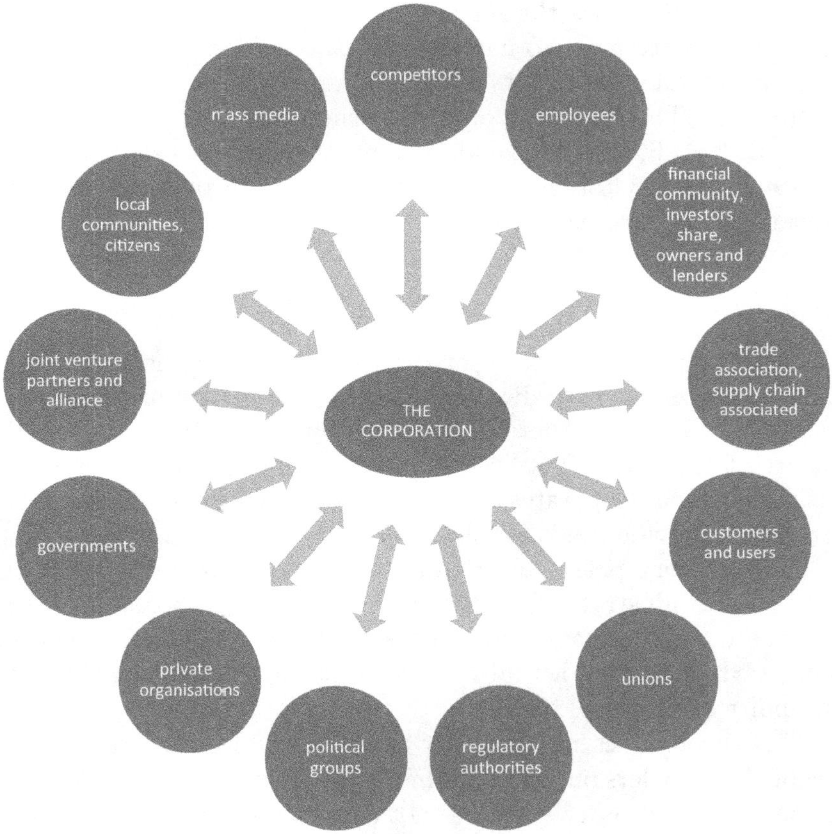

Figure 5.1. Stakeholders.

In addition, Freeman (2010, p. 55) and Post *et al.* (2002, p. 10) asserted that a company has 13 groups of stakeholders, as shown in Figure 5.1, and the firm has to maintain good relationship with them due to the fact that they contribute to firm's sustainability in the future. Therefore, stakeholder theory says that a company is not an entity that only operates for their self but must provide benefits for shareholders, creditors, consumers, suppliers, government, community, and other parties. The company has a moral obligation to maintain the stakeholders' interest.

This theory emphasizes that companies must provide profits and benefits to all parties who contribute to the company. It can be said that an organization must pay attention to stakeholders since they are very important for the survival of the company. Along with that, the company attempts to increase the stakeholders' wealth.

However, all stakeholders mentioned in this theory are on the horizontal side. This theory is only concerned with and pays attention to giving benefits to stakeholders, nevertheless it does not consider nature or the environment. Furthermore, this theory does not consider the vertical stakeholder.

5.4.3 *Entity theory*

Entity theory focuses only to satisfy the shareholders, hence the company activities are only directed to meet the welfare of the owners. This theory explains that the company only pays attention to the welfare of the owner. The traditional form of entity theory is that a business company operates in the interests of the shareholder, as the party who provide funds for the entity.

Entity theory posits an orientation of the company to favor the owners. This illustrates that the company's only responsibility is on how the company maximizes profits to its shareholders. Moreover, doing CSR activities actually incurs costs and will harm business continuity (Friedman, 1970).

This theory does not consider the welfare of other stakeholders except shareholders only. Furthermore, it seems to pay attention only to the horizontal party and does not consider nature or the environment, or even the vertical party.

5.4.4 *Enterprise theory*

Another theory in accounting perspective is the enterprise theory, which emphasizes on company being social institution operating for several interests to achieve the company's performance. This theory states that all stakeholders who have made any contribution to the company's performance will be rewarded (Widayanto, 2005). Moreover, Triyuwono (2001) asserted that enterprise theory merely views that the existence of the company is inseparable from the contribution of the participants (employees, creditors, government, and the community). In other words, a company can exist because it interacts with the community as a consequence of social contract. This theory recognizes that the company's responsibility is not only to the owners but also to broader stakeholder groups. Even though the implementation of this theory is wider than that of entity theory, this theory only pays attention to horizontal stakeholders and does not consider nature as a stakeholder or the vertical stakeholder.

5.4.5 *Legitimacy theory*

Legitimacy theory has always been used as an underpinning theory when discussing about CSR. Guthrie and Parker (1989) mention legitimacy theory as positing that due to using resources, living in the society, and getting support from the public who influence the sustainability and existence of a company, its organization activities are expected to be suitable to social welfare. Legitimacy is a company-oriented management system aligned toward society (society), individual governments and community group (Gray, Owen, & Adams, 1996) Legitimacy theory places the public as its responsibility; therefore, companies should maintain social and environmental performance as a path for companies to maintain or regain their legitimacy from the society point of view.

The legitimacy theory asserts that companies should work with regard to norms in society and the environment. This theory gives attention to the horizontal party and is concerned about the environment. Furthermore, it is also assumed that organizational involvement in the community is important in order to ensure the continuity of its business.

Based on the explanations given earlier, the dimensions of CSR can be determined by internal and external stakeholders as follows:

a. *Internal*: Longo, Mura, and Bonoli (2005) asserted that internal stakeholders are manager, owner or shareholders, employees, etc.

The responsibility of a company to the internal stakeholders can be delivered by enhancing skills and education, workplace safety, working conditions, human rights, equity considerations, equal opportunity, health and safety, and labor rights (Jones *et al.*, 2008; Longo *et al.*, 2005).

b. *External*: Meanwhile, Deakin and Hobbs (2007) mentioned that an organization has to pay attention to external factors, namely economic and social, stakeholders such as suppliers, customer, investor creditor, business partners, and government. Munilla and Miles (2005) added that natural environment must also be considered.

5.5 CSR in Sharia Perspective

It has been mentioned earlier that CSR is the responsibility of an organization for the impact of its decisions and activities on society and the environment, which is realized in the form of transparent and ethical behavior in line with sustainable development and community welfare; stakeholder expectations, in line with established laws and norms of international conduct; and integrated with the organization as a whole (Khatun & Alautiyat, 2012). Thus, CSR is the concern of companies that set aside some of their profits (profit) for the benefit of human development (people) and the environment (planet) in a sustainable manner based on appropriate procedures (procedures) and professionals.

Allah said: "It is not that turning your face to the east and west is a virtue, but it is indeed believing in Allah, in the next day, angels, books, prophets and giving the treasures he loves to his relatives, orphans, the poor, travelers (who need help) and those who ask for; and (free) the servant of sahaya, establish prayers, and perform zakat; and those who keep their promises when they make promises, and those who are patient in narrowness, suffering and in war. These are the righteous. And they are the ones who fear". (QS. Al Baqarah: 177). From the verse, it can be concluded that Islam is a religion that prioritizes the importance of social values in society rather than just turning our faces to the west and east in prayer. Without ruling out the importance of carrying out the obligations of prayer in Islam, the Qur'an integrates the meaning and purpose of prayer with social values.

In addition, to giving the value of faith in the form of faith in Allah SWT, his book, and the Day of Resurrection, the Qur'an affirms that the faith is not perfect if it is not accompanied by social practices in the form of care and service to relatives, orphans, the poor, and travelers and guarantee the welfare of those in need. In this context, CSR from an Islamic perspective is a business practice that has Islamic ethical responsibilities. A company must include Islamic religious norms characterized by a commitment of sincerity in maintaining the social contract in its operations. Thus, business practices within the framework of Islamic CSR include a series of business activities in their form. Although not limited to the amount of ownership of goods, services, and profits, but the ways to obtain and use it are limited by halal and haram rules by Sharia (Al-Abdallah & Ahmed, 2018).

CSR from an Islamic perspective, according to the Accounting and Auditing Organization for Islamic Financial Institutions (AAOIFI), is all activities carried out by Islamic financial institutions to meet religious, economic, legal, ethical, and discretionary responsibilities as a financial intermediary institution for both individuals and institutions (El-Halaby & Hussainey, 2016). In the index, CSR implementation becomes one of the levels of compliance in addition to the Sharia Supervisory Board Report (SSBR) and the presentation of financial statements (FS).

According to Islam, CSR should aim to create virtues that are done not through activities that contain elements of riba but by practices commanded by Allah in the form of zakat, infak, almsgiving, and waqf. CSR must also prioritize the value of generosity and sincerity (Al-Abdallah & Ahmed, 2018). This is what God loves more than worship. The Prophet said, "Fulfilling the needs of a believer is more God loves than doing twenty Hajjs and at each hajj inhaling hundreds of thousands of dirhams and dinars".

In another hadith, the Prophet (Peace Be Upon Him) also said, "If a Muslim walks to meet the needs of his fellow Muslims, it is better for him than to do seventy thawaf in Baitullah". The business ethics perspective of CSR Islamic business ethics is actually taught by the Prophet (Peace Be Upon Him) when conducting trade. The characteristics of the Prophet as a merchant are not only his dedication and tenacity, but also he has the nature of shidiq, fathanah, amanah and tabligh. These characteristics are still coupled with the nature of Istiqamah. Based on these traits, in the context of CSR, business actors or companies are required to act not intentionally between speech and deeds in their business. They are required to be true to promise, on time, admit weaknesses and shortcomings (not covered up), always improve the quality of goods or services continuously, and must not deceive and lie. Business people or organization must have a mandate by displaying attitudes of openness, honesty, optimal service, and ihsan (doing the best) in everything, let alone related to community service. With the nature of trust, business actors have a responsibility to practice their obligations. The nature of tablig can be conveyed by business actors wisely (wisdom). Patience, argumentativeness, and persuasiveness will foster a solid and strong humanitarian relationship. Organizations are required to have awareness of ethics and morals because both are needs that must be owned. Companies that are careless and do not maintain ethics will not lead business properly so that it can threaten social relationships and harm consumers, even themselves. Furthermore, one thing that should be a concern, especially for institutions, is that implementation of CSR must be in accordance with the provisions of the law related to CSR as we see that CSR is the realization of business ethics, especially in Islam, by which our every action must be beneficial for others, especially economic activities.

The implementation of CSR does not only comply with the law but also pays attention to responsibilities in the Islamic religion and in accordance with Islamic law. Islam has many philanthropy forms, namely zakat, donation, alms, and waqf.

From Sharia perspective, CSR is a compulsory activity for individual and corporates. In business, CSR can be meant as ethical businesses and has responsibility in the Islamic way. All activities in Islamic view are parts of good deeds; therefore, all activities should be done rightly and with a right intention. A company has many responsibilities to all of its stakeholders, internal and external. That is why CSR is closely related to "sustainability in development", hence all business processes will affect economic aspects (profit or dividend and social) as well as environment aspects in the short- and long-term visions. CSR in Sharia's view is also linked with "maslahah" (good impact) in the path to reach falah. Falah is success or happiness in short term (world's life) and long term (hereafter's life). Djakfar (2007) explained that CSR in Sharia's perspective should meet some requirements, namely *Al Adl*/Justice (fairness), *Ihsan* (pursuit of excellence), *Beneficial*, Amanah (trustworthiness), and Maqashid:

(1) *Justice:* This means placing things in the rightful place. In Islam, justice is must in all activities, including business activities. There are rights for surroundings, rights for social environment, and right for the environments. All stakeholders should acquire their right for justice.

(2) *Ihsan:* Ihsan is the Muslim responsibility to obtain perfection, or excellence, in worship, such that Muslims try to worship God as if they see him, and although they cannot see him, they undoubtedly believe that He is constantly watching over them. By having the spirit of Ihsan, a person or a company will do the best activities in all aspects of life as there is always a deep feeling that Allah always watches them.
(3) *Beneficial:* A company carries mandate from the community that it should give goodness and benefits to the community. By applying CSR, companies have offered higher values to the stakeholders, and organizations will get good image. The CSR activities carried out by the company must provide benefits to the community and the environment.
(4) *Amanah:* A company should be able to create products or services with good quality. Besides, the company is expected to be trusted and transparent to the community such as in paying employee salaries and tax as well as paying attention to the environment.
(5) *Maqashid:* The comprehensiveness of Sharia objectives includes the perseverance of five fundamental elements in human life that are: *ad-din* (religion), *an-nafs* (life), *al-'aql* (intellect), *an-nasl* (ancestry), and *al-mal* (property or wealth).

Thereby, in Islam, business performance is judged on how well resources are managed to increase benefits to society. The concept of ummah shows that society has rights and interests over whatever a Muslim has. Business organizations are considered human institutions, which are part of the Islamic community. Therefore, moderation and concern for the needs of others, along with one's own, become an integral part of the CSR from an Islamic perspective. Individuals and companies are encouraged to sacrifice, surrender, and spend wealth on the poor and needy while expecting their reward only from Allah. This sense of duty, responsibility, and spirit of sacrifice, nurtured by Islam, really helps eliminate selfishness and greed and promote compassion, care, cooperation, and harmony among people (Dusuki, 2008).

From Shar'ia's perspective, Muslims should believe that all activities are performed in fair ways, with optimum benefit to all stakeholders, with trusted condition to achieve the *maqashid* Sharia. CSR that is directed by these values will create stability and sustainability in all business processes.

According to Jusoh, Ibrahim, and Napiah (2015), CSR action relies on two things: first, accountability as Allah's caliph, humans have certain responsibilities that need to be carried out in this world to ensure justice is continuously upheld. Man is entrusted with trust to be the caliph of Allah and govern the world according to the laws he has established.

In this case, the social responsibility of Muslims can be discussed under the concept of the caliph as an umbrella for a number of viewpoints. As caliph of Allah, a Muslim is bound by the principle of tawhid (the doctrine of "Oneness" of Allah), which guides Muslims to act the right and right to maintain his relationship with Allah and with other human beings and the universe.

Second, CSR is mandatory in Islam, even already embedded in the teachings of Islam fundamentally. Obviously, the concept of caliph is a general concept that can be applied to all people, including entrepreneurs (Jusoh *et al.*, 2015).

Besides all these values, there is one important thing before all activities are performed, which is, a sincere intention or good will. This is the condition where all activities are aimed at Allah SWT to accept all the actions that include CSR. In the Qur'an 38:5, Allah says: "And they have not been commanded except to worship Allah alone, having *ikhlas* (purity of intention) in their Religion and not setting-up partners with Allah in the worship of Him". The presence of these values shows the difference between the normal or conventional CSR and the Sharia perspective of CSR. The concept of CSR from the perspective of Sharia shows how Islamic law represented in Sharia, which consists of a set of rules driven from the Qur'an, Sunnah, Ijma', Qiyas, and other secondary sources, are the general principles of Islam and morality.

Sharia enterprise theory (SET) is a part of enterprise theory combining with Islamic value. Meutia (2009) asserted that there are three categories of stakeholders, namely Allah SWT, humans, and nature. Triyuwono (2007, p. 4) states that apart from those horizontal parties, there is the highest party and the sole purpose of human life, that is Allah SWT, and this is as a form of vertical relationship. The broader vertical and horizontal relationships are mentioned in the SET. In the SET, Triyuwono (2007) explained that companies should not only be responsible to the horizontal accountability, namely to stakeholders and environment, but they must be responsible toward the vertical accountability, that is to the God — Allah SWT, as the highest party and the only aim of human life. Triyuwono (2000) asserted that corporate responsibility is not only about how to generate maximum profits for the benefit of the owner but also that companies should change to zakat-oriented and environment, and stakeholders-oriented.

CSR is not something new in Islam's point of view. Social responsibility has been mentioned in the Qur'an in the Surah Al-Baqarah 205 and Al-A'raaf 56. In the Qur'an, the term social responsibility is often expressed as in the word of Allah Qs. Al-Baqarah: 205, "And if he turns away (from you), he walks on the earth to do damage to it, and destroy crops and livestock, and Allah does not like destruction". Meanwhile, in Qs. Al-A'raaf 56 which means, "And do not make mischief on earth, after (Allah) fix it and pray to Him with fear (will not be accepted) and hope (will be granted). Surely Allah's grace is very close to those who do goodness".

Triyuwono (2001) mentioned that SET pays attention to two aspects, namely vertical accountability to God and the horizontal accountability to direct and indirect stakeholders of humans, the environment, and society. Triyuwono (2001) explains that SET is oriented to providing information to stakeholders and the natural environment as a form of accountability to God, people, and the natural environment. First, God is placed as the highest stakeholder. The consequence of establishing God as the highest stakeholder is the use of sunnatullah as the basis for the construction of Sharia activities, which should only be done based on God's rules or laws. Second, people or humans is the second stakeholder of SET. SET divides human stakeholders into two groups, namely direct and indirect, both in the form of financial contributions and non-financial contributions. Direct stakeholders are those who make direct contributions to the company (such as shareholders, management, employees, creditors, and government), while indirect stakeholders are those who do not directly contribute to the company. Because they have contributed to the company, they have the right to obtain welfare from the company. Meanwhile, indirect stakeholders are those who do not contribute at all to the company (both financially and non-financially), such as someone who receives alms or donation.

The last stakeholder group in the SET is nature. Companies and people cannot live and sustain without nature. Companies exist on the Earth using energy from the planet and nature, exploring raw materials from nature for producing their products and services. The form of welfare distribution to the Earth and nature is the concern of corporates in order to preserve the nature or environment, prevention of pollution, and others.

Furthermore, conducting CSR based on intentions of hoping to achieve blessing from Allah when helping poor people, then it can be categorized as worship. For example, giving zakat as CSR can provide benefits for alleviating poverty. Besides, by doing worship, the subject of the act will be rewarded. More than that, the benefits of doing CSR are that the company not only gaining value and good image but also the manager will get a reward (ajrun) from God. Djakfar (2007) concludes that only organizations that have theological spirit are capable of applying CSR on the basis of ihsan because God teaches that humans must have social interests, be humanistic, help each other in good terms (ta'awun), and be sincere in sharing (ihklas) other virtue values.

Moreover, Jusoh *et al.* (2015) asserted that Islamic organizations have to mandatorily implement CSR similar to an individual. They are not only responsible for the operation of organization but also to conduct worship. An institution is also fundamentally a human organization, where the people in the organization will manage people as well to achieve happiness in this world and the hereafter. This is because humans were created by Allah as caliph, where humans are entrusted to manage this world according to the law which He has established and to manage everything well as well as to maintain good relations between God, humans, and the environment. Jusoh, Ibrahim, and Napiah (2015) also mentioned that the tawhid principle can be implemented in the CSR, where CSR is a part of our responsibility not only to Allah SWT but also to people and the universe. Humans must acknowledge the oneness of God and at the same time believe that everything in this world belongs to Allah. In general, therefore, it seems that caliph has two fundamental responsibilities, namely vertically to Allah SWT and horizontally to people and the environment.

Dusuki (2008) concluded that CSR is activities that encourage organizations to carry out activities that not only fulfill a moral obligation but also a religious one. The activities must be grounded on the belief that organization must do something good for the community and environment and fulfill its responsibility to Allah SWT. This is regardless of negative or positive financial consequences. It can be said that a company should not merely aim to maximize profits but also pursue the highest beatitude of life and the hereafter. Therefore, institutions have to conceive that CSR is a social and moral responsibility for the welfare of stakeholders, including the environment, as well as fulfill responsibility to Allah SWT. This is corresponding to the vicegerency concept (khalifah) in Islam.

All in all, the most appropriate theory for CSR implementation is SET because this theory posits Allah as the main source of trust. Meanwhile, the resources owned by stakeholders are mandated from God in which the responsibility to use is embedded in the manner and purpose that are set by Allah. In addition, SET asserts that relationship is not only with horizontal stakeholder namely, humans and nature or the environment but also with the vertical stakeholder that is the Almighty Allah SWT.

Therefore, any company that claims to base its operations on Sharia principles must naturally practice CSR because it perpetuates the true spirit of Islam. Indeed, Islamic companies should strive to make it central in their business universe, promoting socially good practicing responsibility. In this regard, the assimilation of social and other Islamic responsibilities in meeting customer expectations is worth considering fully because it is a unique and fundamental distinction between Islamic and conventional companies and potentially able to push Islamic corporations to a higher level in securing customer accountability and acceptance.

5.6 Conclusion

CSR arises because corporate responsibility does not only generates profits for their shareholders but also must pays attention to stakeholders and their environment and nature. Some theories only consider stakeholders and nature or the environment. The existing theories, namely agency theory, stakeholder theory, legitimacy theory, entity theory, and enterprise theory, pay more attention to stakeholders and nature on the horizontal side, while the vertical side is not considered.

In agency theory, a manager only considers how to improve the welfare of their shareholders, which may induce conflict of interest. Stakeholder theory considers how a company must provide benefits to stakeholders, such as shareholders, creditors, consumers, suppliers, government, community, and other parties. Entity theory pays attention only to the welfare of the owners. Legitimacy theory has a wider scope by which company should consider not only stakeholders but also the environment.

Based on SET, a company not only considers the horizontal stakeholder and nature but also pays attention to vertical responsibilities, namely responsibility to God Almighty, such as giving zakat, alms, endowments, and waqf. Therefore, organizations should change from being profit-oriented to zakat-oriented and environment, and stakeholders-oriented.

If there is a mismatch between the company's goals and the wishes of stakeholders or if the company does not pay attention to the environment and nature, the company's sustainability can be threatened. However, above all, it is Allah SWT who will govern and determine the sustainability of the organization.

For sustainability of the organization's life in the future, they must maintain a good relationship with the parties of both vertical and horizontal stakeholders. The organization must carry out activities that favor the horizontal parties, such as stakeholders, as the humans, and pay attention to nature and environment. As stated in SET, every organization must not forget God as the vertical party and as the highest stakeholder in all activities.

References

Al-Abdallah, G. & Ahmed, R. (2018). The impact of corporate social responsibility on customer loyalty in the Qatari telecommunication sector. *Journal of Business & Retail Management Research, 13*(1), 253–268. Doi: 10.24052/JBRMR/V13IS01/ART-25.

Deakin, S. & Hobbs, R. (2007). False dawn for CSR? Shifts in regulatory policy and the response of the corporate and financial sectors in Britain. *Corporate Governance: An International Review, 15*, 68–76. Doi: 10.1111/j.1467-8683.2007.00543.x.

Djakfar, M. (2007). *Etika Bisnis Dalam Perspektif Islam*. Malang: UIN-Maliki Press.

Dusuki, A. W. (2008). What does Islam say about corporate social responsibility (CSR)? *Review of Islamic Economics, 12*(1), 1–28.

El-Halaby, S. & Hussainey, K. (2016). Determinants of compliance with AAOIFI standards by Islamic banks. *International Journal of Islamic and Middle Eastern Finance and Management, 9*, 143–168. Doi: 10.1108/IMEFM-06-2015-0074.

Elkington, J. (1998). Accounting for the triple bottom line. *Measuring Business Excellence, 2*(3), 18–22. Doi: 10.1108/eb025539.

Friedman, M. (1970). The social responsibility of business is to increase its Profits. *New York Times Magazine*, September 13: 32–33, 122–124.

Gray, R. H., Owen, D. L., & Adams, C. (1996). *Accounting and Accountability: Changes and Challenges in Corporate Social and Environmental Reporting*. Hemel Hempstead: Prentice Hall Europe.

Gray, R. H., Owen, D. L., & Maunders, K. T. (1987). *Corporate Social Reporting: Accounting and Accountability*. Hemel Hempstead: Prentice Hall.

Guthrie, J. & Parker, L. (1989). Corporate social reporting, a rebuttal of legitimacy theory. *Accounting and Business Research, 19*(76), 343–335.

Januarti, I. & Apriyanti, D. (2005). Pengaruh tanggung jawab sosial perusahaan terhadap kinerja Perusahaan. *Jurnal Maksi, 2*(3), 227–243.

Jensen, M. C. & Meckling, W. H. (1976). Theory of the firm: Managerial behavior, agency costs and ownership structure. *Journal of Financial Economics, 3*(4), 305–360. Doi: 10.1016/0304-405X(76)90026-X.

Jones, P., Wynn, M., Comfort, D., & Hillier, D. (2008). Corporate social responsibility and UK retailers. *Issues in Sustainable and Environmental Accounting, 1*, 244–258. Doi: 10.22164/isea.v1i2.16.

Jusoh, W. N. H. W., Ibrahim, U., & Napiah, M. D. M. (2015). An Islamic perspective on corporate social responsibility of Islamic banks. *Mediterranean Journal of Social Sciences, 6*(2), 308–315.

Khatun, K. M. & Alautiyat, H. (2012). Corporate social responsibility: An Islamic perspective. *International Journal of Business and Technopreneurship, 2*(3), 415–433.

Khurshid, M. A., Al-Aali, A., Soliman, A. A., & Amin, S. M. (2014). Developing an Islamic Corporate Social Responsibility Model (ICSR). *Competitiveness Review, 24*(4), 258–274.

Little, A. D. (2006). The innovation highground — Winning tomorrow's customers using sustainability-driven innovation. *Strategic Direction, 22*(1), 35–37.

Longo, M., Mura, M., & Bonoli, A. (2005). Corporate social responsibility and corporate performance: The case of Italian SMEs. *Corporate*

Governance: The International Journal of Business in Society, *5*(4), 28–42. Doi: 10.1108/14720700510616578.

Meutia, I. (2009). *Shari'ah Enterprise Theory Sebagai Dasar Pengungkapan Tanggungjawab Sosial Bank Syariah.* Universitas Brawijaya Malang, Indonesia.

Munilla, L. & Miles, M. (2005). The corporate social responsibility continuum as a component of stakeholder theory. *Business and Society Review*, *110*, 371–387. Doi: 10.1111/j.0045-3609.2005.00021.x.

Novarela, D. & Sari, I. M. (2015). Pelaporan corporate social responsibility Perbankan Syariah Dalam Perspektif Syariah enterprise theory. *Jurnal Akuntansi dan Keuangan Islam*, *2*(2), 145–160.

Panwar, R., Rinne, T., Hansen, E., & Juslin, H. (2006). Corporate responsibility balancing economic, environmental, and social issues in the forest products industry. *Forest Products Journal*, *56*, 4–12.

Post, J. E., Preston, L. E., & Sachs, S. (2002). Managing the extendend enterprise: The new stakeholders view. *California Management Review*, *45*(1), 6–28.

Rhodes, C. (2016). Democratic business ethics: Volkswagen's emissions scandal and the disruption of corporate sovereignty. *Organization Studies*, *37*(10), 1501–1518. Doi: 10.1177/0170840616641984.

Spitzeck, H. T. (2009). The development of governance structures for corporate responsibility. *Corporate Governance: The International Journal of Business in Society*, *9*, 495–505.

Triyuwono, I. (2001). Metafora Zakat Dan Shari'ah enterprise theory Sebagai Konsep Dasar Dalam Membentuk Akuntansi Syari'ah. *Jurnal Akuntansi Dan Auditing Indonesia*, *5*(2), 131–145.

Triyuwono, I. (2007). *Mengangkat "Sing Liyan" Untuk Formulasi Nilai Tambah Syari'ah.* Paper Presented at the Simposium Nasional Akuntansi X Universitas Hasanudin, Makasar.

Turcsanyi, J. & Sisaye, S. (2013). Corporate social responsibility and its link to financial performance. *World Journal of Science, Technology and Sustainable Development*, *10*, 4–18. Doi: 10.1108/20425941311313065.

WBCSD. (2001). *The Business Case for Sustainable Development: Making a Difference Toward the Johannesburg Summit 2002 and Beyond.* Switzerland: WBCSD.

Widayanto, H. (2005). *Penerapan Enterprise Theory Dengan Menggunakan Laporan Nilai Tambah Sebagai Laporan Pelengkap Dalam Menilai Tanggung Jawab Sosial Perusahaan BUMN (Studi Kasus Di PT. Pal Indonesia (Persero)*. (Doctoral), Universitas Airlangga, Surabaya, Indonesia.

https://doi.org/10.1142/9781800612426_0006

Chapter 6

Forensic Accounting from an Islamic Perspective: A Conceptual Framework from the Jordanian Context

Hashem Alshurafat, Haitham A. Haloush, and Abdallah Bader Mahmoud Alzoubi

Abstract

Forensic accounting is a modern occupation that covers many services, including fraud investigation, IT forensics, litigation support, and business valuation. Few, if any, have come across forensic accounting based on an Islamic perspective. The religion of Islam ascribes to a wide spectrum of the highest morals and virtues. Our research involved a review of the previous research on forensic accounting, and we benchmarked it to the Islamic Sharia and law within the Jordanian context. The findings show that Islamic perspectives would lend robust foundations to forensic accounting in its endeavors to detect and prevent fraud and assist the trier of fact. This chapter contributes to the previous literature on forensic accounting by providing an optimal set of Islamic concepts that might be of benefit to forensic accounting practitioners, academics, and regulators.

Keywords: Islamic Accounting, Forensic Accounting, Jordan.

6.1 Introduction

Since the emergence of Islamic financial institutions, Islamic and other researchers have examined the adoption of different Islamic concepts in the business environment (Kamla, 2009; Velayutham, 2014; Wahyuni *et al.*, 2021). However, until now, forensic accounting remains quite distant from these researchers' investigations. This is despite the fact that forensic accounting techniques and tools have been widely endorsed by accounting practitioners and researchers (Yang & Lee, 2020; DiGabriele & Huber, 2015; Tiwari & Debnath, 2017; Botes & Saadeh, 2018). A forensic accountant is generally recognized as being able to provide professional services in the domains of business litigation matters, fraud investigations, business valuations, and IT forensic accounting (Odia & Akpata, 2021, Arboleda, Guzman-Luna, & Torres, 2018).

The importance of forensic accounting arises from the following reasons. First, with the increasing threat of fraud, forensic accountants can mitigate the fraud risk through fraud detection and investigation services (Lehmann & Heagy, 2017; Vousinas, 2019; Ozili, 2020; Yang & Lee, 2020; Wahyuni *et al.*, 2021). Global fraud surveys show that companies worldwide lose a considerable proportion of their profit due to fraud incidents (Kramer, 2015; Bunn, Ethridge & Crow, 2019). Second, in a complex litigious environment, forensic accountants can simplify the adversarial process through arbitration and mediation process (Durtschi & Rufus, 2017; Tiwari & Debnath, 2017; Alshurafat *et al.*, 2020; Yang & Lee, 2020; Alhusban *et al.*, 2020). Third, the increasing complexity of the financial business environment requires forensic accountants as they can provide business valuation services and hence simplify the process of firm acquisitions and mergers (DiGabriele & Lohrey, 2016; Jalilvand & Kostolansky, 2016; Yang & Lee, 2020). Finally, the increase in financial cybercrime incidents has also heightened the importance of IT forensic accountants (Rezaee & Wang, 2019; Odia & Akpata, 2021) as they enhance firms' cybersecurity which focuses on detecting and investigating such financial cybercrimes.

Islam holds a wide spectrum of the highest morals and virtues. Therefore, triangulating forensic accounting with Islamic concepts and values is expected to yield valuable contributions to forensic accounting practitioners in Islamic regions. In this research, we provide explanations of how Islamic concepts could be tailored to forensic accounting procedures.

Jordan has been considered an appropriate context for this study for multiple reasons. First, Jordan is an Islamic country located at the hub of the Islamic world. Second, Islamic accounting and finance in Jordan is well developed, as 17 Islamic banks are listed on the

Amman stock exchange and it has many Islamic small and medium institutions (Al-Msiedeen, Rashid, & Shams, 2018; Al-Al-Msiedeen & Al Sawalqa, 2021). Third, our case selection process enabled us to identify a complete set of articles of law. Fourth, forensic accounting has been growing recently in the Jordanian context (Alhusban *et al.*, 2020; Alshurafat, Al Shbail, & Almuiet, 2021b). Fifth, the articles of the Jordanian laws and regulations are derived from Islamic notions and principles.

The remainder of this chapter is organized as follows. The next two sections deal with definitions, first of Islamic accounting, then of forensic accounting. The fourth section is a review of prior articles on forensic accounting. In the fifth section, we propose a new definition of Islamic-based forensic accounting. The sixth section gives an illustration of the Islamic perspective on the legal role of forensic accounting. In the seventh, an illustration is provided of the Islamic perspective on the forensic accounting's business valuation role, while in the eighth, the illustration concerns the Islamic perspective on forensic accounting's fraud investigation role. The final section concludes the chapter.

6.2 What Is Islamic Accounting?

In the first instance, the intrinsic aim of Islamic accounting is to conceptualize the accounting profession in terms Islam's social and moral functions (Kamla, 2009; Baehaqi, Birton, & Hudaefi, 2020; Hassan *et al.*, 2021). As the accounting profession touches an aspect of our life of the utmost importance — the financial aspect — and is also known as the language of business, many scholars have emphasized the need to adjust this profession to Islamic to ensure accounting treatments are valid from the Islamic point of view.

It has been argued that the major distinction between conventional and Islamic accounting is a consequence of the difference in philosophical assumptions (Velayutham, 2014). Conventional accounting is based on the principles of individualism, personal interest, and profit maximization. In contrast, Islamic accounting is founded on the social and moral roles of Islam that lead to the tenets of equitable treatment, community interest, and fair profit (Baydoun & Willett, 2000; Velayutham, 2014; Qizam, 2020).

Prior researchers have used two approaches to define Islamic accounting, these are the "spatial or temporal sense" and the "religious sense" (Velayutham, 2014, p. 128). The first centers on "accounting in parts of the world where Islam is the majority religion during periods when Islam has been dominant" (Napier, 2009, p. 124). The second entails developing an Islamic accounting theory and a conceptual framework based on business concepts from the Islamic doctrine, the Qur'an and the Sunnah.[1] The second approach is the most dominant among Islamic accounting authors as it provides a way to address Islamic financial institutions' needs and respond to the requirements of Islamic business concepts such as accountability and *zakat* (Velayutham, 2014; El-Halaby, Albarrak, & Grassa, 2020).

In the literature, it has been evident that culture and religion impact accounting practices (Sulaiman & Willett, 2001; Hassan *et al.*, 2021). In Jordan, as in many Islamic countries, companies' financial reporting is dominated by Western financial accounting systems (Altarawneh & Lucas, 2012; Ghofur & Santika, 2021). Islamic accounting has developed in response to the fact that Western financial accounting systems do not correspond with the values and convictions of Islam (Velayutham, 2014). After the excessive investments in Islamic financial institutions that occurred in the late 20th century, the Accounting and Auditing Organization for Islamic Financial Institutions (AAOIFI) was set up in 1991 to offer these institutions valid accounting treatment for their economic events from an Islamic point of view (Pomeranz, 1997; El-Halaby, Albarrak, & Grassa, 2020).

6.3 What Is Forensic Accounting?

The term "forensic accounting" has been defined using different approaches. These have mainly focused on the services that forensic accountants can provide (Rezaee, Crumbley, & Elmore, 2004; Botes & Saadeh, 2018). Botes and Saadeh (2018) classify these

[1]The Sunnah is "the acts and sayings of the Prophet, as transmitted through traditions known as hadith" (for more information, refer to Ali & Oliver, 2007, p. 45).

approaches into three categories, namely "narrow", "broad", and "comprehensive". The first focuses on forensic accounting's adversarial aspect. Forensic accountants have shown merit in performing mediation, arbitration, and litigation services (Curtis, 2008; DiGabriele & Huber, 2015; Durtschi & Rufus, 2017; Tiwari & Debnath, 2017; Botes & Saadeh, 2018; Alshurafat *et al.*, 2019a; Alhusban *et al.*, 2020). In addition, they engage in business valuation services encompassing the quantification of economic loss and damage, assistance in appraisals, insurance claims, and merger and acquisitions matters (DiGabriele & Lohrey, 2016; Jalilvand & Kostolansky, 2016; Alshurafat *et al.*, 2019a).

The second approach involves the investigative role of forensic accounting, where fraud investigation is recognized as a major role for forensic accountants (DiGabriele & Huber, 2015; Elder & Yebba, 2017; Tiwari & Debnath, 2017; Alshurafat *et al.*, 2019a). They undertake fraud-related examinations, such as financial misstatement investigations, money laundering detection, corruption prevention, asset misappropriations investigations, and financial cybercrime detection (Wahyuni *et al.*, 2021; Ozili, 2020; Akinbowale, Klingelhöfer, & Zerihun, 2020, Yang & Lee, 2020).

Third, the comprehensive approach consolidates the previous two approaches by emphasizing forensic accountants' role in litigation support and fraud investigation (Botes & Saadeh, 2018). For example, Bologna and Lindquist (1995, p. 47) described forensic accounting as:

> the application of financial skills, and an investigative mentality to unresolved issues, conducted within the context of rules of evidence. As a discipline, it encompasses financial expertise, fraud knowledge, and a sound knowledge and understanding of business reality and the working of the legal system. Its development has been primarily achieved through on-the-job training, as well as experience with investigating officers and legal counsel.

In addition, Rezaee, Crumbley, and Elmore (2004, p. 194) defined forensic accounting as:

> the practice of rigorous data collection and analysis in the areas of litigation support, consulting, expert witnessing, and fraud examination.

6.4 Prior Studies on Forensic Accounting

Historically, forensic accounting has been evolving since 1946 when Maurice Peloubet published an article entitled *Forensic Accounting—Its Place in Today's Economy* (Crain *et al.*, 2019, p. 6). Consequently, during the last few decades, forensic accounting has been widely examined by researchers. The main areas of exploration in forensic accounting focused on forensic accounting practice (Arboleda, Guzman-Luna, & Torres, 2018; Akinbowale, Klingelhöfer, & Zerihun, 2020; Dee & Durtschi, 2010; Honigsberg, 2020; Abdulrahman *et al.*, 2020; Heitger & Heitger, 2008; Pearson & Singleton, 2008; Ramamoorti, 2008; Carpenter, Durtschi, & Gaynor, 2011; Kramer, Seda, & Bobashev, 2017; Rezaee, Wang, & Lam, 2018; Alshurafat *et al.*, 2019b, 2020; Rezaee & Wang, 2019), forensic accounting professionalism (Alshurafat *et al.*, 2019a; Alhusban *et al.*, 2020; Yang & Lee, 2020; Alshurafat, 2021; Alshurafat, Al Shbail, & Mansour, 2021b; Huber, 2012), forensic accounting skills (Gbegi & Adebisi, 2014; Carnes & Gierlasinski, 2001; McMullen & Sanchez, 2010; Davis, Farrell, & Ogilby, 2010; Tiwari & Debnath, 2017), and forensic accounting education (Heitger & Heitger, 2008; Pearson & Singleton, 2008; Ramamoorti, 2008; Carpenter, Durtschi, & Gaynor, 2011; Kramer, Seda, & Bobashev, 2017, Rezaee, Wang, & Lam, 2018; Alshurafat *et al.*, 2019b, 2020; Rezaee & Wang, 2019; Arboleda, Guzman-Luna, & Torres, 2018; Akinbowale, Klingelhöfer, & Zerihun, 2020; Dee & Durtschi, 2010; Honigsberg, 2020; Abdulrahman *et al.*, 2020).

Overall, prior studies show that forensic accounting could be of particular assistance in fraud detection and financial litigation. For example, Abdulrahman *et al.* (2020) reported that forensic accounting has a significant impact on the fraud detection process within the banking industry in the UAE. While in the financial litigation process, Abdul-Baki (2019) reported a case where a forensic accountant was able to resolve a conflict between two government agents by using an accounting IT technique (forensic audit).

However, previous researchers indicate that the forensic accounting profession faces various obstacles. Alshurafat, Al Shbail, and Mansour (2021a) illustrate these, which include the misconception of forensic accounting's intrinsic aim, its lack of public recognition, and its occupational reputation. Therefore, there is a need to pay more attention to forensic accounting research, education, and professionalism in different circumstances to enhance the applicability of forensic accounting in different geographical and cultural contexts.

In this chapter, we aim to fill a gap in the forensic accounting literature by highlighting the applicability of forensic accounting within the Islamic accounting context. Our purpose here is to provide an optimal set of Islamic concepts that might be of benefit to forensic accounting practitioners, academics, and regulators. By doing so, this chapter provides a new opportunity to enforce the implementation of fairness to avoid fraud and to simplify the resolution of financial litigation within the Islamic accounting and finance context.

6.5 Islamic-Based Forensic Accounting

Based on the previous Islamic accounting literature, only a few earlier researchers have dealt with financial fraud in Islamic financial institutions. The term "Islamic forensic accounting" has been previously considered by Wahyuni *et al.*, (2021) who acknowledge the lack of literature on Sharia-based forensic accounting or Islamic forensic accounting. They provide a workflow for the procedure of Islamic forensic accounting, as shown in Figure 6.1.

However, no definition for Sharia-based forensic accounting or Islamic forensic accounting has been previously provided. Neither the different roles of litigation support and business valuation in Islamic forensic accounting have been approached. In this chapter, we define the term "Islamic forensic accounting" as follows:

> The application of financial skills and an investigative mentality to unresolved issues, conducted within the context of rules of evidence based on Islamic morals and virtues in the areas of litigation support, consulting, expert witnessing, and fraud examination.

Islamic forensic accounting is presented in this study in order to provide practical implications for policymakers, regulatory authorities, practitioners, and educational in related Islamic accounting and finance institutions. Fraud is a dilemma for individuals and corporations in all countries, from which no one is immune. Therefore, triangulating forensic accounting with the moral and ethical views of

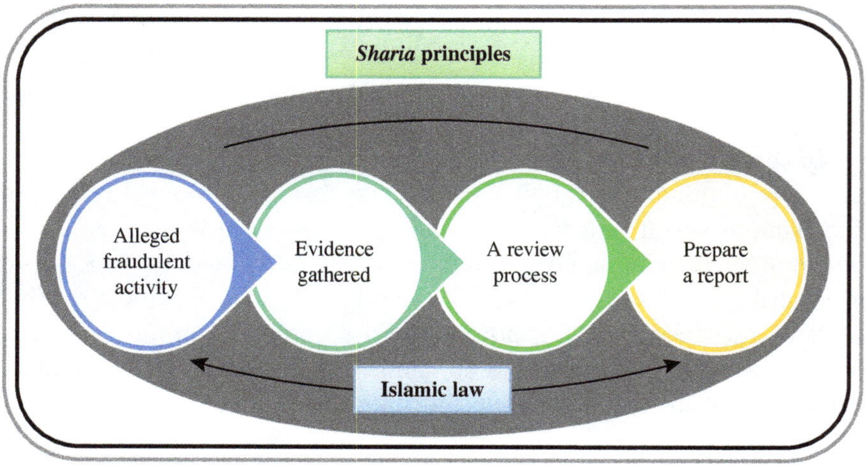

Figure 6.1. Procedure of Islamic forensic accounting.
Source: Wahyuni *et al.* (2021, p. 8).

Islam will provide more immunity for Islamic financial institutions against the dilemma of fraud. Moreover, the business environment nowadays is much more complex than at any other time. Therefore, forensic accountants who are educated in the specialty of Islamic financial requirements are needed to simplify complex legal and financial issues in the context of Islamic financial disputes.

In the following section, the roles of forensic accountants in the areas of litigation support, business valuation, and fraud examination are illustrated.

6.6 Islamic Perspective on the Legal Role of Forensic Accounting

Bearing in mind that forensic accounting is still a newly developed area in Jordan and many other parts of the world, it is imperative to explore the possibility of transplanting deeply rooted theoretical notions of Islam, which collectively echo universal standards of fairness, due process, and efficiency in their legal context. This argument involves a fair, just, and equitable balance between two parameters. The first is the litigious, adversarial nature of court proceedings, including forensic accounting measures. The second comprises general notions of mitigated and less stringent rules commonly associated with less formal methods of dispute resolution, approved by the court system via mediation and arbitration. Striking the right balance between these conflicting notions would be a daunting challenge. In doing so, notions of Islam, with its less formal and stringent rules, might be inserted into the equation. That said, there should be no trade-offs on basic notions on the fairness and efficiency of judicial proceedings.

The *Jordanian Civil Code* provisions are deeply rooted in Islamic principles and notions, as clearly manifested in the *Explanatory Notes* of the Code. Bearing this in mind, it is reasonable to argue for the feasibility of transplanting Islamic notions into the *Jordanian Civil Code*, in order to improve the fairness and efficiency of forensic accounting practice in judicial proceedings in Jordan.

Arguably, this conforms largely with the perception of forensic accounting as a service deploying certain skills to collect, analyze and evaluate the evidential matter, and to interpret and communicate findings in the courtroom. In other words, it is perceived that forensic accountants in Jordan and elsewhere often believe that they have a "common language", which consists of financial statements and annual budgets, notwithstanding that monetary issues must be interpreted and understood in their legal context.

Such interpretation and understanding leaves the gate wide open to incorporate Islamic notions which are thought to be universal in nature. Indeed, it is imperative to reduce the culture of "adversarialism" in litigation, and we hope that increased cooperation between the parties will reduce such a culture. However, efforts to instruct the court's members in cooperative behavior are often exploited by judges who attempt to maintain such adversarial procedure, with a strong legal culture supporting them. Islamic notions have a pivotal compromising and mitigating role to play in this context.

More precisely, *Article 3* of the *Jordanian Civil Code* states clearly that rules and principles of Islam are considered as driving forces in construing and interpreting the aforementioned provisions and theories encapsulated in the Code.

Clearly, one of the recurrent facets of Islamic law is the structure of family law and its correlated implications for the state, society, individuals, and the legal infrastructure. When the subject matter of a contract is intended to create legal effects, this implies that such intention should be capable of being financially assessed in order to consider the contract valid and enable the law to recognize and enforce the provisions of the contract and penalize the non-performers of those provisions. As a result, selling, leasing, and mortgage agreements are contracts because they can be assessed financially while marriage contracts, which are sought as a moral issue rather than a financial issue, are included in family law rather than civil law.

With particular reference to the *Law of Inheritance* in Jordan, according to *Article 206* of the *Jordanian Civil Code*, which stemmed from Islamic principles as argued above, a universal successor can be defined as the person(s) who replaces the deceased in his/her financial patrimony wholly or partially in relation to others. As a result, if the deceased is a seller who did not receive payment for goods or services sold or a buyer who did not receive the goods or services, then universal successors would replace the deceased in claiming such rights. Having said that, it must be clear that with regard to the deceased's financial obligations, these should be executed from the estate before its distribution among inheritors, not from these heirs' financial inheritance after they receive it.

By comparison, in French law, for example, the rights and obligations of the deceased would be transferred to the inheritors, even though this might exceed the amount of inheritance. Consequently, the French legislature gives the choice to the heirs to confine their obligations to their financial amount in the inheritance or refuse to accept the inheritance altogether.

Apparently, contractors might agree that any rights and obligations that are created from the contract would be terminated upon the death of a contractor, e.g., a property owner might agree with his/her tenant that the tenant's right in the subject matter of the contract would not be transferred to the tenant's successors. Also, the law might stipulate certain restrictions on the rights and obligations of the universal successors, e.g., the deceased's will should not be more than a third of the inheritance and the right of "enjoyment of property" would not be transferred.

Bearing in mind that the *Jordanian Civil Code* is derived from Islamic notions and principles, as mentioned earlier, the Jordanian legislature differentiates between taking delivery of the subject matter purchased by the deceased buyer and not taking delivery.

In the first case, the seller cannot detain the subject matter because it is not in his possession anymore and therefore the seller would participate as a normal creditor in the inheritance. In the second case, the seller would be a preferential creditor in the inheritance and would have the right to detaining the subject matter until receiving payment of the contractual price. Apparently, in both cases the buyer has a personal right and not a real right to require the universal successor, which can be defined as the person(s) who replaces the deceased in his/her financial estate wholly or partially in relation to others, to perform the deceased's obligations since the contract has not been concluded since an essential element in a valid contract, i.e., the delivery and not the payment, has been fulfilled.

In addition, the aforementioned article states that with regard to the death of the seller after receiving the payment and prior to delivery to the buyer, the latter would have a real right as a preferential creditor to require the seller's universal successors to perform the deceased's obligation toward the buyer since an essential element in a valid contract, i.e., the payment, and not the delivery, has been fulfilled and consequently the buyer has right of ownership in the sold subject matter which implies a real right.

In the insurance context under the Jordanian law, which is based on Islamic principles, *Article 949* of the *Jordanian Civil Code* provides that the amount of compensation due to a deceased would be excluded from the inheritance of the deceased and therefore the creditors cannot claim their rights from the amount of compensation. In actual fact, the heirs of the deceased insured in this case are thought to be imaginary beneficiaries where their right in compensation derives from the insurance contract with the insurer rather than having the amount of compensation as part of their inheritance which would be subjected to the creditors of the deceased insured.

6.7 Islamic Perspective on the Business Valuation Role of Forensic Accounting

In Jordan, before the enactment of the *Jordanian Civil Code*, the *Legal Rules Periodical*, which was issued under the Ottoman Empire in 1869, was applicable. The *Legal Rules Periodical* is also known as *Al-Majalatu*. This periodical was based on Islamic law. Consequently, *Article 2* of the *Jordanian Civil Code* states clearly that in the absence of a legal rule in the Code that regulates an issue under question, reference must be made to the *Legal Rules Periodical*. Effectively, this means references to Islamic law.

Al-Majalatu was compiled and enacted by the Ottoman Government between 1867 and 1877, to embody the principles of Moslem Sunni law, mainly those of *Al-Hanafi School of Jurisprudence*, which was founded in the eighth century. It was and still is the leading school among the four Moslem jurisprudence schools established in the eighth and ninth centuries AD. *Al-Majalatu* remained effective as the civil law of all Arab countries under Ottoman rule and thereafter until it was gradually superseded by their civil codes, including the present *Jordanian Civil Code* in 1976.

Though this Code preserved the principles of the Moslem Sunni law in some important respects, as is clear from the provisions of Book One of the Code which deals with personal rights, it preserved them to a lesser extent in all other respects or regulated completely new matters, as is clear from the provisions of Book Two which deals with contracts, Book Three which deals with the right of ownership, and Book Four which deals with real securities. This is apparent in matters like aleatory contracts not dealt with in *Al-Majalatu* and company law dealt with therein but not developed to suit modern economic life, for the obvious reason that the Moslem law was developed more than a thousand years before the industrial revolution in Europe.[2]

From this perspective, an important prohibition in this setting is that of *riba* (interest rate) as an unacceptable profit. Of note is that the *Explanatory Notes* in the *Jordanian Civil Code* indicate that, in an early version of the Code, the possibility existed of prohibiting any financial reimbursement for the creditor for late performance by the debtor, notwithstanding any harm reflected, on the assumption that this amounts to *riba*. However, this was deleted, as it offered a potential loophole for contractors to escape liability.[3] Even so,

---

[2]The *Jordanian Civil Code Explanatory Notes*, published in the *Jordanian Official Gazette No. 2645 (1976) 157.*

[3]*Ibid.*, 400.

one might argue that a case of unacceptable financial reimbursement should be acknowledged by the Jordanian courts, in accordance with *Article 3* of the *Jordanian Civil Code.*

Arguably, the Jordanian law is, in theory, opposed to the enforcement of interest rates. This can be explained by the fact that the Jordanian law is based on Islamic law to a large extent, as demonstrated earlier. In practice, however, there appears to be little interest or willingness in Jordan's courts to apply *Article 3* of the *Jordanian Civil Code.* Interest rates constitute a contentious matter under Jordanian law, although *Article 167* of the *Jordanian Civil Procedures Law* caps such interest rates at 9%.[4] Ironically, an interest rate on defaulting payments that are higher than 9% will not be enforceable, and the court will consider it contrary to "public order and morals".

Such a dilemma is not common in Jordan alone. In other Arab countries, this issue has been debated among legal scholars. Other Arab laws are based on Islamic laws also, particularly those of the *Al-Hanafi School of Jurisprudence*, although to a lesser extent in comparison with the Jordanian law. For example, in the United Arab Emirates, the *Penal Code* differentiates between natural and juristic legal persons, whereby the interest rate is prohibited on the former and is subject to a fine and/or imprisonment.[5] The *Kuwaiti Civil Code* explicitly provides that an interest rate is not allowed for non-traders.[6] The *Moroccan Civil Code* allows dealing in interest rates for non-Muslims.[7]

6.8 Islamic Perspective on the Fraud Investigation Role of Forensic Accounting

Corporate frauds and white-collar crimes have prompted the increased demand for forensic accounting practitioners and education in forensic accounting (Pearson & Singleton, 2008; Yang & Lee, 2020; Wahyuni *et al.*, 2021). Islamic financial institutions are

[4] *Article 167* of the *Jordanian Law of Civil Procedures No. 26 of 2002*, published in the *Jordanian Official Gazette No. 4547 (2002).*

[5] *Article 409* of the *UAE Penal Code, No.2 of 1987.*

[6] *Article 547* of the *Kuwaiti Civil Code, No. 15 of 1979.*

[7] *Article 87* of the *Moroccan Civil Code, No. 1 of 1954.*

requested to adopt sound Islamic practices, including accountability and fairness, to prevent fraud from occurring. Islamic morals and virtues provide a wide range of sound principles that a forensic accounting practitioner could adopt to minimize fraud risk.

Fraud specialists have used lots of psychological theories to understand criminal behavior, these theories include fraud triangle theory (Cressey, 1950, 1953), the triangle of fraud action (Dorminey *et al.*, 2012), the fraud scale theory (Albrecht, Howe, & Romney, 1984), the fraud diamond theory (Wolfe & Hermanson, 2004), and the S.C.O.R.E. (stimulus, capability, opportunity, rationalization, ego) model (Vousinas, 2019). All of these focus on the factors that might influence one person's criminal behavior, such as the opportunity to commit fraud, the financial pressure, psychological interpretation and rationalization, the capability of committing fraud, and the behavioral traits of the fraudulent (Bunn, Ethridge, & Crow, 2019; Ozili, 2020; Yang & Lee, 2020).

In this area, Islam contributes to refining human behavior as Islam encourages adopting the noblest qualities, including accountability, fairness, moderation, compliance with truth, honesty, and trust (Ghofur & Santika, 2021; Wahyuni *et al.*, 2021). According to the *Qur'an* and *Sunnah*, all kinds of fraud are prohibited:

> Woe to those who deal in fraud, those who, when they have to receive by measure from men, exact full measure, but when they have to give by measure or weight to men give less than due. Do they not think that they will be called to account on a Mighty Day, a Day when (all) mankind will stand before the Lord of the Worlds?
>
> (Al-Mutaffifin, 83: 1–6)

> And do not consume one another's wealth unjustly or send it [in bribery] to the rulers in order that [they might aid] you [to] consume a portion of the wealth of the people in sin, while you know [it is unlawful]
>
> (Al-Baqarah, 2: 188)

(Ibrahim, Man, & Noor, 2013, p. 449)

> Prophet Muhammad (PBUH) once said in his *hadith* as reported by al-Hakim and al-Bayhaqi, "It is not permissible to sell an article without making everything (about it) clear,

> nor is it permissible for anyone who knows (about its defects) to refrain from mentioning them"
>
> (Al-Qaradhawi, 2001)

Also, Islam provides measures and sanctions to prevent and prosecute fraudulent activities. These measures can be viewed in terms of the corporate perspective. Most Islamic companies, especially those in the financial sector, apply different Islamic measures to minimize fraud risk. These measures include establishing a Sharia compliance board, adopting Sharia compliance procedures, and adopting Sharia corporate governance (Kasim, 2012; Anisykurlillah *et al.*, 2020). Forensic accounting can play role in reviewing and assessing the Sharia compliance level of Islamic financial institutions.

6.9 Conclusion

Based on this review of prior literature, forensic accounting is a new practice area that could be combined with Islamic concepts and perspectives. Islamic morals and values have been previously integrated into accounting practice, and this yields advantages in the Islamic contexts. In this chapter, we used the Jordanian legal and financial context to illustrate how Islamic concepts could be incorporated into forensic acccunting practice. This offers multiple implications for research and practice. In terms of research implications, we introduced and defined a new concept to the forensic accounting literature, Islamic forensic accounting. Future researchers are encouraged to expand investigations into the applicability of this concept. New research could examine where and how to implement Islamic forensic accounting.

In terms of implications for practice, we provided forensic accounting practitioners in the Islamic context with a set of situations where forensic accounting practitioners could utilize the Islamic concepts in their work. As forensic accounting practitioners provide a wide range of services to different businesses' and individuals' financial circumstances, integrating Islamic morals and values would be essential to them. For example, assessing Islamic perspectives would lend the forensic accounting occupation robust foundations in its endeavors to detect and prevent fraud and assist the trier of fact.

As in any research, this research has some limitations. The main one is the type of the research. While we depended mainly on earlier studies in the field of forensic accounting and Islamic accounting, future researchers are anticipated to provide empirical examinations. This can be achieved by examining the applicability of forensic accounting services in the context of Islamic financial institutes using different professional theories. In addition, pedagogical and educational investigations should be conducted by future researchers to examine the best approach to integrate forensic accounting within the Islamic accounting curricula and courses.

References

Abdul-Baki, Z. (2019). The role of accounting in conflicts resolution: The case of PwC's forensic audit of the Nigerian National Petroleum Corporation. *Managerial Auditing Journal*, *36*(2), 261–279. Doi: 10.1108/MAJ-03-2018-1835.

Abdulrahman, M. H. A., Mohd Shukri Ab Yajid, A. K., & SM Ferdous Azam. (2020). The impact of forensic accounting on fraud detection in the UAE banking sector: An empirical study. *European Journal of Social Sciences Studies*, *4*(6), 137–162.

Akinbowale, O. E., Klingelhöfer, H. E., & Zerihun, M. F. (2020). An innovative approach in combating economic crime using forensic accounting techniques. *Journal of Financial Crime*, *27*(4), 1253–1271. Doi: 10.1108/JFC-04-2020-0053.

Al-Al-Msiedeen, J. M. & Al Sawalqa, F. A. (2021). Ownership structure and CEO compensation: Evidence from Jordan. *Asian Economic and Financial Review*, *11*(5), 365–383.

Al-Msiedeen, J. M., Rashid, A., & Shams, S. (2018). Board independence and firm performance: Evidence from Jordan. *Proceedings of Sydney International Business Research Conference 2018*, Novotel Sydney Central, Sydney, Australia, 25–26 March, 2018.

Albrecht, W. S., Howe, K. R., & Romney, M. B. (1984). *Deterring Fraud: The Internal Auditor's Perspective*. Inst of Internal Auditors. Florida, USA.

Alhusban, A. A. A., Haloush, H. A., Alshurafat, H., Al-Msiedeen, J. M., Massadeh, A. A. M., & Alhmoud, R. J. (2020). The regulatory structure and governance of forensic accountancy in the emerging market: Challenges and opportunities. *Journal of Governance and Regulation*, *9*(4), 149–161. Doi: 10.22495/jgrv9i4art13.

Ali, K. & Oliver, L. (2007). *Islam: The Key Concepts*. Routledge, UK.

Alshurafat, H. (2021). Forensic accounting as a profession in Australia? A sociological perspective. *Meditari Accountancy Research*, (ahead-of-print). Doi: 10.1108/MEDAR-04-2020-0865.

Alshurafat, H., Al Shbail, M. O., & Almuiet, M. (2021a). Factors affecting the intention to adopt IT forensic accounting tools to detect financial cybercrimes. *International Journal of Business Excellence*. Doi: 10.1504/IJBEX.2021.10039538.

Alshurafat, H., Al Shbail, M. O., & Mansour, E. (2021b). Strengths and weaknesses of forensic accounting: An implication on the socio-economic development. *Journal of Business and Socio-economic Development*, *1*(2), 135–148. Doi: 10.1108/JBSED-03-2021-0026.

Alshurafat, H., Beattie, C., Jones, G., & Sands, J. (2019a). The domain of forensic accounting services: Evidence from Australia. 19th Asian Academic Accounting Association (FourA) Annual Conference.

Alshurafat, H., Beattie, C., Jones, G., & Sands, J. (2019b). Forensic accounting core and interdisciplinary curricula components in Australian universities: Analysis of websites. *Journal of Forensic and Investigative Accounting*, *11*(2), 353–365.

Alshurafat, H., Beattie, C., Jones, G., & Sands, J. (2020). Perceptions of the usefulness of various teaching methods in forensic accounting education. *Accounting Education*, *29*(2), 177–204.

Altarawneh, G. & Lucas, M. (2012). Understanding the dominance of Western accounting and neglect of Islamic accounting in Islamic countries. *Journal of Islamic Accounting and Business Research*, *3*(2), 99–120. Doi: 10.1108/17590811211265920.

Anisykurlillah, I., Jayanto, P. Y., Mukhibad, H., & Widyastuti, U. (2020). Examining the role of Sharia Supervisory Board attributes in reducing financial statement fraud by Islamic banks. *Banks and Bank Systems*, *15*(3), 106–116.

Arboleda, F. J. M., Guzman-Luna, J. A., & Torres, I.-D. (2018). Fraud detection-oriented operators in a data warehouse based on forensic accounting techniques. *Computer Fraud & Security*, *2018*(10), 13–19.

Baehaqi, A., Birton, M. N. A., & Hudaefi, F. A. (2020). Time value of money in Islamic accounting practice: A critical analysis from maqāṣid al-Sharī'ah. *Journal of Islamic Accounting and Business Research*, *11*(9), 2035–2052. Doi: 10.1108/JIABR-09-2018-0155.

Baydoun, N. & Willett, R. (2000). Islamic corporate reports. *Abacus*, *36*(1), 71–90.

Bologna, G. J. & Lindquist, R. J. (1995). *Fraud Auditing and Forensic Accounting: New Tools and Techniques*. New Jersey, USA: Wiley.

Botes, V. & Saadeh, A. (2018). Exploring evidence to develop a nomenclature for forensic accounting. *Pacific Accounting Review*, *30*(2), 135–154. Doi: 10.1108/PAR-12-2016-0117.

Bunn, E., Ethridge, J., & Crow, K. (2019). Fraud in small businesses: A preliminary study. *Journal of Accounting and Finance*, *19*(3), 24–32. Doi: 10.33423/jaf.v19i3.2030.

Carnes, K. C. & Gierlasinski, N. J. (2001). Forensic accounting skills: Will supply finally catch up to demand? *Managerial Auditing Journal*, *16*(6), 378–382. Doi: 10.1108/02686900110395514.

Carpenter, T. D., Durtschi, C., & Gaynor, L. M. (2011). The incremental benefits of a forensic accounting course on skepticism and fraud-related judgments. *Issues in Accounting Education*, *26*(1), 1–21.

Crain, M. A., Hopwood, W. S., Gendler, R. S., Young, G. R., & Pacini, C. (2019). *Essentials of Forensic Accounting*. New Jersey, USA: John Wiley & Sons.

Cressey, D. R. (1950). The criminal violation of financial trust. *American Sociological Review*, *15*(6), 738–743.

Cressey, D. R. (1953). *Other People's Money; A Study of the Social Psychology of Embezzlement*. New York, USA: Free Press.

Curtis, G. E. (2008). Legal and regulatory environments and ethics: Essential components of a fraud and forensic accounting curriculum. *Issues in Accounting Education*, *23*(4), 535.

Davis, C., Farrell, R., & Ogilby, S. (2010). Characteristics and skills of the forensic accountant. *American Institute of Certified Public Accountants*, *2010*, 11–26.

Dee, C. C. & Durtschi, C. (2010). Return of the Tallahassee BeanCounters: A case in forensic accounting. *Issues in Accounting Education*, *25*(2), 279–321.

DiGabriele, J. A. & Huber, W. M. D. (2015). Topics and methods in forensic accounting research. *Accounting Research Journal*, *28*(1), 98–114. Doi: 10.1108/ARJ-08-2014-0071.

DiGabriele, J. A. & Lohrey, P. L. (2016). The valuation of economic damages: A case study for the forensic accountant. *Journal of Forensic & Investigative Accounting*, *8*(2), 338–348.

Dorminey, J., Fleming, A. S., Kranacher, M. J., & Riley Jr., R. A. (2012). The evolution of fraud theory. *Issues in Accounting Education*, *27*(2), 555–579.

Durtschi, C. & Rufus, R. J. (2017). Arson or accident: A forensic accounting case requiring critical thinking and expert communication. *Issues in Accounting Education Teaching Notes*, *32*(1), 89–105.

El-Halaby, S., Albarrak, H., & Grassa, R. (2020). Influence of adoption AAOIFI accounting standards on earning management: Evidence from Islamic banks. *Journal of Islamic Accounting and Business Research*, *11*(19), 1847–1870. Doi: 10.1108/JIABR-10-2019-0201.

Elder, R. J. & Yebba, A. A. (2017). The Roslyn school district fraud: Improving school district internal control and financial oversight. *Issues in Accounting Education*, *32*(4), 25–39.

Gbegi, D. O. & Adebisi, J. F. (2014). Forensic accounting skills and techniques in fraud investigation in the Nigerian public sector. *Mediterranean Journal of Social Sciences*, *5*(3), 243–243.

Ghofur, R. A. & Santika, A. (2021). The influence of Sharia compliance against fraud on the Sharia banks in Indonesia. Annual Conference of Ihtifaz: Islamic Economics, Finance, and Banking.

Hassan, M. K., Alshater, M. M., Mumu, J. R., Sarea, A. M., & Azad, M. D. K. (2021). Bibliometric analysis of the journal of Islamic accounting and business research: Ten years review. *COLLNET Journal of Scientometrics and Information Management*, *15*(1), 63–88.

Heitger, L. E. & Heitger, D. L. (2008). Incorporating forensic accounting and litigation advisory services into the classroom. *Issues in Accounting Education*. *23*(4), 561–572.

Honigsberg, C. (2020). Forensic accounting. *Annual Review of Law and Social Science*, *16*, 147–164.

Huber, W. (2012). Is forensic accounting in the United States becoming a profession? *Journal of Forensic & Investigative Accounting*, *4*(1), 255–284.

Ibrahim, S. S., Man, N. C., & Noor, A. H. M. (2013). 449. Fraud: An Islamic perspective. *The 5th International Conference on Financial Criminology (ICFC)*.

Jalilvand, A. & Kostolansky, J. W. (2016). Le Beau footwear: A business valuation case for a privately held firm. *Issues in Accounting Education*, *31*(4), 439–447.

Kamla, R. (2009). Critical insights into contemporary Islamic accounting. *Critical Perspectives on Accounting*, *20*(8), 921–932.

Kasim, N. A. A. (2012). Disclosure of Shariah compliance by Malaysian takaful companies. *Journal of Islamic Accounting and Business Research*, *3*(1), 20–38.

Kramer, B. (2015). Trust, but verify: Fraud in small businesses. *Journal of Small Business and Enterprise Development*, *22*(1), 4–20. Doi: 10.1108/JSBED-08-2012-0097.

Kramer, B., Seda, M., & Bobashev, G. (2017). Current opinions on forensic accounting education. *Accounting Research Journal*, *30*(3), 249–264. Doi: 10.1108/ARJ-06-2015-0082.

Lehmann, C. M. & Heagy, C. D. (2017). A case study of fraud concerns at a homeowners' association. *Issues in Accounting Education Teaching Notes*, *32*(1), 42–56.

McMullen, D. A. & Sanchez, M. H. (2010). A preliminary investigation of the necessary skills, education requirements, and training requirements for forensic accountants. *Journal of Forensic & Investigative Accounting*, *2*(2), 30–48.

Napier, C. (2009). Defining Islamic accounting: Current issues, past roots. *Accounting History*, *14*(1–2), 121–144.

Odia, J. O. & Akpata, O. T. (2021). Role of data science and data analytics in forensic accounting and fraud detection. In *Handbook of Research on Engineering, Business, and Healthcare Applications of Data Science and Analytics*, pp. 203–227. IGI Global.

Ozili, P. K. (2020). Advances and issues in fraud research: A commentary. *Journal of Financial Crime*, *27*(1), 92–103. Doi: 10.1108/JFC-01-2019-0012.

Pearson, T. A. & Singleton, T. W. (2008). Fraud and forensic accounting in the digital environment. *Issues in Accounting Education*, *23*(4), 545.

Pomeranz, F. (1997). The accounting and auditing organization for Islamic financial institutions: An important regulatory debut. *Journal of International Accounting, Auditing and Taxation*, *6*(1), 123–130.

Qizam, I. (2020). Identifying a convergence between non-financial information and Islamic accounting for Islamic decision usefulness: A review and synthesis. *Global Review of Islamic Economics and Business*, *8*(2), 59–76.

Ramamoorti, S. (2008). The psychology and sociology of fraud: Integrating the behavioral sciences component into fraud and forensic accounting curricula. *Issues in Accounting Education*, *23*(4), 521–533.

Rezaee, Z., Crumbley, D. L., & Elmore, R. C. (2004). Forensic accounting education: A survey of academicians and practitioners. *Advances in Accounting Education Teaching and Curriculum Innovations*, *6*, 193–231. Doi: 10.1016/S1085-4622(04)06010-9.

Rezaee, Z. & Wang, J. (2019). Relevance of big data to forensic accounting practice and education. *Managerial Auditing Journal*, *34*(3), 268–288. Doi: 10.1108/MAJ-08-2017-1633.

Rezaee, Z., Wang, J., & Lam, B. (2018). Toward the integration of big data into forensic accounting education. *Journal of Forensic and Investigative Accounting*, *10*(1), 87–99.

Sulaiman, M. & Willett, R. J. (2001). Islam, economic rationalism and accounting. *American Journal of Islamic Social Sciences*, *18*(2), 61–93.

Tiwari, R. K. & Debnath, J. (2017). Forensic accounting: A blend of knowledge. *Journal of Financial Regulation and Compliance*, *25*(1), 73–85. Doi: 10.1108/JFRC-05-2016-0043.

Velayutham, S. (2014). "Conventional" accounting vs "Islamic" accounting: The debate revisited. *Journal of Islamic Accounting and Business Research*, *5*(2), 126–141. Doi: 10.1108/JIABR-05-2012-0026.

Vousinas, G. L. (2019). Advancing theory of fraud: The SCORE model. *Journal of Financial Crime*, *26*(1), 372–381. Doi: 10.1108/JFC-12-2017-0128.

Wahyuni, T. D., Sari, I., Haron, H., and Fernando, Y. (2021). The effects of good governance and fraud prevention on performance of the zakat institutions in Indonesia: A Sharī'ah forensic accounting perspective. *International Journal of Islamic and Middle Eastern Finance and Management*, *14*(4), 692–712. Doi: 10.1108/IMEFM-03-2019-0089.

Wolfe, D. T. & Hermanson, D. R. (2004). The fraud diamond: Considering the four elements of fraud. *CPA Journal*, *74*(12), 38–42.

Yang, C.-H. & Lee, K.-C. (2020). Developing a strategy map for forensic accounting with fraud risk management: An integrated balanced scorecard-based decision model. *Evaluation and Program Planning*, *80*, 101780.

Part II

Islamic Accounting: Empirical Perspectives

https://doi.org/10.1142/9781800612426_0007

Chapter 7

The Consequences of AAOIFI Adoption: Countrywide Perspectives

Sherif El-Halaby, Khaled Omair Alotaibi, Ahmad Alqatan, and Alamir Nasser Salim Al-Alawi

Abstract

The Accounting and Auditing Organization for Islamic Financial Institutions (AAOIFI) began to issue standards long ago and by 2021 will mark its 31st anniversary. The existing literature on AAOIFI, which has had its share of supporters and critics, may be categorized into the following three parts: (1) literature evaluating compliance levels, (2) literature examining the AAOIFI determinants, and (3) literature assessing the economic consequences of AAOIFI. Thus far, the third strand in the first research phase has no practical study evaluating the impact of AAOIFI adoption at a national level. Therefore, this report adds to the literature by measuring the macroeconomic effects of AAOIFI on economic size and growth rate based on foreign direct investment (FDI), economic development (ED), corruption, and stock market development (SMD). Data for 150 Islamic banks (IBs) in 22 countries for 10 years (2010–2019) are collected and analyzed using an ordinary least squares (OLS) approach. Our results create indicate that IBs across countries that adopt AAOIFI are further getting an advantage by growing in FDI and GDP than non-adopters. Our results further support the role of AAOIFI adoption by countries rather than adoption by banks on reducing the level of corruption. After applying several robustness checks, our results remain the same, with slight variations. Our results create value for central banks, regulators, setters of an accounting standard as AAOIFI and IASB, investors, and all categories of Islamic Financial Institution (IFI) whether adopters or not by identifying the contributions of AAOIFI adoption. The contemporary international literature is deficient in practical evidence on the consequence of AAOIFI adoption at the macro, such as FDI and corruption. To the author's knowledge, that is one of the original research that provides confirmation of the significance and influences of AAOIFI adoption from a countrywide perspective.

Keywords: AAOIFI, Islamic Banks, FDI, Economic Development, Stock Market Development and Corruption.

7.1 Introduction

The Islamic banking system has come under the attention of academics, investors, and policymakers. As Islamic Financial Institutions (IFIs) grow worldwide, particular accounting standards for IFIs are still in the process of development and distribution by the AAOIFI, which is considered a tool to advance the reporting system quality. In the Islamic banking industry, there is no comparable level of AAOIFI adoption among IFIs and countries, even with the advancement growth and progression of the size of investments and the number of IFIs. Consequently, this phenomenon raises an important question about the purposes behind it, allowing an investigation of the benefits that motivate IFIs and countries to implement these standards.

In the field of accounting, all categories of IFIs, including Islamic banks, (IBs) in various contexts globally adopt a substantial regulatory modification by the standards of AAOIFI. Recently, 550 IFIs across 47 countries deliver Islamic products and comply with Sharia and have started supporting and shifting to adopt, either mandatorily or voluntarily, AAOIFI (AAOIFI, 2021). IFI experts have faith in the AAOIFI adoption to improve transparency, develop comparability, increase reporting quality, and thus advance these institutions. Authorizing AAOIFI makes bank reporting more informative, so the full picture is less doubtful about these anticipations and the principle. However, the effects of adopting AAOIFI are not noticeable and still not yet established. Limited applied investigations have been done about the consent of IBs with this standard. A lot of this literature is concerned with the factors and outcomes associated with the application of international accounting standards like the International Financial Reporting Standards (IFRS) or Generally Accepted Accounting Principles (GAAP).

Current literature associated with AAOIFI can be grouped into three categories. The first one studies the compliance level with AAOIFI (e.g., Brahim & Arab, 2020; Al-Sulaiti *et al.*, 2018). The second group examines the reasons for compliance with AAOIFI (e.g., Elgattani & Hussainey, 2021; Nugraheni & Khasanah, 2019; El-Halaby & Hussainey, 2016). The third group finds the outcomes of AAOIFI adoption (e.g., El-Halaby *et al.*, 2020). Though, the third group is still in the primary research phase. As far as we know, there is no practical research examining the impact of AAOIFI adoption based on country levels in a separate study. Jaeyon *et al.* (2019) recommend that the effects of adopting accounting standards could vary according to country-factor or corporate-factor dynamics. For filling this gap, this study measures the macroeconomic consequences of AAOIFI adoption. The macroeconomic effect involves four factors: openness to the exterior world, which is measured by FDI; economic development, as measured by GDP; corruption; and stock market development (SMD).

There are three accounting standard-setting approaches that explain and justify the mechanism of accounting standards adoption by corporations, which are as follows: (1) approach of co-ordination, (2) naturalistic approach, and (3) particularistic approach. One of the contributions of this study to the theoretical framework is to suggest a novel approach applicable for AAOIFI as well as supported by Sharia and the characteristics of IBs. This approach is called the Common Reference Approach (CRA).

This study is unique in examining the issues relating to accounting standards: (1) Most of the allied literature focuses on international accounting standards, such as IFRS or GAAP (Bin Li *et al.*, 2021), while this study adopts an unlikely set of accounting standards called AAOIFI. (2) Even though numerous studies measure the determinants of accounting standards' adoption (Houqe, 2018), this study measures the consequences of one. (3) The majority of the earlier studies apply their investigations to conventional banks (Eiler *et al.*, 2021), while we used data for IBs. (4) Dissimilar to the earlier studies that examine the consequences of accounting standards among microeconomic levels as earnings management (Noh *et al.*, 2017), we measure the macro factors. (5) The allied literature measures the influence of accounting standards' adoption on one country (Bansal & Garg, 2021), while this study uses data of 20 diverse countries. (6) Dissimilar to some investigations that use data among developed markets (Lenormand & Touchais, 2021), we focused on developing markets. (7) Numerous papers gave attention to non-financial institutions (Wijekoon *et al.*, 2021); conversely, our research sheds light on financial institutions (IBs). (8) While the earlier studies measure the macroeconomic factors of IBs in one country (Abdul Rashid & Jabeen, 2016), our study measures this association for IBs among several countries. (9) While Mohd Zain *et al.* (2021) and El-Halaby and Hussainey (2016) measure the motives for AAOIFI adoption and El-Halaby *et al.* (2020) measure the micro consequences of AAOIFI by focusing on earnings management, this study extends the investigation by measuring the consequences of AAOIFI adoption at the country or macro level.

Consequently, this study seeks to answer the following questions: What is the impact of AAOIFI adoption from the country-level perspective and to what extent this impact differs from the outcomes of IFRS adoption. Here, we apply our analysis based on dynamic panel data for 150 IBs from 22 economies over 10 years (2010–2019). Our analysis shows a positive link between AAOIFI adoption and FDI inflows as well as SMD. Our outcomes furthermore indicate a negative relationship with GDP, whereas corruption is found to have an insignificant effect. Consequently, our analysis indicates that greater implementation of AAOIFI significantly affects outcomes at the countrywide level. The rest of this chapter is arranged as follows. The background of AAOIFI adoption and theoretical framework is presented in Section 7.2, then Section 7.3 reviews the literature and develops the hypothesis. Section 7.4 ascertains the research design, and Section 7.5 presents the findings and robustness analysis. Section 7.6 gives concluding remarks.

7.2 Background of Development and AAOIFI Adoption

The unique products and accounting dealings that the Islamic financial system has are not represented in the international standards like IFRS, which is the reason behind the creation of Islamic standards. The features of IFIs are different from ordinary practices. AAOIFI accounting standards are imitating the distinguishing features of IFIs, and this has become a valued mechanism to meet the various requirements of IFIs. While in 1991, the AAOIFI issue was a primary regulatory development impacting hundreds of IFIs worldwide, its benefits and costs were originally unclear. Rarely, there are opinions about AAOIFI implementation effects that are related to theoretical statements due to lack of data.

IBs among markets can be grouped into the following three groups according to the adopted accounting standards: (1) In some countries, such as Kuwait, KSA, and Egypt, IBs' financial statements are set in the contract with international standards like IFRS. (2) IBs among other places are set in harmony with native standards but with numerous modifications to obey Sharia, as in Iran and Malaysia. (3) Countries such as Bahrain, Qatar, Jordan, Sudan, and Syria, AAOIFI accounting standards have been made a compulsory supervisory obligation, while in other countries, such as Palestine and Yemen, AAOIFI is voluntarily (AAOIFI, 2021). In building the accounting standards for IFIs, the methodology of AAOIFI includes developing standards based on ordinary Western ones, such as IFRS. AAOIFI choose this methodology since the competencies extended from the past work would allow the appropriate application of their standards without collaborating with Sharia.

Thanks to certain rules and standards to sustain good practices, stakeholders were forced to confirm that the system will not be unrestricted in the face of IFIs, growth. (Kabir Hassan *et al.*, 2019). In terms of the ordinary practices of transactions, particularly for the investment account holders, IFI is different, as they have quasi-ownership without the right to vote. So, in this business, founding standard-setting bodies that place importance on these and numerous other hidden concerns have become vital for fair treatment and accountability. Changes between the styles of business practices in Islamic and conventional financial systems require harmonizing standards to direct activities. For Abdel Karim (1995), AAOIFI is not issued as a substitute for IFRS; instead, it is offered in addition to conventional institutions and IFIs.

However, the unique IBs nature demands different accounting and reporting standards. Even the codes of Western accounting, according to Ather and Ullah (2009), which are consistency, conservatism, materiality, and time value of money, are considered to be different in Islamic accounting. Accounting and reporting standards that align with Sharia are energetic demands for IFIs. After studying socio-economic and religious features, Dima *et al.* (2014) declared the need for distinct accounting standards as issued by AAOIFI for Muslims as individuals and corporations. IFIs have solved the problems in adopting standards that are not modified according to Sharia.

The diverse nature of IFIs means that IFRS cannot entirely keep track of IFRS, yet they have been presented as an analogous mutual reporting global standard (Ullah *et al.*, 2018). As IFIs have a certain specific character, according to Ibrahim (2009), they cannot fully achieve ordinary standards, and they have therefore come into collision with IFRS. IFIs also do not work based on the capitalist philosophy that motivates the present IFRS and its objectives, and the settlements accepted through IFIs are different from ordinary ones. Therefore, IBs should reveal certain data that are not necessary from ordinary banks. AAOIFI adoption is therefore the most valid way for IBs. So, we care about the extent IBs need to substitute IFRS or GAAP by AAOIFI.

Two strategies were identified for building Islamic standards and their objectives following discussions by AAOIFI committees: the first was the need of setting aims and create standards that comply with Sharia principles and basics, after concerns about what has been defined by accounting scholars and Western thought. The second policy highlighted the need to set an Islamic standard appraisal related to the known strategies and then approve these in harmony with Islamic rules and improve others that are essential for banks. This method settles the agreement between IFRS and AAOIFI in some of their basics.

AAOIFI gave a relatively restricted indication that has definite significances for the institutions and users that adopt it. The extensive implementation of AAOIFI in several states over a short period is slightly astonishing. One possible explanation that is supported by comparable standards (IFRS) and recognized by Ramanna and Sletten (2014) is that application of IFRS is self-reinforcing. Also, countries reporting financial stalemates showed an increase in benefits relating to the low cost of cross-border transactions than any specified country that use IFRS. Ramanna and Sletten (2014) make clear the ascendancy of IFRS adoption. By verifying through the regulatory bodies, the vast number of IBs and countries that have applied AAOIFI have internationally restructured the map of financial reporting for IFIs. Three stated purposes of AAOIFI application are as follows: (1) compliance with Sharia in all transactions;

(2) improved reporting quality; and (3) improved comparability of financial statements for IFIs (AAOIFI, 2021).

The AAOIFI adoption is found to achieve "an extraordinary score of comparability as well as transparency of financial statements and consequently an operative functioning of the IFIs market" (AAOIFI, 2021). By relying on Western accounting standards, the second approach has been adopted in defining the objectives of accounting standards for IFIs; if these standards comply with Sharia, they are approved. IASB declares that the essential mission of its work is: "To develop a distinct cluster of extraordinary quality, comprehensible, enforceable, and internationally acknowledged financial reporting standards according to clearly articulated ideals. These standards must oblige high quality, transparent and comparable information to support investors and other participants in the global capital markets and other users of financial information to make economic decisions". According to Sharia ideologies, AAOIFI works on developing a collection of extraordinary quality, and rational financial reporting standards validate the accountability of corporations to Allah based on compliance with Sharia and then accountability to society and investors, as well as all stakeholders, for all IFIs. AAOIFI needs a high level of excellence and clear and comparable information to support regulators in international capital markets to make decisions that must obey Sharia.

Across the professional and academic literature, there are three different accounting standard-setting approaches (Tyrrall *et al.*, 2007). The first approach, according to Larson and Kenny (1996), is the approach of co-ordination in which, despite the chronological, geographic, or methodical changes, there are associations between contracts, procedures, and systems that are global in their application. Belkaoui (2002) states that two ways lead to IFRS application as follows: (1) "quick fix", where IFRS is applied as national standards; and (2) leisurely "transfer of technology", where worldwide accounting businesses, global initiatives, and academics engaged in emergent markets apply worldwide accounting approaches. Briston and Wallace (1992) gave a naturalistic second approach, where numerous transactions may be global, with numerous notable environment-based adjustments that must be resolute. Belkaoui (2002) develops the "situationist path", where the emerging markets adopt the accounting techniques through a variety of foundations that apply IFRS. The third approach to standard-setting based on Belkaoui (1988) is "particularistic", where accounting and, consequently, exclusive accounting practices are obligatory in every emerging country affected by definite environment integrally. In the "evolutionary" track developed by Belkaoui (2002), developing markets advance their specific standards regardless of the external impact. Tyrrall *et al.* (2007) selected an approach according to absolute benefits and drawbacks of IFRS versus nationwide definite accounting systems, which may apply standard-setting, nationwide, and corporate scores.

Additionally, an applicable approach according to Islamic standards and concepts, entitled the "Common Reference Approach" (CRA) was presented. While in specific stages, AAOIFI agrees with set international standards like IFRS, the mechanism of AAOIFI issuing Islamic accounting standards are based on a systematic process differs basically in its need to obey the Sharia. However, the Islamic legal reference is firm in its foundations, yet it respects the differences between societies, which appears as differences in many Sharia requirements according to the situation. Therefore, the Sharia boundaries are highlighted and cannot be changed and can be silent or emphatic about what should change and renew, depending on the different situations. Qur'an and Sunnah are the two main organizational sources of Sharia.

Regardless of the different geographical boundaries, legal rules, cultural dimensions, and economic systems, we expect agreement with harmony on the methodology, interpretation, and acceptance of these standards. The Messenger of Allah (may Allah bless him and grant him peace) said, "I have left two matters with you, as long as you hold to them, you will not go the wrong way, they are the Book of Allah (Qur'an) and the Sunnah of His Prophet" (Book 46, Hadith 3). Thus, these standards are accepted and have credibility from both adopters and non-adopters, as Sharia committees now review and approve the process of AAOIFI issuing standards. The content of each standard, which matches with the mechanism of international standards, includes recognition, measurement, and disclosure sections and also includes Sharia jurisprudence and legal foundations upon which it is based. Therefore, this approach assures being supportive and accepting of the content, and it paves the way for quick adoption by all IFIs whose activities require harmony with Sharia.

The adopted mechanism for the formulation of the accounting standards by AAOIFI is unique compared with others, such as IFRS, through the union of the foundations and the simple process of accepting and making them applicable to any setting. The concept of harmonization and universality of application is the main feature of this mechanism without respect to geographical, historical, or systematic variances. Also, it provides a naturalistic approach that is based on the flexibility of these standards to respect all environment-based differences in the formulation process, and it considers the major differences between markets and situation. However, the evolutionary approach is rejected by Islamic values and rules that aim to be stable and standardized for all settings and reject the idea of disintegration and dispersion unless the evolutionary approach updated issues and accpeted any novelties in business practices. This is what AAOIFI declared with continuous issuance of Islamic standards, which considers all developments in the field of Islamic industry and keeps up with all financial and economic developments. Therefore, AAOIFI is more comprehensive than IFRS as it is based on formulation, acceptance, and harmonization that support its orientation toward universality, which calls for more investigation of the outcomes of its adoption at the macro level.

7.3 Literatures and Hypotheses Development

For Ramanna and Sletten (2009), the research of accounting standards application and approval at the countrywide level may progress the academic research sympathetic of the inspirations of accounting standards. The corporate-level literature on nations' decisions to make certain accounting standards obligatory is limited and incentive-related to the application of IFRS and GAAP, while there is a shortage of literature focusing on AAOIFI. There is a conspicuous growth in macroeconomic literature connected with the IFRS and GAAP adoption, as well as the corporate and institutional implications unique to each country using Islamic standards are being distorted. According to Levitt (1998), IFRS adoption can reduce information irregularity across capital markets, promote transparency, encourage international investment, support cross-border comparability, and lower capital costs for implementer countries. This study combines past research on traditional accounting standards, such as IFRS and GAAP, to broaden the argument by examining the repercussions of AAOIFI to see how much of an impact it has on the banks of AAOIFI adopters.

AAOIFI, like IFRS, has the same core aim (to produce a set of high-quality, rational financial reporting standards) and shares the same goals (progress the comparability of financial statements). Furthermore, AAOIFI has a clear process for developing its standards, which includes reviewing existing rules, accepting those that are Sharia compliant, and developing others. The acceptability and harmony between IFRS and AAOIFI are approved by this established mechanism, mission, and objectives. As a result of this harmonization, we expect the same outcomes from the adoption of AAOIFI as from the adoption of IFRS. However, we cannot overlook the fundamental differences between the two sets of standards, as well as the financial systems, in accounting procedures and disclosure, as well as accountabilities, functions, and several other fundamentals that are not reflected in IFRS. These distinctions may allow us to forecast the discrepancies resulting from AAOIFI implementation in comparison to IFRS. As a result, we explore how AAOIFI's repercussions differ from those of IFRS in terms of measured data. The empirical evidence on the relationship between macroeconomic repercussions and accounting standard adoption is available and exists in the IFRS literature. As a result, our contribution was supported by an investigation into the AAOIFI, which is reflected in the global importance and application of this standard as well as the global growth of Islamic banking. This phenomenal increase for AAOIFI and investing in Islamic assets is not reflected in the study, demonstrating the chapter's added value by filling this gap.

AAOIFI has been recognized and permitted to produce various types of Sharia-compliant standards to promote comparable, transparent, and dependable accounting information for users. The laws, commandments, and manner of life that Allah has given to humanity are known as Sharia. Sharia financing and compliance issues impede IFIs' ability to promote their products and services both locally and abroad. As a result, the necessity for Sharia compliance emphasizes the importance of bridging the gap between theory and practice. AAOIFI has produced 63 Sharia norms to address these concerns (AAOIFI, 2021). According to Napier (2009), the advancement of AAOIFI for IFIs satisfies Muslims' desire to apply Islamic concepts in all aspects of their lives, reflecting their obligation to Allah (God). The issue of a truthful representation of financial transactions is crucial for IFIs to win civic confidence and trust. High-quality financial statements are an important tool for IBs to stay competitive in a market where the community trusts that the services they provide are Sharia compliant. The incorporation of Islamic themes into the AAOIFI conceptual framework results in enhanced reporting that aids decision-making (Elgattani & Hussainey, 2021).

AAOIFI's aims and scope are updated on a regular basis to allow new financial instruments to join markets around the world. This symbolizes the importance of Muslim and Arabic regions in the international economy, and it provides its clientele with a diverse choice of items that keep up with new technologies. According to Haniffa and Hudaib (2002), the Islamic accounting system and AAOIFI as standards are a foundation that attempts to offer socio-economic justice through Sharia's methodologies, unbiased measures, reporting, and regulations. According to Sarea (2013), AAOIFI fosters Muslim society's faith in investments and investors. IFIs will suffer in the long run if they do not standardize. Standardization is necessary to avoid disintegration and, eventually, to create a new asset class capable of competing with traditional finance. The major benefits of standardizing, according to Smolo and Habibovic (2010), include increased transparency, uniformity, improved stakeholder confidence, and time and cost savings. The AAOIFI is successful in standardizing IFI rules through harmonization and the establishment of various categories of standards. The AAOIFI standards process strengthens the global position of IFIs and allows for further international expansion and investment.

In comparison to the literature on IFRS, there are only a few articles that look at the effects of AAOIFI. The majority of these researches concentrate on the micro level rather than the macro level. Sarea (2016) investigates the impact of AAOIFI on earnings quality; El-Halaby *et al.* (2020) investigate the impact of AAOIFI on earnings management; Nor Farizal *et al.* (2015) investigate the impact of AAOIFI on reporting; Al-Baluchi (2006) investigates the impact of AAOIFI on disclosure; and Elgattani (2018) investigates the impact of AAOIFI on bank performance. Thus, none of the prior research has looked at the influence of AAOIFI adoption on macroeconomic indicators, such as FDI and stock market growth. The fundamental contribution of our work is to fill these gaps in the literature.

7.3.1 *Accounting standards and foreign direct investment*

Proponents of standards like AAOIFI argue that higher-quality financial reporting and comparability lead to more capital flow and better cross-border financial market integration. Inflows of FDI are widely regarded as a key engine of economic development, particularly in emerging economies. Accounting standards' impact on cross-border capital flows and international investors might make validation easier. This is due to several factors. First, IFRS adoption, according to Amiram (2012), replaces the previous country-detailed reporting rules with a single set of standards that can help overseas investors analyze foreign firms and markets. Second, AAOIFI might increase the transparency of foreign investors and increase their trust in these markets. Chen *et al.* (2014) study the linkage between FDI growth and IFRS adoption across 20 OECD countries. Rakesh and Shilpa (2013) analyze the same association across India. Both research findings are congruent with those of Gordon *et al.* (2012), who claim that nations' FDI inflows can grow if financial statements are prepared under IFRS and are of greater quality than those prepared according to national standards.

To quantify the link between IFRS and FDI growth, Mameche and Masood (2021) specify that the decision of IFRS implementation in the GCC region has a positive influence of 3% on FDI in the short run and leads to a reduction of 10.4% in FDI in the long run. Lasmin (2011) uses the neo-institutional theory. He stated that an increase in FDI increases the likelihood of IFRS adoption in a country. Judge *et al.* (2010) establish the hypothesized link between mimetic pressures caused by FDI growth and the adoption of the IFRS. According to Gordon *et al.* (2012), the adoption of the IFRS has resulted in increased FDI flows, particularly in developing nations. Rakesh and Shilpa (2013) examine Indian firms and conclude that the implementation of the IFRS has been a positive step for India, resulting in increased FDI inflows. In contrast, the adoption of global standards, such as the IFRS, may reduce information barriers across capital markets. In comparison to domestic investors, foreign investors receive smaller informational rewards. As a result, foreign investors' operating costs are higher, resulting in a decrease in FDI inflows. AAOIFI has been identified as a key driver in placing some countries and banks as FDI hubs. We believe that accounting standards are a component of a location's institutional infrastructure and that implementing AAOIFI with government backing will boost FDI by lowering the cost of information processing for foreign investors. However, countries that have hosted IBs and the role of AAOIFI adoption over FDI have received little attention. As a result, we believe that AAOIFI adoption will improve the reliability of financial information, attracting foreign investors and FDI.

H1: Adoption of the AAOIFI increases FDI inflow to countries.

7.3.2 *Accounting standards and corruption*

Tanzi (1998) defines corruption as "an intentional nonconformity with arm's length association aimed at originating some benefit from this behavior for oneself or an associated individual". According to Oshodin and Bakare (2019), corruption can have regulatory effects at several levels and can be used to influence policymakers by exposing them to enticing ideas. As a result, political pressure aimed at combating corruption may have an impact on the adoption of accounting standards. The presence of non-transparent economic methods as well as non-application of laws and ineffective enforcement of legal authorization contribute to the level of corruption (Kythreotis, 2015). While the majority of the literature examines the link between corruption and conformity with international accounting standards, such as IFRS or GAAP, no research has looked at the impact of AAOIFI adoption. Mazzi *et al.* (2018), for example, discover that the level of corruption is highly related to the level of IFRS compliance.

According to Houqe and Reza (2016), the degree of IFRS application is negatively related to perceived corruption. They also discovered that emerging countries that benefit from IFRS have lower levels of corruption. In this chapter, we look at how adopting AAOIFI can help IBs and countries prevent corruption by promoting IBs' ethical image. AAOIFI is built on Islamic ideals, which forbid all forms of immoral behavior such as corruption. The Messenger of Allah (may Allah bless him and grant him peace) said, "I was sent to perfect good character" (Book 47, Hadith 8). In the Holy Qur'an, God Almighty mentions corruption and derivatives of the word in roughly 50 verses. He talked about his lack of corruption, as well as his dissatisfaction with it, saying, "And Allah does not like corrupters" (Qur'an, 5, 64) and "Allah does not like corruption" (Qur'an, 2, 205). As a result, we anticipate that implementing ethical standards, such as, AAOIFI will reduce corruption in nations that have embraced these requirements.

H2: AAOIFI adoption by IBs and countries leads to reduced level of national corruption.

7.3.3 *Accounting standards and economic growth*

According to Coffee (2002), the impact of accounting standards on financial markets is supported by bonding theory, which states that more disclosure caused by the adoption of accounting standards signals to investors an improvement in financial statement quality. As a result, improved financial statements increase the level of transparency that attracts new investors and promotes efficient capital markets (Jermakowicz & Tomaszewski, 2006). As a result, the adoption of accounting standards, such as AAOIFI, should benefit the EG. The fundamental benefit of accounting standards acceptance is that it provides decision-makers with comparable and reliable financial accounts. For example, the adoption of IFRS simplifies the development of global trade, which stimulates EG in the countries where it is used. Global agencies, according to Wyatt and Yospe (1993), highlight the need for stable financial markets to boost EG. Larson and Kenny (1996) support the theory of contingency that identifies the significance and influence of ecological features of accounting standards on EG. According to Schweikart (1985), the theory of contingency admits that such environmental factors are exceptional and interact with the growth and demand of a country's accounting system. The naturalistic technique based on this theory, according to Perera and Baydoun (2007), allows rising countries to deploy an accounting system like AAOIFI, although it requires adjustments to the accounting system to reflect environmental constraints. As a result, AAOIFI deployment should be associated with increased EG.

The literature that emphasizes the link between EG and accounting regulations, such as IFRS, is debatable. Zeghal and Mhedhbi (2006), for example, confirm that IFRS adoption is more appropriate in developing countries (DCs) with a high level of EG. According to Dogan (2015), the implementation of the IFRS has a positive impact on EG in emerging environments. Boukhatem and Ben Moussa (2018) find strong evidence that the development of the financial system motivates EG across selected MENA regions in respect to the Islamic banking business. Furthermore, they argue that while Islamic finance development may improve EG, institutional frameworks that are immature limit its influence. According to Furqani and Mulyani (2009), Islamic financing is favorably connected with EG in Malaysia over time. Finally, the relationship between AD economic progress and the establishment of Islamic banking is bidirectional (Abduh & Omar, 2012). We foresee a beneficial impact on EG in nations that have adopted AAOIFI because it gives all stakeholders an indicator of Sharia compliance, which increases trust and motivates them to invest, resulting in a greater level of EG.

H3: There is a positive association between AAOIFI adoption and the growth of EG.

7.3.4 *Accounting standards and stock market development*

Wilber and Jameson (1979) used the modernization hypothesis to study the link between approved accounting standards and SMD. AAOIFI's accounting standard-setting strategy, like IFRS's, is founded on the following two assumptions: (1) Harmonization is required, implying that financial transactions and processes are used globally in accounting (Tyrrall *et al.*, 2007). (2) Accounting, according to Assenso-Okofo *et al.* (2011), must be internationalized to support the global community. Larson and Kenny (1995) specify that "matching with the projected assistance of coordination is the forecast that SMD and EG should together be better when IFRS are implemented without alteration in emerging countries" (p. 136).

Financial reporting is seen as a vital component of the development of emerging stock markets. According to Al-Akra *et al.* (2009), the type of accounting system has a crucial impact on the stock market's advancement. According to Tyrrall *et al.* (2007), precise accounting data and reliable reporting are essential in sustaining stock market growth. Lee (1987) advocates that "Respectable communication creates it auspicious for the investment of improved quality to facility a greater price and therefore persuades boards to seek funding in a schematized capital market". Accounting's importance as a critical component of SMD is emphasized in the literature. Peng and Smith (2010), for example, suggest that IFRS has contributed to the stock market's expansion. Similarly, Assenso-Okofo *et al.* (2011) discovered that IFRS adoption is associated with receiving various forms of support and awards from multinational firms as well as improved financial market development. Mhedhbi and Zeghal (2016) argue that IFRS adoption is favorably related to the performance of developing capital markets in 31 developing nations. Ben Othman and Kossentini (2015) found that IFRS adoption had a beneficial influence on SMD in 50 emerging economies. Klibi and Kossentini (2014) found that IFRS strongly favors SMD across Middle Eastern and North African (MENA) nations. Based on the idea of modernization, it is possible to forecast that when AAOIFI acceptance rises, the SMD value will rise as well.

H4: There is a positive link between AAOIFI adoption and SMD.

7.4 Research Design

7.4.1 *Sample*

We consider a sample of countries that host IBs from emerging and Muslim countries. We use AAOIFI's official website, which includes profiles of adopted nations and IBs based on the most recent AAOIFI footprint report 2020 (https://aaoifi.com/aaoifi-footprint-report/?lang=en). Bangladesh, Brunei, Iran, Jordan, Kuwait, Oman, Pakistan, Palestine, KSA, Sudan, Qatar, Syria, Egypt, Gambia, Malaysia, Mauritania, Yemen, Nigeria, Tunisia, UAE, and Bahrain are among the 22 nations in the sample, based on data availability. However, due to a lack of data, we have excluded eight countries that host IBs. All of the countries chosen are Islamic or have a Muslim majority, such as Nigeria. At least one IB should have been stationed in each selected country for at least five years of observation. Banks with unpublished annual reports or reports written in a language other than Arabic or English are excluded. These constraints

Table 7.1. Sample selection procedures.

Selection criterion	Total	Sample after filtration	(%)
Total number of countries available in AAOIFI footprint report 2020	30	22	73
Total number of Islamic banks' annual reports and data available	200	150	75
IBs that adopted AAOIFI		66/150	44
IBs that adopted non-AAOIFI		84/150	56

boost the sample's homogeneity. After applying the preceding criteria to a sample of 30 nations and 200 IBs, we arrived at a final sample of 150 IBs from 22 countries across two continents for a period of 10 years (2010–2019), yielding 1450 observations for corporations and 176 observations for countries. We restricted our data until 2019 without adding 2020 and 2021 to neutralize the impact of the COVID-19 pandemic. The future research should consider the impact of this pandemic on the consequences of AAOIFI at the macro level. Table 7.1 presents the sample selection procedures.

Malaysia (19%), Sudan (16.75%), Bahrain (14.50%), and Iran (13.90%) are the countries with the most designated banks in our sample (14.20%). The data in our research are made up of numerous datasets that show the annual country and corporate-feature observations for the last 10 years. To get the countries' data, such as GDP and SMD, we use the World Bank database. We rely on publicly available annual reports for data on corporate governance (CG) and corporate variables. For data on government efficacy, we utilize the Worldwide Governance Indicators project, and for data on business elements, such as assets, we use the Bankscope database. Finally, we gather cultural data from the Green Hofstede website.

7.4.2 *The measurement of variables*

7.4.2.1 *Dependent and independent variables*

Adoption of accounting standards, such as IFRS or AAOIFI, has frequently been operationalized in prior studies by a binary variable that takes 1 if a bank or country adopts the tested standard and

0 otherwise (e.g., Kim & Ryu, 2018; Bonito & Claudio, 2018). As a result, we use the same method to assess AAOIFI adoption as a dichotomous variable. We calculate market capitalization as a percentage of GDP, which corresponds to the literature on SMD (Ben Othman & Kossentini, 2015). Several proxies for economic progress (ED) are used in the literature. The GDP growth rate is used as a surrogate for ED in this case. The market value of manufactured goods and services across the country for a specific period is referred to as GDP. Boukhatem and Ben Moussa (2018) support this measure. FDI, or direct investment equity flows into the economy, is used to gauge the country's openness to the outside world. This metric is used by Zehri and Chouaibi (2013). The corruption perception index, which measures the degree to which civic power is used for private benefit, both large scale and petty, is used to measure corruption. According to Mazzi *et al.* (2018), the score of corruption is calculated using the Worldwide Governance Indicators.

7.4.2.2 *Control variables*

We incorporate a collection of criteria that have been considered based on prior studies about corporate factors, culture, and CG of countries to control the impacts of AAOIFI. Differences in culture, political background, and economic context, according to Clements *et al.* (2010), may affect the adoption and subsequent effective use of accounting standards. According to Zehri and Chouaibi (2013), culture is a key factor in determining which accounting systems are appropriate for each country. Financial reporting, according to Akman (2011), is influenced by culture. Countries with similar social values are more likely to use the same accounting standards. Resistance to implementing accounting standards, such as IFRS, is linked to cultural variables, according to Ding *et al.* (2005). To consider cultural differences statistically, we use the Hofstede model. Individualism, power distance, masculinity, uncertainty avoidance, and long-term orientation are the five traits identified by Hofstede *et al.* (2010).

We keep track of the auditor's size and reputation, both of which are related to business considerations. The log of total assets is used to determine the size of a company. Recognizing the differences in corporate-level reporting enticements connected with the adoption of IAS requires understanding firm size (Daske *et al.*, 2013). One of the characteristics that demonstrate the company's commitment to accounting standards is its size. The auditor has a big role to play in reporting policies and encouraging adoption. Audits are one type of regulating activity that boosts a company's value and reduces difficulties with agency conflict. The big audit firms have strong incentives to show the market that they are of higher quality and to encourage their clients to fully comply with legislation. According to Glaum *et al.* (2013), there is a link between adopting accounting standards and being audited by the Big 4. We regulate domestic credit, which is given by the financial segment and consists exclusively of credit for various subdivisions on a gross basis, because our sample concentrates on the banking business. We also consider the influence of the impact of country CG. Political stability and government effectiveness are priorities for us. These are goals set forward by the project, Worldwide Governance Indicators. The definitions and sources of the variables are included in Table 7.2.

7.4.3 *Research models*

We estimate four models to test our hypothesis. The influence of AAOIFI adoption on FDI, GDP, corruption, and SMD is measured using multiple regression analysis. Each model is used in two ways: First, it is applied based on AAOIFI adoption by the bank, and then, it is applied based on AAOIFI adoption by country. Because the key independent variable — AAOIFI adoption — is measured as a dummy variable, we utilize the following logit models. Because AAOIFI literature is scarce, our models use the same methodology as several other publications that focus on IFRS (e.g., Kaya & Koch, 2015; Zehri & Chouaibi, 2013; Clements *et al.*, 2010).

7.5 Empirical Results and Analysis

7.5.1 *Summary statistics and correlation tests*

Table 7.3 shows the descriptive statistics. These statistics provide useful information on the distribution of variables. The sample of banks contains 44% AAOIFI adopters and 56% non-AAOIFI adopters. AAOIFI has been implemented as an obligatory norm for

Table 7.2. Variables, definitions and sources.

Variables	Symbol	Definitions	Source
Dependent variables			
Economy size and growth rate	GDP	Gross domestic product rehabilitated for global dollars using purchasing power equivalence rates	World Bank database, https://data.worldbank.org/
Stock market development	SMD	Proxy of market capitalization as a proportion of GDP	
International investments	FDI	Foreign direct investments flows in reporting economy which is the amount of equity capital, reinvestment of incomes, and other capital	
Corruption	CORR	Views of level to which public power is exercised for isolated gain, grand forms of corruption, and capture of state through private interests	Worldwide Governance Indicators project, https://info.worldbank.org/governance/wgi/
Independent variables			
Accounting standards	AAOIFI	Dichotomous variable: 1 if adopted standard by bank is AAOIFI and 0 otherwise Dichotomous variable: 1 if adopted standard by country is AAOIFI and 0 otherwise	Annual reports
Control variables for corporate level			
Auditing quality	AUDIT	Dichotomous variable:1 if the auditor is one of the Big 4 and 0 otherwise	Annual reports
Total assets	SIZE	The natural log of total assets	Bank scope database
Control variables for country level			
Government effectiveness	GE	Insights of public services' quality, civil service and level of its freedom from political forces, and reliability of government's obligation to such policies	Worldwide Governance Indicators project, https://info.worldbank.org/governance/wgi/

Domestic credit		DC	Domestic credit delivered through financial segment which comprises whole credit to countless segments on a gross basis	World Bank database, https://data.worldbank.org/
Culture	Power distance	PD	The level to which the less influential members of a society accept as well as anticipate that power is circulated unevenly	Hofstede Model Hofstede (1980, 2001, 2010) https://hi.hofstede-insights.com/national-culture
	Individualism	INDIV	The preference for a loosely knit societal structure in which persons are expected to pay attention of only themselves and their instant relatives	
	Uncertainty avoidance	UA	The level to which the associates feel confused by vagueness and uncertainty	
	Masculinity	MAS	The preference in culture for achievement, bravery, and solid rewards for success	
	Long term orientation	LTO	The great scores take a more practical method: they inspire frugality and efforts in contemporary education as a technique to formulate for the future	
CG	BOD size	BOD.S	Number of BOD members	Annual reports
	BOD independence	BOD.IND	Percentage of number of independent directors over the total number of BOD	
	SSB size	SSB	Number of members in Sharia Supervisory Board	

Table 7.3. Descriptive statistics.

Variable	Minimum	Maximum	Mean	Std. deviation	Skewness	Kurtosis
AAOIFI	0.00	1.00	0.423	0.5774	0.754	−1.809
SMD	0.00	85.19	1.507	1.4216	1.734	5.217
GDP	2.842	3.452	8.25	6.873	1.533	0.636
FDI	0.975	30.296	3.7626	3.6715	2.780	7.614
MC	0.963	172.489	7.6858	5.8129	0.418	−0.934
CORR	−2.760	1.830	−0.4697	0.71277	0.259	−0.960
SIZE	0.783	6.748	4.3843	0.72798	−0.148	−0.257
AUDIT	0	1	0.635	0.5876	−0.439	−1.658
GE	−2.720	2.940	−0.085	0.81764	−0.420	−1.425
DC	−12.151	210.85	76.3347	46.1573	0.489	−0.723
PD	37	114	82.17	15.56	−0.864	0.247
INDIV	20	92	38.26	12.584	2.938	9.834
MASC	45	70	56.687	6.988	0.326	−0.213
UA	38	87	69.577	16.978	−0.734	−0.645
LTO	35	60	24.98	18.749	0.298	−1.844
BOD.S	5	21	9.54	3.451	0.932	1.525
BOD.INDE	0.310	0.95	0.7688	0.562	−1.342	0.977
SSB	1	12	4.854	2.572	1.866	7.781
ADOPT	0.00	1.00	0.498	0.582	0.587	−1.783

Notes: Here, AAOIFI is a dummy variable that equals 1 if the adopted standard by the bank is AAOIFI and otherwise 0. GDP is gross domestic product converted to international dollars using purchasing power parity rates to measure economic growth. FDI is foreign direct investments which reflect the openness to the exterior world and measured as the sum of equity capital and reinvestment of earnings. CORR is control of corruption, which is the perception of the extent to which public power is exercised for private gain, including petty and grand forms of corruption. SMD is stock market development, which is proxy of market capitalization as a percentage of GDP. AUDIT is audit quality, which is a dichotomous variable that equals 1 if auditor is one of the Big 4, and 0 otherwise. SIZE is the natural log of total assets. BOD.INDE is board independence which is the percentage of the number of independent directors over the total number of board members. BOD.S is board size that refers to the number of directors' members in the board. SSB is the value of Sharia Supervisory Board size. Culture is measured depend on Hofstede's model based on five dimensions: PD is power distance, MASC is masculinity, INDIV is individualism, UA is uncertainty avoidance, and LTO is long-term orientation. DC is the domestic credit provided by the financial sector. GE is government effectiveness as a perception of quality of public services, civil service, and degree of its independence from political pressures and credibility of government's commitment to such policies. ADOPT is a country adoption which is dummy variable that equals 1 if the adopted standard by country is AAOIFI and otherwise 0.

all IBs in 43% of the selected nations. A mean FDI of 3.76 is included in the macroeconomic components' mean value. It's worth noting that our sample has an average GDP of USD 8.25 and an average SMD of USD 1.507. Notably, the selected developing countries in our sample had a corruption index of −0.469, indicating a high amount of corruption in our sample. One of the top four auditors oversees is auditing 63% of our banks.

The correlation matrix is shown in Table 7.4. Variance inflation factors (VIFs) were calculated on variables with a correlation of less than 0.5, with the maximum VIF factor being 3.5, well below the crucial threshold of 10, indicating that multicollinearity is unlikely to be a significant issue in our regressions (Groebner *et al.*, 2008). The interplay between AAOIFI and macro variables is of particular interest to us. Several country-level factors are highly associated, which is to be expected given that our sample was limited to 22 nations. We find that AAOIFI adoption is strongly inversely connected to GDP, corruption and stock market development. Our univariate tests show that adoption of AAOIFI correlates positively with the four characteristics of Hofstede's culture but negatively with size, DC, PS, and GE when compared to the control variables.

7.5.2 *Regression results*

The regression findings are presented and interpreted in this section. We estimate four models, starting with Equations 1–4 in Table 7.5 for macrocosmic factors affecting AAOIFI adoption. The influence of AAOIFI adoption on FDI is examined in models 1-1 and 1-2 in Tables 7.5(a) and (b). The FDI coefficient estimate provides statistical evidence of a positive connection with AAOIFI adoption at the 1% significance level. As a result, H1 is recommended. This finding supports the neo-institutional theory. This finding is consistent with that of Mameche and Masood (2021) who determine the extent to which adoption accounting standards has a positive impact on FDI. Okoye *et al.* (2014) also found that adopting IFRS improves financial statements, which assure a corporate entity's information quality, and that this is worth pursuing in our chosen economies. Our findings corroborate the premise that non-local investors prefer a market with high-quality information and support Islamic Sharia compliance because it allows them to evaluate investment possibilities at a lower cost. Our findings support the hypothesis that AAOIFI can lead to

Table 7.4. Pearson correlation matrix.

Variable	AAOIFI	FDI	GDP	CORR	CONS	SIZE	AUD	SMD	DC	GE	PD	INDI	MAS	UA	LTO
AAOIFI	1														
FDI	0.648	1													
GDP	−0.724***	−.27**	1												
CORR	−0.171**	.270**	.817**	1											
CONS	0.618***	−.24***	−.091	−.313**	1										
SIZE	−0.854*	−.28***	.534**	.493**	−.246***	1									
AUD	0.053	.356**	.151	.835**	−.290**	.195**	1								
SMD	−0.292*	.077	.252**	.794**	−.626**	.643**	.586**	1							
DC	−0.294**	.347**	.376**	.322**	−.657**	.378**	.572**	.672**	1						
GE	−0.465***	.272**	.594**	.835**	−.624**	.585**	.726**	.561**	.823**	1					
PD	0.149***	.282**	−.316**	.393**	−.417**	.185*	.528**	.389**	.345**	.713**	1				
INDI	0.463**	−.45**	.428**	.117	−.282	−.29**	−.42**	−.84**	−.113	−.05**	−.24**	1			
MAS	0.549***	−.062	−.312**	.338**	−.169*	−.32**	.551**	.092	−.072	.152**	.291**	.350**	1		
UA	0.451**	−.44**	−.073	−.065	.792**	−.054	.147	−.28**	−.84**	−.93**	−.24**	−.092	.443**	1	
LTO	−0.562***	.158**	.431	.507**	−.632**	.286**	.275**	.425**	.455**	.834**	.241**	−.02**	.280**	−.94***	1

Note: *,** and ***denote significance at the 10%, 5%, and 1% levels, respectively.

Table 7.5. (a) Regression analysis: Macroeconomic consequences of AAOIFI' adoption by bank and (b) Regression analysis: macroeconomic consequences of AAOIFI's adoption by country.

	Model (1): FDI			Model (2): GDP			Model (3): Corruption			Model (4): SMD		
Model	**Beta**	**T**	**Sig.**	**Beta**	**T**	**Sig.**	**Beta**	**T**	**Sig.**	**Beta**	**T**	**Sig.**
(Constant)		7.805	0.000		−2.341	0.078		−7.980	0.000		2.640	0.360
AAOIFI	0.485	7.388	0.000***	0.531	8.461	0.000***	−0.031	−0.393	0.831	0.166	7.910	0.000***
AUDIT	0.367	6.228	0.000***	−0.293	−5.971	0.000***	0.198	8.538	0.000***	−0.093	−2.806	0.088*
SIZE	−0.327	−7.453	0.000***	0.174	4.709	0.004**	−0.821	−5.959	0.000***	0.027	1.054	0.007**
INDIV	−0.422	−5.227	0.000***	0.241	7.798	0.000***	−0.002	−4.124	0.000***	−0.105	−9.084	0.000***
PD	−0.334	−4.109	0.044*	−0.151	−2.148	0.062*	−0.153	−1.180	0.000***	0.245	2.454	0.237
UA	−0.559	−7.526	0.000***	0.344	5.923	0.000***	0.181	9.030	0.000***	−0.357	−1.907	0.162
MAS	−0.369	−3.801	0.009**	0.649	2.960	0.000***	0.341	9.040	0.000***	0.134	0.545	0.341
LTO	−0.108	−0.269	0.345	−0.521	−8.532	0.000***	−0.101	−7.097	0.000***	−0.340	−2.247	0.299
DC	−0.585	−5.604	0.000***	0.314	1.923	0.022*	0.092	4.221	0.009**	0.256	8.026	0.000***
GE	0.666	5.693	0.000***	0.198	7.287	0.000***	0.777	3.095	0.000***	0.107	7.318	0.000***
Adjusted R Square		0.584			0.789			0.680			0.575	
F		37.721			145.87			210.94			89.781	
Sig.		0.000			0.000			0.000			0.000	
(b) Regression analysis: macroeconomic consequences of AAOIFI's adoption by country.												
(Constant)		4.448	0.000		−0.872	0.000		6.963	0.000		2.377	0.004
AAOIFI	0.657	1.482	0.031*	0.642	4.842	0.000***	−0.354	−3.309	0.000***	0.092	0.382	0.082*
DC	−0.051	−0.382	0.679	0.604	5.392	0.000***	0.502	2.783	0.000***	0.266	1.490	0.033*
GE	1.489	0.372	0.822	−1.944	−1.364	0.971	1.158	0.358	0.198	1.416	0.491	0.299
INDIV	−0.165	−1.450	0.279	0.251	1.432	0.007**	0.185	1.041	0.096*	−0.175	−0.549	0.005**
PD	−0.351	−2.755	0.061*	−0.066	−0.496	0.644	0.372	2.518	0.057*	0.339	1.735	0.174
UA	−0.457	−3.264	0.000***	0.355	3.648	0.000***	0.130	1.260	0.376	0.209	1.108	0.000***
MAS	−0.263	−2.312	0.003**	−0.081	−0.477	0.551	0.684	4.743	0.000***	0.548	0.824	0.651
LTO	0.199	1.137	0.214	−0.120	−3.793	0.033*	−0.274	−1.457	0.092*	0.138	0.420	0.324
Adjusted R Square		0.323			0.62			0.698			0.484	
F		8.903			28.681			22.753			8.931	
Sig.		0.000			0.000			0.000			0.000	

Note: *,** and ***denote significance at the 10%, 5%, and 1% levels, respectively.

increased transparency as a result of its perceived superiority over other Islamic norms. The adoption of harmonized accounting rules for IBs may help boost the visibility of investments in remote locations, bringing stocks to the attention of investors. As a result, AAOIFI criteria that are Sharia compliant are the best option for cumulative FDI among Muslim cultures and economies.

At the 1% significance level, the adopted AAOIFI reveals a considerably negative coefficient as related to the developing acceptable GDP ratio for the national adopters, as measured by models 2-1 and 2-2 by GDP, as shown in Tables 7.5(a) and (b). As a result, this finding supports H3, which argues that the more AAOIFI a country or bank adopts, the more likely it is to boost its GDP. This finding backs up contingency theory, which recognizes the impact of accounting norms and EG. This finding is consistent with prior research that has found a link between GDP and accounting standards. According to Daske *et al.* (2008), the strength with which IFRS is applied has a significant impact on economic growth. According to Epstein (2009), IFRS adoption will make cross-border trading easier. According to Zaidi and Huerta (2014), implementing IFRS enhances economic growth rates. Countries that implement the IFRS reap several economic benefits, which are amplified by better enforcement. This finding backs up the idea that by adopting Islamic standards like AAOIFI, we may improve transparency and disclosure, which in turn will improve the quality of financial statements, attracting more investors. This encourages the efficient operation of capital markets.

The level of corruption in the selected nations is negatively but insignificantly related to AAOIFI adoption by the bank non-models 3-1 and 3-2, as shown in Tables 7.5(a) and (b), but the association is significantly unfavorable toward AAOIFI adoption by country. This finding contradicts earlier research that suggests a strong link for this relationship. Agyei-Mensah (2017), for example, finds a substantial link. However, our findings back the findings of Mazzi *et al.* (2018) and Houqe and Reza (2016) who indicated that accounting standards play a significant effect in eliminating corruption, especially in developing nations. As a result, we accept H2 in part. The majority of our sample comes from the MENA region. Even though corruption is common in this region, based on empirical evidence, experts agree that it is deep-rooted and ubiquitous, especially in the state's political architecture and institutional, private, or public infrastructure. As a result, the majority of governments and corporations in this area score low on transparency and accountability indicators. The role, influence, power, and efficacy of accounting standards, such as AAOIFI or even IFRS, in eliminating corruption will be limited due to the high level of corruption. The application and implementation of accounting standards, such as AAOIFI, can be influenced by political pressure brought on by corruption. However, when government regulators, rather than firms, are required to adopt standards, AAOIFI's function in preventing corruption will be activated, as shown in Table 7.5(a).

The influence of AAOIFI adoption over SMD is measured by models 4-1 and 4-2, as shown in Tables 7.5(a) and (b). The positive link is supported by the SMD coefficient estimate, which is consistent with Larson and Kenny's (1996) projections on AAOIFI adoption and SMD for countries at the 1% significance level based on the theory of modernization. As a result, H4 has been approved. Similarly, Hassab-Elnaby *et al.* (2003) support the view that adequately developed accounting standards is a crucial requirement for equity market development since investors strive for reliable accounting information. They discovered a link between SMD and accounting advancement. Overall, our findings are consistent with those of Klibi and Kossentini (2014). Accounting standards are found to have a favorable link with the amount of SMD. The favorable benefits of AAOIFI adoption can be justified based on well-developed accounting standards, which are expected to push countries with IBs to improve the quality of financial reports published. As a result, there is less knowledge asymmetry among stock market participants.

In conclusion, our findings, as shown in Tables 7.5(a) and (b), fully support H1, H4, and H3, indicating that AAOIFI adoption has a good influence on FDI and SMD but a negative impact on GDP. Our findings, on the other hand, somewhat support the dispute over the impact of AAOIFI adoption on the level of corruption control (H2). As a result, IB adoption of AAOIFI has positive economic repercussions for countries, which may encourage governments, regulators, and policymakers to demand greater compliance from adopters' banks as well as encourage non-adopter countries to ask their IBs to adopt these standards.

7.5.3 *Robustness checks*

This section describes a variety of sensitivity analyses that show how reliable our findings are. First, according to Ball (2006), the effectiveness of the CG system influences the positive benefits of accounting standards implementation. We adopt Chen and Zhang's (2010) argument that CG incentives have a significant impact on the outcome of accounting standard adoption. The impact of CG on the macroeconomic repercussions of AAOIFI adoption is investigated. BOD size, BOD independence, CEO duality, and SSB size are the four factors used to calculate CG strength. Overall, the results are qualitatively similar to those of the original study. The analysis, as shown in Table 7.6, supports the favorable impact of AAOIFI adoption on FDI, GDP, and SMD, while finding no evidence of a link to corruption. In terms of CG's direct effect on macro factors, the study reveals a substantial effect (+/−) of the four CG components across the four models. Our findings back the findings of Verriest *et al.* (2013) who discovered that organizations with stronger CG may deliver more transparent information by obtaining higher compliance. Our findings are consistent with those of Mnif and Tahari (2021) who found that CG is positively related to the level of AAOIFI adoption.

Second, as one of the most important country-level fundamentals, inflation volatility increases price erraticism, causing price indicators to change and decrease in the actual EG. Inflation is a challenge for standard-setters, especially in countries with hyperinflationary markets, such as the majority of our chosen countries. We examine the influence of inflation on the relationship between AAOIFI adoption and macroeconomic implications in this study. According to Shima and Yang (2012), inflation is one of the factors that discourages the adoption of accounting standards. Inflation is a recognized feature of company activities in regions such as our chosen countries, and as a result, standard-setters in these marketplaces have updated the setting through more complex rules. As a result, higher inflation is expected to diminish the likelihood of accounting standard implementation. Generally, this analysis provides similar results. As presented in Table 7.7, after controlling the inflation, our analysis supports the positive impact of AAOIFI adoption on FDI, GDP, and SMD.

Table 7.6. Regression analysis for macroeconomic consequences of AAOIFI after controlling CG.

	Model (1): FDI			Model (2): GDP			Model (3): Corruption			Model (4): SMD		
Model	**Beta**	**T**	**Sig.**	**Beta**	**T**	**Sig.**	**Beta**	**T**	**Sig.**	**Beta**	**T**	**Sig.**
(Constant)		8.315	0.000		4.735	0.000		0.827	0.621		1.376	0.095
AAOIFI	0.427	4.801	0.000***	0.958	1.927	0.000***	−0.014	−0.258	0.758	0.254	4.432	0.000***
AUDIT	0.260	3.832	0.000***	−0.292	−2.249	0.003**	0.058	3.470	0.000***	−0.086	−2.641	0.029*
SIZE	−0.338	−5.110	0.000***	0.058	2.281	0.055*	−0.061	−1.867	0.002**	0.174	2.672	0.007**
INDIV	−0.234	−2.125	0.055*	0.148	1.566	0.092*	−0.048	−3.287	0.009**	−0.332	−5.752	0.000***
PD	−0.347	−3.922	0.002**	−0.031	−0.442	0.865	−0.224	−2.491	0.000***	0.073	1.323	0.352
UA	−0.398	−3.336	0.000***	0.662	5.206	0.000***	0.098	4.853	0.000***	−0.125	−0.955	0.590
MASC	−0.424	−5.334	0.000***	0.428	5.386	0.000***	0.221	1.281	0.000***	0.098	1.167	0.225
LTO	−0.142	−0.253	0.452	−0.672	−6.443	0.000***	−0.857	−1.287	0.000***	−0.042	−0.510	0.614
DC	−0.495	−4.693	0.000***	0.783	5.822	0.000***	0.016	0.285	0.358	0.287	5.619	0.000***
GE	0.762	6.319	0.000***	0.370	7.294	0.000***	0.971	4.538	0.000***	0.832	4.342	0.000***
BOD.IND	−0.035	−1.187	0.292	0.037	0.135	0.328	−0.025	−1.561	0.088*	−0.018	−2.681	0.046*
BOD.S	−0.024	−0.325	0.866	−0.053	−2.572	0.008**	0.013	0.540	0.398	−0.090	−2.122	0.029*
SSB	0.118	3.274	0.072*	−0.057	−1.127	0.143	0.043	1.554	0.062*	−0.030	−0.543	0.862
Adjusted R Square		0.548			0.672			0.720			0.592	
F		19.480			68.990			192.94			69.482	
Sig		0.000			0.000			0.000			0.000	

Note: *,** and ***denote significance at the 10%, 5%, and 1% levels, respectively.

Table 7.7. Impact of inflation on the economic consequences of AAOIFI's adoption.

	Model (1): FDI		Model (2): GDP		Model (3): Corruption		Mode SMD	
Model	**Coeff**	**T**	**Coeff**	**T**	**Coeff**	**T**	**Coeff**	**T**
(Constant)		7.495		−3.452		−4.026		3.061
AAOIFI	0.235	4.69***	0.754	2.72***	0.164	1.27	0.492	4.395***
INFL	−0.184	−1.28*	0.362	5.36***	−0.215	−0.74	0.216	2.525***
AUDIT	0.613	6.93***	−0.281	−5.64***	0.307	5.92***	−0.183	−1.428*
SIZE	−0.259	−4.42***	0.143	2.14*	−0.922	−0.39	0.274	2.792**
INDIV	−0.351	−3.81**	0.235	1.37	−0.158	−3.71**	−0.923	−5.164***
PD	−0.194	−2.24*	−0.562	−4.63***	−0.306	−1.82***	0.154	1.579
UA	−0.528	−7.98***	0.387	2.53***	0.136	5.62***	−0.117	−0.914
MAS	−0.248	−3.15**	0.727	5.93***	0.277	8.3***	0.156	1.045
LTO	0.014	0.172	−0.752	−6.28***	−0.138	−3.57***	0.048	0.503
DC	−0.513	−3.93***	0.230	3.78***	0.028	1.35	0.184	8.423***
GE	0.328	1.61**	0.804	5.04***	0.763	9.8***	0.208	4.144***
BOD.IND	−0.126	−0.599	−0.255	−1.70	−0.014	−0.69	−0.096	−3.223*
BOD.S	−0.216	−0.25	−0.184	−3.47***	0.070	3.83**	−0.157	−2.977*
SSB	0.031	0.16	−0.009	−0.18	0.044	1.76*	−0.086	−0.410
Adjusted R Square	0.468		0.712		0.773		0.492	
F	25.880		33.891		176.84		72.462	
Sig	0.000		0.000		0.000		0.000	

Note: *,** and ***denote significance at the 10%, 5%, and 1% levels, respectively.

7.6 Summary and Conclusion

The growing interest in the role of accounting standards, such as IFRS and GAAP in-country practices, prompted this study. Despite the growing demand for investing in Islamic finance around the world, research rarely assesses these benefits based on AAOIFI. We present evidence on the macro factors influencing AAOIFI adoption, including FDI, ED, corruption, and SMD, in this study. For the years 2010–2019, we looked at 150 IBs from 22 different nations. We find a positive correlation between AAOIFI adoption and FDI inflows and SMD, in line with existing work that measures the impact of accounting standards, such as IFRS and GAAP. The data, on the other hand, demonstrate a negative correlation with GDP. Corruption, however, has no substantial implications when AAOIFI is adopted by banks and has a negative impact when AAOIFI is adopted by countries. There are various theoretical, practical, and societal consequences to our study. Our findings corroborate theoretical debates concerning the effects of adopted standards, such as modernization theory for the influence on SMD, contingency theory for the impact on economic growth, and neo-institutional theory for the impact of AAOIFI FDI adoption. Our findings may be of interest to Islamic accounting researchers because they provide an empirical indication of the significant national consequences that may be associated with the adoption of AAOIFI. As a result, our research has the potential to have an impact on the Islamic banking literature by allowing for further research into the consequences of AAOIFI adoption. It is critical to advance the quality of information by supporting total compliance with Islamic standards through full adoption of AAOIFI, which influences investor trust in IFIs to boost the IBs' growth. AAOIFI is currently not obligated to require IFIs to embrace its standards. As a result, it is necessary to maintain the backing of global regulatory organizations to impose these requirements on all types of IFIs. The findings are also relevant to academia in terms of the development of research focused on the influence of accounting standards in general and Islamic standards in particular.

This chapter has numerous policy implications. It is precarious to cultivate the quality of financial data through wholly applying AAOIFI. It is critical for standard-setters and regulators in countries that have not yet implemented AAOIFI to make adoption decisions based on the fact that it is more applicable than other standards, such as IFRS. Furthermore, these findings have implications for central banks as IFI supervisors. For example, the operational implementation of AAOIFI is required to achieve significant improvements in openness. Indeed, studying the effects of AAOIFI acceptance at the country level will make the expansion of AAOIFI standards much easier. Our findings have important implications for countries' standardization organizations that want to implement AAOIFI. Policymakers must explore how AAOIFI can help countries improve their economies.

Similarly, this study has several practical consequences. The hosting nations of IBs should benefit from AAOIFI's good impact on FDI inflows by requiring IBs to adhere to these norms. This requirement may entice foreign investors to participate in emerging countries that are looking for Halal opportunities (complying with Sharia). IBs and other IFIs must take advantage of AAOIFI by conforming to the standards more closely. These favorable outcomes may encourage non-adopters of the AAOIFI to implement the standards in stages, starting with a partial implementation in the short term and then a complete implementation in the long run. Furthermore, our findings suggest that stricter governance standards are more likely to result in greater AAOIFI consequences. We think that the outcomes of this study will be useful for market analysis and the IFI society. The implementation of AAOIFI could be a key factor in attracting global investors to the local market, especially in emerging markets.

However, our findings have several limitations that point to potential areas for further research and examination, such as evaluating adoption using an index rather than a binary measurement to examine how much the amount of adoption influences the macro parameters. Additional effects for AAOIFI adoption based on macroeconomic variables, such as credit rating, may be explored in future research. Several researchers, such as Kossentini and Othman (2014), have included the variable of whether the country has mandated or voluntarily applied standards such as IFRS. To determine the effects of AAOIFI, future studies may divide countries between adopters and non-adopters as well as required and voluntary adopters. Finally, numerous possible research questions appear to be worth looking into, as follows: Does the updated and new content of AAOIFI enable improved accounting information for IBs?

Do new AAOIFI standards support IFIs to confront and overcome the effects of the COVID-19 pandemic? Do other macroeconomic factors, such as education and legal tax rules, have an impact on the adoption of AAOIFI? Does AAOIFI adoption influence the cost of capital? Finally, we consider that the exploration space for the impact of AAOIFI on the expansion of IFIs needs to be expanded and supplemented.

Acknowledgments

This study was supported and financed by the research sector, Arab Open University-Kuwait Branch under decision number 20077.

References

AAOIFI (2021). *Accounting, Auditing and Governance Standards for Islamic Financial Institutions.* Manama, Bahrain: (AAOIFI). Retrieved from www.aaoifi.com.

Abdel Karim, A. (1995). The nature and rationale of a conceptual framework for financial reporting by Islamic Banks. *Accounting and Business Research*, *25*(100), 285–300.

Abduh, M. & Omar, M. (2012). Islamic banking and economic growth: The Indonesian experience. *International Journal of Islamic and Middle Eastern Finance and Management*, *5*(1), 35–47.

Abdul Rashid, A. & Jabeen, S. (2016). Analyzing performance determinants: Conventional versus Islamic Banks in Pakistan. *Borsa Istanbul Review*, *16*(2), 92–107.

Agyei-Mensah, B. (2017). The relationship between corporate governance, corruption and forward-looking information disclosure: A comparative study. *Corporate Governance International Journal of Business in Society*, *17*(2), 284–304.

Akman, N. (2011). The effect of IFRS adoption on financial disclosure: Does culture still play a role? *American International Journal of Contemporary Research*, *1*(1), 6–17.

Al-Akra, M., Ali, M., & Marashdeh, O. (2009). Development of accounting regulation in Jordan. *The International Journal of Accounting*, *44*(2), 163–186.

Al-Baluchi, A. (2006) *The Impact of AAOIFI Standards and Other Bank Characteristics on the Level of Voluntary Disclosure in the Annual Reports of Islamic Banks*, Doctoral thesis, University of Surrey.

Al-Sulaiti, J., Ousama, A., & Hamammi, H. (2018). The compliance of disclosure with AAOIFI financial accounting standards: A comparison between Bahrain and Qatar Islamic bank. *Journal of Islamic Accounting and Business Research*, *9*(4), 549–566.

Amiram, D. (2012). Financial information globalization and foreign investment decisions. *Journal of International Accounting Research*, *11*(2), 57–81.

Assenso-Okofo, O., Ali, M., & Ahmed, K. (2011). The development of accounting and reporting in Ghana. *The International Journal of Accounting*, *46*(4), 459–480.

Ball, R. (2006). International Financial Reporting Standards (IFRS): Pros and cons for investors. *Accounting and Business Research*, *36*, 5–27.

Bansal, M. & Garg, A. (2021). Do high-quality standards ensure higher accounting quality? A study in India. *Accounting Research Journal*, *34*(6), 597–613.

Belkaoui, R. (1988). *The New Environment in International Accounting: Issues and Practices.* West Port, CT: Quorum Books.

Belkaoui, R. (2002). *International Accounting and Economic Development: The Interaction of Accounting. Economic and Social Indicators.* West Port, CT: Quorum Books.

Ben Othman, H. & Kossentini, A. (2015). IFRS adoption strategies and theories of economic development: Effects on the development of emerging stock markets. *Journal of Accounting in Emerging Economies*, *5*(1), 70–121.

Bin, L., Gianfranco, S., & Mohan, V. (2021). Economic consequences of IFRS adoption: The role of changes in disclosure quality. *Contemporary Accounting Research*, *38*(1), 129–179.

Bonito, A. & Cláudio, P. (2018). The macroeconomic determinants of the adoption of IFRS for SMEs. *Revista de Contabilidad – Spanish Accounting Review*, *21*(2), 116–127.

Boukhatem, J. & Ben Moussa, F. (2018). The effect of Islamic banks on GDP growth: Some evidence from selected MENA countries. *Borsa Istanbul Review*, *18*(3), 231–247.

Brahim, N. & Arab, M. (2020). Social disclosure: Compliance of Islamic banks to governance standards No. 7 of AAOIFI (2010). *Journal of Islamic Accounting and Business Research*, *11*(7), 1427–1452.

Briston, R. & Wallace, R. (1992). Accounting education and corporate disclosure regulation in Tanzania. *Research in Third World Accounting*, *1*(2), 281–299.

Chen, C., Ding, Y., & Xu, B. (2014). Convergence of accounting standards and foreign direct investment. *The International Journal of Accounting*, *49*(1), 53–86.

Chen, J. & Zhang, H. (2010). The impact of regulatory enforcement and audit upon IFRS compliance — Evidence from China. *European Accounting Review*, *19*(4), 665–692.

Clements, C., Neil, J., & Stovall, O. (2010). Cultural diversity, country size, and the IFRS adoption decision. *Journal of Applied Business Research*, *26*(2), 115–126.

Coffee, J. (2002). Competition among securities markets: A path dependent perspective. Columbia Law and Economics Working Paper No. 192. https://ssrn.com/abstract=283822 or. Doi: 10.2139/ssrn.283822.

Daske, H., Hail, L., Leuz, C., & Verdi, R. (2008). Mandatory IFRS reporting around the world: Early evidence on the economic consequences. *Journal of Accounting Research*, *46*, 1085–1142.

Daske, H., Hail, L., Leuz, C., & Verdi, R. (2013). Adopting a label: Heterogeneity in the economic consequences around IAS/IFRS adoptions. *Journal of Accounting Research*, *51*(3), 495–547.

Dogan, E. (2015). International Financial Reporting Standards (IFRS) and economic growth: A 326 study of developing countries IFRS: The case of EU commercial banks. *Journal of Financial Services Research*, *40*(1/2), 103–122.

Eiler, L., Miranda-Lopez, J., & Tama-Sweet, I. (2021). The impact of IFRS on earnings management: Evidence from Mexico. *Journal of Accounting in Emerging Economies*, *12*(1), 77–96.

Elgattani, T. (2018). *AAOIFI Governance Disclosure in Islamic Banks: Its Determinants and Impact on Performance*, PhD thesis, Portsmouth University.

Elgattani, T. & Hussainey, K. (2020). The determinants of AAOIFI governance disclosure in Islamic banks. *Journal of Financial Reporting and Accounting*, *18*(1), 1–18.

El-Halaby, S. & Hussainey, K. (2016). Determinants of compliance with AAOIFI standards by Islamic banks. *International Journal of Islamic and Middle Eastern and Management*, *9*(1), 143–168.

El-Halaby, S., Albarrak, H., & Grassa, R. (2020). Influence of adoption AAOIFI accounting standards on earning management: Evidence from Islamic banks. *Journal of Islamic Accounting and Business Research*, *11*(9), 1847–1870.

Epstein, B. (2009). The economic effects of IFRS adoption. *The CPA Journal*, *79*(3). 26–31.

Furqani, H. & Mulyani, R. (2009). Islamic banking and economic growth: Empirical evidence from Malaysia. *Journal of Economic Cooperation and Development*, *30*(2), 59–74.

Glaum, M. Schmidt, P. Street, D., & Vogel, S. (2013). Compliance with IFRS 3- and IAS 36-required disclosures across 17 European countries: Company- and country-level. *Accounting and Business Research*, *43*(3), 163–204.

Gordon, L., Loeb, M., & Zhu, W. (2012). The impact of IFRS adoption on foreign direct investment. *Journal of Accounting and Public Policy*, *31*(4), 374–398.

Groebner, D., Shannon, P., Fry, P., & Smith, K. (2008). *Business Statistics: A Decision-Making Approach*. Prentice-Hall: Upper Saddle River, NJ.

Hassab-Elnaby, H., Epps, R., & Said, A. (2003). The impact of environmental factors on accounting development: An Egyptian longitudinal study. *Critical Perspectives on Accounting*, *14*, 273–292.

Hofstede, G., Hofstede, G., & Minkov M. (2010). *Cultures and Organizations: Software of the Mind*. (3rd edn). USA: McGraw-Hill.

Houqe, N. (2018). A review of the current debate on the determinants and consequences of mandatory IFRS adoption. *International Journal of Accounting & Information Management*, *26*(3), 413–442.

Houqe, M. & Reza, M. (2016). IFRS adoption, extent of disclosure, and perceived corruption: A cross-country study. *The International Journal of Accounting*, *51*(3), 363–378.

Jaeyon, C., Kyongsun, H., & Jinhan, P. (2019). Does a firm's corporate governance enhance the beneficial effect of IFRS adoption? *Sustainability*, *11*(3), 885–901.

Jermakowicz, E. & Gornik-Tomaszewski, S. (2006). Implementing IFRS from the perspective of EU publicly traded companies. *Journal of International Accounting Auditing and Taxation*, *15*, 170–196.

Judge, W., Li, S., & Pinsker, R. (2010). National adoption of international accounting standards: An institutional perspective. *Corporate Governance: An International Review*, *18*(3), 161–174.

Kabir Hassan, M., Aliyu, S., Makeen, H., & Rashid, M. (2019). A survey on Islamic finance and accounting standards. *Borsa Istanbul Review*, *19*, S1–S13.

Kim, S. & Ryu, H. (2018). The impact of mandatory IFRS adoption on capital markets: Evidence from Korea. *International Journal of Accounting and Information Management*, *26*(1), 38–58.

Klibi, M. & Kossentini, A. (2014). Does the adoption of IFRS promote emerging stock markets development? Evidence from MENA countries. *International Journal of Accounting, Auditing and Performance Evaluation*, *10*(3), 279–298.

Kythreotis, A. (2015). The interrelation among faithful representation (Reliability), corruption and IFRS adoption: An empirical investigation. *International Journal of Business and Economic Sciences Applied Research*, *8*(1), 25–59.

Larson, R. & Kenny, S. (1996). Accounting standard-setting strategies and theories of economic development. *Advances in International Accounting*, *9*(1), 1–21.

Lasmin, R. (2011). An institutional perspective on international financial reporting standards adoption in developing countries. *Academy of Accounting and Financial Studies Journal*, *15*(2), 61–71.

Lee, C. (1987). Accounting infrastructure and economic development. *Journal of Accounting and Public Policy*, *6*, 75–85.

Lenormand, G. & Touchais, L. (2021). Does international financial reporting standard 8 improve the firms' information environment? *Journal of Applied Accounting Research*, *22*(2), 383–400.

Levitt, A. (1998). The importance of high-quality accounting standards. *Accounting Horizons*, *12*(2), 79–82.

Mameche, Y. & Masood, A. (2021). Macroeconomic evidence on the impact of mandatory IFRS adoption on FDI in the Gulf Cooperation Council (GCC) countries. *Journal of Accounting in Emerging Economies*, *11*(4), 610–631.

Mazzi, F., Slack, R., & Tsatavoutas, I. (2018). The effect of corruption and culture on mandatory disclosure compliance levels: Goodwill reporting in Europe. *Journal of International Accounting, Auditing and Taxation*, *31*(c), 52–73.

Mhedhbi, K. & Zeghal, D. (2016). Adoption of international accounting standards and performance of emerging capital markets. *Review of Accounting and Finance*, *15*(2), 252–272.

Mnif, Y. & Tahari, M. (2021). The effect of Islamic banks' specific corporate governance mechanisms on compliance with AAOIFI governance standards. *Journal of Islamic Accounting and Business Research*, *12*(1), 21–43.

Mohd Zain, F., Wan Abdullah, W., & Percy, M. (2021). Voluntary adoption of AAOIFI disclosure standards for takaful operators: The role of governance. *Journal of Islamic Accounting and Business Research*, *12*(4), 593–622.

Noh, M., Moon, D., & Parte, L. (2017). Earnings management using revenue classification shifting — Evidence from the IFRS adoption period. *International Journal of Accounting & Information Management*, *25*(3), 333–355.

Nor Farizal, M., Fadzlina, M., & Asyaari, E. (2015). The influence of AAOIFI accounting standards in reporting Islamic financial institutions in Malaysia. *Procedia Economics and Finance, 31*, 418—424.

Nugraheni, P. & Khasanah, E. (2019). Implementation of the AAOIFI index on CSR disclosure in Indonesian Islamic banks. *Journal of Financial Reporting and Accounting*, *17*(3), 365–382.

Nurunnabi, M. (2021). *The Economic Impact of International Financial Reporting Standards (IFRS) Implementation, International Financial Reporting Standards Implementation: A Global Experience (Contributions to International Accounting)*. Bingley: Emerald Publishing Limited, pp. 127–197.

Okoye, P. Okoye, N. & Ezejiofor, R. (2014). Impact of the IFRS adoption on stock market movement in Nigerian corporate organization. *International Journal of Academic Research in Business and Social Sciences, 4*(9), 1–25.

Oshodin, E. & Bakare, I. (2019). IFRS adoption, corruption and quality of financial reporting: A review of literature. *Management Science Review, 10*(1), 149–157.

Peng, S. & Smith, J. (2010). Chinese GAAP and IFRS: An analysis of the convergence process. *Journal of International Accounting, Auditing and Taxation, 19*(1), 16–34.

Qur'an. (2021). https://quran.com/2. Accessed 6/2021.

Rakesh, M. & Shilpa, R. (2013). Effect of IFRS and financial statements: Implications on FDI and Indian economy. *IRACST International Journal of Commerce, Business and Management, 2*(5), 233–241.

Ramanna, K. & Sletten, E. (2009). *Why do Countries Adopt International Financial Reporting Standards*. Working Paper. Boston, MA: Harvard Business School. http://ssrn.com.

Ramanna, K. & Sletten, W. (2014). Network effects in countries' adoption of IFRS. *The Accounting Review, 89*(4), 1517–1543.

Sarea, A. & Hanefah, M. (2013). Adoption of AAOIFI accounting standards by Islamic banks of Bahrain. *Journal of Financial Reporting and Accounting, 11*(2), 131–142.

Sarea, D. (2016). The impact of AAOIFI accounting standards on earnings quality: The case of Islamic banks in Bahrain. *Corporate Ownership & Control, 13*(4), 160–164.

Shima, K. & Yang, D. (2012). Factors affecting the adoption of IFRS. *International Journal of Business, 17*(3), 276–298.

Sunnah. (2021). https://sunnah.com/urn/416890.

Tanzi, V. (1998). *Corruption Around the World: Causes, Consequences, Scope, and Cures*. International Monetary Fund Working Paper.

Tyrrall, D., Woodward, D. & Rakhim, A. (2007). The relevance of international financial reporting standards to a developing country: Evidence from Kazakhstan. *The International Journal of Accounting, 42*(1), 82–110.

Ullah, M., Khanam, R., & Tasnim, T. (2018). Comparative compliance status of AAOIFI and IFSB standards: An empirical evidence from

Islami Bank Bangladesh Limited. *Journal of Islamic Accounting and Business Research*, *9*(4), 607–628.

Verriest, A., Gaeremynck, A., & Thornton, D. (2013). The impact of corporate governance on IFRS adoption choices. *European Accounting Review*, *22*(1), 39–77.

Wijekoon, N., Samkin, G., & Sharma, U. (2021). International financial reporting standards for small and medium-sized entities: A new institutional sociology perspective. *Meditari Accountancy Research*, Vol. ahead-of-print No. ahead-of-print. Doi: 10.1108/MEDAR-06-2020-0929.

World Bank & Islamic Development Bank Group. (2017). *Global Report on Islamic Finance 2016: A Catalyst for Shared Prosperity?* Washington DC: The World Bank. Doi: 10.1596/978-1-4648-0926-2.

Wyatt, A. & Yospe, J. (1993). Wake-up call to American business: International accounting. *Journal of Accountancy*, *175*(7), 80–85.

Zaidi, S. & Huerta, E. (2014). IFRS adoption and enforcement as antecedents of economic growth. *International Journal of Accounting and Financial Reporting*, *4*(1), 1–27.

Zeghal, D. & Mhedhbi, K. (2006). An analysis of the factors affecting the adoption of international accounting standards by developing countries. *The International Journal of Accounting*, *41*(4), 373–386.

Zehri, F. & Chouaibi, J. (2013). Adoption determinants of the International Accounting Standards IAS/IFRS by the developing countries. *Journal of Economics Finance and Administrative Science*, *18*(35), 56–62.

https://doi.org/10.1142/9781800612426_0008

Chapter 8

Disclosure of the Risks of Islamic Financial Instruments (Sukuk)

Omar Ikbal Tawfik and
Hamada Elsaid Elmaasrawy Elsayed Ghazi

Abstract

The study aims to propose a framework for disclosing sukuk risks, show the types of risks to which sukuks are exposed in the various literatures, and how to disclose sukuk risks in international standards such as IFRS, IFSB Standards, and AAOIFI Standards. The chapter deals with the disclosure of the risks of sukuk in the accounting standards divided among the following. First is in IFRS, which focused on the various risks to which conventional Islamic financial instruments are exposed in general, such as market risk, credit risk, liquidity risk, and other risks. Second is AAOIFI Standards that focus on the risks of Islamic financing formulas in general on the basis of which sukuk are issued. Third is IFSB Standards, which focused on the risks of non-compliance with Islamic law and legal risks to which sukuk are exposed. In addition, the chapter deals with a case study of Qatar Islamic Bank, an attempt to obtain field evidence about the level of banks' disclosure of sukuk risks through the annual reports of the Bank. The researchers found that the disclosure of sukuk risks in Qatar Islamic Bank was very limited, as well as the focus on the disclosure of sukuk risks was on quantitative disclosure, while the descriptive disclosure of sukuk risks is very limited. The researchers proposed a framework for disclosing the risks of sukuk, which is divided into quantitative risks and descriptive risks.

Keywords: Sukuk, Sukuk Risk, IFSB, AOIFI, Disclosure of Sukuk Risks, Qatar Islamic Bank.

8.1 Introduction

Islamic finance has emerged as a complementary alternative to conventional finance in line with Islamic principles and teachings. Islamic finance has experienced tremendous growth in recent decades and has been introduced in many countries, not only in the Islamic world but also in Muslim minority countries. Hence, Islamic finance is a potential alternative for developing the economy in these countries (Echchabi *et al.*, 2018).

Worldwide, Islamic financial institutions have contributed to the growth of global banking and the spread of the Islamic banking industry. This growth has partly been driven by the products and services offered by Islamic banks, numerical presence, the value of their business, and profits. This has earned it increasing local and international recognition and prompted many traditional financial institutions to provide Islamic financial services and provide regular commercial, financial services or switch entirely to Islamic finance to meet Muslim clients' growing needs and desires. The financial services provided by Islamic financial institutions are characterized as being compatible with the provisions of Islamic Sharia, such as Mudarabah, Murabahah, Musharaka, Qard Hasan, and leasing of productive assets. Many Muslim and non-Muslim countries have become interested in Islamic banking, with competition increasing to attract and embrace Islamic financial institutions towards becoming an Islamic financial and economic center.

Islamic banking has achieved notable growth in finance and investment, with which development and innovation in Islamic financial instruments have become imperative to devise Islamic financial instruments that serve the purposes of liquidity and profitability for these institutions. Hence, Islamic sukuk emerged as one of the most important products, which could find a foothold in the international financial markets.

Islamic sukuk is a financial instrument that complies with the provisions of the Islamic Sharia. They represent an alternative to bonds in the traditional financial system. They are issued against assets that are often real estate or financial assets with a return over a medium or long term. Islamic sukuk is a focus of interest for many Muslim and non-Muslim investors due to its clear flexibility in terms of return due to the multiplicity of its issuance structures.

Therefore, due to the importance of sukuk, the British Prime Minister announced on October 29, 2013, that the United Kingdom would be the first country outside the Islamic world to issue sukuk (Godlewski *et al.*, 2016). In 2014, Hong Kong, Luxembourg, and South Africa issued sovereign sukuk (Lackmann, 2015).

Islamic sukuk are investment funds that include Murabahah Sukuk, Mudarabah Sukuk, Musharaka Sukuk, Salam Sukuk, Ijara Sukuk, and Istisna Sukuk. Therefore, the process of issuing and trading sukuk in the financial market is a fundamental change in the financing of Islamic banks, as Islamic sukuk can absorb savings according to the desire of its members and provide the necessary financing for projects. This made the issuance of sukuk an appropriate tool for integrating Islamic banking activity and financial markets and integrating with the global market.

The sukuk market has witnessed unprecedented growth all over the world during the past decade. Since the global financial crisis in 2007–2008, the Islamic sukuk market has proliferated with a total global sukuk amounting to USD 346.7 billion at the end of March 2017 (Hasan *et al.*, 2019). Malaysia is the largest market for sukuk, but these securities are also commonly issued in the GCC (Godlewski *et al.*, 2016). In this regard, Echchabi *et al.* (2018) indicate that the United Arab Emirates is the leading country in issuing corporate sukuk in the Gulf region, followed by Saudi Arabia, Kuwait, Qatar, and Bahrain. Bahrain ranks first in terms of sovereign sukuk, followed by the United Arab Emirates, Qatar, and then Saudi Arabia. The Kingdom of Saudi Arabia ranked first in the issuance of semi-sovereign sukuk, followed by the United Arab Emirates, then Kuwait, and finally Bahrain. In general, the United Arab Emirates remains the leading regional issuer of sukuk in terms of the number of issues, followed by Saudi Arabia, Kuwait, Bahrain, and finally Qatar.

These sukuk structures are based on three basic forms of Islamic financing instruments: Mudarabah, Musharaka, and Ijarah/Murabahah, or combinations thereof (Jobs, 2007). In this regard, if the sukuk certificates represent the ownership of the assets or the usufruct right, then they are negotiable and can be traded. On the contrary, if it represents debt or money, it can only be exchanged at face value (Echchabi, 2018).

Sukuk structures undergo a rigorous vetting process by religious advisors to ensure they comply with the Sharia. These instruments must be free from prohibited items such as riba (interest), gharar (uncertainty), and gambling, as well as from activities that are not permitted (e.g., pork investments, drugs, pornography, and military activities). Most importantly, the certificate of sukuk is of paramount importance to investors who must ensure that these securities are Sharia compliant before purchasing them.

In the view of many researchers, sukuk has achieved great success in competing with bonds in many countries, growing from modest and unknown financing instruments to well-established instruments (Azmat *et al.*, 2015; Dimitris *et al.*, 2016; Naifar *et al.*, 2017; Nagano, 2017). However, despite the boom in sukuk issuances globally and the growth and size of the market, like traditional securities (Ibrahim, 2015; Olson & Zoubi, 2017; Bitar *et al.*, 2017), the current work on sukuk is still weak because there are many risks with its structure. These risks differ according to the assets that make them, whether fixed or movable, or benefits or services. Thus, when the risk management tools are weak, the risks are not managed well, and there are weaknesses and defects in the sukuk structures. Furthermore, the sukuk market has not been established on solid foundations of risk management. Several researchers highlighted the risks behind sukuk structures (Majid *et al.*, 2011; Alsaeed, 2012; Alsayed, 2013; Noor & Shahimi, 2013). Zakaria *et al.* (2010) argued that sukuk need to undergo a classification process similar to conventional bonds. This underscores the need for both sukuk issuers and investors to understand sukuk risks. To this end, the research problem aims to answer the following questions:

(1) What is the importance of Islamic sukuk for an Islamic bank?
(2) What are the risks to Islamic sukuk?
(3) Do Islamic banks disclose the risks associated with sukuk?

This research aims to identify the risks of Islamic sukuk, identify how accounting standards deal with the disclosure of sukuk risks, and explore a case study on the disclosure of sukuk risks in Qatar Islamic Bank.

Several factors encouraged the researchers to choose to disclose the risks of the instruments. First, many of the previous studies identified many risks related to sukuk. Second, Islamic sukuk is a new window to provide Islamic banks with long-term sources of financing. The correct use of these sources has a positive impact on the profitability of banks and vice versa. Therefore, it is necessary to increase interest in Islamic sukuk and the necessity of the issuing banks' commitment to disclose any risks they face so that investors can make the right decisions and reduce the risks they may face.

8.2 Nature and Types of Sukuk

8.2.1 *Nature of sukuk*

Transactions in Islam combine stability and flexibility, so monopoly, usury, and fraud are forbidden in every situation until the Day of Resurrection. Early Islamic eras contained numerous forms of financial transactions. The complexity and saturation of economic needs and the different ruling systems for financing and economic exchanges resulted in the need for new financial instruments compatible with the Islamic Sharia. However, it is not enough to provide Islamic financial instruments. These financial instruments must offer advantages equivalent to traditional financial instruments in order to be able to compete in financial markets (Kunduz, 2007).

Under the capitalist system prevailing in the world, large projects are financed by issuing bonds, but bondholders do not go beyond being lenders to the owners of these projects based on interest at a rate compatible with the interest rate in the market. They have no income in the ownership of the project's assets nor in the profit that results from these projects.

The need of the Islamic community for financing sources derived from Islamic law as an alternative to traditional bonds associated with a fixed interest rate, the idea of Islamic sukuk emerged, which is based on the idea of sukuk holders participating in financing the project and participating in profit or loss, which is the basis of Islamic investment. Thus, the sukuk is based on the same idea of shares in contemporary joint-stock companies and the system of investment units in investment funds (Shaheen, 2015, pp. 155–156).

There are two opinions regarding the relationship between sukuk and bonds. The first opinion is closely related to theoretical arguments regarding the relationship between sukuk, stocks, and bonds. Based on this view, Aloui *et al.* (2015a, 2015b) and Kim and Kang (2012) argue that we cannot expect substantial differences between sukuk, stocks and bonds, since sukuk and traditional tawarruq have similar structures (Onder, 2016), and thus, the sukuk is not a financial innovation. Within this trend, Aloui *et al.* (2015b) found that Islamic assets are witnessing similar movements to traditional stocks and bonds. Also, Hassan *et al.* (2018) found that conventional sukuk and bonds follow a similar long-term trajectory in terms of volatility and correlations and that investment-grade conventional sukuk and bonds have less conditional volatility in response to market shocks and higher persistence. The second opinion argues that sukuk differs from traditional bonds. Iqbal and Mirakhor (2007) and Cakir and Raie (2007) argue that Islamic assets differ from traditional assets based on religious instructions and rules. Several principles distinguish Islamic financial products from non-Islamic products. These include the prohibition of explicit interest rates (usury), excessive uncertainty (gharar), the participation of contracting parties in profits and losses, and that operation maintain a direct link with the real economy. In this framework, sukuk are certificates that reflect the rights to participate in the underlying assets that determine the performance of the instruments, potentially acting as a mixture of bonds and stocks. Within this trend, Sulaiman (2020) argues that sukuk represents a common share in the ownership of certain assets or projects and are issued according to Islamic financing formulas. The issuance of sukuk, including the use of funds resulting from the issuance, should not include any of the elements of usury, gharar, and activities prohibited by the Islamic Sharia.

The International Islamic Fiqh Academy (IIFA)[1] presented a definition of sukuk in its Resolution No. 178 (4/19) with a comparison of traditional securitization (bonds). The first paragraph of the council's decision stated:

> "Conventional securitisation Converting debts into securities (bonds) of equal value and negotiable. These bonds represent a debt with interest to the bearer in the custody of their issuer.

[1]The International Islamic Fiqh Academy (IIFA) is a universal scholarly organization. It is a subsidiary organ of the Organization of Islamic Cooperation (OIC). It was established following a resolution at the Third Islamic Summit of the Organization (N.8/3-T/S-I) on 19th–22th Rabi al-Awal 1401H. For more details about the Islamic Fiqh Academy, you can visit the following link: https://www.iifa-aifi.org/ar/%d8%aa%d8%a3%d8%b3%dfilea%d8%b3-d8%a7%.

> These bonds may not be issued or traded, according to the Sharia. As for Sukuk (Islamic securitisation), it is the issuance of financial documents or certificates of equal value that represent common shares in the ownership of assets (principles, benefits, rights, or a mixture of assets, benefits, money and debts) that exist or will be created from the proceeds of subscription".

The Accounting and Auditing Organisation for Islamic Financial Institutions in Standard No. 17, Item 2, defined "Investment Sukuk" as documents of equal value that represent common shares in the ownership of objects, benefits, services, assets of a specific project, or special investment activity, after collecting the value of the sukuk and closing the subscription door, and using it according to the purpose of its issue.

The Islamic Financial Services Board defines in Standard No. (7) defined sukuk as: "certificates, each of which represents a right of ownership of a common percentage in in-kind assets, or a different group of in-kind assets and others, and the assets may be in a specific project or investment activity, and the condition that the project or activity is in accordance with the provisions of Islamic Sharia".

The Accounting and Auditing Organisation for Islamic Financial Institutions defined Investment Sukuk as: "documents of equal value that represent common shares in the ownership of objects, benefits, services, or in the assets of a particular project or a special investment activity, after collecting the value of the sukuk and closing the subscription door and beginning to use it for what it was issued for".

Through this, sukuk can be defined as Islamic Sharia-compliant securities that represent equal ownership shares in assets, benefits, services, or assets of a specific project or activity that achieve a profit or loss for its holder.

In finance theory, a title deed in its essential sense is not a deed. Only the financial asset that is given the right to participate in making basic decisions through the voting process in the general assembly is considered a sukuk, which made the concept of ownership sukuk limited only to common shares (Hindi, 2006). Table 8.1 shows the difference between common shares, sukuk, and bonds.

Table 8.1 shows that Islamic sukuk are similar to traditional securities in that they are tradable securities. It is similar to shares in that it represents a common share in the enterprise's assets and receives a share of the net profit or loss. It is consistent with bonds in being

Table 8.1. Difference between common shares, sukuk and bonds.

Difference	Common shares	Sukuk	Bonds
Concept	Securities representing a title deed in the assets of an enterprise	Documents representing a title deed in the assets of a particular project or a private investment activity	Securities issued by establishments or governments for borrowing, meaning that they represent a credit instrument
Return on investment	Participation in profit or loss, any variable return	Participation in profit or loss, any variable return	Fixed periodic return regardless of profit or loss
Existence of assets	Shares are issued in the enterprise's name as a whole and represent a share in its assets	The necessity of having assets (objects that may be mixed with some debt) for the instrument to be issued and the assets may be in a specific project or investment activity	Bonds are issued in the name of the enterprise, government, or project, and the main component of the securitization process is debts
Compliance with Islamic Sharia	It is compliant with Sharia if the purpose for which the company was established (issuing the share) is legitimate and not prohibited	It is compliant with Islamic law and is carried out under legal supervision	It is not compatible with Islamic law and does not need legal supervision
Securities duration	Indefinite period	Fixed term[a]	Fixed term

Issuer of securities	The issuer must be in the form of a joint-stock company and have a minimum capital	The requirement of a minimum capital does not apply to Islamic financial institutions because the sukuk is not issued based on the financial solvency of the issuing company but rather on the nature and quality of the assets	The issuer must be in the form of a joint-stock company with minimum capital or a government
Appointment of company management (Board of Directors)	The shareholder has the right to appoint and dismiss management	The sukuk holder does not have the right to appoint and dismiss the management	The bondholder has no right to appoint and dismiss management
Guarantee (Safety)	There is no guarantee	There is no guarantee[b]	The issuer is responsible for paying its value in the event of any
Trading timing	Shares are traded at any time and in anyway	Sukuk is traded in any way, but there are specific times when trading may be prohibited[c]	The bond is traded at any time and in any way

Notes: [a]The sukuk market contains some types (although they do not represent a large percentage of the total volume of the sukuk market) with no fixed term at issue.

[b]The sukuk market contains several types — although they do not represent a large percentage of the total size of the sukuk market — and they are the asset-based sukuk, which the sukuk originator undertakes to buy from the owner upon maturity or by mutual consent on an early term at an agreed upon value, which is often equal to the value par for the instrument.

[c]For example, it is not permissible to circulate the deeds of ownership of the usufructs of the properties described in the trust before the asset that receives the benefit is determined. Also, it is not permissible to circulate the title deeds of the services that are fulfilled by a described party before the designation of the party from whom the service is to be fulfilled. Also, the istisna bonds are not negotiable unless the proceeds of the bonds are paid for in a parallel istisna'a or the istisna asset is delivered to the mustasna. At the same time, it is not permissible to trade in salam and murabahah sukuk after the murabahah goods have been delivered to the buyer. As for the muzara'ah and musaqat sukuks, they are not allowed to be traded after the goodness of the crops or fruits have become available (Accounting and Auditing Organization for Islamic Financial Institutions, 2010, pp. 244–245).

a basic financing tool able to control cash flow. It differs from stocks in that it has an expiration date specified in the contract, and from bonds, it represents a right in-kind related to the project's assets, while bonds represent a debt owed by its issuer.

8.2.2 *Types of sukuk*

In the Middle East, most sukuk are either ijarah sukuk or wakala sukuk. But on the other hand, most of the sukuk in Malaysia are sukuk of the type of murabahah (mainly commodity sukuk). One of the reasons why murabahah sukuk is so widely used in Malaysia is that the scheme can also be used by issuers who do not have eligible assets to back the sukuk. On the other hand, there is almost no commodity murabahah sukuk in the Middle East because most Muslim scholars there believe that the scheme is not compliant with Sharia (Lackmann, 2015). Sukuk can be classified according to the nature of the Sharia contract based on which the sukuk is issued and which governs their trading, as follows:

(1) *Ijarah sukuk*: Ijarah is a lease contract. It is based on a similar principle to traditional lease contracts and is therefore familiar to exporters and investors in non-Islamic countries (Lackmann, 2015). Issuance of ijarah sukuk compared to musharaka or mudarabah issuance can be considered a positive sign on the issuer's financial position, although profit and loss instruments are considered more legally in Islamic finance. Godlewski *et al.* (2016) believes that the issuance of ijarah-based sukuk sends a positive signal to market participants compared to other sukuk structures.
(2) *Musharaka sukuk*: They are documents of equal value that are issued to finance the purchase of the murabahah commodity, and the murabahah commodity becomes owned by the holders of the sukuk. The objective of issuing murabahah sukuk is to obtain the necessary liquidity to purchase the murabahah commodity. Murabahah is a scheme often used to purchase assets, products and other commodities under an instalment sale contract. In a murabahah contract, all contract terms are specified in advance, including the repayment period, the number of payments, and the amount of profit margin. Then, the bank issues the sukuk. Using the money obtained, the bank buys the originator's

product and then sells it back to the originator at a predetermined price (Al Kayal, 2017).

(3) *Al Salam sukuk*: They are documents of equal value that are issued to collect the salam capital. The salam commodity becomes owned by the holders of the sukuk (Feigl, 2015). These documents represent a specified commodity that will be delivered at a specified date in the future, with the full price paid immediately by the sukuk holders. Thus, the sukuk holders are entitled to the return resulting from the sale of the commodity (Ben Amara, 2011).

(4) *Istisna sukuk*: They are documents of equal value issued for the use of subscription proceeds in the manufacture of a commodity owned by the holders of the sukuk. It is more flexible than salam sukuk due to the possibility of paying the price of the istisna in instalments. It is also permissible to trade in the istisna sukuk if the subscription proceeds are transformed into assets owned by the sukuk holders during the istisna period. Istisna sukuk can be used to finance real estate facilities and buildings, and the state can also use them to finance infrastructure projects (Qurumi, 2014).

(5) *Wakala sukuk*: Wakala sukuk are agency agreements structured primarily like assets in conventional finance, representing projects or activities managed on the basis of wakala with investment. The investor (owners of sukuk) provides funds to the agent who is called the agent, and the agent invests the funds on behalf of the investor. The sukuk holders own the assets represented by the sukuk, and they are entitled to the participation profit. Wakala sukuk is based on a wakala agreement and backed by investment assets, unlike ijarah sukuk which requires real assets (Lackmann, 2015; Hasan *et al.*, 2019).

Sukuk classifications based on the technical and commercial features are further divided into four main categories:

(1) Nature of issuers (i.e., sovereign, quasi-sovereign, and corporate sukuk);
(2) Complexity of the structure (i.e., convertible, exchangeable, and plain vanilla sukuk);
(3) Underlying assets (i.e., asset-backed, asset-based, and hybrid sukuk); and

(4) Additional features (i.e., subordinated, perpetual, and stapled sukuk) (Hasan *et al.*, 2019).

Sukuk are also classified based on the structure of sukuk into four types:

(1) *Debt-based sukuk*: There are four common types of these sukuk, namely sukuk murabahah, ijarah sukuk, misyarakah sukuk, and mudarabah sukuk (Diaw, 2011). Murabahah for sukuk and leasing of sukuk are classified as debt-based sukuk because of their similarity, in some features, with bonds. Conversely, al-masirah sukuk and mudarabah sukuk are categorized as equity-based sukuk.
(2) *Asset-based sukuk*: They are debt-based sukuk (mostly debt), where there is evidence of indebtedness between the originator and the sukuk holders based on the basic Sharia contract used in the structure of the sukuk (Lahsasna, 2018). According to the Sharia opinion adopted at the level of the Islamic financial industry, this type of sukuk is not based on investment assets but rather takes the assets as collateral or mortgage for the sukuk. This type of sukuk may not be traded because it is debt, and it only leads to the transfer of ownership of the usufruct resulting from the assets and not the ownership of the assets themselves. According to Moody (2006), these sukuk issuers undertake to purchase them from the issuer at maturity or by mutual agreement on an early term at an agreed value. This is often equal to the face value of the sukuk and then the real market value of the sukuk. The promise to buy is meaningless for the sukuk holders. In this case, the bondholders of the sukuk do not have any right over the assets but rather depend entirely on the originator and his financial eligibility for payment, either through his internal resources or through his ability to refinance. Accordingly, if the originator is unable to fulfill its obligations to buy back the assets, the sukuk holders will not be in a preferential position over the rest of the creditors, nor will they be in a weaker position than the unsecured creditors, which confirms that the promise to purchase places on an equal footing the obligations of the originator toward the unsecured sukuk holders, regardless of whether they are a first-class or second-class campaign.

(3) *Asset-backed sukuk*: These sukuk provide a secure structure for sukuk holders, where the real sale takes its toll on the asset. The ownership of the asset is transferred to the sukuk holders. The certificate obtained by the sukuk holders is evidence of legal ownership of the asset. In the event of default, the sukuk holder recourse to the principal and not to the company (Lahsasna, 2018). According to the Islamic Financial Services Board (IFSB) in criterion: (7), asset-backed sukuk are "that meet the conditions required by a recognized external credit rating institution, from which the Sukuk holders will bear any losses in the event of damage to the assets or their depreciation" i.e., the full transfer of legal ownership of the assets under contract. According to Moody (Moody's Investors Service, 2006), asset-backed sukuk are those in which "investors enjoy the support and security of the assets under contract so that they enjoy some form of security over the assets. They are therefore better off than unsecured creditors". In other words, if the issuer defaults or goes insolvent, the sukuk holders can avoid the risks they are exposed to by controlling the assets and then realizing value from them. It also requires the presence of the sukuk element embodied in the real sale and excluding the risk of bankruptcy from the issuer bankruptcy remoteness and the enforcement of the guarantees associated with the issuance process.

The International Academy of Malaysia (ISRA) searched the database obtained from the IFSB. It was found that the number of transactions for asset-backed sukuk is very low for the vast majority of sukuk that are asset-based sukuk, where the property is beneficial ownership. The sukuk was issued after AD 2009, and due to the lack of appropriate sukuk by governments and companies that form the basis for the lease contract and the unwillingness of governments to relinquish public assets because selling such assets to foreign investors may create negative feelings in public opinion, have created new sukuk in which the merger assets are in debt. The percentage of assets at first was a majority. It started decreasing until it became less than a third in some types of sukuk, then it moved, as Rafi Hanif mentioned, to a lower degree than sukuk based on assets, so it became sukuk with light assets (asset-light sukuk) (Bouhrwa, 2015).

(4) *Project-based sukuk*: These are sovereign sukuk intended for project financing. Some countries use these sukuk to finance infrastructure projects. The issuance of sovereign sukuk for project financing is one of the innovations developed by governments in some countries to provide an alternative and effective source of project financing. The main purpose of issuing sovereign sukuk is to finance infrastructure projects that have been allocated in the state budget (Nanaeva, 2010; Kurniawan & Ab Rahman, 2019).

According to Sukuk Holders Financial Reporting Standard No. 34 (in preparation and not yet issued), the sukuk are classified into the following.

- Business sukuk represents a sukuk instrument whereby an underlying business exists, i.e., either of Islamic finance and investment, trade, services, or similar activities.
- Assets sukuk: Any sukuk which is not a business sukuk.

8.3 Islamic Sukuk Risks

Risk is one of the variables of the investment decision. It is a concept used to measure the uncertainties in operations that affect the organization's ability to achieve its goals (Alexandru, 2019), as it means the possibility of loss or volatility in the expected return. Therefore, risk can be viewed as a relative measure of the volatility of the return (cash flow) that will be obtained in the future. Risks are classified based on their causes into unsystematic risks, and they are "represented by fluctuations in the expected return from existing investments" (Usmani, 2002).

8.3.1 *Types of risks to which Islamic financial instruments are exposed*

Financial instruments — whether conventional or Islamic — involve various risks, such as credit risk, market risk, operational risk, and others. These risks differ between traditional financial instruments and Islamic financial instruments, whether in the nature of these risks or how they appear and therefore in the way of dealing with them and hedging against them (Kunduz & Al-Sahlawi, 2017). Although sukuk markets are emerging and attracting increasing interest globally, they still have a long way to go to meet potential demand compared to their conventional counterparts (Hasan *et al.*, 2019). In order to make sukuk attractive to investors, their issuers must deal with all types of risks, uncertainties, and other problems associated with them to facilitate their investment. The knowledge and awareness of sukuk investors of the risks involved in sukuk transactions enable them to make better decisions, and investors can diversify their investment portfolios and achieve good returns.

In addition to the traditional financial and operational risks, Islamic sukuk faces other risks and distinguishes them from other securities (stocks and bonds) stemming from the risks inherent in the financing formulas on which Islamic sukuk are based when they are issued. The origin of the risks in these formulas stems from the fact that some of them are based mainly on sharing in profit and loss, some of them are based on debt, and others are due to not investing in projects whose return may be very large, but these projects may violate the Sharia. At the same time, the risks of the various Islamic financing formulas go beyond the direct sukuk that were issued on their basis through the decrease in their returns in the financial markets (Badran, 2014). In sukuk backed by assets, the sukuk holders are isolated from exposure to any risks related to the originator. This is because their ownership of the specific assets leaves them exposed to losses in the event of damage to the denominated assets. Therefore, the risks of sukuk appear mainly in the risks surrounding Islamic financing formulas with their various characteristics (Ahmed Suleiman, 2020).

The researchers believe that Islamic financial instruments are exposed to both systemic risks and unsystematic risks, and the risks to which securities are exposed can be divided into:

(1) *Systematic risks*: affect all prices and returns of securities and financial instruments as a result of general variables, such as inflation, interest rate risks, exchange rate risks, market risks, political risks, and natural risks.
(2) *Unsystematic risks*: changes in the prices and returns of securities and financial instruments due to variables specific to the

company alone, such as credit risk, operational risk, legal risk, and liquidity risk. Unsystematic risks can be divided into:

A. Unsystematic risks common to conventional financial instruments and investment instruments, such as credit risk, operational risk, legal risk, and liquidity risk.
B. Unsystematic risks, especially sukuk only, which are due to the nature of the sukuk, such as the risks of sukuk issuers, the risks of sukuk in-kind assets, the risks of disposing of receivables accepted by Sharia, the risks of violating the provisions of Islamic Sharia, and the risks of Islamic financing formulas.

Table 8.2 shows the different types of risks that affect Islamic financial instruments.

8.4 Literature Review

Islamic sukuk, like traditional securities, are exposed to many risks in the financial markets. These risks vary according to the assets for which they are made up, whether they are fixed or movable, benefits, or services. This study seeks to identify the risks of Islamic sukuk, as an Islamic financing tool and methods of disclosing the associated risks.

Zakaria *et al.* (2012) aimed to clarify the basic principles of sukuk, the importance of credit rating, and the risks resulting from stopping the payment of sukuk issued by Malaysia. The study followed the descriptive-analytical approach, where data were obtained from observers and official authorities (the Malaysian Securities Commission, the Malaysian Rating Agency, Berhad Company's evaluation, Standard & Poor's report). The study concluded that despite the increasing growth of sukuk in various countries, there are risks that sukuk face due to their weak credit rating, which exposes them to the risk of default. Therefore, sukuk need to undergo a classification process similar to that to which conventional bonds are subject.

Al-Sayed (2013) discussed the concept and meaning of sukuk, the reasons and the mechanism of dealing with its risks and controlling them, focusing on the Islamic perspective and the provisions of Sharia in dealing with these risks. This included highlighting whether sukuk is less risky than conventional bonds or not and to what extent

Table 8.2. Types of risks that affect sukuk.

Risk type	The impact of risks on the sukuk
Interest rate risk	The risks arising from changes in the interest rate and knowing that government regulation of interest rates is part of a broad macroeconomic policy, in particular monetary policy. Sukuk is not directly affected by interest rates because they do not deal in it, but it may be affected if interest rates are taken as a reference rate when financing with murabahah. In general, with other factors remaining the same, the higher the levels of interest rates in the market, the lower the market value of the traded securities and vice versa (Shahin, 2015)
Inflation risk	Risks arising from a decrease in the purchasing power of money. Islamic sukuk consists of money, debts, assets, and assets that are directly affected by inflation as their components of debt and cash increase
Exchange rate risk	Risks arising from fluctuations in the value of the currency against other currencies. It appears when issuing sukuk in a specific currency and investing the proceeds of selling sukuk in other currencies (Shaheen, 2015). Also, in the case of international murabahah, there is an exchange rate risk because the asset is purchased from the issuer in foreign currency (Kunduz & Sahlawi, 2017). It appears when buying commodities or dealing in commodities by the speculator (the other party) in a foreign currency and a decrease in the price of that currency occurs, which leads to losses by the amount of the foreign currency's decline
Market risk	The risks resulting from the rising and falling trends that occur in the market due to economic, political, social, or security factors (Shaheen, 2015). Sukuk are generally exposed to market price risks, not the various forms of Islamic financing, for example: 1. If the mudarabah or musharaka contract is related to trade offers or trading in shares, it may be exposed to the risks of bad market conditions. As well as the risks to the assets of the investment project on which the speculation or participation is based (Kunduz & Al-Sahlawi, 2017) 2. Non-compliance with the promise in the case of murabahah sukuk for the purchase order. It is considered a risk when taking the opinion of not obligating the customer to implement the purchase promise of the commodity after providing it, for reluctance to buy means that the bank is forced to sell it less than its purchase price (Kunduz & Al-Sahlawi, 2017; Al-Ajili, 2016)

(Continued)

Table 8.2. (*Continued*)

Risk type	The impact of risks on the sukuk
	3. In the first stage of the istisna contract (related to the manufacture of the product) exposed to market risks as a result of price fluctuations, scarcity of resources, or any obstacle that raises manufacturing costs (Kunduz & Al-Sahlawi, 2017; Maqalaty, 2015) 4. The value of the lease amounts in lease contracts is defined as periodic payments and is based on a reference index, but if the estimation of the lease amount is not able to meet the actual market requirements, there will be market risks (Maqalaty, 2015)
Political risk	It arises from the prevailing political climate such as power struggle and political turmoil. Issuers of financial instruments may be subject to legislation that permits or requires a national dispute resolution authority to impose losses on holders of certain instruments. For example, the National Authority for Dispute Resolution has the power to reduce the nominal amount of the instrument or convert it to a fixed number of ordinary shares of the issuer. If the National Authority for Dispute Resolution decides that the exporter has severe financial difficulties and needs additional regular capital or decides that it is a failure (IFRS, 9)
Natural risk	All forms of Islamic finance are exposed to the risks of natural disasters because they are transactions based on real assets. Therefore, when any disasters occur, such as floods, earthquakes, or fires, they lead to the destruction of the sukuk's assets. Among the most prominent instruments that are exposed to natural hazards are the instruments of sharecropping, watering, and planting due to the nature of the three formulas closely related to nature — disasters, fires, winds, epidemics, pests, and others — which may lose these instruments their nominal value in the event of force majeure conditions that lead to the depreciation of the assets of the agricultural project completely and failing (Badran, 2014)
Operational risks	It is known that the sukuk are based on assets, and the return on these sukuk results from these assets. Hence, the operational risks resulting from owning these assets are borne by sukuk holders, for example, the environmental damages resulting from factories or ships. (Zameem, 2016). In salam and istisna' contracts, there is a possibility that the received or manufactured goods do not conform to the specifications specified for them, and this failure may

Table 8.2. (*Continued*)

Risk type	The impact of risks on the sukuk
	cause a delay in the delivery of the actual goods after the date of sale and delaying the delivery of goods may lead to a bad reputation and business risks as well as may lead to additional expenses and the possibility of loss (Maqalaty, 2015)
Liquidity risk	It is the inability to dispose of the sukuk quickly and easily, without experiencing a significant decrease in its price compared to the price that was concluded based on the last deal. If the lessee (the lease contract) departs early from the commitment, there will be a loss of the expected payments from the specified payments, as there will be credit risks and liquidity risks, and they are in times of expected cash flows from the instalment amounts or from the expected payments (Maqalaty, 2015). In other words, these risks are related to the ease of disposing of the security and the associated cost (Hindi, 2006)
Sukuk issuers risks	Sukuk issuers are individuals, companies, or governments that issue sukuk and invest the proceeds of their sale
Risks of liquidating real assets	It results from the inability of assets and services that are common ownership assets to generate sufficient cash flows to distribute the expected returns to sukuk holders
The dangers of violating the provisions of Islamic Sharia	There are different forms of the risks of legitimacy for Islamic sukuk, including: 1. Risks related to legal differences between jurists as a result of the absence of unified Sharia standards, and if they exist, they are not binding in application 2. Risks resulting from the non-compliance of the issued sukuk with the legal regulations as a result of the use of sukuk funds in prohibited matters, whether they are prohibited for themselves, such as prohibited goods and services, or forbidden to earn them, such as usury, gambling, fraud, deception, and treason. (Dawaba, 2008) The risks of Islamic financing formulas are the risks of sukuk appear mainly in the risks surrounding Islamic financing formulas with their various characteristics (Sulaiman, 2020)
The risks of securitization of receivables that are acceptable according to the Sharia	Investors face two risks related to the securitization of receivables. It is the risk of delay in payment and the risk of being unable to pay due to financial default or bankruptcy (Zameem, 2016)

traditional strategies can be used to measure and manage sukuk risk. The study concluded that risk tolerance in real assets is a feature of sukuk. Therefore, asset risk management practices should be implemented, Islamic credit rating agencies should be established that classify the asset in accordance with Islamic law, and strict control and auditing of sukuk should be in place.

Noor and Shahimi (2013) studied how to manage credit risk in sukuk and prevent it from defaulting. The results showed that the application of credit risk management used in debt-based sukuk is almost the same as that applied in conventional bonds. The difference occurs only in the methodology used for evaluation at the rating stage by the rating agency for these two instruments. The study recommended that the sukuk issuers strengthen their current indicators in managing the credit risks of sukuk and explore other alternative indicators that are compatible with the provisions of Sharia to secure sukuk financing that defaults do not occur.

Alswaidan (2017) reviewed sukuk risk based on the risk of conventional finance. The finding showed the main sukuk structures, equity-based, debt-based, agency-based, assets-based, and hybrid structures, arise directly from the requirement of sukuk to conform to the Sharia and to the fundamental ethical principles of Islamic finance and business. Furthermore, sukuk risks are directly related to sukuk structures. Thus, sukuk structure risks are essentially Sharia risks.

Ur Rehman *et al.* (2020) dealt with the concepts of corporate governance (CG) and sustainability (CS) as a defense mechanism against sukuk risks. The relationship between them and their relationship to the risk of default was discussed to reach a conceptual framework. It has been observed that governance risk models alone are not sufficient to reach a reasonable conclusion. Sustainability has a direct defensive role against default, but corporate governance has an impact on sustainability oversight. The study showed that corporate governance risk management is better conducted through sustainability performance.

Khan *et al.* (2020) ascertained the credit risk of asset-based sukuk in Pakistan. Various risks related to the sukuk were identified. The study showed that the green clean technology sukuk is a suitable option in the current situation of Pakistan and the need to finance the Demir Bhasha Dam and the Naya Pakistan Housing Program.

Hasan (2019) reviewed the previous literature to analyze the risks of contemporary sukuk and discussed several mechanisms to mitigate these risks. The study showed that sukuk can be good alternatives to traditional bonds. However, the sukuk structures need to be further developed to meet the requirements of Sharia compliance. In-depth knowledge of the risks of sukuk would help academics and investors alike to understand potential problems related to sukuk structures and take precautions at the early stage to prevent the causes of default or bankruptcy.

Chang (2020) provided a critical review on how the sukuk has compared to Malaysia sovereign bonds, Malaysia Islamic sovereign bonds, Malaysia corporate-issued AAA-rated bonds, and other educational, social impact bonds around the world. The study found that the Sustainable and Responsible Investment Sukuk is significantly different from similar AAA-rated corporate bonds, Islamic sovereign bonds, and Malaysia sovereign bonds. The Sustainable and Responsible Investment Sukuk is riskier than Islamic sovereign bond and Malaysia sovereign bond but less risky than similar AAA-rated corporate bonds. There is also a significant difference between Sustainable and Responsible Investment Sukuk and other educational, social impact bonds.

Uluyol (2021) examined previous research to provide some future directions on sukuk. The author had reviewed and examined the following five different aspects of sukuk: (i) the structural and fundamental differences between Islamic and conventional bonds; (ii) empirical research into sukuk; (iii) the choice between sukuk and conventional bond issuance; (iv) Sharia and legal issues of sukuk; and (v) the pricing of sukuk are presented systematically. The study found that most research has been conducted in the area of empirical studies of sukuk, while fundamental research into sukuk is largely ignored.

Several studies examined disclosing the risks of sukuk. Gharib (2016) concluded that there is no model for disclosing the risks of sukuk and the insufficient information that is disclosed in the financial reports of the institutions entrusted with the issuance of sukuk. By presenting the problems of accounting disclosure and proposals for treatment while presenting a suggested entrance to the role of financial engineering in disclosing the sukuk and the risks. Whereas the results of Qizam and Fong (2019) suggest there is a relationship between accounting-based risks (i.e., operating income, leverage, and ROI) and sukuk or bond ratings. Differentiating between sukuk and bond issuers is not empirically proven. Additionally, ancillary evidence that relevance is more pronounced than reliability and bond ratings are more concerned with the variability of financial measures than sukuk is left to further research for confirmation. This is ample evidence for the expanded value-relevance of financial disclosure in the sukuk and bond market.

By reviewing previous studies, we find that most of the previous studies that dealt with the risks associated with sukuk did not address the disclosure of sukuk risks, which is an important matter that helps investors evaluate their investments and take the appropriate decision regarding them. Therefore, the current study seeks to address this gap through a case study to disclose the risks of sukuk in Qatar Islamic Bank. Qatar Islamic Bank is considered one of the largest banks that issue sukuk in dollars. The bank controls 49% of the Islamic banking market in Qatar. The bank has a plan to issue USD 4 billion of sukuk, of which so far it has issued USD 1.5 billion.

8.5 Disclosure of Sukuk Risks

Disclosure aims to distinguish the phenomenon under study, clarify its features to facilitate the understanding of the intended meaning, and is useful in identifying the main trends and topics of importance due to the increasing demand for more disclosure by the different users of information. The importance of accounting disclosure for banks stems from the nature of the financial services provided by this sector, as it is a mediator between savers and investors and its close connection with the development of economic activities and its contribution to maintaining confidence in the monetary system. Also, disclosure is considered one of the main indicators to judge the soundness of the bank's financial position.

The relationship between the Islamic bank that issues the sukuk and the sukuk holders is based on the agency relationship on the basis of the rule of fines or sharing in profits or losses. The investment of the funds of these sukuk is carried out according to Islamic investment and financing formulas that are different from that in which traditional financial instruments such as bonds and treasury bills are invested. Hence, the nature of the assets corresponding to these sukuk varies, and its impact on the measurement of risks and business results of the process subject of the sukuk. In addition, Islamic sukuk exposes to many risks, and these risks directly affect the issuer of the sukuk and negatively affect its returns and allocations, as well as affect the value of real assets by decrease, and affect the nominal value of the sukuk (Al-Beltagy, 2015).

The financial characteristics of sukuk are similar to traditional securities in general. However, there are structures of sukuk that have fundamentally different financial and credit characteristics and risks and therefore require disclosures that reflect those characteristics as well as reflecting any legitimate considerations related to those characteristics (IFSB, 19). Therefore, the sukuk holders need to increase the accounting disclosure of the sukuk they own in terms of quantity, quality, and appropriate timing to obtain information about those sukuk.

The next paragraph deals with the disclosure of the risks of sukuk in the accounting standards for Islamic financial institutions, the international standards for financial reporting, the standards of the IFSB, and they can be stated as follows.

8.5.1 *Disclosure of the risks of sukuk in the accounting standards for Islamic financial institutions*

The accounting standards issued by the above standards, the Accounting and Auditing Organisation for Islamic Financial Institutions (AAOIFI), so far dealt with the risks of the various Islamic financing formulas to which the sukuk is linked, as shown in Table 8.3.

In addition, the AAOIFI is currently preparing each of the following:

(1) ***Financial Accounting Standard No. 29 Sukuk Issuance***: The standard aims to provide guidance for accounting classification and presentation for sukuk issuances primarily based on the sukuk structure, which may include on balance sheet, as well as off-balance sheet accounting. These classifications depend on the

Table 8.3. Disclosure of risks issued in accounting standards for Islamic financial institutions.

Standard	Explanation
Criterion 2 Murabaha, Murabahah for Purchase Order	In the additional notes to the financial statements, the bank must disclose whether it applies in murabahah to the purchase order the principle of obligation in a promise or a commitment promise (Para. 16)
Mudarabah Financing Standard 3	It should be disclosed in the additional notes whether the bank has made a provision for the impairment of the mudarabah assets during that financial period (Para. 19)
Standard 4 Participation Financing	The additional notes must be disclosed whether the bank has made a provision for the depreciation of its share in the joint financing operations during that period (Para. 17)
Standard 10 Istisna'a and Parallel Istisna'	The bank must disclose in the additional notes about: 1. Additional claims under negotiation and any pending fines as a result of penalty clauses for delayed delivery of the manufacture (Para. 42) 2. The method used to determine the percentage of completion in contracts under implementation (Para. 43) 3. The value of parallel istisna contracts that are still under implementation and the time period covered by these contracts (Para. 44) 4. The value of the istisna'a contracts that were contracted during the current financial period and whose implementation has not started, and the time period covered (Para. 45)
Standard 16 Foreign Currency Transactions and Operations	In the supplementary notes, the bank must disclose what is related to the financial period from the total accumulated unrealized gains, the total accumulated unrealized losses related to net investments in foreign currencies separately, in a separate special item within the terms of equity. This is called the cumulative unrealized gains/losses from transferring net investments in foreign currencies (Para. 23) It must also be disclosed for the differences resulting from the conversion (evaluation) of operations carried out based on the speculation or participation contract in a foreign currency into the currency of the financial statements (Para. 24). In addition to that, the policies followed by the bank in the conversion (valuation) of foreign currency must be disclosed in the statements. Financial and the policies it follows in managing foreign currency risks (Para. 27)

control of such assets comprising power to control and nature of control, i.e., for risks and rewards as well as varying benefits to the institution or the fiduciary responsibility on behalf of the sukuk holders.

(2) ***Financial Accounting Standard No. 34 Financial Reporting for Sukukholders***: This standard aims to establish the principles of accounting and financial reporting for assets and business underlying the sukuk to ensure transparent and fair reporting to all relevant stakeholders, particularly sukuk holders.

The AAOIFI issued Financial Accounting Standard No. 34 Financial Reporting for sukuk holders, while Financial Accounting Standard No. 29 Sukuk Issuance is still in preparation. However, Standard 34 and the draft of Standard 29 do not include details of the risks to which Islamic sukuk are exposed and how to disclose them. At the same time, the question is whether these proposed standards are adopted as part of the national legislative standards and frameworks for Islamic financial institutions, but in general, sukuk originators are not always financial services companies, and therefore they will not be required to use AAOIFI standards that Islamic financial institutions in their countries apply.

8.5.2 *International financial reporting standards IFRS*

The IFRS7 standard and the IFRS9 standard dealt with disclosing the various risks to which traditional financial instruments are exposed, such as currency risk, interest rate risk, market risk, liquidity risk, credit risk, and other price risks. Which is the risk that the fair value or future cash flows of a financial instrument will fluctuate due to changes in market prices (other than currency risk and interest rate risk), whether these changes are caused by factors specific to a particular financial instrument or other factors affecting all similar financial instruments traded in the market.

In addition, the risk disclosure is categorized as:

(1) Qualitative disclosure: For each type of risk, a disclosure must be made:

- Exposure to risks and how they arise.
- The objectives, policies, and procedures of risk management and the methods used to measure risks, provided that this disclosure

is in the financial statements or through a reference link between the statements and some other reports such as the management report or the risk report.

(2) Quantitative disclosure: For each type of risk, it must be disclosed:

- A summary of quantitative data regarding its exposure to those risks at the end of the reporting period, and this disclosure should be based on information provided internally to senior management personnel of the facility.

Concentrations of risks arising from financial instruments that have similar characteristics and are similarly affected by changes in economic or other conditions. The disclosure must include:

- A description of how management determines concentrations.
- Describe the common characteristic that defines each concentration (e.g., counter party, geographic region, currency, or market).
- Offer amount of risk associated with all financial instruments that share this feature.

8.5.3 *IFSB standards*

The IFSB issued Standard 19 of 2017, which is the guiding principles for disclosure requirements for Islamic capital market products (sukuk and collective investment programs) to provide a basis for supervisory authorities to set rules and guidelines related to disclosure requirements for Islamic capital market products, especially sukuk and Islamic collective investment programs. The approach of the standard has been adopted that most of the regulatory and supervisory authorities that regulate Islamic capital markets also regulate traditional capital markets and have already adopted regulatory provisions based on those standards, so the standard deals only with areas in which Islamic financial products require additional and different disclosures about those products. Conventional financial by specifying all relevant disclosures common to Islamic and conventional financial products and the standard addresses many risks, including the following:

(1) *The dangers of Islamic law*: Many of the paragraphs dealt with the dangers of non-compliance with Islamic law, including:

Para. 32: Disclosures related to risks should include any risks resulting from non-compliance with the provisions and principles of Islamic Sharia, as well as any other risks, e.g., legal risks. Sufficient disclosures should be made regarding the Sharia aspects of the sukuk to allow for an informed judgement on the initial and continuing compliance with Islamic Sharia provisions.

Para. 62: It happens that there is a need for a legal opinion on the sukuk that may arise after their issuance, for example, when the assets or activities concerned change or if the need for judicial implementation or restructuring arises.

Para. 63: It must be disclosed to investors about how Sharia requirements are taken into account within the state's legal system. This matter may be important even if the investor is not observing the provisions of Islamic Sharia because of the possibility of raising objections to these foundations by others.

Para. 64: The disclosure must specify the Sharia committee or the Sharia advisory bodies that expressed their opinion on the extent of the sukuk's compliance with the provisions and principles of Islamic Sharia and should identify the participating Sharia scholars.

(2) The risks of Islamic financing formulas

Para. 88: The summary of the principal contracts that make up the structure of the sukuk should be disclosed and, in particular, should describe terms of significant Sharia or legal significance and the distribution or transfer of risks (for example, any arrangements relating to surety, guarantee, takaful, or insurance).

(3) *Legal and political risks*: The structure of the sukuk should be described clearly enough to enable the investor to understand and evaluate any risks associated with it, including any legal risks related to the multi-party transactions within the sukuk structure under the agreements.

Para. 82: The right of recourse guaranteed to the holders of the sukuk, the trustee, or any other party acting on their behalf on the assets represented by the sukuk or their returns must be disclosed.

Para. 88: The summary of the principal contracts that make up the structure of the sukuk should be disclosed and, in particular, should describe terms of significant Sharia or legal significance and the distribution or transfer of risks (for example, any arrangements relating to surety, guarantee, takaful or insurance).

Para. 109: The disclosure should state whether the obligor of the sukuk has conventional debts (bank bonds and loans) or not must be disclosed.

A. If the sukuk includes a provision requiring the generalization of default, it will be activated as a result of defaulting on traditional debts.
B. If the traditional debts include a provision for generalizing default, it will be activated as a result of defaulting the sukuk.

Para. 113: The effect of restrictions on property rights in the assets represented by the sukuk structure should be disclosed upon judicial execution, for example, if the assets in question could not be acquired and then sold freely upon judicial execution.

Para. 114: The mechanisms that will be taken to pursue the right of recourse against the obligor of the sukuk or assets upon judicial execution must be disclosed. In addition, the right to dispose of the assets concerned after the occurrence of default should be disclosed (including who is entitled or who will enjoy its use and who may or should transfer and under any conditions).

Para. 115: If there is uncertainty regarding the manner of interpretation or enforcement of key provisions in sukuk contracts that the courts have not legally tested, that risk should be disclosed.

It is clear from the foregoing that the disclosure of the risks of sukuk is distributed between:

(1) IFRS focused on the various risks to which conventional and Islamic financial instruments are exposed in general, such as market risk, credit risk, liquidity risk, and other risks.

(2) Accounting standards for Islamic financial institutions that focus on the risks of Islamic financing formulas in general, on which sukuk are issued.
(3) The standards of the IFSB, which focused on the risks of non-compliance with Islamic law and the legal and legal risks to which sukuk are exposed.

Noting that the accounting standards for Islamic financial institutions and the standards of the IFSB apply to Islamic financial institutions, but in general, the originators of sukuk are not always financial services companies, and therefore, they will not be required to use AAOIFI standards that Islamic financial institutions in their countries apply.

8.6 Case Study

In this study, the researchers address the disclosure of the risks of sukuk by Qatar Islamic Bank. Qatar Islamic Bank is the first Islamic bank in Qatar, which began its work in 1982 and is still the largest Islamic banking institution in the country, as it currently holds 49% of the Islamic banking sector in the country and a share of about 10% of the total banking market. The group has issued permanent sukuk eligible for inclusion in the first tier of capital, amounting to 2 billion Qatari riyals during the year 2015. These sukuk are without collateral, and the dividends are discretionary, non-accumulative, and accumulative. The group has the right not to pay the profits, and the sukuk holders do not have the right to claim the profit on the sukuk. These sukuk have no maturity date and are classified as equity. In the year 2016, the group raised the additional core capital by issuing permanent sukuk in the amount of 2 billion Qatari riyals with an expected, agreed profit rate of 5.25% to be reset every year.

Qatar Islamic Bank has approved a program to issue sukuk in USD, with a total value of USD 4 billion, and it is listed on the Euronext Dublin stock exchange. Qatar Bank is the first Islamic bank in the world market to introduce Islamic instruments through the issuance of sukuk worth USD 800 million listed on the Taipei Stock Exchange. This was the largest amount of its kind issued by the Qatar Islamic Bank to diversify strategic funding sources. In October 2020, it successfully completed the issuance of a five-year sukuk amounting to USD 750 million at a profit rate of 1.95% annually. These sukuk denominated in USD include a fixed and variable profit rate, and the average profit paid in 2020 is 3.47%, while the average profit paid in 2019 is 3.53%. The terms of the two issues include the transfer of some specific assets and include musharaka financing assets and leasehold financing assets and investments that are compliant with Islamic law. The group exchanges any assets to the bank's company for the issuance of limited bonds and the Qatar Islamic Bank for Sukuk Company Limited, which are two subsidiaries of the group.

The annual reports of Qatar Islamic Bank for the years 2019 and 2020 disclosed five types of risks in general: credit risk, market risk, liquidity risk, operational risk, and other risks. As for the sukuk, the bank disclosed its risks as follows:

(1) *Credit risk*: Qatar Islamic Bank disclosed, in a quantitative form, the maximum exposure to credit risks before collateral held or any other credit enhancements (financing assets), exposure to credit risk for assets on the balance sheet, and concentration of credit risk for financial assets with credit risk exposure to geographical sectors. While the bank has disclosed descriptively that all financing assets meet all criteria, all future payments will likely occur.
(2) *Liquidity risk*: The bank disclosed descriptively that the bank maintains a group of high-quality liquid assets, which consist of Qatar Central Bank sukuk, short-term investments, etc., while the bank disclosed in a quantitative form about the maturity analysis of various financial instruments, including sukuk (from three months to three years) and maturity analysis of undiscounted cash flows (from three months to three years).
(3) *Market risk*: Qatar Islamic Bank has disclosed, in a quantitative form, exposure to profit risks for non-trading portfolios (including sukuk), while the bank will not make any descriptive disclosure about the market risks.
(4) Qatar Islamic Bank has not made quantitative and descriptive disclosures about operational risks and other risks to which the sukuk is exposed.
(5) Qatar Islamic Bank disclosed the financing assets related to the issued sukuk (murabahah financing assets — ijarah financing assets). In order to verify the hedging of the sukuk, the

researchers calculated the ratio of the sukuk obligations on the bank to the financing assets related to the sukuk issued by the bank, and they found that the ratio of sukuk obligations to financing assets was 88.23% and 88.75% for the years 2019 and 2020, respectively, which indicates that there is hedging to protect the value of the sukuk until it is filtered.

It is clear from the above that the disclosure of the sukuk was through the disclosure of the risks of assets and liabilities of Qatar Islamic Bank in general and the disclosure of credit risks, liquidity risks, and market risks without other risks. The focus in the disclosure was on quantitative disclosure, while for descriptive disclosure, the risk profile of sukuk was limited. Therefore, the researchers propose a framework for disclosing the risks of sukuk.

8.7 Proposed Framework for Disclosing the Risks of Sukuk

The risks of the various Islamic financing formulas directly infringe on the sukuk dependent on them and thus affect their market value in the financial markets and may lead to the erosion of their nominal value. In accordance with international financial reporting standards, especially IFRS7 and IFRS9, the risks to which financial instruments are exposed are classified into three main categories: credit risk, market risk, and liquidity risk, which must be disclosed. Noting that the IFRS disclosure framework does not cover all the stakeholder needs of Islamic financial institutions, it would be useful if there were additional guidance for preparers of IFRS in two specific areas:

- First, guidance on the application of IFRS when accounting for Islamic financing instruments.
- Second, guidance on additional disclosures should be made for the benefit of stakeholders seeking information about Sharia compliance.

The Asian Oceanian Standard Setters Group has established a working group to communicate with the International Accounting Standards Board on applying IFRS to Islamic finance. This is an important step forward in introducing Islamic finance more clearly within the framework of IFRS. A prime example of this framework developed by the Bahrain-based AAOIFI, which targets these institutions, is an institution that only uses financial instruments that comply with Islamic law. However, IFRS has the advantage of international recognition and use, making it the most appropriate framework for global institutions with multinational stakeholders (PWC, 2019).

IFRS7 and IFRS9 dealt with the disclosure of the various risks to which conventional financial instruments are exposed, such as currency risk, interest rate risk, market risk, liquidity risk, credit risk, and other price risks, which are the risk that the fair value or future cash flows of the financial instrument will fluctuate due to other changes in market prices (other than the risk of currency and interest rate risk), whether these changes are caused by factors specific to a particular financial instrument or an issuer or from other factors affecting all similar financial instruments traded in the market. In addition, risk disclosure has been categorized into qualitative and quantitative disclosure. It is important to note that IFRS does not prohibit entities from making additional voluntary disclosures in their financial statements, provided they are not misleading or do not conflict with the information required by IFRS standards. IFRS requires additional disclosure if compliance with international financial reporting standards alone is not sufficient to enable users to understand the impact of transactions and events on the company. This is similar to the existing paragraphs on the review of public sector units in the international auditing standards. Considering the privacy of Islamic financial instruments and in the absence of a perspective for Islamic financial instruments, the IFRS is applicable in all respects to Islamic financial instruments.

The researchers classified the disclosure of sukuk risks into two types: qualitative or descriptive risks and quantitative risks, as shown in Table 8.4.

8.8 Conclusion and Recommendations

The financial characteristics of sukuk are similar to traditional securities in general, but there are structures of sukuk that have fundamentally different financial and credit characteristics and risks and

Table 8.4. Disclosure of sukuk risks.

Risks	Disclosure rating	Pointer
Credit risk	Qualitative disclosure	• Information on the method used by the entity to disclose defaults on various financial instruments • Assumptions about the recovery rate (i.e., the number of financial assets that have returned to a state of payment) after a default in the payment of a financial asset (pending on the occurrence of recovery) • Information on how the entity monitors the method of measuring the loss allowance that was previously disclosed (information about the compliance of the adjusted financial assets with the controls for which the loss allowance was adjusted to be measured at an amount equal to the expected credit losses over the life (i.e., the rate of deterioration) • Disclosing information about the basis of the inputs, assumptions, and estimation methods used to apply the landing requirements. It may include assumptions and inputs used to measure credit losses since initial recognition such as internal historical information or rating reports, assumptions about the expected life of financial instruments and the timing of the sale of the collateral • Disclosure of the reasons for the changes in the loss allowance, whether it is due to the volume of financial instruments purchased or created or to the severity of the expected credit losses • Disclosure of the names and external credit rating institutions used to determine asset risk weights • Describe the main types of guarantees and other means of mitigating credit risks that banks dealing with sukuk obtain, such as the margin of seriousness, deposit, cash or profit-sharing investment accounts, pledged assets, sukuk, and guarantees provided by a third party
	Quantitative disclosure	• Disclosure of overdue receivables, impaired financial assets, policies, and practices related to forming provisions for financial assets losses

(Continued)

Table 8.4. (*Continued*)

Risks	Disclosure rating	Pointer
		• Total exposure to credit risk and average total exposure to credit risk over the period in terms of geographic region, counterparty, industry, remaining contractual maturity period for each of the sukuk categories and a statement of the percentages of amounts financed from bank capital, current accounts, and profit-sharing investment accounts • Disclosure of the main types of collateral, their size held as collateral and other credit enhancements, and their compliance with legitimacy to mitigate risks along with the policies related to assets leased under Ijarah Muntahia Bittamleek and how important it is in terms of the loss allowance • Describe the main types of guarantees and other means of mitigating credit risks that banks dealing with sukuk obtain, such as the margin of seriousness, deposit, cash or profit-sharing investment accounts, pledged assets, sukuk, and guarantees provided by a third party • Disclosure of the policies and procedures for evaluating guarantees and ensuring their feasibility, along with the policies and procedures for leased assets under Ijarah Muntahia Bittamleek when the assets are not convertible into cash by the issuing bank, and the policies for disposing of these assets or using them in the bank's transactions must be disclosed • Disclosure of the outstanding amounts of total assets according to the type of collateral held by banks. Disclosure of the number of provisions for losses and changes therein during the year
Liquidity risk	Qualitative disclosure	• Clarification of the frameworks used by management in disclosing liquidity risks to deal with risks for each type of sukuk on the basis of total current accounts, unrestricted investment accounts, and restricted investment accounts • Disclosing the policies that deal with liquidity, taking into account the ease of obtaining funds in accordance with the provisions and principles of Islamic Sharia and the diversity of sources of funds

Table 8.4. (*Continued*)

Risks	Disclosure rating	Pointer
	Quantitative disclosure	• Disclosure of an analysis of the maturity of financial obligations, which shows the remaining contractual maturities. In addition, the facility determines the appropriate time ranges, such as not exceeding one or three months • Disclosure of an analysis of the maturity of the financial assets that you hold to manage liquidity such as financial assets that can be sold easily or we expect to generate cash inflows to meet the cash outflows • Disclosure that the entity has borrowing facilities, standby credit facilities, or maintains deposits to meet liquidity needs • Disclosure of indicators of exposure to liquidity risk, such as the ratios of short-term assets to short-term liabilities, ratios of liquid assets or financing fluctuations • Maturity analysis for financing and for the various categories of funds — the current account, the absolute investment account, the restricted investment account — according to the different maturity pools
Market risk	Qualitative disclosure	• Disclosure of an appropriate framework for managing market risks, including preparing reports on all available-for-sale assets, including assets that do not have an active market and that are subject to price fluctuations • Disclosure of indicators of exposure to market risks such as: foreign exchange risk, commodity risk, ratio of net open positions in foreign currencies to capital, ratio of net open positions in commodities to capital, ratio of net open positions in capital contributions to capital, risk capital in the trading book and market risk around the trading positions of the sukuk

(*Continued*)

Table 8.4. (*Continued*)

Risks	Disclosure rating	Pointer
	Quantitative disclosure	• Disclose the sensitivity analysis for each type of market risk (such as the risk of interest rate, equity prices or commodity • Disclosure of sensitivity analysis for each currency to which the entity has significant exposure • Disclosure of the effect of a decrease in a specific stock market index, commodity price, or other risk variables on the increase or decrease of the sukuk or assets to which the guarantee applies. Prices to which the sukuk are exposed, showing how the profit or loss and equity will be affected by changes in the relevant risk variable

Source: Gharib (2016), Hassan (2016); IFRS 7; IFRS 9.

therefore require disclosures that reflect those characteristics as well as reflecting any legitimate considerations related to those characteristics. Conventional bonds, the regulatory and supervisory authorities should make their disclosure requirements based on the principles of disclosure of those traditional bonds (IFSB, 19). Islamic sukuk is exposed to both systemic risks that affect conventional and Islamic securities and financial instruments and unsystematic risks common to conventional financial instruments and investment instruments. Irregular risks, especially sukuk only. Due to the nature of sukuks, such as the risks of sukuk issuers, the risks of sukuk in-kind assets. The requirements for disclosing sukuk in general and sukuk risks were distributed among the IFRS, which focused on the various risks to which conventional and Islamic financial instruments are exposed in general, such as market risks, credit risks, liquidity risks, and other risks. Second, the accounting standards for Islamic financial institutions focused on the risks of Islamic financing formulas in general, on which sukuk are issued. Third, the criteria of the IFSB, which focused on the risks of non-compliance with Islamic law and the legal risks to which sukuk are exposed. All IFRS should be used in the development of accounting standards dealing with Islamic financial instruments, and at the same time, there must be coordination and convergence between international financial reporting standards IFRS and accounting and auditing standards for Islamic financial institutions AAOIFI to enhance Islamic finance at the global level, which increases confidence of investors (Hanefah & Mohammed, 2013).

This study aimed to illustrate the different types of risks to which sukuk are exposed and how to disclose sukuk risks in different international standards such as IFRS, IFSB Standards, and AAOIFI Standards. It attempted to obtain field evidence about the level of banks' disclosure of sukuk risks through studying the annual reports of Qatar Islamic Bank, in addition to trying to propose a framework for disclosing sukuk risks based on previous studies and accounting standards for Islamic financial institutions and international standards for financial reporting. The researchers concluded that the disclosure of sukuk risks is divided between the international financial reporting standards, which focused on the various risks to which conventional and Islamic financial instruments are exposed in general, such as market risk, credit risk, liquidity risk, and other risks. Second, the accounting standards for Islamic financial institutions focus on the risks of Islamic financing formulas on the basis of which sukuk are issued. Third, the standards of the IFSB, which focused on the risks of non-compliance with Islamic law and the legal and legal risks to which sukuk are exposed. Noting that the accounting standards for Islamic financial institutions and the standards of the IFSB apply to Islamic financial institutions, but in general, the originators of sukuk are not always financial services firms and therefore would not be required to use the AAOIFI standards applied by Islamic financial institutions in their countries.

The researchers studied the case of Qatar Islamic Bank when disclosing the risks of sukuk for the years 2019 and 2020 by examining the annual reports and the bank's website. The researchers found that the disclosure of the sukuk was through the disclosure of the risks of assets and liabilities of Qatar Islamic Bank in general and the disclosure of credit risks, liquidity risks, and market risks. Also, disclosure of sukuk risks was limited and were quantitative. The descriptive disclosure of the risks of sukuk is very limited and almost non-existent in the financial reports. The researchers suggest that the disclosure of sukuk and the risks should be in specific paragraphs within the IFRS. Therefore, the international standards for financial reporting must contain paragraphs that take into account the privacy of Islamic financial instruments. In the absence of a perspective for tools of Islamic finance, the IFRS is applicable in all respects to Islamic financial instruments. The researchers classified the disclosure of sukuk risks into qualitative or descriptive risks and quantitative risks.

This study has important implications for academics, investors, policymakers, and regulators. For academics, it contributes to the debate about the risks of sukuk and how the issuing institutions disclose them. Researchers can rely on this research to further investigate the various effects of disclosing the risks of sukuk on financial and investment decisions. Investors and financial analysts who deal with Islamic financial instruments can benefit from the results of this study for the impact of sukuk risks and their disclosure when making their investment decisions. Financial analysts must take into account the various risks to which sukuk are exposed before recommending investment decisions or not. Also, the accounting standard-issuing bodies must disclose the sukuk risks unified in one standard and not separated in the standards of the various standards-issuing bodies around the world. In particular, the AAOIFI should take into account the standards under preparation, such as Financial Accounting Standard No. 29 Sukuk Issuance and Financial Accounting Standard No. 34 Financial Reporting for sukuk holders, when amended in the future. In this way, they would include measurement and detailed disclosures of the risks to which the sukuk is exposed.

Research Limitations: This study is exploratory and therefore seeks to identify the risks related to the issuance of sukuk and to disclose these risks by reviewing the previous literature and accounting standards issued by different authorities. The study also dealt with the disclosure of sukuk risks by only one bank (Qatar Islamic Bank). Given these limitations, future research can study and examine the impact of the nature of the institution's activity issuing the sukuk on the disclosure of sukuk risks and the effect of applying the Financial Accounting Standard No. 34 Financial Reporting sukuk holders on disclosing the risks of sukuk. They could also study the relationship between disclosure of sukuk risks and dividends and the impact of disclosing the risks of sukuk on regulating the liquidity of sukuk in the financial markets.

References

Abdul Karim, K. (2007). Islamic financial engineering. *Journal of King Abdulaziz University: Islamic Economics*, *20*, 3–46.

Abdul-Rahim, A. (2013). An integrative approach for understanding Islamic home financing adoption in Malaysia. *International Journal of Bank Marketing*, *31*(7), 544–573.

Abeer, F. Al-A. (2014). *Managing Financial Risks in Islamic Banking and Finance*. Amman: Dar Al-Fikr for Publishing and Distribution.

Al-Ajili, S. Z. (2016). Financial engineering strategies in hedging and risk management of Islamic sukuk: An applied study on Islamic government sukuk. *Journal of Economics and Business Studies*, *4*(1), 101–128.

Al-Beltagy, M. (2015). Accounting problems related to sukuk issues, tunisian association of Islamic economy, Symposium "Islamic Sukuk between Sharia Controls and Legal and Accounting Provisions" Tunis, 28/29 March, 2015.

Aloui, C., Hammoudeh, S., & Hamida, H. B. (2015a). Co-movement between sharia stocks and Sukuk in the GCC markets: A time-frequency analysis. *Journal of International Financial Markets, Institutions & Money*, *34*, 69–79. Doi: 10. 1016/j.intfin.2014.11.003.

Aloui, C., Hammoudeh, S., & Hamida, H. B. (2015b). Global factors driving structural changes in the co-movement between Sharia stocks and Sukuk in the Gulf Cooperation Council countries. *North American Journal of Economics and Finance*, *31*, 311–329. Doi: 10.1016/j.najef.2014.12.002.

Al Kayal, N. F. (2017). *The Impact of Islamic Sukuk Financing on the Profitability of Islamic Banks: An Applied Study on a Sample of Emirati Islamic Banks, a Project Submitted for Obtaining a License in Islamic Economics*. Balad Al Sham university, College of Sharia and Law.

Alsaeed, K. (2012). *Sukuk Issuance in Saudi Arabia: Recent Trends and Positive Expectations*. Doctoral Thesis, Durham University. Available at Durham E-Thesis, http://ethesis.dur.ac.uk/3502/.

Alsayed, O. (2013). Sukuk risk: Analysis and management. *European Journal of Applied Social Sciences Research (EJASSR)*, *1*(3), 67–76.

Alswaidan, M. W., Daynes, A., & Pasgas, P. (2017). Understanding and evaluation of risk in Sukuk structures. *Journal of Islamic Accounting and Business Research*, *8*(4), 389–405. Doi: 10.1108/JIABR-05-2015-0021.

Azmat, S., Skully, M., & Brown, K. (2015). Can Islamic banking ever become Islamic? *Pacific-Basin Finance Journal*, *34*, 253–272.

Badran, A. J. (2014). *Sukuk as a Tool for Financing Between Theory and Practice*. Egypt: Center for Jurisprudence and Economic Studies.

Ben Amara, N. (2011). Islamic Sukuk and its role in the development of the Islamic financial market the experience of the international Islamic financial market — Bahrain. *Al-Bahith Review, 9*(9), 253–264.

Bitar, M., Hassan, M. K., & Hippler, W. J. (2018). The determinants of Islamic bank capital decisions. *Emerging Markets Review, 35*, 48–68.

Bouhraoua, S. M. (2015). Shari'a problems related to Sukuk issuances" Symposium "Islamic Sukuk between Shari'a Controls and Legal and Accounting Requirements" Tunis 28/29 March, 2015.

Cakir, S. & Raei, F. (2007). Sukuk vs. Euro bonds: Is there a difference in value-at-risk. IMF Working Paper, WP/07/237.

Chang, Z. Y. (2020). *Measuring Risk and Return of Sustainable and Responsible Investment (Sri) Sukuk in Malaysia.* Undergraduate Thesis submitted in partial fulfillment of the requirements for the WHARTON RESEARCH SCHOLARS. University of Pennsylvania.

Diaw, A. K. (2011). *Performance/Commodity-Linked Sukuk for Private and Public Sector Funding: Some Proposed Models* (Doctoral Dissertation). International Centre for Education in Islamic Finance (INCEIF).

Dimitris, K., Naifar, N., & Dimitrios, D. (2016). Islamic financial markets and global crises: Contagion or decoupling? *Economic Model, 57*, 36–46.

Echchabi, A., Aziz, H. A., & Idriss, U. (2018). The impact of sukuk financing on economic growth: The case of GCC countries. *International Journal of Financial Services Management, 9*(1), 60–69.

Feigl, A. H. (2015). *Assessing the Role of Islamic Sukuk in Developing the Islamic Capital Market — The Malaysian Experience as a Model.* Master's thesis, Mohamed Khider University of Biskra, Algeria.

Godlewski, C. J., Turk-Ariss, R., & Weill, L. (2016). Do the type of Sukuk and choice of shari'a scholar matter? *Journal of Economic Behavior & Organization, 132*, 63–76.

Ghareeb, H. A. (2016). Intellectual framework for managing the risks of financial instruments according to the requirements of transparency of financial statements in Islamic banks. *Journal of Accounting Thought, Department of Accounting and Auditing, Faculty of Commerce, 20*(1), 935–986.

Hasan, R., Ahmad, A. U. F., & Parveen, T. (2019). Sukuk risks — A structured review of theoretical research. *Journal of Islamic Accounting and Business Research, 10*(1), 35–49. Doi: 10.1108/JIABR-06-2015-0026.

Hassan, M. Z. F. (2016). The implications of applying the financial engineering approach in increasing the quality of accounting disclosure of financial instruments. *The Scientific Journal of Business and Environmental Studies*, *7*(3), 908–948.

Hassan, M. K., Paltrinieri, A., Dreassi, A., Miani, S., & Sclip, A. (2018). The determinants of co-movement dynamics between Sukuk and conventional bonds. *The Quarterly Review of Economics and Finance*, *68*, 73–84.

Hanefah, M. & Mohammed S. A. (2013). The need of accounting standards for Islamic financial institutions: Evidence from AAOIFI. *Journal of Islamic Accounting and Business Research*, *4*(1), 64–76. Doi: 10.1108/17590811311314294.

Hindi, M. I. (1998). *Managing Markets and Financial Institutions: Commercial Banks, Islamic Banks, Investment Funds, Capital Markets and Choice Markets*. Tanta: Language ASR Center for Computer and Printing.

Hindi, M. I. (2006). Modern thought in financial engineering series 1 risk management using securitisation and derivatives part one: Securitisation. The Ismaili knowledge facility first edition.

Ibrahim, M. H. (2015). Issues in Islamic banking and finance: Islamic banks, Shari'ah-compliant investment and sukuk. *Pacific-Basin Finance Journal*, *34*, 185–191.

Iqbal, M. & Mirakhor, A. (2007). *An Introduction to Islamic Finance: Theory and Practice*. Chichester: John Wiley & Sons.

Khan, A., Saeed, S., Zubair, Z. A., & Hussain, I. (2020). Credit risk in asset based Sukuk. *Journal of Business and Social Review in Emerging Economies*, *6*(1), 239–260.

Khan, T. A. & Ahmad, H. (2003). *Risk Management Analysis of Issues in the Islamic Financial Industry*. Jeddah: Islamic Research and Training Institute, Islamic Development Bank.

Kunduz, A. A. & Al-Sahlawi, A. M. (2017). The risks of Islamic finance tools. Bait Al-Mashura Magazine, Qatar, Issue 7, October.

Kurniawan, T. & Ab Rahman, A. (2019). Project Based Sukuk (PBS) and its implementation in economic development in Indonesia. *AL-'ADALAH*, *16*(1), 41–66.

Lackmann, B. (2015). Types of Sukuk (Islamic bonds) and history of Japanese company issuance. *Nomura Journal of Capital Markets*, *6*(3), 1–20.

Lahsasna, A., Hassan, M. K., & Ahmad, R. (2018). Types of Sukuk, their classification and structure in Islamic capital market. In: *Forward Lease Sukuk in Islamic Capital Markets*. Palgrave Macmillan, Cham., Springer International Publishing, pp. 49–85.

Majid, H. A., Shahimi, S., & Abdullah, M. (2011). Sukuk defaults and its implication: A case study of Malaysian capital market. 8th International Conference on Islamic Economics and Finance, Doha, Qatar.

Maqalaty, K. (2015). *Risk Management of Islamic Financing Formulas, the Case of Al-Baraka Bank of Algeria.* Master's Thesis, Oum El Bouaghi University, Algeria.

Moody's Investors Service (April 2006). A Guide to Rating Islamic Financial Institutions.

Naifar, N., Mroua, M., & Bahloul, S. (2017). Do regional and global uncertainty factors affect differently the conventional bonds and sukuk? New evidence. *Pacific-Basin Finance Journal*, *41*, 65–74.

Nagano, M. (2017). Sukuk issuance and information asymmetry: Why do firms issue Sukuk? *Pacific-Basin Finance Journal*, *42*, 142–157.

Nanaeva, Z. K. (2010). *How Risky Sukuk are: Comparative Analysis of Risks Associated with Sukuk and Conventional Bonds.* Dissertation submitted in partial fulfillment of the degree of MSc in Finance and Banking, British university in Dubai.

Noor, N. & Shahimi, S. (2013). Credit risk management for Sukuk: A case study of debt based Sukuk. *Prosiding Perkem VIII, JILID*, (3), 1259–1271. https://www.pwc.co.uk/assets/pdf/open-to-comparison-islamic-finance-and-ifrs.pdf.

Olson, D. & Zoubi, T. (2017). Convergence in bank performance for commercial and Islamic banks during and after the global financial crisis. *The Quarterly Review of Economics and Finance*, *65*, 71–87.

Onder, Y. K. (2016). Asset backed contracts and sovereign risk. *Journal of Economic Behavior and Organization*, *132*, 237–252. Doi: 10.1016/j.jebo.2016.10.006.

Qurumi, H. (2014). The Islamic Sukuk industry: Reality and prospects, a paper presented to the third international conference on Islamic finance. *The Role of Islamic Finance in Economic and Social Development*, *5*(2), 141–160.

Qizam, I. & Fong, M. (2019). Developing financial disclosure quality in Sukuk and bond market: Evidence from Indonesia, Malaysia, and Australia. *Borsa Istanbul Review*, *19*(3), 228–248.

Reilly, F. K. and Brown, K. C. (2012). *Investment Analysis & Portfolio Management.* (10th ed.). Mason, OH: Cengage Learning.

Reuters, T. (2017). Abu Dhabi's Dana gas to propose $700 million Sukuk restructuring. http://www.reuters.com/article/dana-gas-Sukuk/abu-dhabis-dana-gas-to-propose-700-million-Sukukrestructuring-idUSL8N1JA1I.

Saeed, A. & Salah, O. (2013). Development of Sukuk: Pragmatic and idealist approaches to Sukuk structures'. *Journal of International Banking Law and Regulation*, *28*(1), 41–52.

Suleiman, A. S. (2020). Sukuk risks. *Journal of Islamic Finance, Egyptian Association for Islamic Finance*, *5*, 49–50.

Uluyol, B. (2021). A comprehensive empirical and theoretical literature survey of Islamic bonds (Sukuk). *Journal of Sustainable Finance & Investment*, 1–23.

Usmani, M. T. (2002). *An Introduction to Islamic Finance*. The Hague: Kluwer Law International.

Zakaria, N. B., Isa, M. A. M., & Abidin, R. A. Z. (2012). The construct of Sukuk, rating and default risk. *Procedia-Social and Behavioral Sciences*, *65*, 662–667. https://www.pwc.co.uk/assets/pdf/open-to-comparison-islamic-finance-and-ifrs.pdf.

https://doi.org/10.1142/9781800612426_0009

Chapter 9

Web-Based Corporate Risk Disclosure Practices in Islamic Banks: Empirical Evidence from Listed Islamic Banks in Egypt

Elhassan Kotb Abdelrahman Radwan and Nada Omar Hassan Ali

Abstract

This study explores the status of the online risk disclosure practices on the listed Islamic banks in the Egyptian exchange market. Manual content analysis was employed as a research approach to examine the practices of the online risk disclosure for the three listed Islamic banks in Egypt, and based on a prior study, it developed a risk index composed of 10 main categories and a total of 61 sub-items as a research tool. The empirical analysis presents that all listed Islamic banks in the Egyptian exchange market have websites and all these banks report risk information in their published online reports (full annual report and full financial report). Furthermore, the results provide confirmatory evidence that there is a high adherence by all listed Islamic banks in Egypt to the mandatory risk disclosure requirements on their websites, while there is a low level of voluntary risk disclosure on the websites of these banks as well; in addition, the study pointed out that Al Baraka Bank has the highest average (67.2%) of online risk disclosure level among all Islamic banks, followed by Faisal Islamic Bank with an average of 65.5%, and finally, Abu Dhabi Islamic Bank came in the last place with an average of 60.6%. What's more, the yielded data show that the total average level of online risk disclosure of the Islamic listed banks in Egypt is 64.5%.

Finally, the results of this study outline that there are no significant differences between the levels of online risk disclosure at the level of the common categories for all Islamic listed banks in Egypt. The limitations of this study are as follows: the way the content analysis was conducted; in its reliance on the websites and the published online reports for examining risk disclosure information; due to its focus on the financial and non-financial risks; due to its focus on Islamic listed banks in Egypt; and due to its focus on the context of the Egyptian environment.

Keywords: Islamic, Annual Reports, Content Analysis, Disclosure Index, Bank, Internet Financial Reporting, Websites, Online, Corporate Reporting and Disclosure.

9.1 Introduction

Recently, to satisfy the needs of all interested parties for financial and nonfinancial information, several companies shifted their disclosure from just providing results of financial reporting to a whole other variety of topics, and risk reporting is considered one of these topics (Eccles *et al.*, 2001). Hence, risk disclosure has become a vital component of corporate disclosure practices; recently, examining and investigating corporate risk disclosure (CRD) practices has received huge interest. However, there are many companies and institutions that desire to share the risk information with their stakeholders who need high-quality risk information to evaluate the future economic performance of the company and make their investment decisions. Another key fact to remember is that the information and communication technology sector has witnessed an increasing development in all fields, especially the tremendous expansion of the Internet. Nowadays, about 70% of large companies now rely on the Internet as a medium for information dissemination (Khan, 2006). Hence, the Internet is one of the most used technologies in the current era because of its different benefits in all fields and levels. Regarding the banking institutions, these banks tended to use the Internet intensity to disclose their financial and non-financial information on their websites for several reasons. First, the Internet is a major tool for transmitting information today; second, it is not expensive; third, it deals with a huge number of the national and international audience; fourth, it provides more flexibility in the nature and quantity of the reported information; finally, the Internet introduces the disclosed information to the interested parties at any time and at any place.

Therefore, banks significantly rely on the Internet for reporting their information to help their stakeholders in obtaining the needed information at any time and at any place to make their investment decisions. In Egypt, banks are one of the main financial institutions; furthermore, they are considered one of the most important sectors that affect Egyptian economic life, as their performance represents a major cornerstone of other sectors and the Egyptian environment entirely. Thus, it is important to determine the extent to which the listed Islamic banks in Egypt disclose risk information on their websites that satisfy the needs of Egyptian and foreign interested parties in making their investment decisions rationally and evaluating the future position of these banks in the context of Egyptian environment that may enhance Egyptian financial sector and the national economy as well. So, this work tries to fulfill this gap by answering the following main research question: "What are the levels of online risk disclosure practices by the listed Islamic banks in Egypt?".

This study aims basically to identify the status of the risk disclosure practices on the Internet by the listed Islamic banks in the Egyptian exchange market. To achieve this main objective, this study uses manual content analysis as a research approach and develops a risk index as a research tool composed of 10 main categories and a total of 61 sub-items based on a prior study. In addition, the current study provides a brief overview of the concept and the nature of corporate reporting, internet corporate reporting, CRD, disclosure indices, and the Islamic banking industry, outlines the concept and types of risk, and also reviews the core literature on the internet corporate reporting and corporate risk disclosure in the Egyptian Islamic banking industry.

The findings concluded that Al Baraka Bank has the highest average (67.2%) of online risk disclosure level among all Islamic banks, followed by Faisal Islamic Bank with an average of 65.5%; finally, Abu Dhabi Islamic Bank came in the last place with an average of 60.6%. Additionally, the results also pointed out that the most reported categories by listed Islamic banks on their websites were the financial risks, reserves, and segment information with 100% rate, while the business risks, financial techniques risk of Islamic banks, and operational risks were the lowest reported categories by these banks. The results further revealed that the average level of online risk disclosure of the Islamic listed banks in Egypt was 64.5%. Moreover, the results showed that the highest categories, which were reported by all listed Islamic banks in Egypt, were financial risks, reserves, and accounting policies; however, the least disclosed categories by these banks were business and operational risks. Overall, the results stated that there is a high adherence by all listed Islamic banks in Egypt to the mandatory risk disclosure requirements on their websites, while there is a low level of voluntary risk disclosure on the websites of these banks as well; in addition, financial risk has a higher level of disclosure on the websites of listed banks in Egypt than other risks. Finally, it was confirmed that the overall level of online risk disclosure for all listed Islamic banks in the Egyptian Stock Exchange for all categories was high and that there were no significant differences between the levels of online risk disclosure at all categories levels for all listed Islamic banks on the Egyptian Stock Exchange.

This study makes some important contributions to accounting, both to literature and to practice. To the literature, it contributes by providing an in-depth understanding of the nature of CRD and the Islamic banking industry, also it contributes to existing risk reporting literature and fills one of the research gaps by examining the extent of the internet risk disclosure in Islamic banks in Egypt because there are relatively few such studies in the emerging financial markets. In practice, the results of this study will benefit all the interested parties to obtain the risk information of all listed Islamic banks in Egypt at any time and at any place to help them in making their economic and investment decisions in a suitable time, and also it will help banking by attracting new audiences and increasing the existing investors' confidence.

The rest of the chapter is structured as follows. Section 9.2 discusses the nature of Islamic banking and the risk disclosure in the Egyptian context. Section 9.3 reviews relevant literature on the internet corporate reporting and corporate risk disclosure in the Islamic banking industry. Section 9.4 discusses the research design. Section 9.5 reports the empirical results and discussion, and Section 9.6 reports the conclusion, final remarks, limitations, and recommendations for future research.

9.2 Islamic Banking and Risk Disclosure in the Egyptian Context

The Islamic banking industry has grown rapidly since the early 2000s (Safiullah & Shamsuddin, 2018); moreover, in Egypt, several researchers explored CRD. Thus, in the following sections, we illustrate the nature of Islamic banking and review the risk disclosure in the Egyptian context.

9.2.1 *Islamic banking*

Recently, banks have played a vital and effective role in linking economic processes and commercial transactions to enhance all sectors that contribute to building up the economy of each country. The Egyptian legislator defined the bank in Article No. 19 of Law No. 57 for 1951 as a natural or a legal person whose main job is to accept deposits from the public and pays them on demand or after a period for investments purposes. Meanwhile, El Sabbagh and Abdelkader (2001) mentioned that banks can be classified according to the nature of the activity as follows: central banks, commercial banks, industrial banks, real estate banks, agricultural banks, and Islamic banks, thus Islamic banks are one of the most vital sectors among all other economic sectors in general and among the financial institutions in particular.

Furthermore, based on General Council for Islamic Banks and Financial Institutions in Bahrain, Islamic banking practices began in the 1970s in Egypt, KSA, and UAE. By 2003, Islamic banks became popular in the Arab world and other countries like Malaysia. The numbers of Islamic banks grew to 450 banks by 2009; additionally, more than 300 conventional banks now offer Islamic banking services to their customers. Islamic banks have witnessed one of the fastest growth rates ever with assets that are more than doubled over the last years. Projections made by Islamic Financial Services Board (IFSB) in Malaysia indicated that the volume of Islamic financing is expected to reach USD 1.2 trillion by 2010 with a growth rate ranging from 15% to 20% per annum.

According to Al-Maghzom (2016), an Islamic bank is any bank that operates according to the principles and provisions of the Islamic Sharia in all financing, banking, and investment transactions; it is also subject, as a financial institution, to the supervision and control of the Central Bank. Furthermore, the concept of Islamic banking means that the conducting of the banking operations is in line with the guidance of Sharia law (Islamic jurisprudence laws). Overall, there are three main resources from which the operations of Islamic banks originate; namely, the Qur'an (the holy book of Muslims), Sunnah (the rules or the practices applied by the Prophet Mohammed), Ijma' (the majority of agreeing with people on a specific point or a situation). In addition, an Islamic bank complies with Sharia principles in all the transactions and products it provides to its clients, whether such products are investment deposits, investment certificates, or savings accounts. In addition, Zafar and Sulaiman (2020) pointed out some important issues that distinguish Islamic banks from other banks; in more detail, they stated that these banks introduce the financial products based on the prohibition from the religious point of view and stand on the principle of interest-free, avoids uncertainty in the transaction, prohibits speculation, and invests in halal or Islamic-allowed services and goods. An Islamic bank also meets the client's various financing needs by providing many options that were mentioned by Al-Maghzom (2016) and other Islamic banks academic writings and can be summarized as follows:

(i) *Mudarabah*: A contract between two parties; the first is the client who only owns the money and has no right to interfere in the administration, and the second is called the Mudarib (the Islamic bank) who invests and manages the money for the client. The generated profit is distributed among both parties according to the agreement made now of signing the contract. In case of generating a loss, the client loses his money while the bank loses his work and his efforts. If the capital owner finds the bank to be negligent, he is entitled to rescind the contract.

(ii) *Musharakah*: A contract between two parties, the Islamic bank and the client, each of them participates with a share in the capital of the appointed investment; thus, it is called "Musharakah". In this case, the profit and loss are distributed according to the ratio of each party's share in the capital, and either party can manage the investment in return for a commission or a salary.

(iii) *Murabahah*: A contract between the client who wants to buy a particular asset, such as an equipment or a property, but does not have the ability to buy it, and the Islamic bank (second party), whom the customer asks to purchase that asset from a supplier (third party), as he — the customer — will buy the asset back from the bank with its original cost plus a profit margin for the bank but in installments. Therefore, in this manner, there are two contracts; the first is between the bank and the supplier, and the second is between the bank and the customer. In this case, the relationship between the bank and the customer is an agency relationship to avoid usury and interests because Islam allows for the selling and buying; however, it does not allow usury and interests as they are forbidden.

(iv) *Ijarah* (leasing): A contract between an Islamic bank that provides the asset or the service (the lessor) and the person who benefits from that asset/service (the lessee) with a certain amount of a value (as a rent), but the ownership of the asset remains with the bank.

(v) *Qard Hasan*: Financing granted by the Islamic bank (the lender) to the customer (the borrower) without any interest, in which case the client pays the loan value in addition to some fees for obtaining this loan (not an interest as the Islamic Sharia denies it).

(vi) *Al-Istisna*: A contract in which the customer asks the bank to manufacture a certain commodity somewhere as he obligates to pay the bank the cost of that manufacturing in addition to a profit margin determined by the bank.

(vii) *Salam*: A forward sale contract between the bank, the customer, and the supplier. By this contract, the payment is made in advance at the time of making the contract while the products are delivered later in the future. Therefore, there are here two types of contracts: the first is between the bank and the supplier and the second is between the bank and customer.

(viii) *Wakalah (agency)*: A contract between a client (the principal) who submits his money to a bank (the agent) for investing it in return for certain administrative expenses, and therefore, the client here gains both the profits and losses alone.

(ix) *Sukuk*: An Islamic equivalent of the bonds, but unlike the bonds they are abided by the provisions of Islamic Sharia that prohibits interest, so it gives the investor a share in the assets, in addition to suitable cash flows and risks.

Furthermore, Islamic banks offer, along with the Islamic options, a letter of guarantee, a letter of credit, and covered cards. Islamic bank has a Sharia board composed of Islamic jurists who are continually consulted in all the aspects related to any new banking transactions and also continuously participate in all other banking activities, such as issuing letters of guarantee, opening documentary credits, exchanging currency, collecting commercial paper, and buying and selling securities following the Islamic Sharia.

9.2.2 *Risk disclosure in the Egyptian context*

In Egypt, several researchers explored CRD. For example, Ezat (2014) attempted to study the determinants of risk information disclosure in the listed firms' annual reports in Egypt as well as to explore the potential outcomes of risk disclosure on the Egyptian companies' performance. His study reported that the level of risk disclosure in Egyptian companies is low compared to those of the developed countries. Further, the study also indicated that CRD is significantly associated with the firm size, the board size, diversification variables of the firm, non-executive directors, twofold role, and competitive pressures. In addition, the determinants of internet risk disclosure of Egyptian listed companies were analyzed as well by Khalil and Maghraby (2017) in the context of internet reporting; they concluded that CRD is positively associated with sector type and firm size. They also emphasized that CRD is neither significantly associated with other firm-related characteristics (e.g., cross-listing and risk level) nor the variables of board characteristics (CEO duality, board composition, and board size). Moreover, Marzouk (2016) outlined that there was a high level of disclosure related to monetary, future, and good risk information in the annual reports of listed Egyptian firms during the Egyptian 2011 political instability.

9.3 Empirical Literature Review

Over the past decades, the debate on corporate risk disclosure has received increased interest from global corporations, academic scholars, and other concerned regulators and professional authorities, thus the literature on corporate reporting on the internet and corporate risk disclosure are extensive; subsequently, the key literature of the areas of corporate reporting on the internet and corporate risk disclosure can be presented as follows.

9.3.1 *Corporate reporting on the internet*

The corporate reporting practices on the internet attract the attention of not only the various professional bodies but also the academic researchers. To elaborate, with the great growth in using websites for online reporting, several professional bodies have examined the case of corporate reporting on the internet in the UK, the US, and Canada. These organizations include the Canadian Institute of Chartered Accountants (CICA) in Canada, the Accounting Standards Board (ASB) in the UK, the American Institute of CPAs (AICPA), and the Financial Accounting Standards Board (FASB) in the US (FASB, 2000, 2001; Debreceny *et al.*, 2001).

In the same vein, a large and growing body of researchers has investigated the extent to which companies rely on the internet as a new tool for disseminating information in both developed and developing countries. For example, in the UK, Gowthorpe (2004) indicated that the existing communication methods between the British firms and stakeholders were not affected by the internet-advanced means. In the largest European companies, surveys, such as that conducted by Smith and Pierce (2005) have shown that the governance procedures of online reports are insufficient because they were not paid enough attention. In the US, Ashbaugh *et al.* (1999) pointed out that the vast majority of US companies use the internet to disclose their information. In Japan, Marston (2003) examined a sample of the largest 99 Japanese firms and demonstrated that the Japanese firm size is one of the most important determinants for possession of websites. In Germany, Herzig and Godemann (2010) showed that online reporting is much cheaper than traditional methods for both the firms and the other users.

Concerning the Jordanian companies, Al Khalaileh *et al.* (2005) attempted to explore the current trends in internet environmental reporting practices of these companies. They concluded that nearly half of Jordanian companies use the internet in financial reporting. However, Mohamed *et al.* (2009) pointed out that the practices of internet financial reporting in Oman are quite low. Having said that, another trend of research uses comparisons to explore corporate reporting practices on the internet in different countries. To give an illustration, Khan (2007) examined a sample of 177 companies listed in London and New York Stock Exchange and concluded that London's listed companies had more financial reports than those of New York's. Likewise, Chatterjee and Hawkes (2008) investigated the differences between New Zealand and Indian companies in providing information to their stakeholders via the internet. Al-Jaber and Mohamed (2003) also examined reporting practices on the internet in Egypt, Saudi Arabia, and Kuwait. Finally, Debreceny and Gray (1999) surveyed internet reporting by the top 45 companies listed in France, Germany, and the UK. They stated that approximately 75% of these companies use their websites to publish their annual reports.

9.3.2 *Corporate risk disclosure*

Risk has been discussed by several academic scholars and professional bodies. To give an illustration, Shrand and Elliot (1998) stated that risk includes possibilities, opportunities, and threats. In addition, the ICAEW (1997) illustrated risk as to the uncertainty conditions that should include both the potential good outcomes, such as the gains, and the potential bad outcomes, such as the losses. Furthermore, it is necessary to classify the risks to aid firms in understanding, controlling, managing, and identifying these risks as well as to assist the investors in improving their awareness about the company's economic performance and its risks (Cabedo & Tirado, 2004). For this reason, the different categories of risks, which will be used in this study, can be summarized based on all previous efforts by academic scholars and professional bodies and are explained as follows. First, financial (direct) risks are those related to the potential losses in the firm's finance and the financial markets. They are linked directly and immediately to financial statements and have an explicit influence on a company's assets, liabilities, and cash flow (King Committee, 2002; Cabedo & Tirado, 2004); these risks include credit risk, liquidity risk, market risk, equity risk, and currency risk. Second, non-financial (indirect), which are external and non-monetary risks that have an indirect and longer-term impact on a firm's financial position, such as liabilities/assets on the balance sheet (King Committee, 2002; Cabedo & Tirado, 2004). In this respect, according to Jorion

(1997), King Committee (2002), Cabedo and Tirado (2004), Crouhy *et al.* (2006), Servaes *et al.* (2006), and Vandamaele *et al.* (2009), non-financial risks include business risks, strategic risks, compliance risk, reputation risk, and operational risks; Crouhy *et al.* (2006) divided operational risk into the following three major categories: (i) fraud risk; (ii) human risk; (iii) technology risk. Furthermore, there are several definitions for CRD; however, it is fundamental to adopt a more comprehensive one because the existence of various definitions may result in getting different outcomes. Linsley and Shrives (2006) defined CRD as informing the reader about *any opportunity, chance, danger, or threat that has influenced or will influence the firm itself or the management of these opportunities, chances, or threats.*

In 1998, the Institute of Charted Accountants in England and Wales stressed for the first time the importance of risk disclosure, when it published a discussion paper that suggested for the first time that firms must disclose risk management information in their annual reports (Grassa *et al.*, 2021).

Since the major corporate collapse in 2007–2008, risk disclosure has been of increasing importance in international policy arena and has raised significant interest around the world (Nahar *et al.*, 2020). Moreover, extensive interest has been given to CRD by numerous global accounting regulators such as the FASB, the accounting professional bodies (e.g., the Institute of Chartered Accountants in England and Wales (ICAEW), and the American Accounting Association (AAA). These authorities pointed out the possibility of a gap between preparers and users of risk information due to the inadequately disclosed risk information of the companies (Schrand & Elliott, 1998). The first serious discussions and analyses of CRD emerged during the late 1990s with the benchmarking study of ICAEW (1997), which discussed how companies should provide stakeholders with high-quality risk information and how these risks should be managed. Furthermore, it also suggested that this information should be useful to its preparers and users and should support practices of voluntary risk disclosure by the public limited companies (ICAEW, 1997). On the other hand, CRD practices have also been discussed academically. In more detail, one of the most comprehensive studies that dealt with risk disclosure related to the European insurance industry is that of Stradea (2006); its results indicated a gap between industry-level standards and the level of disclosure-related practices. In addition, the study of Korosec and Horvat (2005) analyzed 36 annual reports of large Slovenian listed companies and pointed out that the practices of CRD in the annual reports of the Slovenian companies are low; also Hassan (2009) indicated that risks and reserves levels play an important role in affecting the risk disclosure index. Furthermore, the study of Linsley and Shrives (2006) looked at the risk disclosure practices in British banks under the Basel-II requirements, the study recommended increasing the level of risk disclosure since it agreed with the results of Stradea (2006), which had focused on the largest European banks and was based on a highly comprehensive sample. Moreover, the results of Sundmacher's (2006) study, which was applied to a group of international banks, was consistent with the results of Oliveira *et al.* (2011), which was applied on the Portuguese banks, as they both confirmed that the quantity and quality of disclosure of operational risks by banks widely vary and that most banks meet the requirements of disclosure only partially.

Further, Moumen *et al.* (2015) investigated the importance and usefulness of the voluntary risk disclosure information for stakeholders in the annual reports in helping them predicting future earnings; they showed that the level of proprietary costs tends to realize the relevance of the risk information. In addition, several other studies focused on identifying the relationship between the risk disclosure and characteristics of the firms. For instance, Naser *et al.* (2006) explored a sample of 21 annual reports of Qatari-listed firms and concluded that there is a positive relationship between the size of firms and leverage on the one hand and risk disclosure on the other hand. Also, Abraham and Cox (2007) pointed out that there is a negative relationship between share ownership in long-term institutions and CRD, and that firms with a lower level of risk disclosure are the more preferred choice of investing to the institutional investor. In addition, Elzahar and Hussainey (2012) assumed that there is no considerable impact of cross-listing, liquidity, profitability, and gearing on narrative risk disclosure; however, industry type and firm size positively affect the narrative risk disclosure level in interim reports.

9.3.3 *Risk disclosure in banking industry*

Risk disclosure of banks has come under scrutiny in the ramification on banks in Europe and Asia (e.g., Royal Bank of Scotland, Bradford

& Bingley, Fortis, Hypo and Alliance & Leicester, BNP Paribas), the aftermath of the major financial crush of several US investments banks (Bear Stearns, Lehman Brothers, Merrill Lynch), and the ensuing turmoil on the global financial markets (Grassa *et al.*, 2020).

Based on the study by Oorschot (2009) in 1997, Basel Committee recommended that banks disclose more information about the risks that they face, as they have analyzed the content of annual reports of about 55 different banks from 13 countries all over the world in the years 1999, 2000, and 2001 to examine the levels of disclosure. In 2001, a survey was prepared that consisted of 104 questions in 12 categories regarding 10 different types of risk (e.g., market risk internal modeling, credit risk modeling, capital structure, and other risks) within the annual reports, it was distributed to national banking supervisors to fill. The committee reported that while there is a lack of credit risk modeling disclosures and internal and external ratings in the annual reports of the year 1999, there was extensive disclosure in the area of the internal models for market risk in 2000 (Basel Committee, 2002, 7 and 3). In addition, in 2001, there was a high increase in the level of risk disclosures related to operational, legal, liquidity, and interest rate. Moreover, the relationship between the level of risk disclosure and banks' governance characteristics was examined by Nahar *et al.* (2020), who concluded that there is a positive relationship between risk disclosure and banks' governance characteristics, such as the presence of various risk committees and a risk management unit. In the context of Islamic banks, Grassa *et al.* (2021) evaluated the effects of deposits structure and ownership concentration on risk disclosure for these banks; they concluded that the level of risk disclosure is lower for Islamic banks with higher ownership concentration, leveraged banks, listed banks, and Islamic banks. However, risk disclosure is higher for Islamic banks with a higher concentration of profit-sharing investment account (PSIA) and higher foreign ownership, large Islamic banks, aged banks, Islamic banks operating in a country with higher country transparency index, positively correlated to gross domestic products and Accounting and Auditing Organization for Islamic Financial Institutions (AAOIFI) adoption, while Grassa *et al.* 2020 examined and compared the relationship between risk disclosure and corporate attributes in Islamic and conventional banks, and they stated that Islamic banks disclose less information about risk compared to conventional banks. Listed banks, larger banks, and aged banks disclose more information about risk than the others; also they pointed out that block holders, foreign ownership, and board size negatively affect risk disclosure.

9.3.4 *Internet corporate reporting in Egypt*

Several scholars have discussed corporate internet disclosure in the Egyptian environment context. For instance, Ezat and El-Masry (2008) examined a sample of 50 Egyptian companies to explore the association between corporate internet reporting and characteristics of firms, they have reported that the timeliness of corporate disclosure via the internet is positively associated with company characteristics (e.g., company size, liquidity, service activity type, ownership framework, board structure, and its size). In addition, they have also indicated that there is no significant link between corporate internet disclosure timeliness and profitability, leverage, stocks issues, and twofold role. Desoky (2009) investigated the internet financial reporting (IFR) practices in Egypt using 88 Egyptian firms. It was found that there is a positive association between IFR and firm size, profitability, foreign listed companies, and ownership composition, while IFR was negatively associated with the legal structure. Furthermore, the study concluded that there was no significant link between the industry type and internet financial disclosure level. Moreover, the corporate internet reporting determinants in listed companies of Egypt were examined by Aly *et al.* (2010); the results pointed out that the amount and presentation style of online disclosed information was positively associated with the industry type, foreign listing, and profitability. In addition, this study summarized that there is no significant association between IFR and leverage, liquidity, auditor, and firm size. Elhelaly and Mohamed (2014) investigated the current trends in internet reporting practices of Egyptian listed companies. They stated that, in Egypt, IFR is still in its infancy and there are several opportunities and challenges in corporate disclosure topic for all the interested parties.

9.3.5 *Research gap*

Based on the above-discussed literature, although there is an extensive amount of literature in each of the areas of corporate risk disclosure and online corporate reporting, we can conclude that the vast majority of the previous risk disclosure studies have concentrated on developed economies only, and to the best of the researchers' knowledge, the prior studies, especially in the Egyptian context, did not represent clear and reliable evidence about the practices of online risk disclosures done by the Islamic banking sectors; hence, the current study tries to fill this gap through investigating the online risk reporting practices in listed Islamic banks in the context of Egyptian environment.

9.4 Research Design

Non-random sampling is the sampling approach that was adopted in this study; all the three listed Islamic banks in the Egyptian stock by the 1st of January 2018 were included in the sample, only the unlisted Islamic banks were excluded. The listing of these banks and the links to their websites are presented in Table 9.1.

Surely, banks are the most appreciate sector to achieve the objectives of the current due to the nature of their business, banks are institutions that primarily face a massive amount of risks such as market, credit, operational, liquidity, compliance/regulatory/legal, and reputation risks; thus, they are called "risk-situated institutions" (Ashfaq *et al.*, 2016); furthermore, this study focused only on the Islamic listed banks and excluded the unlisted Islamic banks because of the following reasons: Listed banks have to fulfill financial regulation as well as the regulations related to risks, risk disclosure, and risk management more than the unlisted banks. After selecting the sample and its criteria, a list of all listed Islamic banks was first compiled from the website of the Egyptian exchange market; afterward,

Table 9.1. Listed Islamic banks in Egyptian stock market.

No.	Name	Website
1	Faisal Islamic Bank of Egypt	http://www.faisalbank.com.eg/FIB/english/index.html
2	Abu Dhabi Islamic Bank — Egypt	https://www.adib.eg
3	Al Baraka Bank of Egypt	http://www.albaraka-bank.com.eg/en

Table 9.2. Number of banks having websites.

All listed Islamic banks in Egyptian exchange market	Number of banks	% of banking industry
Banks that have websites and report risk information	3	100
Banks that have websites but do not report risk information	0	0
Banks that do not have websites	0	0
Total	**3**	**100**

Google and Yahoo search engines were used for determining whether these banks have a website or not; Fisher *et al.* (2004) used a similar sequence for identifying corporate websites. Since all the websites of the listed Islamic banks were available, the researchers then moved to the next stage of the data collection process which involved carefully browsing the entire websites of each bank from the 1st of February 2018 to the 31st of March 2018 to explore whether they report their risk information or not; the location of this information was documented for those with risk information available on their website. The selected banks were classified into three main categories (Oyelere *et al.*, 2003) as follows: first, banks that have websites and report risk information; second, banks that have websites but do not report risk information; and third, banks that do not have websites. As shown in Table 9.2, it can be confirmed that all listed Islamic banks in Egypt have websites, all banks' websites have risk information, and all these websites are active (i.e., none of them is under construction).

Furthermore, the data that were used in this study were collected from the published online reports, in addition to any risk information on the websites of the selected banks. The websites were also revisited in April 2018 as a validity check, and no changes in the banks' websites were found. To investigate the level of the risk disclosure on the websites of the listed Islamic banks in the Egyptian stock market, this study employed a content analysis approach for several reasons. First, it has played a pivotal role in accounting research as it provides the ability to collect rich data and make valid inferences from them because it can reveal relationships the other mechanisms cannot (Krippendorff, 1980; Bowman, 1982; Al-Maghzom, 2016). Second, in the academic literature, content analysis has been adopted as a vital research technique in collecting data, notably that related to risk disclosure (e.g., Beretta & Bozzolan, 2004; Abraham & Cox, 2007; Linsley & Shrives, 2006). Likewise, the content analysis will also be used to measure the content of risk disclosures. Concerning the current study, content analysis was employed because it helps in effectively classifying massive amounts of qualitative data related to risk disclosure (Lajilli & Zeghal, 2005).

To achieve the main objectives of the current study, a risk disclosure index was adopted; disclosure index is a research tool that is used in accounting research to form a list of selected reported items in firms' reports, which assists in measuring the extent of information disclosed in these reports. The items that are included in this index can be applied to a part of the annual report (such as the voluntary or the environmental disclosures), to the overall companies' annual reports, or to some information (such as that related to risk disclosure) (Marston & Shrives,1991; Coy & Dixon, 2004; Hassan & Marston, 2010; Alzead, 2017), In the context of banks, disclosure index is a checklist of various disclosure items included in the annual reports of banks. According to Aly (2008), the following four approaches assist the scholars to construct or select their disclosure index: (i) studying the needs of a selected group of users and construct the disclosure index that meets their needs; (ii) constructing a new index; (iii) using an existing disclosure index; and (iv) amending the content of an existing disclosure index according to the needs and requirements of the study. For the current study, the fourth approach is adopted. For the current study, the Islamic and non-Islamic risk disclosure indices of Al-Maghzom (2016) were used. The indices of Al-Maghzom (2016) consisted of 54 items that were suggested by prior disclosure studies (e.g., ICAEW, 1997, 1999, 2002; Linsely & Shrives, 2006; Lipunga, 2014; Abdallah *et al.*, 2015), in addition to 13 items that were extracted from reviewing the Accounting and Auditing Organisation for Islamic Financial Institutions (AAOIFI, 2014) and Islamic Financial Services Board (IFSB, 2007). Risk disclosure indices of Al-Maghzom (2016) included, among each other, a total of 67 items that were expected to be published in the annual reports of the sample banks, which were divided across 10 categories: accounting policies, financial and other risks, derivative hedging and general risks, financial instruments, reserves, segment information, business risk, compliance with regulations, Islamic bank risk characteristics, and Islamic standards. These disclosure indices were modified and adapted to the Egyptian environment based on the requirements of the Companies Act, Capital Market Law, applicable International Accounting Standards in Egypt, the Central bank of Egypt, and according to the contents of the annual reports of the listed banks in Egypt. For the current study, the unweighted disclosure index is chosen because the study focuses on all interested parties, not a selected group of them, as well as addresses all users of the annual reports, so all of the groups have the same significance and no group is more material (Oliveira *et al.*, 2006; Al-Maghzom, 2016). There are several advantages of using Al-Maghzom's (2016) risk disclosure indices, such as that they are comprehensive indices, as they are based on several corporate risk disclosure studies which, in turn, were based on other studies, as well as the results of these disclosure indices can be compared to other studies too. Moreover, the index was constructed for Islamic banks' disclosure, which suits the current study as the sample of this study includes three Islamic banks (Faisal Islamic Bank of Egypt, Abu Dhabi Islamic Bank, and Al Baraka Bank of Egypt). Thus, for this study, a risk disclosure index was developed, and the risk disclosure index of the current study comprised of 10 main categories and a total of 61 sub-items, see Appendix A.

This study followed the two main steps of validation; the first step is to validate the risk index score (the analytical analysis methodology can be used), and the second step is to get some reviews for the coding scheme by some experts in the field of study (Carmines & Zeller, 1991; Neuendorf, 2002; Bryman & Bell, 2003). Specifically, the current study's index was reviewed by another independent researcher who had previously dealt with Islamic bank reports and was specialized in the area of disclosure and financial reporting, and the content analysis of the online annual reports of the listed Islamic banks in the Egyptian stock market was then performed. Reliability is more concerned with the credibility of the study's results in case the research findings were repeated by different researchers (Collis & Hussey, 2003). The contents of each bank's annual reports were compared to the items listed in the index and based on a dichotomous model, they were coded as 1 if disclosed or 0 if otherwise.

9.5 Empirical Results and Discussion

Based on the descriptive statistics of the risk disclosure by each of the 61 items in the checklist under 10 categories in the Islamic listed banks in the Egyptian stock market, we can note that the highest means (100%) with no standard deviations were recorded by the following items: the description of financial risk management objectives and policies, use of the accounting estimates and assumptions, collateral assets against loans, the impairment of financial and other assets, contingent assets and liabilities, credit risk disclosure and exposure, liquidity and market risk disclosures, description of stress tests and/or sensitivity analyses, pricing and commodity risk, changes in the interest rates risk, currency risk, capital adequacy, equity risk, leverage rate, an explanation of the extent to which financial instruments are used and the associated risks, fair value's cumulative change, operational risk disclosure, communications risk, general legal and other reserves, geographical and sector (business) concentration, diversification, compliance with Egyptian central bank regulation, financial regulations and other regulations and laws, Mudarabah, Musharakah and Murabahah risk, earnings or expenditures prohibited by Sharia instructions (e.g., zakat), the method of allocation the investment profits/loss between unrestricted investment account holders or their equivalent, and the Islamic bank as a Mudarib or as an investment with its own funds by the Islamic bank. This is explained by the fact that all selected Islamic banks mentioned all of these items in their online reports.

In the same way, the descriptive analysis reveals that the outsourcing, performance and efficiency, compliance with Egyptian companies act requirements, litigation risk, and unusual supervisory restrictions items were mentioned by two out of three Islamic banks; subsequently, they had the second-highest means (66.6%) and standard deviations (0.57735). Meanwhile, only a third of the selected Islamic banks reported the items of the objective of holding derivatives and instruments, general financial problems and restricted investments, and financial statements with a mean of 33.3% and a standard deviation of 0.57735. On the contrary, there was no Islamic bank that disclosed the following items: financial derivatives, cash flow hedge, customer satisfaction, competition (service market), reputation risk, technology changes, natural and physical disasters (environmental risks), insurance risk, sustainability risk, regional financial problems, political risk, health and safety, Ijarah risk, Qard Hasan risk, Al-Istisna risk, Salam risk, Sukuk risk, and Wakalah risk; consequently, these items were given the lowest mean (0) between the whole items with lowest standard deviation (0.00000) as well.

According to the statistical information of the total average risk disclosure level per category for each Islamic bank on its website and the total scores achieved per each Islamic bank, we can conclude the following: In the context of *accounting policies* disclosures, Faisal Islamic Bank recorded the highest average (100%), which means that this bank reports all accounting policies on its websites to assist stakeholders in making their investment decisions at anytime and anywhere. Immediately afterward, Abu Dhabi Islamic and Al Baraka Bank have an average rate of 85.7% in that category as well. Faisal Islamic, Abu Dhabi Islamic, and Al Baraka banks have the same average (100%) of disclosure level of *financial risks, segment information, and reserves* categories, as well as, they also have the same averages, 50%, 40%, and 33.3%, in the categories of *the financial instruments and derivatives hedging, business risk, and Islamic finance techniques*, respectively. Moving to *operational, general, and other risk* categories, the highest average (30%) was documented by Abu Dhabi Islamic and Al Baraka banks, while Faisal Islamic Bank achieved only 20%. Moreover, Faisal Islamic and Al Baraka banks came with an average of 83.3% in the *legal risk* disclosures category. And in *the Islamic standards* category, Faisal Islamic Bank came with an average of 75% and Al Baraka Bank with 100%, meanwhile, Abu Dhabi Islamic Bank recorded the same average (50%) in both *legal risk and Islamic standards categories.*

Overall, by looking at the total average risk disclosure per each bank of the three Islamic banks listed on the Egyptian stock market, Al Baraka Bank was the highest among them all with an average of 67.2% and a total score of 41, followed by Faisal Islamic Bank with an average of 65.5% and total score 40, and finally, Abu Dhabi Islamic Bank came in the last place with an average of 60.6% and total score 37; this lowest place by Abu Dhabi Islamic Bank can be explained by the fact that it was the least Islamic bank that disclosed information regarding the compliance with the Islamic standard.

Based on the results of statistical analysis, we can conclude that all listed Islamic banks in the Egyptian stock market report the financial risks, reserves, and segment information with 100% average and with no standard deviation. Furthermore, the accounting policies category was reported with an average of 90.5% and a standard deviation of 0.08248 by all Islamic listed banks in Egypt. In addition, the Islamic standards and legal risks categories were reported with averages of 75% and 72.2% and standard deviations of 0.25000 and 0.19245, respectively, as the third-highest disclosing categories by all Islamic Egyptian listed banks. In a further remark, in light of the findings of the study, the financial instruments and derivatives hedging category was reported with an average of 50% and a standard deviation of 0.00000 by the Islamic listed banks. On the other hand, the results also concluded that the business risks, financial techniques risk of Islamic banks, and operational risks were the lowest reported categories by the Islamic listed banks in Egypt with values of 40%, 33.3%, and 26.6% and standard deviations of 0.00000, 0.00000, and 0.05774, respectively.

By moving to the overall level of risk disclosure on the websites of the Islamic listed banks in the Egyptian stock market, the result indicated that the average of the total risk disclosure scores for the Islamic listed banks is as follows: (i) for the first eight categories, it is about 69.44% with a total standard deviation of 0.02406; (ii) for the eight categories in addition to the two main Islamic categories (financial techniques risk of Islamic banks and Islamic standard, this average is 64.5% with a total standard deviation of 0.03413. This average reflects a bit high level of risk disclosure on the websites of the Islamic listed banks in Egypt. Again, this result is comparable with the study by Al-Maghzom (2016) who reported that the extent of risk disclosure by non-Islamic Saudi Arabian banks is 61%, which was a high result as well.

To sum up, for Islamic banks, there is a greater volume of disclosure in the areas of financial risks, reserves, and segment information than in other categories. Furthermore, the overall level of risk disclosure on the websites of the Islamic listed banks in the Egyptian stock market for the first eight categories combined is 69.44% for the Islamic banks. But as for the 10 categories that contained two main Islamic categories, the overall levels of risk disclosure in the published reports on the websites of the Islamic listed banks in Egypt are 64.5%.

Overall, the results indicate that the most reported categories with the highest averages by the Islamic listed banks in Egypt on their websites were the categories of *financial risks, reserves, accounting policies, segment information, legal risks, and the financial instruments and derivatives hedging.* The possible explanations for these banks' very high averages can be presented as follows. First, these banks operate in the Egyptian economic banking environment; hence, they are subject to the supervision and control of the Central Bank of Egypt. Consequently, these banks prepare their financial statements, accounts, and reports following the provisions, laws, and regulations of the Central Bank of Egypt. Along the same line, the financial statements and the supplementary notes of these banks were prepared based on *The rules and provisions of preparing the financial statements, also the measurement and recognition regulations which approved by the Board of Directors of the Central Bank of Egypt in its session held on 16 December 2008*, these provisions are the models and guides for what the supplementary notes of the financial statements of these banks should contain; for instance, these regulations require from all banks that operate in Egypt to report a set of accounting policies such as financial risk management objectives and policies, the meaning and objectives of the financial instruments, derivatives, hedge accounting, and the risks associated with them. In addition, they must report the types of financial risks that they can be exposed to, such as credit risk, liquidity, market (especially the change in the rate of return and the foreign exchange rate), and the use of accounting estimates and assumptions, which affects the amounts of assets and liabilities disclosed during the next financial year. Equally, they must disclose the contingent liabilities, the impairment losses of the financial and non-financial assets, the reserves hold of profits, whether that reserve was public, for all purposes or under the law (i.e., the 5% statutory reserve that is not available for distribution until the balance equals 100% of the capital), or private for a specific purpose. Also, the most important limits of the bank's credit risk based on the geographical distributions of the areas that involve the bank's customers and according to the activities of those customers too must be mentioned as well.

Second, it was stated in the auditors' report, for most of these Islamic banks, that there has not been any contravention of the

Egyptian local laws, such as Banking and Monetary Institution Law No. 88 of 2003, the Bank Law No. 95 of 1983, and Law No. 159 of 1981 and its executive regulations; therefore, the legal and compliance risks were reported with the highest averages. Third, all Islamic listed banks are obliged to disclose the capital adequacy, the use of regulatory capital, and their leverage rate based on the guidelines developed by the Basel Committee and implemented by the banking supervision unit in the Central Bank of Egypt, thereby all these banks reported the capital adequacy and the leverage rate in their online reports.

On the other hand, the least disclosed categories by these banks were *business, operational, general, and other risks*. The possible explanations for these very low averages are as follows. First, the Central Bank of Egypt places a great emphasis on disclosing the accounting policies, financial, and legal risks, so there is no specific or obliged framework by the Central Bank of Egypt for the disclosure of these risks; accordingly, in the report of the Board of Directors, some banks disclose a large percentage of the operational and business categories, others disclose a small one, such as the performance and efficiency during the year, technology changes risks, outsourcing information (e.g., loans and supporting deposits from others), and the diversification risks (i.e., different types of investment securities, loans, and facilities), while other banks do not disclose any information about these risks at all.

Regarding the overall level of risk disclosure for the Islamic listed banks, for the first eight categories, it is about 69.44%, but it is 64.5% for the eight categories in addition to the main two Islamic categories (financial techniques risk of Islamic banks and Islamic standard), which means that these banks do not disclose all the risks of the financing and facilitating mechanisms; they collectively disclose only the risks of Mudarabah, Murabahah, and Musharakah and ignore the disclosure of other risks associated with the rest of the techniques, such as Ijarah (leasing) and Qard Hasan. Besides, only about one-third of these Islamic listed banks in Egypt disclose their compliance with Islamic standards and are subject to the supervision of Sharia supervisory authorities. More so, there is a low level of disclosure on derivatives by the Islamic banks since these banks do not deal in financial derivatives under their Islamic work system.

Overall, the results stated that most listed Islamic banks in Egypt place a great emphasis on disclosing risks information in their published online reports (full annual report and full financial report). This can be explained by the following possible reasons: These reports are formal, official, and comprehensive means and considered documentation of disclosing information, they are easily downloadable by all stakeholders, the banks use these reports as a basis for making comparisons between sectors and other banks, and these reports assist management of the banks to provide more and comprehensive risk information. Also, findings from the results indicated that there is a high adherence by all listed Islamic banks in Egypt to the mandatory risk disclosure requirements on their websites, while there is a low level of voluntary risk disclosure on the websites of these banks as well; in addition, financial risk has a higher level of disclosure on the websites of listed banks in Egypt than other risks.

To sum up, the current study focused mainly on investigating the level of online risk reporting practices in the Islamic banking context such as an extensive amount of literature (e.g., Grassa *et al.*, 2020, 2021). However, previous risk disclosure studies have concentrated on developed economies, so the current study tries to investigate the online risk reporting practices in listed Islamic banks in Egypt as a developing country. Furthermore, our study introduces more insights related to the theoretical background of the Islamic banking industry and risk disclosure. In addition, our results agree with the results of Grassa *et al.* (2020) who stated that listed banks disclose more information about risk than others, which may result in helping all interested parties to obtain this information at any time and at any place to help them in making their economic and investment decisions in the suitable time, also it will help banking in attracting new audiences and increasing the existing investors' confidence.

9.6 Conclusion

This study aimed basically to identify the status of the corporate risk disclosure practices on the internet by the listed Islamic banks in the Egyptian exchange market. To achieve this main objective, this study was divided into two main parts: theoretical and empirical. First, regarding the theoretical part, a comprehensive theoretical background was established, which included a brief overview of the concept and the nature of corporate reporting, internet corporate reporting, CRD, disclosure indices, and Islamic banking industry, also it outlines the concept and types of risk. The current study stated that most studies have made a distinction between financial or direct risk (e.g., credit, liquidity, and market risk, which are caused by variations in interest rates, exchange/currency rates, commodity prices, and equity prices) and non-financial or indirect risk (e.g., business, underwriting, strategic, compliance, reputation, and operational risks that includes fraud, human, and technology). Then, the core literature on the internet corporate reporting and corporate risk disclosure in the Islamic banking industry was reviewed.

Regarding the empirical part, the manual content analysis approach was employed, and based on the Islamic and non-Islamic risk disclosure indices of Al-Maghzom (2016), this study developed an unweighted (to reduce subjectivity and any potential bias with the score) disclosure checklist by including all items considered as important according to the Egyptian regulation, provisions, and laws. Subsequently, this risk disclosure index was comprised 10 main categories and a total of 61 sub-items; validity and reliability checks were made by two independent researchers. All the listed Islamic banks in Egypt constituted the sample in this study. The results indicated that all listed Islamic banks in the Egyptian exchange market have websites and all these banks report risk information in their published online reports (full annual report and full financial report). Also, the data that were used in this study were collected from the published online reports, in addition to any risk information on the websites of the selected banks.

The findings also concluded that Al Baraka Bank has the highest average (67.2%) of online risk disclosure level among all Islamic banks, followed by Faisal Islamic Bank with an average of 65.5%; finally, Abu Dhabi Islamic Bank came in the last place with an average of 60.6%. Additionally, the results also pointed out that the most reported categories by listed Islamic banks on their websites were the *financial risks, reserves, and segment information* with 100% rate, while the *business risks, financial techniques risk of Islamic banks, and operational risks* were the lowest reported categories by these banks. The results further revealed that the average level of online risk disclosure of the Islamic listed banks in Egypt was 64.5%.

Moreover, the results showed that the highest categories, which were reported by all listed Islamic banks in Egypt, were *financial risks, reserves, and accounting policies*; however, the least disclosed categories by these banks were *business and operational risks.* Overall, the results stated that there is a high adherence by all listed Islamic banks in Egypt to the mandatory risk disclosure requirements on their websites, while there is a low level of voluntary risk disclosure on the websites of these banks as well; in addition, financial risk has a higher level of disclosure on the websites of listed banks in Egypt than other risks. Finally, it was confirmed that the overall level of online risk disclosure for all listed Islamic banks in the Egyptian stock exchange for all categories was high and that there were no significant differences between the levels of online risk disclosure at all categories levels for all listed Islamic banks on the Egyptian stock exchange.

This study has some practical implications; in more detail, the results of this study benefit all the interested parties, such as banks themselves, investors, creditors, financial analysts, auditors, investors, and other users as well. In a broad essence, the findings of this study concluded that all listed Islamic banks in Egypt disclose risk information with high rates on their websites, which may result in helping all interested parties to obtain this information at any time and at any place to help them in making their economic and investment decisions in the suitable time, also it will help banking in attracting new audiences and increasing the existing investors' confidence. The limitations of this study can be summarized in the way the content analysis was conducted and its reliance on the websites and the published online reports for examining risk disclosure information due to the focus on the financial and non-financial risks, the focus also on only the listed Islamic banks in Egypt, and the focus on the context of the Egyptian economic environment. Therefore, there may be several areas for further future research, such as examining the extent of the online risk disclosure for all the 38 Egyptian banks, not only for the listed banks; furthermore, exploring the extent of the online risk disclosure for all listed Islamic and non-Islamic banks in Egypt, also examining the extent of the online risk disclosure for the listed banks in other developing economies and comparing the results with online risk disclosure studies done in developed economies because the vast majority of the previous risk disclosure studies have concentrated on developed economies, as well as investigating the extent of the online financial risk disclosure for the Egyptian listed banks; finally, examining the extent of the online non-financial risk disclosure for the Egyptian listed banks.

References

Abdallah, A. Hassan, M., & McClelland, P. (2015). Islamic financial institutions, corporate governance, and corporate risk disclosure in Gulf cooperation council countries. *Journal of Multinational Financial Management*, *3*, 63–82.

Abraham, S. & Cox, P. (2007). Analysing the determinants of narrative risk information in UK FTSE 100 annual reports. *British Accounting Review*, *39*, 227–248.

Al-Jaber, N. & Mohamed, F. (2003). Disclosing financial reports on the Internet: A survey of Egypt, Saudi and Kuwait. *Working Paper.*

Al Khalaileh, M., Al-Qenae, R., & Abo Farha, H. (2005). A preliminary investigation on the use of the Internet for business reporting: A case study of companies listed on Amman Stock Exchange (ASE). *Journal of Business Administration*, *1*(1), 167–176.

Al Maghzom, A. (2016). *The Determinants and Consequences of Risk Disclosure in Saudi Banks.* A PhD thesis, the School of Business, the University of Gloucestershire.

Aly, D. (2008). *Assessing the Development of Voluntary Internet Financial Reporting and Disclosure in Egypt.* A Thesis for the Degree of Doctor of Philosophy, Department of Accounting and Finance, Hull Business School, the University of Hull.

Aly, D., Simon, J., & Hussainey, K. (2010). Determinants of corporate internet reporting: Evidence from Egypt. *Managerial Auditing Journal*, *25*(2), 182–202.

Alzead, R. S. (2017). *The Determinants and Economic Consequences of Risk Disclosure: Evidence from Saudi Arabia.* A PhD thesis in Accounting and Financial Management at the University of Portsmouth, United Kingdom.

Ashbaugh, H., Johnstone, K., & Warfield, T. (1999). Corporate reporting on the Internet. *Accounting Horizons*, *13*(3), 241–257.

Ashfaq, K., Zhang, R., Munaim, A., & Razzaq, N. (2016). An investigation into the determinants of risk disclosure in banks: Evidence from financial sector of Pakistan. *International Journal of Economics and Financial Issues; Mersin*, *6*(3). Accessed 3 May, 2018. http:// www.econjournals.com.

Beretta, S. & Bozzolan, S. (2004). A framework for the analysis of firm risk communication. *The International Journal of Accounting*, *39*(3), 265–288.

Bowman, H. (1982). Content analysis of annual reports for corporate strategy and risk. *Working Paper*, Alfred P. Sloan School of Management.

Bryman, A. & Bell, E. (2003). *Business Research Methods.* Oxford, New York: Oxford University Press.

Cabedo, J. & Tirado, J. (2004). The disclosure of risk in financial statements. *Accounting Forum*, *28*(2), 181–200.

Carmines, E. G. & Zeller, R. A. (1991). *Reliability and Validity Assessment.* Newbury Park, London: Sage Publications. Accessed 3 May, 2018. https://books.google.hu/books?hl=ar&lr=&id=o5x1AwAAQBAJ&oi=fnd&pg=PA5&dq=Carmines,+E+and+Zeller,+R.+(1991).+Reliability+and+Validity+Assessment.+London:+Sage&ots=2K3IjoGBCZ&sig=_B1GSXNR7qpqBnJZOSMUz9uwlyg&redir_esc=y#v=onepage&q&f=false.

Chatterjee, B. & Hawkes, L. (2008). Does internet reporting improve the accessibility of financial information in a global world? A comparative study of New Zealand and Indian companies. *Australasian Accounting, Business and Finance Journal*, *2*(4), 33–56.

Collis, J. & Hussey, R. (2003). *Business Research, A Practical Guide for Undergraduate and Postgraduate Students* (4th edition). Houndmills: Palgrave Macmillan. [online]. Accessed 3 May, 2018. https://books.google.hu/books?hl=hu&lr=&id=uPgcBQAAQBAJ&oi=fnd&pg=PP1&dq=Collis,+J.+%26+Hussey,+R.+(2003)+Business+Research,+A+practical+guide+for+undergraduate+and+postgraduatev+students,+4th+edition,+Houndmills,+Palgrave+Macmillan&ots=haQn7lUccz&sig=5KFTpmpJr9E86gRxNtQHI0hqtQg&redir_esc=y#v=onepage&q&f=false.

Coy, D. & Dixon, K. (2004). The public accountability index: Crafting a parametric disclosure index for annual reports. *The British Accounting Review*, *36*(1), 79–106.

Crouhy, M., Galai, D., & Mark, R. (2006). *The Essentials of Risk Management.* New York: McGraw Hill.

Debreceny, R. & Gray, G. (1999). Financial reporting on the Internet and the external audit. *The European Accounting Review*, *8*(2), 335–350.

Debreceny, R., Gray, G. L., & Mock, G. L. (2001). Financial reporting web sites: What users want in terms of form and content. *The International Journal of Digital Accounting Research*, *1*(1), 1–23.

Desoky, A. M. (2009). Company characteristics as determinants of internet financial reporting in emerging markets: The case of Egypt. *Research in Accounting in Emerging Economies*, *9*, 31–71.

Eccles, R., Herz, R.. Keegan, M., & Phillips, D. (2001). The risk of risk. *Balance Sheet*, *9*(3), 28–33.

Elhelaly, M. & Mohamed. E. K. A. (2014). A survey of internet financial reporting in Egypt. *International Journal of Accounting and Financial Reporting*, *4*(1), 70–83.

El Sabbagh, A. A. & Abdelkader. Y. (2001). *Accounting Financial Institutions*. Egypt: Faculty of Commerce, Cairo University.

Elzahar, H. & Hussainey, K. (2012). Determinants of narrative risk disclosures in UK interim reports. *Journal of Risk Finance*, *13*(92), 133–147.

Ezat, A. N. M. (2014). Risk disclosure for EGX 100 Egyptian listed companies: Trends, determinants and consequences. *Egyptian Journal of Commercial Studies*, *38*(4), 79–152.

Ezat, A. & El-Masry, A. (2008). The impact of corporate governance on the timeliness of corporate internet reporting by Egyptian listed companies. *Managerial Finance*, *34*(12), 848–867.

FASB (2000). Business reporting research project: Electronic distribution of business reporting information. Steering Committee Report Series, Financial Accounting Standards Board.

FASB (2001). FASB Issues Report on Voluntary Disclosures, *Improving Business Reporting: Insights into Enhancing Voluntary Disclosures.* Financial Accounting Standards Board. Status Report — Financial Accounting Standards Board, No. 333, 4, Norwalk, Connecticut, USA.

Fisher, R., Oyelere, P., & Laswad, F. (2004). Corporate reporting on the Internet: Audit issues and content analysis of practices. *Managerial Auditing Journal*, *19*(3), 412–439.

General Council for Islamic Banks and Financial Institutions in Bahrain (2018). Accessed 2 May, 2018. https://www.linkedin.com/company/cibafi.

Gowthorpe, C. (2004). Asymmetrical dialogue? Corporate financial reporting via the Internet. *Corporate Communications: An International Journal*, *9*(4), 283–293.

Grassa, R., Moumen, N., & Hussainey, K. (2020). What drives risk disclosure in Islamic and conventional banks? An international comparison. *International Journal of Finance & Economics*, *26*(4), 6338–6361. Doi: 10.1002/ijfe.2122.

Grassa, R., Moumen, N., & Hussainey, K. (2021). Do ownership structures affect risk disclosure in Islamic banks? International evidence. *Journal of Financial Reporting and Accounting*, *19*(3), 369–391. Doi: 10.1108/JFRA-02-2020-0036.

Hassan, M. K. (2009). UAE corporations-specific characteristics and level of risk disclosure. *Managerial Auditing Journal*, *24*(7), 668–687. https://doi.org/10.1108/02686900910975378.

Hassan, O. & Marston, C. L. (2010). *Disclosure Measurement in the Accounting Literature: A Review Article*. Brunel University.

Herzig, C. & Godemann, J. (2010). Internet-supported sustainability reporting: Developments in Germany. *Management Research Review, 33*(11), 1064–1082.

ICAEW. (1997). *Financial Reporting of Risk: Proposals for a Statement of Business Risk*. London: Institute of Chartered Accountants in England and Wales.

ICAEW. (1999). *No Surprises: The Case For Better Risk Reporting*. London: Institute of Chartered Accountants in England and Wales.

ICAEW. (2002). No surprises: The case for better risk reporting. *Balance Sheet. The Institute of Chartered Accountants in England and Wales, 10*(4), 18–21.

Jorion, P. (1997). *Value at Risk: The New Benchmark for Controlling Market Risk*. Chicago: Irwin.

Khalil, A. & Maghraby, M. (2017). The determinants of internet risk disclosure: Empirical study of Egyptian listed companies. *Managerial Auditing Journal, 32*(8), 746–767.

Khan, T. (2006). *Financial Reporting Disclosure on The Internet: An International Perspective*, A PhD thesis, Faculty of Business and Law, School of Accounting, Victoria University, Australia.

Khan, T. (2007). Internet financial reporting: Disclosure about companies on websites. *Journal of Business Systems, Governance and Ethics, 2*(2), 37–46.

King Committee. (1994 & 2002). *King Reports on Corporate Governance for South Africa*. Johannesburg: Institute of Directors.

Korosec, B. & Horvat, R. (2005). Risk reporting in corporate annual report. *Economic and Business Review for Central and South-Eastern Europe, 7*(3), 217–237.

Krippendorff, K. (1980). *Content Analysis: An Introduction to its Methodology*. London: Sage.

Lajili, K. & Zeghal, D. (2005). Content analysis of risk management disclosures in Canadian annual reports. *Canadian Journal of Administrative Sciences, 22*(2), 125–142. Accessed 3 May, 2018. https://www.scribd.com/document/270691941/A-Content-Analysis-of-Risk-Management-Disclosures-in-Canadian-Annual-Reports.

Linsley, P. M. & Shrives, P. J. (2006). Risk reporting: A study of risk disclosures in the annual reports of UK companies. *The British Accounting Review, 38*(4), 387–404.

Lipunga, A. (2014). Risk disclosure practices of Malawian commercial banks. *Journal of Contemporary Issues in Business Research, 3*(3), 154–167.

Marston, C. (2003). Financial reporting on the Internet by leading Japanese companies. *Corporate Communications: A International Journal, 8*(1), 23–34.

Marston, C. L. & Shrives, P. J. (1991). The use of disclosure indices in accounting research: A review article. *British Accounting Review, 23*(3), 195–210.

Marzouk, M. (2016). Risk reporting during a crisis: Evidence from the Egyptian capital market. *Journal of Applied Accounting Research, 17*(4), 378–396.

Mohamed, E. K. A., Oyelere, P., & Al-Busaidi, M. (2009). A survey of internet financial reporting in Oman. *International Journal of Emerging Markets, 4*(1), 56–71.

Moumen, N., Othman, H. B., & Hussainey, K. (2015). The value relevance of risk disclosure in annual reports: Evidence from MENA emerging markets. *Research in International Business and Finance, 34*, 177–204.

Nahar, S., Azim, M. I., & Hossain, M. M. (2020). Risk disclosure and risk governance characteristics: Evidence from a developing economy. *International Journal of Accounting & Information Management, 28*(4), 577–605. Doi: 10.1108/IJAIM-07-2019-0083.

Naser, K., Al-Hussaini, A., Al-Kwari, D., & Nuseibeh, R. (2006). Determinants of corporate social disclosure in developing countries: The case of Qatar. *Advances in International Accounting, 19*, 1–23.

Neuendorf, K. A. (2002). *The Content Analysis Guidebook* (2nd edn.). Sage Publications: Cleveland State University, CA.

Oliveira, L., Rodrigues, L. L., & Craig, R. (2006). Firm- specific determinants of intangibles reporting: Evidence from the Portuguese stock market. *Journal of Human Resources Costing, 10*(1), 11–33.

Oliveira, J., Rodrigues, L. L., & Craig, R. (2011). Risk-related disclosure practices in the annual reports of portuguese credit institutions: An exploratory study. *Journal of Banking Regulation, 12*(2), 100–118.

Oorschot, L. (2009). *Risk Reporting: An Analysis of the German Banking Industry*. Master thesis Accounting, Auditing and Control, School of Economics, Erasmus University Rotterdam.

Oyelere, P., Laswad F., & Fisher, R. (2003). Determinants of internet financial reporting by New Zealand companies. *Journal of International Financial Management and Accounting, 14*(1), 26–63.

Safiullah, M. & Shamsuddin, A. (2018). Risk in Islamic banking and corporate governance. *Pacific-Basin Finance Journal, 47*(1), 129–149.

Schrand, C. M. & Elliott, J. A. (1998). Risk and financial reporting: A summary of the discussion at the 1997 AAA/FASB Conference. *Accounting Horizons Sarasota, 12*(3), 271–282.

Servaes, H. Tamayo, A., & Tufano, P. (2006). *The Theory and Practice of Corporate Risk Management Policy.* Deutsche Bank Liability Strategies Group.

Smith, B. & Pierce, A. (2005). An investigation of the integrity of Internet financial reporting. *The International Journal of Digital Accounting Research*, *5*(9), 47–78.

Stradea Consulting (2006). Survey of risk disclosures in the European financial Sector. Accessed 8 May, 2018. http://www.stradea.org/.

Sundmacher, M. (2006). *Consistency of Risk Reporting in Financial Services Firms.* School of Economics and Finance, University of Western Sydney. Available at SSRN: https://ssrn.com/abstract=963245.

Vandemaele, S. Verguawen, P., & Michiels, A. (2009). Management risk reporting practices and their determinants: a study of Belgian listed firms. Accessed 3 May, 2018. https://uhdspace.uhasselt.be/dspace/handle/1942/9392.

Zafar, M. B. & Sulaiman, A. A. (2020). Measuring corporate social responsibility in Islamic banking: What matters? *International Journal of Islamic and Middle Eastern Finance and Management*, *13*(3), 357–388. Doi: 10.1108/IMEFM-05-2019-0227.

Appendix

Appendix A. Risk disclosure index for Islamic banks.

Category	Disclosure Item
Accounting policies	1. Description of financial risk management objectives
	2. Description of financial risk management policies
	3. Objective of holding derivatives/ instruments
	4. Use of accounting estimates and assumptions
	5. Collateral assets against loans
	6. Financial and other assets impairment
	7. Contingent assets and liabilities
Financial risks	
Credit risk	8. Credit risk disclosure
	9. Credit risk exposure
Liquidity risk	10. Liquidity risk disclosure
Market risk disclosures	11. Market risk disclosures
	12. Description of stress tests and/or sensitivity analyses
	13. Pricing and commodity risk
	14. Changes in interest rates risk
	15. Foreign exchange rate risk (Currency risk)
	16. Capital adequacy
	17. Equity risk
	18. Leverage rate

(Continued)

Appendix A. (*Continued*)

Category	Disclosure Item
Financial instruments and derivatives hedging	19. An explanation of the extent to which financial instruments are used and the associated risks
	20. Financial derivatives
	21. Fair value's cumulative change
	22. Cash flow hedge
Operational, general and other risks	23. Operational risk disclosure
	24. Customer satisfaction
	25. Competition (Service market)
	26. Outsourcing risk
	27. Reputation risk
	28. Technology changes
	29. Communications
	30. Natural and physical disasters (Environmental risks)
	31. Insurance risk
	32. Sustainability risk
Reserves	33. General reserves
	34. Legal reserves
	35. Other reserves
Segment information	36. Geographical concentration
	37. Sector (Business) concentration
Business risk	38. General financial problems
	39. Regional financial problems
	40. Political risk
	41. Performance and efficiency
	42. Diversification

Appendix A. (*Continued*)

Category	Disclosure Item
Compliance, legal and regulatory risks	43. Compliance with Egyptian central bank regulation
	44. Compliance with financial regulations
	45. Compliance with Egyptian companies act requirements
	46. Compliance with other regulations and laws (e.g., Egyptian tax laws and regulations)
	47. Litigation risk
	48. Health and safety
The risks of financial techniques in the Islamic bank	49. Mudarabah risk
	50. Musharakah risk
	51. Murabahah risk
	52. Ijarah risk
	53. Qard Hasan risk
	54. Al-Istisna risk
	55. Salam risk
	56. Sukuk risk
	57. Wakalah risk
Islamic standards	58. Unusual supervisory restrictions
	59. Earnings or expenditures prohibited by Sharia instructions (e.g., Zakat)
	60. Restricted investments and finance statement
	61. The method of allocation the investment profits (loss) between unrestricted investment account holders or their equivalent and the Islamic bank as a Mudarib or as an investment with its own funds by the Islamic bank

https://doi.org/10.1142/9781800612426_0010

Chapter 10

An Islamic Perspective on CSR Initiatives and Sustainable Development of Islamic Banks in Egypt

Nada Said Awad Allah Selim

Abstract

Through a case study of three Egyptian Islamic banks, this study examines the concept of corporate social responsibility from an Islamic perspective, the role of Egyptian Islamic banks in social and environmental responsibility, and the extent to which they participate in sustainable development activities. The chapter provides a brief overview of the concept and dimensions of corporate social responsibility as well as the Islamic perspective of social responsibility and its fields and dimensions toward stakeholders, as well as the definition of Islamic banks, their nature, and how they support social activities and sustainability, and the differences between them and traditional banks. According to the report, Islamic banks in Egypt play an effective and pioneering role in sustainable development and social and environmental responsibility, as evidenced by the programs that these banks have established to participate in a variety of social projects and activities as health care, education, charity institution assistance, social housing, persons with special needs, Qard Hasan, the environment, and sustainability.

Keywords: CSR Initiatives, Sustainable Development, Islamic Banks, Egypt.

10.1 Introduction

Corporate social responsibility (CSR) is a widely discussed topic among academics and practitioners alike. It is a strategy that takes into account an organization's economic, legal, estimated, and ethical implications and societal responsibilities (Carroll, 1979). CSR research has expanded in recent years as more organizations understand the value of defining and implementing CSR into all parts of their operations due to the beneficial influence on financial success (Mohammed, 2007). Companies are becoming more conscious of their societal duties, roles, and rights. They are perceived to have implemented actions, procedures, and rules to fulfill their legal, ethical, social, and environmental obligations to stakeholders, including shareholders, employees, customers, suppliers, the environment, and society as a whole (Elasrag, 2015).

CSR in the Islamic world involves the development of an ethical self that identifies good and wrong, and it never forgets its responsibilities to Allah and mankind. Islam as a religion has not lost its general influence on the societies where it is practiced, and it represents a "complete way of life" for its adherents, with specific consequences for economic life, and therefore, the role that ethical business may play in the development of a socially fair community/society/economy and equity ideals rather than efficiency or profit-generating CSR is not the same as charity-giving or philanthropy. In order to achieve long-term growth, it should go beyond that and seek economic, social, and environmental goals (Elasrag, 2015).

Consistent with this, Islamic banks are one of the most significant components of the financial system that have altered their reporting views and released a sustainability report covering a wide range of subjects, including CSR. SR is usually considered to be one of the most significant subjects in Islamic banking, and it investigates how these institutions fulfill their societal obligations through participation in a variety of social activities and initiatives (Kotb *et al.*, 2021). According to Ernst and Young (2013), ethical components should be included in the Islamic banking sector.

CSR activities will increase stakeholder loyalty, confidence, and good reputation as well as improve the bank's investments and deposits (Tuhin, 2014). In general, the Islamic economic system seeks to enable individuals to make a livelihood in a fair and equitable manner and profitably based on Sharia without exploitation of others so that the entire society benefits. Individual rights are also prioritized in Islam over the welfare of the community (Khan & Karim, 2010).

It is worth noting that the debate on CSR has received increasing attention, and as a result, the literature on CSR has become extensive; however, the literature is still inconclusive, and there is a clear lack of research and investigation into the role of Islamic banks in social responsibility in Egyptian studies, as the vast majority of the literature is still inconclusive. According to previous research on CSR in Egyptian banks, they focused on discovering the nature of social responsibility and its determinants, and none of these studies provided clear and comprehensive evidence about discovering the social role of Islamic banks and studying the issues of social responsibility and sustainable development from an Islamic perspective despite the consolidation of its concepts in the teachings of Islamic Sharia, except the study by Kotb *et al.* (2021) which investigated the role of Islamic banks in social responsibility in underdeveloped nations but only looked at one Islamic bank in Egypt.

As a result, this work aims to contribute to the literature by expanding and increasing the sample size to include three Islamic banks in Egypt in order to discover their role in practicing social responsibility activities and to provide a deep understanding of the effective role of Egyptian Islamic banks' participation in these activities and their role in the field of sustainable development using content analysis for Islamic banks in Egypt. To fill this gap, we answer the following research questions:

What is the Islamic perspective of CSR? What is the role of Islamic banks in social responsibility in Egypt? The rest of the chapter is organized as follows. Section 10.2 goes through the theoretical foundation, which includes the idea and aspects of CSR, an Islamic viewpoint on CSR, Islamic bank and social responsibility, and the contrasts between Islamic banks and regular banks. Section 10.3 investigates the literature on CSR and Islamic banking. Section 10.4 goes over the sample and technique. Section 10.5 is the conclusion.

10.2 Theoretical Background

10.2.1 *Concept and dimensions of CSR*

CSR has expanded dramatically in the previous decade as a result of globalization and international commerce, resulting in increasing corporate complexity as well as increasing expectations for greater transparency and corporate citizenship. More firms than ever before are making significant attempts to define and incorporate CSR into all parts of their operations, supported by a growing body of data showing that CSR enhances company economic performance. Dusuki and Wajdi (2008) stated that companies believe that being socially responsible will provide them with a competitive advantage. They anticipate that by effectively communicating their social, environmental, and economic contributions, they will be able to fortify their brand, boost their corporate image with consumers and suppliers, as well as attract and maintain a dedicated and talented staff. Indeed, existing research claims that a commitment to CSR will result in increased profitability and competitiveness and risk management.

In the literature, there are many definitions of social responsibility, but the most comprehensive definitions are provided by Carroll (1999), who defined CSR as the duty of businessmen to seek decisions, policies, and paths of action that are beneficial in terms of social aims and values. According to the World Bank, it is "businesses' commitment to contribute to sustainable development by collaborating with employees, their families, and society to enhance their standard of living in a way that supports both the economy and growth" (United Nations, 2004). And, according to the International Organization for Standardization (ISO, 2010), CSR is defined as making a business accountable for the impact of its activities and operations on society and the environment via ethical behavior and transparency toward stakeholders, compliance with applicable laws and international standards of conduct, and integration of the aforementioned areas into all facets of the facility's business and connections. Finally, the World Business Council for Sustainable Development 2021 (WBCSD, 2021) defines CSR as a company's ongoing commitment to act ethically, contribute to economic development, and strive to improve the quality of life for its employees and their families, the local community, and society as a whole.

Carroll (1979, 1991) indicates that CSR has four dimensions: human, ethical, legal, and economic. These four categories or components of social responsibility can be classified as a pyramid that shows the basic components of CSR, as shown in Table 10.1.

10.2.2 *Islamic perspective of CSR*

The predominant idea of corporate social obligation alludes to the assumptions that society has regarding business in order not to harm it and to make a significant contribution to the prosperity of others. Comparative qualities with highlights of reliability with CSR additionally exist in Islamic qualities and a good way of thinking.

Table 10.1. The pyramid of CSR.

Economic responsibility	It refers not only to profit but also to maintaining a high level of operating efficiency, adherence to ethical practices, and maintaining a competitive position, that is, the organization being useful and economically successful by generating goods and services that society and customers demand while also giving adequate returns to investors
Legal responsibility	Companies adhere to regulations and laws, earn the confidence of people by not engaging in unlawful activities, and deliver goods and services that satisfy the bare minimum of legal standards
Ethical responsibility	In order to achieve the company's goals, the company must recognize and respect the community's ethical standards and prevent violations of those standards. It is also critical for the company to understand that corporate integrity and ethical behavior extend beyond merely adhering to the laws and regulations
Philanthropic responsibility	That the company works in community development and that it provides aid to private and public educational institutions, and the participation of managers and employees in community volunteer and charity activities, as well as voluntarily assisting in projects that enhance people's lives and society

In the Islamic point of view, CSR envelops more extensive importance, accepting the worth of nobility (taqwa) in all circumstances, by which everybody in the association should do his/her jobs and obligations as worker and vicegerent. An individual with honorable esteem comprehends their job in this common life is to oversee and foster the world as per the Sharia rules and worth. The center standards of Islamic CSR are obtained from the Qur'an and Sunnah, While the major pillars of Islamic CSR standards are solidarity, vicegerency and trusteeship, equity and harmony, and rights and duties (Arsad *et al.*, 2015).

The objective of an Islamic social framework depends on falah (human prosperity) and hayat tayyibah (great life), the two of which stress fraternity and social equity. Considering the blessed Qur'an and Hadith, the concept of social responsibility and equity in Islam argues that there is, by all accounts, congruence between ideas in social obligation and equality, as well as deals in Islam that resonate with successful conceptions of CSR (Mohammed, 2013).

This section explains Islam's regulation of the dimensions of the company's social responsibility toward its stakeholders. A company cannot function in a vacuum; it must interact with a variety of stakeholders. Almighty Allah and His Prophet (PBUH) gave detailed instructions for dealing with stakeholders. Stakeholders include employees, debtors, creditors, competitors, the environment, and general society.

10.2.2.1 *Company's social responsibility toward its employees*

Islam emphasizes justice and equality in all human relationships, employees must be treated with respect and humanity, and the Islamic Sharia included controls for preserving the rights of workers, the most important of which are:

- A worker is entitled to a decent standard of living. Allah Almighty has praised the man and exalted him above all other creatures. It is not permissible to deny his dignity because his wages are insufficient to meet his basic needs and the needs of those under his sponsorship. That was confirmed by Allah Almighty, who said "And do not deprive people of their due" (Surat Al'araf, 85).
- The employee's right to freedom, expression of opinion, and participation in decision-making within the framework of the shura

principle, as referred to by Allah Almighty "And those who have responded to their lord and established prayer and whose affair is (determined by) consultation among themselves, and from what we have provided them, they spend" (Surat Alsh-Shuraa, 38).

- That the company guarantees the employee's rights in the event of disability or a crisis. Islam has established a one-of-a-kind social security system that guarantees everyone the right to a decent life. The zakat and social solidarity systems serve as the foundation for this guarantee.
- The principle of Islamic law is that it is based on mercy, kindness, and facilitation, so ease must include work relationships by avoiding everything that leads to exhausting the employee's health while not assigning him what he has no power to do, preserving his rights, and strengthening trust between him and the employer with what he leads them. They achieve their goals in work and production without standing in their way. That disrupts the company's activity.

10.2.2.2 *Company's social responsibility toward its debtor*

In the Western administration style, if a debtor is unable to repay obligations on time, the best alternative is a rescheduling of installment by charging an extra sum that appears to be punishment. Organizations that are more socially conscious may waive the penalty sum and reschedule the first sum. Alternatively, Islam recommended its adherents manage the account holders while acting under the shadow of consideration. "And if someone is in hardship, then (let there be) postponement until (a time of) ease. But if you give (from your right as) charity, then it is better for you if you only know" says the Holy Qur'an (Surat Al-Baqarah, 280).

10.2.2.3 *Relationship with creditors*

Islam provided clear guidelines that must be followed to regulate the relationship between the organization and the suppliers dealing with it. It also calls for fulfilling all obligations toward suppliers and settling them following what was agreed upon before and also creates balance in all things. Debtors are urged to be forgiven in the event of an emergency, while creditors are instructed to not only pay back their debt on time but to pay it back handsomely. There are severe consequences for creditors who do not repay their debts on time for. According to Hadith, narrated Abu Huraira, Allah's messenger stated, "A wealthy person's procrastination (delay) in repaying obligations is injustice".

10.2.2.4 *Company's social responsibility toward its competitors*

In the West, the rival is seen as the most threatening element to the firm's survival. According to Beekun (1997), businesses seek to establish themselves over rivals and destroy them to acquire monopolistic pricing and enjoy above-average profits via hoarding. This phenomenon is categorically condemned by Islam. According to a Hadith, the following is mentioned about hoarding: The Prophet of Allah said, "No one hoards but a sinner" (Sunan Ibn Majah, Sahih).

Competitors also strive to suffocate one another to avoid losing business. The Almighty Allah has advised believers to maintain their faith in Him. If they do, Almighty Allah provides enough for them and showers them with benefits from areas they could never fathom. As a result, a believer should be unconcerned about newcomers and should not try to hurt them in any manner. It is mentioned in the Holy Quran: "And will provide for him from where he does not expect. And whoever relies upon Allah — then he is sufficient for him. Indeed, Allah will accomplish his purpose. Allah has already set for everything a (decreed) extent" (Surat At-Talaq, 3).

10.2.2.5 *Relationship with consumers*

Islam has set a specific ethical framework for trade and exchange operations that guarantees consumer protection, encourages honesty in buying and selling, and imposes penalties for fraud or consumer exploitation. Concerning this, Allah Almighty said: "So fulfill the measure and weight and do not deprive people of their due and cause corruption upon the earth after its reformation That is better for you if you should be a believer" (Surat Al'araf, 85). And Allah's Apostle said, "may Allah's prayers and peace be upon him", said: "Whoever deceives us is not one of us" (Sahih Muslim). And, about the product's quality, he stated, may Allah's blessings and peace be upon him, "Allah likes it whenever one of you accomplishes a task that he masters" (Sahih Al Bukhari).

Islamic Sharia also protects the consumer from the product, as Islam commands the producer (the organization) to perfect the manufacture and increase the quality of the product while rationalizing the expenses so that the prices are suitable for the consumer. Avoid producing and selling taboos.

10.2.2.6 *Relationship with government*

Business organizations are socially responsible toward the government, as they have to pay the imposed taxes and conduct business operations and activities following the laws set by the government, and the organization should participate in social activities and be supportive of policies for economic and social development.

10.2.2.7 *Company's social responsibility toward the environment*

Another essential aspect of social responsibility is voluntarily feeling the obligation to protect the environment. Business organizations must take the necessary steps to protect the environment and avoid contributing to environmental illness.

For such problems, Islam has established clear instructions: protecting the environment from corruption and prohibiting the utilization of resources that would cause damage or inconvenience to the environment and society, even if that destruction is the consumption for a benefit. The Prophet (PBUH) has said: "There is no extension for causing harm in Islam, neither on account of an autonomous activity nor as a response" (Kitab al-Kharaj) (Muhamad, 2008).

In addition to preserving the environment from pollution, excessive consumption and extravagance, whether in water, trees, or other environmental resources, should be avoided. According to Islam, natural resource development should be done with prudence. It is further mentioned in a Hadith: "The blessed Prophet of Allah passed by Sayyiduna Sa'd whilst he was performing wudhu. He asked, 'Why this wastage (of water)?' 'Can a person squander water in wudhu?' said Sayyiduna Sa'd. He replied, "Yes, even if you are on the bank of a flowing river" (Sunan Ibn Majah and Musnad Ahmad). Because natural resources are the shared inheritance of all people, Islamic teachings should be followed in developing them, safeguarding them from harm and degradation, and utilizing them responsibly.

10.2.2.8 *Relationship with general society*

According to Islam, the society in which the company operates should receive a portion of the benefits derived from the company's various activities. This is reflected in urging businesses to support voluntary and charitable works and to finance social projects, as well as to plan and optimize resource use and avoid all commercial transactions that harm society.

There are several Quranic passages and Hadiths in which Almighty Allah and His Prophet (peace be upon him) urge participation in societal welfare. The concept of zakat (obligatory charity) and sadaqah (optional charity) have vast implications in this regard. Allah has strictly instructed us to give 2.5% of our savings to charity, and it is obligatory on every Muslim (Mir *et al.*, 2016).

This concept is mentioned in different places in the Holy Quran: "Take, (O, Muhammad), from their wealth a charity by which you purify them and cause them to increase" (Surat Al-Tawba, 103). "And establish prayer and give zakah and obey the messenger — that you may receive mercy" (Surat An-Nur, 56). As a vicegerent of Almighty Allah, it is the duty of each human to take care of the affairs of his creatures, especially the other people living in society, because whatever humans have belongs to Almighty Allah (Mir *et al.*, 2016).

10.2.3 *Islamic bank and social responsibility*

Islamic banks' activities and operations are not just based on government rules, laws, and regulations but must also adhere to the principles of Islamic law. As a result, Islamic banks' permissible operations are limited in comparison to regular banks, which are not subject to such limitations (Basah, 2013). Islamic banks should seek to participate in society in order to promote economic, financial, political, and social stability based on Islamic principles (Ahmed & Hassan, 2007).

Because Islamic finance is based on religious beliefs, any actions that do not adhere to Islamic norms and principles should be avoided. As a result, Islamic banks should refrain from investing in or financing any entity or corporation that violates human rights or destroys the natural environment. As a result, Islamic banks play a significant role in social responsibility activities (Ullah & Jamali, 2010).

In several ways, social responsibility in Islamic banks differs from established norms in other banks. This distinction is related to the institutional structure of Islamic banking services (Franzoni & Allali, 2018), where Islamic banking is based on observing and executing the responsibilities and principles stated in Islamic Sharia, such as depending on the financial system concept. Islamic banking is interest-free, minimizes transaction uncertainty, forbids speculation, invests in halal or Islamically permissible services and commodities, and does not invest in banned activities and sectors such as gambling, alcohol, and pork (Ullah *et al.*, 2014).

The idea of Islamic banks' commitment to social responsibility may also be defined through the following three key ideologies that differentiate them from regular banks:

- Islamic banks work toward the Islamic economy's vision of a just, equitable, and balanced society. As a result, Islamic banks are not free to conduct anything they choose but must instead blend moral principles with economic activities.
- Islamic banking is founded on the ideals of brotherhood and collaboration as well as a stake-taking and equity-sharing scheme, which strengthens society's economic underpinnings.
- As a system founded on the social and moral framework of Islamic law, Islamic banking is distinguished by moral principles and social duties.

10.2.4 *Distinctions between Islamic and conventional banks*

Islamic banks are distinguished from regular banks by their management structure. Islamic banks have a distinct corporate governance structure since they are required to select a Sharia Supervisory Board (SSB) made up of Islamic experts (Nathan & Ribiere, 2007). The SSB aims to guarantee that Islamic banks follow Sharia law and to decrease risk (Rammal, 2006). The presence of SSB members guarantees that the audit processes of Islamic banks urge them to carefully observe and abide by Islamic standards. Any departure from Islamic standards may result in non-Sharia compliance and harsh fines for Islamic banks. As a result, Islamic banks are expected to demonstrate more comprehensive and active CSR management, particularly in natural environmental risk management.

Table 10.2 compares and contrasts the general similarities and differences between Islamic and conventional banks. This table is based on the research of Ahmad and Hassan (2007), Dusuki (2008), and Basah and Yusuf (2013), who thoroughly studied the features and differences between Islamic and conventional banks.

10.3 Literature Review

Islamic banking is now an undeniable reality. It offers financial services that are based on religious prohibitions. Lewis and Algaoud (2001) defined Islamic bank as "a financial institution that provides a service to its customers free of interest and the giving and taking of interest is prohibited in all transactions". Islamic banking differs from conventional banking in the following three ways: (1) Sharia principles (riba free, extreme uncertainty free, zakat, fairness, justice, and balanced society); (2) offering product structure based on an active partnership between bank and customer's profit and loss, mudarabah, and murabahah; and (3) management structure (Sharia scholar board). Islamic banks are expected to demonstrate more proactive CSR practices due to a focus on Islamic core ethical values and considerations (Dusuki, 2008). Indeed, Islamic banks are required to engage in CSR activities (Jusoh *et al.*, 2015). This is because CSR is a duty for all Muslims (Jusoh *et al.*, 2015; Taman, 2011).

Several researchers (e.g., Dusuki, 2011; Salma Sairally, 2013; Khurshid *et al.*, 2014; Arli & Tjiptono, 2014; Di Bella & Al-Fayoumi, 2016) have examined Islamic banks' CSR operations, demonstrating that they strengthen corporate image and uphold bank duties. Malaysian Islamic banks and financial institutions prioritize people's well-being to preserve morality, justice, and well-being in society (Dusuki, 2011). Islamic financial services should be held accountable for maintaining society's well-being following the purposes of Islamic Sharia (Salma Sairally, 2013). Also, Baghallab and Chaar (2021) investigated four commercial Islamic banks in Saudi Arabia. The findings found that these banks varied in their degrees of participation and implemented the bare minimum of CSR. The findings revealed that they want and wish to contribute to the well-being of humans as a result of their religious beliefs. Nonetheless, only one of the four banks was found to have good strategic thinking in terms of the three dimensions of economic, environmental, and social. As a result of the findings, banks should publish an annual

Table 10.2. Differences between Islamic and conventional banks.

Islamic banks	Conventional banks
Are based on Sharia (Islamic Sharia) principle and Sharia sources (Quran and Sunnah)	Based on artificial principles, secular principles regulate functions and operations, which are not based on religious ideas and ideals
Investment is based on risk-sharing between the capital source (investor) and the fund user (entrepreneur)	The investor receives a set rate of return
Profit maximization is permissible but subject to Sharia constraints	Profit maximization with no limitations
Obligation to pay zakat.	There is no zakat requirement
Investment is based on risk-sharing between the capital source (investor) and the fund user (entrepreneur)	Banks' principal job is to lend money and collect interest on it
Banks are not authorized to levy extra fees to defaulters	Banks may impose an extra fee in the case of a default (compound interest rate)
The PLS banking paradigm necessitates that banks devote more time and effort to developing project appraisals and evaluations	Banks lay minimal attention on building competence in project appraisal and evaluation since advance income is set
The feasibility of projects is more important to Islamic banks	Banks pay a higher focus on the creditworthiness of their customers
The bank–client relationship is seen as a collaborative effort involving partners, investors, and traders	A creditor–debtor relationship exists between a bank and a client
Islamic banks must demonstrate social and economic responsibility by deducting zakat (a religious tax) from earnings	It is not required to carry out charitable activities
Islamic banks are not permitted to engage in immoral or Sharia-prohibited economic activities, such as funding enterprises involving alcohol, prostitution, pork, environmental damage, and so on	There is no such restriction

CSR or TBL report outlining their social and environmental initiatives. Aracil (2019) revealed that Islamic banks have an inherent commitment to CSR activities, whereas traditional banks use CSR techniques. Human resource, philanthropic, human rights, and environmental concerns are all stressed in Islamic banks' CSR efforts, according to Khurshid *et al.* (2014). They investigated the practices and issues arising from CSR of Islamic banks in Malaysia using the interview technique as the research method. They concluded that CSRD, CSR management, and CSR funds are the most critical issues that must be addressed to ensure that CSR is applied effectively in Malaysian Islamic banks and also discovered that Malaysian Islamic banks are not solely concerned with zakat and charitable activities (e.g., Bank Islam Malaysia Berhad (BIMB)).

Bhuiyan *et al.* (2021) discussed CSR practices in Bangladeshi Islamic banks. According to the findings of the study, men are the majority of those who benefit from CSR activities, and the study suggested that Islamic banks in Bangladesh should include CSR activities that encourage females to participate in the development process and change their socio-economic status as well as increase their CSR activities for socio-economic development, such as funding education programs, increasing sponsorship of sporting events, and promoting Bangladeshi arts and culture. In addition, Bakar and Yusof (2016) examined CSR activities from an Islamic perspective using Bank Islam Malaysia Berhad. According to the findings of the research, the bank's CSR efforts have become more structured and well-planned. As a result of the bank's experience with CSR programs, this research offers a management guideline that applies to enterprises that want to do CSR as part of their commitment to being good corporate citizens.

In Egypt, Megeid (2013) investigated CSR implementation in Egyptian Islamic and non-Islamic banks in terms of the impact of bank service quality on customer satisfaction and improving financial performance. Scholars stated that Egyptian traditional banks have a greater spending capacity and commitment to CSR because their financial performance is superior to that of Islamic banks. Furthermore, Kotb *et al.* (2021) investigated Islamic banks and social responsibility, and the empirical part was carried out by using a qualitative case study methodology on the Faisal Islamic Bank of Egypt and exhibiting instances of FIBE-supported social enterprises. The findings verified the importance of Islamic banks in CSR and the growth of social enterprises.

Taking into account the preceding literature, there is a significant amount of literature in both the areas of CSR and CSR in the global Islamic banking industry in general and in Egyptian Islamic banks in particular. The literature is still inconclusive. Due to the presence of a large number of previous studies that were mostly working on CSR in Egyptian banks and focused on exploring the practices, nature, and determinants of CSR reports, there is a lack of research in the field of investigation of the role of Islamic banks in CSR. Previous studies on social responsibility in the Egyptian Islamic banking industry, to the best of the researcher's knowledge, did not provide clear and comprehensive evidence about the role of Islamic banks in CSR in Egypt.

10.4 Methodology and Data

A qualitative case study technique will be utilized to conduct this study and answer the research question, comprehend and explain the idea of CSR, as well as the method of managing its activities from an Islamic standpoint in Egyptian Islamic banks and investigate the extent to which these banks contribute to and engage in CSR activities. It is envisaged that Islamic banks would set an example by implementing social responsibility initiatives under Sharia principles and prioritizing them among their top values and objectives.

This qualitative case study focuses on comprehending and explaining the process under investigation. In previous studies, academics engaged in qualitative research and the social sciences employed the case study technique to explore the development of current life. This study was done on three Egyptian Islamic banks, and data from the sample institutions' annual reports and sustainability and governance reports were collected from 2018 to 2020.

10.5 A Case Study of Islamic Banks in Egypt

10.5.1 *Al Baraka Bank, Egypt*

10.5.1.1 *About Al Baraka Bank, Egypt*

According to the official website of Al Baraka Bank, Egypt, Al Baraka Bank, Egypt, S.A.E, for over 30 years, the company has conducted its many operations and activities following the rules of the tolerant Islamic Sharia.

Al Ahram Bank — an Egyptian joint-stock company — was founded as a commercial bank on March 19, 1980, under Law 43 of 1974 and its amendments. On April 30, 2009, the bank's extraordinary general meeting agreed to change its name to Al Baraka Bank, Egypt. Through 32 branches, the bank provides all corporate and retail banking services as well as investment, following the rules of the Islamic Sharia in the Arab Republic of Egypt. Its headquarters are on El Teseen Southern Street in the Central Area, First Sector, Fifth Settlement of New Cairo. The Egyptian stock exchange lists it as a publicly listed company.

10.5.1.2 *Al Baraka Bank of Egypt's contributions to sustainability and social responsibility*

Since 2012, Al Baraka Bank of Egypt has been a pioneer in realizing and implementing the idea of social responsibility, as it is one of the determinants of the bank's strategy to attain best practices at the local and regional levels, where the bank is trying to bring about a renaissance and growth in all aspects of Egyptian society by promoting and reinforcing the ideals and principles of tolerant Islamic Sharia. This is accomplished by implementing the Al Baraka Social Responsibility Program under an authorized policy and regulation, and the bank has instruments in place to meet the Al Baraka Social Responsibility Program's yearly targets (2016–2020) through the Social Management Committee (Internal), the Committee of Branches, Zakat, and Social Responsibility, which is appointed by the Board of Directors and collaborates with the Al Baraka Social Responsibility Committee.

Al Baraka Program for Sustainability and Social Responsibility:

- Creating 10,000 new job possibilities within the scope of the bank's financing and investment operations, whether individually or through syndicated loans and co-finances.
- Contributing EGP 22 million to the development and purchase of hospital equipment and supplies most needed throughout the

governorates of the Arab Republic of Egypt to offer healthcare to the needy.

- Contributing EGP 7 million through giving financial assistance to new educational institutions and upgrading the infrastructure of current educational institutions, as well as scholarships for the brilliant and needy.
- Donating EGP 11 million to charities and Zakat Institutions interested in giving help and support to poor families, as well as contributing by presenting work possibilities to youngsters through micro, small, and medium enterprises.
- Continued assistance for the Tahya Misr Fund, either for casual labor or for those severely impacted by the epidemic, and recently offering additional help of EGP 15 million to provide COVID-19 vaccination to underprivileged populations.

Allocation of social activities and initiatives of Al Baraka Bank of Egypt (from 2018 to 2020): By establishing the Zakat Fund, as a prominent Islamic Foundation, the Bank has never shied away from its social responsibilities. It has always answered and reacted to the society's financial requirements as it conducts its business on the principles drawn from the merciful Islamic Sharia, while maintaining the highest professional standards ever, enabling it to adhere to the concept of sharing realized profits with its social partners. The total value of the bank's social contributions via the Zakat Fund, as well as its social activities and initiatives over the last three years (from 2018 to 2020) is shown in Table 10.3.

Table 10.3. Total amounts of resources and zakat spent of Al Baraka Bank of Egypt.

Income & expenses account	2018	2019	2020
Total Resources	**8744519**	**16522080**	**12479409**
Zakat Spent			
Hospitals, Foundations & Charitable Associations	8229882	15117450	11756000
Administrative & General Expenses	432	515	210
Total Expenses	**8230314**	**15117965**	**11756210**

Source: The annual reports of the bank for the period from 2018 to 2020.

In 2018, Al Baraka Bank of Egypt contributed around EGP 8.2 million to a variety of social initiatives, including hospitals and medical facilities providing comprehensive health care, charities, subsidizing and funding educational foundations, and the operations of its Zakat Fund. In addition, in collaboration with Al Azhar Al-Sharif, the "Holy Qur'an" competition for all ages is held in Egypt's major cities.

In 2019, within the context of the initiatives established by the Federation of Egyptian Banks, Al Baraka Group sponsored free-of-charge treatment centers, the "Tahya Misr" Fund, and the development of slums. The total amount spent in the framework of social responsibility and aspects of zakat amounted to about EGP 15.1 million.

In 2020, Al Baraka Bank of Egypt spending in the framework of social responsibility and aspects of zakat until the end of 2017 amounted to about EGP 11.8 million.

10.5.2 *Abu Dhabi Islamic Bank — Egypt*

10.5.2.1 *About Abu Dhabi Islamic Bank — Egypt*

According to the Abu Dhabi Islamic Bank (ADIB) of Egypt's official website, under Law No. 43/1974 and its executive rules, ADIB — Egypt (previously National Development Bank) was founded as an Egyptian joint-stock corporation in the Arab Republic of Egypt on April 3, 2013. The bank's main office is located at 9 Rustom Street in Garden City, Cairo Governorate. The bank is listed on the Egyptian stock exchange. ADIB — Egypt, as a financial institution is supervised and controlled by the Central Bank of Egypt (CBE), and the bank adheres to Islamic Sharia rules in all products offered to ADIB clients, whether they be investment deposits, Islamic investment sukuk, or savings accounts. ADIB has a Fatwa and Sharia Supervisory Committee, which is comprised of Sharia jurists with banking, legal, and economic experience and is in charge of issuing fatwas and legal judgments on all aspects of present and future Islamic banking activities. ADIB, — Egypt is an Egyptian joint stock company that provides banking and financial services to individuals and companies through 70 branches.

10.5.2.2 *Abu Dhabi Islamic Bank — Egypt's contributions to sustainability and social responsibility*

The bank has been successful in incorporating community responsibility concepts into its culture and making it a daily activity that is fully linked with the bank's processes and strategy, which act as a support system in addition to the services provided to society. The total value of the bank's social contributions and initiatives over the last three years (2018 to 2020) is shown in Tables 10.4–10.6.

Table 10.4. Allocation social activities and initiatives of ADIB — Egypt in 2018.

NGO	Charity
Misr Al Kheir	During Ramadan, 3,360 food boxes were distributed throughout four governorates
Misr Al Kheir	Resolving debts for 15 persons who were imprisoned for failing to pay arrears
Ministry of Health & Population	The Ministry of Health and Population has launched an endeavor to minimize patient waiting lines
Misr Al Kheir	The first installment of administrative expenditures for 20 community schools in the governorates of Beni Suef, Assiut, and Luxor for one academic year
Orman Healing Hospital in Luxor	The first installment of the cost of constructing and outfitting an operating room at Orman Healing Hospital
Ahl Misr	The first payment toward the cost of constructing an operating theatre and intensive care unit at Ahl Misr Burns Hospital
Family Health Unit in Jirays Village	The expense of medical equipment to completely equip the physiotherapy department in Jirays hamlet and adjacent communities in the governorate of Menoufia to serve patients
Tahya Misr Fund	Contribute to the Tahya Misr Fund for Community Development

Source: The annual reports of the bank 2018.

Table 10.5. Allocation social activities and initiatives of ADIB — Egypt in 2019.

NGO	Donation value (in EGP)	Charity
Misr Al Kheir	2100000	For an academic year, the bank funded the second payment of administrative expenditures for 20 community schools in the governorates of Beni Suef, Assiut, and Luxor
Engaz	500000	In addition to sponsoring the Enactus Sustainability Competition for university students, we are developing innovative techniques to enhance the level of Egyptian schools and institutions
Orman Healing Hospital in Luxor	1570000	The cost of constructing and outfitting an operating room at Luxor's Shefaa Orman Hospital
Ahl Masr Hospital for the Treatment of Burns	1960000	Contributing the funds for the construction of an operating room and an intensive care unit
Misr Al Kheir	1200000	Contributing the cost of three medical convoys in Giza, Luxor, and Assiut governorates
Life Maker Foundation	5250000	Life Makers Foundation receives a donation to cover the costs of renovating and rebuilding four communities in the Qena Governorate
Misr Al Kheir	500000	Pay off debtors
Egyptian Food Bank	1000000	Providing the cost and participating in the distribution of Ramadan boxes to the poor and donating the cost of a fasting breakfast tent in Assiut Governorate for the month of Ramada
Fund Honoring the Martyrs	10000000	Donating to the families of the martyrs, victims, and injured in conflict, terrorism, and security operations
Others	1000000	
Total Donation Value for the Year 2019	**25080000**	

Source: The annual reports of the bank 2019.

Table 10.6. Allocation social activities and initiatives of ADIB — Egypt in 2020.

NGO	Donation value (in EGP)	Charity
Federation of Egyptian Banks	15000000	Financial assistance was provided to day-to-day workers afflicted by the COVID-19 virus as well as equipment and medical supplies to public hospitals with COVID-19 patients
Misr El Kheir	365000	The cost of 146 surgical operations in Assiut's medical caravan
Al-Nour School for the Visually Impaired	406300	The cost of computers, Braille printers, library furnishings, computer lab equipment, and classroom supplies
Al Matareya Educational Hospital	408000	The cost of medical equipment for the Dental Department
Al Qasr Al Einy Hospital	3150000	The cost of a gastroscope for the Gastroenterology Department
Al Joud Association (Al Nas Children's Hospital)	1125000	The cost of a fully equipped ambulance car with an intensive care unit
Magdi Yacoub Heart Hospital	700000	The cost of constructing an outpatient clinic
Raie Misr Organization	3675000	Two fully equipped buses that act as mobile clinics in impoverished areas
Total Donation Value for the Year 2020	**24829300**	

Source: The annual reports of the bank 2020.

10.5.3 *Faisal Islamic Bank of Egypt*

10.5.3.1 *About Faisal Islamic Bank of Egypt*

The Faisal Islamic Bank of Egypt (FIBE) is Egypt's first commercial and Islamic bank. The bank officially opened its doors on July 5, 1979. The Bank was established by Law No. 48 of 1977, which was subsequently confirmed by the Egyptian Parliament, and it was licensed as an economic and social institution in the form of an Egyptian joint-stock company operating under Islamic Sharia principles. The Articles of Incorporation were amended by Law No. 142 of 1981 and again by Law No. 97 of 1996. His Royal Highness Prince Amr Mohammed Al-Faisal Al-Saoud has assumed the role of Chairman of the Board of Directors. Through 36 branches and its headquarters at 3, 26th July St., Cairo, the bank provides all retail and corporate banking services, as well as investment operations, in the Arab Republic of Egypt and abroad.

10.5.3.2 *Contributions of Faisal Islamic Bank of Egypt in the field of social responsibility*

Since its founding in top priority through the legitimate banks of its Zakat Fund and contributions to social activities and initiatives for eligible persons, charities, and institutions, Faisal Islamic Bank of Egypt has led the Egyptian community in the field of social responsibility (Faisal Islamic Bank of Egypt website). Table 10.7 shows the overall value of the bank's social donations through the Zakat Fund, as well as its social activities and projects, over the last five years (from 2018 to 2020).

The bank created the Zakat Fund as a consequence of its view that involvement in community service is needed to develop social solidarity, which is considered as one of the key qualities that distinguish the bank from other comparable institutions. The link between social and economic activity, on the other hand, has a beneficial influence on society's progress toward complete development.

The fund's cumulative resources at the end of 2018 amounted to EGP 386 million, of which EGP 139.5 million reflects the lawfully due zakat on the Bank's funds, The balance is comprised of zakat received from investment account holders and individuals, as well as grants, contributions, charity investment account returns, and other sources. As a consequence, the total real disbursements for the fiscal year was EGP 63.5 million.

The fund's entire resources at the end of 2019 amounted to EGP 500 million, of which EGP 226 million represents the lawfully due zakat on the bank's funds, and the remaining amount reflects zakat from investment account holders and individuals, as well as grants, donations, and charitable investment account returns and others.

Table 10.7. Actual disbursed amount of zakat fund resources from 2018 to 2020.

Spending aspects	Year	Individuals	Students	Mosques	Medical institutions & legally recognized charity associations	Administrative expenses	Total
Amounts	2018	35.299	997	126	26.888	263	63.573
	2019	62.267	3.067	1.467	23.849	0.329	90.979
	2020	52.3	1.5	1.1	95.9	0.4	151.2

Source: The annual reports of the bank for the period from 2018 to 2020.

Thus, the total amount already spent throughout the reporting year was EGP 91 million.

Finally, the Zakat Fund's total collected resources were EGP 623.3 million at the end of 2020, with EGP 325.6 million representing legally due zakat and the rest representing zakat from investment account holders and individuals, as well as gifts, donations, charitable account returns, and other sources. The exact total sum is EGP 151.2 million.

These funds have been allocated to recipients and students in cash and in-kind or through the construction of student housing compounds at universities in some cities (Cairo, Sohag, Assiut, Shebin ElKom, and El Mansoura). Disbursements encompassed the repair of mosques and the provision of medical equipment to public hospitals and medical clinics in all governorates, in addition to the Holy Qur'an competitions and the orphanage, as shown in Table 10.7.

10.6 Conclusion

At the beginning of this work, we discussed the concept and dimensions of CSR and explained the Islamic perspective on the areas of social responsibility and its dimensions toward stakeholders. We then defined Islamic banks and presented their view of social responsibility as well as the differences between them and traditional banks. The experimental part of the study was conducted in the final section of the study by using a qualitative case study methodology on three Islamic banks in Egypt to clarify and display the extent to which these banks contribute to supporting sustainable development and the extent to which they participate in community service activities.

The study concluded that sustainability and social responsibility are naturally commensurate with the ethics of Islamic transactions, where Islamic legislation urged the performance of social responsibility and systems through precisely defined methods, such as the jurisprudence of zakat and rights due to workers, charity, and tolerance with customers, suppliers, charity, and others. It has been shown that Islamic banks play an important role in the field of social responsibility and their participation in social activities and programs that benefit society in addition to their observance of the balance between both economic performance and social performance and taking into account the needs of different stakeholders and this is evident in the sustainability and social responsibility programs during 2018–2020 presented by these banks. It was able to participate in activities that give due attention to the environment and society in various fields and urge them to achieve sustainability, such as providing health-care services by establishing and equipping medical units, providing free treatment services to thousands of poor and needy patients, supporting educational initiatives, providing facilities for researchers and scholars, and participating in many activities and projects, charitable proceeds, and seeking to provide zakat, alms, and legitimate banks for zakat funds, in addition to granting good loans to people with needs and those who suffer from emergency conditions.

The study recommends establishing self-contained departments to implement social responsibility principles within Islamic banks and to better train employees to find out the social responsibility programs and their importance for many stakeholders, including society while developing their religious and moral side by linking transactions with religious and moral values and removing any misunderstanding that may exist during the execution of this idea and the necessity to release sustainability reports separate from financial reporting, in addition to developing plans to discover the effective methods and tools for sustainable development and devising successful strategies for long-term growth.

Finally, this research was carried out in Egypt. In the future, the sample size might be increased and compared to other Islamic banks in Islamic nations and other developing countries, It is also feasible to perform a comparative study of Islamic and conventional banks. The comparative case studies will give further empirical evidence on the advantages of engaging in social responsibility activities as well as the variables and obstacles that might influence these activities in different contextual environments, in addition to learning about and benefiting from other initiatives that promote sustainable development and long-term growth.

References

Abu Bakar, F. & Md Yusof, M. A. (2016). Managing CSR initiatives from the Islamic perspective: The case of Bank Islam Malaysia Berhad (BIMB). *Jurnal Pengurusan*, *46*, 67–76.

Ahmad, A. U. F. & Hassan, M. K. (2007). Riba and Islamic banking. *Journal of Islamic Economics, Banking, and Finance*, *3*(1), 1–33.

Aracil, E. (2019). Corporate social responsibility of Islamic and conventional banks: The influence of institutions in emerging countries. *International Journal of Emerging Markets*, *4*(14), 582–600.

Arli, D. & Tjiptono, F. (2014). Does corporate social responsibility matter to consumers in Indonesia? *Social Responsibility Journal*, *3*(10), 537–549.

Arsad, S., Ahmad, R., Fisol, W. N. M., Said, R., & Haji-Othman, Y. (2015). Maqasid Shariah in the corporate social responsibility of Shari'ah-compliant companies. *Research Journal of Finance and Accounting*, *6*(6), 239–247.

Baghallab, S. M. & Chaar, A. M. (2021). Corporate social responsibility in Islamic commercial banks in Saudi Arabia. *PalArch's Journal of Archaeology of Egypt/Egyptology*, *18*(13), 1373–1382.

Basah, M. Y. A. & Yusuf, M. M. (2013). Islamic bank and corporate social responsibility (CSR). *European Journal of Business and Management*, *5*(11), 194–209.

Beekun, R. I. (1997). *Islamic business ethics* (No. 2). International Institute of Islamic Thought (IIIT). https://l.facebook.com/l.php?u=https%3A%2F%2Fwww.google.com%2Fbooks%3Fhl%3Dar%26lr%3D%26id%3DkiVcCgAAQBAJ%26oi%3Dfnd%26pg%3DPP1%26dq%3DIslamic%2520business%2520ethics%25201997%26ots%3DQTKjvr5zhq%26sig%3DqnsNh7sk7SpzX6JQwTa7_YcmgS4%26fbclid%3DIwAR0bWCGeqQAEf3DF0ob935u5sGRidFfb7zKc8dR4PFxBDPaG9cLjmpSfPHk&h=AT2tF86vVfmlJrNIHjPwF4ylozGjrFqr8FCr56gBDZhllRg_I0ryotc3ukpupcq1TW00N03wUxAAGRwz69QUZgJ948ce0HR_sGmMGfhwn3v-XT4O2_o7q3A8PJ6kW24DfkXD.

Bhuiyan, M., Darda, M., & Hossain, M. (2021). Corporate Social Responsibility (CSR) practices in Islamic banks of Bangladesh. *Social Responsibility Journal, ahead-of-print* (ahead-of-print). Doi: 10.1108/srj-07-2020-0280.

Carroll, A. B. (1979). A three-dimensional conceptual model of corporate performance. *Academy of Management Review*, *4*(4), 497–505.

Carroll, A. B. (1991). The pyramid of corporate social responsibility: Toward the moral management of organizational stakeholders. *Business Horizons*, *34*(4), 39–48.

Carroll, A. B. (1999). Corporate social responsibility: Evolution of a definitional construct. *Business & Society*, *38*(3), 268–295.

Di Bella, V. & Al-Fayoumi, N. (2016). Perception of stakeholders on corporate social responsibility of Islamic banks in Jordan. *Euromed Journal of Business*, *11*(1), 30–56.

Dusuki, A. W. (2008). What does Islam say about corporate social responsibility? *Review of Islamic economics*, *12*(1), 5–28.

Dusuki, A. W. (2011). *Ethical and Social Responsibility Models for Islamic Finance.* ISRA. https://l.facebook.com/l.php?u=http%3A%2F%2Fciteseerx.ist.psu.edu%2Fviewdoc%2Fdownload%3Fdoi%3D10.1.1.627.9647%26rep%3Drep1%26type%3Dpdf%26fbclid%3DIwAR00oJhbOv7VIduvsCCQhY9tHjSLnGg6WQikEvodAj7O71mbZHdod8YVaQI&h=AT2tF86vVfmlJrNIHjPwF4ylozGjrFqr8FCr56gBDZhllRg_I0ryotc3ukpupcq1TW00N03wUxAAGRwz69QUZgJ948ce0HR_sGmMGfhwn3v-XT4O2_o7q3A8PJ6kW24DfkXD.

Elasrag, H. (2015). Corporate social responsibility: An Islamic perspective. *SSRN Electronic Journal.* Doi: 10.2139/ssrn.2603832.

Ernst, Y. (2013). The World Islamic Banking Competitiveness Report, 2013–2014. *The Transition Begins, Ernst & Young, Bahrain.*

Franzoni, S. & Ait Allali, A. (2018). Principles of Islamic finance and principles of corporate social responsibility: What convergence? *Sustainability*, *10*(3), 637.

Iso, B. & Standard, B. (2010). *Ergonomics of Human-System Interaction.*

Jusoh, W. N. H. W., Ibrahim, U., & Napiah, M. D. M. (2015). An Islamic perspective on corporate social responsibility of Islamic banks. *Mediterranean Journal of Social Sciences*, *6*(2 S1), 308.

Khan, M. S. U. & Karim, N. (2010). Corporate social responsibility: Contemporary thought and Islamic perspectives. *Thoughts on Economics*, *21*(1), 45–66.

Khurshid, M. A., Al-Aali, A., Soliman, A. A., & Amin, S. M. (2014). Developing an Islamic Corporate Social Responsibility Model (ICSR). *Competitiveness Review*, *24*(4), 258–274.

Kotb Abdelrahman Radwan, E., Omar, N., & Hussainey, K. (2021). Social responsibility of Islamic banks in developing countries: Empirical evidence from Egypt. *Journal of Sustainable Finance & Investment*, 1–20.

Lewis, M. K. & Algaoud, L. M. (2001). *Islamic Banking.* Cheltenham: Edward Elgar.

Megeid, N. A. (2013). The impact of service quality on financial performance and corporate social responsibility: Conventional versus Islamic banks in Egypt. *International Journal of Finance and Accounting*, *2*(3), 150–163.

Mir, U. R., Hassan, S. M., & Hassan, S. S. (2016). Islamic perspective of corporate social responsibility. *Al-Aẓvā*, *31*(46), 77–90.

Mohammed, J. A. (2007). *Corporate Social Responsibility in Islam* (Doctoral dissertation, Auckland University of Technology).

Mohammed, J. A. (2013). An Islamic perspective of corporate social responsibility. In *Global Conference on Business, Economics and Social*

Sciences Research (GBSR 2013), Kuala Lumpur, Malaysia, 25–26 June 2013.

Muhamad, R., Sukor, M. E. A., & Muwazir, M. R. (2008). Corporate social responsibility: An Islamic perspective. *Asian Journal of Accounting Perspectives*, *1*(1), 43–56.

Nathan, S. & Ribière, V. (2007). From knowledge to wisdom: The case of corporate governance in Islamic banking, *VINE*, *37*(4), 471–483.

Rammal, H. G. (2006). The importance of Shari'ah supervision in Islamic financial institutions. *Corporate Ownership and Control*, *3*(3), 204–208.

Salma Sairally, B. (2013). Evaluating the corporate social performance of Islamic financial institutions: An empirical study. *International Journal of Islamic and Middle Eastern Finance and Management*, *6*(3), 238–260.

Taman, S. (2011). The concept of corporate social responsibility in Islamic law. *Indiana International & Comparative Law Review*, *21*(3), 481–508.

Tuhin, M. H. (2014). Corporate social responsibility expenditure and profitability: An empirical study of listed banks in Bangladesh. *International Journal of Scientific Footprints*, *2*(1), 107–115.

Ullah, S. & Jamali, D. (2010). Institutional investors and corporate social responsibility: The role of Islamic institution. *International Review of Business Research Papers*, *6*(1), 619–630.

Ullah, S., Jamali, D., & Harwood, I. A. (2014). Socially responsible investment: Insights from shari'a departments in Islamic financial institutions. *Business Ethics: A European Review*, *23*(2), 218–233.

United Nations (2004). Revealing data on the impact of firms on society: Trends and current issues. *United Nations Conference on Trade and Development.*

World Business Council for Sustainable Development (2021). Accessed 6 March, 2021. https://www.wbcsd.org/.

https://doi.org/10.1142/9781800612426_0011

Chapter 11

Comparison of Sustainability Performance Reporting Practices in Islamic Versus Conventional Banks: Evidence from the GCC Region

Mohamed Chakib Kolsi and Ahmad Al-Hiyari

Abstract

Islamic banks are presumed to behave ethically toward numerous stakeholders, including investors, customers, governmental authorities, and the public in general, within the Islamic jurisprudence (Sharia) prescriptions. One of the most important pillars of Sharia prescriptions is the protection of all parties, interests rather than the conventional notion of financial performance maximization of shareholders. This principle is the core value of the stakeholder's theory and the derived corporate social responsibility (CSR) notion. In this chapter, we compare CSR practices as proxied by the reported ESG performance score for a sample of both Islamic and conventional banks in the GCC region for the period 2009–2019. Our results show that conventional banks and Islamic banks display different outcomes in ESG performance score, especially in the reporting of individual pillars (environmental, social, and governance). In that, Islamic banks perform *on average* better than conventional banks in most of the ESG performance pillars. Most importantly, our findings show that Islamic banks, and conventional banks, sustainability practices differ when the individual pillars are disaggregated into their main components: emission score, environmental innovation, and resources use for the environmental pillar; human rights, workforce, community, and product responsibility scores for the social pillar; management, CSR strategy, and shareholders scores for the governance score.

Our findings can be helpful to Islamic banks' managers looking for more compliance with sustainability standards and for markets and standardization authorities when issuing new sustainability guidelines.

Keywords: Islamic Banking, Corporate Social Responsibility, GCC Region, ESG Performance Score, Conventional Banks.

11.1 Introduction

Since the occurrence of financial debacles occurrence worldwide at the beginning of the 21st century, the Islamic banking sector has become one of the most important pillars in the financing of the global economy and plays a crucial role in shaping the overall economy at both national and international levels. Islamic finance transactions and the investment in Islamic financial assets have grown at phenomenal rates. According to S&P Global Ratings (2021), "the Middle East, Africa, and South Asia (MEASA) region continues to be a significant contributor to the Islamic finance industry worth more than $2.4 trillion, which grew 11.4% in 2019".[1] Also, Islamic banks alone have recorded 80% of the world Islamic financial assets that accounted for USD 2 trillion at the end of 2014.

Corporate social responsibility (hereinafter CSR) has become very popular during the last decades due to increasing social and environmental issues. Zafar and Sulaiman (2018) added that although the construct of CSR is in great debate with reference to conventional corporates for a long time, the academic debate on CSR reporting, disclosure, a theoretical and empirical narrative with a connection to Islamic corporates, i.e., Islamic banking is relatively young. Socially responsible organizations are presumed to act for the welfare of the public in general that is beyond the narrow notion of profit maximization. This principle is the core value of Islamic banks, where solidarity and community services prevail over other objectives, such as owners' welfare and value maximization. However, due to the convergence of Islamic banking pillars with CSR concepts and principles, scholars in Islamic finance and banking must devote particular

[1] https://www.spglobal.com/_assets/documents/ratings/research/islamic-finance-book-2021-edition.pdf, p. 7.

consideration to CSR and sustainability in this sector. According to Aliyu *et al.* (2017), the sustainability concept has bi-directional (i.e., the institutional and welfarist) perspectives in banking and finance. The institutional scholars are concerned with the long-term viability and survival of the institutions via financial and operational sufficiency (Hartarska & Nadolnyak, 2007). However, the welfarist perspective focus on the banks' capital allocation coupled with financial decisions toward long-run sustainability.

Our research contributes to the current literature on sustainability issues in Islamic banking in several ways. First, while most of the recent studies on CSR focused mainly on manufacturing companies, our research deals with sustainability performance of the Islamic banking sector in the GCC region. Second, while many studies used large sample firms combined with the quantitative CSR measure based on Kinder, Lydenberg, Domini (KLD) database rating (Grougiou *et al.*, 2014), our research used comparative analysis of sustainability practices between Islamic and conventional banks using the actual ESG performance score for a matched sample rather than a qualitative counting of CSR items. Third, most of the CSR-related studies in Islamic banking used a content analysis (Haniffa & Hudaib, 2007) to address sustainability of Islamic banks. However, a major limitation of such an approach is that it simply assesses what people think companies do rather than what they do (Zafar & Sulaiman, 2019). Finally, unlike previous studies that used a set of qualitative items, we compare each individual environmental, social, and governance sub-scores as reported by the two types of banks as well as their main components. The choice of the GCC region is motivated by the fact that banks operate under similar conditions, where corporate governance structures, such as the royal families' ties coupled with public companies' power (ARAMCO, ADNOC, QNB, etc.), largely influence the economic and financial framework of this region. Abduh and Al-Ageely (2015) argued that studies on CSR in Islamic banks are still scanty. Adding to this is the earlier awareness of most of the GCC countries regarding sustainability issues and the creation of mega-sustainable cities (Masdar city in the UAE, Neom city in the KSA, etc.). Finally, there are currently more than 145 major Islamic financial institutions in the GCC countries, meaning that approximately 40% of all Islamic financial institutions are situated in the GCC countries (The Banker's Top Islamic Financial Institutions,

2016). Furthermore, the GCC countries control around 40% of all Islamic financial assets in the world (Akkas, 2017). The aim of this research is to describe and analyze CSR practices of Islamic banks versus conventional ones as proxied by the actual ESG performance score in the GCC region. Specifically, we plan to answer the following question: Do Islamic banks perform better than conventional ones in terms of aggregate ESG score, its main pillars, and other ESG detailed items?

The reminder of this research is organized as follows: First, we present the convergence between sustainability reporting and Islamic banking and finance pillars (Section 11.2). Second, we review some empirical evidence on the relationship between Islamic banking principles and CSR practices (Section 11.3). Third, we describe our sample banks, research variables, and the methodology (Section 11.4). Fourth, we analyze and discuss our results (Section 11.5). Finally, we conclude the chapter and suggest some future research perspectives (Section 11.6).

11.2 Convergence Between CSR and Islamic Finance and Banking Principles

The Islamic banking sector and related transactions are governed by the Islamic jurisprudence (Sharia law) prescriptions that prioritize charitable activities, community services, and stakeholder's well-being in general rather than the maximization of the shareholders' wealth and short-term profitability. Social actions derived from the Sharia prescriptions, such as helping people via *zakat* (financial aid) and environment protections, are the core values of Islamic finance and banking principles. CSR standards and Islamic finance pillars share many similarities and convergences. The latter are derived from the Islamic religion prescriptions. The Islamic religion is a path of life that describes in part how a human should behave in society. Hence, there are clear rules and regulations that Muslims must follow to comply with their religion, including business matters and transactions. Centuries ago, the Holy Qur'an and the Sunnah confirmed that business must be conducted through fair dealings. Also, the Holy Book prohibits interest bearing transactions (*ribaa*) as they cause economic injustice and negative consequences on the society. Other *Sharia* prescriptions toward business matters state not to cheat any parties, not to cause any harm to creatures or to the environment, to maintain equality, to treat matters with justice, to be transparent, to maintain fair prices, and to give charity (*zakat*). Hence, social responsibility is deeply engraved in the Islamic law, and any Islamic corporation that practices business according to *Sharia* naturally implements CSR (Dusuki & Abdullah, 2007). Any non-compliance with even a single aspect of the *Sharia* will affect the company image toward its stakeholders. For instance, there will be serious repercussions if the company does not deliver its due charities in time (*zakat*). Being socially responsible is one of the critical aspects for the success of an Islamic organization. Islamic banks are expected to fulfill not only the shareholders' interest, but rather they shall also consider societal and environmental protections (Haija & Kolsi, 2021). In view of this, Ngalim and Ismail (2014) proposed another construct that includes services offered by the public, environmental protections, service delivery policies, and wealth redistributions. The environmental inclusiveness has similar support from Islamic financial roles in promoting sustainable development goals (Ahmed *et al.*, 2015).

According to a study conducted on the comparison between United Nation's Global Compact and *Sharia* — in terms of business matters — it was found that the 10 principles of UN Global Compact are in proximity with the *Sharia* prescriptions (Williams & Zinkin, 2010). Additionally, results show that the *Sharia* goes above and beyond the minimum standards of UN's Global Compact. *Sharia* regulations have a larger scope and a clearer code of ethical conduct besides the prohibited actions and behavior. Alamer *et al.* (2015) stated that business operations in Islamic entities can never be disconnected from stakeholders' rights and social responsibility and that faith transactions can only generate profits through the utilization of legal methods that can benefit the whole economy. Therefore, the main aim in life according to *Sharia* prescriptions is not only to generate profits but also to behave ethically in all aspects of life and not cause any chaos on the Earth. This portrays the commitment and loyalty that Islamic organizations have toward social responsibility. In sum, whether those principles are pursued, a firm is assumed to be mostly socially responsible, as managers have conscience and the fear of future punishment (Basah & Yusuf, 2013). Ethics in work environment is also an important part of social responsibility in Islamic corporations. According to Gheitani *et al.* (2019), ethical work has a significant impact on employees' motivation, which in turn affects employees' performance. Hence, Islamic organizations must follow Islamic prescriptions during the recruitment process and reward staff complying with those values.

Certainly, there is an abundance of research conducted on CSR issues including the determinants, consequences, and their relationship with firm performance in non-financial sector companies (Huang & Watson, 2015). However, few studies deal with CSR issues in the banking sector, especially Islamic banks, due to the specificities of such entities. Islamic banks are expected to fulfill not only the shareholders' interest, but rather they shall also consider social and environmental issues. In view of this, Ngalim and Ismail (2014) suggested another construct that includes services offered to the public, environmental protections, service delivery policies, and wealth redistributions. The environmental inclusiveness has similar support from Islamic financial roles in promoting sustainability (Ahmed *et al.*, 2015).

11.3 Sustainability Performance in Islamic Banking Sector: A Review of the Empirical Evidence

Culture conveys the essence of the word "Islam" in Islamic banks. Maali *et al.* (2006) suggested a CSR benchmark that is appropriate to Islamic banks by understanding that social concepts of the features of CSR in Islamic banks revert to the conservation of money, humanity, family, life, and religion from the perspectives of the Sharia Law. The main aim of Islamic banks is to create a system of just income distribution rather than unfairly consuming money from debtors. CSR in Islamic banks helps citizens and professionals to measure how much the banking institutions are working toward fulfilling these objectives. CSR activities include paying *zakat* (charity), establishing just policies, enhancing human welfare, and preserving the Islamic accountability, social justice, and ownership from an Islamic perspective. They used a content analysis method for 29 CSR Islamic bank reports. Hassan and Harahap (2010) used the ethical identity index (EII), as developed by Haniffa and

Hudaib (2007), to develop a benchmark used in the analysis of CSR standards through an eight-dimensional score. They concluded that AAOIFI standards should encompass a more comprehensive CSR reporting framework, as for the GRI framework dedicated to Islamic institutions. Similarly, Ayachi *et al.* (2017) measured the sustainability of Islamic banks in Tunisia at both micro and macroeconomic levels with regard to stakeholders. They established a Sharia compliance performance index (SCPI), which was used to value sustainability level. Empirical results showed that Islamic banks are unsustainable, as there is no uniformity in the standards regarding *Sharia* prescriptions across banks. Abbasi *et al.* (2012) reported minor differences in the CSR reporting process between Islamic and conventional banks. They found that the only difference in results is the religious requirements, such as *zakat*, micro-finance, and social justice. Although using a quantitative approach, their CSR disclosure proxy does not measure the quality of the CSR reports. Jusoh and Ibrahim (2017) have found that although Islamic banks are aware of the importance of CSR disclosures, there is a lack of quality in their reports, especially in Malaysia. For instance, many reports usually state CSR activities in a very general sense but do not provide details on when, what, why, and how. And in many other banks, either the CSR disclosure is rather just a paragraph in the financial report without any explanation or the CSR reports of Islamic banks are consolidated with the affiliate conventional bank's reports, where the conventional bank is predominant. Establishing a strong and independent CSR committee and maintaining a separate fund in Islamic banks can result in better autonomous CSR reports and performance. To reach the highest level of social responsibility and commitment, entities should adopt a new business model. Aydi (2015) described a revolutionary social business model that aims to mitigate the risk of failure of free-market capitalism and suggested an Islamic social business model for sustainable development. He argued that, although capitalism has achieved better production, it has failed to deliver subjective well-being, as there is now a wide gap between the rich and poor sectors. For many decades, capitalist failure market was realized, and philanthropists proposed "social business", which is now popular as CSR practices. Aydi (2015) argued that social business model is contradictory to the capitalist society and is not sufficient to reach optimum levels of social responsibility. Furthermore, he proposed the application of a social business model with the Islamic economic system due to their homogenous principles.

However, Meutia and Febrianti (2017) find that commitment to CSR disclosures and standards are at a better level in Indonesian Islamic banks. According to Bahari and Yusuf (2014), there are 34 recommended items and six essential conditions that are crucial for an ideal CSR reporting framework. These six criteria that must be met relate to: monetary equality, welfare assurance, virtuous charity, Sharia compliance, workplace responsibility, and environmental sustainability. Specifically, this means that because of the popularity of Islamic banks, there has been an increased number of debates on CSR items through the conventional business world. Mallin *et al.* (2014) find that the higher quality of CSR disclosures in Islamic banks have resulted in a higher financial performance. Results conducted on a sample of 90 Islamic banks showed that there is a lack of social responsibility toward the environmental factors but a higher concern toward attaining stakeholder satisfaction and complying with Sharia prescriptions. They highlighted that there is a minimum occurrence of voluntary CSR disclosures, whereas all obligatory AAOIFI requirements are met. Results also show a positive relationship between board size and CSR disclosures. Similarly, Platonova *et al.* (2016) reported a positive relationship between CSR and financial performance of Islamic banks in the GCC region, supporting thereby CSR conscience by customers and investors. Helfaya *et al.* (2016) established a comprehensive guideline for environmental CSR and suggested its application in Islamic banks. Their study highly emphasized the importance of environmental sustainability through details from the Holy Qur'an. Musibah and Alfattani (2013) find that higher efficiency of capital employed by Islamic banks lead to a higher CSR for a sample of 53 Islamic banks in the GCC region. Nor and Hashim (2015) designed a different CSR framework for Islamic banks that can potentially narrow the gap between CSR objectives and achievements. He suggested that, instead of plainly handing over zakat and charity, special programs and initiatives must be established to uplift the society. Abduh and Al-Ageely (2015) found a significant positive relationship between corporate governance and CSR disclosures in 17 Islamic banks of GCC. They added that the quality of CSR disclosures is heavily impacted by the efficiency and independence of the board. However, Harun *et al.* (2020) reported that the level of CSR disclosures in GCC Islamic banks is not at an optimal standard. They also reported a significant relationship between CSR disclosures and board size (Abduh & Al-Ageely, 2015). While previous research on CSR issues and sustainability practices in the Islamic banking sector (Khan *et al.*, 2011; Al-Tamimi & Hassan, 2014; Nobanee & Ellili, 2016; Amran *et al.*, 2017; Farouk & Jabeen, 2018; Modugu, 2020; Kotb *et al.*, 2021; Haija & Kolsi, 2021) used qualitative measures of CSR disclosures derived from the GRI standards or the KLD score, our research uses the actual ESG aggregate score, its main pillars, and their sub-scores, as reported by Islamic versus conventional banks in the GCC region for the period 2009–2019.

11.4 Research Methodology

11.4.1 *Sample selection*

In our research, we assess the CSR reporting of Islamic banks in the GCC region and compare the ESG performance score between a sample of Islamic versus conventional banks. The rationale for selecting the GCC region is that the GCC states are the global leaders in Islamic banking and finance (Wilson, 2009). Indeed, the GCC Islamic banking industry controls 31.29% of the assets of the entire region's banking sector (The Banker, 2013). Furthermore, GCC Islamic banks operate under similar economic conditions, making the analysis more homogeneous. The sample for this research consists of Islamic banks from six GCC countries, namely Oman, Bahrain, Saudi Arabia, Qatar, Kuwait, and the United Arab Emirates (UAE). The research study covers 2009–2019, with a total number of 199 years-observations (unbalanced data). This period witnessed an increased awareness of CSR practices among policymakers and regulators worldwide; hence, it is important to examine the impact of such awareness of sustainability issues on the level of CSR disclosure in Islamic versus conventional banks and whether such disclosure is related to financial performance. Our sample encompasses 35 commercial banks operating in the GCC countries: 15 conventional banks and 20 Islamic banks. Saudi Arabia has the highest number of Islamic banks (8 banks), whereas the UAE has the largest

Table 11.1. Sample distribution across countries.

Country	Banks: Conventional	Banks: Islamic	Period (unbalanced)	Number of observations
Saudi Arabia	1	8	2009–2019	42
Qatar	1	5	2009–2018	38
Oman	4	4	2009–2019	55
UAE	6	1	2014–2019	26
Kuwait	2	2	2010–2019	34
Bahrain	1	0	2015–2018	4
Total	**15**	**20**		**199**

number of conventional banks (6 banks). Financial ratio and CSR data, including both the three main pillars and their respective sub-scores, were extracted from the Thomson Reuters Eikon database. Table 11.1 displays the distribution of banks among countries for both Islamic and conventional banks.

11.4.2 *Variables definition*

Table 11.2 displays all explanatory variables used in our research. In addition to the aggregate ESG score, we use the three main pillars (environmental, social, and governance sub-scores), along with their main disaggregated items: emission, innovation, and resource use scores for the environmental pillar; human rights, workforce, community, and product responsibility scores for the social pillar; and finally, management, CSR strategy, and shareholders scores for the governance pillar. All these items or sub-scores are defined by the Thomson Reuters Eikon database for the full period.

11.5 Interpretation of the Results

11.5.1 *Descriptive statistics*

In our research, we first adopt a descriptive analysis of the aggregate ESG performance score and its three main pillars (environmental, social, and governance sub-scores), along with their disaggregated

Table 11.2. Variables' definition.

Variable	Label	Description
Environmental, Social, and Governance combined score	ESG	Environmental, social, and governance sustainability aggregate performance score
1. Environmental score	***ENV***	***Environmental pillar as reported by the bank during the year***
1.1. Emission score	EMI	The emission reduction score measures a company's commitment and effectiveness toward reducing environmental emission in the production and operational processes
1.2. Innovation score	INNO	The innovation score reflects a company's capacity to reduce the environmental costs and burdens for its customers and thereby creating new market opportunities through new environmental technologies and processes or eco-designed products
1.3. Resource use score	RES	The resource use score reflects a company's performance and capacity to reduce the use of materials, energy, or water and to find more eco-efficient solutions by improving supply chain management
2. Social score	***SOC***	***Social pillar as reported by the bank during the year***
2.1. Human rights score	HR	The human rights category score measures a company's effectiveness toward respecting the fundamental human rights conventions
2.2. Workforce score	WF	The workforce score measures a company's effectiveness toward job satisfaction, a healthy and safe workplace, maintaining diversity and equal opportunities, and development opportunities for its workforce
2.3. Community score	CS	The community score measures the company's commitment toward being a good citizen, protecting public health, and respecting business ethics

(*Continued*)

Table 11.2. (*Continued*)

Variable	Label	Description
2.4.Product responsibility score	PR	The product responsibility score reflects a company's capacity to produce quality goods and services, integrating the customer's health and safety, integrity, and data privacy
3. Governance score	***GOV***	***Governance pillar as reported by the bank during the year***
3.1. Management score	MAN	The management score measures a company's commitment and effectiveness toward following best practice corporate governance principles
3.2. CSR strategy score	CSR	The CSR strategy score reflects a company's practices to communicate that it integrates the economic (financial), social, and environmental dimensions into its day-to-day decision-making processes
3.3. Shareholder's score	SHARE	The shareholders score measures a company's effectiveness toward equal treatment of shareholders and the use of anti-takeover devices

Source: All ESG scores are extracted from Thomson Reuters Eikon.

items (emission, innovation, and resources use scores for the environmental pillar; human rights, workforce, community, and product responsibility scores for the social pillar; management, CSR strategy, and shareholders scores for the governance pillar) of Islamic banks compared to conventional banks in the GCC region for the period 2009–2019. Second, we compare the differences in the means of the aggregate ESG score along with the three pillars and their main components for the two kinds of banks.

Table 11.3 shows that Islamic banks perform on average better than conventional banks in terms of the aggregate score of environmental performance (14.023 vs. 6.555). The same result is noticeable for the emission score (80.69 vs. 68.59), innovation score (9.891 vs. 4.577), and resources use score (21.64 vs. 12.08). This last score means that Islamic banks show more efficiency in the resources use

Table 11.3. Environmental pillar and its components (full period 2009–2019).

	Bank							
	Conventional				**Islamic**			
Statistics	**ENV**	**EMI**	**INNO**	**RES**	**ENV**	**EMI**	**INNO**	**RES**
Mean	6.555	8.884	4.577	12.086	14.032	22.990	9.891	21.642
Maximum	54.39	68.59	50.97	58	59.39	80.69	55.7	73.63
Minimum	0	0	0	0	0	0	0	0
Median	4.32	16.78	0	11	6.74	19.04	0	14
Variance	106.26	247.29	85.66	353.38	332.22	675.35	307.49	587.86
STDV	10.30	15.72	9.25	18.75	18.22	25.21	17.53	24.24
1st quartile	0	0	0	0	0	0	0	0
3rd quartile	9.83	16.13	4.46	19.86	22.72	37.67	9.83	42.61

than conventional banks. This result confirms the rational use of resources and the excess use avoidance prescriptions of the Holy Qur'an. It also indicates the deployed efforts of Islamic banks in preserving the environment to comply with Sharia prescriptions. Ngalim and Ismail (2014) argued that being socially responsible is one of the critical aspects of the success of an Islamic organization. Islamic banks are expected to fulfill not only the shareholders' interest, but rather they shall also consider societal and environmental protections. The environmental inclusiveness has similar support from Islamic financial roles in promoting sustainable development goals (Ahmed *et al.*, 2015). Our findings also support those of Helfaya *et al.* (2016), who established a comprehensive guideline for environmental CSR and suggested its application in Islamic banks. Their study highly emphasized the importance of environmental sustainability through details from the Holy Qur'an.

Table 11.4 shows that Islamic banks display on average a better governance score than conventional ones (56.70 vs. 53.74). Similarly, the management performance score is higher in Islamic banks than in conventional ones. In fact, one key feature that distinguishes the two kinds of banks is the Sharia board, which is the main governance structure ensuring that all banks' transactions comply with the Sharia prescriptions. Islamic banks also perform better in terms

Table 11.4. Governance pillar and its components (full period 2009–2019).

	Bank							
	Conventional				Islamic			
Statistics	GOV	MAN	CSR	SHARE	GOV	MAN	CSR	SHARE
Mean	53.74	59.49	27.72	51.91	56.70	62.12	35.81	52.54
Maximum	93	97.06	93.75	98.65	93	97.5	94.4	97
Minimum	8.82	4.55	0	8.33	4.81	2.5	0	3.85
Median	55	62	16	50	60	65	30	54
Variance	372.9	761.13	981	558.6	472.75	711.637	1014	792.23
STDV	19.31	27.58	31.32	23.63	21.74	26.25	31.85	28.15
1st quartile	13.94	5	0	10.71	4.81	2.5	0	3.85
4th quartile	69.2	81.78	0	69	71	85	62.5	75

of CSR strategy score than conventional banks (35.81 vs. 27.72). This score reflects a company's practices to communicate that it integrates the economic (financial), social, and environmental dimensions into its day-to-day decision-making processes. This finding corroborates with that of Mallin *et al.* (2014), who find that there is a lack of social responsibility toward the environmental issues but a higher concern toward attaining stakeholders' satisfaction and complying with Sharia prescriptions. Our findings also corroborate with those of Aydi (2015), who described the revolutionary social business model that has mitigated failed free-market capitalism and suggested an Islamic social business model for sustainable development. Finally, Islamic banks perform better in terms of equal treatment among shareholders (52.54 vs. 51.91) for the shareholders' score, thereby complying with the Islamic pillar of equality among all participants. This finding corroborates with those of Abduh and Al-Ageely (2015), who found a significant positive relationship between corporate governance and CSR disclosures in the 17 Islamic banks of GCC region.

As predicted, Table 11.5 shows that Islamic banks perform better than conventional ones in terms of the aggregate social score (29.42 vs. 25.85). In fact, social actions derived from the Sharia prescriptions, such as helping people via *zakat* (financial aid) and environment protection, are the core values of Islamic finance and

Table 11.5. Social pillar and its components (full period 2009–2019).

	Bank									
	Conventional					Islamic				
Statistics	**SOC**	**HR**	**WF**	**CS**	**PR**	**SOC**	**HR**	**WF**	**CS**	**PR**
Mean	25.85	2.26	32.06	29.61	32.46	29.42	5.75	35.22	31.66	39.52
Maximum	70.13	60.08	83.99	84.23	86.16	72.51	59.48	95.85	96.16	96.72
Minimum	2.26	0	0.86	0.79	0	2.26	0	0.6	0.79	0
Median	22.65	0	28.8	21.68	29.83	2.65	0	28.89	21.62	29.83
Variance	205.68	86.5	542.08	354.76	555.36	352.49	194.07	854.24	783.28	895.04
STDV	14.34	9.3	23.28	18.83	23.56	18.77	13.86	29.22	27.89	29.91
1st quartile	2.26	0	1.78	0.79	0	2.26	0	0.6	0.79	0
3rd quartile	39.75	0	53.21	38.93	58.93	34.89	0	48.19	39.45	41.23

banking principles. Turning to the sub-pillars of the social score, Islamic banks perform better in terms of the human rights respect compared to conventional ones (5.75 vs. 2.26). This finding complies with the principle of profit and loss sharing (PLS) between the bank and its customers and the zakat concept that supports poor people. As suggested by Kotb *et al.* (2021), Islamic banks also enhance the development of social enterprises through the participation in several social initiatives and activities. All other sub-scores (workforce, community, and product responsibility scores) show higher means for Islamic banks than for conventional ones. This finding confirms again the important role of Islamic banks as a central player of charitable actions and community services that largely extends the profit maximization principle of other companies. Finally, since all bank products are approved by the independent Sharia board and comply with the Sharia prescriptions, such products and services reflect the customer's health and safety, integrity, and data privacy.

11.5.2 *Comparison means' T-tests*

In the last step of analysis, we compare the differences in means of the aggregate ESG score along with the three pillars and their main components for the two kinds of banks for the full period (2009–2019).

Table 11.6 displays the differences in means for each ESG score along with its pillars and main components. Results show that both banks display a difference in means regarding the aggregate ESG score. The environmental pillar together with all its components (emission, innovation, and resources use) also display significant differences between Islamic and conventional banks. This is due to the compliance of Islamic banks with the Sharia prescriptions for environmental saving and efficient resources use. However, both governance and social pillars means are not on average different for both kinds of banks. Specifically, management, shareholders, workforce, and community services do not significantly differ in means for the two kinds of banks. This is due the fact that in the GCC region, while Islam is the main religion, all market participants and banks shareholders must comply with Sharia prescriptions regarding social aid (zakat) and other community services. Finally, both kinds of banks display different means of HR score and CSR practices communication score.

Table 11.6. Comparison means-tests of the two kinds of banks (full period 2009–2019).

Item	ESG	ENV	GOV	SOC	EMI	INNO	RES	MAN	CSR	SHARE	HR	WF	CS	PR
Mean DIF	3.88	7.47	2.95	3.56	14.1	5.31	9.55	2.62	8.08	0.63	3.48	3.15	2.04	7.0
Std. error	2.02	2.03	2.95	2.36	2.9	1.91	3.06	3.96	4.58	3.7	1.65	3.74	3.32	3.8
T-test	1.98	3.68	1	1.5	4.48	2.77	3.11	0.66	1.76	0.17	2.11	0.84	0.61	1.8
$P(T>t)$	0.01	0.00	0.15	0.16	0.00	0.003	0.00	0.25	0.03	0.43	0.01	0.2	0.27	0.03

11.6 Conclusion

The aim of this research was to compare sustainability practices as measured by the ESG performance score and its main components of Islamic versus conventional banks in the GCC region. The results were conclusive and show that Islamic banks perform on average better than conventional ones in terms of environmental, social, and governance pillars along with their main components. We attributed these results to the features of the Islamic banking industry based on the Sharia prescriptions, such as solidarity among people and charitable actions, coupled with specific governance structures, such as the Sharia board. However, tests of means' comparisons reveal that both banks display on average the same performance scores, especially for the governance and social pillars, due to the culture of the GCC region shaped mainly by the Islam religion. While previous studies on CSR of Islamic banks adopted a qualitative approach using a simple CSR disclosure index derived mainly from the GRI standards, our research adds to the existing literature by using the actual ESG performance score and its main sub-scores and related items for a sample of GCC Islamic banks. Our research confirmed again previous empirical evidence suggesting that Islamic banks were immunized against the global financial crisis 2008–2009 effects due to the principle of interests' prohibition upon which all banks' transactions must be based. Islamic banks must comply with the Sharia principles of solidarity, people equality, efficiency in resources' use, and transparency. All these concepts are the core values of the ESG sustainability performance score. Future research should address the determinants of specific ESG sub-score reporting by Islamic banks (emission, product innovation, and CSR strategy scores) driven by the bank governance structures. It will be worthwhile then to test the reaction of financial markets' participants (mainly financial analysts) toward such performance reporting scores.

References

Abbasi, T., Kausar, H., Ashiq, A., Inam, H., Nasar, H., & Amjad, R. (2012). Corporate social responsibility disclosure: A comparison between Islamic and conventional financial institutions in Bahawalpur region. *Research Journal of Finance and Accounting*, *3*(3), 51–62.

Abduh, M. & Al-Ageely, H. A. (2015). The impact of corporate governance on CSR disclosure in Islamic banks: Empirical evidence from GCC Countries. *Middle East Journal of Management, 2*(4), 283–296.

Ahmed, H., Mahmoud, M., Jos, V., & Farida, V. (2015). On the sustainable development goals and the role of Islamic finance. *World Bank Policy Research, Working Paper No. 7266.* https://ssrn.com/abstract=2606839.

Akkaş, E. (2017). *An Overview of Islamic Economics and Finance in the GCC Countries (Report No. 3).* İstanbul: Research Center for Islamic Economics.

Alamer, A. R. A., Salamon, B. H., Qureshi, I. M., & Rasli, M. A. (2015). CSR's measuring corporate social responsibility practice in Islamic banking: A review. *International Journal of Economics and Financial Management, 5*, 198–206.

Al-Tamimi & Hassan, H. A. (2014). Corporate Social Responsibility Practices of UAE Banks. *Global Journal of Business Research, 8*(3), 3–106.

Aliyu, S., Hassan, M. K., Yusof, R. M., & Naimi, N. (2017). Islamic banking sustainability: A review of literature and directions for future research. *Emerging Markets Finance and Trade, 53*(2), 440–470.

Amran, A., Fauzi, H., Purwanto, Y., Darus, F., Yusoff, H., Zain, M. M., Naim, D. M. A., & Nejati, M. (2017). Social responsibility disclosure in Islamic banks: A comparative study of Indonesia and Malaysia. *Journal of Financial Reporting and Accounting, 15*(1), 99–115.

Ayachi, A. R., Saidane, D., & Mansouri, F. (2017). Potential of Islamic finance: A survey of Tunisian Northwest companies. *Journal of Emerging Economies & Islamic Research, 5*(2), 28–42.

Aydi, N. (2015). Islamic social business for sustainable development and subjective wellbeing. *International Journal of Islamic and Middle Eastern Finance and Management, 8*(4), 491–507.

Bahari, Z. & Yusuf, M. Y. (2014). Corporate social responsibility in Islamic banking institutions in aceh: Analysis of criteria and perception. *Journal of Educational and Social Research, 4*(2), 390–408.

Basah, A. Y. M. & Yusuf, M. (2013). Islamic bank and Corporate Social Responsibility (CSR). *Islamic Management and Business, 5*(11), 194–209.

Dusuki, A. W. & Abdullah, N. I. (2007). Maqasid al-Shari'ah, Maslahah and corporate social responsibility. *The American Journal of Islamic Social Sciences, 24*(1), 25–45.

Farouk, S. & Jabeen, F. (2018). Ethical climate, corporate social responsibility and organizational performance: Evidence from the UAE public sector. *Social Responsibility Journal, 14*(4), 737–752.

Gheitani, A. Imani, S. Seyyedamiri, N., & Foroudi, P. (2019). Mediating effect of intrinsic motivation on the relationship between Islamic work ethic, job satisfaction, and organizational commitment in banking sector. *International Journal of Islamic and Middle Eastern Finance and Management*, *12*(1), 76–95.

Grougiou, V., Leventis, S., Dedoulis, E., & Owusu-Ansah, S. (2014). Corporate social responsibility and earnings management in U.S. banks. *Accounting Forum*, *38*(3), 155–169.

Haija, E. & Kolsi, M. C. (2021). Corporate social responsibility in Islamic banks: To which extent does Abu Dhabi Islamic bank comply with the global reporting initiative standards? *Journal of Islamic Accounting and Business Research*, *12*(8), 1200–1223.

Haniffa, R. & Hudaib, M. (2007). Exploring the ethical identity of Islamic banks via communication in annual reports. *Journal of Business Ethics*, *76*(1), 97–116.

Hartarska, V. & Nadolnyak, D. (2007). Do regulated microfinance institutions achieve better sustainability and outreach? Cross-country evidence. *Applied Economics*, *39*(10), 1207–1222.

Harun, M. S., Kharuddin, K. A., & Farooque, O. A. (2020). CSR disclosure, corporate governance and firm value: A study on GCC Islamic banks. *International Journal of Accounting & Information Management*, *28*(4), 607–638.

Hassan, A. & Harahap, S. (2010). Exploring corporate social responsibility disclosure: The case of Islamic banks. *International Journal of Islamic and Middle Eastern Finance and Management*, *3*(3), 203–227.

Helfaya, A., Kotb, A., & Hanafi, R. (2016). Qur'anic ethics for environmental responsibility: Implications for business practice. *Journal of Business Ethics*, *150*, 1105–1128.

Huang, X. & Watson, L. (2015). Corporate social responsibility research in accounting. *Journal of Accounting Literature*, *34*, 1–16.

Jusoh, W. N. & Ibrahim, U. (2017). Corporate social responsibility of Islamic banks in Malaysia: Arising issues. *Islamic Economic Studies*, *25*, 155–172.

Khan, H., Azizul Islam, M., Kayeser Fatima, J., & Ahmed, K. (2011). Corporate sustainability reporting of major commercial banks in line with GRI: Bangladesh evidence. *Social Responsibility Journal*, *7*(3), 347–362.

Kotb Abdelrahman Radwan, E., Omar, N., & Hussainey, K. (2021). Social responsibility of Islamic banks in developing countries: Empirical evidence from Egypt. *Journal of Sustainable Finance & Investment*, 1–20. https://doi.org/10.1080/20430795.2021.1949890.

Maali, B., Casson. P., & Napier, C. (2006). Social reporting by Islamic banks. *Abacus*, *42*(2), 266–289.

Mallin, F. H. & Ow-yong, K. (2014). Corporate social responsibility and financial performance in Islamic banks. *Journal of Economic Behavior & Organization*, *103*(supplement), 521–538.

Meutia, I. & Febrianti, D. (2017). Islamic social reporting in Islamic banking: Stakeholders theory perspective. *SHS Web of Conferences. Four A 2016*. https://cyberenlinka.org/article/n/1411617/viewer.

Modugu, K. P. (2020). Do corporate characteristics improve sustainability disclosure? Evidence from the UAE. *International Journal of Business Performance Management*, *21*, 39–54.

Musibah, A. S. & Alfattani, Y. W. B. S. W. (2013). Impact of intellectual capital on corporate social responsibility evidence from Islamic banking sector in GCC. *International Journal of Finance and Accounting*, *2*(6), 307–311.

Ngalim, S. M. & Ismail, A. G. (2014). An Islamic vision development based indicators in analysing the Islamic banks performance: Evidence from Malaysia, Indonesia and selected GCC countries. *IRTI Working Papers WP-1436-02*.

Nobanee, H. & Ellili, N. (2016). Corporate sustainability disclosure in annual reports: Evidence from UAE banks: Islamic vs Conventional. *Renewable and Sustainable Energy Review*, *55*, 1336–1341.

Nor, S. M. & Hashim, N. A. (2015). CSR and sustainability of Islamic banking: The bankers view. *Journal Pengurusan*, *45*, 73–81.

Platonova, E., Asutay, M., Dixon, R., & Mohammed, S. (2016). The impact of corporate social responsibility disclosure on financial performance: Evidence from the GCC Islamic banking sector. *Journal of Business Ethics*, *151*(2), 451–471.

Williams, G. & Zinkin, J. (2010). Islam and CSR: A study of the compatibility between the tenets of Islam and the UN global compact. *Journal of Business Ethics*, *91*, 519–533.

Zafar, M. B. & Sulaiman, A. (2019). Corporate social responsibility and Islamic banks: A systematic literature review. *Management Review Quarterly*, *69*(2), 159–206.

https://doi.org/10.1142/9781800612426_0012

Chapter 12

Implementation of Islamic Ethics in Corporate Governance at PT. Pertamina (Persero) in Indonesia

Lili Wardani Harahap

Abstract

The purpose of this study is to explore the implementation of Islamic ethics and identify *corporate governance*. This study is a qualitative case study using phenomenological approach and paradigm interpretive in which the paradigm focuses on social understanding. The data collection method in this study used secondary data, namely data obtained from the documentation and annual report of PT. Pertamina (Persero). The data analysis technique uses explorative qualitative methods, namely research that aims to map an object in depth. This study uses a content analysis approach. The results of this research consist of the following: (1) PT. Pertamina (Persero) has implemented Islamic ethics in running its business to improve of the company performance; (2) Islamic ethics have been in accordance with the principles of *corporate governance,* which include transparency, accountability, responsibility, independence, and fairness at PT. Pertamina (Persero); (3) honesty, the value of truth (fairness), justice, transparency, accountability, and integrity have been applied at PT. Pertamina (Persero).

Keywords: Islamic Ethics, Corporate Governance.

12.1 Introduction

The business world requires Islamic ethics in realizing a sustainable business to obtain economic benefits which is the goal of the establishment of the business world. The growing business environment with diverse cultural backgrounds makes the principles of Islamic corporate governance (CG) applicable in all conditions. Thus, it is necessary to implement a new rule to deal with quick financial innovation (Mollah *et al.*, 2017). The growing business environment requires companies to compete among other companies. Companies need to change their business strategy in order to survive and be able to compete. The business strategy uses knowledge-based business. According to a previous research by Muhibbai and Basri (2017), Islamic ethical identity provides guarantees to stakeholders for operating activities with the ideal identity that the company must have. The higher the value of Islamic ethical identity, the higher the compliance to Islamic principles run by the company so that it can generate commitment and loyalty from stakeholders in the company with goals that have an impact on improving company performance. According to Marka and Serly (2020), states with disclosure of Islamic ethics identities have a positive and significant impact on the financial performance of financing to deposit ratio (FDR) with the significance of 0.018.

The annual report is used to know the ideal conditions of ethical identity based on an Islamic ethical business framework, so the ethical identity index (EII) is used as the measuring tool for Islamic identity (Haniffa & Hudaib, 2007). Every company that has implemented Islamic ethical principles will be able to develop and produce better company performance, thus to improve sustainable business. PT. Pertamina (Persero) is a world-class national energy company that was established in 1957. PT. Pertamina (Persero) operates in the field of state oil and gas mining in Indonesia. Until now, the Pertamina company is still operating well because PT. Pertamina (Persero) has projected further business development capable of optimizing Indonesia's natural wealth by starting a study on the development of a green refinery in Indonesia. In addition, Pertamina strengthens its commitment to carry out business development in new and renewable energy and business diversification (Annual Report, PT. Pertamina (Persero), 2018). This reason made me interested in carrying out research at Pertamina. So, this research tries to fulfill a gap by answering the following main research question: How is the implementation of Islamic ethics in Corporate Governance at PT. Pertamina (Persero) in Indonesia?

The purpose of this study is to explore the implementation of Islamic ethics and identify CG. This study provides an overview of the concept of Islamic ethics and CG conducted at PT. Pertamina (Persero) in Indonesia. Data analysis in this study used content analysis approach to answer research questions (research gap). In previous research, according to Muhibbai and Basri (2017), the disclosure of Islamic ethical identity provides guarantees to stakeholders for the suitability of operating activities with the ideal identity that the company must have. The strength of this research is it provides benefits to all stakeholders about ethical or behavioral socialization information through the compliance online system portal (Annual Report, PT. Pertamina (Persero), 2018). This research contributes to Indonesia's growth and support sustainable business growth literature.

Pertamina has implemented Corporate Governance, which is a system that directs and controls the company in accordance with the expectations of stakeholders based on the principles of CG, namely transparency, accountability, responsibility, and fairness (Annual Report, PT. Pertamina (Persero), 2018). The principles of CG are in accordance with Islamic ethics. A previous research by Puspa and Yulinda (2019) stated that the effect of implementing good CG on non-financial performance resulted in transparency, accountability, responsibility, independence, and fairness at the B'right PLN Batam company in Indonesia.

Ethics is related to issues of honesty, the value of truth or fairness, fraud, transparency, and accountability in the relationship between workers and the company. Aspects of ethics and morality are considered in economic activities because of ethical values, namely fairness, justice, and honesty which are the basic principles of Islam (Mahfouz, 2016). Fraud is a violation of ethical and moral issues that are important or the main basis for every activity that occurs in the company (Hamel, 2012). Value or ethical issues are sourced from the capitalist economic system which is the basis for the philosophy of activity of most companies in the world (Hamel, 2012). Ethical values are often associated with CG because these values have many types. CG is evaluated through the existence of ethical values in the company. Pertamina needs Islamic ethics in running its business to improve the company's performance. The company's performance is proxied at the level of profitability. Profitability is the level of profit obtained by the company when carrying out its operations. High company profitability will reflect good company prospects. The higher the profitability of the company, the higher the company's efficiency will be so that the company's performance is good too. Profitability shows the company's performance in generating profits.

PT. Pertamina (Persero) must obey with Bank Indonesia Regulation Number 11/33/PBI/2009 about ethical values based on Sharia principles, namely transparency and accountability. Transparency is openness in carrying out the decision-making process and openness in presenting material and relevant information about the company (Decree of the Minister of BUMN Number Kep-117/M-MBUMN/2002). The company should convey to all relevant parties true, accurate, and timely information about the financial condition, company ownership structure, company policies, and changes that occur in the company. Then, company should be accountable for all consequences to the *stakeholders*. In addition, Pertamina's employees are not allowed to embezzle company money, and they are not allowed to divulge company secrets to outsiders or other people.

Based on the description that has been given previously, it shows that the importance of the research model with observing the phenomena that occur and are felt by the community and companies in establishing relationships that exist at PT. Pertamina (Persero). Observation of in depth and continuous Islamic Ethics and CG is done in order to create a model or formulate a concept or theory. This study is intended to understand the meaning of the phenomenon. Disclosure of information presented by informants in the activities carried out by Pertamina companies is very important. This information is needed in formulating the model. Formulation of models and concepts from the results of observations and disclosure of information is a qualitative research.

12.2 Literature Review

12.2.1 *Ethics and morality*

Aspects of ethics and morality are considered in economic activities because of the ethical values, namely fairness, justice, and honesty, which are the basic principles of Islam (Mahfouz, 2016). Fraud is a violation of ethical and moral issues that are important or the main basis for every activity that occurs in the company (Hamel, 2012). Value problems or ethical problems are sourced from the capitalist economic system which is the basis of the philosophy for the companies in the world (Hamel, 2012).

12.2.2 *Islamic corporate governance*

In general, CG is a system that directs and controls company a in line with the expectations of stakeholders based on the principles of CG, namely transparency, accountability, responsibility, and fairness. The principles of CG is the basis for improving the performance of the company which are based on moral values as well as compliance with the law, so it can provide protection and fair treatment for stakeholders (Annual Report, PT. Pertamina (Persero), 2018).

Islamically, the implementation of Islamic Corporate Governance (ICG) has a more obedient scope because it considers religious, ethical, and social aspects (Mansour & Bhatti, 2018). The implementation of ICG at PT. Pertamina (Persero) has been effective and complied Islamic ethical principles which aim to create a PT. Pertamina (Persero) which is strong, healthy, and stable. The implementation of ICG is one of the methods used to ensure the needs of stakeholders are met and form of compliance to applicable regulations. The principles of ICG according to Maradita (2014) are transparency, accountability, responsibility, professionalism, and fairness.

According to Hussainey *et al.* (2021), Islamic banks in general and Faisal Islamic Bank of Egypt (FIBE), in particular, play an effective role in social responsibility (SR) and enhance the development of social enterprises. In addition, FIBE has allocated huge funds for SR through participating in several social initiatives and activities, besides Qard Hasan for needy citizens and its Zakat Fund.

12.2.3 *Legal foundation of Islamic ethics*

The legal foundation is a regulation which is the basis of carrying out certain activities. The discipline in life require the legal foundation based on applicable regulations. The legal foundation of Islamic ethics, namely Bank Indonesia Regulation (PBI) No. 11/33/PBI/2009 on the values of ethics which is based on Islamic principles, namely transparency and accountability. The legal foundation of Islamic ethics based on the Qur'an are:

A. Honest
Surah Hud Verse 85
Syu'aib said: "My people, please fill measures and weights with justice, don't harm the humans against their rights and do not create crime on Earth by doing damage" (Al-Quran Religious Affairs, 2015, p. 231).

B. Justice
Surah At-Taubah Verse 103
Taking zakat from their wealth in order to cleanse and purify their property, so pray for them. Actually, your prayer grows to peace of mind for them (Al-Quran Religious Affairs, 2015, p. 203).

C. Responsibility
Surah Al-Ma'idah Verse 1: The people believers, filling your promise. (Al-Quran Religious Affairs, 2015, p. 106).

D. True and Fairness
Surah At-Taubah Verse 119
The people believers! Have faith for God, and together with the right people (Al-Quran Department of Religion, 2015, p. 206).

12.2.4 *Legal foundation of Islamic corporate governance*

The principle of Islamic CG refers to the Al-Quran and Al-Hadith which makes it unique and different from the concept of CG in the Western worldview. The principles of CG in general are transparency, accountability, responsibility, independence, fairness, and equality. While the principles of Islamic CG, according to Muqorobin (2011), are monotheism, taqwa, ridho, equilibrium (balance and justice), and welfare. The principles of Islamic CG are realized through an Islamic ethical framework in the conduct of business, justice, and equality for the welfare of Allah SWT oriented.

12.2.5 *Islamic corporate governance in Indonesia*

Indonesia as a country where the majority of the population is Muslim must understand and know the principles of Islamic CG. The principles of Islamic CG are not new because these principles have existed for hundreds of years in the form of Islamic management, but with the development of the principles of Western world capitalism, the Islamic principles were thus abandoned by Muslims.

Based on modern terminology, it states that CG is related with the hadith of the Prophet Muhammad which means "Indeed Allah likes it when someone does something well done". Islamic ethics in Indonesia is currently growing. Not only in the field of banking, insurance and companies also enliven the Islamic business. The growing Islamic business has an influence on the implementation of CG. Businesses must adhere to Islamic ethical principles by implementing CG in the business. The development of Islamic business and CG in Indonesia led to the Concept of Good Governance Guidelines for Islamic Business issued by the National Committee on Governance Policy in 2011.

12.2.6 *Research gap*

This study provides an overview of the concept of Islamic ethics and CG conducted at PT. Pertamina (Persero) in Indonesia. Data analysis in this study used a content Analysis approach to answer research questions (research gap). In previous research according to Muhibbai and Basri (2017), the disclosure of Islamic ethical identity provides guarantees to stakeholders for the suitability of operating activities with the ideal identity that the company must have.

12.3 Methodology and Data

The type of research in this study uses a qualitative case study. The case study qualitative research according to Baskarada (2014) states that the sources of data can assist in the exploration of phenomena in certain contexts.

The research location considered was PT. Pertamina (Persero) in Indonesia. The reasons for choosing the research location are as follows: (1) PT. Pertamina (Persero) has the same annual report which has been consolidated with PT. Pertamina (Persero) Center; (2) PT. Pertamina (Persero) was established in 1957 and is in operation until now; (3) PT. Pertamina (Persero) has the characteristic 6C value, namely Clean, Competitive, Confident, Customer focus, Commercial, and Capable.

The sources and types of data in this study are the annual reports from 2014 to 2018. These periods were selected as samples in this study based on the following reasons: (1) the annual report is published through mass media such as the internet in accordance with Law No. 14 of 2008 about the disclosure of public information; (2) the annual reports have information about management, company profile, management analysis, CG, CSR, financial statements, and other information. The data analysis technique uses explorative qualitative methods, namely research that aims to map an object in depth (Arikunto, 2000). This study uses a content analysis approach.

12.4 A Case Study of PT. Pertamina (Persero) in Indonesia

PT. Pertamina (Persero) is a world-class national energy company in accordance with Pertamina's vision and was established in 1957. PT. Pertamina (Persero) operates in the field of state oil and gas mining in Indonesia. Until now, the Pertamina company is still operating well because PT. Pertamina (Persero) has projected further business development capable of optimizing Indonesia's natural wealth by starting a study on the development of a green refinery in Indonesia. In addition, Pertamina strengthens its commitment to carry out business development in new and renewable energy and business diversification. Pertamina has values as the company's foundation to realize its vision and mission based on global standards and the implementation of CG. Pertamina's values, known as 6C, consist of Clean, Competitive, Confident, Customer focus, Commercial, and Capable, must be known and become guidelines for all workers in their daily activities. Understanding and implementing the 6C values will shape the behavior that becomes a culture, as Pertamina's characteristic among other companies. Each individual worker at Pertamina must ensure that they behave in accordance with the 6C values (Annual Report, PT. Pertamina (Persero), 2018).

12.5 Contributions of PT. Pertamina (Persero) in Indonesia

Ethics or morality is important in economic activity because ethical values have the value of truth or fairness, justice, honesty, transparency, accountability, responsibility, independence, and integrity which are the basic principles of Islam and must be implemented by all employees so that Pertamina's company can grow and develop sustainably.

The implementation of Islamic ethics based on the principles of CG at PT. Pertamina (Persero) are as follows:

A. *Honesty and the value of truth (fairness)*: The implementation of honesty, truth value (fairness), discipline, and trust at PT. Pertamina (Persero) produces safety and creates a safe and healthy work environment.

B. *Justice*: PT. Pertamina (Persero) applies justice or avoids discrimination in carrying out its duties and responsibilities in accordance with the duties, principals, and functions of PT. Pertamina (Persero).

C. *Transparency*: PT. Pertamina (Persero) is a world-class national energy company that is growing from year to year. The progress of the company is evidenced by the company's ability to fulfill its obligations as indicated by the ratio of profit to assets and income which shows a positive value and reflects the company's ability to pay its obligations as can be seen in Table 12.1.

   Table 12.1 shows the implementation of transparency at PT. Pertamina (Persero) by publishing an annual report through mass media such as on the internet in accordance with Law No. 14 of 2008 about public information disclosure.

D. *Accountability*: The accountability at PT. Pertamina (Persero) is implemented in accordance with the Minister of BUMN Regulation No. 4 of 2007, namely the partnership program of 2% and environmental development of 2% reported to the Ministry of BUMN with a separate report.

Table 12.1. Graph of profit ratio to total assets and Pertamina's income.

No.	Information	Year 2018	Year 2017	Year 2016	Year 2015	Year 2014
1	Ratio of Profit to Total Assets	3.9	4.56	6.15	3.12	2.85
2	Ratio of Profit to Total Income	4.33	5.63	8.23	3.36	2.06

Source: Annual Report, PT. Pertamina (Persero), 2018.

E. *Responsibility*: The implementation of responsibility at PT. Pertamina (Persero) is in accordance with the Limited Corporate Law No. 40 of 2007, namely the company's moral responsibility or obligation that must be carried out by the company to the society. Through this law, the company must implement CSR programs.
F. *Fraud*: The implementation of Internal Control System at PT. Pertamina (Persero) is used to avoid fraud. Internal Control System is one of the basis for management's evaluation of the effectiveness of the Internal Control System to determine the improvement of management systems or policies effectively in carrying out the company's operational activities. The duties and responsibilities of Internal Control System are to conduct special audits (investigations) to uncover cases that have indications of abuse of authority, embezzlement, and fraud.

Fraud auditing is an effort to detect and prevent fraud in commercial transactions. To be able to conduct fraud audits of bookkeeping and commercial transactions, a combination of two skills is required, namely as a well-trained auditor and a criminal investigator. The next step is to carry out an investigative audit (fraud examination), which is a methodology to resolve clearly problems related to indications of fraud from beginning to end. More specifically, investigative examination includes efforts to obtain various evidences and statements, give testimony, write reports, and assist in detection.

12.6 Conclusion

PT. Pertamina (Persero) has implemented Islamic ethics in running its business to improve the company performance. The implementation of Islamic ethics has been in accordance with the principles of CG, which includes honesty, the value of truth (fairness), justice, transparency, accountability, and responsibility. Practically implications can give to describe that Islamic ethics research and *Corporate Governance* can be practiced at PT. Pertamina (Persero). The research's limitation is that a limited time spent to research directly in the field because of the COVID pandemic. Suggestions consist of the following: (1) the success of implementation of Islamic ethics based on the principles of CG that can give value to all *stakeholders*; (2) Islamic ethics is expected to and can be socialized at PT. Pertamina (Persero) because it is important as evidence shows that the implementation of Islamic ethics can provide positive values; (3) the value of the good of the company through the implementation of Islamic ethics is accepted by all *stakeholders* because the Islamic ethics has the impact on changes in the attitudes and behavior of *stakeholders* which can support the achievement of company goals.

Acknowledgments

The authors like to thank the management of PT. Pertamina (Persero) for publishing the annual reports in a detailed and comprehensive manner on the Pertamina's website, which allows access to data at anytime and anywhere.

References

AlQuran Ministry of Religious Affairs (2015). Surah Hud verse 85, p. 231; Surah At-Taubah verse 103 and 119, pp. 203–206; Surah Al-Maidah verse 1, p. 106.

Arikunto, S. (2000). *Manajemen Penelitian.* Jakarta: Rineka Cipta.

Baskarada, S. (2014). Qualitative case study guidelines. *The qualitative Report* 19, 1–25.

Bank Indonesia Regulation Number 11/33/PBI/2009. (2019). About ethical values base on sharia principles: Transparency and accountability.

Decree of the Minister of BUMN Number Kep-117/M-MBUMN/2002. (2002). "Transparency".

Hamel, G. (2012). *What Matters Now: How to Win in a World of Relentless Change, Ferocious Competition and Unstoppable Innovation at American Multinational Manufacturing Company.* Jossey Bass.

Haniffa, R. & Hudaib, M. (2007). Exploring the ethical identity of Islamic bank via communication in annual report. *Journal of Business Ethics, 76*(1), 97–116.

Kotb Abdelrahman Radwan, E., Omar, N., & Hussainey, K. (2021). Social responsibility of Islamic banks in developing countries: Empirical evidence from Egypt. *Journal of Sustainable Finance and Investment, 11*(21), 1–20.

Laws of the Republic Indonesia No. 14 of 2008 about Public Information Disclosure (2008).

Limited Corporate Law No. 40 of 2007 (2007). *Corporate Social Responsibility* (CSR).

Mahfouz, S.B. (2016). Socially responsible investment and Islamic investment: Is there a difference. In Lehner (Ed.), *Routledge Handbook of Social and Sustainable Finance*. London: Routledge.

Mansour, W. & Bhatti, M. I. (2018). *The New Paradigm of Islamic Corporate Governance in the countries of Islamic finance*. Managerial Finance.

Maradita, A. (2014). Characteristics of good corporate governance in Islamic banks and conventional banks. *Yuridika, 29*(2), 191–204.

Marka, N. & Serly, V. (2020). The effect of disclosure of Islamic ethical identity on the financial performance of Islamic banking in Indonesia. *Journal of Accounting Exploration, 2*(2), 2861–2872.

Minister of BUMN Regulation PER-05/MBU/2007 about the partnership program and environmental development (2007).

Mollah, S., Hassan, M. K., Al Farooque, O., & Mobarek, A. (2017). The governance, risk taking, and performance of Islamic banks. *Journal of Financial Services Research, 51*(2), 195–219.

Muhibbai, A. & Basri, H. (2017). The effect of disclosure of Islamic ethical identity, agency cost and intellectual capital on financial performance. *Scientific Journal of Accounting Economics Students, 2*(1), 30–37.

Muqorobin, (2011). *Governance Fiqh of Profit Organization: An Introduction to Muhammadiyah University*. Purwokerto.

Puspa, S. D. & Yulinda. (2019). The effect of the implementation of good corporate governance principles on non-financial performance at B'RIGHT PLN Batam Company in Indonesia. *Journal of Applied Managerial Accounting, 3*(1), 66–80.

The National Committee on Governance Policy in 2011 at Jakarta about the Concept of Good Governance Guidelines for Islamic Business (2011).

https://doi.org/10.1142/9781800612426_0013

Chapter 13

Integrating Value-Based Intermediation into Business Models: A Proposed Guideline for Islamic Banks

Salaheldin Hamad, Fong-Woon Lai, and Muhammad Kashif Shad

Abstract

The value-based intermediation (VBI) has been recently announced by the Central Bank of Malaysia (Bank Negara) as a vital driver in expanding the responsibilities and influence of Islamic finance in the future. It aims to reinforce the foundations of Islamic finance in social justice and advocate a value-based economy via increased integrity, inclusivity, and sustainable growth. This chapter analyses the current practices of VBI information for Islamic banks operating in Malaysia. Also, it proposes a guideline to communicate VBI information to stakeholders through the bank's business model as the core of integrated reporting (IR). Using a sample of all the 16 Islamic banks operating in Malaysia, content analysis was employed to collect data over a four-year period from 2017 to 2020. The results revealed that the adoption of IR and VBI has seen considerable interest among the research sample. Approximately 82% of all banks in our selection have embedded the VBI information in the recent annual reports of 2020. More than half (7 out of 13) of VBI adopter banks have applied IR to draw and communicate the VBI information to stakeholders. Additionally, the IR framework and business models represent the best strategic tools banks could utilize to provide the VBI progress in a holistic, concise, and useful manner compared to traditional reporting practices. This chapter contributes to the Islamic finance literature by offering vital perceptions to banks' management, analysts, shareholders, and policymakers on the importance of the VBI information disclosures and how to deliver it using the business models.

Keywords: Integrated Reporting, Business Model, Value-Based Intermediation, Sustainable Growth, Islamic Banking.

13.1 Introduction

Islamic finance and banking have grown to be one of the most significant industries as they are critical to a markets' financial stability (Jan *et al.*, 2019; Hoque & Liu, 2021). The year 2020 has seen a negative influence of the COVID-19 pandemic on the global economy, especially the financial system. However, the total worth of Islamic Financial Services Industry (IFSI) reached USD 2.70 trillion in 2020 compared to USD 2.44 trillion in 2019. Hence, the IFSI maintained its upward trend, growing at a rate of 10.7% year over year, and the indicators of financial stability remain adequate (IFSB, 2021). Islamic banks can be found in more than 20 countries; Malaysia is considered one of the pioneers in this industry: It has 16 Islamic banks with a total asset of worth around USD 254 billion in 2019 and total funds account for 38.0% of the total deposits of the banking sector (BNM, 2021). Consequently, this industry occupies a significant position in the Malaysian business context by offering various financial services in line with Sharia principles for a sizable customer base.

Recently, all businesses have become interested in not only achieving financial success but also sustainable growth (Christ & Burritt, 2019). Hence, Islamic banks should change their strategy to investigate new avenues for addressing social and environmental concerns to ensure long-term sustainability, while working side by side with the government to accomplish the "Sustainable Development Goals (SDGs)", which were introduced in 2015 by the United Nations (UN) as part of their global agenda to be achieved by 2030 (United Nations, 2015).

In keeping with this tendency, Malaysia took the lead among other countries with sizeable Islamic banking industries by introducing a new strategy paper, including an initiative known as "Value-Based

Intermediation" in March 2018 by Bank Nigari Malaysia (BNM). It sought to strengthen the Islamic banks' responsibility to positively influence society, economy, and environment. In addition, it aims to generate a solid Islamic financial market that can attain innovation and sustainable growth while maintaining the stockholders' long-term interests (BNM, 2018b).

Integrated reporting (IR) is the most recent corporate reporting which focuses on the value creation process to create sustainable value for shareholders and society through a business model (Hamad *et al.*, 2020; Nwachukwu, 2021). A business model is a tool that allows the organization to illustrate the value creation process to its stakeholders (Norris *et al.*, 2021). While some Islamic banks have responded to the above call to follow the VBI and insert it into their strategy and reporting, the conventional reporting method has many disadvantages since it focuses only on the financial side. Therefore, it is considered an inappropriate way to communicate the VBI disclosures to stakeholders. In this instance, IR and the banks' business model could be the proper way to disclose how banks are aligning their strategy, products, and activities with the VBI as well as show their achievement.

In this chapter, the authors answer two main research questions: First, what are the current practices of VBI disclosures among the Islamic banks in Malaysia? Second, how can these banks utilize the IR and its business models to embed the VBI achievements? Due to the newness and limited spread of VBI globally, only very few prior research have investigated it (Hassan & Nor, 2019; Mahadi *et al.*, 2019; Yusof & Ali, 2021). Additionally, to the best of our knowledge, no investigation has been conducted to present a suitable reporting paradigm to communicate the VBI achievements to stakeholders. Consequently, this chapter provides a novelty and expands on the VBI knowledge by analyzing the current practices of VBI disclosures in the initial stages of implementation and proposing a guideline to communicate VBI disclosures through the bank's business model as the core of integrating reporting. This chapter is constructed as follows: Section 13.2 gives some background; Section 13.3 provides the preliminary guideline; Section 13.4 describes the methodology; Section 13.5 discusses the results; Section 13.6 offers conclusion and future research.

13.2 Background

13.2.1 *Value-based intermediation (VBI) initiative*

The VBI is a recent initiative that emerged in the Malaysian Islamic finance sector in July 2017 as a collaborative work between the BNM and several Islamic bank practitioners. The VBI is defined in the strategy paper in 2018 as *an intermediation function that aims to deliver the intended outcomes of Sharia through practices, conduct, and offerings that generate positive and sustainable impact to the economy, community and environment, consistent with the shareholders' sustainable returns and long-term interests* (BNM, 2018b). This means VBI has two main objectives. First, it assists the financial institution to create positive and long-term influence on the three pillars of sustainability. Second, it strives to satisfy and maintain the interests of shareholders. All of these must happen in line with the Sharia principles and foundations.

Later on, BNM has issued several papers to support and guide Islamic banks in implementing VBI. One of these documents highlighted a framework that gives the main points of VBI, such as the guiding principles, application stages, and the underpinning thrusts (BNM, 2018a). The framework aims to improve the business environment by engaging the key stakeholders to recognize the three pillars of sustainability (people, profit, and plant), encourage innovation, and create long-term value.

Furthermore, BNM provided a "VBI Scorecard" tool to evaluate the Islamic banks' performance by identifying the qualitative and quantitative VBI results, providing a specific score from 0 to 100 to each VBI practitioner in order to indicate the VBI progress (BNM, 2018c). Finally, the last document highlighted the financial risk management issue in Islamic finance. It provided a "VBI Financing and Investment Impact Assessment Framework (VBIAF)" which helps the Islamic banks to create an efficient system for risk management system used in financing products and services that incorporate the VBI concern (BNM, 2019). It accelerates the impact-based risk management system application for evaluating Islamic banks' investment and financing activities following the individual VBI commitments.

The VBI is the most recent initiative that emerged in Islamic finance and banking. Hence, not much academic research has looked into this idea. The study by Arshad *et al.* (2018) was one of the first to use a case study to investigate the benefits of VBI practices highlighted in the BNM's first paper, including efficiency, innovation, and ecosystem.

As a result of the connection between VBI and Sharia principles, various studies focused on addressing the VBI from Maqasid al-Sharia's perspective. Hassan and Nor (2019) reviewed the Sharia principles and objectives that were initiated in VBI. Their results showed certain principles founded in the VBI, e.g., enhancing social responsibility, creating value, and realizing fairness and justice. Consistently, from the same Sharia standpoint, Mahadi *et al.* (2019) observed that applying VBI could allow Islamic financial institutions to offer their consumers valuable products and services through Islamic social finance.

Another study by Sara *et al.* (2019) recommended that Islamic banks apply the VBI and embed it in their strategy to generate sustainable growth over *waqf* projects. Finally, using the qualitative methods of research, Yusof and Ali (2021) studied Sharia governance as one of the VBI determination factors. They mentioned that the combination of the Sharia board and Sharia committee could play a vital role in the success of VBI implementation.

13.2.2 *Integrated reporting in Islamic industry*

Lately, integrated reporting (IR) has earned considerable interest among academics and practitioners as an evolving corporate reporting technique (Hamad *et al.*, 2020; Rinaldi *et al.*, 2018). More than 2000 organizations in over 70 nations use the IR framework to establish their reporting (IIRC, 2020). In Malaysia, the CG monitor highlighted that the number of firms that adopt IR has increased from 97 firms in 2018 to 105 in 2019. Forty of them are classified as large-capital firms, 7 are mid-cap firms, and the remaining 56 are small-cap firms (SCM, 2020).

The prior literature proved several benefits of the IR adoption. It enhances the quality of information by providing a more durable and proficient way of corporate reporting, integrating financial and sustainability disclosures (Adhariani & de Villiers, 2019). IR mitigates information asymmetries and reporting burden (Cortesi & Vena, 2019; Jaffar *et al.*, 2019) and improves the firm's profitability

(Iredele, 2019), especially the return of assets (Albetairi *et al.*, 2018) and earnings per share (EPS) (Cortesi & Vena, 2019). Further, IR plays a major role in reducing the different types of financing costs, whether the cost of equity capital (Vena *et al.*, 2019) or the cost of debt (Raimo *et al.*, 2021). These can make IR accepted generally and may ultimately take the place of current corporate reports in the future (Pavlopoulos *et al.*, 2017).

Despite the importance and advantages of IR to all types of organizations, it is still not commonly employed by Islamic financial institutions. Likewise, less attention has been paid to IR adoption by prior research in Islamic finance and banking. However, Gelmini (2017) claims that Islamic finance is a vitally important area of study for the cultural setting in which IR might be implemented. This study explored the IR of three different Islamic banks from three countries, including South Africa, to determine the motivations behind adopting IR in these banks and measuring the corresponding level of IR disclosure with the Islamic setting and Sharia. In addition, another study explored the elements of IR that are associated with the Islamic NGOs and for Islamic NGOs to improve accountability (Ramli *et al.*, 2018).

Emerging research has focused on how the waqf reporting can be enhanced using the adoption of IR. For instance, Mansor *et al.* (2018) provided a modified waqf reporting in line with the IR and its business model framework to achieve sustainable Islamic social finance. In a similar way, Masruki *et al.* (2020) also suggested a waqf IR model consisting of four discloser scopes to improve the waqf among the waqf institutions.

To explore the market reactions and financial performance in Islamic banks after adopting IR, Buallay *et al.* (2020) studied the effect of IR on the Islamic and traditional banks' performance in the Gulf countries. Results showed that IR does not significantly influence Islamic banks' financial (ROE) and operational (ROA) performance; however, it negatively affects the market (TQ) performance.

13.2.3 *Value-based intermediation and integrated reporting*

VBI is still a relatively new research topic in Islamic finance. Hence, limited prior research work has addressed how to report the VBI initiative information for the financial institutions. In this regard, Ramli and Muhamed (2018) analyzed the IR application in a sample of two Islamic banks in one year. They highlighted that those banks are ready to adopt VBI in their reporting and encouraged them to entrench the VBI in their strategy and reporting. By the same token, using a case study of two Islamic banks in Malaysia, Kasri and Kamal (2021) investigated the application of IR by analyzing these two banks' annual reports and studying how IR supports the concept of Maqasid Sharia. They point out that the role of VBI undertaking by banks in creating values can be improved by using the six capitals and business model of IR.

However, these few prior studies have not addressed the current situation of VBI practices in banks or how to embed and disclose them in their reporting system. Consequently, this chapter aims to fill the above literature gap and contribute not only by exploring the Islamic banks' VBI disclosures but also illustrating how IR can be applied to show the banks' VBI accomplishments. The following sections will go into further detail about it.

13.3 Proposed Guideline

This chapter presents several arguments to prove why Islamic banks should consider the IR framework elements, including the business model, as the best instruments to include the VBI information in their reporting. First, the primary purpose of IR is to maintain "integrated thinking" and clarify in what way organizations can generate value for stakeholders (IIRC, 2021). Likewise, in the Islamic banking industry, the VBI appeared to allocate additional awareness to create value creation to broader stakeholders (BNM, 2018b).

Second, BNM suggested Islamic banks to depend on the IR framework for various purposes. For example, agreeing with the VBI first paper, Islamic banks' self-governance can be assessed using IR as one such method (BNM, 2018b). Also, it improves the disclosures and helps in establishing a suitable environment to apply the VBI. Further, BNM persuaded Islamic financial institutions to apply the IR to disclose the risks in their reporting (BNM, 2019).

Third, VBI and IR are similar in prioritizing the shareholders and their interests; then, the other stakeholders, such as employees, lenders, and depositors, will follow them. Furthermore, the two concepts focus on making a combination of financial and sustainability information (BNM, 2018a; Pavlopoulos *et al.*, 2019). Fourth, the bank's business model is the essence of the IR framework; it allows the bank to demonstrate how value is created to the stakeholders (Norris *et al.*, 2021). Therefore, Islamic banks might employ this model to integrate VBI and demonstrate how to generate sustainable value to stakeholders.

Finally, IR is the most recent corporate reporting and analytical tool which recognizes multiple kinds of disclosures, financial and non-financial, qualitative or quantitative, historical or forward-looking in a condensed manner. Consequently, the VBI disclosures may be enclosed and communicated using the IR and its business model.

The present research suggests a preliminary guideline to disclose the VBI information with the IR framework and its business model for Islamic banks (see Table 13.1). This guideline offers a reporting structure on how the VBI information and achievements will be brought to light utilizing the IR framework. It might present bank executives with new ideas on using the IR framework to improve their VBI disclosures.

13.4 Research Methodology

To achieve the first objective of this chapter, the current practices of VBI information for Islamic banks working in Malaysia are analyzed. We have depended on a sample comprising all the Islamic banks operating in Malaysia based on the Bank Niagara website. The reason behind choosing these banks is that BNM requires only Islamic financial institutions in Malaysia to adopt the VBI in their operations (BNM, 2018b). Due to the different specialized characteristics of Islamic banks, we have excluded the other financial institutions such as Takaful operators. The work has been performed through a deep review of the annual reports, sustainability reports, annual integrated reports, and websites of all 16 Islamic banks for a period of four years from 2017 to 2020. This study has applied a qualitative research method, involving an analysis of all the obtainable literature on IR and VBI as well as the qualitative manual content analysis of all the sample reports to achieve the research objectives.

Table 13.1. Proposed guideline to associate VBI disclosures into the IR.

The VBI essential points	Involving with the IR and business model
1. Financial sustainability It concentrates on profitability and value creation, measured by: • Return on assets • Quality of assets (Impairment ratio) • Strength of capital • Liquidity	• **Performance** Banks could benefit from the various quantitative indicators focusing on the financial capital impact to exhibit the sustainability of the bank's financial situation • **Outlook** To emphasize the expected changes over time
2. Real economy level of support Keep humanity safe and bring benefit to everybody employing innovative Sharia contract implementations, measured by: • Percentage of total financial assets that are used to benefit the real economy directly • Earning produced from such financial intermediation operations • Unique financial instruments aimed at enhancing the efficiency of real economic activities • Managing the liquidity	• **Performance** Banks could benefit from the various quantitative indicators to show how they support the real economy • **Business model** Banks could benefit from business model input, output, and outcome to highlight the financial activities and results that directly or non-directly positively influence the real economy • **Risk and opportunities** Banks can use it to underline the probable real economy risks and opportunities
3. Creating values for a wider group of stakeholders It concentrates on avoidance and reduction of negative impacts and promotes realization of positive impacts for stakeholders, measured by: • Percentage of total financial assets that are used to create values • Determining and monitoring positive and negative impacts of transactions	• **Business model** The core of IR allows the banks to use it as a lens to show how sustainable value is created for the stakeholder by transforming the six capitals into output and outcome • **Strategy and resource allocation** Banks could embed the financial intermediation such as financial intermediation operations • **Governance** Banks use it to show how banks can control the positive and negative impacts of intermediation activities

(Continued)

Table 13.1. *(Continued)*

The VBI essential points	**Involving with the IR and business model**
• Triple bottom line (economic resiliency, social empowerment, and environmental regeneration) • Contributions to SDGs • Maintaining a constant level between the actual and expected effects of intermediation activities	
4. Islamic banks efforts Combination of crucial VBI underpinning thrusts inside six attributes: • Leadership • Products and services • Organizational structure • Human resource instruments • Management systems • Reporting of performance	Banks could depend on the above IR elements to emphasize these six efforts in addition to: • Organizational overview and external environment • Basis of preparation and presentation

Source: Modified from the VBI scoreboard and IIRC framework (BNM, 2018c; IIRC, 2021).

13.5 Findings and Discussion

To draw attention to the current disclosure practices of the VBI initiative, Table 13.2 and Figure 13.1 describe the Islamic banks' participation in the VBI and IR as well as the alignment with the SDGs. The findings showed that the application of VBI is becoming more common among Islamic banks. It goes from 7 in 2017 to 13 Islamic banks in 2020. In other words, almost 82% of all banks in the research sample have implanted VBI information in their 2020 reporting. This result reflects an acceptable rate of response from the Islamic banks to the call of BNM to follow the VBI from 2017. This could happen because of the awareness of participant banks to the benefits of VBI in improving their roles and responsibilities in the Islamic finance intermediation industry toward the stakeholders.

Table 13.2. Alignment of Islamic banks with IR, VBI, and UN SDGs.

No.	Islamic banks	2017		2018		2019		2020			Ownership
		VBI	IR	VBI	IR	VBI	IR	VBI	IR	SDGs	
1	Alliance Islamic Bank	N	N	A	N	A	N	A	N	A	L
2	Affin Islamic Bank	N	N	A	N	A	N	A	N	A	L
3	CIMB Islamic Bank	A	N	A	A	A	A	A	A	A	L
4	AmBank Islamic	A	N	A	A	A	A	A	A	A	L
5	Bank Islam Malaysia	A	A	A	A	A	A	A	A	A	L
6	Bank Muamalat Malaysia	A	A	A	A	A	A	A	A	A	L
7	Hong Leong Islamic Bank	A	N	A	N	A	N	A	N	A	L
8	Maybank Islamic	A	A	A	A	A	A	A	A	A	L
9	Public Islamic Bank	N	N	N	N	A	N	A	N	A	L
10	RHB Islamic Bank	N	N	N	N	A	A	A	A	A	L
11	MBSB Bank	N	N	N	N	A	A	A	A	A	L
12	HSBC Amanah Malaysia	A	N	A	N	A	N	A	N	A	F
13	OCBC Al-Amin Bank	N	N	A	N	A	N	A	N	N	F
14	Kuwait Finance House	N	N	N	N	N	N	N	N	N	F
15	Al Rajhi Banking Malaysia	N	N	N	N	N	N	N	N	N	F
16	Standard Chartered Saadiq	N	N	N	N	N	N	N	N	A	F

Note: A: Applied or adopted; N: Not applied; L: Local, F: Foreign.
Source: Descriptive analysis of banks' annual reports.

By the same token, the application of IR by these banks has also grown. In 2017, the IR framework was adopted by only three banks; however, by 2020, that number has grown to seven banks. It means around 44% of Islamic banks in Malaysia have used the IR framework as a basis for their operations in 2020. The spread of IR adoption among Malaysian Islamic banks is not only because of the awareness of the benefits of IR (Rinaldi *et al.*, 2018) but also the motivation of the governance code and Bursa Malaysia to large Malaysian companies to follow the IR framework in their reporting (Hamad *et al.*, 2020). Finally, according to our analysis, from 2017

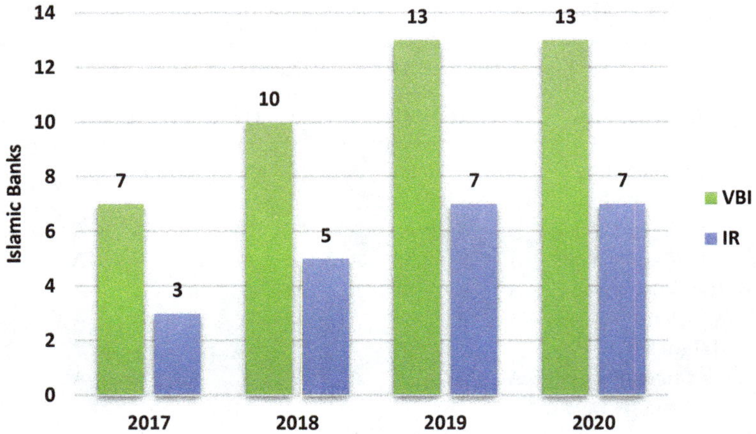

Figure 13.1. Implementation of IR and VBI in the Malaysian Islamic banking industry.

to 2020, the ratio of banks using the IR to publish VBI disclosures grew from nearly 43 to 54%. Furthermore, the local banks are more interested in aligning with the VBI and using the IR framework; on the contrary, only two foreign banks have VBI discourses in their reporting and do not adopt IR.

Regarding the SDGs expected to be achieved by 2030, the Malaysian Government was involved with these goals in 2015 and further combined them into the "11th Malaysia Plan (2016–2020)". So far, Malaysia has made adequate progress in contributing and achieving the SDGs, especially the "SDG 1 No Poverty", in which it was ranked in 65th place out of 165 countries around the world (Sachs *et al.*, 2021). Thus, Islamic banks in Malaysia have to take up a role and cooperate with the government as well as other companies to accomplish the SDGs. They could use the VBI products and services to contribute toward achieving the goals. In this regard, our result revealed that 13 out of 16 Islamic banks in Malaysia (81.3%) mentioned the SDGs in their reporting.

According to the analysis of VBI adopter banks' annual reports from 2017 to 2020, the results showed that most of these banks linked their sustainability efforts not only to the VBI initiative but to the 11th Malaysia Plan and SDGs. They have also embedded the VBI principles into their business practice and approach. While some banks highlighted their commitment to VBI in the CEO/Chairman letter to stakeholders, others showed how their various strategies drive their VBI journey. Likewise, they restated and modified their vision and mission statements to reflect the VBI commitment. To draw attention to the efforts paid by the Islamic banks in the research sample to support the VBI initiative, Table 13.3 shows various activities, products, services, and projects conducted by these banks to be in line with the VBI.

The analysis also showed that not all the banks in the research sample have the same VBI contribution and disclosure level. Around half of the VBI adopter banks made considerable progress from 2017 to 2020. The majority of them were the first to participate and initiate the VBI with BNM. In particular, Bank Islam was one of the pioneers in the VBI disclosures; it integrated the VBI into the heart of its business model and created meaningful progress on its social finance initiatives by building an Islamic crowdfunding platform, Sadaqah House. As a result, Bank Islam came out on top as the most excellent VBI institution in 2018, according to the BNM "VBI Scorecard", reflecting an inclusive evaluation of the institution's overall success with all the VBI criteria and matrices.

Furthermore, some other banks had significant footprints in VBI; in 2019, "HSBC Amanah" was the first to publish a detailed document named "Value-based Intermediation Disclosure" to report and highlight their VBI journey accomplishment (HSBC, 2019). In a different report, Bank Muamalat designed products and services to support the VBI. Similarly, CIMB continued integrating VBI into their business plans to help them make better decisions based on actual cost and benefits to the company and stakeholders.

Concerning the IR adoption among the Islamic banks, the finding revealed that in 2020, of the 13 banks that implemented the VBI, seven (54%) had employed the IR framework to communicate their achievements to stakeholders. The two concepts (VBI and IR) mesh well with the banks' goal of generating value for all stakeholders. More importantly, more than half of IR adopter banks interconnected the VBI into their business models. They showed how the six capitals as the inputs and business activities consisting of sustainable financial products and services could create sustainable value and harmonize with the VBI principles. This value is shown in the form of various indicators in the output and outcome of the business models.

Table 13.3. Examples of VBI activities disclosures by Islamic banks in 2018/2019/2020.

Islamic banks	**Examples of VBI activities in 2019/2020**
Affin Islamic Bank	• Promoted green technology and renewable energy as a financial provider to support VBI
Alliance Islamic Bank	• Issued "Islamic Tier-1 Sukuk Wakalah (AT1 Sukuk)" with a value of RM 100 million to support Sharia-compliant portfolio growth in the VBI and Halal and VBI area
AmBank Islamic	• In serving the real economy as one of our VBI initiatives, they continued to support the SME sector via the provision of credit, enterprise financing program, and other banking facilities
Bank Islam Malaysia	• Contributed to the triple bottom line (TBL) considerations • Embedded the VBI in their business model to create value • Highlighted the VBI journey and correlated it to IR six capitals • Stimulated SME growth (achieved 233 SME account approvals worth RM 954.2 million) to serve the real economy • Set a target of RM 1.76 billion to invest in green financing in 2020
Bank Muamalat Malaysia	• Integrated the VBI principle into the business model • Invested in the world's first UN SDG Sukuk that HSBC Amanah issued • Fostered the growth of local entrepreneurs
CIMB Islamic Bank	• Integrated the VBI approach to the business strategies • Elevated the sustainability agenda to include the VBI (Sustainability Roadmap 2023)
HSBC Amanah Malaysia	• Innovated and offered value-based products and services • Issued the first SDGs Sukuk bond in the world • Aligned the business model with the VBI to create value
Hong Leong Islamic Bank	• Participated in SME sector funding projects and programs • Initiated Islamic Finance Chatbot and article publications

Table 13.3. (*Continued*)

Islamic banks	Examples of VBI activities in 2019/2020
Maybank Islamic	• Introduced one of the first VBI products in the market, called "HouzKEY" is a rent-to-own scheme
Public Islamic Bank	• In 2020, introduced "Energy Efficient Vehicle" with special rates. It has lower fuel consumption and carbon emission levels than regular internal combustion engine vehicles

Source: Islamic banks' annual reports analysis.

Briefly stated, the findings of the foregoing investigation indicate that Islamic financial institutions can benefit from the IR, notably the business model as a useful reporting instrument not only to communicate the VBI accomplishments but to demonstrate their ability to generate sustainable value and produce a positive influence on society, economy, and environment. It could enable banks to disclose their commitment to VBI using a generally recognized reporting structure to satisfy their stakeholders.

13.6 Conclusion

Islamic finance is one of the most significant industries around the world. The global Islamic asset market remained concentrated mainly in Iran, Saudi Arabia, and Malaysia, which together accounted for 66% of the total assets in 2019. Malaysia holds the second-highest Islamic finance assets to GDP at 53%, after Bahrain at 124%. As of late, the VBI has emerged as an Islamic financial and banking initiative seeking to enhance Islamic banks' role toward sustainable growth. Consequently, this chapter investigated the current practices of VBI information for Islamic banks working in Malaysia from 2017 to 2020. In addition, it proposed a primary guideline to communicate VBI information to stakeholders through the bank's business model as the core of IR.

Findings proved a noteworthy surge in the performance of IR and VBI for the Islamic banks in Malaysia. The majority of all Islamic banks and all local banks have responded to the call of BNM to follow and endorse the VBI principles and embed them into their strategy and activities. Also, this upholds the Sharia foundations and principles to create positive and meaningful impacts on their stakeholders. Regarding IR, in 2020, a little over half of VBI adopter banks depend on the IR framework and its business model to exhibit their VBI achievements. Banks can sustain value through the efficient and responsible management of the IR six capitals. Furthermore, incorporating the VBI into banks' business models could boost the real economy via ecosystem play for enterprises.

Besides the interesting prior insights about VBI disclosures which could benefit analysts, shareholders, and policymakers, our reporting proposed guideline contributes to the Islamic finance literature by offering vital perceptions to banks' management that could assist in disclosing the VBI progress information in a holistic, straightforward, and useful manner compared to traditional reporting practices.

The VBI initiative is embraced extensively by the Malaysian Islamic finance industry. However, it is a relatively new concept with a small geographic footprint; it is regarded as a fertile research ground for scholars. Consequently, our study makes certain recommendations for potential research. Future work can consider the anticipated financial and sustainable outcomes of applying the VBI initiative and can also assess the influence of VBI on the financial institutions' value. The factors that could influence the adoption of VBI principles are a respected topic in the Islamic industry. Finally, future research could investigate the possibility of implementing the VBI in other Islamic finance contexts, such as Indonesia, Iran, and Gulf Cooperative Council countries.

References

Adhariani, D. & de Villiers, C. (2019). Integrated reporting: Perspectives of corporate report preparers and other stakeholders. *Sustainability Accounting, Management and Policy Journal, 10*(1), 126–156. Doi: 10.1108/SAMPJ-02-2018-0043.

Albetairi, H. T. A., Kukreja, G., & Hamdan, A. (2018). Integrated reporting and financial performance: Empirical evidences from Bahraini listed insurance companies. *Accounting and Finance Research, 7*(3), 102. Doi: 10.5430/afr.v7n3p102.

Arshad, R., Muda, R., Nair, R., & Baharudin, I. (2018). Value-based intermediation for Islamic banking institutions directed towards sustainable development goals. *International Review of Entrepreneurial Finance*, *1*(1), 1–17. https://revues.imist.ma/index.php/IREF/article/view/12997.

BNM (2018a). *Implementation Guide for Value-based Intermediation.* https://www.bnm.gov.my/index.php?ch=57&pg=137&ac=612&bb=file.

BNM (2018b). *Value-based Intermediation: Strengthening the Roles and Impact of Islamic Finance: Vol. March.* https://www.bnm.gov.my/index.php?ch=57&pg=137&ac=612&bb=file.

BNM (2018c). *Value-based Intermediation Scorecard Consultative Document.* https://www.bnm.gov.my/index.php?ch=en_announcement&pg=en_announcement&ac=670.

BNM (2019). *Value-based Intermediation Financing and Investment Impact Assessment Framework (Consultative Document).* https://www.bnm.gov.my/index.php?ch=57&pg=137&ac=851&bb=file.

BNM (2021). *Bank Negara Malaysia Annual Report 2020.* https://www.bnm.gov.my/bnm-annual-report.

Buallay, A., Al Hawaj, A. A., & Hamdan, A. (2020). Integrated reporting and performance: A cross-country comparison of GCC Islamic and conventional banks. *Journal of Islamic Marketing.* Doi: 10.1108/JIMA-08-2017-0084.

Christ, K. L. & Burritt, R. L. (2019). Implementation of sustainable development goals: The role for business academics. *Australian Journal of Management*, *44*(4), 571–593. Doi: 10.1177/0312896219870575.

Cortesi, A. & Vena, L. (2019). Disclosure quality under Integrated Reporting: A value relevance approach. *Journal of Cleaner Production*, *220*, 745–755. Doi: 10.1016/j.jclepro.2019.02.155.

Gelmini, L. (2017). Islamic banks: Sustainability, integrated reporting and religion. *Corporate Governance and Sustainability Review*, *1*(2), 35–42. Doi: 10.22495/cgsrv1i2p5.

Hamad, S., Draz, M. U., & Lai, F.-W. (2020). The impact of corporate governance and sustainability reporting on integrated reporting: A conceptual framework. *SAGE Open*, *10*(2), 1–15. Doi: 10. 1177/2158244020927431.

Hassan, R. B. & Nor, F. M. (2019). Value-based intermediation: An analysis from the perspective of Shariah and its objectives. *International Journal of Fiqh and Usul Al-Fiqh Studies*, *3*(1), 81–89.

Hoque, H. & Liu, H. (2021). Capital structure of Islamic banks: How different are they from conventional banks? *Global Finance Journal*, *January*, 100634. Doi: 10.1016/j.gfj.2021.100634.

HSBC (2019). *Value-based Intermediation Disclosure a Better & Brighter Future of Banking* (Issue December). https://www.hsbcamanah.com.my/content/dam/hsbc/hbms/documents/amanah-and-me/value-based-intermediation-disclosure.pdf.

IFSB (2021). *Islamic Financial Services Industry Stability Report 2021.* https://www.ifsb.org/download.php?id=6106&lang=English&pg=/sec03.php.

IIRC (2020). *IIRC Integrated Report 2019.* https://integratedreporting.org/integratedreport2019/.

IIRC. (2021). *The International <IR> Framework 2021.* https://integratedreporting.org/wp-content/uploads/2021/01/InternationalIntegratedReportingFramework.pdf.

Iredele, O. O. (2019). Examining the association between quality of integrated reports and corporate characteristics. *Heliyon*, *5*(7), e01932. Doi: 10.1016/j.heliyon.2019.e01932.

Jaffar, N., Nor, A. S. M., & Selamat, Z. (2019). Integrated report content elements effecting value relevance of publicly listed companies in Malaysia. *International Journal of Innovation, Creativity and Change*, *8*(6), 303–318.

Jan, A. A., Tahir, M., Lai, F.-W., Jan, A., Mehreen, M., & Hamad, S. (2019). Bankruptcy Profile of the Islamic banking industry: Evidence from Pakistan. *Business Management and Strategy*, *10*(2), 265. Doi: 10.5296/bms.v10i2.15900.

Kasri, N. S. & Kamal, M. S. (2021). Embracing Maqasid Shari'ah via integrated reporting: The case of Islamic banks in Malaysia. In *Monetary Policy, Islamic Finance, and Islamic Corporate Governance: An International Overview* (pp. 267–290). Emerald Publishing Limited. Doi: 10.1108/978-1-80043-786-920211015.

Mahadi, N. F., Zain, N. R. M., & Ali, E. R. A. E. (2019). Leading towards impactful islamic social finance: Malaysian experience with the value-based intermediation approach. *Al-Shajarah: Journal of the International Institute of Islamic Thought and Civilization (ISTAC), November*, 0–13.

Mansor, N., Jamil, A., & Bahari, A. (2018). Waqf reporting: A modified integrated reporting for sustainable islamic social finance. *International Journal of Academic Research in Business and Social Sciences*, *8*(12), 742–754. Doi: 10.6007/ijarbss/v8-i12/5069.

Masruki, R., Mohd Hanefah, M., & Kamaruddin, M. I. H. (2020). A Waqf-Integrated Reporting (WAQIR) model: Performance, governance, and socio-economic impact. In B. Saiti & A. Sarea (Eds.), *Challenges and*

Impacts of Religious Endowments on Global Economics and Finance (pp. 281–300). Cambridge University, UK: IGI Global.

Norris, S., Hagenbeck, J., & Schaltegger, S. (2021). Linking sustainable business models and supply chains — Toward an integrated value creation framework. *Business Strategy and the Environment*, *30*(8), 3960–3974.

Nwachukwu, C. (2021). Systematic review of integrated reporting: Recent trend and future research agenda. *Journal of Financial Reporting and Accounting*, Doi: 10.1108/jfra-10-2020-0308.

Pavlopoulos, A., Magnis, C., & Iatridis, G. E. (2017). Integrated reporting: Is it the last piece of the accounting disclosure puzzle? *Journal of Multinational Financial Management*, *41*, 23–46. Doi: 10.1016/j.mulfin.2017.05.001.

Pavlopoulos, A., Magnis, C., & Iatridis, G. E. (2019). Integrated reporting: An accounting disclosure tool for high quality financial reporting. *Research in International Business and Finance*, *49*, 13–40. Doi: 10.1016/j.ribaf.2019.02.007.

Raimo, N., Caragnano, A., Mariani, M., & Vitolla, F. (2021). Integrated reporting quality and cost of debt financing. *Journal of Applied Accounting Research*, *23*(1), 122–138. https://doi.org/10.1108/JAAR-04-2021-0097.

Ramli, N. M. & Muhamed, N. A. (2018). Adoption of value-based intermediation through integrated reporting: Evidence from Islamic banks in Malaysia. *6th ASEAN Universities International Conference on Islamic Finance (AICIF)*, Manila, Philippines, December. https://www.researchgate.net/publication/329799176.

Ramli, N. M., Ali, N. S. A. M., & Muhamed, N. A. (2018). *Integrated Reporting based on Maqasid Al-Shariah: A Proposed Framework for Islamic Non-profit Organizations*, *57*(Piceeba), 63–72. Doi: 10.2991/piceeba-18.2018.80.

Rinaldi, L., Unerman, J., & de Villiers, C. (2018). Evaluating the integrated reporting journey: Insights, gaps and agendas for future research. *Accounting, Auditing and Accountability Journal*, *31*(5), 1294–1318. Doi: 10.1108/AAAJ-04-2018-3446.

Sachs, J. D., Kroll, C., Lafortune, G., Fuller, G., & Woelm, F. (2021). *Sustainable Development Report 2021.* Cambridge: Cambridge University Press.

SCM (2020). *Corporate Governance Monitor 2020.* https://www.sc.com.my/api/documentms/download.ashx?id=ff69ce0d-a35e-44d4-996a-c591529c56c7.

United Nations (2015). *Transforming Our World: The 2030 Agenda for Sustainable Development.* Doi: 10.1163/157180910X12665776638740.

Vena, L., Sciascia, S., & Cortesi, A. (2019). Integrated reporting and cost of capital: The moderating role of cultural dimensions. *Journal of International Financial Management and Accounting, 31*(2), 191–214. Doi: 10.1111/jifm.12113.

Yusof, N. A. M. & Ali, M. M. (2021). Shariah Governance in the Face of Value-Based Intermediation: Islamic Banking to Thrive Beyond Halal. In *Enhancing Halal Sustainability* (pp. 129–139). Singapore: Springer.

https://doi.org/10.1142/9781800612426_0014

Chapter 14

Accounting Issue in Cryptocurrency Investment: Islamic Perspective

Qisthi Wajanatin Alfafa and Murniati Mukhlisin

Abstract

The purpose of this chapter is to evaluate how a company should report cryptocurrency investment on their financial statements. In dealing with it, the research problems address the status of positive law and Islamic law in cryptocurrency and how the current economy responds to cryptocurrency. Qualitative descriptive approach and literature review with content analysis method using NVivo 12 plus software are used. The data for this study were obtained from interviews and a review of documents. The finding shows that investments in cryptocurrency held by the companies can be treated as investments in equity with minor adjustments. The content analysis conducted shows that stakeholders are neutral toward this issue. This chapter proposes a standard on how cryptocurrency should be treated in financial report under Indonesian Sharia-based Statement of Financial Reporting Standards/PSAK Syariah since the transaction of cryptocurrency investment has not been accommodated in financial reporting standard in Indonesia.

Keywords: Cryptocurrency Investment, Positive Law, Islamic Law, PSAK Syariah.

14.1 Digital Economy and Cryptocurrency in Indonesia

The accelerating technological advancements bring about rapid change and transformative transformation. Specifically, in economics, technological advances have given rise to a new term known as the digital economy. Digital economy can be summed up as several technologies which have a general purpose in the context of various economic and social activities carried out by people through the Internet and related technologies. The technological facilities present from the innovations themselves bring more to the community as an economy because technological developments play a role as the primary driver of improving the economy both in the real sector and the financial sector (Dahlman *et al.*, 2016).

In trading activities, the digital economy is presented in facilitating the community with e-commerce platforms and digital cross-border trade and investment, where buying and selling and payments are no longer carried out conventionally. However, all are done by utilizing existing technology so that they are no longer limited by distance. Payment systems in online trading depend almost entirely on trusted third-party financial institutions that can process electronic payments (Nakamoto, 2008). The role of technology in the payment system has replaced cash as a means of general payment into non-cash payments (Suharni, 2018). The existence of electronic money now supports the non-cash payment process. Electronic money is a relatively new non-cash payment instrument. Electronic money simplifies transactions, shortens time, and is more efficient than other electronic payment instruments. As a new payment method, electronic money was intended to decrease the growth rate of cash usage. The development of electronic money can create new behavior specifically by using a non-cash method. This trend is called less-cash society (Waspada, 2012).

The development of blockchain technology brings forth the birth of an answer to the barrier on payment systems that depend on third parties (Syamsiah, 2017). Cryptocurrency is the name given to a system that uses cryptography to carry out the process of sending data securely and to carry out the process of exchanging digital tokens in a scattered manner (Dourado & Brito, 2014). By definition, cryptocurrency is a type of digital currency that uses cryptography. Cryptography on digital currency is used for security reasons and as an anti-counterfeiting measure. The public key and private key are often used to transmit cryptocurrency between two individuals. Cryptocurrency has different types, such as currencies of the world and also precious metals. There are various kinds of currencies in the world, such as

Rupiah, Dollar, Euro, and Ringgit. There are also different types of precious metals, such as gold and silver. One type of cryptocurrency best known to the general public is Bitcoin. Besides Bitcoin, there are also several types of cryptocurrency including Ripple, Lisk, Ether, MaidSafeCoin, Litecoin, StorjCoinX, Ethereum, DogeCoin, Dash, Monero, and Zcash.

The term "cryptocurrency" is used because their characteristic use of an encryption system that regulates coin production and transfers must be identified from the perspective of economic analysis. Therefore, it is essential to examine which social, financial, and macroeconomic factors determine the price to determine the scope and economic consequences (Abad & Iyengar, 2017). The existence of Bitcoin is as a transaction tool or currency that has no intrinsic value, and Bitcoin has a place in financial markets and portfolio management classified by Dyhrberg (2016) as between gold and the US dollar on the scale of the means of exchange for exchange rates.

Cryptocurrency is a new innovation in the payment system, but before that, Islam also had a history of payment system developments that had gone a long way. The history of money begins long before the arrival of Islam and Islamic civilization. During the reign of the Prophet Muhammad in Medina, the Prophet Muhammad ordered dirham's use in the number of scales, not numbers. By order, the difference in the size of the Persian dirham which initially consisted of 20 carats, 12 carats, and 10 carats was set in the Islamic dirham to be 14 carats (taken from the average of the three measures of the Persian dirham) or the equivalent of 7 grams today. During the Caliphate, Ummar Bin Khatab in 18 AH, the printing of dirham's money began to be carried out with features describing Islam. The Caliph Ummar also set a standard of dirhams equal to dinar, in which 1 dirham equals 7/10 dinars or equivalent to 2.97 grams with a standard basis of a dinar value of 4.25 grams (Fadilla, 2019).

According to Sharia law, money itself has no intrinsic value. It is a measure of value only, and not valuable in itself. It is simply a medium of exchange. Money and commodities are treated differently in Islam. For example, money cannot directly meet human needs. It must be converted into commodities to serve any purpose. The quality of commodities can be different, while money does not have differential features according to its value. Commodities can be sold or exchanged for transactional purposes at an agreed price/barter between the buyer and seller. The price of commodities also depends on the intrinsic value of the goods involved. In the case of money with no intrinsic value, exchanging money of different values instead of cash will result in usury (interest), which is not allowed under Sharia rules. When money is converted to money, any excess amount collected due to deferred payment is a usurer because the excess amount is collected (Alam *et al.*, 2019).

From an Islamic law point of view, Islam only recognizes commodities that have intrinsic value, such as currency, including gold (dinar), silver (dirham), rice, dates, wheat, oats, and salt. Paper money or electronic money can be used as long as it is backed by a fixed exchange rate for one of the commodities (in other words, paper money is just a contract that stipulates that the carrier can exchange paper money of a fixed size (weight) for specific products). According to the earlier explanation, Islam rejects the view of currency as a commodity. Although currency can play a role in facilitating transactions, currency itself cannot be regarded as an object, so transactions cannot be conducted just because currency will cause usury (Alam *et al.*, 2019).

OneGram has implemented the concept of money in Islam into Cryptocurrency by launching OneGramCoin as a cryptocurrency supported by gold reserves that seek to revolutionize the world of cryptocurrency as well as the Islamic world monetary system. OneGram has partnered with Gold Guard to collect gold that supports each OneGram coin (OGC), so ownership of this coin is considered an asset. For every transaction that uses OneGram, a 1% transaction fee will be charged. Of this fee, 30% will be used for administrative costs, charity, and various other uses. The other 70% of this fee (0.7% of each transaction) will be reinvested in more gold. This means that each OGC will be increasingly backed by more gold but never less than one gram of gold. The maximum transaction fee is 1 OGC (OneGram, 2021).

Cryptocurrency is already widely used globally, although its use in Indonesia is still small, approximately 0.02% of the entire world market share. It can be concluded that there is great potential in the future due to rapid growth in anticipation of technological developments. Some companies now accept cryptocurrencies as payment for specific projects. Some of them also use cryptocurrency as an investment tool. For example, one of the companies that allows Bitcoin as a payment method is Microsoft. Microsoft accepts Bitcoin for certain products at its Xbox Live stores. As businesses begin to accept cryptocurrencies as legitimate payments and investments, businesses need guidance on how to deal with cryptocurrency transactions. However, Indonesian accounting standard setters have not issued any guidance on where to report the use of cryptocurrencies.

The following section explores literature on cryptocurrency followed by research methodology. Next, the result section presents the survey summary and measurement as well as analysis. The final section concludes the study and suggests recommendations for future research.

14.2 Classical vs. Modern Views on Cryptocurrency and Accounting Issues

This section elaborates some definitions, scholars' views, and fatwa regarding cryptocurrency.

14.2.1 *Cash*

According to Berentsen and Schair (2018), cash is represented by physical objects, usually coins or paper money. Indonesian Sharia-based Statement of Financial Reporting Standards (*Pernyataan Standar Akuntansi Keuangan*/PSAK) No. 2 says that cash carrying consists of cash on hand and demand deposits. When cash in physical form/cash is handed over to other individuals, the unit value is also transferred without going through a third party. With cash in physical form, anyone who has a physical object is automatically the owner of the unit of value of the money (Berentsen & Schair, 2018).

According to Takiddin (2014), money in the traditional economy is defined as any generally accepted medium of exchange. The medium of exchange can be any object that can be accepted by everyone in the community in the process of exchanging goods and services. Ilyas (2016) states the concept of money in the perspective of Islamic economics explains that units represent estimates of the value of goods and services, units that are used as standards used to measure the usefulness of goods and labor which are medium of exchange and are called units of money. In the Islamic concept, money is not a commodity and must flow so that it does not cause speculation.

14.2.2 *Ibn Taymiyyah's view of money*

From an economic perspective, money is an item that can be exchanged for other items, it can be used to assess the value of other items, and we can save it. Currency is an object, which can basically be used as: (1) a medium of exchange; (2) a store of value; (3) a unit of account; and (4) a measure of late payment (a standard for late payment) (Solikin, 2002).

Money can be understood from the perspective of Islamic economics: According to Fahmi (2018), specifically, Ibn Taymiyyah mentions the two main functions of money, namely as a measure of value and a tool for the exchange of various commodities. He asserts that: "*Atsmân* (a price or paid as price, money) is intended as a measure of the value of goods (*mi'yar al-amwal*) by which the total value of goods (*maqadir al-amwal*) can be known; and money was never meant for themselves".

In the last sentence, "... and the money was never prepared for themselves" is also in line with another scholar Al-Ghazali who also reveals that he opposed the form of currency trading for profit. Trading currency means making money as a commodity that can be traded, which will deviate from the true purpose of the currency (Fahmi, 2018). Quoting from Nur Chamid (2010), according to Al-Ghazali, currency in Islam is regarded as a tool for trading, not a commodity, for several reasons, namely:

(a) Money does not have an intrinsic satisfaction (intrinsic utility) that can directly satisfy human needs and desires. Therefore, money cannot be traded in Islam.
(b) Commodities have different qualities, but money does not.
(c) Commodities will be accompanied in kind in the purchase and sale operations.

According to Fahmi (2018), Ibn Taymiyyah strongly opposes all forms of money trading. If money is to be exchanged for money, then the exchange must be complete (*taqabud*) and without pause

(*Hulūl*). If two people exchange money, one pays in cash and the other promises to pay later, then the first person cannot use the money promised in the transaction until it is paid. This will cause the first person to lose the opportunity to use the money to meet their needs. That is why Ibn Taymiyyah opposes the buying and selling of foreign currency.

Quoted from Fahmi (2018), Ibn Taymiyyah states that poor-quality money will eliminate good-quality currencies from circulation. He describes this as follows:

> If the authorities cancel the use of certain currencies and print other types of currencies for the people, this will harm the rich people who have money because the fall in the value of the old currency becomes just an item. He means that he has committed wrongdoing because it removes the high value they originally had. Moreover, if the intrinsic value of the currency is different, this will be a source of profit for criminals to collect bad currencies and exchange them for good currencies, and then they will take them to other areas and exchange them for bad currencies. in the area to be brought back to the area. Thus, the value of community goods will be destroyed.

In this statement, Ibn Taymiyyah mentions the consequences of entering bad currency values for those who already own it. If the currency is later announced that it is no longer valid as currency, it means that it is only regarded as an ordinary item, and its value is different from its value as currency. On the other hand, with the emergence of new currency values, people will get lower commodity prices.

According to the money given in the Qur'an, the law stipulates the concept of money in Islam. According to the Qur'an, the money in the hands of people belongs in principle to Allah (God) Himself; Allah says in the Qur'an (24:33) which means *and give them something from the money Allah has given you.* Furthermore, Allah points out that the ownership of wealth is conditional, and mankind cannot do what he wishes with the property he owns. Allah entrusts the use of money to mankind in which he only has the right to discard for the things that Allah has given him and make him prepare for his heir.

14.2.3 *Theory of investment*

Investment can be an investment in one or more assets, which are generally held for a long time, with the hope of making a profit in the future (Sunariyah, 2003, p. 4). According to Samuelson (2004, p. 198), investment includes increasing a country's inventory of goods or capital in one year, such as building production teams and inventory projects. Investing is a step at the expense of future consumption. Based on the above definition, it can be concluded that investment is a type of expense which can be in the form of capital goods, buildings, capital equipment, and inventory items, used to increase the ability to produce goods, serve or increase the productivity of labor, thus improving production.

1. *Neoclassical theory*: Neoclassical theory emphasizes the importance of saving as a source of investment. Investment is considered one of the main drivers of economic growth and development. The faster the rate of investment development, the faster the population growth rate and the faster the capital stock per capita. The higher the capital ratio of each job, the higher the productivity of each worker. In characterizing neoclassical, Sollow and Swan focus on how population growth, capital accumulation, technological progress, and production interact in the process of economic growth (Arsyad, 2010: 8889).

2. *Harrod–Domar's theory*: Harrod and Domar defend previous economists' opinions that is a combination of the opinions of the classics and Keynes, where he emphasizes the role of capital growth in creating economic growth. Harrod–Domar's theory views that capital formation is considered as expenditure which will increase the ability of an economy to produce goods and/or services as well as expenditure which will increase the effective demand of society. If several capital formations are carried out at a certain period, then in the next period, the economy can produce greater goods and/or services (Sadono, 2007, pp. 256–257).

14.2.4 *National Sharia Board of Indonesian Ulema Council Fatwa No. 116 and 117*

National Sharia Council-Indonesian Ulema Council (DSN-MUI) in Fatwa No. 116 of 2017 states electronic money may be used as a means of payment with limitations on the operation and use that must be avoided from:

(1) *riba, gharar, maisîr, tadlîs, risyvah,* and *israf* transactions, and
(2) transactions on illicit or immoral objects.

Quoted from the official website of the West Sumatra MUI, the MUI explains Bitcoin in eleven points in which it is stated that Bitcoin in some countries is classified as a foreign currency. Generally, authorities and regulators are not recognized as official currencies and exchange because they do not represent the value of assets. Bitcoin transactions are similar to forex, so trading is thick with a speculative taste. Bitcoin as an investment is closer to *gharar* (speculation that harms others). Because its existence has no backing assets, the price cannot be controlled and its existence cannot be officially guaranteed, so there is likely to be a lot of publicity in *ḥarām*. Bitcoin as a legal investment is prohibited because it is just a speculative tool rather than an investment, just a profit and loss game, not a business production. National Sharia Board of Indonesian Ulema Council (Dewan Syariah Nasional–Majelis Ulama Indonesia) in Fatwa No. 117 of 2018 states the following:

(1) Information technology-based financing services are allowed on conditions by Sharia principles.
(2) The implementation of information technology-based financing services based on Sharia principles must follow the provisions contained in the fatwa.

14.2.5 *Digital cash*

According to Berentsen and Schair (2018), the ideal payment system is a system where the value of money can be transferred electronically through cash data files. Electronic transactions such as these are used in the form of e-money. According to the Bank for International Settlements, currency means stored value or prepaid products, in which various funds or monetary values are stored in electronic media owned by consumers. This model transaction involves a prepaid software product that involves a computer network by storing cash balance digitally according to the value deposited by the account owner.

14.2.6 *Electronic payment system*

An electronic payment system is a payment mechanism that uses electronic media without involving cash (Hascaryani, 2013). Electronic payment systems can also be defined as types of information between organizations related to transaction systems, linking various associations and connecting to individual clients. The need for complex interactions requires between partners, technology and the environment (Fatonah *et al.*, 2018).

According to the Federal Financial Institution Examination Board (2010), electronic payment is a new retail payment method. Merchants obtain payment information for goods and services and place this information on an electronic platform that creates electronic files for processing via the Internet. Electronic payment services come with a web-based user interface that allows customers to access and manage bank accounts and transactions remotely (Hidayanto *et al.*, 2015). In general, electronic payments refer to electronic payments in the context of electronic commerce online transactions conducted through the Internet (Junadi, 2015).

14.2.7 *Cryptocurrency*

Cryptocurrency is a virtual monetary unit that has no physical representation (Berentsen & Schair, 2018). Cryptocurrency is made on a decentralized transaction system without the presence of a third party that can verify using the digital signature concept on each transaction whose process is designed, among others, to reduce transaction costs created through third parties that validate a transaction (Nakamoto, 2008).

According to Dandapani (2017), cryptocurrency is a decentralized peer-to-peer digital currency based on computer cryptography for security built on a blockchain system. Popular cryptocurrency includes Bitcoin, Lite Coin, Zerocoin, and Peercoin. Cryptocurrency cryptography on digital currencies is used for security reasons and as an anti-counterfeiting measure.

The use of cryptocurrency as a transaction medium is widely used internationally. Reporting from the Yahoo Finance page, a blockchain development company named Bitfury donated the high-capacity computing power it uses to process digital currency transactions for COVID-19 research and participated in the Folding @ Home project to run simulations of the molecular structure of the virus to contribute to the development of effective therapies.

14.2.8 *PSAK 13: Investment*

Investment is an asset used by a company for the growth of wealth (accretion of wealth) through the distribution of investment returns (such as interest, royalties, dividends, and rent), to appreciate the value of an investment or for other benefits for companies that invest as benefits obtained through relationships trading.

14.2.9 *Regulation of the Minister of Trade of the Republic of Indonesia No. 99 of 2018*

Regulation of the Minister of Trade of the Republic of Indonesia No. 99 of 2018, concerning general policies for the implementation of crypto asset trading, implements the following policies:

(1) Crypto assets are defined as commodities that can be used as futures contract subjects traded on the futures exchange.
(2) Further regulation regarding the designation of crypto asset as a commodity that can be used as a futures contract subject traded on the futures exchange, its guidance, supervision, and development is determined by the Head of the Commodity Futures Trading Supervisory Agency.

14.2.10 *CoFTRA Decisions No. 5 of 2019*

Head of CoFTRA Decisions Number 5 of 2019 in Article 16 concerning crypto asset transactions is stipulated as follows:

(1) Crypto asset customers can make transactions if the person concerned has sufficient funds and/or crypto asset balance.
(2) Physical traders of crypto assets are prohibited from facilitating transactions if the customer does not have sufficient funds and/or crypto asset balance.
(3) The Futures Clearing House must verify every transaction made by crypto asset customers facilitated by crypto asset physical traders.

(4) Verification, as referred to in paragraph (3), is carried out by the Futures Clearing House to guarantee and complete transactions to perform the delivery versus payment (DvP) function by:
   (a) ensuring that the funds in the account are separated from the balance or record of ownership of crypto assets;
   (b) recording the transfer of funds and balances or records of ownership of crypto assets;
   (c) asking the crypto asset physical merchant and/or depository manager to change the balance or record of the ownership of the crypto asset stored at the depository; and
   (d) debiting and crediting the financial accounts of crypto asset customers and/or crypto asset physical traders to guarantee and complete transactions.

(5) Physical crypto asset traders and futures clearing institutions submit transaction reports at the end of each trading day to the futures exchange in the context of price reference and market supervision.

14.3 Research Methodology

This research is descriptive exploratory research which is conducted by analyzing the level of description and presenting it systematically so that it is more easily understood and concluded. Explorative research is a type of research that aims to find something new in the form of a grouping of symptoms, facts, and certain diseases. Explorative descriptive research aims to describe the state of a phenomenon. The phenomenon in this research is the existence of cryptocurrency and how positive law and Islamic law on cryptocurrency, measurement, recognition, and presentation, and disclosure of cryptocurrency investments in financial statements and the economic impact caused by cryptocurrency. This research is expected to produce output in the form of the proposed accounting treatment of cryptocurrency investments.

The type of data used in this study is non-financial data that is analyzed qualitatively. Non-financial data were obtained through a thematic interview process with competent parties in the discussion of this study. A literature review is also conducted on the literature related to this research with data sourced from scientific journals, books, and news. This research is conducted by using data as a support. Data were collected through the following ways.

First step is structured interviews. To obtain data to achieve the objectives of the study, primary data and NVivo 12 plus software as tools are used. The data collection technique used is interview method. Interview is a method used to find primary data and is a method that is widely used in interpretive and critical research. Interviews are conducted when researchers want to dig deeper about attitudes, beliefs, behaviors, or experiences of respondents on social phenomena (Bastian *et al.*, 2018). The structured interview aims to obtain information about issues related to the research topic (Sekaran & Bougie, 2016). Interviews in this study aim to explore information and responses from relevant parties regarding the legal status of cryptocurrency, the treatment of accounting for cryptocurrency, and the economic impact caused by cryptocurrency. Interviews are conducted online utilizing available technology. According to Sekaran and Bougie (2016), online interviews require less time and money and cut distance limitations. In this study, the authors selected the interviewees as described in Table 14.1.

The selection of interview sources in this study was carried out based on the involvement of interview sources in reviewing policies

Table 14.1. List of interviewees.

No.	Interviewees	Agencies	Role	Output
1	Two persons	Bank of Indonesia representative	Regulator	Regulatory views regarding positive law and economic impact of cryptocurrency in Indonesia
2	One person	DSN MUI representative	Expert of Fiqh Muamalat	Islamic law views on cryptocurrency in Indonesia
3	One person	Institute of Indonesia chartered accountants representative	Professional organization	A view of accounting treatment of cryptocurrency in Indonesia

regarding cryptocurrency in each institution. Each interviewee is requested to answer research questions related to his respective fields.

Second step is literature review. According to Sekaran and Bougie (2016), a literature review is a step-by-step process involving identification of published and unpublished works from secondary data sources on the topic according to the problem and documentation for the work being carried out.

The data analysis technique used in this study is a qualitative analysis as proposed by Miles and Hubberman (Sugiyono, 2007) that consists of data collection, data reduction, data presentation, and drawing conclusion.

14.4 Result and Discussion

Based on data processing using NVivo 12 plus software on the results of interviews, the authors find that the results had a neutral sentiment on sentiment analysis for all questions asked to all interviewees. Then, all statements in this chapter are made in accordance with the results of data processing.

14.4.1 *Recognition, measurement, presentation and disclosure of cryptocurrency investments in financial statements*

14.4.1.1 *How IFRS account for investment in cryptocurrency*

International Financial Reporting Standards (IFRS) are those that establish international accounting standards. The IFRS foundation has published an acceptable way to report on cryptocurrencies based on existing standards. Table 14.2 is the summary of IFRS treatment for cryptocurrency that have been analyzed by Grant Thornton.

The IAS 7 "Statement of Cash Flows" cannot provide a definition of cash but only states that "cash comprises cash on hand and demand deposits". Regarding the above statement, it is clear that cryptocurrencies cannot be regarded as cash equivalents, as explained in IAS 7, because they are not suitable for the exchange of any goods or services. IAS 7 states that "cash equivalents are short-term, highly liquid investments that are easy to convert into cash of

Table 14.2. How IFRS treat cryptocurrency.

Standard	Categorization	Acceptable under IFRS
IAS 7 statement of cash flows	Cash and cash equivalents	No
IAS 39 financial instruments: Recognition and measurement	Financial asset at fair value through profit or loss	No
IAS 40 investment property	Investment property	No
IAS 16 property, plant and equipment	Property, plant, and equipment	No
IAS 38 intangible assets	Intangible assets	Yes
IAS 2 inventories	Inventories	Yes*

Note: *Under certain conditions.
Source: Grant Thornton (2020).

a known amount and the risk of value changes is negligible". Looking at this statement, since the cryptocurrencies has fluctuated price and ambiguous pricing factor, it is fair enough that cryptocurrencies is not qualified as cash equivalents.

IAS 32 mentions the financial asset with "any asset that is: (1) cash; (2) an equity instrument of another entity; (3) a contractual right; (4) a contract that will or may be settled in the entity's own equity instruments such as a derivative and non-derivative". With that in mind, cryptocurrencies are not equity instruments or contracts to be established in equity instruments.

IAS 40 defines investment property as property held to earn rentals or for capital appreciation. Although the cryptocurrency belongs to certain entities to carry out capital appreciation. Our view is that it is inappropriate for an entity to classify it as an investment property and measure it at fair value that exceeds profit or loss because cryptocurrency is not a tangible asset.

IAS 38 interprets an intangible asset as a recognizable non-monetary asset without physical element. Cryptocurrencies are a structure of digital money with no physical form, and in Grant Thornton's view, intangible assets are appropriate designation for cryptocurrencies.

Proportionate to an entity's business model, theoretically it is related to cryptocurrency according to IAS 2 "Inventory". Regardless of whether the cryptocurrency held meets the definition of intangible assets, IAS 38 confirms that intangible assets owned by entities sold in the standard business sequence are insignificant within the scope of the standard and should be mentioned in IAS 2.

14.4.1.2 *How the Big Four accounting firms account for cryptocurrency investment*

The "Big Four" are the world's four largest accounting firms. They consist of PricewaterhouseCoopers (PwC), Ernst & Young (EY), Deloitte, and Klynveld Peat Marwick Goerdeler (KPMG). These four companies have thousands of customers worldwide. Their discoveries and researches are the foundation of the entire accounting profession. The Big Four trade with companies that are capable of identifying cryptocurrencies. So far, most of its customers do not recognize this cryptocurrency, but this has not prevented the Big Four from investigating it. They have been exposed to cryptocurrencies at some point, and so far, they have made basic conclusions on how in detail they should be (Table 14.3).

(1) *PricewaterhouseCoopers (PwC)*: According to PwC's view on its publication, investment of cryptocurrency cannot be treated by latest standard such as a financial instrument or as an inventory. The cryptocurrency does not meet the requirements of financial instruments.

Table 14.3. How the Big Four accounting firms treat cryptocurrency.

Big four firms	**Cryptocurrency treatment**	**Consideration**
PricewaterhouseCoopers (PwC)	Intangible asset	It is identifiable because it can be sold, exchanged, or transferred individually
Ernst & Young (EY)	—	—
Deloitte	Inventory Financial instrument	Broker company Investment company
Klynveld Peat Marwick Goerdeler (KPMG)	Inventory	Holding it for sale in a normal course of business

Source: Publications of PwC, EY, Deloitte, and KPMG (2020).

That is because cryptocurrency does not represent a contractual obligation to receive cash. In their opinion, cryptocurrency investment cannot be treated as financial instrument. According to IAS 2 "Inventory", if an entity holds cryptocurrency for investment purpose (that is capital appreciation) over extended periods of time, it would likely not meet the definition of inventory, so cryptocurrency investment cannot be treated by IAS 2. PwC concludes that cryptocurrency meet the definition of an intangible asset under IAS 38.

(2) *Ernst & Young (EY)*: EY will not express its own opinions on how to treat cryptocurrency investments. EY is based on guidance provided by other regulatory entities.

(3) *Deloitte*: According to Deloitte, cryptocurrencies should be reported based on their intent, for example: (1) As a broker company that holds cryptocurrency for sale in the ordinary course of business, they should consider cryptocurrency as inventory; (2) As a company that uses cryptocurrency as an investment and hopes to increase its value, they should account for it like any other investment initially and subsequently measured at fair value. Investment or financial instrument is another cryptocurrency account that can be classified in this case.

(4) *Klynveld Peat Marwick Goerdeler (KPMG)*: KPMG published an article on how to report cryptocurrencies. Their opinion approve the guidance that has been given by International Financial Reporting Interpretations Committee (IFRIC). The IFRIC guidance recognizes cryptocurrencies as intangible assets. Cryptocurrency can also be classified as inventory depending on the intent that the company has. The only way to classify cryptocurrency as inventory is holding it for sale in a normal course of business.

14.4.1.3 *How Chartered Professional Accountants (CPA) Canada account for cryptocurrency investment*

CPA states that in certain contracts to buy or sell cryptocurrency in the future (forward contract or options) or other contracts that settle in cash based on movements in a particular cryptocurrency may meet the definition of a derivative and be subject to financial-instrument accounting.

14.4.1.4 *Cryptocurrency as investment*

Hartley (2019) argues that in this era of technology-based society, entities should also keep the cryptocurrency, if they do not want to sell it, hoping that it will appreciate immediately. Cryptocurrency as an asset should be considered as an equity security. Security indicates the total interest of ownership in a company, such as common stock, preferred stock, or other share capital. Cryptocurrency does not meet this definition because its ownership cannot be shared. Many individuals or entities hold into cryptocurrency in hopes that the value will increase, similar to the way people have equity investments. Cryptocurrency can be processed promptly as in the case of securities trading. If an entity intends to hold cryptocurrency, it expect its value to increase, so its basic accounting treatment is similar to that of equities.

14.4.1.5 *PSAK proposal draft of cryptocurrency investment treatment*

The interviewees stated that the accounting treatment of cryptocurrency depends on government regulations, whether the government legalizes cryptocurrency as a medium of exchange or as an investment instrument. If regulations govern cryptocurrency as a medium of exchange, PSAK 10 about foreign currency can be used to present it in the financial statements. If regulations governing cryptocurrency governs cryptocurrency as an investment, PSAK 71 about financial instrument can be used as a basis for the presentation.

Opinions from IAI Indonesia are different when compared with the results of the analysis conducted by Grant Thornton on IFRS, Grant Thornton's analysis results state that cryptocurrency can be treated as intangible assets and inventory. However, the interviewees argued that cryptocurrency could not be considered as intangible assets and inventory.

Due to the many potential usages of cryptocurrency, according to the analysis, the current accounting standards for SAK do not have a suitable way to handle that matter. It differs from the issues that have been through in the past decade. In fact, cryptocurrency is a digital way of trading currencies and in our growing technological era causes a drastic change to our society's trading activities. However, the way we account for such actions does not have any impact at

Table 14.4. A proposal on presentation of cryptocurrency.

No.	Transaction	Long-term investment	Short-term investment
1	Purchase of cryptocurrency at market value	Dr. Cryptocurrency X available for sales Cr. Cash	Dr. Cryptocurrency for trading Cr. Cash
2	Sales of cryptocurrency at higher market value	Dr. Cash Cr. Cryptocurrency X available for sales Cr. Gain on sale of cryptocurrency X	Dr. Cash Cr. Cryptocurrency for trading Cr. Gain on sale of Investment
3	Sales of cryptocurrency at lower market value	Dr. Cash Dr. Loss on sale of cryptocurrency X Cr. Cryptocurrency X available for sales	Dr. Cash Dr. Loss on sale of Investment Cr. Cryptocurrency for trading
4	End year entry	Dr. Cryptocurrency market value adjustment Cr. Unrealized holding gain	

all. With the growth of technological advancements, the community must grow the same rate as well. By that sense, society must use a method that assimilates cryptocurrency's daily usage and other advancements in our currency and trading activities. Through this research, the authors design an accounting presentation model for cryptocurrency investment as follows (Table 14.4 shows the proposal on the presentation of cryptocurrency investment).

1. *Recognition and measurement*: Recognition and measurement of cryptocurrency refers to PSAK 55 about financial instrument: recognition and measurement. Cryptocurrency recognized as an investment that hold by an entity with the expectation that the value will be increase.

a. Recognition:

(1) Entity can recognize the cryptocurrency investment as short-term investment or long-term investment.

(2) Cryptocurrency assets are valued at market prices when first purchased.
(3) Losses are recognized when the disposal price (net of selling costs) is lower than the carrying value.
(4) Investment results, such as the difference between sale and purchase value, can be recognized as income.
(5) Earning from unrealized gains and losses should be reported.

b. Measurement:

(1) Short term and long term of cryptocurrency investment reported at market price.
(2) The amount of earning from unrealized gains and losses measured by the difference between the buying and selling prices.
(3) Gains are recognized when the disposal/selling price (net of selling costs) is higher than the carrying value.

2. *Presentation*: Cryptocurrency investments are presented separately from other investment instruments in the profit and loss statement:

(1) Cryptocurrencies are reported as short-term investments in trading securities.
(2) Cryptocurrencies are reported as long-term investments in sellable securities.

3. Disclosure:

(1) Entity disclose the cryptocurrency investment at profit and loss statement.
(2) Cryptocurrency investment reported in balance sheet and profit and loss statement.
(3) Available-for-sale securities are recorded at fair value and unrealized gains and losses are recorded in other comprehensive income.
(4) Figures 14.1 and 14.2 show the simulation of cryptocurrency investment disclosure on a financial statement.

14.4.2 *Positive law of cryptocurrency based on stakeholder perception*

The interviewee stated that there was no urgency for the issuance of cryptocurrency regulations as a medium of exchange or investment

PT. XXX
Balance Sheet
December 31, 202X

ASSETS		**LIABILITIES**	
Current Asset		Current Liabilities	
Cash and cash equivalents	xxx	Account Payable	xxx
Account Receivable	xxx	Notes Payable	xxx
Inventory	xxx	Long-term Debt	xxx
Investments in Cryptocurrency X - Available for Sale	xxx	Total Liabilities	xxx
Investments in Cryptocurrency X - Trading	xxx		
Total Current Assets	xxx	**EQUITY**	
Fixed Asset		Shareholder's Equity	
Equipment	xxx	Common Stock	xxx
Acc. Depreciation of Equipment	xxx	Retained Earnings	xxx
Building	xxx	Treasury Stock	xxx
Land	xxx	Total Equity	xxx
Total Fixed Assets	xxx	Total Liabilities and Equity	xxx
Intangible Asset			
Goodwill	xxx		
Total Intangible Asset	xxx		
Total Asset	xxx		

Figure 14.1. Balance sheet simulation.

PT. XXX
Comprehensive Profit and Loss Statement
December 31, 202X

Nett Sales	xxx	
Cost of Income	xxx	
Gross Profit/Loss		xxx
Costs:		
Sales Cost	xxx	
Administration Cost	xxx	
Total Cost		(xxx)
Nett Profit/Loss		xxx
Income Tax		(xxx)
Nett Profit/Loss		xxx
Other Comprehensive Income		
Gain/Loss in Investments in Cryptocurrency X - Available for Sale	xxx	
Gain/Loss in Investments in Cryptocurrency X - Trading	xxx	
Total Other Comprehensive Income		(xxx)
Comprehensive Profit/Loss		**xxx**

Figure 14.2. Comprehensive profit and loss statement simulation.

in Indonesia. The interviewee also stated that investment in cryptocurrency is illegal and the government is not responsible for any losses.

The interviewee's statement stating investment in cryptocurrency as an illegal act is contrary to regulations of the Ministry of Trade

Republic of Indonesia Number 99 of 2019 concerning general policy on organizing crypto asset futures trading. As the part of Ministry of Trade Republic Indonesia, Commodity Futures Trading Regulatory Agency (CoFTRA) issued the regulation as follows:

(1) Head of CoFTRA Decisions Number 2 of 2019 concerns with the operation of commodity physical market in futures exchange.
(2) Head of CoFTRA Decisions Number 3 of 2019 concerns with the commodity that can be the subjects of futures contracts in futures exchange, Syariah derivative contracts, and/or other derivative contracts traded on the futures exchange.

    Bappebti Regulation No. 3 of 2019 becomes the legal basis for the determination of crypto assets as one of the commodities that can be subject to futures contracts, and other derivative contracts traded on the futures exchange, by adding commodities in the field of digital assets (digital assets) in the form of crypto assets.
(3) Head of CoFTRA Decisions Number 5 of 2019 concerns with technical provisions of organization of the crypto asset physical market in the futures exchange.

    According to the regulation, several requirements must be obeyed by these digital currency traders, including the following:

    (a) Cryptocurrency trading must be done on a futures exchange.
    (b) The traded cryptocurrency must be based on distributed ledger technology and be in the form of a crypto utility or crypto-backed asset.
    (c) Its market capitalization value is ranked in the top 500 in the market capitalization of crypto assets (coin market cap) for crypto utility assets. It is included in the most significant crypto-asset exchange transactions in the world.
    (d) Crypto asset trading can be facilitated by the futures exchange, which has obtained the approval of the Head of CoFTRA. The condition is that the futures exchange must have a minimum paid-up capital of IDR 1.5 trillion and maintain a final capital balance of at least IDR 1.2 trillion.
    (e) Futures exchanges must also have at least three Certified Information Systems Security Professional (CISSP) employees.

(f) The process of contracting and completing transactions in the trade of crypto assets must be carried out by the futures clearing house which has a capital of at least IDR 1.5 trillion and maintains a final capital balance of IDR 1.2 trillion.
(g) Cryptocurrency transactions on the futures exchange must be facilitated by physical traders of crypto or broker assets with servers in Indonesia. These brokers must have a minimum paid-up capital of IDR 1 trillion while maintaining final equity of at least IDR 800 billion.
(h) Brokerage companies must have a minimum organizational structure with information technology division, audit division, legal division, crypto asset customer complaint division, client support division, and accounting and finance division.
(i) Cryptocurrency brokers must have an online trading system that is used for trading connected to the futures exchange and the futures clearing house.
(j) Brokers must also have a minimum standard operating procedure governing the marketing and receipt of customers of crypto assets, execution of transactions, internal control and supervision, resolution of disputes over crypto asset customers, and implementation of anti-money laundering programs.
(k) Crypto asset customers who will carry out transactions of crypto assets through physical merchants of crypto assets are required to place funds that will be used to carry out operations in separate accounts on behalf of physical merchants of crypto assets for the benefit of the futures clearing house.
(l) Funds placed must use the rupiah currency.

(4) Head of CoFTRA Decisions Number 9 of 2019 concerns with Amendment to Head of CoFTRA Decisions Number 5 of 2019.
(5) Head of CoFTRA Decisions Number 2 of 2020 concerns with Second Amendment to Head of CoFTRA Decisions Number 5 of 2019.
(6) Head of CoFTRA Decisions Number 3 of 2020 concerns with Third Amendment to Head of CoFTRA Decisions Number 5 of 2019.

Previously, Bank Indonesia had issued regulations regarding cryptocurrency viral in Indonesia, as follows:

(1) Article 34 PBI Number 18/40/PBI/2016 Bank of Indonesia Regulation No. 18/40/PBI/2016 concerning processing of payment transactions.
(2) Article 9 paragraph (2) PBI No. 19/12/PBI/2017 concerning technology is prohibited from conducting payment system activities using virtual currency.

Generally, Bank Indonesia prohibits transactions using cryptocurrency included in the virtual currency. However, based on the interview results, Mr. S stated that Bank Indonesia could renew its regulations following the times. However, Indonesia has not been able to become the initiator of cryptocurrency on a large scale because Indonesia's position in international trade is not as strong as China, which has issued its virtual currency.

Contrary to Mr. S, another interviewee from Bank Indonesia, Mr. R, said if Indonesia legalized the use of cryptocurrency, it would violate the law on currency as a symbol of the state. Thus, someday, if it is legalized, it may be necessary to change the current law first.

14.4.3 *Islamic law of cryptocurrency based on stakeholder perception*

MUI, as a regulator, has not issued a specific fatwa regarding crypto currency in Indonesia. According to interviews with informants, a fatwa regarding cryptocurrency can be issued by considering the extent to which this fatwa is needed by the public. MUI also usually issues fatwas on regulations issued by the government based on regulations that have been issued, MUI has just made the same rules in Sharia perspective.

Regarding the fluctuating cryptocurrency values, the interviewee argues that according to economic theory, money, besides having a function of exchange, it must also be able to become a store value and unit of account, if the Bitcoin mentioned is not detrimental and can function like money, then it could be back to the original law of *muamalah*, all are allowed unless there are prohibited elements.

Referring to the classical theory of Ibn Taymiyyah regarding inefficiency, the informant stated that inefficiency can occur in many forms, and it is also very likely to occur in the practice of cryptocurrency, then in Islam there is a *hisbah* (supervision) mechanism in modern Islamic business and financial institutions, there are DPS (Sharia supervisory council) and also required regulations and other law enforcement devices because humans are equally exposed to satanic temptations.

14.4.4 *Cryptocurrency's economic impact*

In the interview process, Mr. S stated that Indonesia still needs a thorough study of the cryptocurrency legalization. However, the currency is not the dominant factor that can influence economic growth. So, economic growth does not depend on the currency in use.

In another interview session, Mr. R stated that if cryptocurrency were legalized in Indonesia, it would have the following impacts:

(1) The loss of the role of sentimental banks in Indonesia.
(2) Measuring instruments in the economy become unclear because there are no measurement tools with fixed values.
(3) Speculation action will be higher and real transactions will be reduced in the community.

14.5 Summary

Investment in cryptocurrency has not been massive. However, as cryptocurrency is increasingly used in the business world, it is not possible that cryptocurrency investments made by an entity will become commonplace in the future. This research produces guidelines to treat cryptocurrency investments in financial statements by modifying existing standards that adopt the nature of cryptocurrency itself.

Indonesia has not legalized cryptocurrency as a transaction tool but has allowed to use cryptocurrency as an investment tool. It is also possible that in the future, Indonesia will apply cryptocurrency as valid transaction tool, following international market trends. In the context of Sharia, cryptocurrency is still forbidden both as a transaction tool and an investment instrument. However, as a regulator, MUI has not issued a fatwa either in the form of a ban or an in-depth study of cryptocurrency investments. If Bank Indonesia, as the central bank, legalizes cryptocurrency as a transaction tool and the use of cryptocurrency as an investment instrument increases, then the economic impact arises from the use of cryptocurrency itself in the form of:

(1) The loss of the role of sentimental banks in Indonesia.
(2) Measuring instruments in the economy becoming unclear because there are no measurement tools with fixed values.

This research suggests a draft accounting treatment for cryptocurrency investments to be immediately reviewed and established to complement existing accounting standards. For regulators, this research is intended as a reference for making comprehensive regulations regarding cryptocurrency in the future.

The pandemic problem caused by the coronavirus (COVID-19) is increasingly affecting the economy on a global scale. Stock values began to decline; investors panicked and sold their assets to hold cash. Reporting from CNBC Indonesia (2020), cryptocurrency is also rapidly becoming an alternative to non-cash transactions such as remittances and cross-border transactions. Encrypted currency with decentralization, transparency, and global blockchain technology is considered to be a solution to various problems faced by traditional financial systems. This cryptocurrency is designed with a layered encrypted security system, is not controlled by a central authority, and is easier to obtain than other currencies.

Head of CoFTRA Decisions Number 5 of 2019 states that cryptocurrency assets are confirmed as commodities that can be traded on futures exchanges. This regulation means that the cryptocurrency industry has clear rules and is increasingly developing in Indonesia. Although it will have various political impacts, cryptocurrency is considered to be a medium for accelerating economic growth during the current pandemic.

According to CNBC Indonesia 2019, Facebook Inc. said it would launch a blockchain-based digital currency (cryptocurrency) called Libra. This currency will be controlled by Facebook and several other large companies that are members of the Libra Association. Libra will be a digital currency backed by a reserve of real-world assets, including bank deposits and short-term government securities, and held by a network of custodians. This structure is meant to attract people's trust and stabilize its value. Libra holders can also convert coins into traditional currency based on the prevailing exchange rates. Indonesia, with the fourth largest number of Facebook users at 120 million, has a great potential to become Libra Coin users.

Beside the launching of Libra Coin, OGC, which launched One-Gram as the first gold-backed cryptocurrency, claims to be the first cryptocurrency that as Sharia-compliant cryptocurrency. By this pandemic situation and the release of Libra Coin, Indonesian people and entity can start to adopt cryptocurrency as an investment instrument. Many cryptocurrencies continue to show positive performance amid the economic slowdown caused by the COVID-19 pandemic. Dogecoin and Aurora, for example, are two crypto assets that experienced an increase of almost 100% and 300%, respectively, in one trading day (CNN Indonesia, 2020). Investors and traders can take advantage of this momentum to reap profits and cover losses due to the decline (sideways) in other investment products' performance due to the COVID-19 outbreak.

References

Alam, N., Gupta, L., & Zameni, A. (2019). Cryptocurrency and Islamic finance. *Fintech and Islamic Finance*, 99–118. Retrieved 23 March, 2020. Doi: 10.1007/978-3-030-24666-2_6.

Arsyad, L. (2010). *Ekonomi Pembangunan.* Yogyakarta: UPP STIM YKPN.

Bandur, A. (2019). *Penelitian Kualitatif-Studi Multi-Disiplin Keilmua dengan NVivo 12 plus.* Jakarta: Mitra Wacana Media.

Bastian, I., Winardi, R., & Fatmawati, D. (2018). *Metoda Wawancara.*

Berentsen, A. & Schar, F. (2018). A short introduction to the world of cryptocurrencies. *Review, 100*(1), 1–19. Doi: 10.20955/r.2018.1-16.

Chamid, N. (2010). *Jejak Langkah Sejarah Pemikiran Ekonomi Islam.* Yogyakarta: Pustaka Pelajar. Yogyakarta.

Cottam, M. L., Diets-Uhler, B., Elena, M., & Preston, T. (2012). *Pengantar psikologi politik.* Jakarta: Raja Grafindo Persada.

CPA (2018). An introduction to accounting for cryptocurrencies.

Dahlman, C., Mealy, S., & Wermelinger, M. (2016). *Harnessing the Digital Economy for Developing Countries.* Paris: OECD. http://www.oecd-ilibrary.org/docserver/download/4adffb24-en.pdf.

Dandapani, K. (2017). Electronic finance — Recent developments. *Managerial Finance, 43*(5), 614–626. Doi: 10.1108/mf-02-2017-0028.

Dourado, E. & Brito, J. (2014). Cryptocurrency. *The New Palgrave Dictionary of Economics*, 1–9. Doi: 10.1057/978-1-349-95121-5_2895-1.

Dyhrberg, A. H. (2016). Hedging capabilities of bitcoin. Is it the virtual gold? *Finance Research Letters*, *16*, 139–144. Doi: 10.1016/j.frl.2015.10.025.

Fadilla, F. (2019). Sejarah Penggunaan Uang Sejak Masa Rasulullah Saw Sampai Sekarang. *Islamic Banking: Journal Pemikiran Dan Pengembangan Perbankan Syariah*, *4*(2), 97–106. Doi: 10.36908/isbank.v4i2.62.

Fahmi, K. (2018). Money function and money banking by ibn Taymiyyah — Munich personal RePEc archive. Retrieved 2 April, 2020, from https://mpra.ub.uni-muenchen.de/87018/.

Fatonah, S., Yulandari, A., & Wibowo, F. W. (2018). A review of e-Payment system in e-commerce. *Journal of Physics: Conference Series*, *1140*(012033). https://doi.org/10.1088/1742-6596/1140/1/012033.

Grant, T. (2018). IFRS viewpoint accounting for cryptocurrencies — The basics.

Hartley, A. (2019). Financial reporting of cryptocurrency. *Honors Theses*. https://scholar.utc.edu/honors-theses/226.

Hidayanto, A. N., Hidayat, L. S., Sandhyaduhita, P. I., & Handayani, P. W. (2015). Examining the relationship of payment system characteristics and behavioral intention in e-payment adoption: A case of Indonesia. *International Journal of Business Information Systems*, *19*(1), 58. Doi: 10.1504/ijbis.2015.069065.

Ilyas, R. (2016). Konsep Uang Dalam Perspektif Ekonomi Islam. *BISNIS Jurnal Bisnis Dan Manajemen Islam*, *4*(1), 35. Doi: 10.21043/bisnis.v4i1.1695.

Junadi & Sfenrianto. (2015). A model of factors influencing consumer's intention to use e-payment system in Indonesia. *Procedia Computer Science*, *59*, 214–220. Doi: 10.1016/j.procs.2015.07.557.

KPMG (2019). Cryptoassets-accounting and tax.

Nakamoto, S. (2009). Bitcoin: A peer-to-peer electronic cash system. Cryptography mailing list at https://metzdowd.com.

Nuraliati, A. & Azwari, P. (2019). Akuntansi Untuk cryptocurrency. *I-Finance: A Research Journal on Islamic Finance*, *4*(2). https://doi.org/10.19109/ifinance.v4i2.2885.

Poyser, O. (2017). Exploring the determinants of Bitcoin's price: An application of Bayesian structural time series. Retrieved 23 March, 2020, from https://arxiv.org/abs/1706.01437.

Procházka, D. (2018). Accounting for bitcoin and other cryptocurrencies under IFRS: A comparison and assessment of competing models. *The International Journal of Digital Accounting Research*, 161–188. Doi: 10.4192/1577-8517-v18_7.

PWC (2019). In depth, a look at current financial reporting issues, cryptograhic assets and related transaction: Accounting considerations under IFRS.

Samuelson, Paul dan Nordhaus William D. (2004). *Ilmu Makroekonomi.* Jakarta: PT Media Global Edukas.

Sekaran, U. & Bougie, R. (2016). *Research Methods for Business: A Skill-Building Approach.* (6th Edition). New York: Wiley.

Sugiyono, (2007). *Metode Penelitian Kuantitatif Kualitatif dan R&D.* Bandung: Alfabeta.

Suharni, (2018). Uang elektronik (e-Money) ditinjau dari perspektif hukum dan perubahan sosial. *Spektrum Hukum, 15*(1), 15. Doi: 10.35973/sh.v15i1.1108.

Sunariyah, (2003). *Pengantar Pengetahuan Pasar Modal.* Yogyakarta: Upp Amp Ykpn Yogyakarta.

Syamsyah, N. O. (2016). Kajian atas cryptocurrency sebagai alat pembayaran di Indonesia — AMIK BSI Jakarta IJNS. *Indonesian Journal on Networking and Security, 6*(1). Doi: 10.55181/ijns.v6i1.1449. Retrieved 25 March, 2020, from https://ijns.org/journal/index.php/ijns/article/view/1449.

Takiddin, T. (2014). Uang Dalam Perspektif Ekonomi Islam. *SALAM: Jurnal Sosial Dan Budaya Syar-i, 1*(2). https://doi.org/10.15408/sjsbs.v1i2.1539.

Waspada, I. (2017). Percepatan adopsi sistem transaksi teknologi informasi untuk meningkatkan aksesibilitas layanan jasa perbankan waspada. *Jurnal Keuangan dan Perbankan, 16*(1). Doi: 10.26905/jkdp.v16i1.1052. Retrieved 18 March, 2020, from http://jurnal.unmer.ac.id/index.php/jkdp/article/view/1052.

Yudhistira, P. A. (2014). Analisis faktor yang mempengaruhi preferensi dan aksesibilitas terhadap penggunaan kartu pembayaran elektronik. Sarjana thesis, Universitas Brawijaya. *Jurnal Ilmiah Mahasiswa,* Feb. Retrieved March 22, 2020, from https://jimfeb.ub.ac.id/index.php/jimfeb/article/view/+1331.

Part III

Islamic Finance: Theoretical Perspectives

https://doi.org/10.1142/9781800612426_0015

Chapter 15

Banking Efficiency: Basic Concepts, Forms, and Specificities of Islamic Finance

Monjia Khalfi and Foued Saâdaoui

Abstract

Islamic finance or Qur'anic finance is an ethical finance based on Sharia, prohibition of riba, prohibition of gharar and maysir, and sharing of losses and profits (3P) because it promotes investment in licit sectors. And, it prohibits investment in illicit sectors. These principles are the main pillars of Islamic banking governance. In this context and given the interest of Quranic finance in this chapter, we sought to highlight the theoretical foundations relating to the notion of efficiency in general and more particularly of its specificity on Islamic finance since the latter has occupied more and more a rather important place in scientific research. We then presented the different forms of banking efficiency. Finally, we presented Islamic banking governance, risk management within Islamic banks, and governance of these banks.

Keywords: Banking Efficiency, Islamic Finance, Literature Review.

15.1 Introduction

Qur'anic finance is one of the most important themes for many researchers in finance and economics (Saâdaoui *et al.*, 2017; Saâdaoui, 2018; Azmat *et al.*, 2021; Bahloul *et al.*, 2021). Although this type of finance is called "Qur'anic" and is based on Islamic law and its principles, it succeeds in attracting the worldwide attention of all who are interested in finance and economics in developed as well as in emerging countries (Islamic and non-Islamic). The main pillars of Islamic finance are the prohibition of interest in all transactions and the prohibition of financing illicit activities that do not respect Islamic law, such as gambling, alcohol, and weapons. According to Beck *et al.* (2010), Sharia-compliant finance does not allow payment of interest (riba), only goods and services are allowed to bear a price; it also does not allow speculation and prohibits the financing of illicit activities.

This finance that offers new products and transaction methods (halal) was positively influenced by the 2007–2009 crisis. This financial crisis has generated serious consequences such as the loss of confidence in the mortgage market in the United States. This crisis has seriously influenced traditional finance and well-defined (enhancing) Islamic finance. Specifically, this financial crisis drew attention to the weaknesses of traditional financial systems and suggested Islamic finance as an alternative (Rosman *et al.*, 2014). Several studies claim that Islamic finance is resistant to shocks due to its inherent stability (Mirakhor, 2008) and that the world of banking and finance without riba (usury) and maysir (gambling) is a better alternative to the current scenario (Siddiqi, 2008). In addition, some researchers, such as Iqbal and Llwellyn (2002), have pointed out that global financial systems can benefit from several financial products and transactions, such as those offered by Islamic banks. These products and operations are characterized by risk-sharing functionalities in all types of contracts. In addition, Hasan and Dridi (2010) highlighted the superior performance of Islamic banks during the crisis. However, Kouran (2004) reported that Islamic banks have no efficiency advantage over traditional banks. Moreover, according to Rosman *et al.* (2014), Islamic banks were successful in supporting operations through the crisis.

Islamic finance has become increasingly important in different countries of the world thanks to the diversity of its products and its social vocation. This finance has had a real onset since the 1970s, especially in the Gulf countries given the economic expansion experienced by the region during this time and the growing awareness of the Muslim community of the advantages offered by this type of financing for the achievement of socio-economic development objectives (Regaieg & Abidi, 2015).

The success rates of Islamic finance around the world, its resilience, and its solidity in the face of global crises motivate researchers to study topics related to this type of finance. In this context and given the interest of Qur'anic finance, we have chosen to theoretically study Islamic banking efficiency to fill the limitations anchored to the importance of the literature in terms of the basic foundations of Qur'anic finance and more particularly the gaps in importance of Islamic banking efficiency (basic concepts and forms). Finally, we explain the importance of governance in the Islamic banking system. Therefore, in this research work, we plan to answer the following questions: What is Islamic finance? What are the forms of Islamic banking efficiency? How important is governance in the Islamic banking system?

Our study seeks to offer a clear vision, to future researchers, on the foundations of Islamic finance in general with a clear explanation of the forms of banking efficiency and the specificities of Islamic banking governance.

Based on a review of the innovative literature, we first examine theoretically the basics of efficiency and present its forms. Next, we present the foundation, principle and reality of Islamic finance. Finally, and more particularly, we study Islamic banking governance.

15.2 Fundamentals of Banking Efficiency

In a climate of financial liberalization, globalization, and particularly with an incessant increase across all countries of the world, of banks in number and size, the study of banking efficiency is mandatory and fundamental for an excellent use of an economy's resources.

According to Scholes *et al.* (1998), efficiency is an internal measure of the performance of the firm, it is assessed in terms of production cost, profit, and productivity, and it designates the quantity of resources used per unit of a good or a service. Moreover, according to Mintzberg *et al.* (1998), efficiency is similar to the terms of standardization and formalization. In general, efficiency is the ability to achieve an optimal performance in a given type of task among which one is banking activity (Banna & Alam, 2020; Ibrahim & Ismail, 2020). A financial market is therefore efficient if it fulfills its task, that is to say it allows the financing of firms[1] (by issuing securities on the secondary market or by merging firms).

Demsetz (1973) confirms in their study that the competitive behavior of financial institutions can be determined by efficiency. Therefore, the most efficient financial institutions are those with the highest profits, which allow them to have a high market share, hence the emergence of less competitive markets. For a better use of the financial resources of an economy, the efficiency of the financial sector becomes very important and even essential. When we discuss the allocation of resources, the first notion that comes to mind is that of efficiency. In addition, when this allocation is efficient, we can estimate the performance as well as the development potential of a company and place it relative to its competitors.

Some banks are more efficient than others, and this primarily comes down to their organization, which enables them to ensure the proper management of financial transformation operations or physical flows. We therefore emphasize that these banks are technically efficient because they have more control over the technical aspects of technical production, and therefore they are able to offer the maximum of services with the minimum of resources.

This concept of efficiency only involves considerations of the physical quantities of resources and the techniques that allow them to be linked. A second concept of efficiency is linked to knowing the prices of resources. Of course, the best banks are those that offer the most profitable and least expensive combination of factors. In addition, they adapt better than others do to price constraints and competition. It is for this purpose that they are referred to as "economically" or "allocatively" efficient. Overall, efficiency encompasses both types of efficiency. On the other hand, a bank can be technically efficient and cannot be economically efficient if it badly foresees the risks and does not use part of its resources or use old and outdated techniques. Nevertheless, there is, of course, a strong link between technical efficiency and allocative efficiency since we can only achieve productivity if we master the technology and ultimately find that the most technically efficient banks are those that are the most economically efficient. "A bank will be globally efficient if it chooses what it has to

[1]Demsetz, H. Information and efficiency: Another viewpoint. *Journal of Law and Economics*, Vol. 12, 1969, pp. 1–22.

do (economic efficiency) and if it does what it chooses to do (technical efficiency)".[2] So the concept of efficiency, is not only interested in the quality of the organization but also it is interested in the market position (market share) and measures the financial and productive performance of banks; this is determined from financial performance indicators, such as return on equity, which focus on short-term performance. While economic and technical efficiency indicators focus on longer-term performance, efficiency indicators focus on the internal determinants of banks, namely:

- Their ability to minimize production and distribution costs by adopting adequate choices of network size and organization;
- Their ability also to optimize the offer or in other words to choose the most suitable prices, the skills used, and the service offered.

The concept of measurement of efficiency is first suggested by Koopmans (1951), and Debreu (1951) was the first to measure it empirically and by introducing the coefficient of resource use which focus on input–output ratio measures (output–input). The concept of efficiency ultimately goes back to the fundamental theoretical work of Farrel (1957). He was the first to distinguish the notion of allocative efficiency and to clearly define the notion of economic efficiency. He also suggested the method of determining the two efficiencies (allocative efficiency and economic efficiency). The immortality of a company is a determinant that measures the efficiency of an institution, but we cannot always say that all organizations that have managed to resist are efficient. According to Scholes *et al.* (2002), efficiency is about offering products and services that meet the needs of their buyers.

15.3 Forms of Banking Efficiency

Achieving better performance is the overarching goal of efficiency. We mainly focus on defining the concept of economic efficiency on

---

[2]Burkart, O. & Gonsard, H. (1999). Cost efficiency and profit efficiency of French credit institutions since 1993. *Bulletin of the Banking Commission*, 20 April, 1999, p. 29.

the one hand and on presenting the analytical framework of efficiency on the other.

15.3.1 *Concept of economic efficiency*

According to microeconomic theory, the main purpose of any investor is to maximize profits. In other words, it arrives at a situation of optimal distribution of inputs, which will lead to an efficient use of resources. So, we can say that the concept of efficiency is considered to be one of the most important neoclassical analyses, which is increasingly taking an important place in the evaluation of the performance of companies. To achieve its objective, the company must master the factors of production, minimize costs, and maximize profits. Therefore, there are three different types of functions; that of production, cost, and profit.

In general, a production function establishes the relation between the factors of production "input" and the final product "output". According to Seiford and Thrall (1990), "according to standard microeconomic theory, the production function is the basis of the description of the relationship between inputs and outputs of a firm. The cost function determines the cost of the bank's outputs. We take as a reference the minimum cost practiced by the best bank, which operates under the same conditions and generates similar outputs. The cost function expresses the price of the banks' inputs. And finally, the profit function indicates the maximum profit that can be achieved taking into account the prices of inputs and outputs".

According to Burkat *et al.* (1999), the notion of efficiency emphasizes the measurement of productive performance. It is not limited to financial performance, usually measured by financial performance indicators.

The explanation of the production function as a frontier for any production entity, is, according to Thiry and Tulkens (1993), "natural as soon as we agree to specify that the production function specifies the maximum quantities d 'output accessible for any level of inputs, and, for any level of output, the minimum quantities necessary to obtain them".[3] It is, therefore, with the objective of taking

[3]Cited in Ambapour (2001).

into account both the possibility of minimizing the means of production and that of maximizing the profit of the product. Consequently, economic theory interprets the concept of efficiency intuitively by interpreting the production function as the production process frontier, which maximizes the level of outputs when the factors of production are given (El Moussawi & Obeid, 2011).

At the firm level, we generally observe two types of efficiency, one looks at competitive prices in markets and the other looks at the physical quantities of resources.

15.3.1.1 *Technical efficiency*

Based on the fundamental theoretical work of Debreu and Koopmans (1951), Farell (1957), Mohd Noor *et al.* (2020) and Ben Mohamed *et al.* (2021), the concept of technical efficiency provides a frontier that measures the performance of firms.

However, Koopmans (2002) is the founder of the definition of technical efficiency. He suggests that "A producer is technically efficient if increasing any output requires decreasing at least one other output or increasing at least one input, and if reducing any input requires the evolution of at least one other input or the reduction of at least one output".[4]

Atkinson and Cornwell (1994) define technical efficiency as follows: "a production unit is said to be technically efficient if for a given level of input that it holds, it produces the maximum possible output or if to produce a given level of outputs, it uses the minimum of inputs".[5] Alternatively and more clearly, we can say that a company is technically efficient if it offers the highest level of output from a given level of input, and this is done by a better mastery of the technical aspects, which makes it possible to link the quantities of resources deployed.

Technical efficiency is decomposed from the work of Banker *et al.* (1984). These authors show that technical efficiency is decomposed into technical efficiency of scale and pure technical efficiency. Regarding the technical efficiency of scale, it reflects whether the bank performs at an optimal scale, which allows it to reduce its costs, and

[4]Cited in Capelle-Blancard and Chaveau (2010).
[5]Cited in Atkinson and Cornwell (1994).

the latter is considered as the best condition under which a company operates if the number of its factors increases relatively. On the other hand, pure technical efficiency means the way of managing the inputs of a bank. Indeed, for a company to be economically efficient, it must be allocatively efficient.

15.3.1.2 *Allocative efficiency*

According to Chaffai (1998), allocative efficiency or price efficiency supposes that a production structure takes the optimal combinations of production factors to reduce total production costs by taking into account prices on the market during production. This efficiency focuses on information on the prices of means and resources of production.

In other words, allocative efficiency is the combination of factors of production (inputs) in an optimal way taking into account their price in the market. Also, Ambapour (2001) suggests that "allocative efficiency implies that the bank on the one hand minimizes its total production costs, and on the other hand it chooses the level of the latter which must be socially optimal (in particular through a policy of selling price or pricing, appropriate)".

15.3.1.3 *Efficiency of scale*

This form of efficiency concerns the case of a company that is in a situation of perfect competition and operates at an appropriate scale. That is, its marginal cost must be equal to the market price of its product (Ambapour, 2001; Idris & Ahmad, 2020; Nugrohowati *et al.*, 2020).

15.3.1.4 *Efficiency, a measure of performance*

Efficiency can be viewed as an indicator that measures the success of a business. Productive performance is usually measured by productivity ratios, determined by the ratio of a quantity of outputs to a quantity of inputs. These ratios nevertheless have the following limits.

It is necessary to master the technology, and therefore, the rapid introduction of technical progress in the production process is a compulsory condition for improving performance. However, ratio analysis requires that the technology remains unchanged over time.

According to Daley and Matthews (2008), the choice of production scale can strongly determine firm productivity. While ratios are useful and they indicate the level and change in efficiency over time, they represent a result and do not identify sources of inefficiency and places where improvements are required.

15.4 Presentation of Islamic Finance: Foundation, Principle, and Realities

Kahf (2002) suggests that: "At the end of the 19th century, the Ottomans introduced a Western style of banking to the Islamic world to finance their spending. While some Islamic jurists have endorsed modern banking practices, the majority has concluded that these practices constitute violations of the Islamic prohibitions against usury (Arabic term: riba, equivalent to Hebrew Ribit, is interpreted in its classical Biblical sense of any interest charge on loans, as opposed to the modern identification of usury with exorbitant interest). This resentment continued during the European colonial period, which lasted until the middle of the 20th century. Islamic Renewal played a central role in the intellectual and social foundations of independence movements of the mid-twentieth century. For many intellectual founders of the movement, political independence had to be complemented with economic independence through the definition of an Islamic economic system".

According to El-Gamal (2006), Islamic finance began as a small industry in some Arab countries in the late 1970s. It differs from conventional finance in its conspicuous adherence to the principles of Islamic law or Sharia law. Also, Ahmed (2010) says that: "The growth of Islamic finance has been accelerated since 2001, in terms of the number of countries in which it operates, as well as the areas of finance in which it has ventured. However, reliable data are not available on Islamic finance at the local, regional, or global level. In recent years, the industry has attracted a number of Western multinational financial institutions, such as Citigroup and HSBC, which have started offering Islamic financial products in some Arab countries (notably, Bahrain and the United Arab Emirates), and to a lesser extent (degree) in the Western world (including the US and UK, where HSBC offers various Islamic financial products in New York and London, including home finance, account verification, etc.)".

A number of Islamic financial products also involve the acquisition of assets (e.g., real estate and small businesses) in the West (including the United States) of "Islamic ally structured" financing offers.

Ahmed (2010) suggests that "the main principles of Islamic finance include the prohibition of interest and profit sharing". In addition, Ghannadian and Goswami (2004) confirm this fact by maintaining that the main Islamic banking principles are the sharing of risk and rewards. Other authors, such as Pollard and Samers (2007), also emphasize the prohibition of interest and absence of interest for all loans.

In the following, we first present the foundations of Islamic finance. Second, we expose the methods of risk management within Islamic banks. Third, we discuss the concept of efficiency in the context of Islamic banking.

15.4.1 *Foundations of Islamic finance*

Traditional finance connects individuals who have a funding requirement and those who have excess liquidity to achieve efficient allocation of financial resources. Nevertheless, Islamic finance explains efficiency differently while integrating ethical criteria.

In general, Islamic finance is based upon economic and social rules that respect Islamic law while offering an ethical and profitable model.

15.4.1.1 *Sources of Sharia*

Islamic law is based on the Holy Qur'an, the Sunnah, the Ijmaa (consensus), the Ijtihad (reasoning effect), and Al Qiyas (reasoning by analogy).

The first source is the Holy Qur'an. Islamic finance offers a new form of partnership governance seeking to bring the principles of Anglo-Saxon finance closer to those of the Qur'an. According to Elkettani (2010), bank managers are subject to governance rules under Islamic law, international law (Basel 1 and Basel 2), shareholding rules and partnership rules.[6]

[6]Elkettani, O. (2010). The governance of Islamic banks. *International Seminar on Financial Services and Risk Management in Islamic Banks*, p. 27.

The Holy Qur'an is the main source of Islamic law, and all other legal sources must conform to the Qur'an.

The second source is the Sunnah. It is the set of words, deeds of the Prophet Muhammad — Blessing and Salvation of God upon him — and which are collected in books called Koutoub al Hadith.

The third source is the Ijmaa. This is an agreement of Muslim jurists on a point of law when no effect of the Qur'an and the Sunnah can resolve in any case.

The fourth source is the Qiyas. It refers to the ways of logical linking of ideas practiced by Muslim jurists in order to find the solution to a problem of law not stipulated by the texts of the Qur'an and the Sunnah.

15.4.1.2 *Pillars of Islamic finance*

The ethical concern is noticed in Islamic finance since it is based on very strong principles. Ethical finance is based on a fundamental principle which is respect for values and this should in no case be ignored even if the objective is to generate profits.

Islamic finance is based on financial mechanisms exercised by investors who manage their investments while respecting Islamic law. It is based on three negative principles, namely prohibition of interest (riba), uncertainty, and illegal sectors, and two positive principles, namely profit and loss sharing and the existence of the underlying asset.

Prohibition of interest (riba): The prohibition of riba stems from verse 275 of the second surah of the Qur'an: "even though Allah has made buying and selling lawful, and interest unlawful". So, we can clearly understand that Islamic law does not prohibit lending, but it prohibits any surplus, increase or increase; this means that Islamic law is not limited to usury, it prohibits any type of interest. In other words, any addition drawn from a transaction based on unreal assets and not previously owned by the seller is illicit (haram). For example, bank loans that do not meet this need, be it business loans or consumer loans, are illicit loans (haram). The ban on riba is considered usurious and attaches great value to receiving a profit even if the underlying asset in which an amount has been invested performs reasonably well. Certainly, the causes of the prohibition of interest have arisen from several researches and studies which have subsequently given several explanations, and among these causes, we can cite the following:

- The interest is contractual remuneration known in advance (fixed rate);
- The risks are fully insured by the borrower; therefore, the interest is unfair;
- The interest is the remuneration of time which should not be the subject of exchanges and Islamic law refuses any form of passive gain achieved without work.

Prohibition of gharar and mayssir (uncertainty, speculation): Uncertainty can be defined as a contract whose results are unknown: As the sale of a lost thing or the sale of a thing that does not hold (e.g., sale of uncaught birds). So, gharar can also be broadly defined as the sale of non-existent assets and their characteristics are unknown; in other words, the existence and characteristics of this asset are uncertain (Al boukari, Muslim).

We also note, and keeping with the same logic, that the prohibition of qimar and mayssir, their prohibition results from the possibility that one of the contracting parties will lose the whole of its participation. Also, the prohibited speculation (mayssir) is that which consists in making plans for the future (uncertainty) and in risking the occurrence of an event in a subjective way, without scientific or rational basis, at the expense of another person (Karich, 2002). In this regard, we can cite the example of games of chance which consist in betting a sum of money or an object of value (the price of the ticket) on the output of certain selected numbers, and the Qur'an strictly forbids this practice (Surate al Maida: verse 90–91).

The difference between riba and gharar: According to Chatti (2010),[7] the ban on riba and uncertainty is caused by the existence of the risk factor (it is a common factor). For riba, the transaction is an example of this factor because the creditor takes zero risk, i.e., he gets his

[7]Chatti, M. A. (2010). Banking diversification, ethical performance: alternative or complementarity? Case of Islamic banks, p. 62.

money back with an addition without incurring any expense. However, the transaction contains a gharar (uncertainty) which exposes itself to almost 100% high risk, as the contractor may have in his possession the object of the action as he may never have. For this reason, Islamic law prohibits both types of risk; the lowest and the strongest and everything else is allowed.

Prohibition and haram: It certainly concerns the activities prohibited by Islamic law, that is to say illicit activities, and according to Islamic jurisprudence (Surat al bakara, verse 168). Moreover, the sectors banned according to Karich (2002) are:

- financial institutions based on riba and gharar, such as conventional banks, leasing companies, insurance companies, and stockbrokers;
- pork, alcoholic beverages, gambling, and all activities related to pornography, weapons, and tobacco.

Profit and loss sharing principle: This principle is considered among the main pillars of Islamic finance, it is also called the "3P" principle, the donor must be a shareholder in the underlying company, an entrepreneur had the right to receive remuneration according to the performance of the underlying asset and that it be invested for losses if any, and as such has the status of shareholder. According to Lacordaire (2005), reciprocally to the traditional system, the Islamic system requires the sharing of profit and risk, favoring the shareholder, who provides the capital, to the detriment of the banker, who only lends while the traditional creditor, who does not is not protected by law, will never provide the loan.

Asset banking: We can also say backing to a tangible asset. Islamic finance, which is based on this pillar, besides the principles already mentioned requires the attachment of any contract to a "palpable" activity that reassures especially as regards the problems of separation of the financial domain from the real domain. Finally, it seems that the strengths of Islamic finance are that it is based on respect for the techniques induced by these pillars or these logics which encourage profitable investments.

15.4.2 *Financing methods offered by Islamic banks*

Islamic banks offer many products. In this context, we will present some products such as Murabahah, Moucheraka, Mudarbah, Ijara, and Qard Hasan. These products are classified according to their categories of financing techniques, namely financing techniques for commercial operations and crowdfunding techniques. In addition, Islamic banks offer these alternative products to interest rate products.

15.4.2.1 *Most popular financing techniques*

Islamic financial institutions offer financing techniques, which respect the principle of Sharia law and which prohibit the interest rate by replacing it with a rate of return applied to "tangible" activities, which allows it to invest their collected resources without riba. In this context, there are two categories of financing techniques: techniques for financing commercial operations and techniques of crowdfunding.

15.4.2.1.1 Techniques for financing commercial transactions

The techniques of financing of commercial operations include all the financing modalities that are based on operations of purchase and sale of several products, the purpose of which is to generate a profit resulting from the difference between the sale price and the price of purchase. Some researchers confirm that these techniques are combinations of traditional banking products and the principles of Islamic law.

Murabahah (sale with deferred payment and margin): According to François Guéranger (2009),[8] "the murabahah is ideal for simple commercial operations but is ill-suited to complex financing such as project financing. It is therefore used for current operating needs (stocks, raw materials, intermediate products, etc.) and even for certain short-term investments. In addition, the fact that the bank acquires the asset on behalf of the customer can be used to preserve the confidentiality of the latter's identity. The principle of murabahah involves a seller and a buyer: a customer contacts a supplier and designates the good he wants to buy from him; the relevant information

[8]Guéranger, F. (2009). Islamic finance: An illustration of ethical finance, p. 93.

such as the cost of the good and the seller's margin were then fixed. After agreement, the good and the ownership thereof are transferred to the buyer who pays the agreed price on the due date (or dates)".

Ijara (rental): According to El Mohandiz (1999),[9] "it is an operation whereby the bank rents equipment to a person who enjoys full rights through usufruct, the rent being considered as a commission. Much of today's Islamic banking activity is based on the rental of capital goods. The bank does not receive any guarantees; it takes into account the client's financial situation and the 'cash flow' estimates relating to the use of the equipment".

Salam: "This is a contract similar to the classic futures contract in function, but it has payment terms. The buyer pays the seller the full-negotiated price of a specific product that the seller promises to deliver on a specified future date. However, unlike a conventional futures contract, the full price is payable at the time of the contract. This forward sale is profitable for both the seller and the buyer. The seller gets the money to invest in the production process and the buyer eliminates the uncertainty about the future price" (Iqbal & Mirakhor, 2011).[10]

Istisna'a: According to Iqbal and Mirakhor (2011), "the istisna'a contract is adapted to facilitate the manufacture or construction of an asset at the request of the buyer. Once the manufacturer agrees to manufacture the asset or property for the buyer, the istisna'a transaction comes into being. Both parties (e.g., the buyer and the manufacturer) agree on the specifics and the price of the asset to be manufactured. At the time of delivery, if the asset does not comply with the specifications, the buyer has the right to withdraw from the contract".

Qard Hasan (interest free loan): This is a loan granted on the only condition, which is the repayment of the nominal amount when the beneficiary is able. It does not assume any profit for the bank and is limited to consumption purposes. The bank grants this loan to

[9]El Mohandiz, A. (1999). The Islamic Banking System, p. 42.
[10]Iqbal, Z. & Mirakhor, A. (2011). *An Introduction to Islamic Finance: Theory and Practice*, Second Edition, p. 79.

customers for the purchase of a consumer good or simply to meet an unforeseen family expense.

We note that Islamic banks only exceptionally grant loans for consumption purposes. However, they lend more readily to clients with whom they are already associated by a Mudarabah or Musharaka contract and follow who have to face "cash-flow" problems, arising during the realization of the project. The Qard Hasan thus serves to support the initial project (El Mohandiz, 1999).

15.4.2.1.2 Crowdfunding techniques

Crowdfunding techniques are long-term financing products in which a capital–labor combination is carried out, the purpose of which is to prohibit interest-bearing loans (riba). This combination of capital and labor coincides with the principle of Islam because the borrower does not have to share the entire risk of failure. In principle, it is about sharing the profit with the donor. There are two participatory financing techniques: the Musharakah and the Mudarbah.

Musharakah: In the musharaka contract, the banker takes a share of the capital of the company, becoming a shareholder and benefiting from a voting right for its management. Thus, the bank can provide sufficient liquidity to the entrepreneur over a long period. In return, it can play the role of an industrial partner, intervening in the management of the company or supervising the management of the company. Financially, this is an advantage for the company because it does not bear the burden of the debt. At the same time, the bank finds an advantage in using its resources in this type of financing, which allows it to obtain regular remuneration for its depositors. This mode of partnership applies especially to project activities in any sector of activity. It seems quite natural for a bank that wishes to support a company for a particular transaction while letting the company run the operations under its supervision. It is for this reason that the musharaka, in conventional finance terminology, is likened to a joint venture. This technique allows the bank to receive regular income. Both profits and losses (which often depend on the skills of the entrepreneur) are shared in proportions of the capital contributions, once the entrepreneur's activity is remunerated (from 20% to 60%). It is well established that the operation is not a bank loan but a participation in the financing of a project. As a result, the bank is a shareholder with the power to direct the project or supervise its conduct. When the bank participates in management, its remuneration is linked to the amount of its investment (profits distributed in proportion to the capital) and to its share of management works (Guéranger, 2009).

Mudarbah: According to Ammar *et al.* (2012),[11] "the obligations of the Mudarbah contract for the different parties respect the following principles:

- The bank provides the client (Moudharib) with the amount of investment needed to finance a project, but the Moudharib does not contribute to the investment. He contributes to the management of the project for which he is responsible;
- The profits obtained are distributed between the bank and the Moudharib according to proportions determined by agreement in advance. However, if the project suffers a loss, the bank bears all losses unless they are the result of negligence or fault on the part of the Moudharib. In other words the bank loses the funds engaged in the operation, while the entrepreneur loses the fruit of his labor (labor) and the time engaged in his activity".

15.4.2.2 *Islamic financial products alternatives to interest rate products*

To respect the principle of Islamic finance, Islamic institutions and subsidiaries of conventional banks have developed legal-financial mechanisms. These are based on the following concepts: Mudarbah, Musharakah, and Murabahah.

Mudarbah: It is a contract that authorizes a promoter to carry out an investment through funds advanced by capital providers whose key to repairing the profits and charges fixed in the contract, the capital providers bear the charges, the promoters do not bear any charge and

[11] Ammar *et al.* (2012), La Pratique Actuelle Des Banques Islamiques Favorise-T-Elle La. Croissance, *Etudes en Economie Islamique*, Vol. 6, Nos. 1 & 2, pp. 57–82. *Mouharram* and *Rajab* 1434 H (November 2012).

only lose the benefit of their project. The partners (entrepreneurs, bank, etc.) participate in both capital and investment management, the fruits of labor are distributed between the parties in predetermined proportions according to the level of participation in the capital.

Musharakah: "Al Musharakah" is the association translation. In this operation, two partners invest together in a project and share the benefits according to the invested capital. In the event of a loss, this is borne by both parties in proportion to the capital invested. The nature of this operation is ultimately akin to a joint venture.

Murabahah: This is a sales contract between seller and buyer, whereby the latter buys the goods requested by a buyer and resells them at a price increased by a profit margin, and the payment period (installment in general) is mentioned in an initial contract.

15.4.3 *Risk management in Islamic banks*

Since the birth of the first Islamic financial institutions in the 1970s, the Islamic finance industry has continued to grow steadily. Important development is taking place in the creation of an interbank money market and an Islamic capital market. This remarkable progress shows that this finance, based on Islamic law, has become an important element in the international financial system.

Islamic finance's dedication to tangible assets and its apprehension of measuring risk contributes to improving market discipline and financial stability. However, the microstructure of the financing techniques offered and the particular type of risk linked to resources and jobs produce systematic risks.

The research studies carried out in the area of Islamic finance contribute to its solidarity and reduce the potential sources of its lack of stability. Good risk management is the important factor determining the development and survival of this industry.

Risk management in the context of Islamic finance is extensive and complex. It is therefore essential to participate in the growth of a financial industry that contributes to the stability and efficiency of international financial markets (Khan & Ahmed, 2001).

15.4.3.1 *Logic of Islamic banks*

Investors and savers are two groups of the main actors in any economy. The second, not knowing, in general, the opportunities of productive investment, have significant funds for the first. The change of funds in the financial market is carried out by the bank, i.e., the bank acts as an intermediary between the saver and the investor. Taking advantage of its location, plus the asymmetry of information in the financial market, the bank can raise questions of alternatives and moral hazard.

The exercise and missions of the bank are efficient and socially desirable, but unfortunately, interest (riba) has an important role in its functioning. Islamic intermediation fulfills its role both by mobilizing savings and allocating them for profitable purposes, replacing interest with other instruments and modes of financing. This provocation considerably develops the logic of the Islamic banking system.

An Islamic bank is an Islamic financial institution that collects deposits and performs all banking activities except lending and borrowing at interest. Liabilities include all funds mobilized according to the logic of Mudharabah or Wakalah. It also authorizes demand deposits considered as interest-free loans (without riba) from customers to the bank, and therefore they are guaranteed. The assets consist of funds based on profit and loss sharing or on indebtedness in accordance with the principles of Islamic law. In this context, the bank plays the role of an investment manager toward depositors whose funds fall under the category of investment deposits. Again, equity participation as well as the financing of current assets (stock of goods) and fixed assets are an integral part of Islamic banking operations (Iqbal & Llewellyn, 2002).

Therefore, the Islamic bank shares its net earnings with its depositors in proportion to the date and value of each deposit. Depositors must be informed in advance of the rationale for sharing profits with the bank.

15.4.3.2 *Nature of the risks incurred by Islamic banks*

According to Arbouna and El Islamy (2008), risk in the context of banking or finance represents the probability of an event that can potentially leave a negative impact on the income and capital of the institution. In general, risks to financial institutions can be initially classified as financial or non-financial risks. Further, Ahmad (2010) suggests that "financial risks can be divided into sub-categories, namely credit risk, market risk, counterparty risk, rate of return risk etc.".

According to Iqbal and Mirakhor (2008), "financial risks are those exposures that result in a direct financial loss to the assets or liabilities of a bank". Schrock (2002) suggests that this risk can be classified as being systematic (which arises from macro sources, e.g., currency risk and equity risk), or unsystematic, such as the risk inherent in commodities or trading assets.

The financial risks incurred by Islamic banks, as discussed by Iqbal and Greuning (2008), have been summarized as follows: credit risk, market risk, and equity risk. Islamic banks are exposed to several risks, such as the following.

15.4.3.2.1 Credit risk

The credit risk is linked to the default of payment, manifesting itself when part of the contract advances funds (e.g., Salam or Istisnaa contract) or delivers a commodity (e.g., Murabahah contract) before receiving the counterpart of its financing and exposes, therefore, to potential losses. In the case of crowdfunding methods (Musharakah or Mudarbah), the credit risk manifests itself in the non-payment of the entrepreneur of the share due to the bank when it becomes due. This problem becomes even more relevant in the case of information asymmetry linked to the ignorance of the real profits made by the company. With regard to the Murabahah contract, the credit risk takes the form of a counterparty risk due to the poor performance of the partner. This poor performance can be of external origin due to systematic causes (Khan & Ahmed, 2001). Moreover, according to Iqbal and Mirakhor (2008) "credit risk arises from the possibilities of the default or failure of counterparty to meet its obligation in agreed terms".

15.4.3.2.2 Market risk

As defined by the World Bank (2009), "Market risk has been defined as the risk of loss of capital resulting from adverse movements in market prices related to commodities, stocks, fixed interest and commodity markets". Market risk arises due to a number of factors such as counterparty risk rate, benchmark risk, and price volatility risk.

Ayub (2004) suggests, "Islamic financial instruments due to being necessarily asset-backed or equity-based face all of these risks and due to their unique characteristics additional risks". Although international financial products do not deal in contracts based on interest, but their debt and leasing-based instruments (e.g., Murabahah, Ijara) are generally benchmarked against London interbank rate (LIBOR). Thus, this practice exposes the Islamic bank to risk as much as its conventional counterparty is exposed to the same interest rate. To explain this problem, Iqbal and Mirakhor (2008) suggest, "In the absence of any Islamic rate of return index, Islamic banks often use LIBOR as a benchmark, which aligns after their market risk with movements in LIBOR rates".

15.4.3.2.3 Liquidity risk

According to Achibane and Cherkaoui (2017), the risk of non-compliance with Sharia is a risk specific to Islamic banking. The compatibility of contracts with the Sharia is therefore a source of liquidity risk. In fact, if this risk arises, depositors may be encouraged to withdraw their deposits, causing a liquidity problem.

According to Sundarajan (2006) and Khan and Ahmed (2001), Islamic banks are exposed to a unique risk which is displaced business risk. This risk resulting from the management of investment accounts is closely related to the liquidity risk.

The Accounting and Auditing Organization for Islamic Financial Institutions (AAOIFI, 1999) identifies this risk as "a risk resulting from the volatility of the returns generated from the assets financed by the investment accounts which may induce the depositors of the bank to withdraw their funds. If their income is lower than that one paid by other banks". Therefore, the appearance of this risk is a materialization of the liquidity risk. However, in order to offer competitive compensation and to convince depositors to keep their funds in the bank, the majority of Islamic banks smooth the rates of return awarded to investment account holders at the expense of profits normally attributed to shareholders under pressure (Khan & Ahmed 2002; Archer & Karim, 2007, 2009).

15.4.4 *Efficiency of Islamic banks*

The role of financial and banking institutions is compulsory for the development of any economy. The narrow link between the development of economies and the banking sector is attracting increasing interest from researchers and economists. Following changes in the banking environment, such as disintermediation and deregulation and the intensification of financial and banking competition, much academic research has focused on studying the impacts of these effects on banking efficiency.

Every bank does seek to maximize its profits and to resist the crisis (Hassan & Rabbani, 2020), and it is as such that it must choose the optimal combination of the means at its disposal for its production. It is as such that a bank's efficiency is not limited only to financial performance, which is usually measured by ratios, but rather involves productive performance. In addition, Burkat *et al.* (1999) announce "that a bank will be globally efficient if it chooses well what it has to do (economic efficiency) and if it does well what it has chosen to do (technical efficiency)". Therefore, a bank is globally efficient, if it allocates its resources efficiently, and this by adopting the best opportunities available to it, then it is allocatively efficient. Indeed, the bank must master the technical aspects, which are a necessary condition for profitability and is called upon to adapt with technical progress to introduce new technologies in order to complete as it chooses. In this case, we can say that the bank is technically efficient.

15.5 Governance of Islamic Banks

The difference, in terms of governance, between Islamic banks and traditional banks is very clear at the level of governance rules applicable by the latter. The governance of conventional banks is made up of four elements (shareholders, partners, board of directors, and management). While Islamic banks apply a fifth rule, which are the fatwa and Sharia Supervisory Board, which ensures compliance, control of the acts of these banks with Sharia.

The rules of governance applied by Islamic banks derive from principles relating to Anglo-Saxon theories of organizations, on the one hand, and Islamic law, on the other. The leaders of Islamic banks are subject to the governance rules of Islamic law, international law (Basel 1 and Basel 2), shareholder rules, and partnership rules (Zied & Pluchart, 2006; Elkettani, 2010; Kusuma & Ayumardani, 2016).

First, the governance rules of Islamic law are, mainly, the prohibition of the practice of an interest rate (riba) assimilated to usury and designating any form of fixed or variable interest, the sharing of losses and profits between the different actors of the financial transaction, the prohibition of speculation (gharar) (the term gharar particularly refers to two hazards, the hazard of the commercial transaction itself and the uncertainty relating to the goods traded as well as the ban on speculating in bankruptcies), the obligation that financing operations relate exclusively to halal assets according to the Sharia and the obligation that any transaction must be underpinned by a tangible asset. Hence, the establishment of a Sharia council aimed at permanently monitoring the legality of banking activities to ensure the legitimacy of banking operations and the development of a solidarity economy. While traditional banking is based on the principle of a fixed and pre-established rate, it does not require the legality of the projects financed (Kusuma & Ayumardani, 2016).

Second, Islamic banks are subject to shareholder governance rules, to control their leaders and to define their discretionary space. In this sense, several rules are applied, in particular the application from the 1980s of the organizational principles and operating rules of boards of directors. Also, the tightening of the rules for controlling accounts, rating and financial communication of listed companies, especially Islamic banks. And the application, by the international accounting regulatory bodies (IAS/IFRS Committee) for listed companies from 2005 of new accounting rules geared toward the defense of shareholders, in particular based on the assessment of elements of assets and liabilities at their market price (fair value). The main objective of these rules is to protect the interests of shareholders (Zied & Pluchart, 2006).

Third, Islamic banks are subject to managerial governance rules that aim to reconcile risk management and minimization with the objective of performance and profitability. These rules differ depending on the nature of Islamic banks (retail banking, investment banking, or Islamic banking). Among the principles that dictate managerial governance, we can cite: the tendency to conduct a risk minimization policy by the priority choice of financing of commercial operations (Murabahah), the Musharakah comes in second position, while the Mudarabah being at the top risk is rather rare (Elkettani, 2010). Also, there are the trend in the financing of consumer loans, the trend for the specialization of banks by sector (agricultural banks, social banks, etc.), and the trend for the development of equity capital (Kusuma & Ayumardani, 2016).

Finally, Islamic banks are subject to rules of partnership governance which are, mainly, the ethics that Islamic banks are supposed to protect the small saver-consumer of banking products. In addition, in the agency relationship that must be established between the bank and its agent, the choice of the entrepreneur is therefore crucial. To ensure a certain control over the activities of the project, the bank, which is a shareholder, always insists on having a seat on the board of directors in addition to imposing certain accounting ratios in terms of management, if necessary. This situation is all the more difficult or even normally unacceptable for applicants. Moreover, the bank does not seem to have any real power of governance over the managers of the firms in which it invests (Elkettani, 2010).

Islamic banks, not being lenders in the classic sense of the word, have no way of disciplining corporate executives as a creditor as if a commercial bank would. This must intervene, for example, when indicators of default on a loan appear. Islamic banks for their part can only intervene as a shareholder through their presence on the board of directors. It remains to be seen whether this presence on the board of directors leads, if necessary, to changes in the management team of the firm (Elkettani, 2010).

Based on financial indicators, the Islamic bank can in principle intervene through its representation on the board of directors, but the real capacity of Islamic banks to discipline senior leaders is not known. Islamic banks do not seem to be the guarantors of corporate governance. They do not appear to be equipped to play an oversight role of senior leaders.

To conclude, in addition to a classic governance structure for financial institutions, Islamic banks have been forced to set up a higher authority, expert in Islamic laws: "the religious council". Faced with this, the managers of Islamic banks find themselves subject to a system of dual governance, that of the board of directors and that of the Sharia committee. One defends the interests of shareholders and the other defends those of Sharia law. Indeed, the first defends the imperatives of the "bottom line", the best return on investment, and the second defends best performance in terms of ethics, respect for the principles of Islamic law, and compliance with Sharia law. Managers are therefore subject to double pressure: on the one hand, pressure from the board of directors who want an improvement in return per share and those from clients who demand very competitive products involving increasingly reduced margins for the bank, and on the other hand, the pressure of the Sharia committee.

15.6 Conclusion

The success of Qur'anic finance and the importance of their interest are the result of the diversity of its products and its resilience in the face of global crises. This finance succeeds in attracting global attention and is defined by researchers as an alternative to traditional finance. So, this type of finance comes to occupy an important place in the banking world and to attract the attention of several researchers in the fields of finance and Islamic economics.

In our study, we have highlighted the theoretical foundations relating to the basics of Islamic finance in general and more particularly the specificities of efficiency (and their forms) and Islamic banking governance.

Recent academic works have succeeded in explaining the basic foundations of Islamic finance, banking efficiency, and its forms and Islamic banking governance, etc. But the studies, which explain the factors of success and the solutions proposed to help Islamic banks established in emerging countries to be successful like those established in developed countries, are very limited. This weakness in studies does not promote the growth and success of Qur'anic finance. In addition, ethical finance remains less important compared to conventional finance.

There also remains the question of the development of Islamic banks in the developed world (challenges and opportunities) which remains embryonic in academic work. This subject is undoubtedly one of the points to be elucidated through further studies.

References

Achibane, M. & Cherkaoui, K. (2017). Problem of refinancing and risk management of Islamic finance: The case of Morocco. *African Management Review, 2*(2), 19–33.

Ahmed, A. (2010). Global financial crisis: An Islamic finance perspective. *International Journal of Islamic and Middle Eastern Finance and Management, 3*(4), 306–320.

Ahmed, A. M. E. T. (2010). *Islamic Banking: How to Manage Risk and Improve profitability.* Hoboken, New Jersey: John Wiley and Sons.

Albouchi, L., Bachta, M. S., & Jacquet, F. (2005). Estimation and decomposition of the economic efficiency of irrigated areas to better manage existing inefficiencies. In *Economic Instruments and the Modernization of Irrigated Perimeters*, Kairouan, Tunisia. p, 19.

Ambapour, S. (2001). Estimation of production frontiers and measures of technical efficiency. *Office for the Application of Statistical and Computer Methods (BAMSI)*, Working Paper, *2*, 27.

Ammar Ayachi, R., Slama, M. B., & Saidane, D. (2012). La pratique actuelle des banques islamiques favorise-t-elle la croissance? *Etudes en Economie Islamique, 6*(1/2), 57–82.

Arbouna, M. B. & El Islamy, H. (2008). Rate of return risk management in Islamic finance: Challenges and propositions. In *Islamic Capital Markets: Products, Regulation and Development*, (Ed.). Salman Syed Ali. Jeddah, Saudi Arabia: Islamic Research and Training Institute. pp. 179–199.

Archer, S. & Karim, R. A. A. (2007). *Specific Corporate Governance Issues in Islamic Banks, Islamic Finance: The Regulatory Challenge.* Singapore: John Wiley and Sons. pp. 310–314.

Archer, S. & Karim, R. A. A. (2009). Profit-sharing investment accounts in Islamic banks: Regulatory problems and possible solutions. *Journal of Banking Regulation, 10*(4), 300–306.

Ariffin, N. M., Archer, S., & Karim, R. A. A. (2009). Risks in Islamic banks: Evidence from empirical research. *Journal of Banking Regulation, 10*(2), 153–163.

Atkinson, S. E. & Cornwell, C. (1994). Parametric estimation of technical and allocative inefficiency with panel data. *International Economic Review, 35*(1), 231–243.

Ayub. M. (2004). Islamic banking and finance: Theory and practice. *Journal of King Abdulaziz University: Islamic Economics, 17*(1), 45–49.

Azmat, S., Hassan, M. K., Ali, H., & Azad, A. S. M. S. (2021). Religiosity, neglected risk and asset returns: Theory and evidence from Islamic finance industry. *Journal of International Financial Markets, Institutions and Money, 74*(101294). Doi: 10.1016/j.intfin.2021.101294.

Bahloul, S., Mroua, M., & Naifar, N. (2021). Are Islamic indexes, bitcoin and gold, still "safe-haven" assets during the COVID-19 pandemic crisis? *International Journal of Islamic and Middle Eastern Finance and Management*. Doi: 10.1108/IMEFM-06-2020-0295.

Banker, R. D., Charnes, A., & Cooper, W. W. (1984). Some models for estimating technical and scale inefficiencies in data envelopment analysis. *Management Science*, *30*(9), 1078–1092.

Banna, H. & Alam, M. R. (2020). Islamic banking efficiency and inclusive sustainable growth: The role of financial inclusion. *Journal of Islamic Monetary Economics and Finance*, *6*(1), 213–242.

Beck, T., Demirguc-Kunt, A., & Merrouche, O. (2010). Islamic vs. conventional banking: Business model, efficiency and stability. *Journal of Banking and Finance*, *2*(37), 433–447.

Ben Mohamed, E., Meshabet, N., & Jarraya, B., (2021). Determinants of technical efficiency of Islamic banks in GCC countries. *Journal of Islamic Accounting and Business Research*, *122*, 218–238.

Burkart, O., Gonsard, H., & Dietsch, M., (1999). Cost efficiency and profit efficiency of French credit institutions since 1993. *Bulletin de la Commission Bancaire*, *20*, 43–66.

Capelle-Blancard, G. & Vandelanoite, S. (2010). Relations intrajournalières entre l'indice CAC 40 et les options sur indice: Quel est le marché préféré des investisseurs informés? *Journal of Environmental Economics and Management*, *59*(2), 192–205.

Chaffai, M., (1998). Estimation des inefficiences techniques et allocatives des banques de dépôts tunisiennes: une frontière de coût fictif, *Économie et Prévision*, *136*(5), 117–129.

Chatti, M. A. (2010). *Diversification Bancaire, Performance, éthique: Alternative ou complémentarité? Cas des banques islamiques*. (Doctoral Dissertation, Paris 10).

Daley, J., Matthews, K., & Whitfield, K. (2008). Too-big-to-fail: Bank failure and banking policy in Jamaica. *Journal of International Financial Markets, Institutions and Money*, *18*(3), 290–303.

Debreu, G. (1951). The coefficient of resource utilization. *Econometrica*, *19*(3), 273–292.

Demsetz, H. (1969). Information and efficiency: Another viewpoint. *Journal of Law and Economics*, *12*(1), 1–22.

Demsetz, H. (1973). Industry structure, market rivalry, and public policy. *The Journal of Law and Economics*, *16*(1), 1–9.

El-Gamal, M. A. (2006). *Islamic Finance: Law, Economics, and Practice*. Cambridge, New York: Cambridge University Press.

El Moussawi, C. & Obeid, H. (2011). Evaluating the productive efficiency of Islamic banking in GCC: A non-parametric approach. *International Management Review*, *7*(1), 10–21.

Elkettani, O. (2010). The governance of Islamic banks, International Seminar on Financial Services and Risk Management in Islamic Banks, April 2010, Sétif, Algeria.

Farrell, M. J. (1957). The measurement of productive efficiency. *Journal of the Royal Statistical Society*, *120*(3), 253–290.

Ghannadian, F. F. & Goswami, G. (2004). Developing economy banking: The case of Islamic banks. *Economics*, *31*(8), 740–752.

Ghayad, R. (2008). Corporate governance and the global performance of Islamic banks. *Humanomics: The International Journal of Systems and Ethics*, *24*(3), 207–216.

Guéranger, F. (2009). *Islamic Finance: An Illustration of Ethical Finance.* Dunod, Paris.

Hasan, M. M. & Dridi, J. (2011). The effects of the global crisis on Islamic and conventional banks: A comparative study. *Journal of International Commerce, Economics and Policy*, *2*(2), 163–200.

Hassan, M. K., Rabbani, M.R., & Ali, M. A. M. (2020). Challenges for the Islamic finance and banking in post COVID era and the role of Fintech. *Journal of Economic Cooperation and Development*, *41*(3), 93–116.

Ibrahim, W. H. W. & Ismail, A. G. (2020). Do regulation, Maqasid Shariah and institutional parameter improve Islamic bank efficiency? *Journal of Islamic Monetary Economics and Finance*, *6*(1), 135–162.

Idris, S. M. & Ahmad, F. A. (2020). Islamic banking efficiency: A systematic literature review. *Journal of Islamic, Social, Economics and Development (JISED)*, *5*(29), 41–50.

Iqbal, M. & Llewellyn, D. T. (2002). *Islamic Banking and Finance: New Perspectives on Profit Sharing and Risk.* Cheltenham, UK: Edward Elgar Publishing.

Iqbal, Z. & Mirakhor, A. (2011). *An Introduction to Islamic finance: Theory and practice*, Vol. 687. John Wiley & Sons.

Iqbal, Z. & Van Greuning, H. (2008). *Risk Analysis for Islamic Banks.* World Bank Publications.

Johnson, G., Scholes, K., & Whittington, R. (2009). *Exploring Corporate Strategy: Text and Cases.* UK: Prentice Hall International.

Kahf, M. (2002). Financing international trade: An Islamic alternative. In "*The Economic and Financial Imperatives of Globalization: An Islamic Response*". Institute of Islamic Understanding Malaysia (IKIM), Kuala Lumpur, Malaysia.

Karich, I., (2002). The Islamic Financial System: From Religion to Banking (vol. 2), Larcier.

Khan, T. & Ahmed, H. (2001). *Risk Management: An Analysis of Issues in Islamic Financial Industry.* The Islamic Research and Training Institute (IRTI), Jeddah.

Koopmas, T. (1951). Efficient allocation of resources. *Econometrica: Journal of the Econometric Society, 19*(4), 455–465.

Kuran, T. (2004). Why the Middle East is economically underdeveloped: Historical mechanisms of institutional stagnation. *Journal of Economic Perspectives, 18*(3), 71–90.

Kusuma, H. & Ayumardani, A. (2016). The corporate governance efficiency and Islamic bank performance: An Indonesian evidence. *Polish Journal of Management Studies, 13*(1), 111–120.

Lacordaire, J. (2005). Bulletin d'histoire des ésotérismes. *Revue des Sciences Philosophiques et Théologiques, 89*(1), 143–187.

Mintzberg, H., Ahlstrand, B., & Lampel, J. (1998). Strategy Safari. A guided tour the wilds of strategic management. New York, USA: The Free Press.

Mirakhor, A. (2008). Lesson of the recent crisis for Islamic finance. *IIUM Journal of Economics and Management, 16*(2), 132–138.

Mohd Noor, N. H. H., Bakri, M. H., Wan Yusof, W. Y. R., Mohd Noor, N. R. A., & Zainal, N. (2020). The impact of the bank regulation and supervision on the efficiency of Islamic Banks. *The Journal of Asian Finance, Economics, and Business, 7*(11), 747–757.

Nugrohowati, R. N. I., Fakhrunnas, F., & Haron, R. (2020). Examining technological and productivity change in the Islamic banking industry. *Pertanika Journal of Social Sciences and Humanities, 28*(4), 3355–3374.

Pollard, J. & Samers, M. (2007). Islamic banking and finance: Postcolonial political economy and the decentring of economic geography. *Transactions of the Institute of British Geographers, 32*(3), 313–330.

Regaieg, B. & Abidi, E. (2015). Les banques islamiques faces à la crise des subprimes: étude de l'x-efficiencepar la méthode SFA (Islamic banks in the time of the credit subprime: A study of the x-efficiency by the SFA method). *International Journal of Innovation and Applied Studies, 10*(1), 45–56.

Rosman, R., Wahab, N. A., & Zainol, Z. (2014). Efficiency of Islamic banks during the financial crisis: An analysis of middle eastern and Asian countries. *Pacific-Basin Finance Journal, 28*, 76–90.

Saâdaoui, F. (2018). Testing for multiufractality of Islamic stock markets. *Physica A: Statistical Mechanics and its Applications, 496*, 263–273.

Saâdaoui, F., Naifar, N., & Aldohaiman, M. S. (2017). Predictability and co-movement relationships between conventional and Islamic stock market indexes: A multiscale exploration using wavelets. *Physica A: Statistical Mechanics and its Applications, 482*, 552–568.

Schrock, R. R. (2002). High oxidation state multiple metal-carbon bonds. *Chemical Reviews, 102*(1), 145–180.

Seiford, L. M. & Thrall, R. M. (1990). Recent developments in DEA: The mathematical programming approach to frontier analysis. *Journal of Econometrics*, *46*(1), 7–38.

Siddiqi, M. N. (2008). Obstacles of research in Islamic economics. *Journal of King Abdulaziz University: Islamic Economics*, *21*(2), 83–95.

Sundarajan, V. (2006). *Systemic Liquidity Infrastructure and Monetary Policy with Islamic Finance. Beirut*: Third Islamic Financial Services Board Summit.

Tulkens, H. (1993). On FDH efficiency analysis: Some methodological issues and applications to retail banking, courts and urban transit. *Journal of Productivity Analysis*, *4*(1/2), 183–210.

Zied, C. & Pluchart, J. J. (2006). *La Gouvernance de la banque Islamique.* Communication à l'IAE Poitiers.

https://doi.org/10.1142/9781800612426_0016

Chapter 16

Islamic Investment and Portfolio Management

Hanaa Abdelaziz Elmoghany

Abstract

Investment in Islamic portfolios and funds must be subject to the provisions of Islamic Sharia standards in all their activities. The main objective of the Islamic investors and Islamic portfolio managers is not only achieving the conventional investment goal but rather achieving this goal in accordance with Sharia standards. In the absence of Islamic financial markets with Islamic financial instruments, Islamic investors and portfolio managers need to know the Islamic criteria for forming and managing different types of Islamic portfolios and funds. This study provides them useful insights and a practical framework for the Sharia standards and Islamic contracts' terms, which are agreed upon by most scholars and Sharia boards, to invest in various types of financial instruments.

Keywords: Islamic Investment, Portfolio Management, Islamic Financial Instruments, Sharia Standards.

16.1 Introduction

Islamic finance is an important component of the global financial system and an outstanding alternative model to conventional finance. With an annual value of more than USD 2 trillion, the share of Islamic finance and investment in the global financial system is increasing exponentially. Islamic finance is now offered in more than 60 countries and over 300 Islamic financial institutions (Erdoğan *et al.*, 2020; Sherif, 2020).

The introduction of Islamic financial instruments around the world has been in response to the growing need of a significant segment of investors who refused to deal with interest-based instruments (Yacout & ElSahn, 2011). The idea of Islamic investment, including investment in Islamic portfolios and funds, is based on the rules of Sharia standards that make the investment acceptable from the Sharia view.

The main problem that Muslim investors and Islamic portfolio managers may face is the absence of Islamic financial markets with Islamic financial instruments. The question is how to form investment portfolios that are consistent with the Islamic Sharia standards within traditional markets? To answer this question, this chapter investigates the Sharia standards for Islamic finance and investment, the Sharia contracts that can be used as Islamic financial instruments, the compatibility and difference of conventional financial instruments to Sharia standards, and the criteria for Islamic portfolios.

The main purpose of this study is to provide a full practical framework for forming and managing different types of Islamic portfolios. The primary motivation for that is to provide useful insights into Islamic investment and portfolio management. This chapter contributes to the literature by identifying the Sharia standards and the terms of Sharia contracts that should be achieved when forming and managing Islamic portfolios. In the field of Islamic portfolio and funds, many studies have been conducted that examine the performance of Islamic portfolios compared to the performance of conventional and socially responsible portfolios (Jawadi *et al.*, 2014; Reddy *et al.*, 2017; Omri *et al.*, 2019; Naveed *et al.*, 2020; Pratama *et al.*, 2021), the different investment strategies of Islamic mutual funds (Hoepner *et al.*, 2011; Othman, *et al.*, 2018; Raza & Ashraf, 2019), or the portfolio diversification benefits of investment in Islamic portfolios (Najeeb *et al.*, 2017; Ali *et al.*, 2021; Bugan *et al.*, 2022), but none of them have fully examined the Sharia standards or the terms of Sharia contracts that should be followed when forming and managing different kinds of Islamic portfolios.

This chapter is organized as follows: First, we explain the concept of Islamic investment, Sharia standards for Islamic finance and investment, the Sharia contracts that can be used as Islamic financial instruments, conventional and Islamic financial instruments, and finally Islamic investment portfolios and funds.

16.2 Concept of Islamic Investment

Islam encourages Muslims to engage in business and share in economic prosperity within the framework of the Sharia rules that govern these activities (Tahir & Brimble, 2011). Islamic investment is the movement and effort to invest and develop money in accordance with Islamic Sharia standards to achieve a halal investment return and attain the goals of the individual investor and society. The main objective of the Islamic investment and Islamic portfolio sector is not only achieving the conventional investment goal which is the maximum return with the least possible risk but rather achieving this goal in accordance with Sharia standards (Elmoghany, 2012).

16.3 Sharia Standards for Islamic Finance and Investment

Sharia compliance refers to compliance to Islamic law based on the teachings of the Qur'an and Sunnah (Ahmed *et al.*, 2021). When Islamic investors invest in various financial instruments, these instruments must be compliant with Islamic law and fulfill the standards of Islamic finance and investment. Linking the investment to a set of standards aims to direct the investor's behavior to achieve the objectives of Islamic Sharia (maqasid al-Sharia). These objectives represented saving and developing halal money, equitable distribution of wealth, achieving the overall well-being of the individual and the society, and carrying out the task of succession and building the land (Rosly, 2010; Elmoghany, 2012). These standards can be explained as follows.

16.3.1 *Ideological (beliefs) standards*

The ideological standards are related to the rules that God imposed on Muslim investors related to their beliefs. According to these standards, the Muslim investors believe that money is the money of

God, and they are committed to preserve and develop this money with what God has permitted and in a way that guarantees the succession and building the land (Sano, 2000, p. 124; Al-Hourani, 2020). The beliefs of Islam include all aspects of a Muslim's life, determining the relationships between man and God and between man and man. They also determine their ethical code as well as giving the framework for daily activities (Ahmed, 2010). These ideological standards combine all the provisions of halal (permissible) and haram (forbidden) things in the Islamic teachings. Therefore, all the following standards fall under these ideological standards (Elmoghany, 2012).

16.3.2 *Financial transactions standards*

The financial transactions standards are related to the rules that God imposed on Muslim investors related to their financial transactions. These standards, such as the prohibition of riba, gharar, najsh, maysir and selling debt, distinct Islamic legal rulings and govern all the investors' financial dealings (Rosly, 2010; Elmoghany, 2019).

16.3.2.1 *Prohibition of riba (Usury)*

God has forbidden riba in the Qur'an. A Sharia term riba refers to the premium that the borrower must pay to the lender on the principal of money borrowed. The Muslim scholars have indicated that a fixed interest in its essence does not differ from riba on debts, and there are main differences between fixed interest and Islamic accepted profit, which are as follows (Ahmed, 2000; Elmoghany, 2019):

- Profit is in exchange for a commodity produced, trade, or productive investment, but fixed interest is in exchange for delaying the payment of capital or money.
- Profit is in return for effort and work, while work is not a primary reason for obtaining interest.
- Dealing with interest does not involve a real risk, but in Islamic investment, the financiers bear the risk of losses, and in return for this risk, they get profits.

Based on this rule, Islamic investors cannot conclude contracts that require obtaining a fixed interest or predetermined payment which is not a function of realized profits and losses. Islam considers money as a medium of exchange and it will not be treated as a commodity (Mirakhor & Zaidi, 2007; Razak & Saupi, 2017; Rabbani *et al.*, 2020).

16.3.2.2 *Prohibition of gharar sale*

Gharar is a term for sales that involve ignorance, deception, and ambiguity since their delivery is not trusted and may lead to unfairness and risk. The sale of ambiguity is a false sale. The Qur'an has clearly forbidden all business transactions, which cause injustice for any of the contract parties. Prohibition of gharar is another important rule that governs all transactions in Islamic contracts (Obaidullah, 2005; Uddin & Ahmad, 2020). A clear example of those contracts in the current financial markets is dealing in financial derivatives such as option, future, and swap contracts. These transactions occur to take advantage of the price difference without bringing the securities that are the subject of the transaction, so neither the seller hands over what he sold, nor the buyer receives what he bought (Dowabah, 2006, p. 135).

16.3.2.3 *Prohibition of najsh sale*

Najsh sale is bidding to raise the price without intention to buy. In Najsh, while a transaction is in the progress between the seller and the buyer, a third party interferes intending to increase the price over the buyer. This sale is considered deceiving for the buyer, and Islam rejects this false deception (Al-Dalaa & Al-Dhaina, 2021). Najsh sale appears in the stock markets through false rumors to control stocks' prices. Muslim investors must avoid falling into such corrupt sales (Sano, 2000, p. 147).

16.3.2.4 *Prohibition of gambling (Maysir)*

Gambling or maysir refers to the ease of acquiring money or wealth by chance, even if it deprives others of their rights. Islamic Sharia prohibits all transactions or contracts involving gambling (Uddin & Ahmad, 2020). Based on this rule, it is not permissible for the Muslim investor to engage in investment activities that may involve gambling, such as investing in hotels that have gambling halls, and any other investments that include gambling in their activities or transactions (Obaidullah, 2005).

16.3.2.5 *Prohibition of selling debt*

Most of the Muslim scholars and the Islamic Fiqh Academy have agreed that it is not permissible to convert receivable debts into securities and trade them in the market, like loan bonds.[1] They clarified that it is not permissible to sell the deferred debt to someone other than the debtor for immediate cash because it leads to riba (Elmoghany, 2019; Uddin & Ahmad, 2020).

16.3.3 *Ethical standards*

Islamic investment is distinguished from other investments by the obligation to follow the ethics of honesty, justice, loyalty, and other values that Islam considered as religious constants (Sano, 2000, p. 129). Islamic investors should consider these ethical and moral concerns in their allocation decisions (Tahir & Brimble, 2011). These values of Islamic ethics guarantee that Islamic investors will not enter investments that conflict with Islamic ethical rules or make any dealings that are harmful or dangerous to human life. These investments include inaccurate advertising, pornography, weapons, and tobacco (Chong & Anderson, 2008; Al-Hourani, 2020).

16.3.4 *Socio-economic standards*

Islamic financial paradigms concentrate on socio-economic development aimed at achieving Sharia objectives (maqasid) (Hassan *et al.*, 2019). From an Islamic socio-economical perspective, an investment is a means to achieve economic and social well-being for individuals and society. So, the Islamic investor, in addition to his investment responsibility, has a socio-economic responsibility to achieve general societal interests, even if there is a special interest for the investor himself. These standards include investing in accordance with Islamic priorities and generating sufficient livelihood for the largest number of community members (Elmoghany *et al.*, 2012; Al-Hourani, 2020).

---

[1]Decisions of the Islamic Fiqh Academy, session of the 11th conference in Manama, 1998.

16.4 Sharia Contracts that Can Be Used as Islamic Financial Instruments

The acceptance of a Muslim investor to invest in various financial instruments, whether traditional or new, depends on the compliance of these instruments with Islamic Sharia standards as well as taking a form of Sharia-compliant contracts (Elmoghany, 2012). While most of the conventional financial instruments are fixed-interest debt instruments, Islamic instruments should be free of the elements of riba, gharar, and gambling and based on a system of sharing ownership and risk between the investors and lenders or borrowers (Fauzi *et al.*, 2016; Ahmed & Elsayed, 2019). Instead of using one standardized contract, like the classical loan contract in conventional finance, Islamic finance uses instruments based on numerous Sharia contracts (Al-Jarhi, 2017). Some of these Sharia contracts are discussed in the following.

16.4.1 *Musharka*

In musharka contract, the Islamic investor participates with one or more parties to establish a business, commercial, industrial, or agricultural project to make a profit. Each partner shares the capital of the company in equal or different proportions. The profit is distributed among the partners according to the agreement, and the losses must be shared in the proportion of investors' capital. This contract is suitable for long-term financing. (Al-Zuhaili, 2002, p. 431; Ebrahim & Abdelfattah, 2021).

16.4.2 *Modaraba*

It is a mode of financing contract through which an owner of capital (investor) can provide a fund for a worker or moda-rib (Entrepreneur, Fund Manager) who provides professional, managerial, and technical expertise for initiating and operating the business. The profit is distributed between them according to a pre-agreed ratio. As for the loss, if it occurs, it will be on the owner of the capital alone, and the speculator will lose his time and effort or work (Al-Zuhaili, 2002, p. 432; Ahmed, 2017).

16.4.3 *Murabahah*

A contract of sale between the Islamic Investor, like Islamic bank, and their client at a price plus an agreed profit margin for the Islamic bank. The contract involves the purchase of goods by the bank which then sells them to the client at an agreed mark-up in price. Thus, Murabahah is known as a mark-up sale. Repayment is usually on a deferred payment basis in installments (Al-Zuhaili, 2002, p. 68; Ahmed, 2017; Suzuki & Miah, 2021).

16.4.4 *Ijarah (Leasing)*

Leasing is an agreement that permits one party (the lessee) to use an asset or property owned by another party (the lessor) for an agreed price over a fixed period. It is a form of asset finance that has the benefit of using assets without the requirements of ownership or borrowing with interest. The lessee receives the benefits of use while the lessor receives the value of regular rental payments for a specified period plus the residual value of the asset. The lessor will bear all asset ownership risks including the responsibility for any damages, repairs, and insurance. (Al-Zuhaili, 2002, p. 72; Ebrahim & Abdelfattah, 2021).

16.4.5 *Bai Salam*

Bai Salam is a form of forward sale contract when the price of assets or goods is paid upfront with the assets or goods to be delivered later. The type and the amount of salam capital (the amount paid) are required to be known. The assets or goods are required to be a debt, disciplined in character, can be found in the market, and can be delivered (Al-Zuhaili, 2002, p. 298; Ahmed, 2010).

16.4.6 *Istisna'a*

It is a contract with a maker to manufacture a certain thing or a commodity as a debt, with an obligation from the manufacturer or producer to deliver them to the customer upon completion. The manufactured thing and its raw materials will be from the maker. In contrast to the salam contract, the key advantage of an istisna'a contract is that it can provide flexibility to the customer. In istisna'a contract, payments can be made in installments, the period of manufacturing or the time of delivery is not required, the manufactured thing should not be a form of what is found in the market (Al-Zuhaili, 2002, p. 56; Elmoghany, 2019).

16.5 Conventional and Islamic Financial Instruments

The possibility of dealing with traditional financial instruments in Islamic investment depends on the compatibility of these instruments or securities with the previous basic standards of Islamic investment, the Sharia contracts terms, and the work nature of the company issuing the security (Elmoghany, 2012).

16.5.1 *Common stock*

Common stock is a security that represents ownership in a corporation. The common stockholders in a speculation company have a common percentage of profit not a specific amount of return. So, common stock securities do not include any special privilege and do not include any fixed interest. Although the common stock from this perspective is considered acceptable security from the viewpoint of Sharia standards, other controls must be included to make these common stocks acceptable and tradable. First, the main activity of the company issuing these stocks must be halal in compliance with the Sharia standards. Second, the companies issuing these stocks must not borrow or invest in fixed interest. Third, to make common stock tradable, the majority of the company's assets must be formed of real assets and services, not of cash or debts (Elmoghany, 2012; Ho, 2015; Ahmed & Elsayed, 2019).

16.5.2 *Preferred stocks*

Like common stock, preferred stock is an ownership share with a face value, book value, and market value. The holder of the preferred share has a priority over common shareholders in the case of the company's liquidation. He or she also has the right to get determined annual dividends as a fixed percentage of the share's par value. With this definition, there is a conflict between preferred stocks and Sharia rules, whereby the preferred shareholders get a special privilege over other shareholders and they also get a specific fixed share of profit not a common percentage of profits. Accordingly, scholars do not permit dealing with preferred stocks (Al-Zuhaili, 2002, p. 337; Mustafida & Fauziah, 2021).

16.5.3 *Bonds and Islamic sukuk*

Bonds are investment securities where an investor lends money to a company or a government for a set period in exchange for regular fixed interest coupon payments. Once the bond reaches maturity, the bond issuer returns the par value of these bonds. With this definition, there is a conflict between bonds and Sharia rules, whereby a bond is purely a debt contract that guarantees the return and guarantees the principal capital. Hence the opinion of most scholars, regarding these traditional bonds, is that they are forbidden, and it is not permissible to deal with bonds either by sale or purchase (Al-Zuhaili, 2002, p. 487; Uddin *et al.*, 2022).

As a result, the Fiqh Academy provided an alternative to these traditional bonds, which are named sukuk. The Islamic Fiqh Council permitted the issuance of sukuk as Islamic financial instruments under the following foundations and conditions[2]:

- It is required that Islamic sukuk be linked to real assets, not to debts, so that the bearer of these sukuk has the right to take a part of the profit or the rent as an owner of these assets, and he is also entitled to trade these sukuk.
- The Islamic sukuk must be based on profit and loss sharing not based on fixed interest.
- Like common stocks, the activity portfolio by the Islamic sukuk must be halal activity in compliance with the Sharia standards.
- There is no pledge to purchase sukuk from its bearers at their nominal value in the maturity date, but it is permissible to pledge to purchase based on the market value or at a price agreed upon amortization.

[2]Decisions of the Islamic Fiqh Academy, session of the fourth conference in Jeddah, 1988.

According to the previous conditions, sukuk are defined by the Accounting and Auditing Organization for Islamic Financial Institutions (AAOIFI) as "securities of equal denomination representing common shares (undivided) in the ownership of assets, usufructs, services, or in the assets of a particular project or special investment activity" (Bhuiyan *et al.*, 2020). Sukuk by this definition must be subject to compliant contract, asset-backed security, based on speculation or participation in a specific project or an investment activity, and income from these securities must be related to the purpose for which the funding is used. The sukuk's owners do not guarantee any interest or lump sum benefit, but rather they have a part of the profit and they do not obtain this profit unless it is realized (Radzi, 2018). Based on these previous requirements regarding the nature of Islamic sukuk, Islamic scholars have strived to find alternatives to traditional bonds, such as modaraba sukuk, musharaka sukuk, and ijarah sukuk[3] (Elmoghany, 2012; Uddin *et al.*, 2022).

16.5.3.1 *Modaraba sukuk*

Modaraba sukuk are standard value documents issued in the name of their owners, in exchange for the modaraba capital they provide to the moda-rib. (entrepreneur). The holders of modaraba sukuk provide funds to the sukuk issuer, who acts as an entrepreneur and manager of the business venture. The returns to modaraba sukuk holders would be a specified percentage of the project's profits. Modaraba sukuk offer non-fixed cash flows to their holders because they are based on the partnership contract (Uddin *et al.*, 2022). Modaraba sukuk can be restricted or absolute. As for the restricted, the modarib uses the proceeds of those sukuk to finance a specific project or activity, and the owner of the sukuk gets a specific percentage of the profit for this project. As for the absolute modaraba sukuk, the proceeds of those sukuk are used to finance various investments of the company, and the holders shall have the right to obtain a common percentage of the profit from these various investments (Elmoghany, 2012).

[3]Sharia Standard No. (17) Approved by AAOIFI in 2003, concerning the Investment Sukuk.

16.5.3.2 *Musharaka sukuk*

Musharaka sukuk do not differ from modaraba sukuk except in the relationship organized between the sukuk issuer and the sukuk holders. The holders of musharakah sukuk participate in a joint venture with the sukuk issuer. The issuer of musharaka sukuk is one of the participants of the sukuk holder, where the sukuk issuers form a committee of participants to make investment decisions. Profits or losses are distributed between sukuk holders according to musharaka contract terms. Musharaka sukuk offer non-fixed cash flows to their holders because they are based on the partnership contract (Elmoghany, 2012; Uddin *et al.*, 2022).

16.5.3.3 *Ijarah sukuk*

Ijarah sukuk are documents that represent equal shares in real estate or leased assets. These sukuk give their owner the right to own and obtain rent according to the ijarah contract. The ijarah sukuk holders dispose of their properties in a manner that does not harm the rights of the lessee, and they will bear all maintenance consequences of the leased assets. Ijarah sukuk offer fixed cash flows (rent) to their holders because they are based on the ijarah contract (non-partnership agreements). Ijarah sukuk are the most widely used sukuk (Elmoghany, 2012; Uddin *et al.*, 2022; Ebrahim & Abdelfattah, 2021).

16.5.4 *Short-term financial instruments*

Short-term financial instruments are instruments that are dealt within the money market. All securities in the money market are fixed-interest loans that give their holders the right to obtain the principal value of the loan at the maturity date, in addition to an agreed fixed interest value. By this definition, short-term securities are like fixed-interest loans and bonds, so scholars do not permit dealing with the money market instruments. Therefore, various financial institutions, such as Islamic banks and funds, use other short-term instruments that are acceptable from Sharia's viewpoint, like murabahah sukuk, salam sukuk, and istisna'a sukuk. But these short-term sukuk cannot be traded between investors in the secondary market because these sukuk are related to owed debts, and the Islamic scholars stipulated that the tradable sukuk must be related to real assets' ownership, not to debt[4] (Hammoud, 1998; Bukhari *et al.*, 2014; Ulusoy & Ela, 2018; Radzi & Muhamed, 2019).

16.5.5 *Derivatives*

Derivatives are financial instruments that are linked to a specific instrument like stock, index, or commodity. Financial derivatives are used for several purposes such as hedging against risks and speculation.

16.5.5.1 *Option contracts*

An option is defined as a contract that represents the buyer's right to oblige the seller to sell or buy a certain thing at a specific price (execution price) during a specific period, in exchange for an amount of money to a seller called a premium. Most Islamic scholars view that dealing in these contracts is forbidden for the following reasons (Elmoghany, 2012):

- Options do not include any ownership of assets or commodities, but they make the will subject to contract. Sharia does not allow these rights to be subject to exchange, even if they are with the consent of the seller and the buyer. This consent has no value because it loses the meaning of trading.
- Options involve selling what a person does not own and there will be no delivery or receipt of any assets. So, most options are not executed, rather the contracts are often settled in cash by arithmetic settled, that the option writer paying the bearer the price difference.
- Options include a great ambiguity, which is represented in ignorance, anticipation, and waiting for a rise or fall in market prices. This leads to an unfairness resulting from giving one contractor the opportunity to make profits at the expense of another contractor. These ambiguity and unfairness lead to the spoilage of the contract itself.

According to the previous reasons, scholars have indicated that options contracts include gharar, gambling, and a sale of debt

[4]Sharia Standard No. (17) Approved by AAOIFI in 2003, concerning the Investment Sukuk.

(Abu-Munis, 2014; Ahmed & Elsayed, 2019; Hanini, 2020; Rabbani *et al.*, 2020). But given the importance of options contracts in the financial markets for the purposes of hedging and speculation, some scholars have permitted dealing in these contracts under some conditions and restrictions. They stipulated that these contracts must be compatible with one of the Sharia contracts (immediate or forward), represent real or financial assets that comply with Sharia standards, all the options' transactions should end with the delivery of assets but not by arithmetic settled, and finally the exchange management should guarantee the real application of these Sharia terms (Hanini, 2020).

16.5.5.2 *Forward and future contracts*

Forward and future contracts are agreements between sellers and buyers to exchange assets, whether a commodity or a financial asset, on a future date at an agreed price upon the present time. Most Islamic scholars prohibited future contracts due to selling nonexistent things, deferment in both payment and delivery, gharar, excessive risk-taking, and selling debt for debt (Uddin & Ahmad, 2020). They also indicated that some of these contracts are clearly prohibited, such as the futures related to prohibited commodities or financial instruments that are not Sharia permissible, such as interest rate or bonds. Islamic scholars also prohibited the futures related to indices because an index is not an asset but is a statistical number that is calculated to identify the change in the value of different markets. Buying and selling this indicator is pure gambling, and it is an imaginary sale that cannot exist (Al-Zuhaili, 2002, p. 512). Some scholars have permitted dealing in forward or future contracts if they are associated with goods, commodities, or stocks that comply with Sharia standards and are compatible with one of the Sharia contracts that are like forward contracts, such as salam or istisna'a contracts (Elmoghany, 2012).

16.6 Islamic Investment Portfolios and Funds

Islamic portfolios and funds are considered of great importance in the modern Islamic financial industry. Islamic portfolios differ from traditional portfolios where Islamic portfolios are subject to the provisions of Islamic Sharia standards in all their activities. The objectives of the Islamic portfolios are not only achieving financial criteria but also achieving these criteria in accordance with Islamic Sharia standards (Derigs & Marzban, 2008). The year 1986–1987 witnessed the first appearance of the Islamic investment portfolios, through the Islamic Development *Bank*. Since then, the number of Islamic portfolios and funds has increased in many Islamic and non-Islamic countries (Elmoghany, 2012). Along with the emergence of new financial products as alternatives to traditional investment instruments, Islamic share markets also emerged in the financial markets (Tuna, 2019). The growth of Islamic investment around the world has led to the emergence of global Islamic indices, such as the Dow Jones Islamic Market Index (DJIMI), Financial Times Islamic Index Series (FTSE Sharia), Standard & Poor Sharia Index (S&P Sharia), and Morgan Stanley Capital International Islamic Index (MSCI Islamic) (Ho *et al.*, 2014). This emergence of Islamic indices offers a diversification opportunity for Muslim and non-Muslim investors and portfolio managers, as they can provide a better alternative during financial stress and crisis periods because they rely on risk-sharing (Mensi *et al.*, 2017). These Islamic indices have significantly helped the rapid growth of Islamic investment portfolios and funds around the world, which requires defining the criteria of forming and managing Islamic portfolios and funds (Elmoghany *et al.*, 2012).

16.6.1 *Criteria of forming and managing Islamic portfolios and funds*

In addition to traditional investment requirements and conventional portfolio management rules, Islamic investors are only willing to invest their capital in investments that comply with their religious standards. These standards restricted the universe of investments to a set of compliant Sharia investments which is convenient for Islamic portfolios and funds (Derigs & Marzban, 2008). The Sharia standards pose challenges to the portfolio managers. Sharia-compliant portfolio managers should be aware of the Sharia criteria that determine the procedures for the portfolio investments screening and the frequency of portfolio rebalancing (Ashraf & Khawaja, 2016). Determining the Islamic criteria that must be followed when forming and managing different types of Islamic portfolios and funds (as shown in Figure 16.1) is the basis to accept these portfolios from

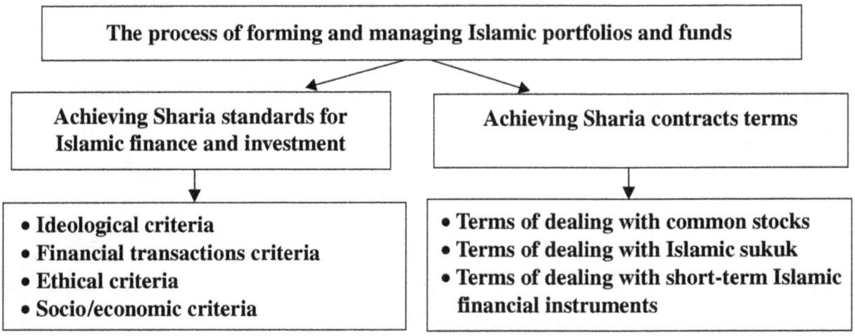

Figure 16.1. Criteria of forming and managing Islamic portfolios and funds.

the Sharia view. The process of forming and managing Islamic portfolios is subject to Sharia standards for Islamic finance and investment and Sharia contracts terms. Although there are some jurisprudential differences among scholars about some of these criteria, most of the fatwa and Sharia Supervisory Boards have agreed on basic Sharia criteria for forming and managing Islamic portfolios and funds (Elmoghany *et al.*, 2012).

16.6.1.1 *Achieving ideological criteria*

In accordance with these ideological standards, the Islamic portfolio manager must be committed to implementing the Sharia standards related to halal and haram rules as follows (Ahmed, 2010; Elmoghany *et al.*, 2012):

- Exclude any investments that deal in the production or provision of forbidden drinks such as wine and other alcoholic products.
- Exclude any investments that deal in forbidden food such as pork or pork products.
- Exclude any investments that deal in forbidden services, such as hotels, bars, casinos, some restaurants, and tourism establishments, that depend on any services, like serving alcohol, gambling, offering pork, and offering entertainment programs, that do not follow Sharia.

16.6.1.2 *Achieving financial transactions criteria*

In accordance with these controls the Islamic portfolio manager must be committed to implementing the following indicators (Rosly, 2010; Elmoghany*et al.*, 2012):

- Not dealing in any contracts or instruments that include any kind of riba or interest.
- Not dealing in any investments where the primary activity is dealing with interest, like conventional financial institutions.
- Not dealing in any contracts or instruments that include gharar or gambling, such as derivatives, short sales, or marginal purchase.

16.6.1.3 *Achieving ethical criteria*

In accordance with these controls, the Islamic portfolio manager must be committed to implementing the following indicators (Chong & Anderson, 2008; Elmoghany*et al.*, 2012):

- Exclude goods and services that are harmful to human health, such as cigarettes and tobacco companies.
- Exclude goods and services that are dangerous to human life, such as weapons, trading in goods with expired validity dates, and building housing units that are subject to collapse.
- Exclude any audio, visual, or print media that present what contradicts the ethical standards.

16.6.1.4 *Achieving socio/economic criteria*

In accordance with these controls, the Islamic portfolio manager must commit to directing his resources to the best possible uses to benefit the individual and general societal interests, such as the following (Elmoghany *et al.*, 2012; Al-Hourani, 2020):

- Prefer investments that achieve public interest and are provided for the largest number of people.
- Prefer investments that achieve Islamic priorities and development.

16.6.1.5 *Achieving terms of dealing with common stocks*

The criteria agreed by scholars when dealing in stocks are as follows (Elmoghany *et al.*, 2012; Ho, 2015; Ahmed & Elsayed, 2019):

- The activities of the company issuing the stocks must be halal in compliance with the Islamic investment standards.
- The majority of the company's assets must be formed of real assets and services, not of cash or debts.

- The companies issuing these stocks must not borrow or invest in fixed interest.

If there are not enough companies that do not deal in prohibited activities or do not borrow or invest in fixed interest, then most fatwa and Sharia supervisory bodies agreed on the following criteria[5]:

- Ensure that the prohibited activities or dealing with fixed interest are not the main activities of the company.
- The percentage of borrowing with fixed interest must be less than 30% of the company's market value.
- The percentage of depositing with fixed interest must be less than 30% of the company's market value.
- The revenues from prohibited sub-activities or fixed interests do not exceed 5% of the company's total revenues, with those revenues being disposed of.

16.6.1.6 *Achieving terms of dealing with Islamic sukuk*

The criteria agreed by scholars when dealing in Islamic sukuk are as follows (Elmoghany *et al.*, 2012; Radzi, 2018)

- The activity financed by the sukuk must be halal in compliance with the Sharia standards.
- The sukuk must represent a common share in real ownership and be linked to real assets or services, not to debts.
- The sukuk are based on profit and loss sharing, bearing full investment risks.
- The sukuk manager is a trustee who does not guarantee the value of the instrument except by infringement, default, or violation of investment conditions.
- It is stipulated not to purchase sukuk from its bearers at their nominal value in maturity date, but it is permissible to pledge to purchase based on the market value or at a price agreed upon amortization.
- If the sukuk represent a mix of real assets, cash, debts, and services, then it is permissible to trade sukuk in case that most assets are real assets or services.

[5]Sharia Standard No. (21) Approved by AAOIFI in 2004, concerning the Provisions of companies' stocks.

16.6.1.7 *Achieving terms of dealing with short-term Islamic financial instruments*

The scholars stipulated the following conditions for investing in these tools (Elmoghany *et al.*, 2012; Ulusoy & Ela, 2018; Radzi & Muhamed, 2019):

- These tools must be based on Sharia accepted contracts such as murabahah, salam, and istisna'a sukuk.
- The commodities, assets, or activities that these tools finance are halal things in compliance with the Islamic investment Sharia standards.
- It is not permissible to sell goods that could not be sold on credit, such as gold and silver.
- Murabahah, salam, and istisna'a sukuk cannot be traded in the secondary market because they are related to owed debts, and sukuk must be related to assets' ownership, not to owed debt to be traded.

16.7 Conclusion

Islamic investment sector has become one of the important sectors in several world countries. The main objective of the Islamic investment sector is not only achieving the conventional investment goal but rather achieving this goal in accordance with Sharia standards and terms of Sharia contracts. Investment in Islamic portfolios and funds must be subject to the provisions of Islamic Sharia standards in all their activities. In the absence of Islamic financial markets with Islamic financial instruments, this study provides useful insights to Islamic investors and portfolio managers. Islamic investors and portfolio managers within traditional financial markets need to know the Islamic criteria for forming and managing different kinds of Islamic portfolios and funds. This study provides them a practical framework for the Sharia standards and Islamic contracts' terms, which are agreed upon by most scholars and Sharia boards, to invest in different kinds of financial instruments. Finally, the field of Islamic finance and investment still needs more attention and research to develop an integrated and applied framework for global Islamic financial markets, in which Islamic Sharia standards are achieved and Islamic financial instruments are available.

References

Abu-Munis, R. N. (2014). The possibility of dealing options rights in the Islamic economic activities. *ISRA International Journal of Islamic Finance*, *5*(2), 111–148.

Ahmed, A. Y. (2000). Islamic banks foundations, work mechanisms, and development necessities. Working Paper, *Islamic Financial Industry Symposium*, Alexandria, Egypt.

Ahmed, A. (2010). Global financial crisis: An Islamic finance perspective. *International Journal of Islamic and Middle Eastern Finance and Management*, *3*(4), 306–320.

Ahmed, H. & Elsayed, A. H. (2019). Are Islamic and conventional capital markets decoupled? Evidence from stock and bonds/Sukuk markets in Malaysia. *The Quarterly Review of Economics and Finance*, *74*, 56–66.

Ahmed, M. (2017). Building social business with Islamic fund. *Journal of Islamic Economics, Banking and Finance*, *13*(4), 11–18.

Ahmed, S., Mohiuddin, M., Rahman, M., Tarique, K. M., & Azim, M. (2021). The impact of Islamic Shariah compliance on customer satisfaction in Islamic banking services: Mediating role of service quality. *Journal of Islamic Marketing*, Ahead-of-print. Doi: 10.1108/JIMA-11-2020-0346.

Al-Dalaa, M. & Al-Dhaina, I. (2021). The implications of the differences of jurists in the criteria affecting the value. *Journal of the College of Education (Assiut)*, *3*(2), 204–238.

Al-Hourani, Y. M. (2020). Financial investment: Its reality, purposes, and controls. *Journal of Humanities and Social Sciences*, *34*(6), 271–312.

Al-Jarhi, M. A. (2017). An economic theory of Islamic finance. *ISRA International Journal of Islamic Finance*, *9*(2), 117–132.

Al-Zuhaili, W. (2002). Contemporary financial transactions. Damascus, Syria: Dar Al-Fikr.

Ali, M. H., Uddin, M. A., Khan, M. A. R., & Goud, B. (2021). Faith-based versus value-based finance: Is there any portfolio diversification benefit between responsible and Islamic finance? *International Journal of Finance & Economics*, *26*(4), 5570–5583.

Ashraf, D. & Khawaja, M. (2016). Does the Shariah screening process matter? Evidence from Shariah compliant portfolios. *Journal of Economic Behavior & Organization*, *132*, 77–92.

Bhuiyan, R. A., Puspa, M., Saiti, B., & Ghani, G. M. (2020). Comparative analysis between global sukuk and bond indices: Value-at-risk approach. *Journal of Islamic Accounting and Business Research*, *11*(6), 1245–1256.

Bugan, M. F., Cevik, E. I., & Dibooglu, S. (2022). Emerging market portfolios and Islamic financial markets: Diversification benefits and safe havens. *Borsa Istanbul Review*, *22*(1), 77–91.

Bukhari, S. M. H., Nawaz, H., & Sair, A. (2014). Compliance of investment Sukuk with Shariah, *Science International*, *26*(4), 1697–1706.

Chong, R. & Anderson, A. (2008). Ethical investment vs Islamic investment: Will the two ever converge in the globalized world? *In International Trade and Finance Association Conference Papers*, p. 29.

Derigs, U. & Marzban, S. (2008). Review and analysis of current Shariah-compliant equity screening practices. *International Journal of Islamic and Middle Eastern Finance and Management*, *1*(4), 285–303.

Dowabah, A. (2006). *Investment Funds in Islamic Banks Between Theory and Practice*. Egypt: Dar Al Salam for Printing and Publishing.

Ebrahim, A. & Abdelfattah, T. (2021). The substance and form of Islamic finance instruments: An accounting perspective. *Journal of Islamic Accounting and Business Research*, *12*(6), 872–886.

Elmoghany, H. A. (2012). *Performance Evaluation of Financial Islamic Portfolios Compared to Traditional Portfolios*. Ph.D. *Thesis, Department of Business Administration*, Faculty of Commerce, Alexandria University, Egypt.

Elmoghany, H. A., El-Hennawy, M. S., & Ismail, E. A. (2012). Criteria for evaluating Islamic financial portfolios from sharia's viewpoint. *The proceedings of the 3rd World Islamic Marketing Conference*, Cairo, Egypt, pp. 118–134.

Elmoghany, H. A. (2019). Risk, profitability and market value ratios of Islamic banks in Egypt: A comparative study with conventional banks. *Journal of the faculty of Commerce for Scientific Research. Alexandria University*, *56*(1), 1–43.

Erdoğan, S., Gedikli, A., & Çevik, E. İ. (2020). Volatility spillover effects between Islamic stock markets and exchange rates: Evidence from three emerging countries. *Bosra Istanbul Review*, *20*(4), 322–333.

Fauzi, P. N. F. N. M., Rashid, K. A., Sharkawi, A. A., Hasan, S. F., Aripin, S., & Arifin, M.A. (2016). Takaful: A review on performance, issues and challenges in Malaysia. *Journal of Scientific Research and Development*, *3*(4), 71–76.

Hammoud, S. (1998). Development through Islamic financing tools. *The Fifth Jurisprudence Symposium*, Kuwait Finance House, Kuwait.

Hanini, M. (2020). Islamic financial options design for speculation and risk management, studies. *Sharia Sciences and Law*, *47*(1), 155–176.

Hassan, M. K., Aliyu, S., Huda, M., & Rashid, M. (2019). A survey on Islamic finance and accounting standards. *Borsa Istanbul Review*, *19*, S1–S13.

Ho, C. S. F. (2015). International comparison of Shari'ah compliance screening standards. *International Journal of Islamic and Middle Eastern Finance and Management*, *8*(2), 222–245.

Ho, C. S. F., Abd Rahman, N. A., Yusuf, N. H. M., & Zamzamin, Z. (2014). Performance of global Islamic versus conventional share indices: International evidence. *Pacific-Basin Finance Journal*, *28*, 110–121.

Hoepner, A. G., Rammal, H. G., & Rezec, M. (2011). Islamic mutual funds' financial performance and international investment style: Evidence from 20 countries. *The European Journal of Finance*, *17*(9–10), 829–850.

Jawadi, F., Jawadi, N., & Louhichi, W. (2014). Conventional and Islamic stock price performance: An empirical investigation. *International Economics*, *137*, 73–87.

Mensi, W., Hammoudeh, S., Sensoy, A., & Yoon, S. M. (2017). Analyzing dynamic linkages and hedging strategies between Islamic and conventional sector equity indexes. *Applied Economics*, *49*(25), 2456–2479.

Mirakhor, A. & Zaidi, I. (2007). Profit-and-loss sharing contracts in Islamic finance. *Handbook of Islamic Banking*, *49*(1), 2–37.

Mustafida, R. & Fauziah, N. N. (2021). Implementing ESG concept in Sharia stock screening process. *Hasanuddin Economics and Business Review*, *5*(1), 1–7.

Najeeb, S. F., Bacha, O., & Masih, M. (2017). Does a held-to-maturity strategy impede effective portfolio diversification for Islamic bond (Sukuk) portfolios? A multi-scale continuous wavelet correlation analysis. *Emerging Markets Finance and Trade*, *53*(10), 2377–2393.

Naveed, F., Khawaja, I., & Maroof, L. (2020). Are Islamic mutual funds exposed to lower risk compared to their conventional counterparts? Empirical evidence from Pakistan. *ISRA International Journal of Islamic Finance*, *12*(1), 69–87.

Obaidullah, M. (2005). Islamic financial services, working paper, Islamic Economics Research Center, King Abdulaziz University, Jeddah, Saudi Arabia.

Omri, A., Soussou, K., & Ben Sedrine Goucha, N. (2019). On the post-financial crisis performance of Islamic mutual funds: The case of riyad funds. *Applied Economics*, *51*(18), 1929–1946.

Othman, A. H. A., Aziz, H. A., & Kassim, S. (2018). Identification of macroeconomic determinants for diversification and investment strategy for Islamic unit trust funds in Malaysia. *International Journal of Emerging Markets*, *13*(4), 653–675.

Pratama, M. R., Pusparini, M. D., & Andriansyah, Y. (2021). Financial performance of Islamic and conventional mutual funds in Indonesia stock exchange. *Advances in Economics, Business and Management Research*, *168*, 322–327.

Rabbani, M. R., Abdulla, Y., Basahr, A., Khan, S., & Moh'd Ali, M. A. (2020). Embracing of Fintech in Islamic finance in the post COVID era. *In International Conference on Decision Aid Sciences and Application (DASA)*, 1230–1234, IEEE.

Radzi, R. M. (2018). Evolution in the sukuk (Islamic bonds) structure: How do market demands and Shariah (Islamic Law) solutions shape them. *Journal of Islamic Banking and Finance, 6*(1), 16–28.

Radzi, R. M. & Muhamed, N. A. (2019). Are Sukuk debt or equity? A classification of sukuk by regulatory bodies and credit rating agencies. *Journal of Emerging Economies and Islamic Research*, *7*(2), 75–84.

Raza, M. W. & Ashraf, D. (2019). Does the application of smart beta strategies enhance portfolio performance? The case of Islamic equity investments. *International Review of Economics & Finance*, 6046–6061.

Razak, L. A. & Saupi, M. N. (2017). The concept and application of ḍamān al-milkiyyah (ownership risk): Islamic law of contract perspective. *ISRA International Journal of Islamic Finance*, *9*(2), 148–163.

Reddy, K., Mirza, N., Naqvi, B., & Fu, M. (2017). Comparative risk adjusted performance of Islamic, socially responsible and conventional funds: Evidence from United Kingdom. *Economic Modelling*, *66*, 233–243.

Rosly, S. A. (2010). Shariah parameters reconsidered. *International Journal of Islamic and Middle Eastern Finance and Management*, *3*(2), 132–146.

Sano, Q. (2000). Investment: Its provisions and controls in Islamic jurisprudence. Amman, Jordan: Dar Al-Nafees for Printing, Publishing, and Distribution.

Sherif, M. (2020). The impact of Coronavirus (COVID-19) outbreak on faith-based investments: An original analysis. *Journal of Behavioral and Experimental Finance*, *28*, 100403, Doi: 10.1016/j.jbef.2020.100403.

Suzuki, Y. & Miah, M. D. (2021). Shari'ah-compliant benchmark and Shari'ah-based "*raf'al-haraj*" benchmark on prohibition of *riba*. *International Journal of Islamic and Middle Eastern Finance and Management*, *14*(1), 151–163.

Tahir, I. & Brimble, M. (2011). Islamic investment behavior. *International Journal of Islamic and Middle Eastern Finance and Management*, *4*(2), 116–130.

Tuna, G. (2019). Interaction between precious metals price and Islamic stock markets. *International Journal of Islamic and Middle Eastern Finance and Management*, *12*(1), 96–114.

Uddin, M. A. & Ahmad, A. U. F. (2020). Conventional futures: Derivatives in Islamic law of contract. *International Journal of Law and Management*, *62*(4), 315–337.

Uddin, M. H., Kabir, S. H., Kabir Hassan, M., Hossain, M. S., & Liu, J. (2022). Why do Sukuks (Islamic bonds) need a different pricing model? *International Journal of Finance & Economics*, *27*(2), 2210–2234.

Ulusoy, A. & Ela, M. (2018). Secondary market of Sukuk: An overview. *International Journal of Islamic Economics and Finance Studies*, *4*(2), 17–32.

Yacout, O. M. & ElSahn, M. F. (2011). 15 customer-based brand equity of Islamic banks in Bahrain: An empirical investigation. In O. Sandikci & G. Rice (Eds.), *Handbook of Islamic Marketing*. UK: Edward Elgar Publishing Ltd., pp. 274–299.

https://doi.org/10.1142/9781800612426_0017

Chapter 17

Role of Blockchain in Enhancing Islamic Crowdfunding Mechanisms

Bassam Said Mohamed Bayomi

Abstract

In this study, we discussed several aspects, including the definition of the general concept of traditional crowdfunding, which aims to finance emerging small projects and innovative ideas as well as financing medium-sized projects that cannot provide sufficient guarantees for banks to obtain the necessary liquidity for their projects. These companies use crowdfunding to obtain this required liquidity for new projects through electronic platforms. In the same context, some of the challenges facing these companies when obtaining crowdfunding from these electronic platforms were discussed, with the presentation of the regulatory framework for crowdfunding in light of Islamic funding standards, which differ from traditional funding in that it is essentially non-profit as much as it targets charitable and social work as well as it regulates the collection of funds and the distribution of profits to the principles of Islamic finance. On the other hand, the general concept of blockchain, its general characteristics, and working mechanisms were discussed. Then, the reasons that may lead to the shift from traditional models in Islamic crowdfunding to the use of blockchain in enhancing Islamic crowdfunding mechanisms were discussed through exposure to the Ventera project model of crowdfunding using blockchain technology as a model as well as exposure to other models of Islamic crowdfunding, where the study suggests that it can improve their performance through the use of blockchain technology as it may bring them a number of benefits and help them overcome a number of challenges. This chapter aims to explore the impact of the application of blockchain technology in Islamic crowdfunding operations and also bridge the gap between the academic side and the applied professional side in the field of using modern technologies, such as blockchain as a safer, faster, and lower-cost alternative in Islamic finance projects, as there are only few studies that dealt with this area despite its importance. This chapter discusses the benefits of blockchain in Islamic crowdfunding with an illustration of some projects as an applied model, after identifying the challenges facing traditional Islamic crowdfunding and the advantages of developing it using blockchain applications; this study ends with presenting models of Islamic crowdfunding projects that can be developed using blockchain technology.

Keywords: Blockchain Applications, Decentralization, Trust, Smart Contracts, Islamic Crowdfunding.

17.1 Introduction

The knowledge resulting from reliable accounting information is a way for economic institutions today to compete in light of what is known as the fourth industrial revolution, which is concerned with the applications of modern technologies, such as big data analysis, cloud computing, the internet of things, artificial intelligence and others, and perhaps the emergence of what is known as blockchain technology is one of the most important developments are in what is known as fin-tech, as this technology was found primarily to solve the problems of the finance sector.

Blockchain can be defined according to Al-Shater (2018) as a decentralized ledger that allows peer-to-peer transactions between two parties without the presence of intermediaries with the availability of transparency and privacy characteristics in the distributed ledger between the parties. Also, it represents a database consisting of a group of computers distributed across the world and is continuously updated and transactions are carried out on it, and these transactions may be a transfer of money, assets, transfers, and settlements in what is known as the exchange of value.

As a consequence, according to Manula (2019), the blockchain applications are with the availability of stability and encryption properties of the data after verification in a decentralized manner by the majority of members, with more than 51% of the participants in that network in what is known as the consensus mechanism; it can enhance trust in these applications without the presence of an intermediary so that some studies called them "chains of trust" after there was a need for a third party to achieve that trust, such as banks and regulatory and legal bodies, this trust became stemming from the consensus mechanism in those networks or the distributed ledger.

At the same time, according to Berrahlia (2019), crowdfunding is considered one of the most important financial technology techniques that increased interest in it after the global financial crisis in 2008 and the loss of confidence in the central banking sector. So, the World Bank expects to double this value to USD 90 billion during 2020. The importance of this type of financing is due to emerging companies and medium-sized companies that are looking for financing systems that reduce the guarantees that banks require from these companies, with the inability of these companies to provide those guarantees.

Also, according to Felicia *et al.* (2021), the benefits of blockchain in Islamic finance is presenting an illustration of the smart contract as privacy and transparency, after it identified the advantages of Islamic development financial technology (i-FinTech), and this study presented a discussion of two challenges that must be addressed to enhance the development of a real and sustainable Islamic financial technology, which is the extent to which verifications in blockchain comply with Sharia compliance and determine whether these transactions are Islamic in nature as well as how to reduce environmental pollution resulting from the large use of electricity in blockchain mining operations. Furthermore, according to the recommendations of the Islamic financial services board report in 2018, the crowdfunding technique allows investors to obtain the necessary liquidity for their projects away from traditional financial restrictions.

However, Nor *et al.* (2021) clarified that the perceptions of zakat institutions and the intention of the community toward the application of blockchain technology in zakat management and the results of this study provide a positive view for zakat institutions to embrace the use of the blockchain in its management; however, there are many concerns that must be addressed such as job loss and application problems. This study concluded that a special model for the use of blockchain in zakat can be developed that can enhance the characteristics of privacy and transparency in a way that supports the fair distribution and collection of zakat.

As result, based on the foregoing, the study concludes that there can be a strong role for blockchain in supporting crowdfunding projects, which was confirmed by Sasy (2019). It was confirmed that the applications of the blockchain, with its decentralization, transparency, and privacy characteristics, can provide confidence and security in Islamic crowdfunding transactions and can also be controlled according to the principles and provisions of Islamic finance.

This study contributes to the formation of the body of knowledge in Islamic crowdfunding through incorporating blockchain technology. In addition, this study also adds value to complete literature examining the acceptance of technology for users in crowdfunding management, in addition to the values of trust, and the practical meaning of this study indicates that the integration of the blockchain would enhance good governance and sustainability in managing crowdfunding in support of the Islamic goal economics, and the research also contributes to clarifying the challenges and opportunities for Islamic crowdfunding using the blockchain.

In the same context, the study reviews the role of blockchain technology in enhancing the technology of Islamic crowdfunding by presenting the following points in more detail:

(1) What is crowdfunding?
(2) What is the regulatory framework for crowdfunding in light of Islamic finance standards?
(3) The general concept of blockchain.
(4) General characteristics of blockchain.
(5) Types, components, and generations of blockchain.
(6) Mechanisms of blockchain.
(7) The role of blockchain in strengthening crowdfunding mechanisms.
(8) Project Ventera Islamic crowdfunding using blockchain technique as a model.
(9) Findings and recommendations of the study.

17.2 What Is Crowdfunding?

The concept of crowdfunding began in 2005 in the United States by providing one of the electronic online platforms through which small companies collect the necessary funds to turn their studies, projects, and ideas into actual implementation (Roberto, 2016).

In the same time, one of the studies describes crowdfunding as a type of project financing by raising funds from individuals and institutions through dedicated participatory platforms available online (Enrique, 2012).

Crowdfunding can also be defined as an opportunity to raise funds from electronic platforms to support new initiatives and ideas that collectively represent entrepreneurship, and at the same time, the platform charges fees ranging from 5 to 5.2%, and in the event that if the full amount of funding is not collected, the platform will refund amounts previously collected without these online platforms collecting any fees (Cento, 2015).

Through the previous definitions, the study can propose the definition of crowdfunding as websites for financing small and medium enterprises that cannot obtain financing and provide the necessary liquidity for their projects through the traditional banking system, and these funds are collected in the form of individual and collective donations and contributions.

17.3 What Is the Regulatory Framework for Crowdfunding in Light of Islamic Finance Standards?

Islamic crowdfunding is based on the same principles as traditional crowdfunding, except the following two main points:

(1) Money investment tools represent tools correspond with principles of Islamic Sharia, such as speculation and participation, the rate of return on investment in these funds is not a fixed percentage, in contrast to traditional investment with a fixed rate of return in cases of profit or loss.
(2) Complete finance projects that agree with Islamic law like housing projects with low cost (Malak, 2020).

At the same time and according to Angel (2020), there is a set of crowdfunding models that are compatible with the principles of Islamic Sharia:

(a) Donation platforms: It includes electronic platforms that serve charitable and social causes, where the donors represent benefactors and they donate without expecting any direct return or rewards, so there is personal freedom in the value and method of donation, and

from this, the study concludes that this system is similar to zakat through these electronic platforms, as it aims to provide support and solidarity. This is in accordance with the principles of the Islamic religion, so these funds are provided without any return.

(b) Reward platforms: It includes industrial and service projects that provide a specific product or service and require financing, so they can obtain it in return for a reward that the participants get as result of their finance, such as benefits, company products, and rewards.

(c) Lending platforms: These platforms offer loans to owners of small companies and projects with great facilities in interest rates or without interest at all, and the study concludes that loans can be given in this case with the interest rate fixed and the investor bears his share of the loss, as he receives interest in the event of profit, until there is compatibility with the principles of Islamic law.

(d) Stock platforms: The donors in these projects receive compensation for their contribution in the form of equity shares in these projects and companies that they have donated to, and therefore, the study concludes that this type of Islamic crowdfunding results in the distribution of ownership among its participants, which achieves the principle of fair and equal distribution according to the participation of each of them.

17.4 General Concept of Blockchain

According to Sudi (2019), blockchain can be defined as a set of blocks that contain transactions that were recorded in them and are linked to each other and contain fully encrypted and secure data (Al-Shater, 2019).

In the same context, the blockchain can be described as an electronic record or a decentralized and distributed ledger in which data is recorded in a historical and sequential manner and all parties participating in the network can verify those transactions, then identical copies of this ledger are distributed after it is updated.

Consequently, the study concludes that the blockchain is a global decentralized ledger in which a set of transactions is recorded without a third party or intermediary, and the participants verify those transactions and then record them within decentrally distributed blocks while ensuring that these records are not tampered with through the encryption and transparency mechanisms available in this network.

17.5 General Characteristics of Blockchain

There are a set of characteristics that characterize blockchain applications as a decentralized ledger, which can be exposed as follows (Al-Shater, 2019):

(a) Decentralization: There is no central authority that controls the network data, such as the presence of a central server in one of the central authorities, but rather there are a number of nodes or devices participating in a ledger distributed across the world in which transactions are made from person to person peer to peer without any intermediaries. The study concludes from this that through this method, it is possible to maintain identical copies of the data and continuously update the participants in that network.

(b) Immutable: The blockchain ledger record cannot be modified without verifying it through the consensus mechanism and recording it within the blocks, and also this data cannot be deleted, modified, falsified, or manipulated.

(c) Verification: The validity of the transaction is verified through the consensus mechanism, and the private key of the person who deals within the network is used to digitally sign those transactions, which means his approval of them.

These main characteristics of the blockchain can be illustrated in Figure 17.1.

Also, according to Puthal (2018), there are other characteristics of the-blockchain, as follows:

- *Open-source network*: Blockchain applications are an open-source network in which anyone can participate and use those applications.
- *Transparency*: Information about transactions made via the blockchain ledger is available to everyone in the form of mirrors and updated periodically, which means transparency while preserving

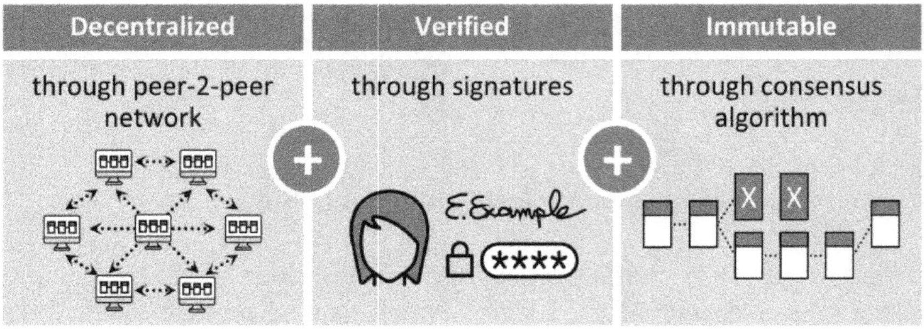

Figure 17.1. Characteristics of the blockchain (euromoney.com).

privacy, as the transaction is via the public key without announcing the identity of the original people.
- *Real-time settlement*: Transactions within the blocks are settled instantaneously after verification processes are carried out through the consensus mechanism, which means that transactions are recorded, reviewed, verified, then recorded and encrypted all in a very short time.

According to a study (Ibrahim, 2020), blockchain applications can also save a lot of transaction processing costs and transfers, which means increasing operational efficiency while reducing operational expenses while reducing fraud because there are no intermediaries, and this reduces human errors in recording transactions, which enhances customers' confidence in this system through the security systems available in it, especially with the use of smart contracts.

17.6 Types, Components, and Generations of Blockchain

There are two main types of blockchain, the difference between them can be explained by Figure 17.2.

It is clear from the previous figure that there are two types of blockchain networks: the private and the public, as the private is the most important thing that distinguishes it that no one can participate in it without the approval of a certain party. And there are federated networks that can be represented by a group of institutions such as banks that want to join several private blockchain networks with each other to make inter-settlement.

Blockchain types

	Public	Consortium/private
Permissions	Permissionless	Permissioned
Participation	Anyone, free	Requires access
Location	More decentralized	More centralized
Currency	Typically native	Typically does not have native
Examples	Bitcoin, Ethereum, Litecoin	Hyperledger, Corda, Quorum

Figure 17.2. Types of blockchain.
Source: AICPA (2019).

In the same context, there is a question about the compatibility of Islamic finance and these types of blockchain, and the answer is that there is convergence, although public cryptocurrency networks, such as Bitcoin, are still under discussion among Islamic scholars, but private and consortium network types are compatible with the Islamic finance system. There are many interesting applications of blockchain in Islamic finance because it is a peer-to-peer system of transactions and depends on a fully distributed system through an autonomous process (AI). Islamic finance is about implementing righteous behavior, and blockchain is about "coding" these behaviors into an entire system of artificial intelligence, which will then ensure that these behaviors are adhered to independently, without additional interference from another party. Then, it becomes self-executing, self-regulating, self-correcting, and self-performing (Nor, 2021).

Also there are several components of a blockchain that can be illustrated in Figure 17.3.

It is clear from Figure 17.3 that blockchain applications consist of several components.

Blockchain consists of several components, which include the transaction that takes place in the form of an exchange of value, whether it is money or assets, as well as the block that collects a number of transactions, and there is the so-called mining, which

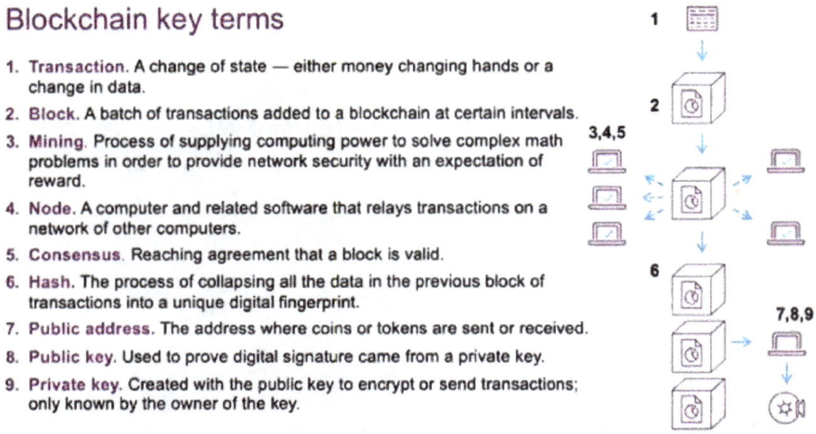

Figure 17.3. Components of blockchain.

Source: AICPA (2019).

is responsible for creating blocks, producing cryptocurrencies, and verifying transactions between the group of participating nodes, which represent devices, the computers shared in the network, and those transactions are verified through a consensus mechanism, which means that more than 51% of the network subscribers confirm the validity of the transaction, and the transaction data is encrypted after verification using what is known as the hash generated by the transaction, where each block contains a hash. A precursor of the previous block and a current hash of the current block represent the chain, transactions are made through the public key and public address with anonymity as well as a private key for the digital signature of the transaction owner for approval (Alidin *et al.*, 2018).

Also, the applications of the blockchain went through three stages, which can be clarified through Figure 17.4.

It is clear from Figure 17.4 that blockchain applications have gone through three phases, starting with the first generation in 2009 of cryptocurrencies such as Bitcoin and Ethereum. There are different views and opinions of scholars on compliance with Islamic law in cryptocurrencies. The Egyptian Grand Mufti rejected cryptocurrencies on the grounds that they violated the basic principles of Islam as it provides transactions that are prohibited under Sharia because the basic principles of finance state that gharar is contrary to Sharia and it is forbidden. It cannot be a store of value and there is no

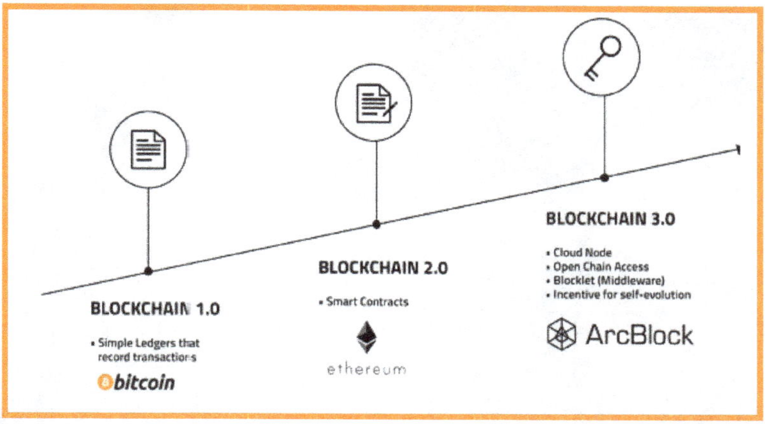

Figure 17.4. Blockchain generations.

Source: get7keys.com.

supervision from the central bank and thus can easily be abused; it also violates the basic principle of Islamic economics of social justice. For these reasons, Bitcoin is considered to be against Sharia and should be banned (Mohamed *et al.*, 2018).

Then, there was the second generation for smart contracts via the Ethereum network in 2014, which were used in the financial and insurance sectors to a large extent, ending with the third generation of open-source applications for the blockchain, such as applications in the field of health, education, tourism, and real estate, as shown in Figure 17.5 for the applications of blockchain technology.

17.7 Mechanisms of Blockchain

There are several steps to complete transactions via the blockchain, where two parties or people who want to conduct a transaction are announced via the blockchain ledger, and in case these people own property and funds as announced, the validity of the transaction is validated, a group of participating devices (miners) validate the transactions and the correctness of the numbers contained in them, and therefore, the hash that represents the solution of the arithmetic equation for the information of this transaction was found, and thus new blocks are added, and these blocks are linked to each other through a series of hashes, and public and private encryption

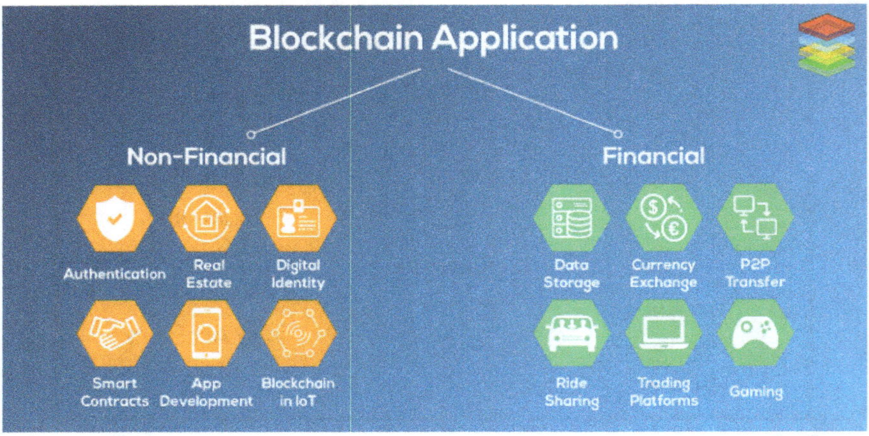

Figure 17.5. Blockchain applications (pianoroll.com).

keys are used to sign the approval of the transaction, although it is possible to know the characteristics of all participants in the transactions, but their identity and privacy are preserved, and thus the amount of assets and money owned by everyone can be determined (Khal, 2020).

As a consequence, the working mechanism of blockchain is as expressed in Figure 17.6.

It is clear from Figure 17.6 that a person via the blockchain network submits a request to perform a transaction over the network, then the transaction is spread across the network among the individuals participating in it, then the individuals participating in the network validate the transaction. Then, the transaction hash is generated and a new block is added, and then the adding verified transactions to those previous blocks and linking them together through a chain of hashes, where each block contains its own current hash and the previous hash of the previous block which represents the block chain.

17.8 Role of Blockchain in Strengthening Crowdfunding Mechanisms

According to bbvaopenmind.com, although the current crowdfunding platforms provide support for financing small and medium

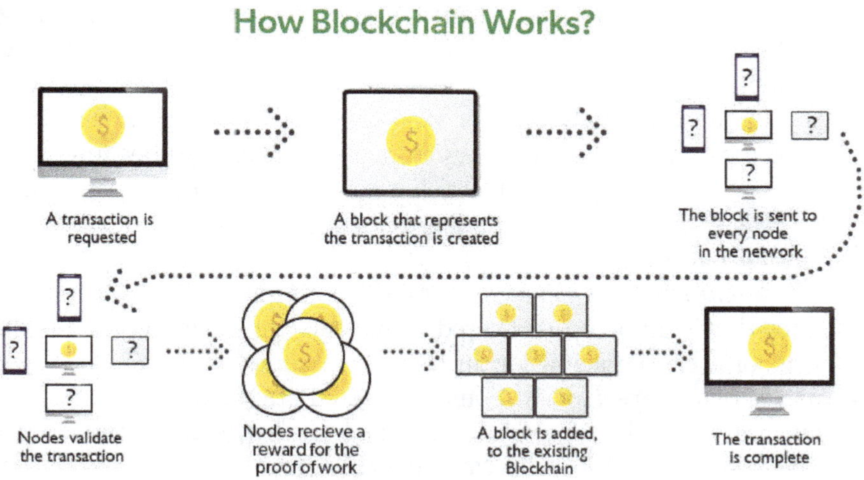

Figure 17.6 Blockchain working mechanism.

Source: arabiangazette.com.

enterprises in innovative ways, there are some challenges that these platforms face when providing this service within FinTech technologies, as follows:

- *High fees*: Crowdfunding platforms charge a fee for each project that is included in them, although these fees can be reduced, but some platforms require a high percentage of the total revenue collected by contributors, and this leads to funds that may lead to the failure of the crowdfunding project as these projects may be small ones which need every dollar and cannot bear the exorbitant fees.
- *Platforms' rules and regulations*: Not all platforms accept services as a potential project or just an innovative idea or a new initiative by requesting real, tangible products, and this weakens crowdfunding for projects, outstanding ideas for entrepreneurship, and the production of new products and services.
- *Marketing and advertising*: With a few exceptions, platforms will not help spread the word about new startups that need startups

to pay for marketing and advertising because online crowdfunding platforms only provide financial support and do not contribute to marketing the products and ideas of these companies that offer creative and innovative ideas, and the study concludes that this represents an additional pressure on these companies because they bear the marketing and advertising costs despite their weak financial resources, which is the reason for which they resorted to crowdfunding platforms.

- *Fraudulent startups*: Do some scam startups and not produce something that cannot be recovered? Investors for their money in the event of their participation in these companies.
- *Intellectual property risk*: Some protected startups cannot protect their intellectual property rights, which makes them vulnerable to experienced investors who can take the idea and enter the market early with all the resources at their disposal so that they cannot wait to raise funds through crowdfunding platforms and time that can be spent until the required funding is achieved.

As a result of the above, the availability of blockchain technology with its decentralization, transparency, privacy, and low-cost properties can support crowdfunding as follows:

- *Decentralization*: Startups will not rely on any central platform or group of platforms to enable creators to raise funds, startups are no longer bound by the rules and regulations of the most popular crowdfunding platform on the Internet through a decentralized blockchain, and as a result, with that technology, any project has a chance to emerge and get funded, and it also removes the fee problem as crowdfunding via the blockchain requires less money, so it will significantly reduce transaction fees. This makes crowdfunding less expensive for creators and investors.
- *Tokenization*: It is used in blockchain instead of using crowdfunding to enable pre-orders for upcoming tangible products, the blockchain could rely on asset tokenization to provide investors with equity or some similar concept of ownership, such as an initial coin offering (ICO).

  Thus, in this way, investors will see success commensurate with the company's ultimate success. This can open up whole new worlds of investment opportunities. Startups can save money on hiring employees by partially compensating them in partial ownership of the company and turning it into an employee-owned company. Asset tokens become their own form of currency in this model, enabling organizations to do more like hiring professionals like marketers and advertisers.

- *Instant savings*: Any project that uses a blockchain-based crowdfunding model can anyone with an internet connection contribute to these projects. And blockchain-based crowdfunders will not have to worry about the "fraud" that has plagued crowdfunding projects in the modern era. Instead, contributors will immediately receive partial ownership or partial ownership of the product.
- *Smart contracts*: It enforces funding terms: There are several ways in which smart contracts that support blockchain can provide greater accountability in crowdfunding. These contracts will provide milestones that will prevent funds from being released without a source related to the legitimacy of the project or campaign. This would prevent large sums of money being wasted by those who had no ill intent or were unqualified to run a crowdfunding campaign in the first place.

As a consequence, the role of blockchain in promoting crowdfunding technology can be illustrated as shown in Figure 17.7.

In the same previous framework and according to bbvaopenmind, it is possible to support blockchain technology for crowdfunding technology by providing the following features (blockchain.oodles.io):

- *Improved access to stocks*: It provides blockchain mechanisms to encrypt assets which makes it easy to tokenize assets for investors. An entrepreneur who intends to use the funds to develop several new products may give each new investor a small ownership stake in the business in proportion to his contribution in the form of opening new investment opportunities.
- *Availability of blockchain platforms distributed around the world*: Increasing the success rate of a crowdfunding model based on a blockchain system has a chance of success because such projects can be contributed by anyone with an internet connection and this is not available in centralized crowdfunding platforms tied to specific geographies.

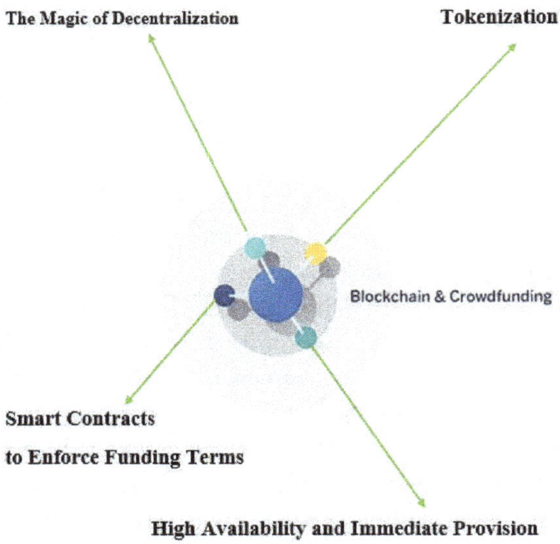

Figure 17.7. Blockchain in crowdfunding.

Source: mobilecoderz.com.

- *Transactions take place in real time*: In light of the use of blockchain in crowdfunding, there will be no waiting for weeks or months for fundraising for funders, but rather donors get immediate ownership or ownership of certain products.
- *Peer-to-peer transactions*: Shares of the company or funded products can be exchanged from person to person directly just like cryptocurrency which provides greater fluidity for the contributors participating in these platforms, and therefore, it can be an effective way to get people interested in the project as a whole yama. It can lead to the emergence of a new form of market.
- *Campaigns marketing*: All campaign data marketing and goals and strategies and materials ad and legal documents can be registered and controlled in blockchain distributed ledger because it is tamper-proof and securely accessible, and therefore, investors can use it to verify the campaign process marketing and comply with the requirements.
- *Decentralized fundraising*: Fundraising processes are clear and compliant with know your customer (KYC) technology through smart contracts powered by blockchain as possible plural money

for entrepreneurs whose meet the specified criteria, and then, stakeholders may vote in full democracy on the legality of each project separately through consensus algorithms.

- *Low operating costs*: Operations can be simplified and limbs removed argument using smart contracts, saving fundraising money and letting them spend only the amount they planned to invest.
- *Enhance privacy for funders*: Complete private messages encrypted with public keys to communicate with groups and issue advertisements and these messages visible to senders and recipients only in order to support the privacy of these funders by not disclosing their identity.
- *Flexibility in crowdfunding management*: Crowdfunding operations are managed safely and transparently through the guarantee enabled by blockchain, messaging, deposit, withdrawal of digital assets, and other resources leading to access of many new financing technologies, such as scheduled transfers or monthly payments.
- *Additional financing options*: Real-world asset tokenization and fast, low-cost, cross-border transactions are just two examples of how digital assets based on blockchain in ways of financing and investing that were previously impossible.

17.9 Project Ventera Crowdfunding Islamic Using Blockchain Technique as a Model

It is a company established in Geneva, with branches in Singapore, Hong Kong, Abu Dhabi, and New York, and this company offers a blockchain application, which is known as the platform for the electronic development of assets generated by Islamic endowments so that the lost confidence in the management of these Islamic endowments can be restored, as they were managed by political parties and controlled by personal interests that lead to the loss of the funds of these endowments.

At the same time, this platform aims to take advantage of the untapped assets in Islamic endowments, where the company has developed a crowdfunding platform that uses blockchain technology to create smart contracts linked to the management of a group of Islamic endowments by providing effective means of raising funds by receiving donations from Muslim individuals to run social projects, such as mosques, schools, welfare programs, and social solidarity, to develop these projects and improve their management as Islamic endowments using blockchain technology.

As a result of the foregoing, this platform is managed by a banking entity represented by a Sharia committee that conducts audits and ensures the compatibility of this platform and the projects available to it with the provisions and principles of Islamic Sharia, such as the decisions of the organization of the authority. The Islamic Conference and Accounting and Auditing Organization for Financial Institutions (AAOIFI) standards and their compatibility with the guidance of the Islamic Financial Services Board and the International Islamic Financial Market Standards. It is run via smart contracts as a blockchain application.

Thus, the process of Islamic crowdfunding via the blockchain platform can be done through the following steps:

(1) The body representing the ministry of endowments in a specific country identifies land that can be used as an Islamic endowment on which this body wishes to establish a project and then prepares a detailed economic feasibility study and the financing tools recommended for the project.
(2) One of the financial auditors reviews and confirms the project proposal submitted by the Ministry of Awqaf.
(3) A letter is sent to the management of the fund designated for this project, which is located in an Islamic bank, to launch ICO to develop the Islamic endowment project by selling distinctive tokens for investors participating in this platform.
(4) Ventera platform gives an automatic token to these projects equal to the total capital value and is called waqf chain.
(5) Investors buy tokens as crowdfunding for those projects launched by the fund management in the Islamic bank, and they are allowed to choose between the four funding methods available through that platform (the cash endowment): waqf cash Islamic loan, speculation, and sukuk.
(6) A contracting company is assigned through the fund management to carry out the construction work for the project after

completing the amount of capital required through crowdfunding on the platform.

(7) The fund management assigns project management to carry out the operation and maintenance of the asset after the contracting company has completed the construction of the project.

(8) The fund's management collects the revenues generated from operating the assets and then distributes them to investors in accordance with the principles, terms, and conditions of Islamic finance.

At the same time, Abojeib (2021) shows that blockchain and smart contracts are shaping a new business registration and management system with less need for intermediaries while achieving a higher level of governance with lower transaction cost compared to traditional technologies, more transparency, and greater trust, thus enhancing business resilience and market access especially in Islamic finance in general and finance Islamic social in particular.

In the same context as the previous, Chong (2021) believes that blockchain technology and smart contracts in the context of Islamic finance support rejecting wrong behavior, coding these wrong behaviors in a fully automated system to ensure that these behaviors are followed automatically without third-party intervention, as well as achieving a number of advantages, such as transparency, reducing human errors, speed, and democratization of Islamic finance, that contribute to the principles promoted by Islamic finance.

As a result of the above, the study concludes that the development of current models of Islamic finance using blockchain technology through smart contracts can reduce the costs of financing operations and increase the speed of time with writing all the terms of the crowdfunding contract in the form of software codes that are executed automatically, which prevents human errors, and these transactions are not subject to modification or fraud, which enhances confidence in the use of smart contracts as one of the applications of the blockchain in Islamic crowdfunding.

Also, in connection with the foregoing, there are many projects related to Islamic crowdfunding, but they are not based on blockchain technology, which is considered as opportunities available to develop these platforms using blockchain technology and benefit from characteristics of these applications, including the following (Saloua, 2020):

(a) Chakra model for Islamic crowdfunding: Chakra is an electronic platform that supports Islamic crowdfunding, in particular projects that link innovators with new ideas to investors.

The project financing ranges from USD 50,000 to USD 300,000. These projects are announced through social media with marketing advertising campaigns. The following is noted on this platform:

- The platform lacks the basic skills and requirements that make it more reliable.
- The funding cycle on the platform takes about 60 days on average.
- The platform needs legal documentation of its work periodically through a body designated for this.
- The financier needs a periodic meeting for investors to agree on their shares of shares and other agreements related to financing and the resulting distributions through a set of reports and monitoring.

(b) Egyptian model Yomken: This platform targets the processes of new innovations as a means to push the Egyptian economy toward progress, so it is based on the following:

- The platform allows all creators from individuals, companies, university students, and others to publish their technological and innovative ideas through the platform, such as posting ideas to improve available products or create a new product or service, and gives these innovators benefits and rewards for that.
- A group of financiers come forward to purchase this new innovation and offer rewards to its owners, then they collect the necessary amount to launch the project.

In the same context, Shifa (2021) indicates that the use of blockchain supports good governance and sustainability in Islamic economic institutions, such as zakat institutions, and that blockchain may be a good way to solve issues of financial and social inclusion, which helps improve the efficiency of the processes of collection and distribution of zakat in order to support the provision of societal welfare and improve the economy of Muslims.

The study concludes from the foregoing that these previous platforms, such as Chakra, can make use of the blockchain technology to overcome a number of challenges it faces, as blockchain technology can help these platforms to speed up the time in conducting financing operations with its cost reduced to a minimum, in addition to bearing the costs of marketing and the necessary legal documentation, which means more reliability and confidence in these transactions, and attracting more financiers when crowdfunding platforms are based on blockchain technology.

After presenting these previous projects, the most important challenges and opportunities for using financial technology such as blockchain in Islamic finance must be presented, as shown in the Table 17.1.

From Table 17.1, FinTech such as blockchain offers great opportunities for Islamic finance as Islamic FinTech companies can greatly assist new startups by providing innovative products that provide a cost-effective solution to financial services, enhance transaction transparency, are accessible, user friendly, and can easily gain customers' trust.

In the same context, blockchain financial technology faces many challenges in Islamic finance, including the lack of good and real research in the Islamic financial technology sector, with the lack of trained human resources, the lack of a clear policy from the government, and other challenges as Islamic FinTech must maintain stability, investors must be protected, and institutions from fraudulent practices.

17.10 Findings

The findings of this study provide a positive view for the role of blockchain in enhancing Islamic crowdfunding mechanisms; however, there are several concern that needs to be addressed such as the design of blockchain applications, which should conform to the principles of Islamic Sharia and the strengthening of the internal control

Table 17.1. Islamic FinTech: Opportunities and challenges.

Islamic FinTech opportunities	Islamic FinTech challenges
Islamic FinTech companies can help the new startups in a big way	Lack of good and authentic research in the Islamic FinTech sector
Islamic FinTech companies can provide a wide range of innovative products and services	Developing the Islamic FinTech has been the lack of trained human personnel and clear policy from the government
It provides an option to the customers to use both traditional financial services as well as new and innovative services	Educational intuitions must bring good researches and provide trained personnel and academic researches must provide good research
It can provide cost-effective solution to the financial services and will give a lifeline to traditional Islamic banks to go digital and provide financial services at a low cost	Islamic FinTech needs to keep itself at pace with the rapid development going in the conventional finance world
Islamic FinTech is transparent, accessible and easy to use and can gain customer confidence easily	Islamic FinTech must maintain the stability and must protect the investors and institutions from the fraudulent trade practices
It can be linked to the cryptocurrencies, blockchain and other areas such as cross border payments	The banks are exposed at every level as technology brings more transparency
It can easily gain the confidence of Muslim investors as it is in accordance with the rules prescribed by the Sharia	Since, Islamic FinTech is still new and investors are not able to make sure how much investments are worth investing

Source: Mustafa Raza (2020).

system to protect the participants in these applications from fraud, while training the operators of these applications well, and the governance of these applications in a way that helps protect privacy and transparency and reduce crowdfunding costs.

- *Practical implications*: This study provides new insights to the body of knowledge especially in the Islamic crowdfunding and blockchain. Besides, from a managerial aspect, this study contributes to the new practices that could be implemented in Islamic institutions for crowdfunding via blockchain as blockchain applications provide confidence, transparency, and privacy for the transactions that take place through them, whether those transactions are money transfers, assets, settlements, or others. Also, blockchain applications have a decentralized and distributed network across the world, in which people from different regions can participate; however, crowdfunding is concerned with financing operations based on individual or collective initiatives outside the framework of traditional systems and guarantees that small and emerging institutions and owners of creative ideas cannot fulfill, so they have resorted to these platforms.

- *Social implications*: Many small- and medium-sized companies and charitable projects based on Islamic Sharia principles are unable to obtain the necessary liquidity and financing from official agencies, such as banks, which pushes them to methods such as crowdfunding, which makes blockchain technology a safe and reliable platform for Islamic crowdfunding important to help in social and economic development. The time has come for Islamic crowdfunding platforms to implement blockchain especially during the crisis due to the COVID-19 pandemic that requires a more contactless approach to ensure health and safety.
- *Originality/value*: This study is important to encourage Islamic social finance institutions to adopt blockchain technology in providing an effective service for social and economic development, where traditional crowdfunding agrees with Islamic crowdfunding in the goal, which is to raise the funds needed to launch some small start-up projects and support the innovative ideas for which the funds were raised, But crowdfunding via electronic platforms faces several challenges, including the high costs of marketing campaigns, theft of intellectual property rights sometimes, and the length of the cycle of collecting funding operations at other times, so blockchain technology enhances crowdfunding platforms with the characteristics of trust, transparency and speed of transactions, processing and settlement, making them a better alternative. There are successful models of Islamic crowdfunding using blockchain technology, such as the Ventera project, and there are

other models of Islamic crowdfunding, such as the Chakra project, that can use blockchain technology to improve its performance.

17.11 Future Research

- The study recommends conducting more studies on the use of blockchain technology in crowdfunding operations due to the scarcity of studies in this field.
- The study recommends holding media seminars in professional unions and universities to raise awareness of the importance of blockchain technology because it represents the next generation of accounting generations, represented by the triple entry technology as an alternative to the double entry that has been known for hundreds of years.
- Integrating the use of artificial intelligence techniques with the blockchain is a way to automate financial operations in crowdfunding, so it is recommended to conduct more studies on this.
- The internal control of projects based on blockchain technology must be controlled and studied in terms of benefit and return before launching, including protection from cybersecurity risks.

17.12 Conclusion

From the results achieved, it appears that there is a great potential for Islamic crowdfunding platforms to embrace blockchain in their management system. There are many benefits that these platforms can enjoy and improve the efficiency of operations, especially in collecting and distributing the financing and liquidity necessary for the establishment of these projects. Thus, the ultimate goal of crowdfunding can be embodied in providing liquidity for new projects and ideas that can help improve the economy of Muslims.

At the same time, the second objective of this study is to try to bridge the gap between the academic and applied professional sides in the use of blockchain applications in Islamic crowdfunding operations by identifying the potential effects of these applications, including trust, credibility, and speed of time to collect the necessary funding with a significantly lower cost of raising such funds. With the need to increase knowledge and training, the community needs to know the benefits and ease of using the blockchain in Islamic crowdfunding.

Also, the future direction of this study should be toward developing a blockchain model of Islamic crowdfunding that can benefit society. This study should include important stakeholders, i.e., government agencies, zakat institutions, Islamic finance organizations, professional organizations based on Islamic Sharia principles and FinTech experts, to build a comprehensive blockchain model for Islamic crowdfunding that can enhance its effectiveness under blockchain technology.

References

Abojeib, M. & Habib, F. (2021). Blockchain for Islamic social responsibility institutions. In I. Management Association (Ed.), *Research Anthology on Blockchain Technology in Business, Healthcare, Education, and Government* (pp. 1114–1128). IGI Global. https://doi.org/10.4018/978-1-7998-5351-0.ch061.

Al-Shater, M. M. (2019). Blockchain technology and the challenges of Islamic finance. Islamic economic studies. *The Islamic Institute for Research and Training*, *25*, 1–55.

Alidin, A. A., Ali-Wosabi, & Yusoff, Z. (2018). Overview of Blockchain implementation on Islamic finance: Saadiqin experience. *Cyber Resilience Conference (CRC)*. 1–2. Doi: 10.1109/CR.2018.8626822.

Berrahlia & Badreddine. (2019). The legal and regulatory framework for crowdfunding in the UK and France: A mechanism to support Islamic finance. 2.

Chong, F. H. L. (2021). Enhancing trust through digital Islamic finance and blockchain technology. *Qualitative Research in Financial Markets*, *13*(3), 328–341.

Enrique Estellés-Arolas & Fernando González-Ladrón-De-Guevara. (2012). Towards an integrated crowdsourcing definition. *Journal of Information Science*, *38*(2), 9–10.

Hastig, G. & Sodhi, M. (2019). Blockchain for supply chain traceability: Business requirements and critical success factors. *Production and Operations Management Journal*, *29*(4), 935–954.

Ibrahim, R. (2020). The effect of adopting blockchain technology Blockchain on reducing and upgrading the cost of banking services in Egyptian banks: A field study. *Journal of Accounting Fikr: Ain Shams University, Egypt*, *24*, 1–40.

Malak, S. & Bukhari, L. M. (2020). Islamic crowdfunding platforms between theory and practice with reference to some successful models in the Arab world. Economic Visions'. *Journal: El-Wadi University — Faculty of Economic, Commercial and Management Sciences, 10*, 251–267.

Mohamed, H. & Ali, H. (2018). *Blockchain, "Fintech, and Islamic Finance: Building the Future in the New Islamic Digital Economy"*. Berlin, Boston: De Gruyter. Doi: 10.1515/9781547400966.

Nkhal, A. M. S. (2020). The impact of using digital blockchain technology (Block Chain) on the accountability of the auditor. *Journal of Accounting Fikr — Ain Shams University, 24*, 743–801. Doi: 10.21608/atasu.2020.78522.

Nor, S. M., Abdul-Majid, M., & Esrati, S. N. (2021). The role of blockchain technology in enhancing Islamic social finance: The case of Zakah management in Malaysia. Foresight.

Puthal, D., Malik, N., Mohanty, S. P., Kougianos, E., & Das, G. (2018). Everything you wanted to know about the blockchain: Its promise, components, processes, and problems. *IEEE Consumer Electronics Journal, 7*(4), 6–14.

Rabbani, M. R., Khan, S., & Thalassinos, E. I. (2020). FinTech, blockchain and Islamic finance: An extensive literature review.

Roberto, B. & Pichler, F. (2016). *Crowdfunding for SMEs: A European Perspective.* Palgrave Macmillan Studies in Banking and Financial Institutions. https://www.worldcat.org/title/crowdfunding-for-smes-a-european-perspective/oclc/951434428.

Saloua, M. & Boukhari, L. (2020). Islamic crowd funding platforms between theory and practice with reference to some successful models in the Arab World. *Economic Roaa Journal*, University of Bordj Bou Arréridj — Algeria, https://www.asjp.cerist.dz/en/article/129910.

Sasy, H. F. A. (2019). Use of blockchain applications in developing waqf: A platform by Finterra companies as a modal study. *Journal of Islam in Asia, 16*(3), 141–160. Doi: 10.31436/jia.v16i3.907.

Sento, I. W. & Marina, A. (2015). Islamic crowdfunding (alternative funding solution, 1st World Islamic Social Congress (WISSC2015), Putrajaya, Malaysia.

Websites

https://arabiangazette.com/blockchain-solution-social-impact-finterra/ (Accessed on 10 July, 2021).

https://www.bbvaopenmind.com/en/economy/business/how-blockchain-is-revolutionizing-crowdfunding/ (Accessed on 10 July, 2021).

https://blockchain.oodles.io/blog/developing-advanced-crowdfunding-platform-blockchain/ (Accessed on 12 july, 2021)

https://www.kau.edu.sa/Files/320/Researches/72780_45937 (Accessed on 15 July, 2021).

https://ethiscrowd.com/ (Accessed on 25 July, 2021).

https://www.euromoney.com/learning/blockchain-explained/what-is-blockchain, (Accessed on 1 August, 2021).

http://pianoroll.it/update/block-apps-blockchain-8914, (Accessed on 5 August, 2021).

Part IV

Islamic Finance: Empirical Perspectives

https://doi.org/10.1142/9781800612426_0018

Chapter 18

Capital Adequacy in Conventional Versus Islamic Banks According to Basel III and Islamic Accounting Standards and Its Impact on Financial Stability: Empirical Evidence from the Kingdom of Saudi Arabia

Nahla Mohamad El Sayed Ibrahim, Mahmoud Mohamed Elsayed Ibrahim, and Mohamed Abd Elmoneim Abou ElSoud Zaied

Abstract

This study aims to compare capital adequacy and financial stability in Islamic and conventional Saudi banks and investigate the impact of capital adequacy on the financial stability of a bank. Our study uses the annual data of five conventional banks and four Islamic banks listed on the Saudi Stock Exchange for the period 2016–2020. The Z-score has been computed and used as the measure of the stability of listed Saudi Islamic and conventional banks for the period 2016–2020. This study uses ordinary least square regression to investigate the impact of capital adequacy on the financial stability of banks. The researchers adopt the development of research hypotheses in the light of the theory of stakeholders and the foundations of Islamic law. The findings indicated that, first, there are significant differences in the capital adequacy ratio between conventional and Islamic banks. This difference is due to the increase in the mean capital adequacy ratio of Islamic banks over conventional banks. Second, our result found significant differences in financial stability between conventional and Islamic banks. This difference is due to the increase in the mean of the Z-score for Islamic banks over conventional banks. Third, our result refers to significant negative impacts of capital adequacy ratio on financial stability. Our study applied to listed Saudi banks from 2016 to 2020. The empirical results of our study are very useful for supervisors, banks management, investors, bank customers, and policymakers. The results contribute to knowing the unexpected negative effects of increased capital adequacy and its negative impact on the bank's profits and the threat to financial stability, in addition to knowing the main indicators of capital adequacy and financial stability for Islamic and conventional banks in a way that helps bank supervisors, policymakers, and investors in rationalizing. Their decisions are specific to both Islamic and conventional banks, in addition to identifying the factors that help to enhance the financial stability process. This study is among a few studies that provide empirical evidence for the claim that the increase in capital adequacy rates is always one of the positive indicators to achieve financial stability, in addition to the great role of Islamic banks in achieving this. The study found a rejection of the validity of this claim and reached unexpected results.

Keywords: Financial Stability, *Z*-score, Capital Adequacy, Islamic versus Conventional Banks, IFSB, Basel III, Capital Structure, Bank Performance.

18.1 Introduction

Financial stability has recently become one of the most important issues of concern to many parties, as financial stability is the basis for the stability of the banking structure, and the banking sector plays a major role in countries through its large role in money formation, mobilization of domestic and foreign savings, and investment financing. Hence, achieving more growth and economic development and having a financially stable banking sector contributes to managing banking risks well, eliminating financial imbalances in light of exposure to market shocks, and thus reducing the impact of financial crises (Koske, 2020). Islamic banks are considered one of the main important components of the banking sector, which has seen a significant growth in the past two decades, especially after the financial crisis of 2007–2008 and their ability to withstand the effects of that crisis. For instance, estimates of the Islamic Financial Services Board (IFSB) indicate a growth in total assets from USD 195 million in 2000 to USD 2.19 trillion in 2018, this is expected to further increase to USD 2.71 trillion by 2021. The growth and great spread of

Islamic banks contributed to increasing the focus of academic efforts on researching the issue of financial stability for Islamic banks compared to other traditional banks (Safillah, 2021).

In the context of the banking sector facing many crises over different periods, the Basel Committee on Banking Supervision (BCBS) is interested in developing its rules and standards to limit the occurrence of such crises. After Basel I accord (1988) and Basel II accord (2004), a set of rules and guidelines was agreed upon for reforming the banking sector through good regulation and supervision and limiting the risks facing this sector. These rules and guidelines were represented in the issuance of Basel III, where the Basel Committee published the first version of this agreement in late 2009 in order to overcome the deficiencies in Basel I and Basel II, which were one of the main reasons for the occurrence of the global financial crisis in 2008. This was especially the case when facing credit and liquidity risks, when banks are required to keep a proper capital adequacy ratio with a high-quality capital base and supplementing this ratio with proper leverage ratios (Elbadry, 2016). The capital adequacy ratio measures a bank's capital to its risk-weighted assets. The capital-to-risk-weighted-assets ratio promotes strong capitalization and better financial resilience of banks throughout the world to resist economic and financial shocks and crises. Under Basel III, total regulatory capital will consist of the sum of the following elements: Tier 1 Capital (Common Equity Tier 1 and Additional Tier 1) and Tier 2, Common Equity Tier 1 which must be at least 4.5% of risk-weighted assets at all times. Tier 1 Capital must be at least 6.0% of risk-weighted assets at all times. Total Capital (Tier 1 Capital plus Tier 2 Capital) must be at least 8.0% of risk-weighted assets at all times; in addition, the capital conservation buffer of 2.5% of risk-weighted assets should apply at all times and has to be met with a capital of the highest quality: Common Equity Tier 1 (Basel Committee on Banking Supervision, 2011).

As a result of the rapid growth of Islamic banks in recent times, and because of the different nature of their work and financing formulas from those of conventional banks, and as they operate under products and tools that are compatible with Islamic Sharia, there was a need to integrate this type of bank into the national and global systems in the light of a set of rules and standards that reflect the specific operational features of Islamic finance (Archer *et al.*, 2010).

As a result, the IFSB, which is based in Kuala Lumpur, was officially inaugurated on November 3, 2002 and started operations on March 10, 2003. It serves as an international standard-setting body of regulatory and supervisory agencies that have a vested interest in ensuring the soundness and stability of the Islamic financial services industry, which is defined broadly to include banking, capital market, and insurance. In advancing this mission, the IFSB promotes the development of a prudent and transparent Islamic financial services industry through introducing new or adapting existing international standards consistent with Sharia principles, and recommends them for adoption, so the work of the IFSB complements that of the Basel Committee on Banking Supervision, International Organization of Securities Commissions, and the International Association of Insurance Supervisors (IFSB). With regard to the regulation of capital adequacy in Islamic banks, the Islamic Financial Services Board issued in 2005 Standard No. 2 entitled "Capital Adequacy Standard for Institution (Other than Insurance Institution) Offering Only Islamic Financial Services". The purpose of this standard is providing controls and requirements related to capital adequacy for institutions (other than insurance institutions) offering only Islamic financial services (IFS). In light of Basel II, this standard explains the minimum capital requirements for each type of credit risk and market risk for each of the financial instruments that comply with Islamic Sharia, these financial instruments include: murabahah and murabahah for the purchase ordered; salam and parallel salam; istisna and parallel istisna; ijarah and ijarah muntahia bittamleek; musharakah and diminishing musharakah; mudarabah; and sukuk held as investment. The minimum capital adequacy requirements for IIFS shall be a capital adequacy ratio (CAR) of not lower than 8% for total capital. Tier 2 capital is limited to 100% of Tier 1 capital (IFSB-2, 2005).

As a result of the financial and economic crisis that began in 2007, the global regulatory landscape witnessed several developments which resulted in the issuance of numerous publications by global standard-setting bodies such as the Financial Stability Board (FSB), the BCBS, the International Organization of Securities Commissions (IOSCO) and the International Association of Insurance Supervisors (IAIS). Among other things, these global regulatory reforms included the issuance by the BCBS of several documents collectively labelled Basel III, in line with the IFSB mandate to develop prudential standards and guidelines to promote the soundness and stability of the Islamic financial services industry (IFSI). In December 2013, the Islamic Financial Services Board issued Standard No. 15 entitled "Revised Capital Adequacy Standard for Institutions Offering Islamic Financial Services [Excluding Islamic Insurance (TAKĀFUL) Institutions and Islamic Collective Investment Schemes]". According to this standard, the eligible capital requirements for IIFS shall not be less than 8% of total RWA at all times. IIFS shall maintain CET1 capital of at least 4.5% of RWA at all times. Tier 1 capital (CET1 plus AT1) must be at least 6% of RWA at all times. Total capital (Tier 1 capital plus Tier 2 capital) must be at least 8% of RWA at all times. In addition, IIFS shall be required to maintain a capital conservation buffer and a countercyclical buffer, as stipulated by their respective supervisory authorities; this is consistent with what Basel III, which is indicated regardless of the different details of each type of Islamic financial instrument. The application of this standard began in January 2015 (IFSB-15, 2013).

Saudi Arabia is the largest market for Islamic finance globally and is poised to become a leader in the Islamic financial services industry on a global level. According to the report issued by the Islamic Research and Training Institute (IRTI) in 2020 entitled "Islamic Finance in Saudi Arabia: Leading the Way to Vision 2030", by the end of 2018, in total, Islamic financial assets in Saudi Arabia reached a remarkable USD 879.2 billion (SAR 3,297 billion). Furthermore, the return on assets of Islamic banks in Saudi Arabia consistently outperforms their peers in the G20, namely Indonesia and Turkey, as well as Malaysia, which makes Saudi Arabia the largest global Islamic finance market. Islamic banks are one of the main components of the banking system in the Kingdom of Saudi Arabia. According to this report, by the end of 2018, the overall assets of the financial system were valued at SAR 4.75 trillion. The banking sector is valued at SAR 2.36 trillion, out of which Islamic banks and windows account for 65%, and the conventional banks make up the remaining 35% (IRTI, 2020).

The previous introduction reflects the importance of Islamic finance, specifically Islamic banks, in the Saudi financial system. Therefore, this study aims to investigate the expected role of both Islamic and conventional banks in achieving financial stability in light of the capital adequacy rate maintained by these banks. This will be achieved by comparing the adequacy rate capital and financial stability in both Islamic and conventional banks and determining the impact of the capital adequacy ratio on financial stability in the banking sector.

Following the above discussion, the researchers conclude that there are some gaps in the general literature review regarding capital adequacy and financial stability, there is fairly extensive literature on financial stability and capital adequacy from several sources. However, it has focused on assessing the implications for the conventional banks and has not addressed the issues for Islamic banking, specifically in Saudi Arabia, which is no doubt understandable given the relative size of the Islamic banking sector compared to that of the conventional banks in Saudi Arabia. In addition, this study represents a good scientific contribution to addressing capital adequacy in light of the latest publications of the Basel Committee, which are the decisions of Basel III, in addition to the new IFSB 15 issued by the IFSB, which began its application in January 2015 and which adds scientific importance to the results of that study. This is in light of keeping pace with the international rules and guidelines regulating both Islamic and conventional banks. Also, this study covers the latest available period from 2015 to 2020, which includes the period of the COVID-19 pandemic, which can give greater strength to the results of the study by including the period of the COVID-19 crisis in terms of capital adequacy in both Islamic and conventional banks and its reflection on achieving financial stability.

18.2 Literature Review and Hypotheses Development

18.2.1 *Capital adequacy in conventional and Islamic banks*

Since the early 1980s, many developed and developing countries have faced many severe financial crises, the most important of which is the global financial crisis in 2007–2008 which resulted in the bankruptcy of many major banks. These banks were not expected to have this fate, for example, the bankruptcy of Lehman Brothers in the United States. The main reason for these crises is that banks face many risks such as credit risk, liquidity risk, market risk, operational risk, and other risks, which if not managed and controlled will affect the financial stability of the bank and reduce its ability to withstand shocks (Louati *et al.*, 2015). Since then, the BCBS has developed many standards for banking supervision and made several amendments to Basel II due to its inability to succeed in facing crises. In light of this, the BCBS in December 2010 issued a Basel III document entitled "A global regulatory framework for more resilient banks and banking systems". One of the main pillars on which Basel III relied is to strengthen the global capital framework, specifically the capital adequacy standard, by raising the quality and quantity of the regulatory capital base and enhancing the risk coverage of the capital framework. Then, the bank's regulatory capital will have greater quality than the above and strengthen the bank's ability to withstand shocks (BCBS, 2011).

The CAR is one of the important and main tools that is used to monitor and follow up the financial condition of the bank, regulators use the CAR as an important measure of the "safety and soundness" of banks because they consider capital a safety margin capable of absorbing potential losses, so, this ratio is given great attention by the international regulatory authorities (Mili *et al.*, 2017). Hence, the regulatory authorities, headed by the Basel Committee, from time to time determine the capital adequacy ratio and improve its quality in a manner sufficient to face most banking risks, such as credit, liquidity, and operational risks. This ratio is calculated according to total capital/total risk assets (Khan & Jabeen, 2011). Under Basel III, the focus was on strengthening the stability of the financial system. Specifically, enhancing the quality and quantity of capital requirements by increasing the Tier-1 capital requirements to 6% from 4%, and adding common equity requirements from Level 1 (CET1) at 4.5%, and in addition applies the capital conservation buffer of 2.5% of risk-weighted assets at all times and has to be met with capital of the highest quality. Total Capital (Tier 1 Capital plus Tier 2 Capital) must be at least 8.0% of risk-weighted assets at all times. Basel III also focused on enhancing risk coverage more comprehensively than Basel II. Banks will be subject to a countercyclical buffer that varies between zero and 2.5% to total risk-weighted assets to reducing procyclicality, supplementing the risk-based capital requirement with a leverage ratio, introducing a global liquidity standard, liquidity coverage ratio (LCR) and net stable funding ratio

(NSFR). All of these prudential procedures contribute to enhancing the safety and stability of the banking sector (BCBS, 2011).

With the recent spread of the phenomenon of the growth of Islamic banks, the interest has also increased in these banks for them to maintain sufficient capital requirements to face the risks in light of the diversity of Islamic financial instruments. The Islamic banking system, mainly the investment loss and profit-sharing, fosters the investor's participation in equity, which promotes the assiduity in the investment management and proper monitoring. Furthermore, the other Islamic financial mechanisms (such as murabahah, ijara, and istisna) require the involvement of investors in the real economy; as a result, financial transactions are fully backed by real assets (Louati *et al.*, 2015). On the other hand, such instruments change the nature of risks that Islamic banks face compared to conventional banks. For example, credit risk in murabahah contracts arises in the form of the counterparty defaulting in paying the debts in full and on time. Non-payment may be the result of external reasons or willful default, and in Islam, the reasons for that default must be determined as to whether they are intentional or not because Islamic banks do not allow debt restructuring on the basis of compensation unless the default is willful Therefore, the credit risks faced by face Islamic banks here may be larger in light of the asymmetry of information to determine the real reasons and the participation for the customer in the profit and loss in such contracts. Therefore, we can say that Islamic banks may face greater risks than conventional banks in light of the different nature of their work, which requires more quality of capital adequacy requirements in line with the nature of the work of Islamic banks (Ahmed & Khan, 2007). As a result, the regulatory authorities interested in Islamic finance have developed a set of standards that regulate Islamic finance in light of the requirements of Islamic law, foremost among them Accounting and Auditing Organization for Islamic Financial Institution (AAOIFI), established in 1991 and based in Bahrain. In addition, the IFSB, which was officially opened in 2003 in Kuala Lumpur, aims to promote and enhance the soundness and stability of the Islamic financial services industry by issuing global prudential standards and guiding principles for the industry, broadly defined to include banking, capital markets, and insurance sectors.

The IFSB explains and determines the requirements for Islamic banks capital adequacy through Standard No. 2 issued in 2005 entitled "Capital Adequacy Standard for Institution (Other than Insurance Institution)". Offering only Islamic financial services, after that, the IFSB supplemented IFSB-2 with a number of other publications (March 2008: GN-1, January 2009: IFSB-7, December 2010: GN-2, December 2010: GN-3 March 2011: GN-4), and in subsequent years, this was related to the calculation of capital adequacy requirements in IIFS in order either to cover additional products and services offered by IIFS or to provide further guidance on the application of various aspects of the current IFSB standards. After the global crisis in 2007–2008 and Basel III was issued, and in line with the IFSB mandate to develop prudential SAGs to promote the soundness and stability of the IFSI, the council of the IFSB approved the a revision of IFSB-2 and IFSB-7 and the formation of the Revised Capital Adequacy Standard Working Group and issue Standard No IFSB-15, issued in December 2013, entitled "Revised Capital Adequacy Standard for Institutions Offering Islamic Financial Services [Excluding Islamic Insurance (TAKĀFUL) Institutions and Islamic Collective Investment Schemes". This standard aims to assist the IIFS and their supervisory authorities in the implementation of a capital adequacy framework that will ensure effective coverage of risk exposures of the IIFS and allocation of appropriate capital to cover these risks, thus enhancing the resilience of the IFS. The eligible capital requirements for IIFS shall be not less than 8% of total RWA at all times, this requirement is consistent with Basel III (IFSB-15, 2013).

Many studies in the literature on IF have examined the unique situation of Islamic banking, specifically capital adequacy, such as Smaoui *et al.* (2020), who investigated the determinants of capital ratios in contemporary Islamic banking. The results show that Islamic banks capital ratios are persistent over time. In addition, protection of shareholder rights seems to have a positive and robust effect on Islamic banks capital holdings, whereas bank size, deposit structure, and bank competition are significantly negatively related to Islamic banks capital ratios. In regard to the impact of capital adequacy on the financial performance of banks, many studies such as Al-Kayed *et al.* (2014), Hafeez *et al.* (2018), and Qayyum and Noreen (2019) have examined the effect of capital structure on Islamic banks' performance, and studies indicate that Islamic banks' performance responds positively to an increase in capital ratio. Boukhatem and Djelassi (2020) examined the liquidity risk of Islamic and conventional banks in the Saudi banking system, the result shows that the liquidity risk indicators of Islamic banks are affected differently from those of conventional banks. For example, one indicator for liquidity risk used in this study was the loan-to-deposit indicator. Larger Islamic banks have, on average, a narrower funding gap than their smaller counterparts. In addition, larger conventional banks have more vulnerable funding structures than larger Islamic banks. Finally, Islamic and conventional banks that are more oriented toward traditional intermediation activities (i.e., financing/loans) have wider funding gaps. Bita *et al.* (2019) examined efficiency in Islamic versus conventional banking; the role of capital and liquidity findings support the view that the constraints imposed by Sharia law may widen the efficiency gap between the two bank types at the expense of Islamic banks. In addition, the efficiency of conventional banks not only depends on bank capital and liquidity but also on the level of bank efficiency, while the relationship is inconclusive for Islamic banks. These findings refer to higher capital and liquidity buffers serving as a constraint on policymakers and which may function very differently depending on the level of bank efficiency regard facing the crisis in 2008. Zopounidis *et al.* (2017) and Wahab *et al.* (2017) compared the stability and efficiency for Islamic and conventional banks pre and post crisis 2008, the result refers to Islamic banking having more efficacy and stability during the 2008 crisis. Louati *et al.* (2015) suggested that capital regulatory requirements have a significant impact on the credit behavior of Islamic and conventional banks. Korbi and Bougatef (2017) examined regulatory capital and stability of Islamic and conventional banks in the Middle East and North Africa region. The comparative analysis reveals that Islamic banks seem to be less stable than their conventional peers. Concerning the determinants of bank stability, the findings suggest that the regulatory capital represents the primordial factor that reinforces the soundness of banking systems. Conversely, Aldeen *et al.* (2020) argue that Islamic banks were better in terms of capital adequacy, efficiency, risk management, and liquidity.

The researchers in the development of H1 also based their work on Islamic Sharia, where the nature of work in Islamic banks is based on Islamic Sharia in the first place and on which the various foundations of financing in Islamic banks are based on traditional banks, where the work of Islamic banks is based on participation in profits and losses, unlike traditional banks that depend on interest without looking at profit and loss (Salman & Nawaz, 2018). This may expose Islamic banks to greater risks than traditional banks, so the researchers put their hypothesis related to comparing capital adequacy in conventional and Islamic banks that Islamic banks will perform more hedging and have capital adequacy and higher money compared to traditional banks.

Following the above discussion, we predict that there are significant differences between Islamic and conventional banking capital adequacy. Hence, we formulate the following hypothesis:

H1. There are no significant differences in the capital adequacy ratio between conventional and Islamic banks.

18.2.2 *Financial stability in conventional and Islamic banks*

The interest in the issue of financial stability has increased recently, especially after the events of the global financial crisis in 2008 and its negative effects on all countries of the world, which called for focusing attention on issues of financial stability. Broadly, according to the IMF (2004), financial stability can be thought of in terms of the financial system's ability: (a) to facilitate both an efficient allocation of economic resources — both spatially, especially inter temporally — and the effectiveness of other economic processes (such as wealth accumulation, economic growth, and ultimately social prosperity); (b) to assess, price, allocate, and manage financial risks; and (c) to maintain its ability to perform these key functions — even when affected by external shocks or by a build-up of imbalances — primarily through self-corrective mechanisms. Financial stability can be also defined as the smooth operation of all segments of the financial system (Ramlall, 2018). Financial stability is also defined as a situation where financial shocks could be resisted by a financial system that consists of financial markets, intermediaries, and infrastructures (Saha & Dutta, 2021). Ramlall (2018) suggested that there is a three-pronged approach to financial stability for financial markets, which are the ability to allocate resources efficiently, ability to manage risks, and ability to absorb shocks. The World Bank (2015) suggests that a stable financial system is capable of efficiently allocating resources, assessing and managing financial risks, maintaining employment levels close to the economy's natural rate, and eliminating relative price movements of real or financial assets that will affect monetary stability or employment levels, instability, and that the system will absorb the shocks primarily via self-corrective mechanisms, preventing adverse events from having a disruptive effect on the real economy or on other financial systems. The importance of financial stability is due not only to price stability but also to its significant role in achieving sustainable development of the economy because financial instability entails high costs for the economy, as the fluctuations of price variables in financial markets increase and financial institutions or companies may go bankrupt. In addition, economic development can be limited at such a time, as economic actors find it difficult to make rational decisions and the efficiency of resource allocation decreases (Bank of Korea). The banking sector is considered one of the main components of the financial system in any country. Hence, achieving financial stability for the banking sector contributes to achieving financial stability at the macro level. Therefore, this study is concerned with studying the levels of financial stability of Islamic and conventional banks.

Many studies in the literature have investigated financial stability in Islamic and conventional banks. The study of Sarpong-Kumankoma *et al.* (2020) aimed to analyze the potential implications of economic freedom and competition for bank stability. Applying to 139 banks across 11 Sub-Saharan African (SSA) countries during the period 2006–2012, the results show evidence of the competition-fragility hypothesis in SSA banking but suggests that beyond a set threshold, increases in market power may also be damaging to bank stability. Financial freedom has a negative effect on bank stability, suggesting that banks operating in environments with greater financial freedom generally tend to be less stable or riskier. The authors also find evidence of a conditional effect of economic freedom on the competition–stability relationship, implying that bank failure is more likely to occur in countries with greater economic freedom but with low competition in the banking sector. Nair and Anand (2020) probed into the employability of monetary policy as a tool to achieve financial stability by comparing between interest rates obtained from the standard Taylor rule and asset price augmented Taylor rule in the Indian context. The results suggest that targeting asset prices can be one of the effective ways to contain financial instabilities and consequent economic slumps. Barra and Zotti (2019) explored the relationship between bank market power and stability of financial institutions in Italy. The empirical evidence shows that the inefficiency of financial stability is found to be U-shaped related with respect to the measure of market power. Bank size is an essential factor in explaining the relationship between bank market power and risk-taking. Cooperative banks have fewer incentives to gain market power to better perform in terms of risks. Lassoued (2018) examined the relationship between corporate governance and financial stability of the Islamic banking institutions in Malaysia. The study found that the percentage of independent members in the board of directors has a significant positive impact on the financial stability of the IBS. However, the Sharia board size and the size of the board are found to have no influence on financial stability. Safiullah (2021) examined the financial stability efficiency of Islamic and conventional banks from 28 countries over the period 2003–2018. The result shows that Islamic banks have 5.3% higher stability efficiency compared to conventional banks. This is consistent with the study by Fadoua and Brahim (2020), where it was found that Islamic banks outperformed conventional banks in the MENA region concerning capitalization efficiency and profitability during the financial crisis. On the contrary, Abrar *et al.* (2018) analyzed the financial stability of Islamic versus conventional banks in Pakistan from 2012 to 2016. The result showed that, first, conventional banks are more financially stable than Islamic banks. Second, large conventional banks are more financially stable than large Islamic banks.

The researchers also rely on developing H2 on the basis of Islamic Sharia, and that it is more of a hedging risk due to the different nature of its work from traditional banks and its participation in most of its business on profit and loss sharing, and therefore, it will maintain higher rates of capital adequacy. Islamic Sharia is also characterized by the presence of an ethical dimension in all aspects of its work, which researchers expect to achieve greater financial stability for Islamic banks compared to conventional banks (Mansour *et al.*, 2015).

Following the above discussion, we predict that there are significant differences between the financial stability of Islamic and conventional banks. Hence, we formulate the following hypothesis:

H2. There are no significant differences in financial stability between conventional and Islamic banks.

18.2.3 *Capital adequacy and financial stability*

The banking sector is one of the main sectors of the financial system of any country, and this sector plays a vital role in achieving financial stability for both developed and developing countries, hence the need for continuous monitoring and implementation of appropriate policy measures to enable the sector to carry out its functions effectively and efficiently (Igbinosa & Naimo, 2020). Capital adequacy is considered one of the basic criteria that expresses the efficiency and ability of banks to maximize their returns and face and control banking risks. Capital adequacy contributes to improving the pricing of banking services, maximizing bank returns, and developing the necessary procedures to face risks, in a way which reflects on strengthening the competitive position (AlAli, 2019). Moreover, applying minimum capital adequacy ratios according to Basel III serves to promote the stability and efficiency of the financial system by reducing the likelihood of banks becoming insolvent (Ogere *et al.*, 2013). Given the importance of the issue of achieving financial stability at the world level, especially after the global financial crisis, many regulatory agencies led by the BCBS and the FSB are constantly developing their issuance and guidance in a way that enhances the achievement of financial stability at the global level to reduce falling into more crises.

A few studies in the literature have investigated the relationship between capital adequacy and financial stability in Islamic and conventional banks. Kombo and Njuguna (2016) investigated the effects of the Basel III framework on capital adequacy requirement in commercial banks in Kenya. The findings show that capital adequacy requirement is important in commercial banks because it leads financial stability in the Kenyan economy, improves credit risk management techniques as poor credit risk management requires more capital and leads to reduced vulnerability to liquidity shocks due to sound capitalization policies being implemented under the Basel III framework. Rupeika-Apoga *et al.* (2020) examined the determinants of bank stability in a small post-transition economy, based on the case of Latvia. The result found a positive significant relationship between capital adequacy and bank stability. Mohamad *et al.* (2018) examined the impact of characteristics of Islamic and conventional bank on the stability of Malaysia banking sector, the result indicated that the characteristics of a bank do influence a bank's performance. There are significant differences in financial ratios between Islamic and conventional banking, the findings also indicated that only 8 Islamic banks and 11 conventional banks are highly stable banking institutions in Malaysia.

Daoud and Kammoun (2020) researched the determinants of financial stability in Islamic banking established in 22 counties from 2010 to 2014, the result indicated that the capital ratios (non-risk-weighted capital ratio and risk-weighted capital ratio), banks' size, loans to total assets, total deposit to total assets, and overhead cost to total assets represent important predictors of bank stability in the Islamic banking industry. Hossain and Imam (2017) found that Islamic banks are financially more stable than conventional banks, and the presence of Islamic banks increases the stability of all banks in the system, including their conventional peers. On the other hand, Odour *et al.* (2017) found that increased capital beef-up significantly increases financial instability in Africa (except in big banks) implying that higher capital requirements did not make African banks safer.

The researchers adopted the stakeholders theory in developing the main hypothesis of study, H3, which is related to the impact of capital adequacy ratio on financial stability. The stakeholders theory, which was developed originally by Freeman (1984), is used as a managerial instrument (Klimczak, 2007). The main idea of this theory is based on the fact that the organization is based on a network of relationships among various stakeholders, and then in the light of this theory, managers seek to create value for stakeholders by achieving a kind of harmonization and balance between all stakeholders and not favoring one stakeholder category over another (Horisch *et al.*, 2020). This theory explains the vision adopted by researchers from the perspective that capital adequacy can contribute to achieving financial stability, as capital adequacy is one of the basic indicators that expresses the ability of institutions to hedge against the risks that they may face, as it is concerned with achieving a kind of balance between lenders and creditors who wish to have a guarantee against potential losses, and shareholders who focus on the return on capital. This contributes to achieving financial stability for institutions.

Following the above discussion, we predict that there are significant impacts of the capital adequacy ratio on financial stability. Hence, we formulate the following hypothesis:

H3. There is no significant impact of the capital adequacy ratio on financial stability.

18.3 Data and Methodology

18.3.1 *Data and sample*

According to the objective of the study, the differences between conventional and Islamic banks are related to both capital adequacy and financial stability, in addition to studying the impact of capital adequacy in both conventional and Islamic banks and applying this to banks in the Kingdom of Saudi Arabia, the data were collected from a sample of listed Islamic and conventional banks on the Saudi Stock Exchange. All data have been collected from "TADAWL" website as this is the formal website of Saudi stock market. The Saudi banking system is composed of a total of 11 banks, including two distinguished groups, Islamic and conventional. Four banks were classified as Islamic banks, according to the non-interest financing practice of this group of banks, The other seven banks are conventional banks (Ghassan & Taher, 2019). The sample size consists of four Islamic banks and five conventional banks listed on the Saudi financial market for which data are available for analysis. The period is from 2016 to 2020, as this period is considered the most recent period for the study, in addition to the start of the IFSB 15 application starting from January 2015.

18.3.2 *Variables measurements*

18.3.2.1 *Dependent variable (Financial stability)*

To measure banks' financial stability, a wide range of indicators were devised such as Z-score, probability of bankruptcy, a standard deviation of return on assets, NPL ratio, and so on, among which the Z-score is very common and used by many researchers (Barra & Zotti, 2020; Sarpong-Kumankoma *et al.*, 2020; Igbinosa & Naimo, 2020; Saha & Dutta, 2021). So, we use the Z-score to measure banks' financial stability as follows:

$$Z\text{-score}_{it} = \text{ROA}_{it} + \text{E/TA}_{it}\, \sigma\text{ROA}_{it}.$$

Here, ROA is the return on assets, E/TA refers to the bank equity to total assets ratio, and σROA represents the standard deviation of return on assets, Z-score measures the insolvency risk of a bank; a larger value indicates a lesser risk of bankruptcy and higher bank stability.

18.3.2.2 *Independent variable (Capital adequacy)*

Capital adequacy in this study was measured by the capital adequacy ratio. According to Basel III, the capital adequacy ratio is calculated by dividing a bank's capital by its risk-weighted assets. The capital used to calculate the capital adequacy ratio is divided into two tiers: (BCBS, 2011):

$$\text{CAR} = \text{Tier 1 Capital} + \text{Tier 2 Capital Risk Weighted Assets (RWA)}.$$

So, we can investigate this independent variable in more detail as follows:

- Tier 1 Capital Ratio: wish calculated by dividing Tier 1 Capital/ Risk-weighted Assets.
- Tier 2 Capital Ratio: wish calculated by dividing Tier 2 Capital/ Risk-weighted Assets.
- CAR Ratio: wish calculated by dividing Tier 1 Capital + Tier 2 Capital/Risk-weighted Assets.

The researcher predicts Ratio Tier 1 more sensitively to financial stability compared with Tier 2 Ratio because Tier-1 capital is used to absorb losses and does not require a bank to cease operations. Tier-1 capital is the capital that is permanently and easily available to cushion losses suffered by a bank without it being required to stop operating.

18.3.2.3 *Control variables*

A control variable is anything that is held constant or limited in a research study. It is a variable that is not of interest to the study's aims but is controlled because it could influence the outcomes. Many literature reviews suggest using many variables as a control variables for financial stability. Raouf and Ahmed (2020) suggest that gross domestic product (GDP) growth rate is used to control economic growth, which is also used by Saha and Dutta, (2020), and Korbi and Bougatef (2017). Alshubiri (2017) suggests that bank size, which is defined as the natural logarithm of total assets, is one of the most important determinants of financial stability. Rashid *et al.* (2017) and Salamat and Al-Kharouf (2021) argue that the inflation rate is considered one of the important determinants of financial stability. Chauhan and Ramesha (2016) argue that the interest rate is one of the most important financial stability determinants. Igbinosa and Naimo (2020) suggest that assets quality ratio and liquidity bank can be used as a control variable for financial stability. Assets quality ratio can be calculated as ratio of non-performing loans to gross or total loans, where liquidity bank measures the ability of banks to meets its short term maturing obligations. It is captured here LCR ratio according to Basel III.

Following the above discussion, we suggest using the following control variables:

- Bank size
- Product growth rate (GDP)
- Inflation rate
- Interest rate
- Islamic financial institutions (IFIs)
- Assets quality ratio.

In general, we used financial stability (FS) in this study as a dependent variable and CAR as an independent variable to investigate the impact of CAR on FS with controls variables according to

Table 18.1. Variables and definitions.

Variables	Abbreviations	Definitions
Dependent Variable		
Financial stability	Z-score	$Z\text{-score} = \frac{\text{ROA}_{it}+\text{E/TA}_{it}}{\sigma\text{ROA}_{it}}$
Independent Variables		
Tier 1 adequacy ratio	T1AR	Tier 1/Risk Weighted Assets
Tier 2 adequacy ratio	T2AR	Tier 2/Risk Weighted Assets
Capital adequacy ratio	CAR	Tier 1+ Tier 2/Risk Weighted Assets
Control Variables		
Bank size	Size	Natural logarithm of total assets
Product growth rate	GDP_ratio	Gross domestic product growth rate
Inflation rate	INF	Inflation rate
Interest rate	INRate	One year market interest rates (nominal)
Islamic financial institution	IFIs	An indicator variable that captures whether the bank is an IFIs, with a value of 1 for bank classified as IFIs, and 0 otherwise.
Assets quality ratio	ASQ	Ratio of non-performing loans to gross or total loans, NPL/TL

the literature review. Table 18.1 explains all variables abbreviations, and their definitions are as follows.

18.3.3 *Research model*

The objectives of this study are comparing the difference between Islamic and conventional banks and capital adequacy and financial stability. These goals can be achieved through by testing hypotheses H1 and H2. We can do that through showing descriptive statistics and using appropriate statistical techniques to determine the difference between two independent samples. These techniques depend on the availability or non-availability of the conditions of the parametric tests; in the event that the conditions of the parametric tests are available, one of the techniques of the parametric tests can be used to compare the differences in the case of two independent samples, where a test can be used independent sample T-test. However, in the absence of those conditions, one of the techniques is nonparametric tests which can be used to compare differences between two independent samples such as the Mann–Witney test and Kolmogrov–Smirnov Z-test. The impact of CAR on FS can be predicted through testing H3 by using multiple regression analysis.

Figure 18.1 indicates a summary of the theoretical model.

The following regression equation was used to investigate the impact of CAR for Islamic and conventional banks on bank financial stability:

$$\begin{aligned} Z\text{-score} = {} & \text{B0} + \text{B1(T1AR)} + \text{B2(T2AR)} + \text{B3(CAR)} + \text{B4(Size)} \\ & + \text{B5(GDP)} + \text{B6(INF)} + \text{B7(INRate)} + \text{B8(ASQ)} \\ & + \text{B9(IFIs)} + \text{it}, \end{aligned}$$

where Z-score: refers to bank financial stability, T1AR: Tier 1 adequacy ratio, T2AR: Tier 2 adequacy ratio, CAR: capital adequacy ratio (Tier 1 + Tier 2/RWA), Size: natural logarithm of total assets, GDP: product growth rate, INF: inflation rate, INRate: interest rate, IFIs: an indicator variable that captures whether the bank is an IFIs, with a value of 1 for bank classified as IFIs, and 0 otherwise, ASQ: assets quality ratio.

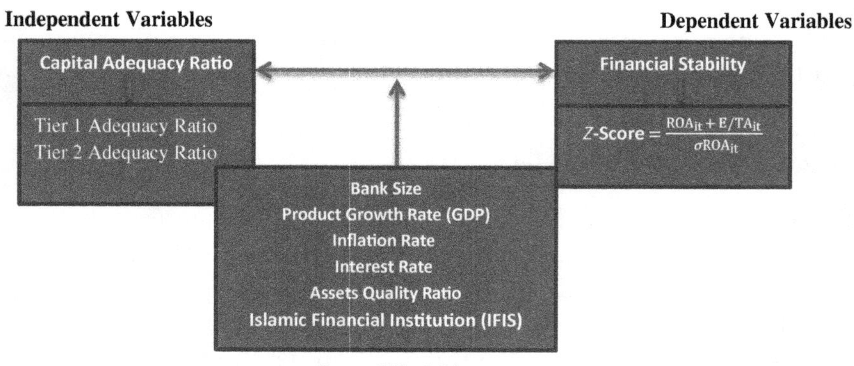

Figure 18.1. Conceptual model.

18.4 Empirical Results

18.4.1 *Descriptive statistics*

Table 18.2 reports descriptive statistics for the variables used in this study at the level of all banks as a whole and at the level of both conventional and Islamic banks. Descriptive statistics at the level of banks as a whole indicate that the average capital adequacy amounted to 19.98%, where the average capital adequacy of Tier 1 (T1AR) was 17.65% and the average capital adequacy of Tier 2 (T2AR) was 2.33%. This indicates that the Saudi banks have maintained a CAR higher than what was approved by the BCBS (Basel III) in a way that provides the bank with sufficient capital in the event of any shocks at the level of Islamic banks the average capital adequacy of Islamic banks was relatively higher than that of conventional banks. The capital adequacy of Islamic banks is 20.68% and in conventional banks is 19.42%, and this is reflected in the enhancement of capital adequacy levels in the Saudi banking system.

With regard to the financial stability of the banking sector in the Kingdom of Saudi Arabia, expressed in Z-score, descriptive statistics in Table 18.2 indicate that the average value at the level of banks as a whole was 27.60%, a value that indicates that Saudi banks have a good level of financial stability, and statistics indicate and also that the average value of this value in Islamic banks is higher than that of conventional banks, where the average value of Z-score in Islamic banks was 31.51%, while it reached 24.48% in conventional banks, and this indicates that Islamic banks have a better level of financial stability than conventional banks. Figures 18.2–18.7 also explain capital adequacy and financial stability in Islamic and conventional banks.

Figure 18.2 illustrates the comparison of the average CAR in both conventional banks and Islamic banks and for banks overall, and also through the figure, it is clear that the average CAR of Islamic banks is higher than that of conventional banks, where the average capital adequacy in Islamic banks was 20.68% and 19.4% in conventional banks.

Figure 18.3 shows a comparison of the average value of Z-score as an indicator of financial stability in both conventional banks and Islamic banks and for banks overall, and through the figure, it is

Table 18.2. Descriptive statistics.

Variables	Valid N (listwise)	Mean	Minimum	Maximum	Std. deviation	Range	Variance
All Bank							
T1AR	45	17.6502	12.92	22.93	2.26407	10.01	5.126
T2AR	45	2.3331	0.78	5.26	1.30869	4.48	1.713
CAR	45	19.9833	16.47	27.48	2.11020	11.01	4.453
Z-score	45	27.6066	1.41	133.61	26.25680	132.20	689.419
GDP_Ratio	45	−0.0820	−4.10	2.43	2.31173	6.53	5.344
INF	45	1.2960	−2.09	3.50	2.34481	5.59	5.498
INRate	45	2.1500	1.75	2.60	0.35323	0.85	0.125
ASQ	45	0.0229	0.01	0.19	0.03035	0.18	0.001
Size	45	8.2061	7.28	9.54	0.40709	2.25	0.166
IFIs	45	0.4444	0.00	1.00	0.50252	1.00	0.253
Islamic Bank							
T1AR	20	17.9745	12.92	22.93	2.95596	10.01	8.738
T2AR	20	2.7100	1.00	5.26	1.73550	4.26	3.012
CAR	20	20.6845	17.33	27.48	2.51828	10.15	6.342
Z-score	20	31.5120	1.68	50.52	15.83335	48.84	250.695
GDP_Ratio	20	−0.0820	−4.10	2.43	2.34528	6.53	5.500
INF	20	1.2960	−2.09	3.50	2.37884	5.59	5.659
INRate	20	2.1500	1.75	2.60	0.35836	0.85	0.128
ASQ	20	0.0184	0.01	0.12	0.02414	0.11	0.001
Size	20	8.1550	7.73	9.54	0.43212	1.81	0.187
IFIs		1.0000	1.00	1.00	0.00000	0.00	0.000
Conventional Bank							
T1AR	25	17.3908	14.62	20.56	1.52403	5.94	2.323
T2AR	25	2.0316	0.78	3.54	0.73646	2.76	0.542
CAR	25	19.4224	16.47	23.03	1.55105	6.56	2.406
Z-score	25	24.4822	1.41	133.61	32.28916	132.20	1042.590
GDP_Ratio	25	−0.0820	−4.10	2.43	2.33304	6.53	5.443
INF	25	1.2960	−2.09	3.50	2.36642	5.59	5.600
INRate	25	2.1500	1.75	2.60	0.35649	0.85	0.127
ASQ	25	0.0265	0.01	0.19	0.03460	0.18	0.001
Size	25	8.2470	7.28	9.28	0.38997	2.00	0.152
IFIs	25	0.0000	0.00	0.00	0.00000	0.00	0.000

clear that the average financial stability of Islamic banks is higher than that of conventional banks, where the value of Z-score in Islamic banks reached 31.5% and 24.48% in conventional banks.

Figure 18.4 shows a comparison of the average capital adequacy at the level of all the banks of the study sample, where the largest capital adequacy ratio for Bank AlJazira was 23.3%, followed by

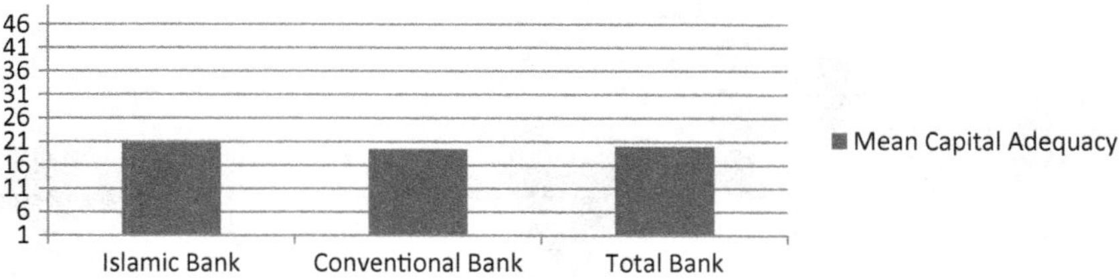

Figure 18.2. Means of capital adequacy in Islamic and conventional banks and whole banks.

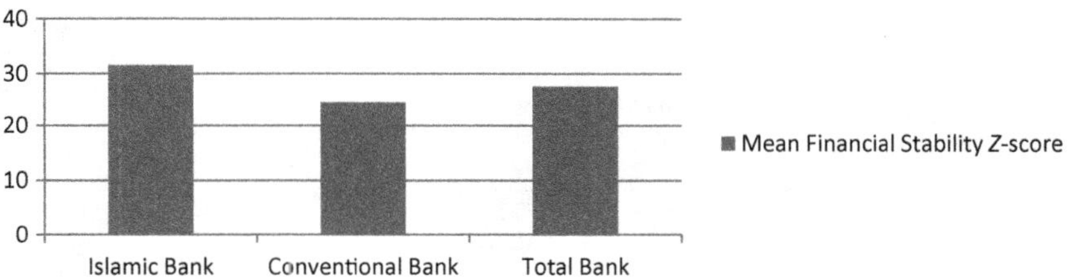

Figure 18.3. Means of financial stability in Islamic and conventional banks and whole banks.

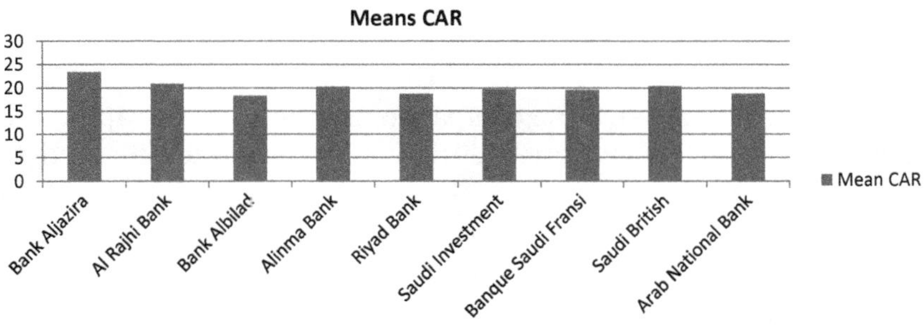

Figure 18.4. Means of capital adequacy of the studied sample banks.

Al Rajihi Bank 20.87%, down to the lowest CAR for Bank Albilad, which reached 18.35%.

Figure 18.5 shows a comparison of the average value of the Z-score as an indicator of financial stability at the level of all the banks of the study sample, where the largest value of financial stability belonged to Alinma Bank and its value was 46.7, followed by Bank Albilad with 44.35, to reach the lowest value of financial stability for Al Rajhi Bank and its value was 9.85.

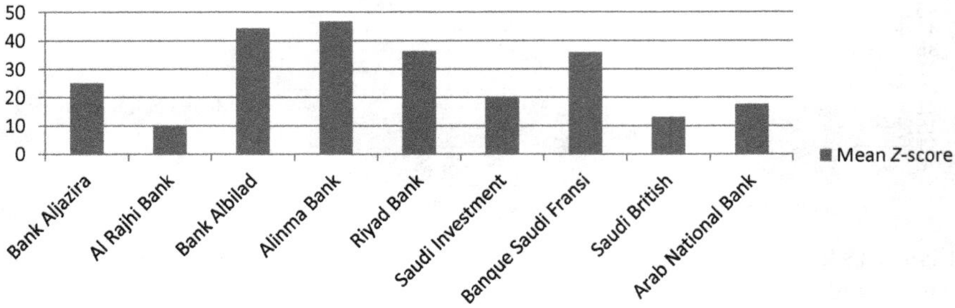

Figure 18.5. Means of financial stability of the studied sample banks measured by Z-score.

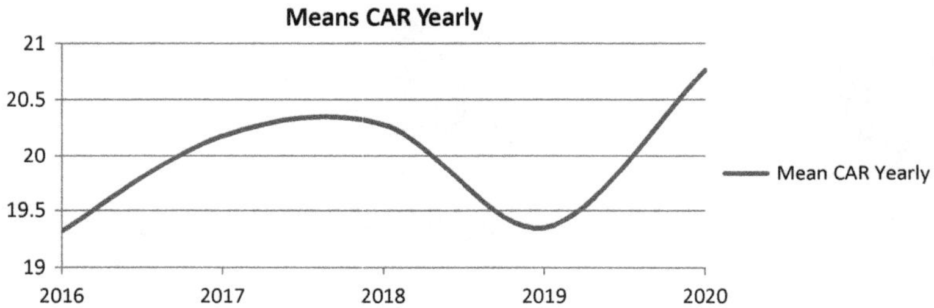

Figure 18.6. Means of capital adequacy during the period of study from 2016 to 2020.

Figure 18.6 illustrates the comparison of the average capital adequacy during the study period 2015–2016, where they reached the largest value of the average capital adequacy of 20.76% in 2020, followed by the year 2018, where the average value of capital adequacy reached 20.28%, and the lowest value average capital adequacy was 18.09% in 2016.

Figure 18.7 shows a comparison of the average value of the Z-score as an indicator of financial stability during the study period 2015–2016, where the highest value of the mean Z-score was 35.69 in 2017, followed by 2019 where the value of the Z-score was 35, and the lowest value of the mean Z-score was 18.88 in 2018.

18.4.2 *Result of tests of H1*

In this section, we discuss the result of test H1 related to the differences in the capital adequacy ratio between conventional and Islamic

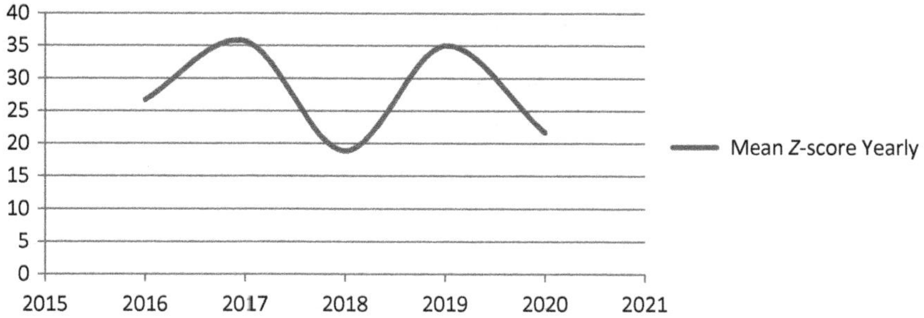

Figure 18.7. Means of financial stability during the period of study from 2016 to 2020 measured by Z-score.

Table 18.3. Group statistics.

Bank	Islamic/ conventional	*N*	Mean	Std. deviation	Std. error mean
CAR	Islamic	20	20.6845	2.51828	0.56310
	Conventional	25	19.4224	1.55105	0.31021

banks. To determine the appropriate statistical test to determine the differences between two independent samples to verify the validity of this hypothesis, we use the Kolmogorov–Smirnov to test normality distribution for this variable. The p-value for this test is equal to 0.117 (p-value > 0.05). Thus, we accepted the normality distribution for this variable. As a result, we use here one of the appropriate parametric tests to test this hypothesis, the parametric test suitable to determine the difference between two independent samples is independent-samples t-test.

Tables 18.3 and 18.4 present the result of the independent-sample t-test. Table 18.3 provides basic information about the group comparisons, the main result in this table regarding capital adequacy refers to Islamic banks ($\text{mean} = 20.68, \text{SD} = 2.51$) and conventional banks ($\text{mean} = 19.42, \text{SD} = 1.55$), this means that CAR in Islamic banks is greater than that of conventional banks, but both of them are in compliance with Basel III CAR. Looking at the results of Table 18.4, the independent-samples test displays the results most relevant to the independent samples t-test. There are two parts that provide

Table 18.4. Independent samples test.

Assumption		Levene's test for equality of variances		*T*-test for equality of means						
									95% confidence interval of the difference	
		F	Sig.	*t*	*df*	Sig. (2-tailed)	Mean difference	Std. error difference	Lower	Upper
CAR	Equal variances assumed	2.662	0.110	2.066	43	0.045	1.26210	0.61077	0.03036	2.49384
	Equal variances not assumed			1.963	30.088	0.059	1.26210	0.64290	–0.05071	2.57491

different pieces of information: Levene's test for equality of variances and t-test for equality of means. The p-value for Levene's test > 0.05 equals 0.110 (not significant), so we accepted null of Levene's test, thus we depending on equal variances assumed" output in Table 18.4, this output reported that $t = 2.066$, $df = 43$, sig. (2-tailed) $= 0.045$, this result refers to the significant difference between Islamic and conventional banks CAR, where p-value ≤ 0.05, therefore we rejected null hypothesis H1 which states that there are no significant differences in the CAR between conventional and Islamic banks and accepted alternative hypothesis which refer to that there are significant differences in the CAR between conventional and Islamic banks. This difference is due to the increase in the mean CAR of Islamic banks over conventional banks. The results are consistent with previous study results (Louati *et al.*, 2015; Dodoev, 2018; El-Ansary *et al.*, 2019).

18.4.3 *Result of tests of H2*

In this section, we discuss the result of test H2 related to the differences in financial stability between conventional and Islamic banks. To determine the appropriate statistical test to determine the differences between two independent samples to verify the validity of this hypothesis, we use Kolmogorov–Smirnov to test normality distribution for this variable. The p-value for this test is equal to 0.000 (p-value $\leq$ 0.05). Thus, we rejected the normality distribution for this variable. As a result, we use here one of the appropriate non-parametric tests to test this hypothesis. The non-parametric test suitable to determine the difference between two independent samples is Mann–Whitney test.

Table 18.5 presents the result of the Mann–Whitney test regarding test H2 related to the differences in financial stability measured by Z-score between conventional and Islamic banks, the result shows that ranks for Islamic banks are mean rank $= 28.45$ and sum of rank $= 569$, and the ranks of conventional banks are mean rank $= 18.64$ and sum of rank $= 466$. These results indicate that the mean of financial stability in Islamic banks is higher than the mean of financial stability in conventional banks. Also, the Mann–Whitney test shows that Mann–Whitney $U = 141$, Wilcoxon $W = 466$, $Z = -2.49$, Asymp. Sig. (2-tailed) $= 0.013$, where p-value ≤ 05, this means that

Table 18.5. Mann–Whitney test result.

Ranks				
Z-score	Islamic/conventional	N	Mean rank	Sum of ranks
	Islamic	20	28.45	569.00
	Conventional	25	18.64	466.00
	Total	45		
Test statistics Z-score				
Mann–Whitney U	Wilcoxon W		Z	Asymp. Sig. (2-tailed)
141.000	466.000		–2.490	0.013

there are significant differences in financial stability between conventional and Islamic banks, therefore we rejected null hypothesis H2 which states that there are no significant differences in financial stability between conventional and Islamic banks and accepted the alternative hypothesis which refers to significant differences in financial stability between conventional and Islamic banks. This difference is due to the increase in the mean of Z-score for Islamic banks over conventional banks according to the result of Table 18.5. The results are consistent with previous study results (Rashid *et al.*, 2017; Ghassan & Krichene, 2017; Fadoua & Brahim, 2020; Safiullah, 2021).

18.4.4 *Result of tests of H3*

Before using multiple linear regression analyses to test H3 related to the impact of the capital adequacy rate on the financial stability of banks, it is necessary to ensure the availability of special assumptions using this model, the most important of which is the normal distribution of the research variables. Through the study and tests of the study variable normality, it became clear to us that normality for some variables and non-normality for others variables are used to overcome this problem. Before using the research model, the researchers transformed the variables non-normality into normality variables by using the transform tools in SPSS program. Moreover, the researchers checked multicollinearity using statistical collinearity: variance inflation factor (VIF) and tolerance for all variables of

Table 18.6. Collinearity test statistics.

Variables	Tolerance	VIF
T1AR	0.717	1.394
T2AR	0.652	1.534
GDP	0.423	2.366
INF	0.782	1.279
IN Rate	0.445	2.246
ASQ	0.740	1.351
IFis	0.847	1.180
Size	0.808	1.237

the model. Table 18.6 presents collinearity test statistics VIF and tolerance. Also, Table 18.7 presents a correlation matrix to identify multicollinearity for the research model. The result shows the range of VIF is (1.1: 2.3). Also, the correlation coefficients between the independent variable are weak and less than 0.80, this means that there is no multicollinearity between variables. As a result, multiple linear regression analysis by the ordinary least squares (OLS) method can be used to study the impact of capital adequacy on the financial stability of banks.

Table 18.8 presents the regression result for Model Equitation. A significant regression equation was found (F(8,36) = 53.257, p-value = 0.000, $p \leq 0.05$), with an R2 of 0.922. Model Summary Model $R = 0.960$, R square adjusted = 0.905, R square = 0.922, std. error of the Estimate = 0.28048, ANOVA a model sum of squares $df = (8, 36)$, mean squares = 4.190, $F = 53.257$, Sig. = 0.000, regression residual total = 2.3832. All of these statistics refers to power and robustness model studied to predict the impact of capital adequacy (Tier 1 adequacy + Tier 2 adequacy) on the financial stability of banks. The result of this model according to adjusted R square is 0.905, which means that independent variables explained 0.90% changes in financial stability measured by Z-score.

Table 18.8 also presents the result of the estimated coefficient for all variables of the OLS model to examine the impact of CAR (Tier 1 adequacy + Tier 2 adequacy) on financial stability banks measured by Z-score, with control variables (size of bank, GDP ratio, inflation rate, interest rate, assets quality ratio, Islamic

Table 18.7. Correlations matrix.

	Bank	T1AR	_T2AR	Size	GDP	INF	INRate	ASQ	IFis	*Z*-score
T1AR	Pearson Correlation	1	−0.445	0.285	−0.170	0.020	−0.062	−0.038	0.130	−0.233
	Sig. (2-tailed)		0.002	0.058	0.263	0.896	0.686	0.803	0.396	0.124
	N	45	45	45	45	45	45	45	45	45
T2AR	Pearson Correlation	−0.445	1	−0.336	0.014	0.173	−0.148	0.122	0.106	0.118
	Sig. (2-tailed)	0.002		0.024	0.925	0.255	0.333	0.425	0.487	0.438
	N	45	45	45	45	45	45	45	45	45
Size	Pearson Correlation	0.285	−0.336	1	−0.018	0.148	0.031	−0.057	−0.114	−0.914
	Sig. (2-tailed)	0.058	0.024		0.906	0.331	0.838	0.711	0.458	0.000
	N	45	45	45	45	45	45	45	45	45
GDP	Pearson Correlation	−0.170	0.014	−0.018	1	−0.248	0.690	−0.363	0.000	−0.029
	Sig. (2-tailed)	0.263	0.925	0.906		0.101	0.000	0.014	1.000	0.850
	N	45	45	45	45	45	45	45	45	45
INF	Pearson Correlation	0.020	0.173	0.148	−0.248	1	−0.390	−0.008	0.000	−0.156
	Sig. (2-tailed)	0.896	0.255	0.331	0.101		0.008	0.958	1.000	0.307
	N	45	45	45	45	45	45	45	45	45
INRate	Pearson Correlation	−0.062	−0.148	0.031	0.690	−0.390	1	−0.153	0.000	−0.049
	Sig. (2-tailed)	0.686	0.333	0.838	0.000	0.008		0.317	1.000	0.750
	N	45	45	45	45	45	45	45	45	45
ASQ	Pearson Correlation	−0.038	0.122	−0.057	−0.363	−0.008	−0.153	1	−0.256	−0.017
	Sig. (2-tailed)	0.803	0.425	0.711	0.014	0.958	0.317		0.089	0.914
	N	45	45	45	45	45	45	45	45	45
IFis	Pearson Correlation	0.130	0.106	−0.114	0.000	0.000	0.000	−0.256	1	0.266
	Sig. (2-tailed)	0.396	0.487	0.458	1.000	1.000	1.000	0.089		0.078
	N	45	45	45	45	45	45	45	45	45
Z-score	Pearson Correlation	−0.233	0.118	−0.914	−0.029	−0.156	−0.049	−0.017	0.266	1
	Sig. (2-tailed)	0.124	0.438	0.000	0.850	0.307	0.750	0.914	0.078	
	N	45	45	45	45	45	45	45	45	45

Table 18.8. Result of impact of capital adequacy on financial stability.

	Unstandardized coefficients		Standardized coefficients		
Variables	***B***	**Std. error**	**Beta**	***t***	**Sig.**
(Constant)	22.364	1.060		21.098	0.000
T1AR	−0.050	0.022	−0.124	−2.248	0.031
T2AR	−0.451	0.091	−0.285	−4.954	0.000
Size	−2.130	0.116	−0.954	−18.437	0.000
GDP	−0.040	0.084	−0.035	−0.484	0.631
_INF	0.015	0.061	0.013	0.254	0.801
INRate	−0.225	0.385	−0.041	−0.585	0.562
_ASQ	−0.010	0.074	−0.008	−0.139	0.890
IFIs	−0.365	0.091	−0.202	−3.992	0.000
Model Summary					
R Square	Adjusted *R* Square		*F*	Significance	
0.922	0.905		53.257	0.000	

financial institution). The result of the model indicates a negative and significant effect of CAR (T1AR, T2AR). That means the higher degree of Tier 1 capital adequacy and Tier 2 capital adequacy in Saudi banks reduces the degree of financial stability for banks, therefore we rejected null hypothesis H3, which states that there are no significant impacts of CAR on FS and accepted the alternative hypothesis which refers to significant impacts of CAR on FS, but this impact is a negative impact.

The researchers consider that this result seems somewhat strange but that the negative effect can be justified because of increasing capital adequacy may lead to a negative impact on the ability of the banking system to provide credit, and this may lead to the risk-adjusted market return on bank loans being insufficient to cover this artificially high cost of capital and thus reduce bank lending activities, which threatens the financial performance of banks in a way that may be reflected in the threat to the financial stability of the banking system. The researchers also confirmed the capital adequacy of the bank, which faces an alternative opportunity cost to obtain returns, and therefore the excessive use of this tool may threaten the performance of the bank and its ability to continue. We cannot imagine working in light of the excessive adherence to a manner that negatively affects the stability of the banking sector, which is the main objective of maintaining capital adequacy, but exaggerating too much may lead to negative results, the opposite of what we expect. Odour *et al.* (2017) also justified this result in viewpoint that capital beef-up requirements forces banks to hold more risky assets by understating their risks through the use of complex in-house risk assessment models. As a result, banks hold less regulatory capital than they are legally supposed to hold and therefore exposing the entire financial sector to instability. Hakenes and Schnable (2011) argue that capital regulation may destabilize the banking sector through its effect on banking competition. The results are consistent with the previous study that predicted and showed the impact of capital adequacy on financial stability (Hakenes & Schnable, 2011; Oduor *et al.*, 2017; Igbinosa & Naimo, 2020), which found a negative significant effect of capital adequacy on the financial stability of banks.

The result also indicated negative significance for the Islamic financial foundation compared with a conventional foundation. The researcher justified this result due to Islamic banks facing greater risks than conventional banks because of their different financing formulas from traditional banks and their participation in profit and loss in many financing formulas, unlike the system of traditional banks that operate on the interest system. The results are consistent with previous study results (Chakroun & Gallali, 2015; Korbi & Bougatef, 2017; Ghassan & Taher, 2019).

18.5 Conclusion

Financial stability is one of the main determinants that contribute to achieving economic stability in a way that contributes to achieving real and sustainable economic development. The financial stability of the banking sector contributes to raising the capacity and efficiency of the banking sector's work and increasing its ability to withstand and absorb shocks. Many international scientific and professional institutions have given more attention to the issue of achieving financial stability, specifically after the negative effects of the global financial crisis in 2008 and the consequent bankruptcy of many banks due to the inability of those banks to meet the sudden demands of their customers and their failure to maintain a level of sufficient capital to face such crises.

Since then, the spread of Islamic banks has increased, which is no longer only limited to Islamic countries, but many countries have adopted that model and applied many of their transactions in their banking systems, where most of the transactions of Islamic banks are based on the principle of sharing risks and profits. In theory, this principle should reduce the risks incurred by Islamic banks (Louati *et al.*, 2015). In light of this, researchers have a strong motivation to study this Islamic model and compare it with conventional banks in terms of capital adequacy rates and their impact on financial stability. Another motivation for choosing the Saudi Arabia banking system to implement this study is due to the Saudi banking system being one of the most important regulations that contains a large volume of Islamic finance assets, as reports indicate that these assets amounted to more than USD 879.2 billion by the end of 2018 which constituted another impetus for the application to the Saudi banking system (IRTI, 2020).

The study aimed to compare the level of capital adequacy and financial stability in both conventional and Islamic banks and investigate the impact of the capital adequacy rate on the financial stability. This was applied to Islamic and conventional banks listed on the Saudi Stock Exchange for which data are available during the time period 2016–2020.

Our results show that there are significant differences in the CAR between conventional and Islamic banks. This difference is due to the increase in the mean capital adequacy ratio of Islamic banks over conventional banks, our result also found significant differences in financial stability between conventional and Islamic banks, This difference is due to the increase in the mean of Z-score for Islamic banks over conventional banks. Contrary to what was expected, the study also found significant negative impacts of CAR on FS. Through these results, we can conclude that increasing capital adequacy more than necessary is not always positive, as this is reflected in the decrease in the bank's performance and its ability to finance, in addition to the high cost of financing for banks that have a greater CAR, which is reflected in the decrease in banks' profits and threatening the financial stability of the bank.

This study contributes to the enriching literature review with modern scientific results that is consistent with some studies (Chakroun & Gallali, 2015; Korbi & Bougatef, 2017; Ghassan & Taher, 2019), in light of the application in the latest period

2016–2020, which contributes to the impact of accounting literature review on the issue of financial stability for Islamic and conventional banks.

Our findings have an important implication. It offers useful insight for supervisors, banks management, investors, bank customers, and policymakers. Where these results contribute to knowing the unexpected negative effects of increased capital adequacy than what is required and its negative impact on the bank's profits and the threat to financial stability, in addition to knowing the main indicators of capital adequacy and financial stability for Islamic and conventional banks in a way that helps bank supervisors, policymakers, and investors in rationalizing their decisions are specific to both Islamic and conventional banks, in addition to identifying the most factors that help to enhance the financial stability process. Our findings support theoretical arguments that Islamic banks have higher capital adequacy rates and financial stability than conventional banks, and this is consistent with the assumption that Islamic Sharia is more hedging in financial transactions. The results also differ with the stakeholders' theory adopted by the researchers, assuming that increasing capital adequacy leads to achieving financial stability, which contributes to achieving balance among all stakeholders. The researchers explained this by the fact that excessive capital adequacy affects profitability and upsets the balance between stakeholders, especially investors.

In measuring capital adequacy, our chapter uses capital adequacy ratio, including Tier 1 and Tier 2 included in the financial reports of banks, and not to address the details of the capital base. The study also depends on measuring financial stability based on the Z-score value without exposure to other measures.

Future research could be carried out to look at the issues related to banking risks faced by both conventional and Islamic banks, and the extent of the impact of the application of Islamic financial accounting standards, the quality of financial reports, and rationalization of investor decisions.

References

Ahmed, F. & Kashif, M. (2018). Financial stability of Islamic versus conventional banks in Pakistan. *Journal of Islamic Economics*, *10*, 341–336.

Ahmed, H. & Khan, T. (2007). Risk management in Islamic banking. In M. Kabir Hasan and Mervyn K. Lewis (Eds.), *Handbook of Islamic Banking*. UK: Edward Elgar, pp. 144–160.

Abd Wahab, N., Rosman, R., & Zainol, Z. (2017). How efficient were Islamic banks during the financial crisis? Empirical evidence from Asian countries. *Intelektinė Ekonomika Intellectual Economics*, *11*(1), 44–62.

Alali, S. (2019). Influence of capital adequacy on financial stability indexes a field study in commercial banks in Jordan. *Academy of Accounting and Financial Studies Journal*, *23*(4), 1–10.

Aldeen, K., Shah, S., Agawany, Z., Heriangrum, S., & Sukmana, R. (2020). Performance comparison of Islamic and conventional banks: Empirical evidence from Syria. *International Business Management*, *14*(5), 164–171.

Alshubiri, F. (2017). Determinants of financial stability: An empirical study of commercial banks listed in Muscat Security Market. *Journal of Business and Retail Management Research (JBRMR)*, *11*(4), 192–200.

Al-Kayed, L., Zain, S., & Duasa, J. (2014). The relationship between capital structure and performance of Islamic banks. *Journal of Islamic Accounting and Business Research*, *5*(2), 158–181.

Archer, S., Ahmed Abdel Karim, R., & Sundararajan, V. (2010). Supervisory, regulatory, and capital adequacy implications of profit-sharing investment accounts in Islamic finance. *Journal of Islamic Accounting and Business Research*, *1*(1), 10–31. https://0810bota8-1103-y-https-doi-org.mplbci.ekb.eg/10.1108/17590811011033389.

Barra, C. & Zotti, R. (2020). Market power and stability of financial institutions: Evidence from the Italian banking sector. *Journal of Financial Regulation and Compliance*, *28*(2), 235–265. https://0810bpmz 5-1103-y-https-doi-org.mplbci.ekb.eg/10.1108/JFRC-05-2019-0055.

Basel Committee on Banking Supervision. (2011). Basel III: A global regulatory framework for more resilient banks and banking systems. https:www.bis.org/publ/bcbs189.pdf.

Boukhatem, J. & Djelassi, M. (2020). Liquidity risk in the Saudi banking system: Is there any Islamic banking specificity? *The Quarterly Review of Economics and Finance*, *77*, 206–219.

Chakroun, M. & Gallali, M. (2015). Islamic banks and financial stability: An empirical analysis of the Gulf Countries. *International Journal of Business and Commerce*, *5*(3), 64–87.

Chauhan, G. & Ramesha, K. (2016). Macroeconomic determinants of financial stability in a business cycle evidence from India. *The Indian Economic Journal*. *63*(4), 702–724.

Daoud, Y. & Kammoun, A. (2020). Financial stability and bank capital: The case of Islamic banks. *International Journal of Economics and Financial Issues*, *10*(5), 361–369.

Dodoev, K. (2018). Comparative analysis of Islamic and conventional banks in camel model: In case of Malaysia. *Global Journal of Management and Business Research: C Finance*, *18*(6), 29–33.

El-Ansary, O., El-Masry, A., & Yousry, Z. (2019). Determinants of Capital Adequacy Ratio (CAR) in MENA region: Islamic vs. conventional Banks. *International Journal of Accounting and Financial Reporting*, *9*(2), 287–313.

Elbadry, A. (2016). Bank's financial stability and risk management. *Journal of Islamic Accounting and Business Research*, *9*(2), 119–137.

Fadoua, J. & Brahim, D. (2020). Financial stability of Islamic and conventional banks of the MENA region: Post and pre-crisis of camels framework.*International Journal of Islamic Banking and Finance Research*, *4*(2), 38–48.

Ghassan, H. & Krichene, N. (2017). Financial stability of conventional and Islamic banks: A survey. https://mpra.ub.uni-muenchen.de/82372/ MPRA Paper No. 82372, posted 7 November, 2017 14:51 UTC.

Ghassan, H. & Taher, F. (2019). Financial stability of Islamic and conventional banks in Saudi Arabia: Evidence using pooled and panel models. https://mpra.ub.uni-muenchen.de/92889/ MPRA Paper No. 92889, posted 31 March, 2019 04:41 UTC.

Hafeez, M., Khan, H., Majeed, F., & Azeem, A. (2018). Impact of capital structure on Islamic banks performance: Evidence from Asian country. *Global Journal of Management and Business Research: C Finance*, *18*(3), 49–53.

Hakenes, H. & Schnable, I. (2011). Capital regulation, bank competition, and financial stability. *Economics Letters*, *113*(3), 256–258.

Horish, J. Schaltegger, S., & Freeman, E. (2020). Integrating stakeholder theory and sustainability accounting: A conceptual synthesis. *Journal of Cleaner Production*, *275*, 1–12.

Hossain, E. & Imam, M. (2017). Financial stability of Islamic and conventional banks in Bangladesh: Revisiting stability measures and analyzing stability behavior. *Journal of Islamic Monetary Economics and Finance*, *3*(2), 293–314.

IFSB-2 (2005). Capital adequacy standard for institution (Other than insurance institution) offering only Islamic financial services, https://www.ifsb.org/ar_published.php.

IFSB-15 (2013). Revised capital adequacy standard for institutions offering Islamic financial services [Excluding Islamic insurance (TAKĀFUL) institutions and Islamic collective investment schemes. https://www.ifsb.org/ar_published.php.

IFSB. https://www.ifsb.org/ar_background.php.

Igbinosa, S. & Naimo, F. (2020). Capital adequacy and bank stability/soundness in sub-Saharan Africa. *European Journal of Accounting, Finance and Investment*, *6*(5), 38–54.

IMF (2004). Defining financial stability. working paper, WP/04/187. https://www.imf.org/external/pubs/ft/wp/2004/wp04187.pdf.

IRTI (2020). Islamic finance in Saudi Arabia: Leading the way to vision 2030. https://irti.org/product/islamic-finance-in-saudi-arabia/.

Khan, S. & Jabeen, Z. (2011). Comparative study of assessment of Capital Adequacy Ratio (CAR) for Islamic banks in Pakistan under Basel II and IFSB formulae for capital adequacy. Working Paper, 8th International Conference on Islamic Economics and Finance, Center for Islamic Economics and Finance, Qatar Faculty of Islamic Studies, Qatar Foundation.

Klimczak, K. (2007). Risk management theory: A comprehensive empirical assessment, MPRA Paper No. 4241, posted 24 July UTC, Online at https://mpra.ub.uni-muenchen.de/4241/.

Kombo, K. & Njuguna, A. (2016). Effects of Basel III framework on capital adequacy of commercial banks in Kenya. *International Journal of Finance and Accounting*, *1*(1), 61–74.

Korbi, F. & Bougatef, K. (2017). Regulatory capital and stability of Islamic and conventional banks. *International Journal of Islamic and Middle Eastern Finance and Management*, *10*(3), 312–330.

Koskei, L. (2020). Determinants of banks' financial stability in Kenya commercial banks Asian *Journal of Economics, Business and Accounting*, *18*(2). Article no. AJEBA.60317, 48–57.

Lassoued, M. (2018). Corporate governance and financial stability in Islamic banking. *Managerial Finance*, *44*(5), 524–539. https://0810bpmz5-1103-y-https-doi-org.mplbci.ekb.eg/10.1108/MF-12-2016-0370.

Louati, S., Abida, I., & Boujelbene, Y. (2015). Capital adequacy implications on Islamic and non-Islamic bank's behavior: Does market power matter? *Borsa Istanbul Review*, *15*(3), 192–204.

Mansour, W., Jedidia, K., & Majdoub, J. (2015). How ethical is Islamic banking in the light of the objective of Islamic law. *Journal of Religious Ethics*, *43*, 51–77.

Mili, M., Sahut, J., Trimeche, H., & Teulon, F. (2017). Determinants of the capital adequacy ratio of foreign banks' subsidiaries: The role of interbank market and regulation. *Research in International Business and Finance*, *42*, 442–453.

Mohamad, A., Mohamad, M., & Hashim, S. (2018). Islamic versus conventional banking. In A. A. Rahman (Ed.), *New Developments in Islamic Economics*. Bingley: Emerald Publishing Limited. pp. 119–214.

Nair, A. & Anand, B. (2020). Monetary policy and financial stability: Should central banks lean against the wind? *Central Bank Review, 20*, 133–142.

Odour, J., Ngoka, K., & Odongo, M. (2017). Capital requirement, bank competition and stability in Africa. *Review of Development Finance, 7*(1), 45–51.

Ogere, A., Peter, Z., & Inyang, E. (2013). Capital adequacy ratio and banking risks in the Nigeria money deposit banks. *Research Journal of Finance and Accounting, 4*(17), 17–25.

Qayyum, N. & Noreen, U. (2019). Impact of capital structure on profitability: A comparative study of Islamic and conventional banks of Pakistan. *Journal of Asian Finance, Economics and Business, 6*(4), 65–74.

Ramlall, I. (2018). Concept of financial stability demystified. understanding financial stability. In *The Theory and Practice of Financial Stability*, Vol. 1. Bingley: Emerald Publishing Limited. pp. 13–31. https://0810bpm7o-1103-y-https-doi-org.mplbci.ekb.eg/10.1108/978-1-78756-833-420181013.

Raouf, H. & Ahmed., H. (2020). Risk governance and financial stability: A comparative study of conventional and Islamic banks in the GCC. *Global Finance Journal.* Available online 13 December, 2020, 100599, 1–12.

Rashid, A., Yousaf, S., & Khaleequzzaman, M. (2017). Does Islamic banking really strengthen financial stability? Empirical evidence from Pakistan. *International Journal of Islamic and Middle Eastern Finance and Management, 10*(2), 130–148. https://0810bpynx-1103-y-https-doi-org.mplbci.ekb.eg/10.1108/IMEFM-11-2015-0137.

Rupeika-Apoga, R., Romānova, I., & Grima, S. (2020). The determinants of bank's stability: Evidence from latvia, a small post-transition economy*. In Grima, S.,Özen, E., & Boz, H. (Eds.), *Contemporary Issues in Business Economics and Finance (Contemporary Studies in Economic and Financial Analysis*. Vol. 104. Bingley: Emerald Publishing Limited. pp. 235–253. https://0810bpw3t-1103-y-https-doi-org.mplbci.ekb.eg/10.1108/S1569-375920200000104016.

Safillah, M. (2021). Financial stability efficiency of Islamic and conventional banks. *Pacific-Basin Finance Journal, 68*, 1–12. Available online 2 June. Doi: 10.1016/j.pacfin.2021.101587.

Saha, M. & Dutta, K. D. (2021). Nexus of financial inclusion, competition, concentration and financial stability: Cross-country empirical evidence. *Competitiveness Review*, *31*(4), 669–692. https://0810bpm7o-1103-y-https-doi-org.mplbci.ekb.eg/10.1108/CR-12-2019-0136.

Salamat, W. & Al-Kharouf, S. (2021). The determinants of financial stability: Evidence from Jordan. *International Journal of Business and Social Science*, *12*(1), 25–35.

Salman, A. & Nawaz, H. (2018). Islamic financial system and conventional banking: A comparison. *Arab Economic and Business Journal*, *13*(2), 155–167.

Sarpong-Kumankoma, E., Abor, J. Y., Aboagye, A. Q. Q., & Amidu, M. (2020). Economic freedom, competition and bank stability in Sub-Saharan Africa. *International Journal of Productivity and Performance Management*, 1510–1527. https://0810bpmz5-1103-y-https-doi-org.mplbci.ekb.eg/10.1108/IJPPM-06-2019-0310.

Smaoui, H., Salah, I., & Diallo, B. (2020). The determinants of capital ratios in Islamic banking. *The Quarterly Review of Economics and Finance*, *77*, 186–194.

World Bank (2015). Global financial development report 2015/2016: Long-term Finance Global Financial Development Report. Washington, DC. ©World Bank. https://openknowledge.worldbank.org/handle/10986/22543 License: CC BY 3.0 IGO.

Zopounidis, C., Lemonakis, C., Voulgaris, F., & Stylianos, C. (2017). Islamic banking vs conventional banking during the crises period: Evidence from GCC and MENA banking industries. *Jarr B Economics, Business, Social Sciences and Education*, *XVI*(1), 1–13.

https://doi.org/10.1142/9781800612426_0019

Chapter 19

Banks' Capital Structure Determinants: A Comparative Analysis Between Islamic and Conventional Banks Based on Corporate and Regulatory Approaches

Kaouther Toumi

Abstract

The research aims to empirically investigate the banks' capital structure determinants by considering 386 listed and unlisted banks categorized into 74 Islamic banks, 256 conventional banks, and 56 hybrid banks from 20 countries for 2008–2016 based on corporate and regulatory approaches. The main findings are interesting. From a corporate approach, we find differences between IBs, CBs, and HBs regarding the determinants of their capital structure which offer an empirical confirmation of the reduced information asymmetry in an Islamic finance context. From a regulatory approach, the findings show similarities regarding the negative impact of deposit insurance schemes on the regulatory capital for all types of banks. When focusing on IBs, we evidence that banks subject to Sharia-compliant deposit insurance schemes hold lower capital than those subject to conventional deposit insurance schemes.

Keywords: Capital Structure, Islamic and Conventional Banks, Information Asymmetry, Deposit Insurance Schemes.

19.1 Introduction

Banks' corporate governance has become an important area attracting much international attention, especially after the 2008 financial crisis (De Haan & Vlahu, 2016). Understanding capital structure is essential for banks as it affects their stability and ability to provide liquidity and credits effectively (Diamond & Rajan, 2000). The past quarter-century of deregulation and the globalization of financial markets, combined with the rapid pace of financial innovation and the moral hazard caused by frequent government bailouts, caused a devastating financial crisis (Crotty, 2009). Excessive leverage is one of the major causes of bank fragility during the financial crisis (Crotty, 2009). This crisis also highlights the importance of considering banks' business models (Köhler, 2014).

From a theoretical perspective, capital structure has always been a fundamental dimension of financial analysis, starting from the famous proposition of Modigliani and Miller (1958). When dealing with banks, the corporate approach of capital structure is observed to explain the capital structure of these financial institutions (Berger *et al.*, 1995; Gropp & Heider, 2010; Octavia & Brown, 2010). Based on the regulatory approach, regulation and safety nets also significantly impact banks' capital structure (Diamond & Dybvig, 1983; Berger *et al.*, 1995; Gropp & Heider, 2010; Octavia & Brown, 2010; Allen *et al.*, 2014). The existing empirical literature on banks are limited in scope concerning geography, for instance, the study of Gropp and Heider (2010) for listed US and UE banks and Berger *et al.* (1995) for listed US banks; or economic context (e.g., Octavia & Brown (2010) for banks in developing countries).

Islamic banks (hereinafter, IBs) capital structure is different in nature. IBs respect specific ethical principles (e.g., profit and loss sharing, ban on dealing with interest, tangibility and transparency requirement, ban on speculation and high risk-taking) making them distinctive. Such unique characteristics may influence IBs capital structure. Capital structure is a well-investigated area for conventional banks. For IBs, the capital structure is also important, and few researches have been conducted on the capital structure. To the best of our knowledge, no existing study compares IBs' capital structure with that of conventional banks (hereinafter, CBs) and hybrid banks (hereinafter, HBs). For IBs, empirical studies regarding financial decisions are emerging, and the existing literature considers mainly the corporate approach to explain IBs' capital structure (Bitar *et al.*, 2018; Meslier *et al.*, 2020; Guizani, 2021; Guizani & Ajmi, 2021). Hoque and Liu (2021) recently considered the regulatory approach, but their study lacks considering the impact of safety nets and deposit insurance schemes on IBs capital structure. We complement the existing literature first by comparing three types of banks: IBs, CBs and HBs (conventional banks with Islamic windows) and second by considering the regulatory approach of capital structure with taking into consideration the impact of *Sharia*-compliant deposit insurance schemes on IBs regulatory capital.

The research aims to empirically investigate the banks' capital structure determinants by considering three types of banks. Our sample consists of 386 listed and unlisted banks categorized into 74 IBs, 256 CBs, and 56 HBs from 20 countries for 2008–2016. Depending on the considered approach, we integrate several measures of capital structure. Based on the corporate finance approach, we identify profitability, market-to-book ratio, dividend, collaterals, and size as bank-specific determinants of banks' leverage. When considering the regulatory approach, we add regulation and deposit insurance schemes, conventional and *Sharia*-compliant ones, as additional determinants of banks' regulatory capital.

The main findings are interesting. From a corporate approach, we find differences between IBs, CBs, and HBs regarding the determinants of their capital structure which offer an empirical confirmation of the reduced information asymmetry in an Islamic finance context. From a regulatory approach, the findings show similarities regarding the negative impact of deposit insurance schemes on the regulatory capital for all types of banks. When focusing on IBs, we evidence that banks subject to Sharia-compliant deposit insurance schemes hold lower capital than those subject to conventional deposit insurance schemes.

Our results contribute to the literature on Islamic banking, developing markets, and the broader corporate finance capital structure literature in several important ways. First, no other study addresses a world-level test of bank determinants of the capital structure under the three categorizations of IBs, CBs, and HBs. Making several sub-samples to examine the determinants of bank capital structure contributes to a better understanding of whether Islamic ethical principles affect financial decisions. Second, the research considers separately listed and unlisted banks and contributes to the scarce literature dedicated to the capital structure of unlisted banks. The previous research focused mainly on listed banks (Caglayan & Sak, 2010; Gropp & Heider, 2010; Octavia & Brown, 2010) or listed non-financial firms (Booth *et al.*, 2001; Antoniou *et al.*, 2008; Frank & Goyal, 2009). Third, with using common bank-level measures, we empirically investigate the determinants of IBs financial decisions and find that standard and regulatory capital structure theories and empirical results can be applied to IBs.

The rest of this chapter is organized as follows. Section 19.2 gives the literature review. Section 19.3 specifies the research design. Section 19.4 describes the empirical results, and Section 19.5 concludes.

19.2 Islamic Banks' Capital Structure and Its Determinants

19.2.1 *Corporate approach*

The corporate finance theories on firm capital structure identified mainly taxation, bankruptcy costs, information asymmetries, and conflicts of interest as main drivers of firms' financial structure. These same theories are also considered to explain banks' capital structure (Berger *et al.*, 1995; Gropp & Heider, 2010; Octavia & Brown, 2010). Considering the Islamic finance ethics in the classical theories of capital structure could lead to different conclusions for IBs. Toumi *et al.* (2012) conduct a first theoretical explanation of IBs' capital structure from a corporate approach and suggest that the trade-off arguments are similar, but the pecking order arguments are weaker compared to CBs.

The trade-off theory suggests that the optimal capital structure results from a trade-off between tax benefits and expected bankruptcy costs (Modigliani & Miller, 1958; Myers, 1984). Considering the Islamic finance context, the level of bankruptcy costs could be theoretically lower compared with CBs. On the one hand, the religious beliefs of IBs customers may induce loyalty and decrease default and bankruptcy costs (Abedifar *et al.*, 2013). On the other hand, several features related to Islamic finance make IBs conceptually less vulnerable to risk and thus reduce default costs (e.g., the traceability requirement in Islamic financial transactions, the profit and loss sharing scheme, limited access to speculative and risky asset classes). Based on the trade-off theory contributions, Toumi *et al.* (2012) suggest that the capital ratio is lower theoretically due to decreased bankruptcy costs in IBs and that the tax burden related to liabilities is calculated similarly for both IBs and CBs.

The pecking order theory suggests that firms prefer internal to external financing and debt to equity due to information asymmetry between firm insiders and outside investors (Myers, 1984; Myers & Majluf, 1984). From this perspective, banks are highly leveraged as these institutions are known to be opaque institutions, especially with respect to asset and loan portfolio risk characteristics and quality (Mülbert, 2009). However, information asymmetries are addressed differently when considering Islamic finance ethics (Toumi *et al.*, 2012). Transparency in financial contracts and agreements is mandatory, and all stakeholders need to be morally responsible with respect to each other to avoid a situation of incomplete information (Toumi *et al.*, 2012; Abdelsalam *et al.*, 2016). All players are required to fulfill the religious obligation of amana (trust), forcing them to behave with respect to justice (adl), balance (qist), and perfection (ihsaan) principles. This feature permits each stakeholder to benefit from equal, adequate, and accurate information, thus reducing information asymmetries. Furthermore, the traceability requirement in Islamic arrangements, the strong link with the real economy, and the restricted set of investment opportunities allow outside investors to have a clearer view of IB assets quality (Toumi *et al.*, 2012). The Sharia governance ensured by SSB also plays a central role in reducing information asymmetries in IBs since it ensures that the financial interests of all stakeholders are protected, that IB behavior complies with Islamic finance ethics, and that the transparency principle is respected (Toumi *et al.*, 2012; Abdelsalam *et al.*, 2016; Farag *et al.*, 2017). Based on the contributions of pecking order theory, Toumi *et al.* (2012) suggest that pecking order arguments are weaker in IBs as lower information asymmetries is expected in this context, and thus IBs should have a higher capital ratio compared to CBs.

Third, the agency theory states that firms face a trade-off between equity and non-equity financing due to agency costs. The optimal capital structure is obtained by arbitration between debt benefits that reduce agency conflicts between shareholders and managers, and agency costs of debt resulting from asset substitution effect and conflict of interest between shareholders and debt holders (Jensen & Meckling, 1976; Myers, 1977; Jensen, 1986; Williamson, 1986; Harris & Raviv, 1990). For IBs, the agency structure is more complex since the corporate structure deviates from the conventional forms and managers act in a Sharia-compliant manner besides maximizing their shareholders' wealth (Archer *et al.*, 1998), as revealed in Table 19.1. Based on the agency theory, Toumi *et al.* (2012) suggest that the optimal capital structure in IBs will be obtained by trading off between benefits and costs related to different agency relationships. They conclude that IBs should have a different capital ratio compared with CBs when considering the new and the classical agency relationships.

Based on the corporate approach, the empirical literature identified mainly market-to-book ratio, profitability, collaterals, size, and dividend payout as standard determinants that are reliably related to firm leverage (Titman & Wessels, 1988; Harris & Raviv, 1991; Rajan & Zingales, 1995; Frank & Goyal, 2009). Similar recent studies using the same variables have emerged for banks (Gropp & Heider, 2010; Octavia & Brown, 2010).

Regarding *profitability*, more profitable firms will have more internal funding, decreasing the need for external financing. Following pecking order, a negative relationship between leverage and profitability is expected. Trade-off theory suggests the opposite result. Trade-off theory suggests that profitable firms increase debts because, first, they find interesting tax shields and, second, they face lower expected bankruptcy costs. The most profitable firms have more facilities to take on more debt since the probability of repayment is higher. As for IBs the pecking order arguments are weaker, we expect a higher impact of profitability on the leverage ratio for IBs than for CBs.

For *collaterals*, a high proportion helps firms raise more debts secured by these assets based on trade-off theory. Based on agency theory, using assets as collaterals limits the ability of shareholders to engage in risk-taking behavior that significantly reduces debtholders' exposure to asset substitution effect and increases leverage (Jensen & Meckling, 1976). Pecking order theory suggests that firms with a high proportion of collaterals are less sensitive to information

Table 19.1. Agency relationships in IBs.

Nature (1)	Agency relationship identified in the literature for IBs and comparison with CBs (2)		Potential impact on IB capital structure (3)
Traditional	**Shareholders-liability claim holders** (Archer *et al.*, 1998; Safieddine 2009; Toumi *et al.*, 2012; Abdelsalam *et al.*, 2016; Farag *et al.*, 2017)	**Lower** agency costs in IBs because of the limited possibilities of wealth transfers from shareholders to claim holders due to the impossibility for shareholders to engage in speculative and highly risky projects (Toumi *et al.*, 2012)	**Favoring liabilities claim holders**
	Shareholders-managers (Archer *et al.*, 1998; Safieddine, 2009; Toumi *et al.*, 2012; Beck *et al.*, 2013; Abdelsalam *et al.*, 2016; Farag *et al.*, 2017)	**Lower** agency costs in IBs result from higher moral accountability and required transparency that encourages managers to be morally responsible with respect to shareholders (Toumi *et al.*, 2012; Abdelsalam *et al.*, 2016)	**Favoring equity**
New (with PSIA depositors)	**PSIA depositors-managers** (Archer *et al.*, 1998; Safieddine 2009; Toumi *et al.*, 2012; Abdelsalam *et al.*, 2016; Farag *et al.*, 2017)	**Additional** agency costs in IBs since managers act as agents of PSIA depositors (Toumi *et al.*, 2012). Managers are free to decide how PSIA funds are invested and do not empower PSIA depositors to monitor their investment through representation in the board of directors (Abdelsalam *et al.*, 2016). Even if the depositors' means of pressure to control managers appear to be more limited than those of shareholders, they nevertheless have others mean through the threat of withdrawing funds; PSIA holders also exert disciplinary control on managers via shareholders (Toumi *et al.*, 2012)	**Favoring equity**

(*Continued*)

Table 19.1. (*Continued*)

Nature (1)	**Agency relationship identified in the literature for IBs and comparison with CBs (2)**		**Potential impact on IB capital structure (3)**
	PSIA depositors-shareholders (Toumi *et al.*, 2012)	**Additional** agency costs in IBs. Agency conflicts regarding the bank risk level exist between PSIA depositors and shareholders, but they are far less important than those between shareholders and debt holders (because of the similarities of their incentives). An increase in risk could generate a wealth transfer from debt holders to shareholders, but for PSIA holders, the problem is only of non-optimal risk level (Toumi *et al.*, 2012)	**Favoring PSIA deposits**
New (with the Sharia Supervisory Board)	**Managers-Sharia Supervisory Board** (Toumi *et al.*, 2012; Abdelsalam *et al.*, 2016)	**Additional** agency costs in IBs result from difficulties for the SSB to exert control on managers to ensure that they operate in accordance with Islamic finance ethics. These difficulties should be of the same type and magnitude as those extensively studied in the literature on the board of directors (Toumi *et al.*, 2012). The existence of this second layer of governance is expected to limit opportunities for financial misstatements and consequently moderate the higher agency costs in IBs (Abdelsalam *et al.*, 2016). The committee is expected to act in the best interests of all stakeholders (shareholders, PSIA depositors, claimholders) (Toumi *et al.*, 2012)	**Favoring non-equity or equity financing**

asymmetries, thus favoring equity. As for IBs, the pecking order arguments are weaker; for IBs, we expect a lower impact of tangibility on the equity ratio than for CBs.

With regards to *size*, large banks would be exposed to a low risk of bankruptcy that favors leverage following trade-off theory. Large firms have easier access to bank credit market. Gropp and Heider (2010) and Octavia and Brown (2008) confirm this result for the banking sector. Following pecking order theory, information asymmetries is lower in large firms which should encourage equity financing. As for IBs the trade-off arguments are similar and asymmetry is lower, we expect that size will have a greater positive impact on the leverage ratio.

Finally, with regards to *dividend*, the pecking order theory suggests that paying dividends helps to reduce information asymmetries since it allows information to be conveyed, thus increasing equity. Dividend-paying firms transmit a good signal regarding future prospects and could easily attract investors (Lintner, 1965). Following agency theory, shareholders may use dividends as a strategic weapon to discipline managers and align with their interests. As asymmetry of information and agency conflict should be less important in IBs, we expect that the impact of dividends should be lower on the equity ratio than the one expected for CBs.

Regarding *market-to-book ratio*, a high value reflects greater investment opportunities that give shareholders greater choices for future investments. According to the trade-off theory, firms with high growth investment opportunities have higher bankruptcy costs that limit leverage. Regarding agency theory, growth options promote the alignment of interests, and equity financing is thus a choice (Jung *et al.*, 1996). However, if growth opportunities are low, debt is the appropriate vehicle to discipline managers (Jensen, 1986; Stulz, 1990). From a pecking order perspective theory, firms with high growth opportunities and significant funding requirements will primarily use external financing, which is less subject to asymmetric information (Myers, 1984; Myers & Majluf, 1984). We expect that the impact of market-to-book ratio on equity ratio will be higher for IBs than for CBs.

From a corporate approach, as the trade-off arguments are similar and the pecking order arguments is weaker for IBs, *we expect thus a different impact of standard corporate determinants (size, market to book, profitability, collaterals, dividend payout) on IBs' capital structure, compared to conventional banks (H1).*

19.2.2 *Regulatory approach*

Banks differ substantially from non-financial firms by the nature of debts and the special treatment in the form of government safety net and prudential regulation (Merton, 1977; Diamond & Dybvig, 1983; Berger *et al.*, 1995; Miller, 1995; Macey & O'Hara, 2003; Gropp & Heider, 2010; Octavia & Brown, 2010; Allen *et al.*, 2014). Such protection from bankruptcy and the costs of financial distress affects capital requirements for banks (Berger *et al.*, 1995). From a regulatory point of view, regulators could force riskier banks to hold more regulatory capital to protect themselves against costs of financial distress (Berger *et al.*, 1995; Gropp & Heider, 2010; Octavia & Brown, 2010).

In the Islamic banking context, the ability to engage in reckless economic behavior as well as the incentives shareholders to increase risks are limited first by the requirement to conform to Islamic finance morals and second by the availability of SSB in the governance structure that guarantees to all stakeholders' compliance with Islamic finance rules. The business model of IBs should conceptually allow IBs to pass through adverse shocks more easily, thereby decreasing the costs of financial distress. *We expect a lower impact of risk on IBs' regulatory capital than CBs (H2).*

The government safety net includes deposit insurance, unconditional payment guarantees, and the entire panoply of regulation and supervision that is not directly related to capital (Berger *et al.*, 1995; Calomiris, 1999). Banks resort to safety nets as a means of extreme liquidity risk management that stabilizes the financial system and protects small and uninformed depositors from adverse shocks and associated costs (Diamond & Dybvig, 1983). Safety net policies limit depositors' tendency to overreact by changing the incentives of depositors (Calomiris, 1999). Safety nets tend to reduce the bank level of capital requirement since their introduction reduces the likelihood of bank failure and isolates banks from the potential market discipline (Berger *et al.*, 1995). Higher deposit insurance coverage is thus associated with higher leverage and lower capital requirement in banks than others with similar portfolios not subject to deposit insurance.

IBs hold safer portfolios and, consequently, less regulatory capital is theoretically required than CBs. IBs do not have to provide liquidity insurance to mudarabah-based profit-sharing investment account holders. However, several studies highlight the divergence between the treatment of investment accounts in practice and the theoretical conception (Archer & Karim, 2006, 2009; El-Hawary *et al.*, 2007; Farook *et al.*, 2012; Toumi & Viviani, 2013) When IBs' returns on investment accounts are weak, their depositors could exercise power over the IB managers due to their ability to withdraw their deposits (Toumi *et al.*, 2012; Aysan *et al.*, 2016). To avoid massive withdrawal of funds and market discipline that IBs' depositors could exercise upon negative information indicating poor investment returns, IBs may be constructively obliged to manage the payout of profits to investment account holders, mainly with the absence of adequate tools for that purpose compared with CBs (Farook *et al.*, 2012; Toumi *et al.*, 2018).

Most IBs do not benefit from Islamic protection schemes in several jurisdictions, and their deposits are mostly protected under conventional schemes.[1] Aysan *et al.* (2016) observe that deposit insurance affects the incentives of IBs' depositors to exert market discipline as in a conventional context. More interestingly, their study reveals that the nature of deposit insurance, being Islamic or conventional, impacts the intensity of the market discipline of IBs' depositors. Conventional deposit insurance schemes appear to increase the market discipline of IBs' depositors, compared with a situation where IBs are protected by *Sharia*-compliant deposit insurance schemes (Aysan *et al.*, 2015, 2016). IBs' depositors show a greater tendency to discipline their banks if the deposit insurance lacks religious quality and is not compliant with Islamic finance rules.

We expect, thus, a different impact of the Sharia-compliant deposit insurance schemes on the regulatory capital of IBs, compared to conventional deposit insurance schemes (H3).

[1]Main differences exist with conventional schemes (IFSB, 2011). First, products covered under deposit insurance are Islamic deposits and may be extended to PSIAs. Second, members are IBs. Third, premiums are paid from IBs' funds. In the case of PSIAs, premiums may be paid from PSIAs funds. Finally, expenses incurred and any investment of premiums should comply with ethical principles of Islamic finance.

19.3 Research Design

19.3.1 *Sample*

We consider three categories of banks: IBs, CBs, and HBs (CBs with Islamic windows). We consider both listed and non-listed banks. In contrast to the literature, which usually examines listed banks (Berger *et al.*, 1995; Gropp & Heider, 2010; Octavia & Brown, 2010), we include unlisted banks to give a more representative picture of the banking sector.[2]

We collect data from the Bankscope database. We considered banks with codes C1, C2, and C* as they publish consolidated financial statements (Mollah *et al.*, 2016). Then, we checked for the categories of banks. We note that first, some IBs are mistakenly classified as CBs. Second, Bankscope does not classify HBs as a third category. To solve this problem, we manually scanned the financial services provided by banks through consulting their websites. We then filtered the remaining banks by considering only countries having both Islamic and conventional banks.

Our final sample covers 386 banks implemented in 20 countries over the period 2008–2016. Banks are categorized into 74 IBs, 256 CBs, and 56 HBs (see Table 19.2).

19.3.2 *Variables specification*

From a corporate finance approach, the empirical literature identified mainly market-to-book ratio (MTB), profitability (Prof), collaterals (Coll), size, and dividend payout (Div) that are reliably related to firm leverage (Frank & Goyal, 2009; Harris & Raviv, 1991; Rajan & Zingales, 1995; Titman & Wessels, 1988). Similar recent studies have emerged for CBs (Gropp & Heider, 2010; Octavia & Brown, 2010).

[2]Listed banks are typically larger, have significantly higher non-deposit funding, and are usually more closely monitored by the market than banks that could force managers to expand into more risky non-interest income activities (Köhler, 2014). Listed banks are also controlled by institutional investors with greater expertise in processing information and monitoring managers and can exert greater control than atomistic shareholders (Köhler, 2014). Furthermore, listed banks usually have a more dispersed ownership structure giving their managers greater scope to generate private benefits of control than unlisted banks (Barry *et al.*, 2011).

Table 19.2. Country-wise distribution of the sample, period: 2008–2016.

	Panel A: Islamic banks (IBs)		Panel B: Conventional banks (CBs)		Panel C: Hybrid banks (HBs)		Panel D: All banks			
Countries	**Listed**	**Unlisted**	**Total**	**Listed**	**Unlisted**	**Total**	**Listed**	**Unlisted**	**Total**	**Total**
Bahrain	4	3	7	4	4	8	1	1	2	17
Brunei Darussalam	0	1	1	0	1	1	0	0	0	2
Egypt	3	0	3	8	10	18	1	3	4	25
Indonesia	1	5	6	23	21	44	12	5	17	67
Iraq	1	2	3	5	0	5	0	0	0	8
Jordan	2	1	3	9	0	9	0	0	0	12
Kuwait	3	0	3	4	1	5	0	0	0	8
Lebanon	0	1	1	4	29	33	1	1	2	36
Malaysia	1	16	17	3	18	21	0	5	5	43
Oman	0	0	0	1	0	1	4	1	5	6
Qatar	3	1	4	3	1	4	2	0	2	10
Saudi Arabia	4	0	4	3	0	3	4	0	4	11
Singapore	0	1	1	4	9	13	0	0	0	14
Syria	2	0	2	7	1	8	0	0	0	10
Thailand	0	1	1	9	8	17	0	1	1	19
Tunisia	0	1	1	10	4	14	0	0	0	15
Turkey	3	1	4	12	14	26	0	0	0	30
UAE	6	2	8	5	1	6	7	1	8	22
UK	2	0	2	7	11	18	1	5	6	28
Yemen	0	4	4	0	2	2	0	0	0	6
Total	**35**	**39**	**74**	**121**	**135**	**256**	**33**	**23**	**56**	**386**

From a regulatory approach, we also consider the bank risk (*Risk*) and the availability of an explicit conventional deposit insurance scheme (*DepIns*) and an Islamic deposit insurance scheme (*ShDepIns*). We also consider the following control variables, the gross domestic product per capita (*GDP*) and inflation (*Inf*), as in Gropp and Heider (2010) and Bitar *et al.* (2018). As for the macroeconomic factors, they reflect the environment in which banks operate. In order to avoid effect of outliers, all variables are winzorized at 0.5% and 99.5% (see Table 19.3).

19.3.3 *Econometric modeling*

We run first the corporate standard regression on *Leverage* of IBs, CBs, and HBs as in Gropp and Heider (2010). The corporate literature consider market-to-book, profitability, collaterals, size, and dividend payout as the main variables explaining firm's capital structure (Gropp & Heider, 2010; Octavia & Brown, 2010; Frank & Goyal, 2009; Harris & Raviv, 1991; Rajan & Zingales, 1995; Titman & Wessels, 1988) (see Equation 19.1).

$$\begin{aligned}\text{Leverage}_{i,t} = \beta_0 &+ \beta_1\,\text{MTB}_{i,t-1} + \beta_2\,\text{Prof}_{i,t-1} + \beta_3\,\text{Coll}_{i,t-1}\\ &+ \beta_4\,\text{Size}_{i,t-1} + \beta_5\,\text{Div}_{i,t} + \text{GDP}_t + \text{Inflation}_t + \varepsilon_{i,t}.\end{aligned} \tag{19.1}$$

We then break it down into *Deposits* and *NDeposits* to test the standard regression on leverage components of banks. The corporate finance literature does not explicitly distinguish between debt and non-debt liabilities. However, the financial structure of banks differs from non-financial firms by including deposits, a source of financing generally not available to firms (Miller, 1995). We also consider listed and unlisted banks separately.

In Equation 19.2, we investigate the regulatory approach of bank capital structure, and we test the potential effect of *Risk* and the availability of an explicit deposit insurance scheme (*DepIns*) on the regulatory capital (*RegCapital*) and leverage. For IBs, we test the impact of introducing the Islamic explicit deposit insurance scheme (*ShDepIns*) to capture the impact of IB depositors' market discipline. We also regress the same variables of Equation 19.2

Table 19.3. Variables definitions.

Variables	Definitions	Sources
Leverage	1-Equity to total assets	Bankscope
RegCapital	Tier 1 capital divided by risk-weighted assets	Bankscope
Deposits	Total customer deposits (current, saving, and term) to total assets. For IBs, deposits correspond to mudharaba and non-mudharaba based deposits: unrestricted PSIAs + murabahah deposits, medium-term wakalah financing + Saving accounts + Current accounts	Bankscope
NDeposits	Leverage ratio minus deposits ratio	Author's calculation from Bankscope
MTB	Market value of assets to book value of assets	Bankscope
Prof	Return on average assets	Bankscope
Coll	Total securities + Cash and due from banks + Derivatives + Land and buildings + Other tangible assets. For IBs, there are no conventional derivatives	Author's calculation from Bankscope
Size	Ln (Total assets)	Bankscope
Div	Dummy variable that takes the value of 1 if the bank pays a dividend in a given year, zero otherwise	Bankscope
DepIns	Dummy variable that takes the value of 1 if explicit deposit insurance is available and zero otherwise	International Association of Deposit Insurers, www.iadi.org
ShDepIns	Dummy variable that takes the value of 1 if there is separate deposit protection for IBs and CBs in a given jurisdiction and the value of 0 if there is a single conventional deposit protection scheme for all banks	International Association of Deposit Insurers, www.iadi.org and IFSB website, www.ifsb.org

(*Continued*)

Table 19.3. (*Continued*)

Variables	Definitions	Sources
Risk	ln(Z-score). The value is equal to ln [(return on average assets + Capital to assets ratio)/Standard deviation of return on average assets over three years]	Author's calculation from Bankscope
GDP	The annualized growth rate of GDP per capita	World Bank database
Inflation	Inflation rate	World Bank database

on leverage and the component of leverage.

$$\begin{aligned}\text{RegCapital}_{i,t} &= \beta_0 + \beta_1\,\text{MTB}_{i,t-1} + \beta_2\,\text{Prof}_{i,t-1} + \beta_3\,\text{Coll}_{i,t-1}\\ &\quad + \beta_4\,\text{Size}_{i,t-1} + \beta_5\,\text{Div}_{i,t} + \beta_6\,\text{Risk}_{i,t} + \beta_7\,\text{DepIns}_{i,t}\\ &\quad + \text{GDP}_t + \text{Inflation}_t + \varepsilon_{i,t}. \qquad (19.2)\end{aligned}$$

19.4 Regression Results

19.4.1 *Descriptive statistics*

Table 19.4 provides descriptive statistics. Descriptive analysis reveals that, although IBs hold on average a lower proportion of deposits (65.52% vs. 66.88% for CBs and 70.53% for HBs), they are observed to have the highest capital ratio (15.8% for IBs vs. 13% for CBs and 12.23% for HBs). Similarly, the regulatory capital ratio for IBs is 17.53% compared with 16.37% for CBs and 14.17% for HBs. Results also show that IBs record on average lower return on assets (1.10% vs. 1.26% for CBs and 1.77% for HBs). Regarding the market-to-book ratio, IBs are observed to have a higher value compared with CBs (1.73% vs. 1.49%) and a lower value than that of HBs (1.93%). Furthermore, the value of collaterals is lower in IBs (47.89%) compared with CBs (51.08%). HBs are observed to have, on average, a lower proportion of collaterals (41.11%). Regarding bank size, IBs are relatively smaller (14.57) compared with CBs (14.98). Results regarding risk indicate that IBs have the lowest value on average (3.31 for IBs vs. 3.73 for CBs and 3.79 for HBs).

Table 19.4. Descriptive statistics.

	Panel A: Islamic banks (IBs)		Panel B: Conventional banks (CBs)		Panel C: Hybrid banks (HBs)		Panel D: All banks			
Variables	**Mean**	**SD**	**Mean**	**SD**	**Mean**	**SD**	**Mean**	**SD**	**Max**	**Min**
RegCapital	17.53	8.42	16.37	7.42	14.17	4.31	16.18	7.23	51.04	4.67
leverage	84.19	10.70	87	8.24	87.76	6.41	86.61	8.57	96.96	40.09
NDeposits	20.93	20.57	20.84	17.37	17.22	13.79	20.30	17.55	94.18	0.24
Deposits	65.52	21.18	66.88	18.42	70.53	15.04	67.21	18.52	95.46	2.25
MTB	1.73	1.24	1.49	0.88	1.93	1.02	1.62	1.001	7.96	0.02
Prof	1.10	2.47	1.26	1.64	1.77	1.28	1.31	1.78	11.17	−10.3
Coll	47.33	21.40	51.08	21.64	41.11	13.48	48.93	20.88	99.48	8.48
Div	0.48	0.46	0.47	0.34	0.56	0.29	0.48	0.37	1	0
Size	14.57	1.50	14.98	2.06	15.68	1.6	15.01	1.94	21.55	7.81
Risk	3.31	1.11	3.73	1.11	3.79	1.02	3.67	1.11	6.91	0.14
Inflation	4.78	4.34	4.44	3.57	4.83	3.44	4.56	3.71	26.17	−15.1
GDP	5.04	5.39	5.4	4.32	5.28	3.58	5.32	4.46	53.23	−10.1

Table 19.5 provides the matrix of Pearson correlation coefficients and indicates a relatively weak association between the variables on average. *MTB* appears to be positively correlated to *Prof* implying that banks with high market-to-book ratio tend have high profitability. Besides, a positive relationship is observed between *Prof* and *Div* suggesting that banks with high profitability tend to pay high dividend. A similar relationship is detected between *Prof* and *Risk* showing that high profitable banks tend to be riskier. Furthermore, greater banks (*Size*) tend to pay more dividends (*Div*) and record higher levels of *Risk*. Finally, the negative correlation between *DepIns* and *Risk* highlights that riskier banks tend to benefit more from deposit insurance schemes. Finally, we note that no problem of multicollinearity is detected based on VIF tests.

19.4.2 *Regression results: The standard corporate approach*

Table 19.6 presents the results related to capital structure determinants based on the corporate approach. Models 1 and 2 give results related to the determinants of banks' leverage, whereas Models 3–6 present results related to leverage components.

Models 1 and 2 give results on the determinants of leverage for listed and unlisted banks, respectively. When considering listed banks, the findings show the significance of all variables at 1% and 5% levels and suggest that the standard determinants of capital structure apply to listed banks. These findings align with those of Gropp and Heider (2010) for listed US and EU large banks and those of Octavia and Brown (2010) for banks in developing countries. A pure regulatory view is thus observed to be not the only explanation for the capital structure of listed banks; the standard corporate approach also contributes to it.

Globally, we find that larger listed banks with the greater market-to-book ratio, greater dividend payout, lower profitability, and lower collaterals tend to be more leveraged. Our results align with those of Octavia and Brown (2010) for listed banks in developing countries but are slightly different from those of Gropp and Heider (2010) for listed banks from developed countries. For instance, one possible explanation for the positive relation between market-to-book ratio and bank book leverage is that a high value reflects overpricing in

Table 19.5. Correlation matrix.

Variables	MTB	Prof	Coll	Size	Div	DepIns	Risk	Inflation	GDP
MTB	1								
Prof	0.12**	1							
Coll	−0.11**	−0.05**	1						
Size	0.02	−0.001	−0.22**	1					
Div	−0.01	0.18**	0.009	0.17**	1				
DepIns	−0.12**	−0.12**	0.09**	−0.02	−0.10**	1			
Risk	−0.09**	0.18**	−0.04*	0.11**	0.23**	0.07**	1		
Inflation	0.16**	0.18**	0.022	−0.14**	−0.01	−0.034*	0.05**	1	
GDP	−0.05	0.09**	0.037	−0.19**	0.001	−0.28**	−0.08**	0.15**	1

Note: ***, **, and *correspond respectively significance at 1%, 5%, and 10%.

Table 19.6. Capital structure determinants for all banks during the period 2008–2016.

	Leverage		**Deposits ratio (Deposits)**		**Non-deposits ratio (Ndeposits)**	
Variables	**Listed**	**Unlisted**	**Listed**	**Unlisted**	**Listed**	**Unlisted**
	(1)	(2)	(3)	(4)	(5)	(6)
MTB_{t-1}	1.02***		−0.12		0.75***	
(Std. err.)	(0.2)		(0.3)		(0.2)	
$Prof_{t-1}$	−0.86***	−0.08*	−0.4***	0.45	−0.31	−0.49
	(0.1)	(0.1)	(0.3)	(0.5)	(0.3)	(0.55)
$Coll_{t-1}$	−0.001*	−0.01	−0.07**	−0.06	0.03**	0.06
	(0.02)	(0.01)	(0.05)	(0.05)	(0.04)	(0.05)
Div	1.50***	−0.6	0.06	−0.07	0.75	−7.9
	(0.6)	(0.5)	(0.8)	(2.12)	(0.8)	(2.00)
$Ln(size)_{t-1}$	2.30***	3.6***	0.54**	0.24	4.21***	3.64*
	(1.2)	(0.5)	(1.7)	(2.1)	(1.6)	(2.1)
Inflation	−0.07**	0.04	0.06	−0.15	−0.01	0.19
	(0.05)	(0.07)	(0.05)	(0.1)	(0.06)	(0.1)
GDP	−0.01	0.09	−0.09	−0.25	−0.01***	0.35
		(0.07)	(0.1)	(0.2)	(0.09)	(0.18)
Constant	49.5***	32.2***	65.2**	65.7**	−52.7**	−37.4*
	(5.98)	(8.7)	(3.7)	(33.2)	(26.54)	(8.92)
R^2	0.33	0.38	0.17	0.06	0.21	0.03
Wald Chi2	1.24***	1.50***	3.48***	7.06***	9.6***	7.15***
N. Obs.	805	596	800	582	800	590

Note: ***, **, and *denote statistical significance at 1%, 5%, and 10% level, respectively.

the capital market. As suggested by the pecking order theory, the high degree of information asymmetry between the bank insiders and the market therefore results in banks issuing more debt Octavia & Brown, 2010). In addition, the positive relation between dividends and bank book leverage indicates the relatively higher cost of having equity. Banks that commit to paying out dividends to their shareholders prefer to finance their operations with debt. Furthermore, the negative association of profitability with leverage could be explained under the pecking order theory that argues that firms prefer internal financing over external funds, allowing more profitable firms to be less levered over time. Finally, the negative impact of collaterals could also be explained under the pecking order theory that suggests that banks with a high proportion of collaterals are less sensitive to information asymmetries, thus favoring equity and lowering leverage.

Regarding unlisted banks, the standard corporate regression explains less bank leverage ratio with only profitability and size having a negative and positive impact respectively at the 5% and 1% significance levels. Larger unlisted banks with lower profitability tend to be more leveraged than listed banks. Our results are in line with Bitar *et al.* (2018), suggesting that the effect of classical determinants on the capital ratios of banks is also driven by the disciplinary role that the financial markets play in the capital structure decisions of publicly listed banks, compared to unlisted banks.

When splitting the sample into IBs, CBs, and HBs as shown in Table 19.7, the results confirm the contribution of the standard corporate approach in explaining leverage mainly for listed banks. We observe some differences between all categories of banks confirming the Hypothesis 1. Globally, we find that larger listed IBs and CBs with greater market-to-book ratio, greater dividend payout, lower profitability, and lower collaterals tend to be more leveraged, which aligns with those of Octavia and Brown (2010) for listed banks in developing countries. The results for IBs are consistent with Bitar *et al.* (2018) when focusing in the impact of size, profitability, and collaterals on leverage. Our results for IBs are also similar to Hoque and Liu (2021) findings regarding profitability, size, collaterals, and MTB.

Furthermore, compared to listed CBs, market to book and collaterals are observed to have approximately the same significant impact on non-equity financing of listed IBs. By contrast, size and profitability have a significantly greater impact on leverage (Models 1 and 3, Table 19.7). As for IBs, the trade-off arguments are similar, and asymmetry is lower, size appears to have a greater positive impact on leverage for IBs than CBs and HBs for both listed and unlisted banks. Similarly, we find a higher impact of profitability on leverage for IBs than for CBs due to the weaker arguments of the pecking order theory in IBs. For the same arguments, dividend payout has a lower impact (insignificant) on leverage in IBs than CBs. Finally, when focusing on unlisted banks, the standard corporate approach appears to explain better IBs' capital structure (Model 2).

Table 19.7. Corporate finance approach for the period 2008–2016. The dependent variable is leverage.

	Panel A: (IBs)		**Panel B: (CBs)**		**Panel C: (HBs)**	
Variables	**Listed**	**Unlisted**	**Listed**	**Unlisted**	**Listed**	**Unlisted**
	(1)	(2)	(3)	(4)	(5)	(6)
MTB_{t-1}	0.78**		0.74***		0.47**	
(Std. err.)	(0.4)		(0.2)		(0.2)	
Prof_{t-1}	−0.54***	−0.41	−0.15	0.09	0.18	0.06***
	(0.1)	(0.3)	(0.20)	(0.5)	(0.4)	(0.3)
Coll_{t-1}	−0.06**	−0.06**	−0.06***	0.03	0.13***	−0.02
	(0.04)	(0.03)	(0.02)	(0.04)	(0.8)	(0.02)
Div	0.23	−2.48**	0.85*	0.04	−0.36*	1.48*
	(0.9)	(0.9)	(1.1)	(1.2)	(0.5)	(0.80)
Size_{t-1}	5.53***	5.00**	1.39***	3.00*	−1.27**	0.64
	(0.66)	(1.8)	(2.08)	(1.6)	(1.5)	(1.2)
Inflation	−0.15***	0.05	−0.10***	0.02	0.06	0.004
	(0.09)	(0.1)	(0.06)	(0.08)	(0.08)	(0.07)
GDP	0.01***	−0.04	0.08	0.21**	−1.18***	−0.14
	(0.15)	(0.1)	(0.06)	(0.08)	(0.06)	(0.08)
Constant	13.2	15.62	66.5***	37.9***	102.8***	78.9***
	(13.5)	(27.9)	(7.4)	(3.26)	(8.75)	(19.4)
R^2	0.47	0.45	0.35	0.43	0.19	0.53
Wald Chi2	1.87***	11.48∗	1.008***	3.64***	2.6***	1.65***
N. Obs.	160	138	519	376	126	82

Note: ***, **, and *denote statistical significance at the 1%, 5%, and 10% level, respectively.

Models 1 to 12 in Table 19.8 present the estimation results of the standard corporate regression on deposit and non-deposit ratios for IBs, CBs, and HBs. Empirical results show an effective substitution between deposit and non-deposit liabilities.

Globally, we find that the corporate approach works less for the components of leverage, and the variables of the standard corporate finance approach do not retain their importance. When considering the R^2 in Table 19.6, we observe that values are higher for regressions on bank leverage than regressions on bank deposit and non-deposit liabilities. The standard corporate models' weak explanation power is also confirmed when we consider each bank type separately, where fewer variables are significant in the standard corporate approach

Table 19.8. Corporate finance approach for IBs, CBs, and HBs during the period 2008–2016. The dependent variables are deposits and non-deposits liabilities.

	Panel A: Islamic banks (IBs)				Panel B: Conventional banks (CBs)				Panel C: Hybrid banks (HBs)			
	Listed		Unlisted		Listed		Unlisted		Listed		Unlisted	
	Dep (1)	NDep (2)	Dep (3)	NDep (4)	Dep (5)	NDep (6)	Dep (7)	NDep (8)	Dep (9)	NDep (10)	Dep (11)	NDep (12)
MTB_{t-1}	0.5	0.12			−0.30	0.88**			0.21	0.26		
(Std. err.)	(0.6)	(0.5)			(0.3)	(0.4)			(0.5)	(0.4)		
$Prof_{t-1}$	−0.02	−0.51	0.71	−1.04	0.11	−0.29	0.76	−0.63	−1.02*	1.08	1.8**	−1.76
	(0.4)	(0.4)	(1.5)	(1.3)	(0.3)	(0.4)	(0.5)	(0.4)	(0.8)	(0.77)	(1.7)	(1.5)
$Coll_{t-1}$	−0.16**	0.10	−0.44**	0.36*	0.01	−0.05	0.18**	−0.10	0.06	0.04	−0.01	−0.01
	(0.07)	(0.06)	(0.2)	(0.1)	(0.05)	(0.05)	(0.08)	(0.08)	(0.19)	(0.14)	(0.1)	(0.1)
Div	0.68	−0.56	−3.45	1.28	−1.17	1.89	−0.06	−0.07	−0.97	0.74	4.63	−3.15
	(2.04)	(1.7)	(3.5)	(3.8)	(1.1)	(1.3)	(1.7)	(1.7)	(0.87)	(0.87)	(3.3)	(2.6)
$Ln(size)_{t-1}$	−1.24	−0.14**	−11.7	16.09*	−0.73	4.30*	1.40	2.15	−5.47*	5.25**	2.98	−2.3***
	(4.03)	(0.99)	(10.03)	(9.03)	(2.1)	(2.1)	(3.1)	(3.04)	(3.07)	(2.23)	(3.00)	(2.3)
Inflation	−0.04	−0.10	−0.36	0.45	−0.09	−0.02	−0.24**	0.26*	0.09	−0.02	0.77*	−0.76**
	(0.1)	(0.14)	(0.6)	(0.53)	(0.06)	(0.07)	(0.1)	(0.5)	(0.09)	(0.09)	(0.3)	(0.3)
GDP	−0.1***	0.07	−0.64	0.65	0.07	−0.01	−0.20	0.39	0.003	−0.19	−0.94	0.80
	(0.3)	(0.25)	(1.14)	1.02	(0.1)	(0.1)	(0.3)	(0.2)	(0.1)	(0.14)	(0.7)	(0.7)
Constant	96.8	−81.1*	26.37	−23.56	80.8**	−50.1	33.59	−5.50	99.1***	−79.6**	16.44	62.4
	(21.16)	(41.5)	(15.8)	(14.31)	(34.4)	(36.0)	(48.6)	(46.2)	(45.8)	(33.8)	(46.3)	(34.5)
R^2	0.34	0.13	0.16	0.05	0.23	0.33	0.10	0.06	0.16	0.13	0.34	0.23
Wald Chi2	3.4***	2.4***	5.8***	4.17	5.1***	5.5***	7.1***	4.2***	5.8***	1.3***	3.7***	9.3***
N. Obs.	160	160	131	135	514	514	369	373	126	126	82	82

Note: ***, **, and * denote statistical significance at the 1%, 5%, and 10% level, respectively.

(see Tables 19.7 vs. 19.8). These results are consistent with regulation as a second approach to explain capital structure. Our results are in line with Berger *et al.* (1995) and Gropp and Heider (2010), who argue that corporate capital structure theories cannot be fully applied to banks due to regulation and the specific capital structure of banks where deposits are an essential component in financing sources.

19.4.3 *Regression results: The regulatory approach*

Tables 19.9 and 19.10 report results based on the regulatory approach. The variables *Risk* and the availability of deposit insurance schemes are added to all regressions as explanatory variables.

As shown in Models 5–8 in Table 19.9, *Risk* is observed to have a significant positive (negative) impact on deposit liabilities (respectively non-deposits). The higher risk the outside investors face, the more discount they demand on the price of issued securities. Consequently, banks will prefer financing through free-risk debt or low risk-debt instead of equity. However, when splitting the sample into IBs, CBs, and HBs (Table 19.10), we find that risk drives the regulatory capital only for conventional banks. The impact of risk appears lower for IBs, confirming our second hypothesis (H2). From a regulatory point of view, regulators could force riskier banks to hold more regulatory capital to protect themselves against costs of financial distress (Berger *et al.*, 1995; Gropp & Heider, 2010; Octavia & Brown, 2010). In the Islamic banking context, the ability to engage in reckless economic behavior as well as the incentives shareholders to increase risks are limited, first, by the requirement to conform to Islamic finance morals and, second, by the availability of SSB in the governance structure that guarantees to all stakeholders' compliance with Islamic finance rules.

Besides, results in Table 19.9 reveal that deposit insurance schemes are negatively associated with the regulatory capital at 5% and 1% levels for listed and unlisted banks, respectively (Models 1 and 2). We also find that listed banks under the protection of deposit insurance schemes tend to have higher leverage (Models 3 and 4). Our results are consistent with the related theory on the effect of regulation and safety nets on capital structure. Safety nets tend to reduce the bank level of capital requirement since their introduction

Table 19.9. Regulatory approach for all banks during the period 2008–2016.

	Regulatory capital		Leverage		Deposits ratio		Ndeposits ratio	
	(1) Listed	(2) Unlisted	(3) Listed	(4) Unlisted	(5) Listed	(6) Unlisted	(7) Listed	(8) Unlisted
MTB_{t-1} (Std. err.)	0.02		0.76***		2.64***		−1.94***	
	(0.17)		(0.2)		(0.4)		(0.37)	
$Prof_{t-1}$	0.56***	1.45***	−2.01***	−1.24***	−2.31***	−1.61**	0.41***	0.63
	(0.15)	(0.26)	(0.14)	(0.21)	(0.3)	−(0.71)	(0.29)	(0.66)
$Coll_{t-1}$	0.04***	0.04***	−0.001	−0.01	−0.01	−0.05	−0.005	0.03
	(0.01)	(0.01)	(0.01)	(0.01)	(0.02)	(0.04)	(0.02)	(0.04)
Div	0.19	−0.09	0.97*	0.12	2.71**	7.04***	−1.64	−6.85***
	(0.5)	(0.73)	(0.5)	(0.65)	(1.21)	(2.28)	(1.05)	(2.15)
$Size_{t-1}$	−0.61***	−1.14***	1.01***	1.96***	−1.85***	2.04***	2.57***	0.01
	(0.11)	(0.19)	(0.13)	(0.17)	(0.24)	(0.57)	(0.22)	(0.53)
$Risk_{t-1}$	−0.06	−0.26	0.24	−0.13	1.67***	1.82**	−1.41***	−2.56***
	(0.18)	(0.27)	(0.19)	(0.24)	(0.19)	(0.86)	(0.37)	(0.79)
DepInsurance	−0.65**	−1.51***	0.75**	0.45	−1.61**	−1.86	2.38***	2.47*
	(0.3)	(0.27)	(0.3)	(0.41)	(0.71)	(1.47)	(0.64)	(1.4)
Inflation	0.03	0.04	−0.13***	0.13*	−0.01	0.50	−0.15*	0.50
	(0.04)	(0.09)	(0.04)	(0.07)	(0.09)	(0.28)	(0.08)	(0.28)
GDP	−0.13***	−0.11	0.36***	0.06	0.55***	−0.15	0.20**	−0.15
	(0.04)	(0.11)	(0.04)	(0.07)	(0.11)	(0.28)	(0.1)	(0.28)
Constant	22.69***	31.7***	73.05***	60.03***	88.7***	28.02***	−13.1***	33.68***
	(2.04)	(3.37)	(1.87)	(2.85)	(4.38)	(2.85)	(3.9)	(9.42)
Wald Chi2	45.5***	86.03***	260.9***	164.7***	31.4***	71.85***	−13.1***	71.85***
R^2	0.10	0.23	0.29	0.30	0.20	0.07	0.20	0.05
Number of banks	189	197	189	197	189	197	189	197

Table 19.10. Regulatory approach for IBs, CBs and HBs capital structure determinants during the period 2008–2016. The dependent variable is the regulatory capital (RegCap).

	Panel A: Islamic banks (IBs)				Panel B: Conventional banks (CBs)		Panel C: Hybrid banks (HBs)		Panel D: All banks	
	Listed		Unlisted		Listed	Unlisted	Listed	Unlisted	Listed	Unlisted
	(1)	(2)	(3)	(4)	(5)	(6)	(7)	(8)	(9)	(10)
MTB_{t-1} (Std. err.)	−0.13	−0.003			−0.56**		−0.39*		−0.46*	
	(0.63)	(0.5)			(0.2)		(0.2)		(0.2)	
$Prof_{t-1}$	0.86**	0.88**	0.28	0.4*	0.002	1.33**	0.83	−0.31	0.53**	0.68***
	(0.4)	(0.3)	(0.25)	(0.24)	(0.3)	(0.5)	(0.5)	(1.5)	(0.2)	(0.2)
$Coll_{t-1}$	−0.04	−0.04	0.03	0.07	0.05	0.002	0.02	0.08	0.02	0.02
	(0.03)	(0.03)	(0.04)	(0.05)	(0.03)	(0.03)	(0.05)	(0.06)	(0.02)	(0.03)
Div	1.87*	2.01*	0.27	1.41	−0.02	−3.5**	−2.29**	0.3	0.19	−1.02
	(1.06)	(1.07)	(1.1)	(1.22)		(1.5)	(0.9)	(1.9)	(0.6)	(0.9)
$Size_{t-1}$	−3.56**	−3.4**	−1.14	−0.25	−0.81*	−2.32***	−0.93	−0.89*	−1.1***	−2.12***
	(1.6)	(1.6)	(1.08)	(1.02)	(0.4)	(0.5)	(0.6)	(0.6)	(0.4)	(0.4)
$Risk_{t-1}$	−0.27	−0.26	0.76	0.41	0.46**	0.41	−0.6**	0.7	−0.06	0.33
	(0.4)	(0.5)	(0.67)	(0.58)	(0.2)	(0.4)	(0.3)	(0.8)	(0.2)	(0.2)
Dep Insurance	−1.46		−2.9***		−0.60	−0.67	−0.68	−0.86	−0.89**	1.46**
	(1.3)		(1.33)		(0.9)	(1.1)	(1.1)	(2.7)	(0.7)	(0.7)
ShDep Insurance		−0.51		−5.48**						
		(2.06)		(1.1)						
Inflation	−0.04	−0.03	−0.17	−0.15	0.13***	0.19*	−0.10	0.20	0.06	0.04
	(0.1)	(0.1)	(0.2)	(0.3)	(0.04)	(0.11)	(0.1)	(0.2)	(0.04)	(0.09)
GDP	−0.4***	−0.4***	−0.6	−0.99**	−0.13	−0.31*	0.03	−0.16	−0.13**	−0.23
	(0.1)	(0.1)	(0.4)	(0.4)	(0.09)	(0.18)	(0.1)	(0.1)	(0.07)	(0.1)
Constant	75.8***	72.4***	33.2*	19.3	25.3***	52.6***	33.2***	21.5***	33.8***	47.4***
	(26.5)	(26.4)	(17.2)	(17.2)	(2.45)	(10.5)	(11.2)	(9.08)	(6.8)	(7.7)
R^2	0.38	0.37	0.46	0.35	0.14	0.44	0.28	0.21	0.13	0.23
Wald Chi2	5.08***	5.16***	25.5***	50.79***	11.05**	6.1*	8.86*	74.73***	13.5**	14.8**
Number of banks	117	117	78	78	345	213	108	52	566	335

Note: ***, **, and *denote statistical significance at the 1%, 5%, and 10% level, respectively.

reduces the likelihood of bank failure and isolates banks from the potential market discipline (Berger *et al.*, 1995). The introduction of deposit insurance schemes in banks leads thus to lower capital levels and higher leverage compared to banks with similar portfolios not subject to deposit insurance (Berger *et al.*, 1995). Our result is consistent with these banks having better access to debt markets because they may be less likely to default as we observe a significant positive impact on non-deposit liabilities for listed and unlisted banks (Models 7 and 8, Table 19.9).

However, when considering the different categories of banks, the significant negative impact of explicit deposit insurance schemes on the regulatory capital is only confirmed for unlisted IBs (see Table 19.10). Regarding IBs, the *Sharia*-compliant deposit insurance scheme has a more pronounced significant negative impact on the regulatory capital than the conventional deposit insurance scheme, confirming our third hypothesis (H3). Our results indicate that IBs under *Sharia*-compliant deposits insurance scheme tend to have lower capital requirements (Models 3 and 4, Table 19.10). Our findings are in line with Aysan *et al.* (2016), who found that conventional deposit insurance increases IBs depositors' market discipline, compared with a situation where IBs are under the protection of Islamic deposit insurance. In light of this conclusion, IBs subject to Islamic deposit insurance face lower market discipline and thus the related liquidity problems which le-ad to lower capital requirement compared with banks subject to conventional deposit insurance schemes.

19.5 Conclusion

The objective of the chapter is to understand the capital structure of IBs, CBs, and HBs. We build on the theoretical contributions of the classical financial theories to explore the impact of Islamic principles on the capital structure of banks. We have considered both corporate finance and regulatory approaches. We empirically investigated factors that significantly affect IBs, CBs, and HBs capital structure by considering listed and unlisted banks. Depending on the approach considered, we integrate several measures of capital structure.

Regarding the corporate approach, we identify profitability, market-to-book ratio, dividend, collateral, and size as specific bank determinants of capital structure. When considering the regulatory approach, we add risk and deposit insurance schemes as additional determinants. To conduct our analysis, we make several sub-samples and run panel regressions. The sample includes 386 banks categorized into 74 IBs, 256 fully CBs, and 56 HBs from 20 countries for 2008–2016. In sum, from a corporate finance approach, we assumed that the trade-off arguments are similar but that the pecking order arguments are weaker due to lower information asymmetries in the Islamic finance context. The differences captured between the regression results for IBs, CBs, and HBs offer a first empirical confirmation that the information asymmetries are less important in IBs, thus changing the equity and non-equity financing level and the extent of the impact of determinants. When considering the regulatory approach, we find that impact of Islamic deposit insurance is observed to be negatively and significantly important, revealing that IBs subject to Islamic deposit insurance hold lower capital requirement levels than other IBs subject to conventional deposit insurance.

The results presented extend the literature on bank capitalization in developing and Islamic financial markets and has important policy implications. As current international financial markets and regulatory standards evolve in order to develop sound financial systems and bank governance, our results help explain how Islamic bank managers choose between debt and equity financing, especially in developing countries.

For research limitations, the study has not constructed a new capital structure theory specific to IBs but only apply the classical concepts and theories of capital structure (information asymmetry, agency theory, trade-off theory, and pecking order theory) to the Islamic context. Despite these interesting results, the determinants of capital structure of IBs cannot probably be explained only by traditional capital structure theories.

For future research, specific theories should be developed to discover specific determinants of IBs' capital structure. Exploring these new determinants requires considering the presence of dual governance systems and the ethical constraints. This specific framework is necessary to avoid applying models grounded on expected utility maximization choice theory in a context where ethical objectives and constraints are important.

References

Abdelsalam, O., Dimitropoulos., P., Elnahass, M., & Leventis, S. (2016). Earnings management behaviors under different monitoring mechanisms: The case of Islamic and conventional banks. *Journal of Economic Behavior and Organization*, *132*, 155–173.

Abdul Karim, M., Hassan, M. K., Hassan, T., & Mohamad, S. (2014). Capital adequacy and lending and deposit behaviors of conventional and Islamic banks. *Pacific-Basin Finance Journal*, *28*, 58–75. Doi: 10.1016/j.pacfin.2013.11.002.

Abdullah W. A. W., Percy, M., & Stewart, J. (2015). Determinants of voluntary corporate governance disclosure: Evidence from Islamic banks in the Southeast Asian and the Gulf Cooperation Council regions. *Journal of Contemporary Accounting & Economics*, *11*, 262–279. Doi: 10.1016/j.jcae.2015.10.001.

Abedifar, P., Molyneux, P., & Tarazi, A. (2013). Risk in islamic banking. *Rev Financial*, *17*, 2035–2096.

Allen, F., Carletti, E., & Marquez, R. (2014). Deposits and bank capital structure. *Journal of Financial Economics*, *118*, 601–619. Doi: 10.1016/j.jfineco.2014.11.003.

Antoniou, A., Guney, Y., & Paudyal, K. (2008). The determinants of capital structure: Capital market-oriented versus bank-oriented institutions. *Journal of Financial and Quantitative Analysis*, *43*, 59–92. Doi: 10.2307/27647340.

Archer, S. & Karim R. A. A. (2006). On capital structure, risk sharing and capital adequacy in Islamic banks. *International Journal of Theoretical and Applied Finance*, *9*, 269–280.

Archer, S. & Karim, R. A. A. (2009). Profit-sharing investment accounts in Islamic banks: Regulatory problems and possible solutions. *Journal of Bank Regulation*, *10*, 300–306.

Archer, S., Karim, R. A. A., & Al-Deehani, T. (1998). Financial contracting, governance structures and the accounting regulation of Islamic banks: An analysis in terms of agency theory and transaction cost economics. *Journal of Management and Governance*, *2*, 149–170. Doi: 10.1023/A:1009985419353.

Athari, S. A., Adaoglu, C., & Bektas, E. (2016). Investor protection and dividend policy: The case of Islamic and conventional banks. *Emerging Markets Review*, *27*, 100–117. Doi: 10.1016/j.ememar.2016.04.001.

Aysan, A. F., Disli, M., Ozturk, H., & Turhan, I. (2015). Are Islamic banks subject to depositor discipline? *Singapore Economic Review, 60*, 1550007. Doi: 10.1142/S0217590815500071.

Aysan, A. F., Disli, M., Duygun, M., & Ozturk, H. (2016). Islamic banks, deposit insurance reform, and market discipline: Evidence from a natural framework. *Journal of Financial Services Research, 51*(2), 1–26.

Barry, T. A., Lepetit, L., & Tarazi, A. (2011). Ownership structure and risk in publicly held and privately owned banks. *Journal of Banking and Finance, 35*, 1327–1340.

Basel Committee on Banking Supervision, (2011). Basel III: A global regulatory framework for more resilient banks and banking systems (Bank for International Settlements, December 2010; revised June 2011).

Beck, T., Demirgüç-Kunt, A., & Merrouche, O. (2013). Islamic vs. conventional banking: Business model, efficiency and stability. *Journal of Banking and Finance, 37*, 433–447.

Berger, A., Herring, R., & Szegö, G. (1995). The role of capital in financial institutions. *Journal of Banking and Finance, 19*, 393–430. Doi: 10.1016/0378-4266(95)00002-X.

Bitar, M. & Madiès, P. (2017). What makes Islamic banks different? A multivariate approach. *Economic Systems, 41*, 215–235.

Bitar, M. & Tarazi, A. (2018). Creditor rights and bank capital decisions: Conventional vs. Islamic banking. *Journal of Corporate Finance, 55*, 69–104.

Bitar, M., Kabir Hassan, M., & Hippler, W. J. (2018). The determinants of Islamic bank capital decisions. *Emerging Markets Review, 35*, 48–68. Doi: 10.1016/j.ememar.2017.12.002.

Booth, L., Varouj, A., Asli, D-K., & Vojislav, M. (2001). Capital structure in developing countries. *Journal of Finance, 56*, 87–130.

Caglayan, E. & Sak, N. (2010). The determinants of capital structure: Evidence from the Turkish banks. *Journal of Money, Investment Banking, 15*, 57–65.

Calomiris, C. W. (1999). Building an incentive-compatible safety net. *Journal of Bank Finance, 23*, 1499–1519. Doi: 10.1016/S0378-4266(99)00028-X.

Čihák, M. & Hesse, H. (2010). Islamic banks and financial stability: An empirical analysis. *Journal of Finance Service Research, 38*, 95–113.

Crotty, J. (2009). Structural causes of the global financial crisis: A critical assessment of the 'new financial architecture. *Cambridge Journal of Economics, 33*, 563–580.

De Haan, J. & Vlahu, R. (2016). Corporate governance of banks: A survey. *Journal of Economic Surveys, 30*, 228–277. Doi: 10.1111/joes.12101.

Diamond, D. & Dybvig, P. (1983). Bank runs, deposit insurance, and liquidity. *Journal of Political Economy, 91*, 401–419.

Diamond, D. & Rajan, R. (2000). A theory of bank capital. *Journal of Finance, 55*, 2431–2465.

Dietrich, A. & Wanzenried. G. (2011). Determinants of bank profitability before and during the crisis: Evidence from Switzerland. *Journal of International Financial Markets, Institutions & Money, 21*, 307–327.

El-Hawary, D. (2004). Regulating Islamic financial institutions: The nature of the regulated. *World Bank Policy Research Working Paper*, 3227: Doi: 10.1596/1813-9450-3227.

El-Hawary, D., Grais, W., & Iqbal, Z. (2007). Diversity in the regulation of Islamic financial institutions. *Quarterly Review of Economics and Finance, 46*, 778–800.

Farag, H., Mallin, C., & Ow-Yong, K. (2017). Corporate governance in Islamic banks: New insights for dual board structure and agency relationships. *Journal of International Financial Markets, Institutions & Money, 54*, 59–77.

Farook, S., Hassan, M. K., & Clinch, G. (2012). Profit distribution management by Islamic banks: An empirical investigation. *Quarterly Review of Economics and Finance, 52*, 333–347.

Frank, M. Z. & Goyal, V. K. (2009). Capital structure decisions: Which factors are reliably important? *Financial Management, 38*, 1–37.

Giordana, G. & Schumacher, I. (2013). What are the bank-specific and macroeconomic drivers of banks' leverage? Evidence from luxembourg. *Empirical Economics, 45*, 905–928. Doi: 10.1007/s00181-012-0643-8.

Gropp, R. & Heider, F. (2010). The determinants of bank capital structure. *Rev Financial, 14*(4), 587–622.

Guizani, M. (2021). The determinants of capital structure of Islamic and conventional banks: An autoregressive distributed lag approach. *Journal of Islamic Accounting and Business Research, 12*, 131–147. Doi: 10.1108/JIABR-06-2020-0177.

Guizani, M. & Ajmi, A. N. (2021). The capital structure decision of Islamic and conventional banks: Empirical evidence from Malaysia. *Asia-Pacific Journal of Business Administration, 13*, 216–234. Doi: 10.1108/APJBA-06-2020-0218.

Haniffa, R. & Hudaib, M. (2007). Exploring the ethical identity of Islamic banks via communication in annual reports. *Journal of Business Ethics, 76*, 97–116.

Harris, M. & Raviv, A. (1990). Capital structure and the informational role of debt. *Journal of Finance, 45*, 321–349.

Harris, M. & Raviv, A. (1991). The theory of capital structure. *Journal of Finance*, *46*(1), 297–355.
Hoque, H. & Liu, H. (2021). Capital structure of Islamic banks: How different are they from conventional banks? *Global Finance Journal*, 100634.
Jensen, M. (1986). American economic association agency costs of free sash flow, corporate finance, and takeovers authors: Michael, C. Jensen, source. *The American Economic Review*, *76*(2). Papers and Proceedings of the Ninety-Eighth Annual Meeting of the American Economic Review, 76: 323–329.
Jensen, M. & Meckling, W. (1976). Theory of the firm: Managerial behavior, agency costs, and ownership structure. *Journal of Financial Economics*, 53–82.
Jung, K., Kim, Y., & Stulz, R. (1996). Timing, investment opportunities, managerial discretion, and the security issue design. *Journal of Financial Economics*, 159–185.
Kabir, M. N., Worthington, A., & Gupta, R. (2015). Comparative credit risk in Islamic and conventional bank. *Pacific Basin Finance of Journal*, *34*, 327–353.
Köhler, M. (2014). Which banks are more risky? The impact of business models on bank stability. *Journal of Financial Stability*, *16*, 195–212.
Lintner, J. (1965). The valuation of risk assets and the selection of risky investments in stock portfolio and capital budgets. *Review of Economics and Statistics*, 13–37.
Macey, J. & O'Hara, M. (2003). The corporate governance of banks. *Economic Policy Review*, *9*, 91–107.
Merton, R. (1977). An analytic derivation of the cost of deposit insurance and loan guarantees: An application of modern option pricing theory. *Journal of Banking and Finance*, *1*, 3–11.
Meslier, C., Risfandy, T., & Tarazi, A. (2020). Islamic banks 'equity financing, Shariah supervisory board, and banking environments. *Pacific-Basin.Finance Journal*, *62*, 101354.
Miller, M. H. (1995). Do the M Propositions apply to banks? *Journal of Banking and Finance*, *19*, 483–489.
Modigliani, F. & Miller, M. (1958). The cost of capital, corporation finance, and the theory of investment. *American Economic Review*, *48*, 261–297.
Mokni, R. B. S. & Rachdi, H. (2014). Assessing the bank profitability in the MENA region: A comparative analysis between conventional and Islamic bank. *International Journal of Islamic and Middle Eastern Finance and Management*, *7*, 305–332.

Mollah, S. & Zaman, M. (2015). Shari'ah supervision, corporate governance and performance: Conventional vs. Islamic banks. *Journal of Banking and Finance*, *58*, 418–435.

Mollah, S., Hassan, M. K., Al Farooque, O., & Mobarek, A. (2016). The governance, risk-taking, and performance of Islamic banks. *Journal of Financial Services Research*, 1–25.

Mülbert, P. (2009). Corporate governance of banks. *European Business Organization Law Review*, *10*, 411–436.

Myers, S. C. (1977). Determinants of corporate borrowing. *Journal of Financial Economics*, *5*(2), 147–175.

Myers, S. C. (1984). The capital structure puzzle. *Journal of Finance*, *34*, 575–592.

Myers, S. C. & Majluf, N. (1984). Corporate financing and investment decisions when firms have information that investors do not have. *Journal of Financial Economics*, *13*, 187–221.

Octavia, M. & Brown, R. (2010). Determinants of bank capital structure in developing countries: Regulatory capital requirement versus the standard determinants of capital structure. *Journal of Emerging Markets*, *15*, 50–62.

Olson, D. & Zoubi, T. (2008). Using accounting ratios to distinguish between Islamic and conventional banks in GCC region. *International Journal of Accounting*, *43*, 45–65.

Olson, D. & Zoubi, T. (2017). Convergence in bank performance for commercial and Islamic banks during and after the global financial crisis. *Quarterly Review of Economics and Finance*, *65*, 71–87.

Rajan, Z. (1995). What do we know about capital structure? Some evidence from international data. *Journal of Finance*, *50*, 1421–1460.

Safieddine, A. (2009). Islamic financial institutions and corporate governance: New insights for agency theory. *Corporate Governance*, *17*, 142–158.

Shibani, O. & De Fuentes, C. (2017). Differences and similaritites between corporate governance principles in Islamic banks and conventional banks. *Research in International Business and Finance, 42*, 1005–1010. Doi: 10.1016/j.ribaf.2017.07.036.

Stulz, R. (1990). Managerial discretion and optimal financial policies. *Journal of Financial Economics*, *26*, 3–27.

Titman, S. & Wessels, R. (1988). The determinants of capital structure choice. *Journal of Finance*, *43*, 1–19.

Toumi, K. & Viviani, J.-L. (2013). Le risque lié aux comptes d'investissement participatifs: Un risque propre aux banques islamiques. *Rev des Sci Gest*, *48*, 131–142.

Toumi, K., Louhichi, W., & Viviani., J-.L. (2012). Alternative financial decision principles: Theoretical foundations of Islamic banks' capital structure. *Recent Development Alternative Finance Empirical Assessments Economic Implications* (International Symp Econ Theory Econom Vol 22) William A Barnett, Fredj Jawadi Emerald Gr Publ. Ltd. 22, 157–172.

Toumi, K., Viviani, J.-L., & Chayeh, Z. (2018). Measurement of the displaced commercial risk in Islamic Banks. *Quarterly Review of Economics and Finance*, *74*, 18–31.

Williamson, S. D. (1986). Costly monitoring, financial intermediation, and equilibrium credit rationing. *Journal of Monetary Economics*, *18*, 159–179.

https://doi.org/10.1142/9781800612426_0020

Chapter 20

Banking Performance in MENA Region: A Comparative Study Between Conventional and Islamic Bank Systems

Asma Sghaier and Asma Guizani

Abstract

This study aimed to analyze the profitability in Islamic banks and conventional ones in the Middle East and North Africa (MENA) region. After restatement, our sample consisted of 184 banks (132 conventional banks and 52 Islamic banks) in 11 countries in the MENA region. For our analysis period of 11 years (from 2009 to 2019), we collected 2024 observations. We noticed that the profitability of Islamic banks was significantly different from that of conventional ones. After examining bank risk, asset quality, environmental influences such as the level of interest rate, and country effect, we found that the cost and profit efficiencies of Islamic banks are similar to those of conventional banks. Our results suggest that the country-specific variables have a significant impact on the cost and profit efficiencies of banks operating in the MENA region, and we have confirmed that Islamic banks are more profitable than conventional ones, whereas the total loan to total assets for Islamic banks is higher than that of conventional banks. Based on regression test, return on asset (ROA) is a factor of profitability for conventional banks and Islamic banks. ROA has an important relationship with the independent variable, total equity to total asset. The deterioration of the bank's profitability poses a threat not only to the interests of consumers and internal staff but also affects investors who may equally suffer from significant financial losses. It is important to establish an effective system that assists investors in their investment choices. In prior literature, traditional models were developed but achieved short-term performances. This chapter applies a data analysis method to distinguish between conventional and Islamic banks in the MENA region. This method can successfully identify nonlinearity and correlations between the financial indicators used. The results demonstrate the superior performance of the proposed method.

Keywords: Principal Component Analysis, MENA, Profitability, Global Financial Crisis.

20.1 Introduction

Nowadays, the world faces many economic and social problems which increase the intensity of poverty in most countries, particularly the developing ones. These problems urged the international community to organize the Millennium Summit in September 2000 at the United Nations headquarters in New York. This summit set among its eight Millennium Development Goals (MDG), the elimination of extreme poverty and famine.

To achieve these goals, most countries have set up a road map that includes public and private financial structures and mechanisms to meet the needs of the poorest social categories as well the needs of the micro-entrepreneurs. As a result, conventional microfinance has emerged as an effective and flexible tool for addressing inequalities of poverty and encouraging economic growth in neglected areas in the world (Rhanoui & Belkhoutout, 2017).

However, the Consultative Group to Assist the Poor (CGAP) and Andhra Pradesh (2010) showed that conventional microfinance did not fully achieve its objectives such as reaching the needy. In addition, a crisis has emerged since 2010 endangering many International Monetary Funds (IMFs) around the world.

Faced with this reality, Islamic finance was better than conventional finance around the world.

Islamic finance is based on viable structures and mechanisms, such as waqf, qard al hassan, zakat, and takaful, which could be the solution to give access to financial services for millions of people excluded from the conventional financial system.

Since Islamic microfinance is intended by several economists as an effective solution for the alleviation of poverty, especially for all developing countries, our research will be concentrated on the region of the Middle East and North Africa (MENA) because of Tunisia's membership in this region and also to properly invest experiences from other countries.

In the same strategy of regional choice, the 13 MENA developing countries have a population of more than 355 million, with the vast majority living in middle-income countries. At the outbreak of the Arab Spring, this region had multiple assets: a young population (30% of its population is 14 years old or less and it is educated), a strong resource base, and resilience to economic shocks, which allowed it to overcome the international financial crisis of 2008–2009.

In this context, our work aims at assessing the performance of Islamic banks by using key financial indicators, such as liquidity, credit risk and credibility, capital adequacy, operational efficiency, and resources allocation efficiency, which measure the performance of Islamic banks in the MENA region.

In our work, we focused on two parts. First, we theoretically discussed the performance measurement of Islamic banks compared to the conventional ones. Second, we tested and evaluated the financial indicators based on adequate tests in our empirical study.

Several studies have been conducted in different contexts and have identified different factors that influence consumers' decision to accept the use of Islamic banks. For example, in Uganda, Kaawaase *et al.* (2019) conducted a study on the determinants of intention to adopt Islamic banking in a non-Islamic developing country. The study showed that attitude and religion are significant influencing factors on the intention to adopt, as opposed to subjective norms that have no impact. Albaity and Rahman (2019) carried out a study on the intention to adopt Islamic banking in the United Arab Emirates (UAE).

Mamun *et al.* (2018), examined the role of stock markets in the economic growth of four Asian countries, namely Bangladesh, India, Malaysia and China. In the short term, they noticed that the stock markets also have a positive relationship with economic growth in all countries.

This chapter conducts the first empirical examination of the relationship between performance risk and Islamic banks ownership. The authors examine simultaneously the effect of franchise value and owner/manager problem on Islamic bank risk-taking behavior. They consider separately the impact on total risk, systematic risk, and bank-specific risk.

This chapter applies a data analysis method to distinguish between conventional and Islamic banks in the MENA region. This method can successfully identify nonlinearity and correlations between the financial indicators used. We try to improve the accuracy of interpretations and conclusions found by the estimation of profitability (ROA) for the two subsets by the weighted least squares method to perform the results find in other works.

The main contribution of this study is to improve the estimation of profitability by using the weighted least squares method and compare the performance of conventional and Islamic banks.

This chapter is organized as follows: Section 20.2 reviews the literature to state the current problem. Section 20.3 describes the sample, data sources, and explains the empirical model used in the study. Section 20.4 reports the empirical results. Finally, Section 20.5 concludes the chapter with essential remarks.

20.2 Literature Review

Our theoretical analysis allowed us to conclude that Islamic and conventional banks have different capital structures and profitability. We used conventional arguments to explain these differences. The review of the empirical literature also allowed us to identify the classic internal determinants which affect the bank's profitability and efficiency and that could explain the differences that exist between Islamic banks and those of their conventional counterparts.

Many empirical studies focused on comparing the profitability of Islamic and conventional banks. Some studies revealed that Islamic banks were more profitable than conventional ones (Hassoune, 2002; Rosly & Bakar, 2003; Olson & Zoubi, 2008). However, other empirical studies found different results (Ahmed & Hassan, 2007; Kader & Asarpota, 2007).

Olson and Zoubi (2008) compared 28 conventional banks to 16 Islamic banks in the Gulf region over the period 2000–2005.

Their study confirmed that Islamic banks were more profitable and showed that the return on assets (ROA) and the return on equity (ROE) are significantly higher in Islamic banks. The ratio of the net interest margin (NIM) is twice as high for Islamic banks as for conventional ones, and the difference is significant. Their study also revealed that Islamic banks pay their shareholders greater dividends than their conventional counterparts.

Rosly and Bakar (2003) showed that the ROA and the profit margin of Islamic banks were higher in Malaysia during the period 1996–1999. Based on this empirical literature, the difference in profitability between Islamic and conventional banks could be explained by the difference of these determinants of profitability between the two types of banks.

Several researchers studied the role of Islamic banks in 18 countries between 1993 and 2004 (Čihák & Hesse, 2008). They analyzed the financial stability using the Z-score model. Their results indicate an interesting difference in the stability of small and large Islamic banking institutions. Smaller banks were found to be much more stable than those operating on a larger scale. They explained that Islamic banks tended to have a difficulty in monitoring credit risk when the business became larger and therefore more complex.

A number of authors analyzed the bank's performance by using data from several countries, such as Molyneux *et al.* (1992), Goddard *et al.* (2004), and Athanasoglou *et al.* (2006), others, such as Berger *et al.* (1987) (banking system in the United States), Barajas *et al.* (1999) (Colombia). Mamatzakis and Remoundos (2003) (Greece) and Garcia Herrero *et al.* (2009) (China) investigated the data analysis of specific countries.

Analyses of the bank's performance determinants were a fundamental research component in many countries, and they investigated both categories of banks: on the one hand, Islamic banks (Bashir, 1999; Bashir & Hassan, 2003; Sanusi & Ismail, 2005; Srairi, 2009), and on the other hand, conventional banks (Pasiouras & Kosmidou, 2007; Athanasoglou *et al.*, 2008; Olson & Zoubi, 2008; Srairi, 2009; Sghaier *et al.*, 2016).

Empirical investigations are based on the internal factors related to the bank's specific characteristics and on the external factors related to the banking industry and economy.

Overall, the most used internal factors that have significant effects on profitability are size, capital structure, bank asset liquidity, credit risk, and deposit volume. About the external determinants, we can mention competition, concentration, market share, inflation, and real GDP.

We summarize our literature review in Table 20.1.

We focus our study on internal and external characteristics. Our choice is justified by the fact that these determinants consider the specificities of the bank; we can thus detect the "Islamic" character of Islamic banks.

First, the relationship between the size variable (in terms of total assets) and the profitability variable is an important part of the firm's theory. Indeed, we raised the problem of the optimal size of a firm that maximizes profitability. The impact of size on the bank's profitability differs according to the studies. Dietrich and Wanzenried (2011) showed that size positively affected profitability. Bashir and Hassan (2003) found the same result for Islamic banks. This can be explained by the fact that larger banks have more opportunities to grant more loans and financing to their clients than smaller banks, which increases their ROA. However, the study by Athanasoglou *et al.* (2008) demonstrated that the size of the bank did not matter on the profitability. This result shows that small banks usually try to grow faster, even at the expense of their profitability. The financial system also takes advantage of increased higher Islamic banks productivity and then uses the untapped potential profits by expanding into those regions with restricted supply, such as the African countries (Kamarudin *et al.*, 2017; Khasawneh, 2016). Credit risk has some serious impacts on financial institutions' results, contributing to economic and financial turmoil (Kamran, Omran, & bin Mohamed Arshad, 2018, 2019). To spotlight this important problem, the study examined bank-related and macroeconomic factors of credit risk, denoted by their amount of nonperforming debts (Jabbouri & Naili, 2019).

Throughout the last couple of years, the Islamic financial system in the MENA region reported a fast expansion of 10–12% on a yearly basis and expanded coverage of Sharia principles enforcement by financial institutions, equity markets, and insurance agencies (Mrad & Mateev, 2020). The results suggest that financial performance decreases substantially the amount of liquidity and credit risks (Abdelaziz, Rim, & Helmi, 2020). It was anticipated that banks in the MENA region have higher profits in a lesser competitive environment and different natures of risk, such as insolvency, capital, liquidity, and credit-related risks, are linked strongly to bank's profitability (Moudud-Ul-Huq, Halim, & Biswas, 2020). Similarly, the

Table 20.1. Literature review of empirical analysis of conventional and Islamic banks.

Authors	**Papers**	**Method & model**
Mohammed, Dzuljastri, & Taib (2008)	Performance measures of Islamic banks based on maqashid framework	Maqashidindeks and simple additive weighting (SAW)
Mohammed & Taib (2009)	Performance test measured based on the maqashid al-Sharia model (PMMS) (24 Islamic and conventional banks)	Maqashidindeks, Mann–Withney U-test and SAW
Shaukat Mughess (2008)	The recent financial growth of Islamic banks and their realization of maqashid al-Sharia Gap analyzes	Maqashidindeks, SAW, and Gribd matrix
Shahul Hameed *et al.* (2004)	Replacement information and performance measures for Islamic banks	The comparison on Islamicity disclosure indeks
Kuppusamy, Saleha, & Samudhram (2010)	Measuring the performance of Islamic banks using sharia compliance and the profitability model	Sharia conformity and profitability (SCnP)
Ben Ali & Sghaier (2012)	Comparison between competition and the efficiency of Tunisian commercial banks during the period 2000–2006, (for a sample of 10 Tunisian banks)	• Test of Panzar and Rosse (1987) • Stochastic frontier models (SFA & DEA) for Translog & Cobb–Dauglass models
Sghaier *et al.* (2015)	Measure of banking performance	Profitability models
Sghaier *et al.* (2016)	Measuring the performance of Islamic banks using sharia compliance and the profitability model	Stochastic frontier models (SFA and DEA)
Sghaier *et al.* (2016)	Measuring competition in BIs and conventional ones	Modèle of Panzar & Rosse

Islamic system of banking as a comparison of conventional banking is more exposed toward credit risk, more liquid, more solvent, less profitable, less stable, and are more capitalized (Neifar, 2020). Banks significantly contribute to economic growth, mainly in developing nations, whereby they highlight the different mechanisms for the movement of cash.

Furthermore, the performance of the banking industry has become a quality management practice in order to improve the efficacy and stability of banking. The internationalization of financial institutions, which has already been preceded by government privatization, financial innovations, the knowledge uprising, and changes in technology, have changed the competitive financial sector and altered the banking sector (Hussain *et al.*, 2020; Alaeddin *et al.*, 2018).

Owing to these innovations and improvements in the current banking market, banks are required to improve organizational performance in terms of value and benefit to remain competitive (Otero *et al.*, 2020).

Other studies found that credit risk negatively affects the banks' profitability. Srairi (2009), Olson and Zoubi (2011), and Dietrich and Wanzenried (2011) revealed that the credit risk negatively affected the ROA of conventional banks. The capital ratio also determines the bank's profitability. Athanasoglou *et al.* (2008), Rouisi *et al.* (2010), and Olson and Zoubi (2011) illustrated that capital had a positive effect on the bank's ROA and the net margin. The study by Olson and Zoubi (2011) demonstrated that the volume of deposits positively affected the ROA of Islamic banks. Dietrich and Wanzenried (2011) stated that the volume of deposits had a significant negative impact on the ROA and the net margin ratio of conventional banks.

Mehta and Bhavani (2017) stated that there are several internal and external variables that are determinants of the profitability of the banks in the UAE. Most notable among these were the cost-efficiency ratio, adequate capital adequacy ratio, and improvement in the asset quality ratio.

Based on this empirical literature, the difference in profitability between Islamic and conventional banks could be explained by the difference of these determinants of profitability between the two types of banks.

Concerning earning ability in our model, we have focused on this parameter by using three major indicators since most studies have focused on the profitability (earnings) by using three earning indicators of ROA, ROE, and net profit margin (NPM) as proxies for the financial performance of banking and finance, ROA and ROE based on the literature (Yazdani, 2011; Khan *et al.*, 2014; Adekola, 2016; Djalilov & Piesse, 2016; Rabaa & Younes, 2016; Zarrouk *et al.*, 2016; Alharbi, 2017; Olson & Zoubi, 2017; Setyawati *et al.*, 2017; Tabash, 2019), in which higher ratios of ROA and ROE indicate better performance (Zarrouk *et al.*, 2016).

The third indicator is NPM (or net revenue margin), according to the studies of (Yazdani, 2011; Zarrouk *et al.*, 2016; Alharbi, 2017; Olson & Zoubi, 2017; Tabash, 2019) in which NPM explores the effectiveness of bank investment decisions related to its debt situations and represents the efficacy of the intermediation of bank funds (Zarrouk *et al.*, 2016). Thereby, the higher NPM ratio also reveals better financial performance. Whereas, the remaining parameters of the model were adopted by a single individual indicator based on the previous studies as shown in (Table 20.1).

The economic growth variable: All reviews in this study have settled on the use of GDP as a proxy for economic growth when it is analyzed with the financial performance of Islamic finance. Thus, this empirical study has adopted the GDP as a proxy-independent variable for economic growth. In our chapter, we try to test the following hypothesis (Ali Sulieman Alshatti, 2016):

H1: A significantly positive link between performance, cost to income ratio (COSR), and GDP growth. We estimate the profitability by OLS by using financial indicators and try to explain the link between COSR and GDP growth.

20.3 Method

20.3.1 *Data and sample procedures*

In our sample construction, we considered the MENA countries in which banking data were published regularly for the period 2009–2019.

The search results on Bankscope gave us 158 Islamic banks. The unavailability of data forced us to limit our analysis to 52 Islamic banks and 132 conventional ones. We retained only 100%

Islamic banks. We eliminated the "Islamic Windows". Banks that were classified "Islamic" by "Bankscope" but did not have a Sharia advisory board on their websites were also eliminated.

The availability of useful statistical data is a necessary condition for conducting empirical and analytical studies in any field. Our study focuses on the case of Islamic banks. The observation of this study subject is not an easy task because of the unavailability of statistical data. First, there are few specialized or general databases, offering information and data on Islamic banks. Famous databases, such as Datastream or Bankscope, certainly provide some data on these institutions (ROA, ROE), but some variables needed for our study were not available for some banks.

Clearly, bank profitability matters for financial stability. Profits are the first line of defense against losses from credit impairment. Retained earnings are an important source of capital, enabling banks to build strong buffers to absorb additional losses.

Second, the banks' annual reports were not always available. Even the big Islamic banks did not have a complete set of annual reports.

There were limitations related to the lack of standardization of the financial statements of Islamic banks. These banks did not yet use a unified accounting and the same communication and disclosure code for financial statements (as for conventional banks). Thus, the annual reports could vary considerably from one bank to another, both in their presentation and in the terminology used, that is why we limited the choice of our sample and even limited the study period according to the availability of data and annual reports.

There were limitations related to the lack of standardization of the financial statements of Islamic banks. These banks did not yet use a unified accounting and the same communication and disclosure code for financial statements (as for conventional banks). Thus, the annual reports could vary considerably from one bank to another, both in their presentation and in the terminology used, that is why we limited the choice of our sample and even limited the study period according to the availability of data and annual reports.

20.3.2 *The study period*

The initial idea of this research was to study a sample of Islamic banks for at least 10 years. Indeed, data on conventional banks are available for a long time. In the same way, this period of study makes our analysis quite rich and leads us to representative results of the current strategies and trends of banks. Several elements led us to reconsider this choice.

First, most Islamic banks were created only recently, in the 2000s. Many of them only started operating in 2005. In addition, for banks that existed before the year 2005, several annual reports were missing, which indicates the problem of the transparency of Islamic financial institutions. The preceding elements forced us to limit the length of our study to the period extending from 2009 to 2019. This period is of major importance.

The duration of our study can be considered relevant because if we compare our analysis to other research dealing with Islamic banks, we find that it is among the longest (11 years), and the other research considered one, two, or three years at most.

In addition, the period 2009–2019 witnessed several important financial events, including:

- 2007: The financial crisis recorded some strains on liquidity;
- 2008: The purely financial liquidity crisis evolved toward a crisis of confidence paralyzing all banks leading to a crisis of the real economy;
- 2009: The "subprime" crisis spread to all sectors of finance and the real economy, the first actions of public authorities arose to contain the crisis;
- 2010: The influx of liquidity raised the fears of bursting new bubbles in real estate, stock markets, and government bonds. It was the financial crisis in the background (Boyer, Dehove, & Plihon, 2004).

Our analysis focused on the crisis period of "subprime" (2009–2019), the economic crisis that shook finance, and more broadly the global economy between 2007 and 2010.

20.3.3 *Data sources*

We used the "Bankscope" database to collect accounting, financial, and managerial data about the banks in our sample. This database is almost concerned with all banking firms in the world. It includes the balance sheet data, income statements, activity reports, annual reports, and abridged statements of the banks in question. These different reports can be downloaded directly from the website of the database. For our sample, we selected all the banks for which data are available and then excluded the firms for which data are missing.

After restatement, our sample consisted of 184 banks (132 conventional banks and 52 Islamic banks) in 11 countries in the MENA region. For our seven-year analysis period, we collected 2024 observations. These panel data allow us to take advantage of the individual and temporal dimensions of the information available. All amounts are expressed in thousands of US dollars (MUSD). To convert the currencies the exchange rate was used on 31/12 of each year.

20.3.4 *Models, variables, and methodology*

Table 20.2 shows variables' definitions and the expected effect of the independent and control variables on the dependent variable. The mathematical formulation of the model is as follows:

$$\mathbf{ROA}_{i,t} = \beta_0 + \beta_1\mathbf{LLR}_{i,t} + \beta_2\mathbf{EA}_{i,t} + \beta_3\mathbf{COSR}_{i,t} + \beta_4\mathrm{NLA}_{i,t} + \beta_5\mathbf{GDP}_{i,t} + \beta_6\mathbf{CPI}_{i,t} + \mu_{i,t} + \varepsilon_{i,t}.$$

Dependent variable:
• ROA = Profitability

Independent variables:
• LLR = Loan loss reserves to gross loan ratio
• EA = Total equity to total assets ratio
• COSR = Cost to income ratio
• NLA = Net loans to total assets ratio
• GDP = GDP growth rate
• CPI = Consumer price index

We can notice from the results of Table 20.1, the weakness of the scope of Islamic finance in the MENA countries, especially in terms of microfinance and the refusal of suppliers to provide Islamic microfinance services. When analyzing the behavior of target groups in the region and their orientation toward the demand of Islamic finance, we found that studies showed that the demand for Islamic microfinance tools indicates that nearly two-thirds of the microfinance clients in

Table 20.2. Definitions, rating, and expected effect of the explanatory variables of bank performance.

Variables	Description	Rating	Expected effect
A. Dependent variable	Return on average assets	ROA	
B. Independent variable			
Specific to banks			
Assets Quality	Loans loss reserves/ gross loans	LLR	Positive
Capital	Equity to total assets	EA	Positive
Efficiency	Cost to income ratio	COSR	Negative
Liquidity	Net loans to total assets	NLA	Negative
Macroeconomic			
GDP growth	GDP growth	GDP	Positive
Inflation	Consumer price index	CPI	Positive

Sources: Melaty Binti Ghazali, 2008. The bank-specific and macroeconomic determinants of Islamic bank profitability: Some international evidence.

the Islamic world insisted on Islamic finance. Table 20.3 shows the scope of microfinance institutions in each country.

For example, 60% of low-income participants in the Gaza Strip and the West Bank preferred Islamic financing instruments, even if the cost is higher. Further, studies in Jordan conducted by the United States Agency (USAID) showed that 32% of these respondents indicated religious reasons for not obtaining loans from the Foundation for International Community Assistance (FINCA) in Jordan, while in Yemen 40% requested Islamic services, regardless of the cost, and in Syria also, 43% of participants believed that religious reasons were the biggest obstacle for microfinance. We noted that many clients refused services not compliant with Sharia (Sghaier *et al.*, 2016).

Market analysis is very important to assess, study, and understand the needs, behaviors, estimates, and expectations of a target population. It includes several techniques such as quantitative techniques which can be manifested in some forms of investigation and documentation.

Then, we tested the classical assumptions of the application of ordinary least squares methods for the estimation of our model. We began by testing the multicollinearity of the variables, then the heteroskedasticity and the autocorrelation of errors to decide on the choice of the most efficient estimation method.

Table 20.3. Scope of the MFI.

Region	No. of institutions covered	% of women (average)	Total no. of customers	Total outstanding loan portfolio (US$)	Average loan balance (US$)
Afghanistan	4	22	53,011	10,347.290	162
Bahrain	1	n.d	323	96,565	299
Bangladeshi	2	90	111,837	34,490.490	280
Indonesia*	105	60	74,698	122,480.000	1,640
Jordan	1	80	1,481	1,619.909	1,094
Libanon	1	50	26,000	22,500.000	865
Mali	1	12	2,812	273.298	97
Pakistan	1	40	6,060	746.904	123
West Bank and Gaza**	1	100	132	145.485	1,102
Saoudi Arabia	1	86	7,000	586.667	84
Somalia	1	n.a	50	35.200	704
Sudan	3	65	9,561	1,891.819	171
Syrian Arab Republic	1	45	2,298	1,838.047	800
Yemen	3	58	7,031	840.240	46
Total	**126**	**59**	**302,303**	**197,891.882**	**541**

Notes: *Microcredits and rural banks only. **In the West Bank and Gaza seven MFIs granted. Thanks to training and financing facilities offered by the Islamic Development Bank, a total of 578 Islamic loans between 2005 and 2006. The table only contains data relating to one of these MFIs. The other six have granted Islamic loans for an average amount of more than 250% of the gross domestic product per capita of the region.
Source: The Islamic Banking System-Trade Center.

We started by testing the correlations of the explanatory variables via the analysis of the correlation matrix.

To be more efficient in our study, we consider the significant explanatory variables.

We noted that from Table 20.4, there is a strong correlation between the performance variables. Table 20.5 presents a symmetric square matrix that describes the correlation between the variables of this study.

The COSR variable (cost to income ratio = total cost/total assets), which refers to the efficiency of the firm, is significantly negative for the equity to total assets (EA). Most of the other

Table 20.4. Correlation matrix of explanatory variables.

	Correlation matrix												
Variables	ROAA	Asset	Equity	EA	Share_ Cap	NLA	Nllnc	OtOpe	TOperln	LN	Dep STF	Cust Dep	Dep
ROAA	1.0000	−0.0138	0.0068	0.2688	0.0402	0.1202	0.0305	0.0187	0.0270	−0.0114	−0.0140	−0.0115	−0.0084
Asset	−0.0138	1.0000	0.8742	−0.1443	0.5978	0.0963	0.6366	0.8275	0.8422	0.8935	0.9767	0.9739	0.7800
Equity	0.0068	0.8742	1.0000	−0.0715	0.5606	0.0766	0.7395	0.7460	0.8573	0.8074	0.8287	0.8311	0.8728
EA	0.2688	−0.1443	−0.0715	1.0000	−0.0782	−0.2055	−0.1129	−0.1100	−0.1336	−0.1659	−0.1404	−0.1331	−0.1289
Share_Cap	0.0402	0.5978	0.5606	−0.782	1.0000	0.2215	0.5991	0.4789	0.6389	0.6493	0.5798	0.5529	0.4633
NLA	0.1202	0.0963	0.0766	−0.2055	0.2215	1.0000	0.1033	0.827	0.1122	0.1614	0.1016	0.1002	0.0793
Nllnc	0.0305	0.6366	0.7395	−0.1129	0.5991	0.1033	1.0000	0.4484	0.8563	0.6710	0.5671	0.5554	0.6677
OtOpe	0.0187	0.8275	0.7460	−0.1100	0.4789	0.0827	0.4484	1.0000	0.8216	0.6672	0.8284	0.8330	0.6883
TOperln	0.0270	0.8422	0.8573	−0.1336	0.6389	0.1122	0.8563	0.8216	1.0000	0.7962	0.8135	0.8079	0.8066
LN	−0.0114	0.8935	0.8074	−0.1659	0.6493	0.1614	0.6710	0.6672	0.7962	1.0000	0.8885	0.8713	0.8235
DepSTF	−0.0140	0.9767	0.8287	−0.1404	0.5798	0.1016	0.5671	0.8284	0.8135	0.8885	1.0000	0.9975	0.7694
CustDep	−0.0115	0.9739	0.8311	−0.1331	0.5529	0.1002	0.5554	0.8330	0.8079	0.8713	0.9975	1.0000	0.7654
Dep	−0.0084	0.7800	0.8728	−0.1289	0.4633	0.0793	0.6677	0.6883	0.8066	0.8235	0.7694	0.7654	1.0000

Table 20.5. Correlation matrix: Total sample.

	Eigenvalues of the correlation matrix			
	Eigenvalue	**Difference**	**Proportion**	**Cumulative**
1	7.82381845	6.55029987	0.6018	0.6018
2	1.27351857	0.12582433	0.0980	0.6998
3	1.14769424	0.35745268	0.0883	0.7881
4	0.79024156	0.16391454	0.0608	0.8489
5	0.62632702	0.11616590	0.0482	0.8970
6	0.51016111	0.14980532	0.0392	0.9363
7	0.36035580	0.12457480	0.0277	0.9640
8	0.23578100	0.09915441	0.0181	0.9821
9	0.13662659	0.07586118	0.0105	0.9927
10	0.06076541	0.03805863	0.0047	0.9973
11	0.02270679	0.01210430	0.0017	0.9991
12	0.01060249	0.00920151	0.0008	0.9999
13	0.00140097	—	0.0001	1.0000

variables have a negative relationship with COSR, including the measure of profitability, ROA. This is consistent with the results obtained by Heffernan and Fu (2008). There is a positive relationship between the variable, net loans to total assets (NLA), and the ROA profitability ratios. The same positive aspect applies to the relationship between the loans loss reserves (LLR) and the ratio (COSR), while there is a negative relation between the variables LL, COSR, and the ratio (EA), which suggests an increase in liquidity. On the other hand, the NLA is negatively correlated to EA and the consumer price index (CPI).

Gross domestic product (GDP) growth affects many factors related to the supply and demand of loans and deposits. From the correlation matrix, we find that the GDP has an inverse relationship with most variables such as ROA, EA, and CPI, while it is positively correlated with the LLR, COSR, and NLA. This is consistent with the study by Kosmidou (2008) who stated that GDP harmed the ROA.

The inflation variable, which is represented by the CPI, has a positive effect on the ROA and EA and a negative impact on the other variables.

Table 20.6. Correlation matrix.

Variables	ROA	ROE	llpr	EA	COSIR	NLA	GDP	CPI
ROA	1.0000							
ROE	0.6299	1.0000						
llpr	−0.0599	−0.0419	1.0000					
EA	0.2688	−0.0558	−0.1044	1.0000				
COSIR	−0.3098	−0.2962	0.0300	−0.0446	1.0000			
NLA	0.1207	0.1735	0.0541	−0.2047	0.3404	1.0000		
GDP	−0.0838	−0.0142	0.1810	−0.0832	0.2394	0.1700	1.0000	
CPI	0.1211	0.0674	−0.0761	0.1115	−0.116	−0.0649	−0.0555	1.0000

The link between the ROA, ROE and EA, and the inflation index is positive. The most important correlation coefficient is found between the ROA profitability ratio and the liquidity ratios.

We show that there is a problem of multicollinearity. So, to recall this problem, we can analyze the principal components. The number of extracted components in a principal component analysis (PCA) is equal to four main components (Ax 1, Ax 2, Ax 3, Ax 4) which contain 84.89% of the total variation. Component 1 explains 60.18% of the variation, component 2 explains 9%, component 3 explains 8%, and component 4 explains 6%.

Finally, we transform the 12 original variables into four main components.

To create a description of each factor, the highest load variables on each factor are summarized, as shown in Table 20.6.

According to Table 20.7, we can define the four axes as follows:

- **Axis 1:** total assets of the firms;
- **Axis 2:** total liabilities of firms;
- **Axis 3:** banking liquidity;
- **Axis 4:** debt situation of firms.

In Figures 20.1 and 20.2, we projected the explanatory variables on the axes to confirm the interpretation we gave for each one of them.

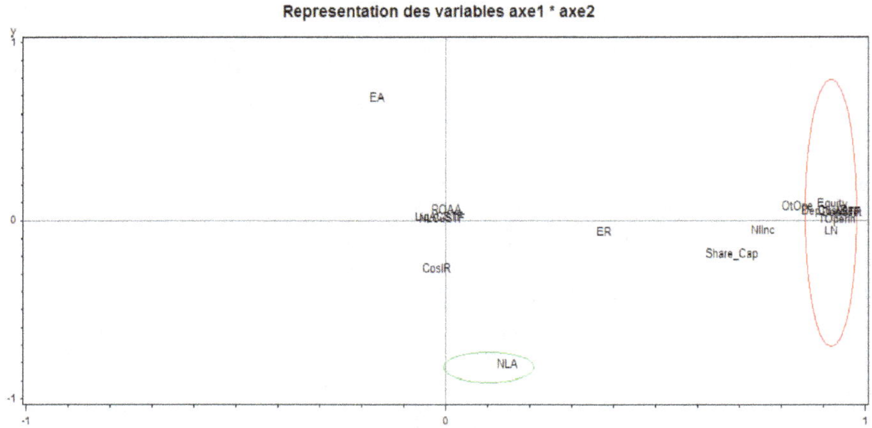

Figure 20.1. Representation of variables Axis 1 vs. Axis 2.

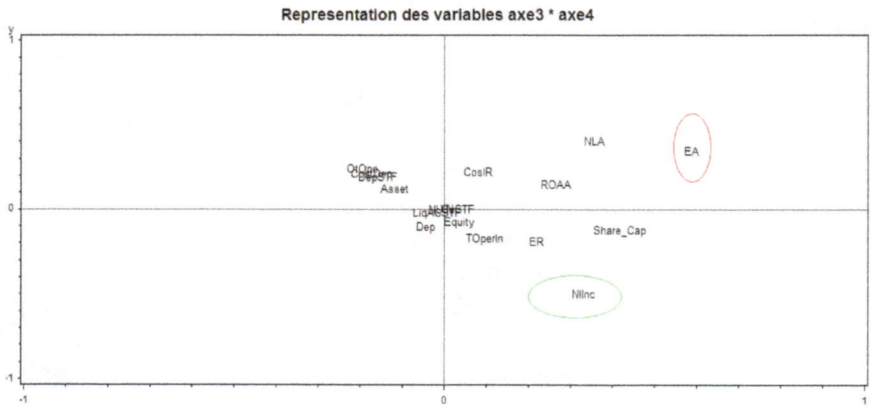

Figure 20.2. Representation of variables Axe 3 vs. Axe 4.

20.3.5 *Regression*

Once the multicollinearity problem is solved by the principal component analysis method, we proceed to the estimation of the model.

We have a linear model to estimate ROA by using four principal components:

$$\text{ROAA} = \beta_0 + \beta_1 \text{axe}_1 + \beta_2 \text{axe}_2 + \beta_3 \text{axe}_3 + \beta_4 \text{axe}_4 + \varepsilon.$$

We divide our sample into two subsamples: one specified to Islamic banks and the other for conventional ones.

Table 20.7. Correlation of variables with the different main axes.

	Axe 1	Axe 2	Axe 3	Axe 4
Asset	0.96086			
Equity	0.92334			
EA		0.70121	0.58965	
Share_cap	0.68277			
ER				
NLA		−0.79455		0.41158
CosIR				
NIInc	0.75777			−0.48817
Otope	0.83935			
TOperln	0.93453			
LN	0.92111			
LiqACSTF				
NLCuSTF				
DepSTF	0.94488			
CustDep	0.93851			
Dep	0.87133			

We note $\text{ROA}_{(0)}$ for Islamic banks and $\text{ROA}_{(1)}$ for conventional banks.

Number of observations for Islamic banks	572
[2]**Number of observations for conventional banks**	1452

Table 20.8 shows the R-square and F-values of the models. Table 20.9 shows the white test and Breusch–Pagan test. The values of the estimated parameters give the equation for the fitted model:

$$\begin{aligned}\text{ROAA}_{(1)} &= 2.32150 - 0.01179\,\text{axe }1 + 2.68418\,\text{axe2} + 1.56463\,\text{axe3}\\ &\quad + 0.60189\,\text{axe4},\end{aligned}$$

$$\begin{aligned}\text{ROAA}_{(0)} &= 2.31941 + 0.13434\,\text{axe }1 + 3.16705\,\text{axe2} + 3.46282\,\text{axe3}\\ &\quad + 1.81682\,\text{axe4}.\end{aligned}$$

We can visualize the distribution of residuals in the model by plotting them by QQ-Plot — "Normal Probability Plot" (see Figure 20.3). We see a bad-looking normal quintile plot. Therefore, it is incompatible with the normal distribution.

Table 20.8. Characteristics of OLS models.

			Interpretation	
	ROAA$_{(1)}$	**ROAA$_{(0)}$**	**ROAA$_{(1)}$**	**ROAA$_{(0)}$**
R^2	0.7132	0.9059	A good fit	A very good fit
$\overline{R}^2$	0.7120	0.9048	A good fit	A very good fit
F-value	p-value <0.0001	p-value <0.0001	This causes a rejection of the null hypothesis at the 5% level. It indicates that at least one coefficient beta is not zero so the model is significant	

Table 20.9. The white test and Breusch–Pagan test.

Heteroskedasticity Test					
Equation	**Test**	**Statistique**	**DDL**	**Pr > Khi-2**	**Variables**
ROAA(0)	White's Test	139.2	14	<0.0001	Cross of all vars
	Breusch–Pagan	54.92	4	<0.0001	axe 1, axe 2, axe 3, axe 4, 1
ROAA(1)	White's Test	825.6	14	<0.0001	Cross of all vars
	Breusch–Pagan	152.6	4	<0.0001	axe 1, axe 2, axe 3, axe 4, 1

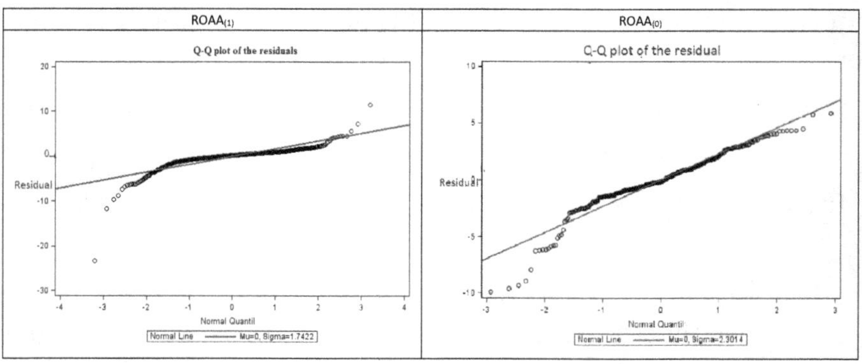

Figure 20.3. Evolution of profitability indicators by type of bank.

We can conclude, also, that all these tests show there is heteroskedasticity in the two models.

Finally, the residue study confirms the absence of the first-order autocorrelation for the two models.

To solve the problem of heteroskedasticity and the non-normality of errors, we modified the model by using the weighted least squares (WLS) method to get the estimators. The results are shown in the following.

20.4 Results and Discussion

Table 20.10 shows the results found when estimating our model by using the WLS method, considering the ROA ratio as the variable to be explained for the two subsets: Islamic banks and conventional ones.

We note that Islamic banks present a more efficient model than conventional ones and this is by comparing their explanatory powers. This explains that despite the intense competition and the relentless evolution of the economic environment, Islamic banks are still performing well.

Our study shows that unconventional banks perform much better based on their return on assets than on their return on equity.

So, we can say that banks are increasingly profitable that they develop other activities or that they are getting bigger (which is the

Table 20.10. Weighted least squares method.

			Interpretation	
Coefficient	**ROAA$_{(1)}$**	**ROAA$_{(0)}$**	**ROAA$_{(1)}$**	**ROAA$_{(0)}$**
R^2	0.8679	0.8863	A good fit	A very good fit
$\overline{R}^2$	0.8673	0.8851	A good fit	A very good fit
F-value	1509.31	699.83	This causes a rejection of the null hypothesis at the 5% level. It indicates that at least one coefficient beta is not zero so the model is significant	

case of conventional banks). These results were also found by Bourke (1989) and Molyneux *et al.* (1992).

To summarize, the overall conclusion (Saibal Ghosh, 2015) reached in the analysis was that the Arab Spring exerted an asymmetric impact on the MENA region, both across banks and countries. Although the magnitude of the impact on profits was not sizeable, there was, however, quite a discernible impact on the bank's solvency. Further research would of course be necessary to understand whether the impact differed across oil importers and exporters and if so, to what extent, given their differential fiscal space, especially after the crisis. Additionally, given the duration of the Arab Spring was also different across the affected countries, it remains a moot question as to how far this had a role to play in affecting the bank's performance. Addressing these questions comprises elements for future research.

For the dependent variables, the author has chosen OA. The dependent variable corresponds to studies made by Pradhan and Shrestha (2016) which stated that management efficiency has a positive strong correlation to bank's performance. While macroeconomic factors are important, they do not play a vital role in the impact of the individual performance of the bank. The study further revealed that ROA and NIM could be decisive factors affecting bank's performance.

Menicucci and Paolucci (2016) further investigated the relation between bank-specific factors with profitability in the European banking sector to ascertain the role of internal factors in achieving higher profitability. Their analysis used a regression model for 35 banks based on capital ratios and loan loss provision ratios on the efficiency of the banks over the period 2009–2013. Their study suggested that banks with higher deposits and loan ratios are more profitable, but their effect was statistically insignificant to compare the efficiency of these banks.

Abobaker's (2018) study stated that high profitability can be achieved by increasing the bank assets, capital ratio, and operating income. Consequently, the profitability is reduced as non-interest income increases over time. Following the same concepts for conventional and Islamic banks as provided in Table 20.2, there is a nominal deviation in ROA, NIM, and capital adequacy of the conventional and Islamic banks in the UAE. The reason could include those banks in the UAE apply similar interest rates and have sufficient liquid assets within the UAE without considering macroeconomic factors.

There is significant variation in PEA and the reason could be the Sharia requirements that need to be followed by the Islamic banks as these are more conservative in their lending practices.

For independent variables, the table reveals a range of variation. The most notable variation is seen in ROE, ED, TLSC, and RETA. The reason for the large difference in the means is due to the size and composition of the banks' balance sheet. Also, some banks have been in existence for a longer time than others conventional banks in the UAE. While other independent variables indicate insignificant variation, it signifies consistency of the business model between Islamic and conventional banks. It must be known that UAE is an over-banked market with 22 local national banks, 27 branches of foreign banks, and 11 wholesale foreign bank branches as of June 30, 2019. Further, even though there is demand for Islamic products, UAE Islamic banks enjoy a relatively small market share as compared to their conventional counterparts as stated by the study conducted by Kapur (2020).

20.5 Conclusion

Through the above theoretical analysis and model estimation of the ROA ratio for the two subsets: Islamic banks and conventional ones, it is shown that, first, the weakness of the scope of Islamic finance in the MENA countries, especially in terms of microfinance and the refusal of suppliers to provide Islamic microfinance services. Second, the estimation of profitability (ROA) by WLS method to solve the problem of heteroskedasticity and the autocorrelation to perform the first results find.

In this chapter, the principal component analysis method and the WLS method are used to improve the accuracy of interpretations and conclusions found previously.

The results verify that this estimation method is effective and applicable and gives good results. We note, also, that Islamic banks present a more efficient model than conventional ones, and this is by comparing their explanatory powers. This explains that despite the intense competition and the relentless evolution of the economic environment, Islamic banks are still performing well. This chapter develops a model to identify a set of specific and macroeconomic determinants of bank profitability for conventional and Islamic banks in the MENA region.

We adopted several ratios from the empirical literature on bank profitability. The findings show that specific and macroeconomic factors have a significant effect on bank profitability. Based on a dynamic model specification, empirical analysis results reveal that the determinants' significance varies between Islamic banks and conventional banks. Profitability seems to be quite persistent in the MENA region, reflecting a higher degree of government intervention and may signal barriers to competition.

We find that banking capital is important in explaining conventional bank profitability. The efficiency of expenditure management is negatively linked to Islamic bank profitability.

Additionally, the ownership status of banks is significant for Islamic banks in explaining profitability, denoting that Islamic banks make relatively higher profits.

Furthermore, for the macroeconomic control variables, economic growth affects the performance of conventional banks. Overall, our findings provide some evidence into the factors that explain the profitability of conventional banks and Islamic banks in the MENA region. First, our estimation results concur with the previous studies on bank profitability. Second, we consider a large set of the bank- and industry-specific determinants.

To enhance academic understanding of this study, this research can be extended particularly by studying a larger sample size, hence the sample size used in this study might be relatively limited, and many important banks were omitted from the study, which can significantly affect the findings. In addition, future studies could be conducted for specific MENA countries to identify the profitability in each of these countries separately; this could not be achieved by the current study due to the nature and size of the sample studied. Also, future studies should attempt to extend the study by introducing other alternatives of bank performance and the impact of insurance and agency rating agencies to solve the risk problems.

The future avenues of the study are to include control variables in our regression analysis to verify the results found.

In addition, we consider more factors and variables to be used to evaluate profitability in Islamic finance in the future.

References

Abaoub, E., Homrani, K., & Gamra, S. B. (2013). The determinants of earnings management: Empirical evidence in the Tunisian banking industry (1999–2010). *Journal of Business Studies Quarterly, 4*(3), 62–72.

Abdel Karim, R. A. (1990). The independence of religious and external auditors: The case of Islamic banks. *Accounting, Auditing & Accountability Journal, 3*(3), 34–44.

Abdelaziz, H., Rim, B., & Helmi, H. (2020). The interactional relationships between credit risk, liquidity risk and bank profitability in MENA region. *Global Business Review*, 1–23. Doi: 10.1177/0972150919879304.

Abdul Rahman, R. (2012). *Religious Ethical Values and Earnings Quality: Some Evidence from Malaysia*, PhD Dissertations, Massey University, Albany, New Zealand.

Abdullah, N. & Tan, Y. (2017). Profitability of commercial banks revisited: New evidence from oil and non-oil exporting countries in the MENA region. *Investment Management and Financial Innovations, 14*(3), 62–73.

Abobaker, M. J. (2018). Bank specific, industry concentration and macroeconomic determinants of Egyptian bank profitability. *International Journal of Accounting and Financial Studies, 8*(1), 380–397.

Africa Region, *Comparative Economic Studies, 52*(3), 287–323.

Aharony, J., Wang, J., & Yuan, H. (2010). Tunneling as an incentive for earnings management during the IPO process in China. *Journal of Accounting and Public Policy, 29*(1), 1–26.

Ahmad, A. U. F. & Hassan, M. K. (2007). Regulation and performance of Islamic banking in Bangladesh. *Thunderbird International Business Review, 49*(2), 251–277.

Ahmed, A. S., Takeda, C., & Thomas, S. (1999). Bank loan loss provisions: A reexamination of capital management, earnings management and signaling effects. *Journal of Accounting and Economics, 28*(1), 1–25.

Ahrens, B. (2010). *Capital Market Implications of Earnings Quality.* Lohmar-Koln Josef Eul Verlag GmbH.

Akande, J. O., Kwenda, F., & Ehalaiye, D. (2018). Competition and commercial banks risk-taking: Evidence from Sub-Saharan Africa region. *Applied Economics*, *50*(44), 4774–4787. Doi: 10.1080/00036846.2018.1466995.

Akhtar, M. H. (2002). X-efficiency analysis of commercial banks in Pakistan: A preliminary investigation. *The Pakistan Development Review*, *41*(4). 567–580.

Albaity, M. & Rahman, M. M. (2019). The intention to use Islamic banking: An exploratory study to measure Islamic financial literacy. *International Journal of Emerging Markets*, *14*(15), 988–1012.

Al-Jarrah, I. & Molyneux, P. (2003) *Efficiency in Arabian banking*. Paper presented at the International Conference on Financial Development in Arab Countries, Abu Dhabi, UAE.

Altamuro, J. & Beatty, A. (2010). How does internal control regulation affect financial reporting? *Journal of Accounting and Economics*, *49*(1), 58–74.

Alves, S. (2012). Ownership structure and earnings management: Evidence from Portugal. *Australasian Accounting, Business and Finance Journal*, *6*(1), 57–74.

Anandarajan, A., Hasan, I., & McCarthy, C. (2007). Use of loan loss provisions for capital, earnings management and signaling by Australian banks. *Accounting and Finance*, *47*, 357–379.

Ariff, M. (2007). Islamic banking: a variation of conventional banking. *Monash Business Review*, *3*(1), 1–8.

Ashraf, A., Hassan, M. K., & Basher, S. A. (2015). Loan loss provisioning in OIC countries: Evidence from conventional vs. Islamic banks. *Journal of King Abdulaziz University: Islamic Economics*, *28*(1), 23–59.

Athanasoglou, P., Brissimis, S., & Delis, M. D. (2008). Bank-specific, industry-specific and macroeconomic déterminants of bank profitability. *Journal of International Financial Markets Institutions and Money*, *18*(2), 121–136.

Athanasoglou, P., Delis, M. D., & Staikouras, C. (2006). Determinants of bank profitability in the South Eastern European Region.

Barajas, A., Steiner, R., & Salazar, N. (1999). Interest spreads in banking in Colombia, 1974–96. *IMF Staff Papers*. *46*(2), 196–224.

Bashir, A.-H. M. (1999). Risk and profitability measures in Islamic banks: The case of two sudanese banks. *Islamic Economic Studies*, *6*, 1–24.

Beatty, A. L., Ke, B., & Petroni, K. R. (2002). Earnings management to avoid earnings declines across publicly and privately held banks. *The Accounting Review*, *77*(3), 547–570.

Beaver, W. & Engel, E. (1996). Discretionary behavior with respect to allowances for loan losses and the behavior of security prices. *Journal of Accounting & Economics*, *22*(1–3), 177–206.

Ben Ali, M. S. & Sghaier, A. (2012). Competition and banking efficiency evidence from Tunisian banking industry. *Journal of Islamic Economics, Banking and Finance*, *8*(1), 53–70.

Ben Othman, H. & Mersni, H. (2014). The use of discretionary loan loss provisions by Islamic banks and conventional banks in the Middle East region: A comparative study. *Studies in Economics and Finance*, *31*(1), 106–128.

Berger, A., Hanweck, G., & Humphrey, D. (1987). Competitive viability in banking: Scale, scope and product mix economies. *Journal of Monetary Economics*, *20*, 501–520.

Biurrun, M. V. (2010). *Bank Earnings Management: Costs, Drivers and Remedies*, Doctoral Dissertation, WHU.

Bo, X. H. & Wu, L. S. (2009). The governance roles of state-owned controlling and institutional investors: A perspective of earnings management. *Economic Research Journal*, *2*, 81–91.

Bourke, P. (1989). Concentration and other determinants of bank profitability in Europe, North America and Australia. *Journal of Banking & Finance*, *13*(1), 65–79.

Bouvatier, V., Lepetit, L., & Strobel, F. (2014). Bank income smoothing, ownership concentration and the regulatory environment. *Journal of Banking & Finance*, *41*, 253–270.

Boyer, R., Dehove, M., & Plihon, D. (2004). *Les Crises Financières. La Documentation Française*. La Documentation française. Paris, 2004, ISBN: 2-11-005815-3.

Burgstahler, D. & Dichev, I. (1997). Earnings management to avoid earnings decreases and losses. *Journal of Accounting and Economics*, *24*(1), 99–126.

Busta, I., Sinani, E., & Thomsen, S. (2014). Ownership concentration and market value of European banks. *Journal of Management & Governance*, *18*, 159–183.

Caprio, G., Laeven, L., & Levine, R. (2007). Governance and bank valuation. *Journal of Financial Intermediation*, *16*, 584–617.

Chen, C. W. K. & Yuan, H. (2004). Earnings management and resource allocation: Evidence from China's accounting-based regulation of rights issues. *The Accounting Review*, *79*(3), 645–665.

Chen, K. Y., Lin, K. L., & Zhou, J. (2007). Audit quality and earnings management for Taiwan IPO firms. *Managerial Auditing Journal*, *20*(1), 86–104.

Chniguir, M., Sghaier, A., Soufeljil, M., & Mighri, Z. (2016). The degree of home bias in the holding of share portfolio: Case of American investors. *International Journal of Sustainable Economies Management*, *6*(3), 10–25.

Čihák, M. & Hesse, H. (2008). Islamic banks and financial stability: An empirical analysis. *Journal of Financial Services Research*, *38*(2), 95–113.

Cihák, M., Demirgüç-Kunt, A., Pería, M. S. M., & Mohseni A. (2012). Banking regulation and supervision around the world: A crisis update, World Bank Policy Research Working Paper 6286, December.

Conroy, S. J. & Emerson, T. L. N. (2004). Business ethics and religion: Religiosity as a predictor of ethical awareness among students. *Journal of Business Ethics*, *55*, 373–386.

Cornett, M. M., McNutt, J. J., & Tehranian, H. (2009). Corporate governance and earnings management at large US bank holding companies. *Journal of Corporate Finance*, *15*(4), 412–430.

Curcio, D. & Hasan, I. (2015). Earnings and capital management and signaling: The use of loan-loss provisions by European banks. *The European Journal of Finance*, *21*(1), 26–50.

Dechow, P., Ge, W., & Schrand, C. (2010). Understanding earnings quality: A review of the proxies, their determinants and their consequences. *Journal of Accounting and Economics*, *50*(2–3), 344–401.

Dechow, P., Sloan, R., & Sweeney, A. (1996). Causes and consequences of earnings manipulations: An analysis of firms subject to enforcement actions by the SEC. *Contemporary Accounting Research*, *13*(1), 1–36.

Demerjian, P. R., Lev, B., Lewis, M. F., & McVay S. E. (2012). Managerial ability and earnings quality. *The Accounting Review*, *88*(2), 463–498.

Demsetz, H. & Lehn, K. (1985). The structure of corporate ownership: Causes and consequences. *Journal of Political Economy*, *93*, 1155–1177.

Dietrich, A. & Wanzenried, G. (2011). Determinants of bank profitability before and during the crisis: Evidence from Switzerland. *Journal of International Financial Markets*, *21*(3), 307–327.

Ding, Y., Hope, O., Jeanjean, T., & Stolowy, H. (2007). Differences between domestic accounting standards and IAS: Measurement, determinants and implications. *Journal of Accounting and Public Policy*, *26*(1), 1–38.

Dyreng, S., Mayew, W. J., & Williams, C. D. (2012). Religious social norms and corporate financial reporting. *Journal of Business Finance and Accounting*, *39*(7–8), 845–875.

El Hawary, D., Grais, W., & Iqbal, Z. (2008). Regulation Islamic financial institutions: The nature of the regulated, World Bank Policy Research Working Paper.

Fan, J. P. H. & Wong, T. J. (2002). Corporate ownership structure and the in formativeness of accounting earnings in East Asia. *Journal of Accounting and Economics*, *33*(3), 401–425.

Fang, Y., Hasan, I., & Li, L. (2014). Banking reform, risk-taking and earnings quality-evidence from transition countries. Bank of Finland BOFIT- Institute for Economies in Transition, Discussion paper 19/2014.

Farazi, S., Feyen, E., & Rocha, R. (2011). *Bank Ownership and Performance in the Middle East and North Africa*, Policy Research Working Paper 5620, Washington, DC, United States: World Bank.

Fonseca, A. R. & Gonzalez, F. (2008). Cross-country determinants of bank income smoothing by managing loan-loss provisions. *Journal of Banking & Finance*, *32*, 217–228.

Francis, J., LaFond, R., Olsson, P. M., & Schipper, K. (2004). Costs of equity and earnings attributes. *The Accounting Review*, *79*(4), 967–1010.

Gaio, C. & Raposo, C. (2011). Earnings quality and firm valuation: International evidence. *Accounting and Finance*, *51*, 467–499.

Garcia Herrero, A., Gavilá, S., & Santabárbara, D. (2009). What explains the low profitability of Chinese banks? *Journal of Banking & Finance*, *33*(11), 2080–2092.

Ghosh, S. (2014). *Risk, Capital and Financial Crisis*. MPRA Paper 65246, University Library of Munich, German.

Goddard, J., Molyneux, P., & Wilson, J. O. S. (2004). The profitability of European banks: A cross-sectional and dynamic panel analysis. *The Manchester School*, *72*(3), 363–381.

Hamdi, F. M. & Zarai, M. A. (2012). Earnings management to avoid earnings decreases and losses: Empirical evidence from Islamic banking industry. *Research Journal of Finance and Accounting*, *3*(3), 88–107.

Hasan, M. et Dridi, J. (2010). The effects of global crisis on Islamic and conventional banks: A comparative study, IMF Working paper 10/201.

Hassan, M. K. & Bashir, A. M. (2003). Determinants of Islamic banking profitability. ERF paper.

Hassan, M. K., Samad, M., & Islam, M. M. (2003). The performance evaluation of the Bahraini banking system. University of New Orleans: Working Paper.

Hassoune, A. (2002). Islamic banks' profitability in an interest rate cycle. *Arab Bank Review, International Journal of Islamic Financial Services*, *4*(2).

Haw, I. M., Ho, S. S. M., Hu, B., & Wu, D. (2010). Concentrated control, institutions, and banking sector: An international study. *Journal of Banking & Finance*, *34*(3), 485–497.

Hussain, H. I., Kamarudin, F., Thaker, H. M. T., & Salem, M. A. (2019). Artificial neural network to model managerial timing decision: Non-linear evidence of deviation from target leverage. *International Journal of Computational Intelligence Systems, 12*(2), 1282–1294.

Hussain, H. I., Kot, S., Kamarudin, F., & Mun, W. C. (2020). The nexus of competition freedom and the efficiency of microfinance institutions. *Journal of Competitiveness, 12*(2), 67–89.

Ibrahim, M. (2020). Islamic banking and bank performance in Malaysia: An empirical analysis. *Journal of Islamic Monetary Economics and Finance, 6*(3), 487–502. Doi: 10.21098/jimf.v6i3.1197.

Illiashenko, P. & Laidroo, L. (2020). National culture and bank risk-taking: Contradictory case of individualism. *Research in International Business and Finance, 51*, 101069. Doi: 10.1016/j.ribaf.2019.101069.

Iqbal, M. (2001). Islamic and conventional banking in the nineties: A comparative study. In *Islamic Economic Studies*. The Islamic Research and Training Institute (IRTI), Vol. 8, pp. 1–27.

Isenmila, P. A. & Elijah, A. (2012). Earnings management and ownership structure: Evidence from Nigeria. *Research Journal of Finance and Accounting, 3*(7), 24–36.

Jaouadi, S. & Zorgui, I. (2014). Exploring effectiveness and efficiency of banks in Switzerland. *International Journal of Academic Research in Business and Social Sciences, 4*(4), 313–325.

Jensen, M. & Meckling, W. (1976). Theory of the firm: Managerial behavior, agency costs and ownership structure. *Journal of Financial Economics, 3*, 305–360.

Jung, K. & Kwon, S. Y. (2002). Ownership structure and earnings in formativeness evidence from Korea. *The International Journal of Accounting, 37*(3), 301–325.

Kaawaase, T., Juma, B., Kwizina, T. P., & Nabaweesi, J. (2019). Intellectual capital and performance of small and medium audit practices the interactive effects of professionalism. *Journal of Accounting in Emerging Economies.*

Kader, J. M. & Asarpota, A. K. (2007). Comparative financial performance of Islamic banks vis-à-vis conventional banks in the UAE, chancellor's undergraduate research award. The first annual student research symposium.

Kanagaretnam, K., Lim, C. Y., & Lobo, G. J. (2011). Effects of national culture on earnings quality of banks. *Journal of International Business Studies, 42*, 853–874.

Kanagaretnam, K., Lim, C. Y., & Lobo, G. J. (2014). Effects of international institutional factors on earnings quality of banks. *Journal of Banking & Finance, 39*, 87–106.

Kanagaretnam, K., Lobo, G. J., & Mathieu, R. (2004). Earnings management to reduce earnings variability: Evidence from bank loan loss provisions. *Review of Accounting and Finance*, *3*(1), 128–148.

Kapur, M. (2020). Performance of conventional and Islamic banks in the UAE: A comparative graphical ratio analysis. *International Journal of Accounting & Finance Review*, *5*(2), 50–63.

Kennedy, E. J. & Lawton, L. (1998). Religiousness and business ethics. *Journal of Business Ethics*, *17*, 163–175.

Khan, M. & Porzio, M. (2009). *Islamic Finance and Banking in the European Union: A Challenge*. Northampton, MA, USA: Edward Elgar. pp. 22–32.

Khawla, B. & Mahmoud, S. (2013). Islamic and conventional banks' soundness during the 2007–2008 financial crisis. *Review of Financial Economics*, *22*, 68–77.

Kobeissi, N. & Sun, X. (2010). Ownership structure and bank performance: Evidence from the middle East and North. *Comparative Economic Studies*, *52*, 287–323.

Kosmidou, K. (2008). The determinants of banks' profits in Greece during the period of EU financial integration. *Managerial Finance*, *34*(3), 146–159.

Kung, F. H., Cheng, C. L., & James, K. (2010). Effects of corporate ownership structure on earnings conservatism. *Asian Journal of Finance & Accounting*, *2*(1), 47–67.

Leventis, S. & Dimitropoulos, P. (2012). The role of corporate governance in earnings management: Experience from US banks. *Journal of Applied Accounting Research*, *13*(2), 161–177.

Mamatzakis, E. C. & Remoundos, P. (2003). Determinants of Greek commercial banks profitability, 1989–2000. *Spoudai*, *53*(1), 84–94.

Mamun, A., Muniady, R., Bin Ibrahim, M. A., & Binti Che Nawi, N. (2018). Effect of economic vulnerability on entrepreneurial competencies among Malaysian micro-entrepreneurs. *Asia Pacific Journal of Innovation and Entrepreneurship*, *12*(2), 223–237.

McGuire, S., Omer, T. C., & Sharp, N. Y. (2012). The impact of religion on financial reporting irregularities. *The Accounting Review*, *87*(2), 645–673.

Mohamed Khaled I., Bader Shamsher Mohamad et Taufiq Hassan. (2009). Efficiency of conventional versus Islamic banks: International evidence using the Stochastic Frontier Approach (SFA). *Journal of Islamic Economics, Banking and Finance*, *4*, 107–130.

Molyneux, P. & Thornton, J. (1992). The determinants of European bank profitability. *Journal of Banking and Finance*, *16*, 1173–1178.

Molyneux, P. & Thornton, J. (1992). Determinants of European bank profitability: A note. *Journal of Banking & Finance, 16*(6), 1173–1178.

Monzer, K. (1982). Saving and investment functions in a two- sector Islamic economy. In *International Centre for Research in Islamic Economics*. Jeddah, KSA: King Abdulaziz University.

Mrad, F. & Mateev, M. (2020). Banking system in the MENA region: A comparative analysis between conventional and Islamic banking in the UAE. *Sustainable Development and Social Responsibility, 1*, 61–85. Doi: 10.1007/978-3-030-32922-8_6.

Naciri, A. (2008). *Comparative Corporate Governance: The MENA Countries National Systems of Corporate Governance*. New York: Routledge Studies in Corporate Governance.

Narayan, P. K. & Phan, D. H. B. (2019). A survey of Islamic banking and finance literature: Issues, challenges and future directions. *Pacific–Basin Finance Journal, 53*, 484–496.

Neifar, M. (2020). Interest-free versus conventional banks-a comparative study using linear and nonlinear panel regression: Empirical evidence from Turkey and 6 MENA countries. Munich Personal RePEc Archive (MPRA), 1–48.

Olson, D. & Zoubi, T. A. (2008). Using accounting ratios to distinguish between Islamic and conventional banks in the GCC region. *The International Journal of Accounting, 43*(1), 45–65.

Otero, L., Razia, A., Cunill, O. M., & Mulet-Forteza. C. (2020). What determines efficiency in MENA banks? *Journal of Business Research, 112*, 331–341. Doi: 10.1016/j.jbusres.2019.11.002.

Pasiouras, F. & Kosmidou, K. (2007). Factors influencing the profitability of domestic and foreign commercial banks in the European Union. *Research in International Business and Finance, 21*(2), 222–237.

Penman, S. & Zhang, X. (2002). Accounting conservatism, the quality of earnings, and stock returns. *The Accounting Review, 77*(2), 237–264.

Rhanoui, S. & Belkhoutout, K. (2017). Islamic banking in Morocco: The factors of a promising future. *Journal of Islamic Banking and Finance, 5*(1), 7–14.

Rosly et Bakar. (2003). Performance of Islamic and mainstream banks in Malaysia. *International Journal of Social Economics, 30*(12), 1249–1265. Doi: 10.1108/03068290310500652.

Rosly, S. A. & Bakar, M. A. A. (2003). Performance of Islamic and mainstream banks in Malaysia. *International Journal of Social Economics, 30*(12), 1249–1265.

Samad, A. & Hassan, M. (2001). The performance of Malaysian Islamic bank during 1984–1997. *An Explanatory Study, Economics, 10*(1&2), 7–26.

Sanusi, N. & Ismail, A. (2005). A panel data analysis of the determinants of Malaysian Islamic bank returns: 1995–2004. Paper in Islamic Economics and Finance No. 0508.

Sghaier, A, Sekrafi, H., & Mighri, Z. (2016). Comparative study on performance of Islamic and conventional banks in MENA region. *Journal of Business Management and Economics*, *7*(2), 72–88.

Shehzad, C. T., De Hann, J., & Schltens, B. (2010). The impact of bank ownership concentration on impaired loans and capital adequacy. *Journal of Banking & Finance*, *34*, 399–408.

Siddiqi, M. (2008). The current financial crisis and Islamic economics. *Journal of Economics of Management*, *16*(2), 125–132.

Soufeljil, M., Sghaier, A. Kheireddine, H., & Mighri, Z. (2017). The financial structure of the Tunisian listed businesses: An application on panel data. *Journal of Global Entrepreneurship Research*, *7*(1), 1–25. (http://www.springeropen.com/journals).

Srairi, S. (2009). A comparison of the profitability of Islamic and conventional banks: The case of GCC countries study. *Studies in Economics and Finance*, *31*(1), 106–128.

Yudistira, D. (2003). Efficiency in Islamic banking: An empirical analysis of 18 banks. *Islamic Economic Studies*, *12*(1), August 2004.

Zhong, K., Gribbin, D. G., & Zheng, X. (2007). The effect of monitoring by outside blockholders on earnings management. *Quarterly Journal of Business and Economics*, *46*(1), 1–37.

https://doi.org/10.1142/9781800612426_0021

Chapter 21

Determinants of Islamic Banks Profitability in MENA Region Before and During the COVID-19 Pandemic Period

Hani El Shaarani

Abstract

The first objective of this research is to explain and analyze the financial indicators of the Islamic banking sector in the Middle East and North Africa (MENA) countries before and over the COVID-19 pandemic period, and the second objective is to explore the key determinant that might affect Islamic banks performance before and during COVID-19 pandemic period. Orbis Bank Focus database and annual financial reports are used to collect financial information of Islamic banks in MENA countries over two years: 2019 and 2020. Descriptive statistics, t-test, and multiple regression are employed to analyze the financial structure and performance of Islamic banks before and during COVID-19 pandemic period. The results of this study reveal that there is a sharp drop in financial indicators in Islamic banks during the pandemic period, liquidity risk, bank size, managerial efficiency ratio, and oil price shocks are the determinants of Islamic banks profitability before the appearance of COVID-19. The credit risk, bank size, liquidity risk, managerial efficiency, inflation, and oil price shocks are the determinants of Islamic banks profitability during the pandemic period. Finally, there is no significant impact of GDP and capital structure on Islamic banks profitability before and during the COVID-19 pandemic period.

Keywords: Islamic Banks, Performance, Financial Risk, Capital Structure, Oil Price.

21.1 Introduction

Islamic banks are considered to be more resistant during unstable and uncertain periods than their non-Islamic counterparts. Several studies have shown that Islamic financial institutions performed better than non-financial institutions during the international financial crisis of 2008–2009 (Beck *et al.*, 2013; Alqahtani *et al.*, 2017; Nurfalah *et al.*, 2018). El-Chaarani and Ragab (2018) argued that Islamic banks succeeded to control their liquidity risk and managing their profitability during the Arab political crisis in several Middle East and North Africa (MENA) countries.

Nowadays, Islamic banks over the world are facing a new type of crisis. The development of coronavirus cases across the globe and the long lockdown period have declined the economic development and increased the risk level of Islamic financial institutions. A huge number of banks customers are not able to pay back their credits because they lost their jobs during the quarantine period (Hasan, 2020). Many Islamic banks are struggling with various macroeconomic risks (Fakhrunnas *et al.*, 2021) and huge withdrawals of funds by their depositors (Cahyono *et al.*, 2021).

Hidayat *et al.* (2020) argued that the COVID-19 pandemic has raised the financial risk of the Islamic banking system in Indonesia. They stated that the economic, health, and social conditions led numerous MSMEs to announce their bankruptcy and many employees to lose the total or a part of their income. As a result, Islamic banks are facing a lack of funds and a high level of non-performing loan.

In MENA countries, the pressure of the international health crisis on the economic situation and Islamic financial system started with the enormous development of COVID-19 cases in the United Arab Emirates by March 2020. According to a World Bank report (2021), the pandemic period has caused deep damage to many economic sectors such as oil, tourism, transportation, and banking in MENA countries.

For Hassan *et al.* (2021), the economic, financial, and social influence of COVID-19 has increased the pressure on the Islamic financial institutions in the MENA region. Mihajat (2021) and Almonifi *et al.* (2021) also confirmed the negative influence of COVID-19 crisis on Islamic banking institutions in MENA countries. They argued that Islamic banks should manage and control their liquidity buffer and capital structure to deal with various economic challenges during the COVID-19 outbreak.

Despite the financial damage caused by COVID-19 to Islamic financial institutions, Hassan *et al.* (2021) argued that Islamic banks will have a highly important role during and after the lockdown period in MENA countries. They stated that Islamic banks can sustain and mitigate the negative financial impact of the pandemic on SMEs, entrepreneurs, and people.

Several other scholars revealed that Islamic financial systems and products (like sukuk) can persist during and after the COVID-19 pandemic crisis (Yarovaya *et al.*, 2021) because they are based on the Islamic principle of sharing losses and profit — PLS (Farooq & Zaheer, 2015). They stated that Islamic banks showed a quick response to the crisis and a high level of financial resistance and profitability (Almonifi *et al.*, 2021; Rizwan *et al.*, 2021).

Thus, based on the above discussion, two questions arise. First, what is the financial impact of the COVID-19 crisis on the Islamic banking industry in MENA countries? Second, what are the determinants that lead Islamic banks to perform and sustain in the MENA region before and during the pandemic crisis? These two research questions provide new insights and need further analysis to reduce the knowledge gaps.

The first research objective is to investigate the influence of the COVID-19 crisis on financial and operational indicators of Islamic banks, namely liquidity risk, capital structure, credit risk, managerial efficiency, and profitability. The second objective is to reveal the determinant of Islamic bank's performance before and during the last healthcare epidemic period. This research is different from previous studies since it examines a new type of crisis and a large sample of Islamic banking firms in MENA countries.

This research is different from previous empirical studies since it assesses a recent period (2019 and 2020) and a broader sample of Islamic banking firms in the MENA region in which the largest Islamic population and most important Islamic financial institutions work.

Based on our knowledge, no prior research explored the impact of the COVID-19 crisis on Islamic bank valuation, structure, and risk behavior. Therefore, this research provides several contributions to the literature of Islamic financial institutions in different ways. First, it develops the extant literature and theories of Islamic banks by exploring the key determinant of Islamic banks' performance before and during the COVID-19 pandemic period. No prior research has explored and compared the success factors of Islamic bank's performance before and during the COVID-19 pandemic crisis. Second, this chapter compares different financial indicators of Islamic banks before and during the development of the global healthcare crisis. It helps to explore and analyze the impact of the healthcare crisis on the financial return, risk, and structure of Islamic banks. Third, the empirical result of this research will be helpful for CEOs and executives to optimize the financial behavior and structure of Islamic banking firms in the MENA region mainly throughout the post-COVID-19 period.

The rest of this research is presented as follows: Section 21.1 presents Islamic banking principles and determinants of banks profitability. Section 21.3 presents the research data, sample, variables, and methodology. Section 21.4 provides the empirical findings, and finally, Section 21.5 of this research concludes this research.

21.2 Literature Review

21.2.1 *Islamic financial institutions: Basic principles and financial resistance during the crisis*

Islamic financial institutions have raised during the last years across the globe and mainly in Islamic countries like KSA, Indonesia, Malaysia, Qatar, Oman, and the United Arab Emirates. Nowadays, the majority of international conventional banking firms are providing Islamic financial products and services in several Islamic countries located mainly in the MENA region.

Islamic finance is based on Islamic rules, regulations, and principles that are consistent with Islamic law (Sharia), and it is different from traditional finance widely used in conventional banks. The first regulation source of Islamic finance is the Holy Qur'an that includes well-defined principles related to commercial and economic activities. The second regulation source largely applied in Islamic banks is the Sunnah that includes several commercial principles based on the Holy Prophet's sayings and habits. All Islamic commercial activities are founded on the respect of fair dealing, transparency, justice, fair pricing, honesty, sincerity, levy, and elimination of misleading marketing.

Modern Islamic finance employs many financial products such as musharakah (financing based on equity participation), mudarabah (profit and loss sharing partnership), murabahah (trade financing based on a sales contract), and wakalah (managing customers portfolio based on fixed fees). All Islamic financial products are employed and activated after the acceptance of the Sharia controlling board (SCB) to verify their compliance with Islamic laws.

There is a consensus that Islamic financial products and activities elaborated based on the Holy Qur'an and Sunnah can raise profitability, reduce risk, and resolve uncertainty problems during the crisis period. The empirical studies on assessing the risk and overall performance of Islamic financial institutions have showed that Islamic banks have a high capacity to resist during the crisis (Abdulle & Kassim, 2012; Rafiuddin & Alam, 2012; Mansor & Syed-Aun, 2017; Mihajat, 2021). They also revealed that Islamic banking institutions perform better than their conventional and commercial counterparts during instability (Ftiti *et al.*, 2013; El-Chaarani & Ragab, 2018; Almonifi *et al.*, 2021).

Mokhtar and Laldin (2009) argued that Islamic bankers can reduce the financial risk level because they work based on assets market principle, whereas non-Islamic banks operate based on money market principle. They stated that Islamic banks do not have any problem related to transparency and information asymmetry since they follow Islamic laws that prevent any doubt and uncertainty. However, the major problem during the financial crisis of 2008 was related to the lack of transparency in conventional banks.

Some scholars consider that Islamic banks have a high capacity to resist during crisis periods because they are considered equity-based institutions (Abdul-Majid *et al.*, 2017). In Islamic financial institutions, depositors are considered as shareholders since their investment deposits do not rely on any type of assets guarantee or fixed interest rate. Islamic banks depositors receive a pre-defined percentage of bank revenue in case of profit. In the opposite case, depositors must share the loss with the Islamic bank.

Several studies reveal that the nature of Islamic financial contracts and financing methods used during the crisis is the reason behind the financial resistance of Islamic banks (Husain *et al.*, 2015). The implementation of the profit and loss sharing principle through Islamic financial contracts can mitigate the financial risk and improve the overall performance of Islamic banks (Hassan & Kayed, 2009).

In the Malaysian context, Husain *et al.* (2015) showed that the use of loss- and profit-sharing contracts, such as musharakah and mudarabah, can enhance the productivity of Islamic banking institutions during the crisis. Abusharbeh (2014) revealed that murabahah's funding methods enhanced the profitability of Indonesian banks. For the author, a murabahah contract has low credit risk compared to other financing methods employed by conventional banks.

Throughout the COVID-19 pandemic period, the Islamic financial institutions in the MENA region and other countries like Indonesia and those in Africa are highly affected by the economic recession and long lockdown periods. Hasan *et al.* (2021) have explored the impact of the healthcare crisis on the stock markets of Islamic financial institutions. They showed that the Sharia screening process failed to provide immunity to Islamic stock markets during the economic turmoil. They recommended bankers to be precautious in employing future financial management measures to boost market confidence.

Salsabilla *et al.* (2021) studied the financial shock of the COVID-19 outbreak on Indonesian Islamic banks. They showed that Islamic financial establishments in Indonesia succeeded to sustain their returns during the last healthcare sector. They indicated that Islamic banks can manage their risk and by doing so, they can mitigate the negative impact of any crisis. Nugroho *et al.* (2020) had confirmed the negative influence of COVID-19 on Indonesian Islamic banks. They recommended bankers to improve the liquidity level and restructure the capital of Islamic banks to reduce their financial risk throughout COVID-19.

In KSA, Almonifi *et al.* (2021) revealed that the long COVID-19 pandemic period had a marginal influence on Islamic banks. They argued that Islamic banks can mitigate any economic and financial crisis.

Akkas and Al Samman (2021) showed that Islamic banking firms in the Gulf Cooperation Council (GCC) countries are less exposed to the negative financial impact of COVID-19 than commercial and conventional banks. However, the resilience of the Islamic banking sector during the pandemic period is not as high as that in the case of the international financial crisis of 2008–2009. The authors recommended bankers and regulators in GCC countries that they have to implement reforms and regulations to enhance the resilience of Islamic banks.

Despite the existence of several studies that reveal the financial impact of the COVID-19 crisis on the overall performance of Islamic banks, the literature review does not present any research that explores the determinant of Islamic banks' performance in the MENA region. Similarly, there is no extant research examining the impact of the COVID-19 crisis on the financial indicators of Islamic banks in MENA countries. Therefore, this chapter fills these knowledge gaps by addressing the impact of COVID-19 on different financial indicators of Islamic banks and by exploring the key success factors of Islamic banks' profitability during the epidemic period.

21.2.2 *Determinant of bank performance*

Berger (1995) was the first scholar who stated that bank revenues are influenced by several internal and external factors. He argued that the key success factors of each bank could vary due to many reasons like economic conditions and bank characteristics.

For pecking order, agency, and trade-off theories, the profitability of any firm is highly correlated with its capital structure and financial management system (Kraus & Litzenberger, 1973; Jensen & Meckling, 1976; Myers & Majluf, 1984; Myers, 1984).

Thus, to enhance the profitability of financial institutions, managers must optimize their capital structures and decrease their financial risks. Jensen and Meckling (1976) revealed that a high level of debt could lower agency costs because debtholders can monitor the manager and lead him to cut off his private benefits.

Under the market power (MP) and structure conduct performance (SCM) hypotheses, the efficiency of any financial and non-financial institution is also the result of its collusion with industry and economic conditions (Bain, 1956; Berger, 1995; Berger & Hannan, 1997). Therefore, it is impossible to analyze the profitability of banking firms without considering the impact of the external environment.

This research evaluates the impact of the following factors on the financial profitability of Islamic banks in the MENA region.

21.2.2.1 *Internal determinants*

21.2.2.1.1 Capital adequacy and structure

Capital structure and capital adequacy ratios show the available capital of banks that can be employed to protect depositors. These ratios ensure the stability of the Islamic financial system. An Islamic bank characterized by a high capital level is considered safe and able to absorb the negative impact of any financial difficulties (Masood & Ashraf, 2012). The bankruptcy risk is considered very low when capital adequacy ratios are above the minimum requirement fixed by international regulators like Basel committee.

The majority of empirical findings showed a significant positive correlation between capital adequacy and financial revenue of the banking sector (Sufian 2012; Ben Ameur & Mhiri, 2013). They showed that the higher the capital adequacy and structure ratios in bank, the higher the level of profitability.

During the COVID-19 pandemic crisis, all Islamic banks with high capital adequacy and structure ratios should have the ability to resist and mitigate the negative shocks. Thus, the first hypothesis is presented as follows:

H1: There is a positive relationship between capital adequacy and Islamic banks financial return during the COVID-19 pandemic period.

21.2.2.1.2 Liquidity risk

The liquidity risk of Islamic banks is defined as the failure to face short-term debts. Several financial specialists, researchers, and regulators recommend Islamic banks to keep a minimum level of liquid assets to avoid insolvency and liquidity risks mainly during unstable periods (Curak *et al.*, 2012; Adusei, 2015). Basel III committee has recommended banks to manage liquidity needs and liquidity risk exposure.

During the COVID-19 pandemic period, Islamic banks are facing a slowdown in funding activities and excess cash withdrawals because many people became jobless and many companies stopped their business activities. Thus, they should keep a comfortable level of liquid assets to meet their financial and business obligations. However, the level of liquid assets should not exceed certain limits because it can lead to a decrease in banks activities and leading therefore to a reduction in banks profitability (Marijana *et al.*, 2012).

Alexiou and Sofoklis (2009) stated that a bank with an acceptable liquidity risk ratio will be able to meet its short-term financial obligations and enhance its profitability. Petria *et al.* (2015) confirmed that a financial institution with a proper liquidity risk will have the financial capacity to resist during crisis. Based on the reviewed literature, the second hypothesis in this research is stated as follows:

H2: There is a positive relationship between liquidity risk and Islamic banks financial return during the COVID-19 pandemic period.

21.2.2.1.3 Credit risk

Credit or financing risk in Islamic banks refers to the loss probability of banks when their borrowers fail to meet their obligations and repay their loans. The level of non-performing loans is employed as a proxy to measure banks' credit risk. Islamic and conventional banks that are exposed to a high financial credit risk must increase their loan loss provision.

After the appearance of COVID-19, all banks across the globe were highly affected by the socio-economic impact of the long lockdown period. Several banks suffered from the increasing of non-performing loans during the pandemic period of COVID-19 because many firms failed to sustain (Korzeb & Niedziółka, 2021). In the case of Islamic banks, Hasan (2021) reported an increasing in credit risk level because a lot of their customers lost their jobs during the long period of social distancing. He argued that Islamic banks are struggling with high non-performing loans.

Several studies reported a negative impact of a high level of credit risk exposure on banks revenues. Athanasoglou *et al.* (2008) revealed that a high level of loss provisions is correlated to a low level of profitability. Likewise, Dietrich and Wanzenried (2014) and Le and Ngo (2020) reported that high credit risk exposure leads to a decrease in banks profitability.

By considering the literature review presented above, the third hypothesis of this research is presented as follows:

H3: There is a negative relationship between credit risk and Islamic banks financial return during the COVID-19 pandemic period.

21.2.2.1.4 Managerial efficiency

Managerial efficiency is considered as the ability of the financial institution to control its total costs and revenues. It is defined as operational costs divided by incomes of the bank. The lower the total cost relative to bank revenue, the higher the bank profitability is. On the other hand, higher ratios indicate lower efficiency.

Many Islamic banks around the world have experienced a decrease in business activities and revenues with the spread of COVID-19. However, their operational costs are almost stable and thus lead banks to be in a highly risky situation. To sustain and resist, Islamic banks must implement a low-cost strategy. They have to minimize their operational costs to meet their obligations during extended lockdowns.

Several scholars such as Akbas (2012), Salike and Ao (2017), and Petria *et al.* (2015) showed in their studies a negative correlation between managerial efficiency ratio and bank revenues measured by both ROA and ROE. They stated that the managerial efficiency ratio is a key determinant factor of bank profitability during unstable periods because it measures the capacity of banks in monitoring and minimizing their operational costs.

Taking into consideration the literature review, the fourth hypothesis in this research is stated as follows:

H4: There is a negative relationship between managerial efficiency and Islamic banks financial return during the COVID-19 pandemic period.

21.2.2.1.5 Bank size

Bank size is considered (among) the internal determinants of bank revenue. A large bank can generate synergetic effects and economies of scale (Adusei, 2015). In addition, large banks have massive number of ATMs and branches that can attract more customers, and therefore, increase profitability (Pervan *et al.*, 2010).

Despite the social distancing during the pandemic period of COVID-19, large banks succeeded to serve their customers remotely due to the employed updated technology. Their massive number of ATMs and branches also kept their customers well-served and satisfied during extended lockdowns. These arguments have been confirmed by Mirzaei *et al.* (2013) who stated that large commercial and conventional banks are able to control their risks during crisis due to their diversified portfolio, technology, and competitive advantage.

Many scholars studied the link between bank size and financial profitability in different European, Asian, and African regions (Flamini *et al.*, 2009; Bertay *et al.*, 2013; Petria *et al.*, 2015; Al-Harbi, 2019). They found in their studies a positive influence of large-sized bank on the performance and profitability during stable and unstable periods.

Taking into consideration the literature review, the fifth hypothesis is stated as follows:

H5: There is a positive relationship between size and financial return in Islamic banks during the COVID-19 pandemic period.

21.2.2.1.6 Non-traditional Islamic activities

The profitability in Islamic banks has two different sources. The first income source is provided through traditional Islamic activities based on PLS contracts. The second income source is generated through non-traditional business activities such as restricted mudarabah contracts (restricted investment accounts), guarantee and letter of credit (Ma'in *et al.*, 2015).

The non-traditional activities (shareholders and depositors' investments) can be developed by Islamic banks during the COVID-19 pandemic period to generate additional revenues and compensate the drop of their revenues from traditional Islamic contracts.

Many studies confirmed the positive impact of off-balance sheet (non-traditional Islamic operations) activities on the profitability during stable and unstable periods (Petria *et al.*, 2015; Saona, 2016). They stated that off-balance sheet assets generate additional revenues for the banking sector and enhance the overall financial performance of banking firms.

Taking into consideration the literature review, the sixth hypothesis in this study is defined as follows:

H6: There is a positive relationship between non-traditional Islamic activities and financial returns during the COVID-19 pandemic period.

21.2.2.2 *External determinants*

21.2.2.2.1 Growth domestic product

Growth domestic product (GDP) reflects the business cycle and economic growth. The GDP is affected by numerous factors like supply and demand. In case of the banking sector, GDP can influence the level of loan, deposit, and profitability. For example, higher economic growth can develop loans and deposits activities, thus leading to enhance banks performance. On the other hand, higher economic growth can develop business activities and competition between banks, and therefore leads to a decrease in banks profitability.

During the COVID-19 period, the majority of countries in the MENA region (KSA, Kuwait, Tunisia, Morocco, the United Arab Emirates, and Oman) has experienced a decrease in GDP and business activities due to the long quarantine period. During this health crisis, the level of bankruptcy and non-performing loans have increased which leads to a decrease in banks profitability. Thus, it is expected in this research a positive correlation between GDP ratio and bank financial revenue.

Several studies revealed this positive correlation between bank financial performance and GDP (Saona, 2016; Mungly *et al.*, 2016; Yahya *et al.*, 2017). When economic activities develop, the demand for loans and deposits increase and positively affect banks profitability (Sufian & Chong, 2008). Therefore, the seventh hypothesis in this research is defined as follows:

H7: There is a positive relationship between GDP and Islamic banks financial return during the COVID-19 pandemic period.

21.2.2.2.2 Inflation

Inflation is the variation of consumer price index (CPI) for services and foods. The inflation ratio has a direct impact on the consumer behavior and thus on bank activities. Higher inflation rate can decrease the purchasing power of customers and therefore leads to lower banks loans and revenues. On the other hand, higher inflation rate can raise loans interest rate and thus leads to an increase in banks profitability.

In the MENA region, it is not clear how the COVID-19 pandemic period has affected the inflation rate. Some countries like the United Arab Emirates and Oman have experienced a decrease in inflation rate, whereas some other countries like Saudi Arabia and Kuwait have faced a development of inflation percentage. The consumer behavior has dramatically changed in the MENA region.

In this research, it is supposed that the development of the inflation rate without any increase of wages, like the current situation in MENA countries during the health crisis, can reduce all banks activities. The literature review shows different outcomes regarding the influence of inflation rate on banks performance; however, the majority of recent empirical findings showed a negative correlation between inflation rate and bank performance (Al-Homaidi *et al.*, 2020; Yao *et al.*, 2018; Abel & Le-Roux, 2016). Thus, the hypothesis related to the inflation rate can be formulated as follows:

H8: There is a negative relationship between inflation and bank financial return during the COVID-19 pandemic period.

21.2.2.2.3 Oil price

Several countries in the MENA region like Saudi Arabia, Kuwait, Qatar, the United Arab Emirates are large oil producers. Their economies and government's expenditures rely mainly on oil production and exports.

The combination of COVID-19 with lockdowns has created an unexpected crisis for the oil industry. During 2020, crude oil prices decreased several times below USD 20 due to the imbalance between demand and supply. All oil producers in MENA countries have faced serious financial crisis. As a result, banks loans and profitability decreased because the majority of bank deposits in the MENA region come directly and indirectly from oil sales (Berument *et al.*, 2010).

Saif-Alyousfi *et al.* (2018) indicated that the overall performance of banking firms in the MENA region is highly affected by the fluctuation of oil prices since it is considered the main source of economic development for many countries. Ayu-Effendi (2019) showed that oil revenues are highly correlated with banks reserves in oil-producing countries. Lower oil prices can decrease the economic growth of oil-exporting and producing countries and thus lead to a decrease in the liquidity level of the banking sector. El-Chaarani (2019) also found a direct correlation between oil prices and banks performance in several MENA countries like Bahrain and Oman. Two other research papers (Poghosyan & Hesse, 2009; Imam & Kpodar, 2010) also confirmed the positive correlation between oil prices and Islamic bank performance in the MENA region. They stated that any raise in oil prices can enhance banks liquidity and deposits.

Based on the previous literature review, the final hypothesis of this study is presented as follows:

H9: There is a positive relationship between oil prices and bank financial return during the COVID-19 pandemic period.

21.3 Methodology, Sample, and Variables Definition

The first empirical goal of this research is to explore the financial determinants of Islamic banks profitability in MENA countries before and over the COVID-19 pandemic period.

The second empirical goal is to reveal the influence of the COVID-19 crisis on several financial indicators of Islamic banks. Thus, two different years are considered in this study (2019 and 2020). The influence of the development of COVID-19 cases on the financial profitability of the Islamic banking sector must be observed during 2020.

T-test and multiple regression models are employed in this research to reveal and compare both external and internal determinants of Islamic banks profitability before and during the development of COVID-19.

Table 21.1. Distribution of sample in MENA countries.

Country name	Total number of banks	Percentage per country (%)
Saudi Arabia	4	8.89
Qatar	6	13.33
Oman	4	8.89
The United Arab Emirates	7	15.56
Bahrain	11	24.44
Kuwait	5	11.11
Egypt	4	8.89
Morocco	2	4.44
Tunisia	2	4.44
Total	**45**	**100**

The data of the banking sector in the MENA region is collected from different databases and sources, mainly the Orbis Bank Focus database and Islamic banks annual reports.

The population of this study includes all Islamic banks from 20 countries located in the MENA region.[1] To eliminate any bias, some countries like Palestine, Djibouti, Lebanon, Syria, Yemen, Iraq, Iran, Libya, and Algeria are excluded from this study due to their economic, financial, and political instability. Malta is also excluded since it is considered as a member of the European Union and its banking system is highly influenced and supported by European Commissions.

From the main population, a number of banks have been also excluded due to missing financial data. In total, the number of Islamic banks explored in this study is 45 from nine countries (KSA, Egypt, Morocco, Bahrain, Qatar, the United Arab Emirates, Tunisia, Kuwait, and Oman). Table 21.1 presents the sample of this research.

In this research, three categories of financial and economic variables are employed. The first category of variables includes the internal financial and managerial factors that could affect Islamic banks profitability. The second category of variables covers the

[1]The definition of MENA region is based on the classification of the World bank. data.worldbank.org. Retrieved 16 July 2021.

Table 21.2. Key ratios.

Category	Ratio	Formula	Symbol
Internal determinants	Credit risk	($\sum$ Nonperforming loan)/($\sum$ loans)	NPL
	Liquidity risk	($\sum$ loans)/($\sum$ deposits)	LTD
	Size	Natural logarithm of total assets	SIZ
	Capital structure	($\sum$ equity)/($\sum$ assets)	CAS
	Managerial efficiency	($\sum$ cost)/($\sum$ net income)	MAE
	Non-traditional Islamic activities	($\sum$ non traditional Islamic income)/($\sum$ average assets)	DIV
External determinants	GDP	Gross domestic product rate per capital	GDP
	Inflation	GDP deflator variation rate	INF
	Oil price	Annual variation of oil price	OIL
Performance	Return on assets	($\sum$ net income)/($\sum$ assets)	ROA
	Return on equity	($\sum$ net income)/($\sum$ equity)	ROE

external factors that could affect Islamic banks profitability. The third category of variables contains the dependent variables. The three categories of variables are defined and presented in Table 21.2.

The model of this research is illustrated in Figure 21.1.

21.4 Empirical Findings

21.4.1 *Descriptive analysis*

With the spread of the COVID-19 pandemic, all MENA countries are facing a decrease in their macro indicators (Table 21.3) due to the interruption of supply chains, long lockdown periods, and decline of oil and tourism revenues. The average of GDP in MENA countries decreased from 0.67 to –2.91, whereas the inflation rate increased from 2.019 to 9.505. The average crude oil price also decreased from USD 64.34 in 2019 to USD 41.47 in 2020.

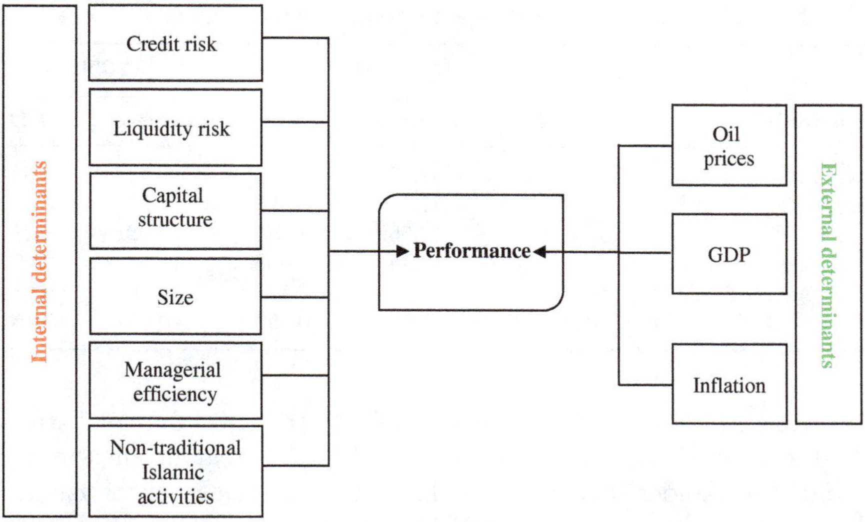

Figure 21.1. Model of the research.

Table 21.3. Average and standard deviation of external determinants.

	2019		2020	
Variable	Average	SD	Average	SD
GDP	0.672	1.841	−2.913	1.255
Inflation	2.019	2.502	9.505	6.331
Oil prices	64.34	2.68	41.47	15.06

Table 21.4. Average and standard deviation of profitability.

	2019		2020	
Variable	Average	SD	Average	SD
Return on assets (ROA)	0.18	1.019	−0.35	1.331
Return on equity (ROE)	3.27	2.422	2.04	1.441

Islamic banks profitability in the MENA region was negatively influenced by the appearance of COVID-19 (Table 21.4) and the drop of economic indicators. The average rate on assets of Islamic banks decreased from 0.18 in 2019 to −0.35 in 2020, whereas the average rate on equity declined from 3.27 in 2019 to 2.04 in 2020.

Table 21.5. Average and standard deviation of internal determinants.

	2019		2020	
Variable	**Average**	**SD**	**Average**	**SD**
Credit risk	7.37	3.727	8.19	3.531
Liquidity risk	77.16	6.502	78.51	5.603
Size	12.569	2.093	13.021	3.236
Capital structure	19.18	2.608	15.58	2.075
Managerial efficiency	0.322	0.121	0.109	0.018
Non-traditional Islamic activities	0.067	0.592	−0.021	0.661

Table 21.5 indicates that the COVID-19 triggered financial stress on the Islamic banking industry in the MENA region. On the one hand, the pandemic period amplified the financial risk of Islamic banks. The credit risk increased from 7.37 in 2019 to 8.19 in 2020, whereas liquidity risk increased from 77.16 in 2019 to 78.51 in 2020. On the other hand, many Islamic banks in MENA countries suffered from a sharp drop in capital structure, managerial efficiency, and non-traditional Islamic activities ratios. First, the capital structure ratio decreased from 19.18 in 2019 to 15.58 in 2020. Second, the managerial efficiency ratio declined from 0.322 in 2019 to 0.109 in 2020. Finally, the non-traditional Islamic activities dropped from 0.067 in 2019 to −0.021 in 2020. However, the assets of Islamic banks developed slightly by 0.452 between 2019 and 2020.

The T-test results in Table 21.6 show the comparison of financial indicators (means) in Islamic banks between 2019 and 2020. The majority of means differences are significant except capital structure ratio and non-traditional Islamic activities. Thus, the results confirm the negative impact of the last health crisis period on almost all financial indicators of the Islamic banking sector in the MENA region.

21.4.2 *Regression analysis*

The multivariate regression models are employed in this research to reveal the external and internal key success factors of Islamic bank profitability in MENA countries before and during the COVID-19

Table 21.6. Comparison of the Islamic banking sector before and during the COVID-19 pandemic period.

Ratio	Symbol	2019 Mean	2019 *N*	2020 Mean	2020 *N*	Mean difference	Significance
Credit risk	NPL	7.37	45	8.19	43	−0.82	(**)
Liquidity risk	LTD	77.16	45	78.51	43	−1.35	(**)
Size	SIZ	12.569	45	13.021	43	−0.452	(***)
Capital structure	CAS	19.18	45	15.58	43	3.6	(n.s)
Managerial efficiency	MAE	0.322	45	0.109	43	0.213	(**)
Non-traditional Islamic activities	DIV	0.067	45	−0.021	43	0.088	(n.s)
Return on assets	ROA	0.18	45	−0.35	43	0.53	(***)
Return on equity	ROE	3.27	45	2.04	43	1.23	(***)

Note: (***): 1% → significance level; (**): 5% → significance level; (n.s): → no significance level.

pandemic period. Before running the regression models, the variance inflation factor (VIF) levels of independent variables were examined. Since the values of VIF are less than 10, the results do not reveal any collinearity problem between independent variables, and thus, they can be implemented in the same regression model.

The multivariate regression models of this research that will be employed during two different years (2019 and 2020) are developed as follows:

$$1 - \text{ROA} = \beta_0 + \beta_1.\text{NPL} + \beta_2.\text{LTD} + \beta_3.\text{SIZ} + \beta_4.\text{CAS} + \beta_5.\text{MAE} + \beta_6.\text{DIV} + \beta_7.\text{GDP} + \beta_8.\text{INF}\beta_{9.}\text{OIL} + \varepsilon.$$

$$2 - \text{ROE} = \beta_0 + \beta_1.\text{NPL} + \beta_2.\text{LTD} + \beta_3.\text{SIZ} + \beta_4.\text{CAS} + \beta_5.\text{AE} + \beta_6.\text{DIV} + \beta_7.\text{GDP} + \beta_8.\text{INF} + \beta_{9.}\text{OIL} + \varepsilon.$$

The profitability (ROE and ROA) of Islamic financial institutions in MENA countries does not have the same determinant before and over the COVID-19 epidemic period. During the healthcare crisis period, the impact of several internal and external factors became significative whereas some others became non-significative. Thus, Islamic banks have to change their financial strategies in light of COVID-19.

The level of non-performing loans shows a negative influence on the profitability level of Islamic banks in MENA countries during the pandemic period whereas this variable does not reveal any significant impact during 2019. The quick spread of the COVID-19 in MENA countries has increased the credit risk level and leading therefore to a reduction in the financial return of Islamic banks. Thus, the hypothesis (H3), suggesting the presence of a negative relationship between credit risk and Islamic bank financial return during the COVID-19 pandemic period, is supported.

The impact of liquidity risk on Islamic banks financial performance is non-consistent. Before the pandemic period, the impact of loan to debt ratio (LTD) is positive whereas this impact becomes negative and significant during the pandemic period. Accordingly, an adequate level of LTD ratio can develop the profitability of Islamic banks during normal periods while in case of crisis and pandemic periods Islamic banks must minimize their liquidity risk to enhance their profitability. Thus, the second hypothesis (H2) suggesting the presence of a positive association between liquidity risk and Islamic bank financial return over the COVID-19 pandemic period, is not supported.

A large Islamic bank has a high capacity to resist and generate profit during the last healthcare crisis. Table 21.7 shows that the size of the assets of the Islamic bank has a positive influence on its ROA and ROE during the pandemic period. It is also noticed that there is a positive impact of the size variable on the return on assets during 2019. Therefore, the hypothesis (H5), suggesting the presence of a positive relationship between the size of Islamic banks and their financial return during the COVID-19 pandemic period, is supported.

Islamic financial industry in MENA countries is highly influenced by the ratio of managerial efficiency. The impact of the MAE variable is negative and significant before and during the pandemic period. With the spread of COVID-19, the impact of managerial efficiency becomes higher than that during the pre-COVID period. This result indicates that is very important to control and minimize Islamic banks costs mainly during the pandemic period. Accordingly, the hypothesis (H4), suggesting that "there is a negative relationship between managerial efficiency and bank financial return during the COVID-19 pandemic period" is supported.

The capital structure and non-traditional Islamic activities have no significant impact on the profitability of the banking sector in MENA countries before and during the pandemic period. Thus, the first hypothesis (H1), suggesting that "there is a positive relationship between capital adequacy and Islamic bank financial return during the COVID-19 pandemic period", and the sixth hypothesis (H6), suggesting that "there is a positive relationship between non-traditional Islamic activities and financial returns throughout the COVID-19 pandemic period", are not supported.

As for external determinants of Islamic banks profitability, the result of multiple regression models presented in Table 21.7 reveals that during the COVID-19 pandemic period two factors have negatively affected the return on equity and the return on assets. The inflation rate and oil prices variation have a negative relationship with Islamic banks financial returns (ROE and ROA) during 2020.

The Islamic banks profitability is highly influenced by the volatility of crude oil prices. This result is very normal since the oil sector

Table 21.7. Regression results.

	2019				2020			
	ROA		ROE		ROA		ROE	
	Coefficient value	Significance	Coefficient value	Significance	Coefficient value	Significance	Coefficient value	Significance
Constant value	1.554	(***)	1.744	(***)	1.664	(***)	1.978	(***)
NPL	−0.018	(ns)	−0.031	(ns)	−0.112	(**)	−0.154	(**)
LTD	0.121	(***)	0.142	(***)	−0.134	(**)	−0.158	(**)
SIZ	0.011	(*)	0.028	(ns)	0.012	(*)	0.035	(**)
CAS	0.082	(ns)	0.093	(ns)	0.112	(ns)	0.126	(ns)
MAE	−0.093	(***)	−0.103	(***)	−0.239	(**)	−0.206	(***)
DIV	0.023	(ns)	0.048	(ns)	0.012	(ns)	0.055	(ns)
GDP	0.045	(ns)	0.053	(ns)	0.013	(ns)	0.025	(ns)
INF	−0.131	(ns)	−0.148	(ns)	−0.174	(***)	−0.201	(***)
OIL	−0.028	(**)	−0.046	(***)	−0.192	(**)	−0.107	(**)
$R^{(2)}$	0.5622		0.5441		0.507		0.492	
Adjusted (R^2)	0.5163		0.4983		0.443		0.424	
Fisher-stat	6.774		6.652		5.832		5.736	
N	45		45		43		43	

Note: (***): 1% → significance level; (**): 5% → significance level; (*): 10% → significance level; (^{ns}): → no significance level.

is considered a basic source of revenues and activities for several countries in the MENA region. During 2020, the negative impact of oil price variation was higher than its impact in 2019 due to the sharp drop in oil prices and the long lockdown period. Thus, the hypothesis (H9), suggesting that "there is a positive relationship between oil prices and bank financial return during the COVID-19 pandemic period", is supported.

As for the inflation rate impact, Tables 21.7 and 21.3 indicate that the spread of COVID-19 cases in 2020 increased the inflation rate and thus leading to a reduction in Islamic banks activities and revenues. As a result, the hypothesis (H8), suggesting that "there is a negative relationship between inflation and bank financial return during the COVID-19 pandemic period", is supported.

On the other hand, the result does not indicate any substantial impact of GDP on the financial returns of Islamic in MENA countries during the pandemic period. Thus, the seventh hypothesis (H7), suggesting that "there is a positive correlation between GDP and bank financial return during the COVID-19 pandemic period", is not supported.

Before the socio-economic shock of COVID-19, only the oil price has shown a negative impact on Islamic banks financial return. However, there are no impacts of GDP and inflation on Islamic banks profitability during 2019.

21.5 Discussion and Conclusion

This research sheds light on Islamic banks profitability (ROE and ROA) in the MENA region before and during the crisis of the COVID-19 epidemic period. The findings reveal that several external and internal factors significantly affect both ROE and ROA of Islamic banks. Before the appearance of COVID-19, liquidity risk, bank size, managerial efficiency ratio, and oil price shocks influenced Islamic banks profitability. During the pandemic period, credit risk, liquidity risk, bank size, managerial efficiency, inflation, and oil price shocks affected Islamic banks profitability. The study also does not reveal any impact of GDP and capital structure on Islamic banks profitability.

This study delivers new contributions to the literature and financial theories that assess the key success factors of Islamic banks. First, the findings of this research validate some previous results on conventional and Islamic banks profitability. Second, this scientific research reveals the determinants of Islamic banks profitability throughout the pandemic period. Third, the results provide practical insights for bankers during and post-COVID-19 periods.

According to this study, Islamic banks must manage and analyze their financial activities differently during and post-COVID-19 pandemic period. Executives in Islamic banks have to reduce their lending portfolio to face the huge cash withdrawals and minimize the level of non-performing loans. They must implement new strategies to reduce the overhead cost and increase the overall bank performance. To make their customers satisfied and close during extended lockdowns, they have to upgrade the digitalization level of their procedures and services. Finally, it is recommended for Islamic banks in the MENA region to diversify their portfolio and reduce their high dependence on the oil sector. They can increase their investments in new technologies, R&D, and international activities to reduce risks and improve the quality of their portfolio.

Local and international regulators in the banking sector should consider the socio-economic impact of COVID-19 on Islamic banks. They must improve their supervision actions and support for the banking sector. During a crisis, regulatory authorities in MENA countries need to motivate Islamic banks to enhance their deposits insurance, develop their capital requirement and avoid the excessive lending strategy.

This research presents several limitations. First, this study is conducted during a very short period (one year before the pandemic and one year during the pandemic). Second, the number of Islamic banks considered in this research is relatively small. Third, this research does not consider the implication of COVID-19 on Islamic banks in each country. Fourth, this study omits many other internal and external factors of bank profitability, such as ownership structure, level of legal protection in each country, and unemployment rate.

Therefore, it is suggested to conduct future research that includes extended periods based on a larger sample of Islamic banks. Also, future research can study the situation of the Islamic banking industry in each country among MENA countries. Finally, some other external and internal determinants of Islamic banks financial returns could be explored and covered in future research.

References

Abdjul-Majid, M., Falahaty, M., & Jusoh, M. (2017). Performance of Islamic and conventional banks: A meta-frontier approach. *Research in International Business and Finance*, *42*, 1327–1335.

Abdulle, M. Y. & Kassim, S. H. (2012). Impact of global financial crisis on the performance of Islamic conventional banks: Empirical evidence from Malaysia. *Journal of Islamic Economics, Banking and Finance*, *8*(4), 9–20.

Abel, S. & Le Roux, P. (2016). Determinants of banking sector profitability in Zimbabwe. *International Journal of Economics and Financial Issues*, *6*(3), 845–854.

Adusei, M. (2015). The impact of bank size and funding risk on bank stability. *Cogent Economics and Finance*, *3*(1), 1–19.

Akbas, H. E. (2012). Determinants of bank profitability: An investigation on Turkish banking sector. *Öneri Dergisi*, *10*(37), 103–110.

Akkas, E. & Al Samman, H. (2021). Are Islamic financial institutions more resilient against the COVID-19 pandemic in the GCC countries? *International Journal of Islamic and Middle Eastern Finance and Management*. Available at https://doi.org/10.1108/IMEFM-07-2020-0378.

Al-Homaidi, E. A., Almaqtari, F. A., Yahya, A. T., & Khaled, A. S. (2020). Internal and external determinants of listed commercial banks' profitability in India: Dynamic GMM approach. *International Journal of Monetary Economics and Finance*, *13*(1), 34–67.

Alexiou, C. & Sofoklis, V. (2009). Determinants of bank profitability: Evidence from the Greek banking sector. *Economic Annals*, *54*(182), 93–118.

Almonifi, Y., Rehman S., & Gulzar R. (2021). The COVID-19 pandemic effect on the performance of the Islamic banking sector in KSA: An empirical study of Al Rajhi Bank. *International Journal of Management* (IJM), *12*(4), 533–547.

Alqahtani, F., Mayes, D. G., & Brown, K. (2017). Reprint of economic turmoil and Islamic banking: Evidence from the Gulf cooperation council. *Pacific-Basin Finance Journal*, *42*, 113–125.

Athanasoglou, P. P., Brissimis, S. N., & Delis, M. D. (2008). Bank-specific, industry-specific and macroeconomic determinants of bank profitability. *Journal of International Financial Markets, Institutions and Money*, *18*(2), 121–136.

Ayu-Effendi, K. (2019). Oil prices and macroeconomic on the Islamic banking performance in OPEC member countries. *International Journal of Energy Economics and Policy*, *9*(1), 200–204.

Bain J. (1956). *Barriers to New Competition*. Cambridge, Mass: Harvard University Press.

Beck, T., De Jonghe, O., & Schepens, G. (2013). Bank competition and stability: Cross-country heterogeneity. *Journal of Financial Intermediation, 22*(2), 218–244.

Ben Ameur, I. & Mhiri, S. (2013). Explanatory factors of bank performance evidence from Tunisia. *International Journal of Economics, Finance and Management, 2*(1), 1–11.

Berger, A. (1995). The profit-structure relationship in banking — Test of market power and efficient-structure hypotheses. *Journal of Money, Credit and Banking, 27*(2), 404–431.

Berger, A. & Hannan, T. (1997). Using measures of firm efficiency to distinguish among alternative explanations of the structure-performance relationship in banking. *Managerial Finance, 23*, 6–31.

Bertay, A. C., Demirgüç-Kunt, A., & Huizinga, H. (2013). Do we need big banks? Evidence on performance, strategy and market discipline. *Journal of Financial Intermediation, 22*(4), 532–558.

Berument, H., Ceylan, N., & Dogan, N. (2010). The impact of oil price shocks on the economic growth of selected MENA countries. *Energy Journal, 31*(1), 149–176.

Cahyono, K. E., Sudarmiatin, K., & Wahyuni, D. U. (2021). The development strategy for preparing the Asean economic community of small and medium enterprises (UMKM) to get business credit in kelurahan medokan ayu surabaya. *International Journal of Academic Research in Business and Social Sciences, 11*(4), 833–844.

Curak, M., Poposki, K., & Pepur, S. (2012). Profitability determinants of the Macedonian banking sector in changing environment. *Procedia—Social and Behavioral Sciences, 44*, 406–416.

Dietrich, A. & Wanzenried, G. (2014). The determinants of commercial banking profitability in low, middle, and high-income countries. *Quarterly Review of Economics and Finance, 54*(3), 337–354.

El-Chaarani, H. (2019). The impact of oil prices on the financial performance of banking sector in Middle East Region. *International Journal of Energy Economics and Policy, 9*(5), 148–156.

El-Chaarani, H. & Shaker, N. (2018). Financial resistance of Islamic banks in Middle East Region: A comparative study with conventional banks during the Arab crises. *International Journal of Economics and Financial Issues, 1*(3), 207–218.

Fakhrunnas, F., Tumewang, Y., & Hendrie-Anto, M. B. (2021). The impact of inflation on Islamic banks' home financing risk: Before and during the COVID-19 outbreak. *Banks and Bank Systems, 16*(2), 78–90.

Farooq, M. & Zaheer, S. (2015). Are Islamic banks more resilient during financial panics? *Pacific Economic Review, 20*(1), 101–124.

Flamini, V., McDonald, C., & Schumacher, L. (2009). *The Determinants of Commercial Bank Profitability in Sub-Saharan Africa.* Working Paper No. 09/15. International Monetary Fund.

Ftiti, Z., Nafti, O., & Sreiri, S. (2013). Efficiency of Islamic banks during subprime crisis: Evidence of GCC countries. *The Journal of Applied Business Research*, *29*(1), 285–304.

Hasan, B., Mahi, M., Hassan, K., & Bhuiyan, A. (2021). Impact of COVID-19 pandemic on stock markets: Conventional vs. Islamic indices using wavelet-based multi-timescales analysis. *The North American Journal of Economics and Finance*, *58*, 1–11.

Hasan, Z. (2020). The impact of COVID-19 on Islamic banking in Indonesia during the pandemic era. *Journal of Entrepreneurship and Business*, *8*(2), 19–32.

Hassan, M. K. & Kayed, R. N. (2009). The global financial crisis, risk management and social justice in Islamic finance. *ISRA International Journal of Islamic Finance*, *1*(1), 33–34.

Hassan, M. K., Rabbani, M. R., & Abdullah, M. (2021). Socioeconomic impact of COVID-19 in MENA region and the role of Islamic finance. *International Journal of Islamic Economics and Finance*, *4*(1), 51–78.

Hidayat, S. E., Farooq, M. O., Nasution, A., & Sari, C. A. (2020). COVID-19 and its impacts on the Islamic financial industry in the OIC countries. In the impact of COVID-19 outbreak on the Islamic finance in the OIC Countries. e-book available at: https://www.salaamgateway.com/story/covid-19-and-its-impacts-on-the-islamic-financial-industry-in-the-oic-countries .

Husain, A., Affandi, S., & Shukur, N. A. (2015). The internal determinants of Islamic banks' profitability in Malaysia. *Journal of Basic and Applied Scientific Research*, *5*(7), 17–21.

Imam, P. & Kpodar, K. (2010). *Islamic Banking: How has it Diffused.* IMF Working Paper 10/195.

Jensen, M. & Meckling, W. (1976). Theory of the firm: Managerial behavior, agency cost and ownership structure. *Journal of Financial Economics*, *3*, 305–360.

Korzeb, Z. & Niedziółka, P. (2020). Resistance of commercial banks to the crisis caused by the COVID-19 pandemic: The case of Poland. *Equilibrium, Quarterly Journal of Economics and Economic Policy*, *15*(2), 205–234.

Kraus, A. & Litzenberger, R. (1973). A state-preference model of optimal financial leverage. *Journal of Finance*, *28*, 911–922.

Le, T. D. & Ngo, T. (2020). The determinants of bank profitability: A cross-country analysis. *Central Bank Review*, *20*(2), 65–73.

Ma'in, M., Misni, L., & Siti S. (2015). Off-balance sheet income activities for Islamic and conventional banks. *Journal of Emerging Economies and Islamic Research*, *3*(3), 1–10.

Mansor, H. & Syed, A. R. (2017). Bank lending, deposits and risk-taking in times of crisis: A panel analysis of Islamic and conventional banks. *Emerging Markets Review*, *12*(2), 296–309.

Marijana, Č., Poposki, K., & Pepur, S. (2012). Profitability determinants of the Macedonian banking sector in changing environment. *Procedia-Social and Behavioral Sciences*, *44*, 406–416.

Masood, O. & Ashraf, M. (2012). Bank-specific and macroeconomic profitability determinants of Islamic banks. *Qualitative Research in Financial Markets*, *4*(2–3), 255–268.

Mihajat, M. (2021). Islamic banking performance amidst COVID-19 outbreak: Prospects and challenges. *Journal of Economics and Business*, *6*(1), 38–51.

Mirzaei, A., Moore, T., & Liu, G. (2013). Does market structure matter on banks' profitability and stability? Emerging vs advanced economies. *Journal of Banking and Finance*, *37*(8), 2920–2937.

Mokhtar, S. & Laldin, M. A. (2009). *Risk Management in Islamic Finance.* Harvard-LSE Workshop on Risk Management, London School of Economics, 26 February.

Mungly, Y., Seetanah, B., Babajee, R., & Maraye, N. (2016). *Determinants of Mauritian Commercial Banking Profitability. Proceedings of the Fifth Asia-Pacific conference on Global Business, Economics, Finance and Social Sciences.*

Myers, S. C. (1984). The capital structure puzzle. *The Journal of Finance*, *39*(3), 574–592.

Myers S. C. & Majluf N. (1984). Corporate financing and investment decisions when firms have information that investors do not have. *Journal of Financial Economics*, *13*, 187–221.

Nugroho, L., Utami, W., Harnovinsah H., & Doktoralina, C. (2020). COVID-19 and the potency of disruption on the Islamic banking performance (Indonesia Cases). *International Journal of Economic and Business Applied*, *1*(1), 11–25.

Nurfalah, I., Aam, R., Nisful, L., & Eko F. (2018). Early warning to banking crises in the dual financial system in Indonesia: The markov switching approach. *Journal of King Abdulaziz University*, *31*(2), 133–156.

Pervan, M., Pervan, I., & Guadagnino, A. (2010). Market structure and profitability of Croatian commercial banks. *The Business Review*, *20*(1), 209–216.

Petria, N., Capraru, B., & Ihnatov, I. (2015). Determinants of banks' profitability: Evidence from EU 27 banking systems. *Procedia Economics and Finance, 20*, 518–524.

Poghosyan, T. & Hesse, H. (2009). Oil prices and bank profitability: Evidence from major oil exporting countries in the Middle East and North Africa. IMF, working paper series, No. 09/220.

Rafiuddin, A. & Alam, Z. (2012). Islamic banks and conventional banks in the QATAR before and after the recession. *International Journal of Financial Management, 1*(1), 50–59.

Rizwan, R. (2021). Performance comparison of Islamic banks and conventional banks in Pakistan. *International Journal of Islamic Banking and Finance Research, 5*(1), 34–41.

Saif-Alyousfi, A., Md-Rus, R., & Mohd, K. N. (2018). Oil price and banking sectors in gulf cooperation council economies before and after the global financial turmoil: Descriptive analysis. *International Journal of Energy Economics and Policy, 8*(6), 89–101.

Salike, N. & Ao, B. (2018). Determinants of bank's profitability: Role of poor asset quality in Asia. *China Finance Review International, 8*(2), 216–231.

Salsabilla, A., Azhari A., Wahyudi, R., Pambudi, Riduwan. (2021). Impact of the COVID-19 pandemic on the profitability of Islamic banks in Indonesia. Annual Conference on IHTIFAZ: Islamic Economic, Finance and Banking(ACI-IJIEFB). http://seminar.uad.ac.id/index.php/ihtifaz/article/view/6008.

Saona, P. (2016). Intra-and extra-bank determinants of latin American banks' profitability. *International Review of Economics and Finance, 45*, 197–214.

Sufian, F. (2012). Determinants of bank profitability in developing economies: Empirical evidence from the South Asian banking sectors. *Contemporary South Asia, 20*(3), 375–399.

Sufian, F. & Chong, R. R. (2008). Determinants of banks profitability in a developing economy: Empirical evidence from the Philippines Asian Academy of Management. *Journal of Accounting and Finance, 4*(2), 91–112.

World Bank Report (2021). The World Bank Group's response to the COVID-19 (coronavirus) pandemic. https://www.worldbank.org/en/who-we-are/news/coronavirus-covid19.

Yahya, A. T., Akhtar, A., & Tabash, M. I. (2017). The impact of political instability, macroeconomic and bank-specific factors on the profitability of Islamic banks: En empirical evidence. *Investment Management and Financial Innovations, 14*(4), 30–39.

Yahya, A. T., Akhtar, A., & Tabash, M. I. (2017). The impact of political instability, macroeconomic and bank-specific factors on the profitability of Islamic banks: An empirical evidence. *Investment Management and Financial Innovations*, *14*(4), 30–39.

Yao, H., Haris, M., & Tariq, G. (2018). Profitability determinants of financial institutions: Evidence from banks in Pakistan. *International Journal of Financial Studies*, *6*(2), 53–62.

Yarovaya, L., Elsayed, A. H., & Hammoudeh, S. M. (2020). Searching for safe havens in the COVID-19 pandemic: Determinants of spillovers between Islamic and conventional financial markets. *Finance Research Letters*, *3*(5), 27–41.

https://doi.org/10.1142/9781800612426_0022

Chapter 22

Investigating Bank-Specific and Macroeconomic Factors Affecting the Liquidity Position of Islamic Banks in Pakistan

Muhammad Tahir, Fong-Woon Lai, Ahmad Ali Jan, and Syed Quaid Ali Shah

Abstract

Today, not only the financial but also the non-financial attributes are considered vital for the financial health of the banks. To validate this argument, the current study investigates factors affecting the liquidity position of banks and examines its impact along with the moderation of the Sharia board on the liquidity of Islamic banks in Pakistan. Collecting panel data, this study applied a fixed-effect model on Pakistani Islamic banks for the post-financial crises period 2009–2020. Empirical findings revealed that total assets and profitability are positively and significantly linked to the liquidity position of Islamic banks. However, the deposits and capital adequacy ratios were found to have a negative influence on the Islamic banks' liquidity. Among the macroeconomic factors, none has established significant nexus with the liquidity of Islamic banks in Pakistan. Interestingly, the insignificant relationship between funding cost became significant with the moderating factor of Sharia board size. The study provides important insights for the shareholders, customers, investors, and policymakers of Islamic banks. The empirical findings offer practical guidance for the regulators of Islamic banks to strengthen their Sharia boards to manage the liquidity position by regulating the funding costs. The Islamic banks' liquidity position can also be managed by generating high profits, maintaining capital adequacy ratio, and increasing deposits. To the best of the authors' knowledge, this is the first empirical study that investigates the moderating role of Sharia governance in managing the liquidity of Islamic banks in Pakistan. This research offers a new and most important direction for future studies to investigate the role of non-financial attributes along with the financial indicators in evaluating the financial soundness of Islamic banks.

Keywords: Agency Theory, Sharia Governance, Liquidity, Economic Growth, Insolvency Risk.

22.1 Introduction

The banking industry not only sustains economic growth in economies but also serves as a financial mediator between the borrower, lenders, and investors (Jan *et al.*, 2021). Banking institutions are considered as the sole organized source in providing funds from depositors to investors. Banks play a dominant role in developing economies where capital markets are weak in performing their part. Nevertheless, in recent years, several banking institutions faced liquidity issues owing to poor liquidity management. The banks' liquidity problems came into the spotlight when several big commercial banks went bankrupt due to substantial liquidity issues during the global financial crisis (GFC) (Bhati *et al.*, 2015). For instance, the GFC also affected the performance of large Islamic banks such as Al Rajhi Bank, Kuwait Finance House, Noor Islamic Bank, and Al Hilal Bank (Jan *et al.*, 2019).

The aforementioned cases, so far, reflect only a small portion of the broader Islamic banking sector, which has been unaffected by the GFC. There were two main reasons behind the resilience of Islamic banking. First, the strong principles of Islamic banks, such as the prohibition of interest and speculation, for example, the Islamic banks cannot perform activities that do not comply with Islamic principles. The second and the main reason was the unique characteristics of Sharia governance that protected the majority of Islamic banks from the aftershocks of the GFC (Abd Razak, 2018). Islamic banks usually establish a Sharia Supervisory Board acting as an internal check and balance tool, which ensures the Sharia compliance of a product or service. The explicit codes of conduct and unique characteristics of Islamic banking have led to exceptional variances amongst Islamic and conventional banking (Mollah *et al.*, 2017). Islamic banking promotes property rights, profit and loss sharing, and the sanctity of contracts (Zaher & Kabir Hassan, 2001). Unlike the traditional banking system, Islamic banks have developed a Sharia-compliant substitute to replace the interest rate in the banks' operations. Therefore, Islamic banks due to Sharia supervision are less exposed to financial shocks. Islamic financial contracts provide a wider range of risk and responsibility sharing agreements between the bank and its clients, making Islamic banks less prone to insolvency than conventional banks.

To effectively deliver the responsibilities, Islamic banks need to be financially healthy. For financial strength, liquidity may be considered one of the important concerns of the Islamic banking administration. One important reason why banks might not be financially sound is their contribution to maturity transformation and the provision of insurance for possible liquidity demands of depositors (Yimer, 2016). In addition, Basel (2008) on banking surveillance highlighted that commercial bank stability is determined by its liquidity position and the appropriate management of liquidity risk. To ensure investor security, administrative agencies must settle some institutions' basic liquidity breaking points (Bagh *et al.*, 2017). Since liquidity may be considered as a basic aspect for financial institutional soundness, especially in the banking sector (Assfaw, 2019). Liquidity risk in the banking sector, before the global financial crisis, was mainly regarded as a secondary issue (Sheefeni & Nyambe, (2016). Nevertheless, after the global financial upheaval, the serious consequences of liquidity risks were attributed to the financial institutions, which was supposed to be the fundamental reason for their low solvency. The financial crisis of 2007–2008 raised the question of improved awareness of the problems provided by the management of liquidity risk and underlined the relevance of liquidity in the proper operation of the financial market and banking sector.

The banks' failure to manage their funds was caused by the mismanagement of liquidity risks (Munteanu, 2012), and despite a lot of assets, unexpected withdrawals and liquid money led to considerable losses due to emergency lending several profitable banks (Assfaw, 2019). The proper management of liquidity risk helps in protecting the ability of the bank to meet its liable obligations and reduces the likelihood that a liquidity crisis can have serious systemic consequences in the banking sector in emerging economies, where the banking sector acts like a predominant financial intermediary (Sopan & Dutta, 2018). Liquidity plans and execution flaws nonetheless impact the operations of banks and might have a long-term economic impact; this might influence the revenue and capital of a bank and may in extreme circumstances lead to a collapse of a bank (Berihun-Engida, 2015). Liquidity risk not just influences a bank's performance but also its reputation (Jenkinson, 2008). Consequently, banks need to retain a significant liquid reserve to prevent such a crisis and preserve financial stability.

Today, not only the financial but also the non-financial attributes, such as Sharia governance and corporate governance, are considered vital for financial stability. Nevertheless, the role of the Sharia Supervisory Board in managing the Islamic banks' liquidity risk is an unexplored area of research. Furthermore, the majority of the empirical studies on Pakistani Islamic banks mainly focused on the banks' profitability and gave limited attention to the Islamic banks' liquidity and their determinants. To fill the current information gap, this study aims to investigate the determinants of Islamic banks' liquidity in the Pakistani context for the post-financial crises period. Accordingly, this study sets two objectives, i.e., to investigate bank-specific factors and macroeconomic factors affecting the liquidity position of Pakistani Islamic banks. Second, to investigate the moderating role of the Sharia Supervisory Board on the nexus of bank-specific and macroeconomic factors with the liquidity position of Pakistani Islamic banks. The introduction of the Sharia Supervisory Board would shed light on the egalitarian role of non-financial attributes in managing the liquidity position of banks.

The current study contributes to the existing body of knowledge on Islamic banking and finance by giving a shred of an empirical investigation on the liquidity position and the determinants of Islamic banks' liquidity in Pakistan. This study claims novelty by examining the moderating role of Sharia governance on the nexus of bank-specific factors and macroeconomic factors and Islamic banks' liquidity position in Pakistan. This research also adds contribution to the theoretical perspective of agency theory, theory of financial ratios, and buffer theory by testing their perspective in the Islamic banks' liquidity context. The findings of this study provide insights to the policymakers, regulators, practitioners, and academics on the liquidity position of Pakistani Islamic banks and open a new debate on investigating the role of corporate governance in managing the liquidity risk.

The rest of this research is outlined as follows. Section 22.2 sheds some light on the banks' liquidity, theoretical background is highlighted in Section 22.2.1, while the conceptual framework and hypotheses development are presented in Section 22.2.2. Section 22.3 discusses the methodological procedures, data and sampling, modeling, and estimating methods. Results and discussions are provided in Section 22.4, and the last section concludes the chapter.

22.2 Literature Review

Contemporary financial theories recognize that banks have two primary functions: liquidity creation and risk transformation (Berger & Bouwman, 2017). Undeniably, banks, as a financial mediator, play a vital role by converting customer deposits into customer loans (Dietrich *et al.*, 2014; Bonfim & Kim, 2012). In general, the liability is formed when depositors deposit any cash and when the funds are extended to borrowers, assets are created on the balance sheet of banks (Hartlage, 2012). Therefore, banks need to manage their assets and liabilities to justify additions and withdrawals, while maintaining optimum liquidity requirements to fulfill the regulatory requirements.

Liquidity refers to *the capability of a bank to meet its obligations due at any time, especially to repay customer deposits or to make a payment on the client's order* (Vodova, 2016). Banks are vulnerable to risks especially when depositors start a sudden withdrawal of their funds (Gatev *et al.*, 2007). As a consequence, banks are inevitably exposed to liquidity risk as an effect of re-financing (Bonfim & Kim, 2012). In severe cases, the lack of liquidity might lead to bankruptcy (Jan *et al.*, 2019).

22.2.1 *Theoretical background*

The theory of financial ratios presented by Wilcox (1971) indicates that financial ratios are the best indicators of a corporate's financial health. Since the financial ratios are derived from the financial statements of firms, thereby, the easiest way to determine a corporate's financial health is to look at its financial statements. Financial ratios provide managers with information about the corporate's financial health. Accordingly, ratios are the best predictors of banks' liquidity position. Deposits, funding cost, profitability, total assets, and capital adequacy ratio are good prognosticators of liquidity position. It becomes difficult for banks to swiftly raise its liquidity. At the time of crisis, banks resiliency was largely supported by the customer deposits. Hence, the deposits inflow assists banks in mitigation of liquidity issues. Bank size is another determinant of strengthening the banks liquidity position. There are two views to support the nexus between bank size and liquidity. In line with the view of "too big to fail", large size banks usually are bestowed with more resources and do less focus on liquidity due to its easy access to capital markets. On the contrary, small banks struggle to maintain its liquidity position due to intermediation and transformation activities. Hence, positive nexus might be expected between total assets and bank liquidity. According to theory of financial ratio, profitability and liquidity are crucial elements in determining the performance and survival of firms. The banks can have a sound liquidity position in case of high profitability. Moreover, on the basis of "expected bankruptcy cost hypothesis", banks with more liquidity assets have lower financial cost and boosting profitability. Hence, profitability is crucial indicator of bank's liquidity.

Buffer theory is introduced by Calem and Rob (1996) to support the high capital adequacy ratio to reduce not only the potential risks but also to improves liquidity position of banks. Maintaining the capital adequacy ratio (CAR) provides incentives to banks in the form of reduced regulatory costs and boost its capital. Lower CAR impedes the liquidity position of banks and exposes it to liquidity and other financial risks. Hence, high CAR is the best response to avoid all the risks and strengthening bank's liquidity position.

Sharia governance, a non-financial attribute, is carried in the study to examine its impact as a moderator on the liquidity of Pakistan's Islamic banks. Agency theory describes the role of agents (Sharia board) working in the interest of the principal (stakeholders) (Jan *et al.*, 2021). The main focus of the Sharia board is to ensure that the banking operations are performed under the Sharia rules and ethics, which restrict the opportunistic behavior and excessive risk-taking behavior of managers. The efficient monitoring role of the Sharia board minimizes agency costs and control the financial as well as the non-financial activities of banks. Consequently, it can be argued that the Sharia board plays an important role in the banks' liquidity management and prevent them from any potential crises. Thus, the moderating role of the Sharia board is supported by agency theory, which is expected to improve the liquidity position of Islamic banks.

22.2.2 *Conceptual framework and hypotheses development*

Past literature indicates that banks' liquidity has been examined by numerous scholars using bank-specific and various macroeconomic factors. The conceptual framework of the study has combined three different variables as the independent variables, the moderating variable, and the dependent variable. This study has utilized bank-specific and macroeconomic factors as the explanatory variables and introduced the Sharia Supervisory Board as a moderating factor, where the liquidity of Islamic banks is the dependent variable of the study (see Figure 22.1). All these factors and their expected effects are discussed in the following.

22.2.2.1 *Bank-specific factors*

22.2.2.1.1 Total assets

Total assets, in general, being described as net assets of a bank taken into account to reflect the economies or diseconomies of scale (Yitayaw, 2021). Several scholars have taken the log of total assets (Singh & Sharma, 2016). In line with the theory, larger banks can easily manage its liquidity as compared to small banks in terms of total assets. Its easy access to capital market helps in strengthening the position of liquidity. Moreover, the hypothesis "too big to fail" supports that large bank do not focus on liquidity because of its easy access to sources of funding and dependence of lender of last resort. The argument on the relationship between total assets and liquidity is mixed in both the theoretical as well as empirical research. For example, past research conducted by Laximikantham (2015), Shah *et al.* (2018), and Al-Homaidi *et al.* (2019) disclosed a positive association

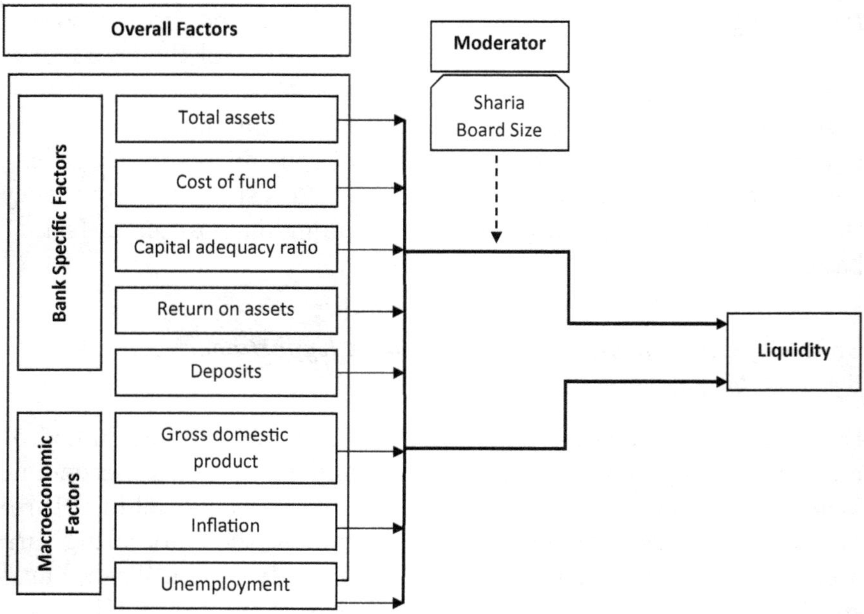

Figure 22.1. Conceptual framework of the study.

between the size of banks and liquidity. These studies support the argument that large banks have greater liquidity than smaller banks. Nevertheless, several studies revealed a negative nexus of total asserts with bank's liquidity (Singh & Sharma, 2016). Therefore, consistent with prior empirical findings, this study hypothesizes that:

H1: Significant positive nexus exists between total assets and liquidity of Pakistan's Islamic banks.

22.2.2.1.2 Funding cost

As per financial intermediation theory, funding cost, referring to paid interest rate, has a link with liquidity risk. The banks with high funding cost create lower profit which leads to failure of repayment on the loans borrowed. Hence, funding cost has an influence over the banks' liquidity. If these costs rise, the banks need to refinance in liquid assets and not to rely on the interbank funds. A rise in funding costs enables financial institutions to preserve high liquid assets. Numerous empirical researches are conducted for inspecting the linkage between funding cost and liquidity. For instance, Alger and Alger (1999) revealed a significant positive connection between funding cost and liquidity, while Singh and Sharma (2016) failed in demonstrating any relationship between the funding cost and banks' liquidity. Therefore, consistent with the theory of financial ratios and past empirical findings, this study hypothesizes that:

H2: Significant positive nexus exists between the cost of funds and liquidity of Pakistan's Islamic banks.

22.2.2.1.3 Profitability

Numerous researchers consider profitability to be a key factor in determining a bank's liquidity. According to theory of financial ratio, profitability and liquidity are crucial elements in determining the performance and survival of firms. The banks can have a sound liquidity position in case of high profitability. Moreover, on the basis of "expected bankruptcy cost hypothesis", banks with more liquidity assets have lower financial cost and boosting profitability. Hence, profitability is a crucial indicator of bank's liquidity. With the intent to make a profit on the shareholders' investments, banks play a role in transferring the depositor's money as a lender to borrowers in various ways, such as credit services, whereas depositor withdrawal actions may negatively impact the bank's financial soundness. Given that the banks' profitability affects the liquidity, numerous studies in this regard have demonstrated that bank's profitability has a negative association with the banks' liquidity (Delechat *et al.*, 2012). Nevertheless, empirical findings indicated a positive impact on the profitability of liquidity (Laximikantham, 2015). In light of theory and above findings, this study hypothesizes that:

H3: Significant positive nexus exists between profitability and liquidity of Pakistan Islamic banks.

22.2.2.1.4 Deposits

Deposit is counted as an influencing factor of banks' liquidity. The desire for higher liquidity arises mostly when the deposits become scant (Assfaw, 2019). Deposits have been utilized for the resiliency of banks during great financial crisis. Higher inflow of deposits increases the liquidity of banks. On contrary, large withdrawal of deposits might also lead to liquidity shortage. Hence, it is expected that banks effort to increase their deposits inflow with cushion them from liquidity risk. In an empirical investigation, Al-Homaidi *et al.* (2019) disclosed a positive relationship between deposits and liquidity. These studies indicate that a rise in the deposit's demand increases the liquid assets of the banks. Nonetheless, studies conducted by Assfaw (2019) and Shah *et al.* (2018) revealed that deposits negatively affect the liquidity of banks. However, based on the summaries of prediction-based theories and consistent with the past literature, this study hypothesizes that:

H4: Significant positive nexus exists between deposits and liquidity of Pakistan's Islamic banks.

22.2.2.1.5 Capital adequacy ratio

Capital is counted as a vital determinant that maintains the stability of the banks and the preservation of the industry by preventing any unexpected losses faced by the banks (Moh'd Al-Tamimi & Obeidat, 2013). CAR is considered an important factor for the banks' liquidity management. It is argued that an increase in CAR strengthens the risk-bearing capacity of banks (Berger & Bouwman, 2017). In line with buffer theory, CAR overcomes the financial risks and creates bank liquidity. Similarly, the hypothesis of "risk absorption" also increases the banks capacity to cope with risks and create liquidity through high CAR. On the contrary, "financial fragility/crowding-out" hypothesis adds that CAR negative influence the bank liquidity. (Al-Harbi, 2017). The nexus of CAR and banks' liquidity has been explored by several studies and revealed fascinating results. For instance, Al-Homaidi *et al.* (2019) indicate that the CAR has a positive effect on liquidity because it has the capability of engrossing risk. In this vein, Gorton and Winton (2000) contend a reduction in liquidity creation by "the crowding out of deposits" when CAR is high. Moreover, Moussa (2015) and Bhati *et al.* (2015) disclosed a negative relationship between capital adequacy and banks' liquidity. Hence, in line with the foregoing discussion and perspective of the theory of financial ratios, this study hypothesizes that:

H5: Significant positive nexus exists between CAR and liquidity of Pakistan's Islamic banks.

22.2.2.2 *Macroeconomic factors*

22.2.2.2.1 Inflation

Inflation replicates a situation where the demand for products and services exceeds the supply in an economy. Inflation adversely affects lending to clients, which reduces the value of money and raises bank's vulnerability. During inflation, loan repayments are negatively influenced and savings are discouraged, which affects the banks' liquidity. In line with the informational friction theory, high inflation leads to lower financial performance of banks, not just return on money but also on assets. Since the lower return exacerbates credit markets friction which drives to credit rationing due to inflation rising. Consequently, banks reduce the loans which in turn increase bank liquidity (Fola, 2015). In this esteem, several pieces of the research argue that due to inflation, the living cost increases that decrease the deposits of banks and thereby negatively affects the banks' liquidity. Research conducted by Malik and Rafique (2013) and Vodova (2016) disclosed that inflation has a negative effect on the banks' liquidity. Whereas, Singh, and Sharma (2016) indicated a positive impact of inflation on liquidity. On the basis of informational friction theory and above-discussed evidence, this study hypothesizes that:

H6: Significant positive nexus exists between the inflation rate and liquidity of Pakistan's Islamic banks.

22.2.2.2.2 Gross domestic products growth

Gross domestic product growth (GDPG) is an indicator of a country's financial health. At the time of economic expansion, banks become more hopeful and increase their long-term investments while decreasing their liquid assets; however, during a recession, the opposite is true. Based on the theory of liquidity and financial fragility, GDPG has a negative effect on the liquidity of financial institutions (Al-Harbi, 2017). During the economic expansion, banks are more concerned in rising their investment to generate high profit. Banks reduce their focus on liquidity creation and givers more attention to risky capitals for the sake of high returns. In such an environment, financial entities have fewer liquid assets and make short-term loans with high interest rates. Hence, it can be argued that GDPG negatively links to bank liquidity. Though, when the economy is in a slump, banks may favor high liquidity over low liquidity. On the contrary, GDPG has a considerable positive influence on the liquidity of banks (Mazreku *et al.*, 2019; Zaghdoudi & Hakimi, 2017; Bunda & Desquilbet, 2008). Besides, Al-Harbi (2017) in line with theory postulated a positive significant nexus between GDPG and banks liquidity. Nevertheless, Singh, and Sharma (2016) and Sheefeni and Nyambe (2016) revealed that GDPG has a negative relationship with the liquidity of banks. Consistent with the past research, this study hypothesizes that:

H7: Significant positive nexus exists between GDPG and liquidity of Pakistan's Islamic banks.

22.2.2.2.3 Unemployment rate

Unemployment has a substantial effect on the lending portfolios of banks. The extent of unemployment unfavorably affects the customers' demand for loans (Singh & Sharma, 2016). Consequently, a decrease in the unemployment rate leads to a rise in loan demand, which forces banks to maintain greater liquidity. Hence, the higher demand for loans weakens the banks' liquidity position. On the contrary, there is also a possibility of liquidity rise in case of unemployment. Banks grant loan on the basis of some guarantee paying installments which would be impossible for borrower due to unemployment. Therefore, banks might be discouraged in issuance of loans at time of unemployment. Hence, the decrease in loans issuance booms the bank liquidity (El-Chaarani, 2019). The role of unemployment with liquidity was tested by Horváth *et al.* (2014), who disclosed a negative relationship between unemployment and liquidity. However, Munteanu (2012) revealed a positive relationship between unemployment and the liquidity of banks. Therefore, based on the above arguments and prior studies, this study hypothesizes that:

H8: Significant positive nexus exists between unemployment and liquidity of Pakistan's Islamic banks.

22.2.2.3 *Moderating factor*

22.2.2.3.1 Sharia Supervisory Board

This study has introduced the Sharia Supervisory Board (SSB) as the non-financial and the most dominant factor to manage the liquidity of the Islamic banks in Pakistan. It is considered one of the most dominant check and balance tools that improve the overall performance of the industry. SSB ensures the Sharia compliance of the products and services to confirm the banking operations are performed according to Islamic law (Jan *et al.*, 2020). It prohibits *riba* (interest) and *gharar* (contracting vulnerability) and encourages the profit and loss sharing concept (Jan *et al.*, 2021). The consensus on the relationship between SSB size and firm performance is mixed. For example, Hakimi *et al.* (2018) studied the impact of SSB size on firm performance and disclosed an insignificant relationship between SSB size and firm performance. Farag *et al.* (2018) reported that SSB has a positive relationship with firm performance. However, empirical evidence on the role of the Sharia board on liquidity management is limited. Therefore, consistent with the agency theory perspective, this study aims to test the nexus of Sharia board and liquidity in Islamic banks and hence hypothesizes that:

H9: Sharia board moderates the significant positive nexus that exists between total assets and liquidity of Pakistan's Islamic banks.

22.3 Methodology

This study intends to inspect the determinants affecting the liquidity of Islamic banks in Pakistan for the post-financial crises span. Since liquidity is influenced by several internal and external factors as well as governance attributes, this study considers both the internal and external factors along with the role of the Sharia Supervisory Board.

22.3.1 *Data and sampling*

This research utilized panel data of seven Islamic banks operating in Pakistan for 12 years during the period 2009–2020. However, few Islamic banks with incomplete data were excluded. Based on past literature, the study selected the most important factors that are expected to have a significant influence on the liquidity of the Islamic banks in Pakistan. The internal factors include total assets, funding cost, ROA, ROE, net operating profit, deposits, and CAR, whereas external factors include Inflation, gross domestic product, and unemployment. This study collected the data on internal factors and the Sharia board from embedded reports of the selected Islamic banks. The data for inflation, GDPG, and unemployment was collected from world development indicators (WDI).

22.3.2 *Regression modeling*

To investigate the effect of various factors on the liquidity of Islamic banks, this study specifies a regression model as follows:

LIQ: $\alpha + \beta_1$LNTA $+ \beta_2$COF $+ \beta_3$ROA $+ \beta_4$DEPOSIT $+ \beta_5$LNCAR $+ \beta_6$INF $+ \beta_7$GDPG $+ \beta_8$UNEM $+$ Ut (Model 1),

LIQ: $\alpha + \beta_1$LNTA $+ \beta_2$COF $+ \beta_3$ROA $+ \beta_4$DEPOSIT $+ \beta_5$LNCAR $+ \beta_6$INF $+ \beta_7$GDPG $+ \beta_8$UNEM $+ \beta_9$SSB $+ \beta_{10}$SSB*LNTA $+ \beta_{11}$ SSB*COF $+ \beta_{12}$SSB*ROA $+ \beta_{13}$SSB*DEPOSITS $+ \beta_{14}$SSB* LNCAR $+$ Ut (Model 2),

where $\beta 1$, $\beta 2$, ..., $\beta 14$ are the coefficients of the determinant variables and ε is the error term. In this model, the banks' liquidity is represented by LIQ, which is the dependent variable of the study, it can be calculated as liquid assets over total assets. Whereas, the independent variable, total assets being represented by LNTA is measured by taking the natural log of the total assets. FC is used to denote the funding costs, which is measured by the formula = total interest expense/total liabilities. ROA represents the return on assets, it can be calculated as net income/total assets. DEP represents the banks' deposits which are measured by deposits over total assets. CAR represents the capital adequacy ratio (capital adequacy ratio Tier-I); however, GDPG is used for gross domestic product growth, INF for the inflation rate, and UNE is used to represent the unemployment rate. Lastly, the SSB represents the Sharia board size, which has been utilized as the moderating variable in the model.

22.3.3 *Estimating methods*

This study has selected panel data, which is a mix of time and cross-section dimensions. For estimating panel data, the Hausman test is applied, which suggests the appropriateness between a fixed effect or random effect estimation model (Tahir *et al.*, 2018). In case, factors of liquidity are serially correlated with the error term, then a fixed effect is appropriate. Besides, the random effect model is best to utilize in the absence of serial correlation amid liquidity factors and standard errors. This study employs a fixed-effect model for the analysis.

22.4 Results and Discussions

22.4.1 *Descriptive statistics*

Table 22.1 depicts the descriptive analysis of the current research. The data shows that the liquidity of Islamic banks has a mean value of 1.163 ranging from 1.46 to 1.04 with a standard deviation of 0.097. The minimum ratio of liquidity requirement is 104% (1.04 × 100), which is greater than the required threshold of 100% by the State Bank of Pakistan. The observed mean value of total assets is 19.39 with a standard deviation of 1.028. Moreover, COF, CAR, ROA, and deposits has a mean value of 0.0452, 16.59, 0.0059, and 0.8009 with a standard deviation of 0.0137, 0.829, 0.0070, and 0.0591, respectively. The average value of CAR is 16.59% which is above the 8% required

Table 22.1. Descriptive statistics.

Variables	Observations	Mean	Maximum	Minimum	Std. dev.
LIQ	84	1.163	1.467	1.048	0.097
LNTA	84	19.399	21.143	16.799	1.028
COF	84	0.045	0.075	0.020	0.013
CAR	84	16.592	19.162	15.052	0.829
ROA	84	0.005	0.024	−0.028	0.007
DEPOSITS	84	0.800	0.887	0.636	0.059
SBS	84	2.53	4	1	1.091
GDPG	84	3.57	5.83	0.52	1.770
UNEMP	84	2.26	4.08	0.54	1.247
INF	84	8.23	13.64	2.52	3.626

by the State Bank of Pakistan. The mean value of GDP growth is recorded as 3.57 with a standard deviation of 1.77. The unemployment rate is 2.66 on average with a standard deviation of 1.24. On average, the inflation rate is 8.23 ranging from 2.59 to 13.64 with a standard deviation of 3.62. The maximum number of Sharia directors on board is four and a minimum of one person over the span of 2009–2020.

22.4.2 *Correlation matrix*

Table 22.2 depicts the correlation matrix between variables. The highest correlation is observed between CAR and LIQ, i.e., 0.657. All variables are negatively correlated to LIQ except CAR, ROA, and TA. Besides, COF, SBS, INF, and GDPG show an insignificant correlation with LIQ.

22.4.3 *Regression results*

Analyzing the effect of various factors on the liquidity of Islamic banks in Pakistan, a fixed-effect model is utilized. Since the outcome obtained by Hausman tests shows the probability of less than 5%, which indicates the appropriateness of the fixed-effect model.

The results reported in Table 22.3 shows that LNTA and LIQ, expectedly, are positive and statistically significant. This means, to be specific, a 1% increase in total assets leads to a 0.0894% increase in the liquidity of Islamic banks. Islamic banks in Pakistan are smaller in terms of total assets as compared to non-Islamic banks. Delechat *et al.* (2012) argued that small banks have limited resources, therefore, requires to hold more liquidity when their assets increase. The constant increase in total assets of Islamic banks would not lead to liquidity shortage and thereby preventing the liquidity risks. Thus, our findings are in line with argument that small banks need to hold more total assets to cope with liquidity risks due to its fewer approach to capital markets (Al-Harbi, 2017). The finding is similar to the outcome of Shah *et al.* (2018). Profitability measured through ROA plays a vital role in meeting the liquidity demands of the entities. In other words, Islamic banks can hold more liquid assets when they perform well in terms of profitability. However, an increase in the ROA of banks is linked to the investment in risky assets. For risky

Table 22.2. Correlation matrix.

Variables	LIQ	CAR	COF	DEPOSITS	ROA	TA	SBS	UNEMP	GDPG	INF
LIQ	1									
CAR	0.657[a]	1								
COF	−0.039	−0.270[b]	1							
DEPOSITS	−0.830[a]	−0.542[a]	−0.088	1						
ROA	0.315[a]	0.513[a]	−0.180	−0.118	1					
TA	0.627[a]	0.867[a]	−0.287[a]	−0.474[a]	0.515[a]	1				
SBS	−0.063	0.209[c]	−0.411[a]	0.094	0.067	0.151	1			
UNEMP	0.269[a]	0.478[a]	−0.609[a]	−0.162	0.237[b]	0.446[a]	0.397[a]	1		
GDPG	−0.008	−0.125	−0.548[a]	0.090	−0.020	−0.085	0.010	0.295[a]	1	
INF	−0.137	−0.182[c]	0.729[a]	0.001	−0.158	−0.207[b]	−0.220[b]	−0.711[a]	−0.779[a]	1

Notes: The significance level for 1%, 5%, and 10% are represented by a, b, and c, respectively.

Table 22.3. Fixed-effect regression model (dependent variable).

Independent variables	Model 1	Model 2
LNTA	0.0894*** (0.0120)	0.1572*** (0.01138)
COF	−0.1143(0.2428)	−0.7435*** (0.2686)
LNCAR	−0.0896*** (0.0143)	−0.1967*** (0.0170)
ROA	0.7941*** (0.2233)	−0.4143(1.1366)
DEPOSITS	−1.5495*** (0.0524)	−1.6328*** (0.0932)
UNEMP	−0.0003(0.0030)	−0.0012(0.0031)
GDPG	0.0003(0.0019)	$6.97E-05$(0.0019)
INFL	−0.0004(0.0011)	−0.0011(0.0013)
SBS		−0.1430** (0.0556)
LNTA*SBS		−0.0253*** (0.0078)
COF*SBS		0.2274*** (0.0672)
LNCAR*SBS		0.0361*** (0.0102)
ROA*SBS		0.3987(0.4438)
DEPOSITS*SBS		0.0341(0.0272)
C	2.1615	2.7219
R-squares	0.9717	0.9773
Adjusted R-squared	0.9660	0.9701
F-statistic	169.45	135.79
Prob (F-statistic)	0.000	0.000

Note: The numbers in the parenthesis are standard errors. ***, **, and * show significance level at 1%, 5%, and 10%, respectively.

investment, banks are required to hold liquidity buffers as per standard of Basel III accord. Interestingly, this study investigates positive association between ROA and LIQ at a standard significance level. It implies that 1% increase in ROA raises the liquidity of Islamic banks by 0.7941%, respectively. Moreover, it is indicated that Islamic banks in Pakistan are involved in risky investments to increase their profitability and liquidity. For risky investment, Islamic banks have a minimum liquidity cushion of 104% depicted in the descriptive statistics of the study. These findings are in harmony with theory of financial ratio and the findings of Al-Harbi (2017) and Singh and Sharma (2016). Nevertheless, the results show that CAR negatively affects the liquidity (LIQ) of Islamic banks at 1% significance over the period of study. In other words, a 1% increase in CAR lessens the liquidity of Islamic banks by 0.0896%. This implies that Islamic banks with higher capital ratios reflect their strong liability structure. Thus, it reduces the need for liquidity holdings (Smith *et al.*, 2019).

Moreover, higher capital ratios reduce the chances of bank failure. Therefore, Islamic banks prefer to lower their liquidity in case of higher CAR. These results are against the buffer theory and risk absorption hypothesis. But supported with crowding effect hypothesis and the results of Al-Harbi (2017) and Shah *et al.* (2018). Also, the findings indicate that deposits and LIQ are statistically significant at 1% but in a negative way. In other words, a 1% increase in deposits reduces the bank liquidity by 1.5495%. These findings are in line with that of Shah *et al.* (2018) and Dinger (2009). This implies that when banks get higher deposits, they do less investment in the liquid assets. This is because liquid assets produce low profitability. The banks are however entitled to pay some interest to the depositors for the money they deposited in the banks. Therefore, liquidity of Islamic banks decline when the banks receive more deposits. Furthermore, the inverse association amid COF and LIQ is noteworthy but due to insignificance level, it is negligible. Amongst the macroeconomic factors, none of them demonstrates significant nexus with the liquidity of Islamic banks. But the relationship between LIQ and GDPG is positive, while the nexus of LIQ with UNEMP and INF is reported with negative coefficients. Greater value of R-squared 0.9717 shows the model fitness.

In Model 2, the Sharia board size (SBS) is used as a moderating variable with the bank's specific liquidity factors. The concept of Baron and Kenny (1986) advocates that it is a third variable that strengthens or weakens the relationship between dependent and independent variables. The condition for this variable as per Barron's concept is that the interacting term, the product of independent and moderating variables, should be significant. The findings indicate that SBS plays an important role in affecting the liquidity of banks by managing the total assets. Results revealed that LNTA × SBS has a negative and significant relationship with banks' liquidity. This means that Sharia board members keep the liquidity of banks when their total assets are growing. By keeping the liquidity low, the banks can enjoy sound profitability. Moreover, COF × SBS shows a positive and significant relationship with liquidity. Banks support their liquidity position either from deposits or from outside funds. Thus, when the cost of funds increases, the Sharia board members increase the liquidity of banks in order to prevent the shocks of increased funding costs. The association between LNCAR × SBS and

LIQ is positive and significant. Sharia board members manage the banks' liquidity through the CAR. The positive nexus reflects that when banks are facing liquidity risk, Sharia board members stress increasing CAR, which ultimately increases the liquidity of banks. Moreover, findings revealed that Sharia board members do not influence the liquidity of banks by total assets and deposits. Thereby, an insignificant impact of LNTA × SBS and DEPOSITS × SBS is observed on LIQ.

22.5 Conclusion

This study investigated the bank's specific and macroeconomic factors affecting the liquidity of Pakistani Islamic banks over the period 2009–2020. Specific factors are total assets, deposits, cost of funding, profitability, and CAR. While macroeconomic indicators are GDPG, inflation, and unemployment. Furthermore, the study has introduced Sharia board size as a moderating factor to strengthen the nexus between banks specific factors and liquidity. The study used the fixed-effect estimation technique for the analysis. Empirical findings revealed that bank-specific factors such as total assets and profitability positively and significantly impact the liquidity position of Pakistani Islamic banks. Whereas, the deposits and capital adequacy ratio significantly impact the liquidity position but with a negative coefficient. The cost of the fund has no significant association with liquidity. However, when the moderating role of Sharia board size was tested, the cost of funds signifyingly influence the liquidity position of Pakistani Islamic banks in a positive way. Moreover, among the macroeconomic indicators, none has established significant nexus with the liquidity position of Islamic banks in Pakistan.

Based on the findings, this study provides operational and policy recommendations. The liquidity of the bank was largely influenced by internal variables according to the findings of the research. Since the banks' management has control over the particular banking (internal) variables, greater attention may be given to recognized elements to increase the bank's liquidity. Islamic banks must have a liquidity strategy, should effectively manage liquidity risk, and should determine their optimum level of liquid investment by weighing their marginal costs and benefits to enable them to pay their commitments and decrease the likelihood of a liquidity crisis.

This study has important implications for the bankers, customers, regulators, and policymakers of Islamic banks to manage the liquidity position of Islamic banks by using the total assets, generating high profitability, maintaining the capital adequacy ratio, and increasing the deposits. Also, the Islamic banks need to enlarge the Sharia board size in order to manage the liquidity position by controlling the cost of funds. The Central Bank of Pakistan should evaluate and constantly review their bank liquidity regulations, and urge banks to maintain central bank and international liquidity standards in order to strengthen the sector's viability.

22.5.1 *Limitations and future directions*

This study has certain limitations. For instance, only restricted bank and macroeconomic variables are identified in this study, more research must be conducted to incorporate more variables, macroeconomic variables, and regulatory issues that impact the liquidity position of Pakistani Islamic banks. Since the study only focused on Islamic banks operating in Pakistan. Future studies are motivated to test these variables in other Islamic banks operating in various countries. Future studies are encouraged to introduce other variables in the model and test the moderating role of other corporate governance attributes. Future studies can also be conducted using other measuring ratios of liquidity, such as short-term borrowing ratios or liquid assets to total assets, not included in the study.

Acknowledgments

The authors would like to thank the Management and Humanities Department of Universiti Teknologi PETRONAS (UTP), Malaysia.

References

Abd Razak, A. H. (2018). Centralisation of corporate governance framework for Islamic financial institutions. *ISRA International Journal of Islamic Finance*, *10*(1), 36–51.

Al-Harbi, A. (2017). Determinants of banks liquidity: Evidence from OIC countries. *Journal of Economic and Administrative Sciences*, *33*(2), 164–177.

Al-Homaidi, E. A., Tabash, M. I., Farhan, N. H., & Almaqtari, F. A. (2019). The determinants of liquidity of Indian listed commercial banks: A panel data approach. *Cogent Economics & Finance*, *7*(1), 1616521.

Alger, G. & Alger, I. (1999). *Liquid Assets in Banks: Theory and Practice.* Boston College Department of Economics.

Assfaw, A. M. (2019). Firm-specific and macroeconomic determinants of banks liquidity: Empirical investigation from Ethiopian private commercial banks. *Journal of Accounting, Finance and Auditing Studies*, *5*(2), 123–145.

Bagh, T., Razzaq, S., Azad, T., Liaqat., I., & Khan, M. A. (2017). The causative impact of liquidity management on profitability of banks in Pakistan: An empirical investigation. *International Journal of Academic Research in Economics and Management Sciences*, *6*(3), 153–170.

Berger, A. N. & Bouwman, C. H. S. (2017). Bank liquidity creation, monetary policy, and financial crises. *Journal of Financial Stability*, *30*, 139–155.

Berihun-Engida, B. (2015). *Determinants of Banks Liquidity and Their Impact on Profitability: Evidence from Eight Commercial Banks in Ethiopia.* Unpublished PhD Thesis, Addis Ababa: Addis Ababa University.

Bhati, S. A., Zoysa, D., & Jitaree, W. (2015). Determinants of liquidity in nationalised banks of India.

Bonfim, D. & Kim, M. (2012). Liquidity risk in banking: Is there herding. *European Banking Center Discussion Paper*, *24*, 1–31.

Bunda, I. & Desquilbet, J.-B. (2008). The bank liquidity smile across exchange rate regimes. *International Economic Journal*, *22*(3), 361–386.

Calem, P. S. & Rob, R. (1996). The impact of capital-based regulation on bank risk-taking: A dynamic model. *Finance and Economics Discussion Series*, *96*(12), 1–47.

Delechat, C., Henao, C., Muthoora, P., & Vtyurina, S. (2012). *The Determinants of Banks' Liquidity Buffers in Central America.* IMF, Washington, DC.

Dietrich, A., Hess, K., & Wanzenried, G. (2014). The good and bad news about the new liquidity rules of Basel III in Western European countries. *Journal of Banking & Finance*, *44*, 13–25.

El-Chaarani, H. (2019). Determinants of bank liquidity in the Middle East region. *International Review of Management and Marketing*, *9*(2), 64–75.

Farag, H., Mallin, C., & Ow-Yong, K. (2018). Corporate governance in Islamic banks: New insights for dual board structure and agency relationships. *Journal of International Financial Markets, Institutions and Money*, *54*, 59–77.

Fola, B. (2015). *Factors Affecting Liquidity of Selected Commercial Banks in Ethiopia*. Masters of Science in Accounting and Finance Thesis.

Gatev, E., Schuermann, T., & Strahan, P. E. (2007). Managing bank liquidity risk: How deposit-loan synergies vary with market conditions. *The Review of Financial Studies*, *22*(3), 995–1020.

Gorton, G. & Winton, A. (2000). Liquidity provision and the social cost of bank capital. Working Paper.

Hakimi, A., Rachdi, H., Ben Selma Mokni, R., & Hssini, H. (2018). Do board characteristics affect bank performance? Evidence from the bahrain Islamic banks. *Journal of Islamic Accounting and Business Research*, *9*(2), 251–272.

Hartlage, A. W. (2012). The Basel III liquidity coverage ratio and financial stability. *Michigan Law Review*, *111*(3), 453–483.

Horváth, R., Seidler, J., & Weill, L. (2014). Bank capital and liquidity creation: Granger-causality evidence. *Journal of Financial Services Research*, *45*(3), 341–361.

Jan, A. A., Lai, F.-W., & Tahir, M. (2021). Developing an Islamic corporate governance framework to examine sustainability performance in Islamic Banks and Financial Institutions. *Journal of Cleaner Production*, *315*, 128099.

Jan, A. A., Lai, F. W., Isa, M. P. B. M., & Hamad, S. (2020). The structure of Shariah governance in Islamic banking industry: A theoretical review. *International Journal of Psychosocial Rehabilitation*, *24*(6), 10465–10476.

Jan, A. A., Tahir, M., Lai, F.-W., Jan, A., Mehreen, M., & Hamad, S. (2019). Bankruptcy profile of the Islamic banking industry: Evidence from Pakistan. *Business Management and Strategy*, *10*(2), 265–284.

Laximikantham, N. M. D. (2015). Assessment of banks liquidity: Empirical evidence on Ethiopian commercial banks. *Assessment*, *5*(21), 21–30.

Malik, M. F. & Rafique, A. (2013). Commercial banks liquidity in Pakistan: Firm specific and macroeconomic factors. *Romanian Economic Journal*, *16*(48).

Mazreku, I. F., Morina, V. Misiri, J. V., Spiteri, & Grima, S. (2019). Exploring the liquidity risk factors in the balkan region banking system. *European Research Studies Journal*, *XXII*(1), 91–102. Doi: 10.35808/ersj/1409.

Moh'd Al-Tamimi, K. A. & Obeidat, S. F. (2013). Determinants of capital adequacy in commercial banks of Jordan an empirical study. *Dirassat Journal Economic Issue*, *4*(2), 267–280.

Mollah, S., Hassan, M. K., Al Farooque, O., & Mobarek, A. (2017). The governance, risk-taking, and performance of Islamic banks. *Journal of Financial Services Research*, *51*(2), 195–219.

Moussa, M. A. B. (2015). The determinants of bank liquidity: Case of Tunisia. *International Journal of Economics and Financial Issues*, *5*(1), 249.

Munteanu, I. (2012). Bank liquidity and its determinants in romania. *Procedia Economics and Finance*, *3*, 993–998.

Shah, S. Q., Khan, A. I., Shah, S. S. A., & Tahir, M. (2018). Factors affecting liquidity of banks: Empirical evidence from the banking sector of Pakistan.*Colombo Business Journal*, *9*(1), 1–18.

Sheefeni, J. P. & Nyambe, J. M. (2016). Macroeconomic determinants of commercial banks' liquidity in Namibia.

Singh, A. & Sharma, A. K. (2016). An empirical analysis of macroeconomic and bank-specific factors affecting liquidity of Indian banks. *Future Business Journal*, *2*(1), 40–53.

Smith, J., Arnould, A. G., Milonas, K., & Vo, Q.-A. (2019). Capital and liquidity interaction in banking. *Bank of England Working Paper No. 840.*

Sopan, J. & Dutta, A. (2018). Determinants of liquidity risk in Indian banks: A panel data analysis. *Asian Journal of Research in Banking and Finance*, *8*(6), 47–59.

Tahir, M. S., Shah, Q. A., Khan, M. M., & Afridi, M. A. (2018). Intellectual capital and financial performance of banks in Pakistan. *Dialogue (Pakistan)*, *13*(1), 105–118.

Vodova, P. K. (2016). Bank liquidity and profitability in the polish banking sector. *Scientific Journal of Bielsko-Biala School of Finance and Law*, *20*(1), 19–33.

Wilcox, J. W. (1971). A simple theory of financial ratios As predictors of failure. *Journal of Accounting Research*, *9*(2), 389–395.

Yimer, M. S. (2016). *Determinants of Liquidity in Commercial Banks of Ethiopia: The Case of Selected Private Banks.* Addis Ababa University, Ethiopia.

Yitayaw, M. K. (2021). Firm-specific and macroeconomic determinants of commercial banks liquidity in Ethiopia: Panel data approach. *Cogent Business & Management*, *8*(1), 1956065.

Zaghdoudi, K. & Hakimi, A. (2017). The determinants of liquidity risk: Evidence from Tunisian banks. *Journal of Applied Finance and Banking*, *7*(2), 71.

Zaher, T. S. & Kabir Hassan, M. (2001). A comparative literature survey of Islamic finance and Banking. *Financial Markets, Institutions & Instruments*, *10*(4), 155–199.

https://doi.org/10.1142/9781800612426_0023

Chapter 23

Blended Islamic Finance: A Tool for Poverty Reduction

Sahar Munir, Resul Sapar, and Muhammad Imran Majeed

Abstract

The objective of this research is to answer the main question of how to integrate Islamic redistribution instruments with other developmental aids in addressing the persistent poverty issues in Pakistan. Data were collected from both government and private organizations. Thematic analysis was done on the data. The results indicate that in Pakistan, zakat is the most important driving tool, whereas Islamic microfinance, mainly interest-free loans are making a place in the market. However, waqf still needs to make a place in the private ownership. Moreover, no major role is being played by waqf properties for poverty elimination. Being a new and emerging topic in Islamic finance, no proper definition is available for blended Islamic finance (BIF). However, it can be said to be the utilization of Islamic social finance funds, such as waqf, sadaqah, qard hasan, and zakat, and government development aids in mobilizing resources from private sector, including institutional impactful investors, in financing sustainable development initiatives in developing countries. Moreover, BIF can be used to attain the ultimate maqasid Sharia, which is well-being of the people, with focus on poor and needy.

Keywords: Zakat, Waqf, Blended Islamic Finance.

23.1 Introduction

23.1.1 *Background*

Poverty is a global phenomenon and a major challenge of this era. It has always been of prime importance for policy makers as it is directly connected to population welfare (Chen & Ravallion, 2013). One of the solutions in combating poverty is through economic development, especially for developing countries (Kwon & Yi, 2009).

According to Awojobi and Bein (2010), being a multifaceted term, poverty has numerous definitions, surrounding both economic and social aspects, which cannot be easily measured. However, economic development is possible by having a focused program for poverty reduction. The United Nations provided two definitions of poverty in 1995, one for absolute poverty, which was defined as:

> a condition characterised by severe deprivation of basic human needs, including food, safe drinking water, sanitation facilities, health, shelter, education and information. It depends not only on income but also on access to services.

Second one is overall poverty, which is defined as, takes various forms, including:

> lack of income and productive resources to ensure sustainable livelihoods; hunger and malnutrition; ill health; limited or lack of access to education and other basic services; increased morbidity and mortality from illness; homelessness and inadequate housing; unsafe environments and social discrimination and exclusion. It is also characterised by lack of participation in decision making and in civil, social and cultural life. It occurs in all countries: as mass poverty in many developing countries, pockets of poverty amid wealth in developed countries, loss of livelihoods as a result of economic recession, sudden poverty as a result of disaster or conflict, the poverty of low-wage workers, and the utter destitution of people who fall outside family support systems, social institutions and safety nets (UN, 1995).

Fosu (2015) observed that in the case of sub-Saharan countries, economic growth played a critical role for poverty eradication. The study conducted portrayed that in the mid-1990s, an average progress was made in poverty reduction. Mainly, an increase in income resulted in poverty reduction. Moreover, a decline in inequality also contributed to decrease poverty.

According to the estimation of World Bank, it is expected that an additional number of 40–60 million will fall below the poverty line in 2020 as compared to 2019 due to COVID-19 pandemic. The global state of poverty might get worse as a result of job loss, inflation, disturbance in supply chain, and decease in remittances, education, and health services (Pakistan Economic Survey, 2019–2020).

23.1.1.1 *Poverty eradication and Pakistan*

According to the Economic Survey of Pakistan (2019–2020), Pakistan is committed to comply to with SDG 1 which is poverty alleviation by 2030. However, it is expected that the COVID-19 will have a negative impact on the Pakistan's economy, and the existing figure of people living below poverty line might increase from 50 million to 60 million.

Over the years, poverty in Pakistan has seen a decline from almost 30% in 2013 to 24% in 2019. The annual percentage of poverty in the country is provided in Table 23.1.

Like other countries, Pakistan had undertaken various measures to combat poverty over the last six decades. These measures are highlighted in Table 23.2.

Along with the organizations discussed above, many others are also providing services in Pakistan, such as USAID. But still a lot needs to be done. According to the Economic Survey of Pakistan 2018–2019, 24% of Pakistanis are living below the poverty line (Pakistan Economic Survey, 2018–2019). As efforts for poverty eradication are being done globally, likewise they need to be done in Pakistan.

Table 23.1. Poverty rate in Pakistan.

Sr. No.	Year	Poverty rate (%)
1	2013–2014	29.5
2	2014–2015	38.8
3	2015–2016	24.3
4	2016–2017	24.3
5	2017–2018	24.3
6	2018–2019	24
7	2019–2020	24.3

Source: Pakistan Economic Survey (2013–2020).

Table 23.2. History of government and private plans for poverty eradication.

Sr. No.	Name	Year	Main objective
1	Edhi foundation	1951	Founded in 1951 by Abdul Sattar. The Edi Foundation was a non-profit private social welfare program. Along with having the world's largest private run ambulance network, it provides services such as homes and orphanage services, education, graveyard, education, and children services
2	Agha Khan foundation	1967	Agha Khan Foundation provided numerous services in Pakistan especially facilities for the poor in the remote areas
3	Oxfam	1973	Oxfam has been working in Pakistan since 1973, with a special focus on women and girls. The main objective was to enable them to exercise their rights and have access to basic services and economic resources
4	The Zakat and Ushr department	1980	Zakat is an essential of Islamic faith. In 1980, The Zakat and Ushr Department was established, aimed at distributing zakat collection to the deserving people through the State Bank of Pakistan
5	Pakistan Bait-ul-Mal (PBM)	1992	Pakistan Bait-ul-Mal (PBM) was founded as an autonomous corporate body in 1992. PBM has various functions, such as provision of health facilities, education assistance, woman empowerment, credit facilities for small businesses, education stipend, and orphanage
6	Pakistan poverty alleviation fund (PPAF)	1997	In 1997, the government founded Pakistan Poverty Alleviation Fund (PPAF) to provide the poor with financing facilities. Currently, it is working with the World Bank for the provision of micro credit facilities for the poor
7	Saylani foundation	1999	Established in May 1999 by famous spiritual and religious scholar Maulana Bashir Ahmed Farooqui. *Saylani* Welfare International Trust provided numerous services such as education medical, welfare, clean drinking water, food provision, and few others for the poor and needy

Table 23.2. (*Continued*)

Sr. No.	Name	Year	Main objective
8	Khushhali bank	2000	Government of Pakistan also took initiative in microfinance. With the assistance of Asian Development Bank, Khushhali Bank was established in 2000. The main objective was to finance income generating activities for the poor such as small-scale businesses
9	Akhuwat foundation	2001	Akhuwat is a non-profit company founded in 2001 for the assistance and betterment of the poor and needy. It is currently providing several programs such as Islamic microfinance, education facilities, health facilities, and a clothes bank. It is also providing services for transgenders
10	Benazir income support program	2008	Benazir Income Support Program was launched in 2008 to enhance the standard of living, predominantly for women, with provision of money for the basic needs. It has dual objective of poverty eradication and woman empowerment
11	PM Nawaz Sharif health programme	2016	The PM's National Health Programme scheme was launched in 2016 for the provision of health facilities of the poor
12	Ehsaas	2019	The Division of Poverty Alleviation and Social Safety established with the sole objective to initiate Ehsaas program, which was launched on March 27, 2019. The main objective of Ehsaas was to reduce income inequality, invest in people, and lift lagging districts. Ehsaas is about the creation of a "welfare state" by promoting financial inclusion and access to digital services, empowerment of women

23.1.1.2 *Blended finance*

Myriad institutions are working to combat poverty. Organizations like World Bank have set targets to eradicate it. Initially, Millennium Development Goals (MDGs) were defined, which expired at the end of 2015 without achieving the desired goals. After this, in 2015,

Figure 23.1. 17 Sustainable Development Goals (SDGs).
Source: www.un.org.

the Sustainable Development Goals (SDGs) were introduced, which are provided in Figure 23.1.

In comparison to the eight goals outlined in the MDGs, a more comprehensive set is defined in the 17 major goals of the SDGs (Sachs, 2012). In both the MDGs and SDGs, the utmost priority is given to poverty elimination (UN, 2015a).

The SDGs are expected to be achieved in 15 years, ending 2030. There are 17 SDGs provided by the UN for the betterment of the future generations. It is believed that with the help of blended finance, these SDGs can be achieved with an optimum and better resource mobilization.

According to an estimate of the United Nations (UN), approximately an annual development fund of USD 5 trillion is needed to attain the goals of SDGs by 2030. UN estimated that the development funds from governments and international aids agencies are inadequate to achieve the SDGs by USD 2.5 trillion, annually. With trillions of deficits, the need of the time is to come up with innovative ideas to gather funds from the private sector (Badjie, 2019). Most private investors are reluctant to invest in development program of emerging markets due to high risk and low return, such as the SDG development-related investments. To attract private sector to participate in the SDG-related investment, blended finance can be a feasible option (OECD, 2018).

Blended finance can be defined as "the strategic use of development finance for the mobilization of additional finance towards sustainable development in developing countries" (OECD, 2018, p. 13). It can be used to blend concessionary funds (including philanthropic funds) together with private sector and impact investor to undertake SDGs development initiatives, hence overcoming the funding gap of USD 2.5 trillion mentioned earlier.

Blended finance can contribute significantly to the well-being of the society by undertaking sustainable or impact development investment in the developing countries that create new job opportunities, upskilling and enhancing human capital development. Blended finance can capitalize on the development funds from philanthropic, government, international aids (UNCHR, OECD, and IsDB) and subsequently entice private sector and impact investor to participate actively. Despite the effort of blended finance, the SDGs might not be achieved by 2030, mainly due to global inequalities, susceptibility in societies, especially Muslim countries, and high rate of poverty (Badjie, 2019).

23.1.1.3 *Blended finance and maqasid al Sharia*

In comparison to the 17 SDGs of UN, there are five components of maqasid al Sharia, which serve the same purpose, that can be described as follows:

(1) Protection of religion — includes protecting one from blasphemy and to give the basic rights to practice religion.
(2) Protection of life — consists of maintaining the honorable rights to live, provision of healthcare, and road safety.
(3) Protection of intellect — preserving the human intellect from all that is harmful because unsound mind is the source of affliction and ailments.
(4) Protection of ancestry — focusing on welfare of people, orphans, and homeless, including to strive, to raise, to educate offspring honorably and to protect the environment for future generation.

(5) Protection of wealth — provision of job opportunities, improvement in standard of living, to acquire and maintain the property in a way that is halal and beneficial to all without tyranny and persecution.

The focus of SDGs is to enhance the quality of life, conserve the planet, and increase the economic growth, which are consistent with the maqasid al Sharia. As cited in Chapra (2008, p. 4), Al-Ghazali stated that, "The very objective of the Sharia is to promote the well-being of the people, which lies in safeguarding their faith (din), their self (nafs), their intellect ('aql), their posterity (nasl), and their wealth (māl). Whatever ensures the safeguard of these five serves public interest and is desirable, and whatever hurts them is against public interest and its removal is desirable".

Basically, both frameworks emphasize on human capital development (Badjie, 2019). The focus of Sharia is on enablement of comfort and elimination of difficulties for any person. This understanding enables one to understand that the setup and principles of SDGs is consistent with the basic principles of maqasid al Sharia. Both share the features of elimination of numerous types of deprivations, such as provision of a good standard of living, education, and opportunity to grow (Al-Ahsan, 2015).

Islamic Finance instruments has the potential of being a source of development finance too. Sekreter (2017) defines Islamic finance as, "Islamic finance is an economical and financial system that approved by Sharia law or Sharia principles". Moreover, Sharia contains five prohibition, i.e., riba, gharar, maysir, rishwah, and jahl.

Islamic finance has been growing on a rapid pace and has achieved a major share in various countries. The current value of global assets is estimated to be USD 3 trillion (IFSB, 2019). Still, it is not playing a pivotal role for poverty alleviation, which it can play. Moreover, The Organisation of Islamic Cooperation (OIC) countries should also address this issue at emergency basis (Hydara, 2020). Moreover, It is believed that a vital role can be played by Islamic finance in bridging the gaps in SDGs financing (Ahmed *et al.*, 2015). The main tools available for poverty eradication are zakat, waqf, qard e hassan, and sadaqah.

23.1.2 *Motivation of the study*

Poverty is a global phenomenon and a problem faced by every country, especially the developing ones. UN has committed to fulfill its SDGs by 2030, for which various measures are being taken. Along with conventional finance, Islamic finance can also play a role, as it also has the potential and solutions, which when applied can assist in achieving the SDGs.

23.1.3 *Contribution*

This study is first of its nature in Pakistan to study the distribution mechanism proposed by Sharia for poverty eradication. Various tools of Islamic redistribution instruments, such as zakat, waqf, qard hasan, and sadaqah, have been previously used, but none of them were used holistically for eradication of poverty in Pakistan.

The focus of this research is to highlight the issue of ineffective measures taken by the Pakistan's government and private sectors in addressing the persistent poverty. Thus, this study is about understanding and investigating or examining the failure of the poverty eradication measures.

In the current scenario, the main obstacle in attaining the goal of SDGs is the issue of efficient allocation of resources. Moreover, despite efforts done by various institutions in Pakistan to curb poverty, it persists even though reduced. So, it is intended to propose a mechanism to address this issue.

We subsequently propose a new conceptual model that would complement the past and current poverty eradication measures by integrating the Islamic redistribution instruments such as zakat, qard hasan, waqf, and sadaqah together with other contemporary impact investment instruments.

23.2 Literature Review

23.2.1 *Poverty eradication tools provided by Sharia*

As discussed in the introduction, poverty alleviation is on the priority list of SDGs of the UN. Along with conventional solutions for

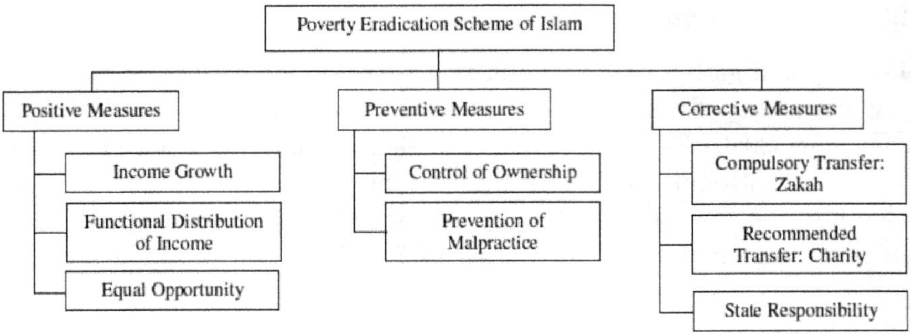

Figure 23.2. Poverty alleviation tools available in Sharia.
Source: Sadeq (1995).

poverty alleviation, Sharia has offered various solutions for the same. A basic structure for poverty eradication is discussed by Sadeq (1995) and shown in Figure 23.2.

Moreover, according to Khan (2010), the poverty mitigation measures are multi-dimensional, mainly being charity, which can be further discussed as:

(a) compulsory charity: zakat and fitrah;
(b) optional charity: sadaqah;
(c) perpetual charity: waqf.

A comparison is done by Hassan (2008) of the major methods of charity in Islam, as provided in Table 23.3.

As provided in this section, the main options available in Islamic finance are zakat and waqf, which can be helpful in poverty eradication.

23.2.2 *Zakat as a tool for poverty alleviation*

Rahman and Najib (2010) state that zakat has the potential to develop and grow the economy. Zakat holds the position of a tool for compulsory charity, which can be used for eight motives, among which five are used for poverty eradication. Based on this, it is believed that zakat can help in poverty eradication if managed properly by the responsible authorities (Hassan, 2010).

Table 23.3. A comparison of Islamic charity tools.

Factors	Waqf	Zakat	Liliah
Nature	Voluntary	Compulsory	Voluntary
Rate	Any amount	Fixed rate	Any amount
Expense categories	Flexible expense categories. Donor can decide	Eight fixed expense categories	Flexible expense categories. Donor can decide
Spend	Generally capitalized	Generally spent in one year	Generally spent in one year
Investments	Invested in social or economic asset	Generally not invested — needs to be discharged as soon as possible	Generally not invested — may be discharged according to need and mandate
Sharia governance: Liability	Donor must be sane, of age, male or female	Liability for payment is governed by Sharia	Any person can give
Mutawallee	Must appoint mutawallee (trustee)	Mutawallee not necessary	Mutawallee not necessary
Document	No document necessary	No document necessary	No document necessary
Sadaqah jariya	Always a continuous charity and continuous reward	Generally not continuous	Generally not continuous
Capital base	Forms a capital base for sustainable community development	Not a capital base	Not a capital base
Beneficiaries	May be applied to all irrespective of creed	Applied only to Muslims	May be applied to all irrespective of creed
Time for payment	Can be paid at any time	Generally paid in Ramadan	Can be paid at any time
How payment is effected	Can take the form of any asset — cash, land, coins, jewellery	Generally paid in cash or stocks	Can take the form of any asset

Source: Hassan (2008).

Zakat is one of the five pillars of Islam on which the code of life is governed. Zakat is believed for the welfare of the society based on Sharia. The most critical area is zakat management, in which the disbursement holds immense importance. Zakat is a portion of wealth for the poor (Bagus, Kusuma, & Sukmana, 2010).

Two of the most important redistribution instruments provided by Islam are zakat, also known as obligatory charitable wealth tax, and waqf, an irrevocable and inalienable endowment in perpetuity. The spending on zakat is used for self-purification. In the second decade of Islam (AD 622), zakat became compulsory transfer system (Hassan, 2006). Similarly, the recipients are purifying from the sentiments of jealousy from the well-off (Benthall, 1999).

The collection of zakat differs among various countries (Ahmed *et al.*, 2015). The governments of countries, such as Yemen, Saudi Arabia, Malaysia, Pakistan, and Sudan, enacted laws for the collection of zakat on an obligatory basis (Kahf, 1989). Whereas, few other countries have instituted government agencies entrusted to collect and distribute zakat without making its payment to these bodies obligatory, such as Jordan, Kuwait, Qatar, Iraq, Bahrain, Bangladesh, Indonesia, Oman, Egypt, and Morocco.

According to Obaidullah (2008), by the permanent provision of zakat, nonetheless, it is feared to increase financial dependence by the zakat recipient. So, it is encouraged to invest in sectors like health, education, and various inclusive and sustainable social impact projects of economic development.

Zakat assists soul purification of the payer while providing economic growth and better standard of living to the recipient (Qardhawi, 2009). It ensures distributional justice by allocating a portion of wealth of the financially able person for the basic needs of the poor (Kahf, 2014).

According to Badjie (2019), zakat plays a twofold role in maqasid e Sharia: first, provision of basic needs (Hifzu Nafs) and second, betterment of standard of living (Hifzu Maal). Three of the SDGs, namely no poverty, zero hunger, and reduced inequality, are in line with zakat's twofold role in maqasid e Sharia. Moreover, by these provisions for social welfare and economic growth, it can help break the vicious circle of poverty.

23.2.3 *Waqf as an instrument for poverty eradication*

Waqf can be defined as, "Appropriation or tying up a property in perpetuity for specific purposes. No property rights can be exercised over the corpus. Only the usufruct is applied towards the objectives (usually charitable) of the waqf" (Obaidullah & Khan, 2008).

Kinds of Waqf: Khan (2010) has discussed three kinds of waqf as follows:

(1) *Religious Waqf*: This waqf is based on properties for religious purposes, such as mosques, madrassah (religious school), Muslim burial grounds, and for the maintenance of waqf properties. Thus, it is a social welfare instrument of redistribution for the benefit of society by and large for religious purposes.
(2) *Philanthropic Waqf*: It focuses on the support of the deprived sector and provision of needs on education, health services, microfinance loans, and building of infrastructure, such as parks, bridges, and roads.
(3) *Posterity or Family Waqf*: It was initiated after the death of the Holy Prophet (Peace Be Upon Him) in the regime of Hazrat Umar (635–645). Waqf must be used first for the members of one's own family, such as children and descendants. The remaining should be appropriated to the poor.

Cash Waqf: Classical waqf are generally in the form of land and building. However, these days, cash waqf is also gaining importance, mainly because of the ease of donation and usage. The funds are mainly collected from the rich with the issuance of certificates of waqf to document the act of endowment. The funds are redistributed directly or indirectly to the poor and for funding the development of waqf properties that benefit the Muslim and non-Muslim. In addition, waqf of intellectual property is also classified under this category (Khan, 2010).

Basically, the main purpose of waqf is philanthropy. Awqaf certificates are used to evidence the donation of cash waqfs. Moreover, awqaf mutual funds can be designed, and the proceeds can be utilized for charitable purposes (Sadeq, 1995).

Awqaf funds hold an importance presence in the society as it can complement government expenditure for public services. Nowadays, waqf is used for provision of shelters, basic infrastructure of an area, and supply of food for the needy (Hasan, 2006; Ahmed *et al.*, 2015).

Cash waqf is gaining popularity as people find it easy to donate with the banking system provides facilities in support of waqf (Cizakca, 1995). Moreover, apart from the provision of social services, waqf is also being used for environmental protection, etc. (Kahf, 2000).

Cash waqf can be used for providing interest-free loans and investment purposes, by which the proceeds are distributed to the beneficiaries. Hence, it holds a vital position for poverty eradication (Cizakca, 2002).

According to Shahidah (2011), waqf assets are irrevocable, inalienable, and perpetual. The waqf properties cannot be seized, transferred, sold by any individual or the government. In view of these restrictions, a waqf assets and its benefit will last forever as long as the assets are well maintained. Hence, it is also considered as sadaqah jariya (continuous charity). As opposed to zakat, waqf is a voluntary act. (Obaidullah, 2008).

23.2.4 *Use of Islamic redistribution instruments to develop models for poverty alleviation*

A model was proposed by to Hydara (2020), according to which the proposed model will deploy the Islamic social finance (ISF) tools, using a combination of waqf, sadaqah, and takaful. As it is expected that waqf might not be able to address the issue properly, so a combination of saqaqah and takaful can have better results.

Waqf, sadaqah, and profit and loss sharing contracts can be developed (Qardhawi, 2009). Zakat can be said to be an instrument based on Sharia for the equal distribution of wealth. Moreover, it can help for provision of basic needs of life for the deserving cluster of the society. Whereas, waqf can be used for developmental purposes with provision of services for a longer period. In addition, Islamic microfinance can provide opportunities to the beneficiaries for wealth creation and employment options. Consequently, all three can be used for resource mobility to achieve SDGs, mainly poverty eradication (Badjie, 2009). This setup can be defined as blended Islamic finance.

Abdullah (2018) investigated the role of waqf in realizing the maqasid e Sharia and SDGs and proposed a development framework based on waqf, which can be connected to the SDGs of 2030. Payment from the rich students can be utilized for waqf framework in the provision of education and research, where the poor can be benefit from it. Thus, the waqf facilities can be connected to SDG 4 which is quality education and SDG 8 which is decent work and economic growth.

For the well-being of public, a combination of zakat, waqf, sadaqah and profit and loss micro-finance sharing contracts can be developed (Qardhawi, 2009). Zakat can be an effective instrument for the provision of the basic needs of the deserving cluster that lives on the fringe of the society. Whereas, waqf can be used for a short- and long-term developmental purpose. Islamic microfinance can provide opportunities for wealth creation and employment options. Consequently, all three can be used for resource mobility to achieve SDGs, mainly poverty eradication (Badjie, 2019).

Shirazi and Yasin (2010) explained the setup created by the management state of Swat, Pakistan based on ushr. The main source of income was ushr on agricultural production. The system of collections and distributions were well organized. The collection and distribution mechanism had certain unique and interesting features. Enough revenue was collected, which was employed widely on public expenditure, both developmental and non-developmental.

An integrated framework based on zakat, awqaf and Islamic microfinance was proposed by Hassan (2010). The key features of the proposed framework are:

(a) collection and management of zakat from expected donors and zakat institutions;
(b) collection and management of waqf funds from expected donors and awqaf institutions;
(c) provision of Sharia-compliant microcredit financing to the deserving recipient.

Initially, the NGO can focus on provision of micro-finance and collection of funds from various zakat- and awqaf-based organizations. However, as the organization becomes mature, it may engage in the management of zakat and awqaf funds and use them as a stable source of funds (Hassan, 2010).

Zakat and waqf can be used to decrease the financial services cost, by which the poor and needy can be helped (Ahmed, 2002, Kahf, 2014). Explicitly, charity funds can be used channelize the funds through both commercial and non-profit organizations to help the deserving. However, to get complete benefits from Islamic finance for achieving SDGs would necessitate a creative combination of products and a proper legal and governing framework (Ahmed *et al.*, 2015).

Ahmad (2004), Cizakca (2004), Elgari (2004), and Kahf (2014) proposed a model based on cash waqf, which can be used to provide micro-finance to the needy. Elgari (2004) suggested a setting up of a non-profit financial institution to offer interest-free loans (qard hasan) to the beneficiaries (poor and needy). The funds will mainly come from the cash waqf. The cash waqf can be used for impactful development sectors (Ahmed, 2004; Kahf, 2014).

Moreover, capital markets can assist in the development of residential and commercial sectors. A successful example is the use of sukuk proceeds for the development of waqf properties in Mecca. A structured sukuk, known as sukuk aliIntifa'a was sold to investors that generate sukuk proceeds of USD 390 million to finance the construction cost Zam Zam Tower, situated adjacent to the Holy Mosque, Makkah (Ahmed, 2004). The concession period of 24 years was given to sukuk al intifa holders. Upon maturity of the sukuk al intifa, the whole Zam Zam Tower was returned to the Ministry of Awqaf, Saudi as the trustee of waqf.

According to Aliman (2017), Sukuk Ihsan program is being run under sukuk program to finance Yayasan Amir Trust Schools Programme, which is a non-profit institution imitated in 2010 for improvement of quality of education in government schools, with the help of public–private partnership under the Education Ministry. RM 100 million worth sukuk were issued, with the proceeds to finance the program. The main organizer and controller is CIMB Investment Bank, jointly managed by Maybank Investment Bank and RHB Investment Bank.

A model was developed by Yumna and Clarke (2011) in which zakat and Islamic charities were unified with micro-financing for poverty eradication in Indonesia. They tested their model in Indonesia's Baitul Maal Muamalat and Baitul Qiradh Baznas. The results showed that this cohesive merger can result in resolving issues of poverty for the deserving.

Correspondingly, Obaidullah (2008) also suggested a combined setup with focus on the key non-profit modes based on Sharia instruments, mainly zakat, waqf, and qard hasan. He integrated the guarantee (kafala) facility for the financing, which is believed to be the first of its type in helping the poor and needy.

Hassan (2010) introduced an arrangement of merging non-profit and commercial processes. Initially the proceeds of zakat can be used for basic needs provision and microfinance loans. Moreover, he proposed the use funds of waqf for financing working capital with the help of murabahah. In addition, investments to be made in bonds and other Islamic financial sources for earnings. Furthermore, the proceeds can be reinvested. Similar models were suggested by Alpay *et al.* (2015), Mohammed *et al.* (2014), and Haneef *et al.* (2015), who tested on Bangladesh and got similar results.

One of the World Humanitarian Summit 2016 outcomes indicate the use of social and faith-based financing such Islamic social finance to increase resources to meet humanitarian needs and reduce in risk and vulnerability of the less-fortunate peoples. The motive was to restructure and mobilize local resources in critical zones through equitable, dignified, and accountable partnerships. The model integrates Islamic social funds to pool private investors funding through social impact sukuk. The basic motive was to make internationals donors and private investors attracted toward financing in crisis zones. Islamic microfinance, development of human resource and takaful were the investment modes used to fulfill this purpose (Badjie, 2019).

23.2.5 *Gaps identified*

Even though, various tools are available and possible solutions are proposed, there is lack of any literature especially in the context of Pakistan. No literature discusses the concept of blended Islamic finance for poverty alleviation. It is intended to explore the possible solution with the help of blended Islamic finance.

The gaps identified by the researcher are as follows:

(1) No major relevant literature is available in the context of Pakistan on blended Islamic finance.

(2) To the best knowledge of the researcher, though various integrated models have been proposed, few practical examples are available.

23.3 Research Methodology

23.3.1 *Theoretical approach adopted by the researcher*

Several authors such as Burrell and Morgan (1979), Laughlin (1995), and Ryan *et al.* (2002) have explored numerous methodological approaches (cited in Rosmilla, 2009). The implementation of an interpretivist position supports to eradicate the restrictions of the positivist position (Rosmilla, 2009).

According to interpretivist approach, it is believed that not only one mental construction exists. Instead, the world can be construed in a unique perspective by each individual and cluster.

Over the last few decades, an addition is made in the human race described as "post-modernism" (Montagna, 1997). Post-modernism can be defined as, "an approach to the development of society, or societies or (indeed) cultures, which asserts that we have gone beyond the stage of modernism".

The researcher has developed a theoretical foundation, provided in Figure 23.3.

According to Figure 23.3, the researcher has taken the position of an interpretivist adopting a post-modernism as the research theory.

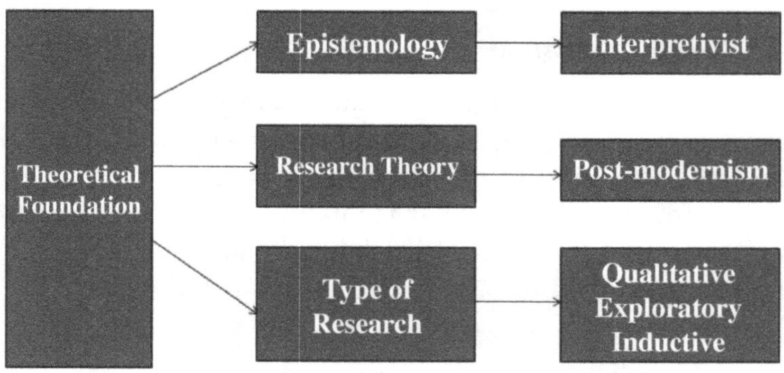

Figure 23.3. Theoretical foundation.

As the topic under study is in infancy, the study will be exploratory and inductive. For the data analysis, a qualitative approach will be taken.

23.3.2 *Sampling*

The study is based on secondary data mainly collected from the online sources of the sample size. For a qualitative study there is no particular rule for a sample size (Patton, 1990). Additionally, the researchers can identify few main persons for the sample size and afterward they can link the researcher to other individuals who can be added into the sample size (Bernard, 2000).

As the study is based on the institutions available in Pakistan which are working for poverty eradication, so the sample size includes the organizations listed in Table 23.4, which includes both government and private institutions.

As the study is based on secondary data, the reports and documents issued by the above provided organizations will be used and analyzed.

23.3.3 *Research administration*

As provided in the Figure 23.3, it is intended to propose a model by using blended Islamic finance for the welfare of the poor and needy

Table 23.4. Sample size.

Sr. No.	Name	Year
1	Edhi Foundation	1951
2	Agha Khan Foundation	1967
3	Oxfam	1973
4	The Zakat and Ushr Department	1980
5	Pakistan Bait-ul-Mal (PBM)	1992
6	Pakistan Poverty Alleviation Fund (PPAF)	1997
7	Saylani Foundation	1999
8	Khushhali Bank	2000
9	Akhuwat Foundation	2001
10	Benazir Income Support Program	2008
11	PM Nawaz Sharif Health Programme	2016
12	Ehsaas	2019

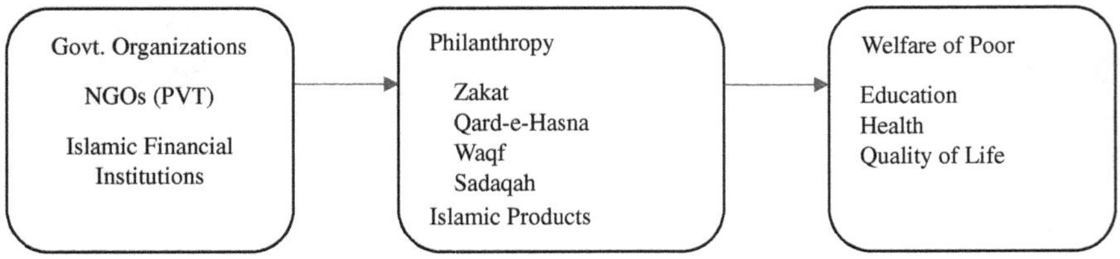

Figure 23.4. Proposed conceptual framework.

through philanthropic activities such as zakat, qard e hasna, waqf and sadaqah, and Islamic products through the government institutions and private philanthropic organizations.

Figure 23.4 proposes to highlight the role of government organizations, NGOs, and Islamic financial institutions which can work on the welfare of the poor for poverty eradication through Islamic finance tools.

23.3.4 *Data analysis*

The method selected for analysis is thematic analysis. According to Bryman (2008), it is one of the widely used method for qualitative research.

It can be further discussed as follows:

> Thematic analysis focuses on identifiable themes and patterns of living and/or behaviour (Aronson, 1994, p. 3).

According to Miles and Huberman (1994, p. 56), "Coding is analysis". The perks of coding with the assistance of thematic analysis are emphasized by Denzin and Lincoln (2000, p. 781) as they discuss as follows:

> No matter how the researcher actually does inductive coding, by the time he or she has identified the themes and refined them to the point where they can be applied to an entire corpus of texts, a lot of interpretive analysis has already been done.

Boyatzis (1998, p. 145) reviews thematic analysis consistent for getting results:

> Thematic analysis with reliability allows the interpretive social scientist to generate qualitative hypotheses that provide a basis for a positivist social scientist to conduct qualitative or quantitative hypothesis testing as part of the building process of science.

23.4 Findings and Discussion

23.4.1 *Profile of organizations*

The profile of organizations under study are divided into two lists, one is the organizations including both public and private organizations which are dealing with either zakat, waqf, or Islamic microfinance. The second list of Table 23.5 comprises of Islamic financial institutions (IFIs) that are authorized to collect zakat.

23.4.2 *Findings and discussion*

This study was carried out with the objective to examine the effectiveness of poverty eradication measures taken by the Pakistan's government and private sector. Subsequently, we propose a new conceptual model that would complement the past and current poverty eradication measures by integrating the Islamic redistribution instruments, such as zakat, qard hasan, waqf, and sadaqah, together with other contemporary impact investment instruments.

The researcher has organized the findings according to the redistribution instruments available in the country for poverty alleviation.

23.4.2.1 *Role of zakat for poverty alleviation*

23.4.2.1.1 Findings

The findings showed that zakat was channelized through many private institutions along with the efforts done by the main institute of the government, known as Pakistan Bait ul Maal. Many functions were taken out by them mainly for the education of the needy, women empowerment, and helping with medical needs. Zakat and Ushr department also work with them to provide the needy with necessities.

Table 23.5. List of organizations and departments.

Sr. no.	Name	Year	Main objective
1	Edhi Foundation	1951	Founded in 1951 by Abdul Sattar, the Edhi Foundation is a non-profit private social welfare program. Along with having the world's largest private run ambulance network, it has services such as homes and orphanage services, education, graveyard, education, and children services
2	Agha Khan Foundation	1967	Agha Khan Foundation is providing numerous services in Pakistan, few of which are provision of facilities for the poor especially who belong to remote areas
3	Oxfam	1973	Oxfam is working in Pakistan since 1973 to ensure that its people, with a special focus on women and girls. The main objective is to enable them to exercise their rights and have access to basic services and economic resources
4	The Zakat and Ushr Department	1980	Zakat is an essential of Islamic faith. In 1980, the Zakat and Ushr Department was established, which had the aim to channel the zakat paid to the deserving people through the State Bank of Pakistan
5	Pakistan Bait-ul-Mal (PBM)	1992	Pakistan Bait-ul-Mal (PBM) was founded as an autonomous corporate body in 1992. PBM has various functions, such as provision of health facilities, education assistance, woman empowerment, credit facilities for small businesses, education stipend, and orphanage
6	Auqaf & Religious Affairs Department-Punjab		Auqaf & Religious Affairs Department is chaired by the Secretary Auqaf & Religious Affairs. This department runs as a self-fund-raising body. Mainly from donation and funds collected by waqf properties
7	Auqaf Department KPK		Auqaf Department is an autonomous body of the provincial government. Its main source of income is from waqf properties, which is then used on repair/maintenance, constructions of mosques and shrines. It is run by chief administrator and supporting staff known as administrator auqaf

Table 23.5. (*Continued*)

Sr. no.	Name	Year	Main objective
8	Religious Affairs & Inter-Faith Harmony Department, Balochistan	2007	This department is run as a self-fund generating department. The main source of income is income raised from waqf properties
9	Sindh Auqaf Department	1970	The main functions of the department are maintenance of waqf properties. By provision of food and water at shrines and mosques. Along with building of musafir khanas, langar khanas, and toilets at the shrines. It generates income from waqf properties. It maintains agricultural land and commercial properties
10	Pakistan Poverty Alleviation Fund (PPAF)	1997	In 1997, the government founded Pakistan Poverty Alleviation Fund (PPAF) to assist the poor by providing loans. Currently, it is working with the World Bank for the provision of credit facilities for the poor
11	Saylani Foundation	1999	Established in May 1999 by famous spiritual and religious scholar Maulana Bashir Ahmed Farooqui, *Saylani* Welfare International Trust is providing numerous services such as education medical, welfare, clean drinking water, food provision, and few other for the poor and needy
12	Khushhali Bank	2000	Government of Pakistan also took initiative in microfinance. With the assistance of Asian Development Bank, in 2000, Khushhali Bank was established in 2000. The main objective was to provide income-generating activities for the poor such as small-scale businesses
13	Akhuwat Foundation	2001	Akhuwat is a non-profit company founded in 2001 for the assistance and betterment of the poor and needy. It is currently providing several programs such as Islamic microfinance, education facilities, health facilities, and a clothes bank. It is also providing services for transgenders

(*Continued*)

Table 23.5. (*Continued*)

Sr. no.	Name	Year	Main objective
14	Benazir Income Support Program	2008	Benazir Income Support Program was launched in 2008 to enhance the standard of living. predominantly for women, with provision of money for the basic needs. It has dual objective of poverty eradication and woman empowerment
15	PM Nawaz Sharif Health Programme	2016	The PM's National Health Programme scheme was launched in 2016 for the provision of health facilities of the poor
16	Ehsaas	2019	The Division of Poverty Alleviation and Social Safety established with the sole objective to initiate Ehsaas program, which was launched on March 27, 2019. The main objective of Ehsaas is to reduce inequality, invest in people, and lift lagging districts. Ehsaas is about the creation of a "welfare state" by countering elite capture promoting financial inclusion and access to digital services, supporting the economic empowerment of women
17	Wasil Foundation	1992	With its inception, Wasil has focused on poverty eradication. It runs with the ideology of "Potential Poor"

Table 23.6. Islamic financial institutions (only full-fledged IFIs).

Sr. no.	Name of Islamic financial institutions	No. of branches
1	Al Baraka Bank (Pakistan)	181
2	Bank Islami	227
3	Dubai Islamic Bank Pakistan	210
4	Meezan Bank	802

The results include the details of amount of zakat disbursed by the government organizations in the last five years, which is provided in Tables 23.7–23.11. Table 23.6 comprises of Islamic financial institutions (IFIs) that are authorised to collect Zakat.

According to the officials at Pakistan Bait ul Maal, the zakat funds are mainly employed in assisting the poor and needy, especially

Table 23.7. Disbursement of zakat, 2015–2016.

S. no	Provinces/other areas	Disbursed amount (Rs. Million)
1	Punjab	2784.83
2	Sindh	1190.40
3	Khyber Pakhtunkhwa	693.85
4	Balochistan	256.55
5	FATA	174.93
6	ICT	132.79
7	Gilgit-Baltistan	70.18
	Total	**5303.53**

Source: Ministry of Religious Affairs.

Table 23.8. Disbursement of zakat, 2016–2017.

S. no	Provinces/other areas	(Rs. Million)
1	Punjab	4,038.687
2	Sindh	1,669.408
3	Khyber Pakhtunkhwa	973.059
4	Balochistan	359.792
5	ICT	186.230
6	Gilgit-Baltistan	98.414
7	FATA	245.320
	Total	**7,570.910**

Source: Ministry of Religious Affairs and Inter-Faith Harmony.

orphans and widows, along with disabled persons. Moreover, many projects are run by the organization, such as shelter homes, free education, and hospital facilities. In addition to this, necessities for disabled like wheelchair and other assistance equipment are provided by the funds.

For the financial year 2020 from July to March, Pakistan Bait ul Maal has distributed a sum of PKR 2.705 billion for its main projects, which include:

(i) *Individual Financial Assistance (IFA)*: Through this program education, medical and general assistance is provided for the poor, orphans, widows, and disabled persons. Any family which has two or more special (disabled) children are declared "Special

Table 23.9. Disbursement of zakat, 2017–2018.

Federal areas/ provinces	**% Share**	**Allocated budget 2017–2018**
Federal Areas	7% of total zakat collection has been distributed amongst federal areas	
ICT	35.14% of 7%	197.024
Gilgit Baltistan	18.57% of 7%	104.119
FATA	46.29% of 7%	259.541
Total Federal		**560.684**
Provincial	Share of provinces after deduction of above federal payment is as per their share	
Punjab	57.36% of 93%	4272.796
Sindh	23.71% of 93%	1766.178
Khyber Pakhtunkhwa	13.82% of 93%	1029.464
Balochistan	5.11% of 93%	380.648
Total Provincial		**7449.086**
G. Total		**8009.770**

Source: Ministry of Religious Affairs and Inter-Faith Harmony.

Table 23.10. Disbursement of zakat, 2018–2019.

Federal areas/ provinces	**% Share**	**Allocated budget 2018–2019**
Federal Areas	7% of total zakat collection has been distributed amongst federal areas	
ICT	35.14% of 7%	181.476
Gilgit Baltistan	18.57% of 7%	95.902
FATA	46.29% of 7%	239.059
Total Federal		**516.437**
Provincial	Share of provinces after deduction of above federal payment is as per their share	
Punjab	57.36% of 93%	3935.608
Sindh	23.71% of 93%	1626.800
Khyber Pakhtunkhwa	13.82% of 93%	948.224
Balochistan	5.11% of 93%	350.609
Total Provincial		**6861.241**
G. Total		**7377.678**

Source: Ministry of Religious Affairs and Inter-Faith Harmony.

Table 23.11. Disbursement of zakat, 2019–2020.

Federal areas/ provinces	% Share	Allocated/released budget 2019–2020
Federal Areas	7% of total zakat collection is distributed amongst federal areas	
ICT	35.14% of 7%	227.70
Gilgit-Baltistan	18.57% of 7%	120.33
FATA	46.29% of 7%	299.94
Total Federal		**647.97**
Provincial	Share of provinces after deduction of above federal payments	
Punjab	57.36% of 93%	4,937.94
Sindh	23.71% of 93%	2,041.12
Khyber Pakhtunkhwa	13.82% of 93%	1,189.72
Balochistan	5.11% of 93%	1,189.72
Total Provincial		**8,608.69**
G. Total		**9,256.66**

Source: Poverty Alleviation and Social Safety Division.

Family" by the government and are provided assistance of PKR 25,000 per annum and a family with one child is given PKR 10,000 annually. An amount of PKR 1,387 million has been disbursed during the financial year July to March.

(ii) *Child Support Programme (CSP)*: Under this program, a monthly cash incentive is given to the parents for educating and sending children to schools. A monthly PKR 300 is given to a family with one child going to school and for families having two or more children PKR 600 is given. During the financial year July till March 2020, a sum of PKR 35 million has been disbursed.

(iii) *Schools for Rehabilitation of Child Labour (SRCLs)*: 159 Schools for Rehabilitation of Child Labour (SRCLs) have been established by the Pakistan Bait ul Maal for the primary education. It focuses on the children aged 5–6 years with a provision of books, stationery, and uniform. During the financial year July 2019–March 2020, a total amount of PKR 421 million has been distributed.

(iv) *Women Empowerment Centres (WEC)*: Vocational training centers established in 1995 are now named as Women Empowerment Centres; 154 centers are providing training to poor girls, orphans, and widows for various skills with free training material. A sum of PKR 354 million has been disbursed during July 2019–March 2020.

(v) *Dar-ul Ehsaas/Pakistan Sweet Homes*: Thirty-five Pakistan Sweet Homes, which are orphanages, are formed for the orphans. They are provided with free food, boarding and lodging, medical assistance, and free education. During the financial year July 2019–March 2020, a sum of PKR 484 million has been utilized.

(vi) *Pakistan Great Homes (PGH)*: Currently two Pakistan Great Homes have been established on test basis in Karachi and Lahore. Senior citizens, above 60 years, are provided with free lodging, boarding, and medical care.

In addition to the above efforts, the present government has launched a program mainly for poverty eradication, known as Ehsaas. It has initiated numerous programs for poverty eradication and social welfare. The main programs are listed in Table 23.12.

Along with them other institutions such as Edhi Foundation, Agha Khan Foundation, Saylani, Akhuwat and few other private organizations collect zakat and provide mainly food and other needs.

Moreover, IFIs also use the charity amount collected by them for the needy. Details of charities provided and utilized by the full-fledged IFIs in Pakistan are discussed in Tables 23.13–23.16.

23.4.2.1.2 Discussion

The results agree with Rahman and Omar (2010), Qardhawi (2009), and Hassan (2010) that zakat helps grow the economy and can assist in poverty eradication if managed properly by the responsible authorities. Moreover, the findings also are in accordance that zakat should also be invested in sectors such as health and education to reduce financial dependence.

Table 23.12. Programs under the Ehsaas Program.

Ehsaas Kafaalat program	It is a cash transfer program which is unconditional, with the main objective of assisting women through one woman one bank account policy
Ehsaas Emergency Cash	Ehsaas Emergency Cash program is focused on assisting the needy who have been hit by the COVID-19 pandemic. The main aim is to get them food. Till now this program has facilitated 15 million families, by giving PKR12,000 per family with a total budget of PKR 203 billion
Ehsaas Rashan Portal	The Ehsaas Rashan Portal is basically a donor–beneficiary linkup system for distribution of rashan. It has been initiated to facilitate the private sector and civil society organizations to assist the most vulnerable and deserving beneficiaries and provide them food rashan packs or cash equivalent in the wake of the COVID-19 crisis
Ehsaas Nashonuma	It is a health and nutrition conditional cash transfer program, which focuses on the children under 23 months of age. In August 2020, in the first phase, the prime minister launched Nashonuma in nine districts of the country
Undergraduate student scholarships	This program is launched on improving access to higher education over the next four years with the help of awarding 50,000 scholarships of worth PKR 20 billion to undergraduate students, in which 50% to girls, from disadvantaged families and areas, over the next four years
Education CCT	Since 2012, an educational program is being run in selected districts with a conditional cash transfer for primary school going children known as Waseela-e-Taleem. Now, this program has been reformed and expanded nationwide as "Waseela e Taleem Digital"
Commercialization policy for specialized nutrition food	A policy is in process to be developed to ensure access to specialized nutrition food
Orphanages policy and reform	The orphanages policy is currently under review

(*Continued*)

Table 23.12. (*Continued*)

Schools for the marginalized	This program is focused on the revamping of 150 schools run by Pakistan Bait ul Maal
Women's centers	Under this program, free trainings will be provided to widows, orphans, and underprivileged girls to gain various skills, i.e., cutting, drafting sewing, hand and machine embroidery, and knitting
Graduation and interest free loans	Under the Ehsaas National Poverty Graduation initiative, interest-free loans of PKR 80,000 monthly are being paid nationwide with the span of four years
Ehsaas Amdan (Income) Programme	Ehsaas Amdan (Income) Programme aims on providing assets to assist the deprived to start small businesses and skills training and business planning
Ehsaas Langar	It is targeted to open 112 langars nationwide over a two-year period through public–private partnerships arrange meals for the needy and most deprived segments of society
Ehsaas food card	It is under planning to devise a system for ration distribution, with the help of public–private partnership. The procurement process has been started to identify potential private partners
Ehsaas online education	This program focuses on the online education content as a public good for K12 to provide them with quality education
Ehsaas micro-credit for daily wage workers	Under this program, online mirco-credit facilities will be provided for the unbanked and poor daily wage workers for monthly rations

23.4.2.2 *Role of waqf for poverty alleviation*

23.4.2.2.1 Findings

The results indicate that waqf is being done only on the government levels with having provincial division and management of the waqf properties, which mainly consist mainly of mosques and shrines. Moreover, commercial and agricultural properties also are categorized as waqf properties, which are under the government control and the proceeds from them are used for the maintenance of mosques and shrines.

Table 23.13. Al Baraka Bank charity details.

Particulars	2015	2016	2017	2018	2019
	Rupees in '000				
Opening balance as of January 1	57,742	47,763	49,928	76,218	46,736
Additions during the year	26,321	15,085	58,876		
Received from customers on delayed payment				51,570	49,198
Dividend purification amount				1,773	382
Non-Sharia income					1,186
Transfer upon amalgamation		13,377			
Others				417	5
Less: Distribution of charity	36,300	26,297			
Education			7,801	16,007	6,818
Health			13,607	32,824	25,782
Ramzan Rashan drive			3,313		
Infrastructure and development				7,500	2,520
Mass wedding			1,350	1,530	1,635
Others			6,865	25,382	14,401
Closing balance as of December 31	47,763	49,928	76,218	46,736	46,351

Table 23.14. Meezan Bank charity details.

Particulars	2015	2016	2017	2018	2019
	Rupees in '000				
Opening balance as of January 1	11,899	10,851	1,637	2,398	1,086
Additions during the year					
Received from customers on delayed payment	43,562	24,899	29,502	32,376	49,110
Dividend purification amount	2,666	2,587	1,937	3,396	9,847
Non-Sharia compliant income	1,526	712	—	1,150	5,269
Profit on charity saving account	775	405	172	166	238
Less: Distribution of charity					
Education	40,427	32,867	26,450	30,250	38,100
Health	7,200	2,900	2,700	5,050	4,450
Islamic microfinance	1,950	100	—		
Community development		1,950	1,900	3,100	7,300
Closing balance as of December 31	10,851	1,637	2,398	1,086	15,700

Table 23.15. Bank Islami charity details.

Particulars	2015	2016	2017	2018	2019
	Rupees in '000				
Opening balance as of January 1			2,145	2,679	12,966
Additions during the year					
Received from customers on delayed payment	6,800	7,160	8,864	51,213	29,248
Non-Sharia compliant income	168		239	2,773	4,727
Profit on charity saving account	270	238	81	101	964
Less: Distribution of charity	9,060	9,210			
Education			3,400	1,700	1,000
Health			2,300	37,500	18,300
Islamic Microfinance			700	500	1,000
Community development			2,250	4,100	6,000
Closing balance as of December 31			2,679	12,966	21,605

Table 23.16. Dubai Islamic Bank charity details.

Particulars	2015	2016	2017	2018	2019
	Rupees in '000				
Opening balance as of January 1	11,244	10,071	3,373	16	154
Additions during the year	4,627	3,352	1,943		
Received from customers on delayed payment				4,010	11,482
Profit on charity fund				28	55
Less: Distribution of charity	5,800	10,050	5,300		
Education				1,000	4,350
Health				2,900	6,450
Closing balance as of December 31	10,071	3,373	16	154	891

The findings depict the provincial-wise details of waqf properties, which are discussed in Table 23.17.

According to the findings, no private known waqf is present currently in Pakistan.

Table 23.17. Province-wise details of waqf properties.

Sr. no	Province	Waqf properties	Number of properties
1.	Khyber Pakhtun Khawa KPK	Mosques	87
		Shrines	5
		Agricultural properties	49
		Commercial properties	104
2.	Sindh	Mosques	84
		Shrines	80
		Agricultural properties	—
		Commercial properties	30
3.	Balochistan	Mosques	2
		Shrines	—
		Agricultural properties	—
		Commercial properties	1
4.	Punjab	Mosques	24
		Shrines	37
		Agricultural properties	—
		Commercial properties	15

23.4.2.2.2 Discussion

The results disagree with Foyasal (2010) as till now no cash waqf is available in the country. Moreover, only the basic structure of waqf is available in which mosques and shrines are waqf properties. In addition, the properties available for agricultural or commercial purposes are used to maintenance of mosques and shrines. So, it can be said that the findings agree with Raissouni (2001) that the properties are future philanthropy.

The findings are not in accordance to Sadeq (1995), as no waqf mutual funds are available in the country.

The results agree with Hasan (2006) and Ahmed *et al.* (2015) that waqf properties are used for shelter and food for the needy which is mostly available at shrines.

The findings do not agree with Cizakca (1995) and Kahf (2000), as no model is present where waqf is done through banking facilities nor it is used for environmental protection.

Shahidah (2011) stated that waqf asset are considered as sadaqah jariya (continuous charity), which is true.

23.4.2.3 *Role of microfinance for poverty alleviation*

23.4.2.3.1 Findings

A major step taken by the previous governments was provision of cash amounts as a monthly stipend to the needy, especially widows. According to results institutes especially Akhuwat is providing zero-percent loans to the deprived and needy for education and self-employment. In the time span of 19 years under, its Islamic microfinance program Akhuwat has distributed PKR 120 billion as interest-free loans with assisting over 4.2 million families. The details of loans provided over the past few years is provided in Table 23.18.

Moreover, the network of Akhuwat has grown rapidly over the last decade due to the increase in the amount of loans disbursed. The details of branch network are presented in Table 23.19. Table 23.20 provides more details on the position of Islamic microfinance loans till December 2020 by Akhuwat.

Table 23.18. Year-wise amount of loans disbursed by Akhuwat.

	Indicators		
Year	**No. of loans**	**Amount disbursed**	**% of recovery**
2001–2002	192	1,895,000	100
2002–2003	282	2,791,300	99.90
2003–2004	832	8,504,000	99.90
2004–2005	3,124	31,811,000	99.90
2005–2006	6,264	66,020,700	99.90
2006–2007	8,674	89,935,600	99.80
2007–2008	11,388	122,445,242	99.80
2008–2009	13,821	164,226,000	99.80
2009–2010	21,073	251,808,800	99.80
2010–2011	34,194	418,211,100	99.80
2011–2012	67,683	1,137,684,000	99.83
2012–2013	159,138	2,580,467,000	99.82
2013–2014	234,883	4,047,109,100	99.85
2014–2015	367,798	7,310,527,000	99.92
2015–2016	496,458	11,205,522,500	99.92
2016–2017	619,396	16,585,952,800	99.96
2017–2018	731,302	21,607,796,495	99.99

Table 23.19. Branch network of Akhuwat.

	Indicators		
Year	**Cites**	**No. of branches**	**No. of employees**
2001–2002	1	1	3
2002–2003	1	2	3
2003–2004	1	4	12
2004–2005	1	7	32
2005–2006	6	11	50
2006–2007	10	18	75
2007–2008	10	20	76
2008–2009	11	22	101
2009–2010	24	36	186
2010–2011	33	60	343
2011–2012	105	81	615
2012–2013	165	169	869
2013–2014	219	271	1549
2014–2015	233	357	2013
2015–2016	291	500	3497
2016–2017	386	683	5693
2017–2018	435	791	4,427

Table 23.20. Position of Islamic microfinance loans till December 2020 by Akhuwat.

Progress indicator	**Total**
Total benefiting families	4,525,914
Total loans disbursed — Males	2,629,020
Total loans disbursed — Females	1,896,894
Amount disbursed PKR	128,347,435,826
Percentage recovery	99.92%
Active loans	814,722
Outstanding loan portfolio PKR	19,376,447,080
Number of branches	838

In addition to Akhuwat, Wasil Foundation has also initiated Islamic microfinance products. They are currently offering three products, murabahah, salam, and ijarah.

23.4.2.3.2 Discussion

The findings have been organized according to the tools under study. Thematic analysis was used as the analysis technique by the researcher, so three main themes were made, and the results were accordingly explained.

The findings are divided according to the redistribution tools available in Pakistan, i.e., zakat, waqf, and Islamic microfinance products. The findings showed that zakat was channelized through many private institutions along with the efforts done by the main institute of the government, known as Pakistan Bait ul Maal. Many functions were taken out by them mainly for the education of the needy, women empowerment, and helping with medical needs. Zakat and Ushr department also works with them to provide the needy with necessities.

According to the officials at Pakistan Bait ul Maal, the zakat funds are mainly employed in assisting the poor and needy, especially orphans and widows, along with disabled persons. Moreover, many projects are run by the organization, such as shelter homes, free education, and hospital facilities. In addition to this, necessities for disabled like wheelchair and other assistance equipment are provided by the funds.

The results agree with Rahman and Omar (2010), Qardhawi (2009), and Hassan (2010) that zakat helps grow the economy and can assist in poverty eradication if managed properly by the responsible authorities. Moreover, the findings also are in accordance that zakat should also be invested in sectors like health and education to reduce financial dependence.

The results indicate that waqf is being done only on the government levels with having provincial division and management of the waqf properties, which mainly consist mainly of mosques and shrines. Moreover, commercial and agricultural properties also are categorized as waqf properties, which are the government control and the proceeds from them are used for the maintenance of mosques and shrines.

The results disagree with Foyasal (2010) as till now no cash waqf is available in the country. Moreover, only the basic structure of waqf is available in which mosques and shrines are waqf properties. In addition, the properties available for agricultural or commercial purposes are used to maintenance of mosques and shrines. So, it can be said that the findings agree with Raissouni (2001) that the properties are future philanthropy.

The findings are not in accordance to Sadeq (1995), as no waqf Mutual Funds are available in the country.

The results agree with Hasan (2006) and Ahmed *et al.*, (2015) that waqf properties are used for shelter and food for the needy which is mostly available at shrines. The findings do not agree with Cizakca (1995) and Kahf (2000) as no model is present where waqf is done through banking facilities nor it is used for environmental protection. Shahidah (2011) stated that waqf asset are considered as sadaqah jariya (continuous charity), which is true.

A major step taken by the previous governments was provision of cash amounts as a monthly stipend to the needy, especially widows. According to results, institutes especially Akhuwat is providing zero-percent loans to the deprived and needy for education and self-employment. In the time span of 19 years under its Islamic microfinance program, Akhuwat has distributed PKR 120 billion as interest-free loans assisting over 4.2 million families.

The setup of Islamic microfinance is in accordance to Yumna and Clarke (2011) who discussed a similar model in Indonesia.

However, no setup or model is present which are discussed by Badjie (2009), Qardhawi (2009), Abdullah (2018), Shirazi and Yasin (2010), Hassan (2010), Ahmad (2004), Cizakca (2004), Elgari (2004) and Kahf (2014) Alpay *et al.* (2015), Mohammed *et al.* (2014), and Haneef *et al.* (2015).

Overall, the results indicate that in Pakistan, zakat is the most important driving tool, whereas Islamic microfinance, mainly interest-free loans are making a place in the market. However, waqf still needs to make a place in the private ownership. Moreover, no major role is being played by waqf properties for poverty elimination.

23.5 Conclusion

Overall, the results indicate that in Pakistan, zakat is the most important driving tool, whereas Islamic microfinance, mainly interest-free loans are making a place in the market. However, waqf still needs to make a place in the private ownership. Moreover, no major role is being played by waqf properties for poverty elimination.

23.5.1 *Summary of findings*

This study was based on exploring that how to integrate Islamic redistribution instruments with other developmental aids in addressing the persistent poverty issues in Pakistan?

The findings are divided according to the redistribution tools available in Pakistan, i.e., zakat, waqf, and Islamic microfinance products. The findings showed that zakat was channelized through many private institutions along with the efforts done by the main institute of the government, known as Pakistan Bait ul Maal. Many functions were taken out by them mainly for the education of the needy, women empowerment, and helping with medical needs. Zakat and Ushr department also work with them to provide the needy with necessities.

According to the officials at Pakistan Bait ul Maal, the zakat funds are mainly employed in assisting the poor and needy, especially orphans and widows, along with disabled persons. Moreover, many projects are run by the organization, such as shelter homes, free education, and hospital facilities. In addition to this, necessities for disabled like wheelchair and other assistance equipment are provided by the funds.

The results indicate that waqf is being done only on the government levels with having provincial division and management of the waqf properties, which mainly consist mainly of mosques and shrines. Moreover, commercial and agricultural properties also are categorized as waqf properties, which are the government control and the proceeds from them are used for the maintenance of mosques and shrines.

A major step taken by the previous governments was provision of cash amounts as a monthly stipend to the needy, especially widows. According to results, institutes especially Akhuwat is providing zero-percent loans to the deprived and needy for education and self-employment. In the time span of 19 years under its Islamic microfinance program, Akhuwat has distributed PKR 120 billion as interest-free loans with assisting over 4.2 million families

Overall, the results indicate that in Pakistan, zakat is the most important driving tool, whereas Islamic microfinance, mainly interest-free loans are making a place in the market. However, waqf still needs to make a place in the private ownership. Moreover, no major role is being played by waqf properties for poverty elimination.

23.5.2 *Contribution of the research*

To highlight the contribution to literature, first the gaps identified by researcher are provided in the following:

(1) No major relevant literature is available with the context of Pakistan on blended Islamic finance.
(2) To the best knowledge of the researcher, though various integrated models have been proposed, few practical examples are available.

The contributions of this research to the existing literature are as follows:

(1) It is understood to be the first of its nature to no instruments available are connected to blended Islamic finance for poverty alleviation, whereas the components are discussed and practiced individually.
(2) No existing integrated model is practically being used for poverty elimination in Pakistan. This study proposes financing based on blended Islamic finance, which can be used for poverty elimination.

23.5.3 *Research limitations*

This study is the first of its nature, especially in the context of Pakistan. The main limitations are listed as follows:

(1) The concept of integrated Islamic redistribution tools is a new phenomenon for the Pakistani market, so limited understating and literature is available. As the market for *Islamic* banking was new in the country, the available literature was very limited.
(2) The main limitation faced by the researcher was constraint of interviewing and collecting responses at a larger level, mainly due to COVID-19. This limited the effective size of the sample of those willing to cooperate.

(3) Moreover, this study had to completed in the time span of one year, so time constraint was another limitation.

23.5.4 *Research implications*

This study has various implications:

(1) It can be used a benchmark for future studies on tools for poverty elimination.
(2) Poverty elimination is a global fact, this study can be used for policymaking by the government, where the understanding and practical application of blended Islamic finance can be used and policies and frameworks can be designed.
(3) This study can be addition to existing literature and can be used to understand the role of blended Islamic Finance in poverty eradication.

23.5.5 *Recommendations/suggestions for further research*

During the last decade, Islamic finance has grown in Pakistan, still many concepts and model areas are new to the country, hence lacking in literature also. This study can be used a benchmark for future studies. However, this study can be further based on the following recommendations and suggestions.

Being a new and emerging topic in Islamic finance, no proper definition is available for blended Islamic finance. According to Figure 23.5, it is believed that the utilization of Islamic social finance funds, such as waqf, sadaqah, qard hasan and zakat, and government development aids in mobilizing resources from private sector, including institutional impactful investors, in financing sustainable

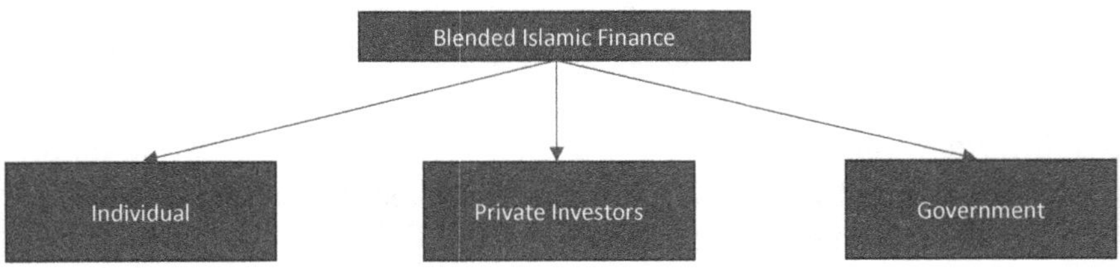

Figure 23.5. Sources for blended Islamic finance.
Source: Badjie (2019).

development initiatives in developing countries. Moreover, BIF can be used to attain the ultimate maqasid Sharia, which is well-being of the people, with focus on poor and needy.

According to Badjie (2009), Islamic blended finance can be defined as "an optimal mixture of Islamic social funds like zakat, waqf, sadaqah and penalties from delinquency with financial instruments for the purpose of financing socially responsible and positively impactful businesses for SDGs".

The main components used for blended Islamic finance are zakat, waqf, sadaqah, qard hasan. According to Qardhawi (2009), the zakat system, waqf, aadaqah, and profit and loss sharing contracts are practical activities to for betterment of quality of life, provision of social justice, equality, and social solidarity.

During the last decade, Islamic finance has grown in Pakistan, still many concepts and model areas are new to the country. Furthermore, this study can be sued as benchmark or future studies for tools for poverty elimination. Poverty elimination is a global fact, this study can be used for policymaking by the government, where the understanding and practical application of blended Islamic finance can be used and policies and frameworks can be designed. This study can be addition to existing literature and can be used to understand the role of blended Islamic finance in poverty eradication.

Being a new and emerging topic in Islamic finance, no proper definition is available for blended Islamic finance. However, it can be said to be the utilization of Islamic social finance funds, such as waqf, sadaqah, qard hasan and zakat, and government development aids in mobilizing resources from private sector, including institutional impactful investors, in financing sustainable development initiatives in developing countries. Moreover, BIF can be used to attain the ultimate maqasid Sharia, which is well-being of the people, with focus on poor and needy.

References

Abdullah, M. (2018). Waqf, Sustainable Development Goals (SDGs) and Maqasid al-Shariah. *International Journal of Social Economics*, *45*(1), 158–172.

Ahmed, H. (2002). *Financing Microenterprises: An Analytical Study of Islamic Microfinance.* Islamic Research and Training Institute, Jeddah, Kingdom of Saudi Arabia.

Ahmed, H. (2004). *Role of Zakat and Awqaf in Poverty Alleviation.* Islamic Development Bank, 30–72. Islamic Research and Training Institute, Jeddah, Kingdom of Saudi Arabia.

Ahmed, H., Mohieldin, M., Verbeek, J., & Aboulmagd, F. (2015). *On the Sustainable Development Goals and the Role of Islamic Finance.*

Aliman, K. H. (2017). *The Edge Markets.* https://www.theedgemarkets.com/article/going-listing-ihsan-sukuk-good-cause.

Alpay, S. & Haneef, M. A. (2015). *Integration of Waqf and Islamic Microfinance for Poverty Reduction: Case Studies of Malaysia, Indonesia and Bangladesh.* Gombak, Kuala Lumpur: The Statistical, Economic and Social Research and Training Centre for Islamic Countries (SESRIC) and International Islamic University Malaysia (IIUM).

Aronson, J. (1994). A pragmatic view of thematic analysis. *The Qualitative Report*, *2*(1), 3.

Awojobi, O. & Bein, M. A. (2011). Microfinancing for poverty reduction and economic development: A case for Nigeria. *International Research Journal of Finance and Economics*, *72*, 159–168.

Badjie, F. (2019). *Islamic Blended Finance for Funding Small and Medium Enterprises: Special Reference To The Gambia.* Unpublished Thesis.

Bagus, D., Kusuma, W., & Sukmana, R. (2010). The power of Zakah in poverty alleviation. *Seventh International/Conference The Tawhidi Epistemology: Zakat and Waqf Economy.* Malaysia Bank, pp. 30–72.

Bernard, H. (2000). *Social Research Methods: Qualitative and Quantitative Approaches.* London: Sage.

Boyatzis, R. E. (1998). *Transforming Qualitative Information Thematic Analysis and Code Development.* Thousand Oaks, CA: Sage Publications.

Burrell, G. & Morgan, G. (1982). *Sociological Paradigms and Organisational Analysis.* London: Heinemann.

Chapra, M. U. (2008). The Islamic vision of development in the light of Maqasid al-Shariah, Occasional Paper, *The International Institute of Islamic Thought*, London.

Chen, S. & Ravallion, M. (2013). More relatively-poor people in a less absolutely-poor world. *The Review of Income and Wealth*, *59*(1), 1–28.

Cizakca, M. (1995). Cash Waqfs on Bursa. *Journal of Economic and Social History of the Orient*, *38*(3), 313–54.

Cizakca, M. (2002). Latest developments in the western non-profit sector and the implications for Islamic awqaf. *Islamic Economic Institutions and The Elimination of Poverty*, 263–287.

Cizakca, M. (2004). Incorporated cash waqfs and mudaraba, Islamic non-bank financial instruments from the past to the future. *Munich Personal RePEc Archive*, 1–14.

Denzin, N. & Lincoln, Y. (2000). *The Handbook of Qualitative Research.* (2nd edn.), London: Sage.

ElGari, M. A. (2004). "The qard hassan bank", Paper Presented in the International Seminar on Nonbank Financial Institutions: Islamic Alternatives, 1–3 March, 2004, Kuala Lumpur, jointly organized by Islamic Research and Training Institute, Islamic Development Bank and Islamic Banking and Finance Institute Malaysia.

Fosu, A. K. (2015). Growth, inequality and poverty in Sub-Saharan Africa: Recent progress in a global context. *Oxford Development Studies*, *43*(1), 44–59.

Haneef, M. A., Ataul, P. H., Mohammed, M. O., Amin., M. B., & Muhammad, A. D. (2015). Integration of waqf-Islamic microfinance model for poverty reduction: The case of Bangladesh. *International Journal of Islamic and Middle Eastern Finance and Management*, *8*(2), 246–270.

Hassan, M. K. (2006). *The Role of Zakat in Poverty Alleviation in Bangladesh*, In a conference in Dhaka, November, 24–26.

Hassan, M. K. (2008). *Estimation of Zakah in Bangladesh With Secondary Macrodata.* http://centerzakatmanagement.org.

Hassan, M. K. (2010). An integrated poverty alleviation model combining zakat, awqaf and micro-finance. Mangi: Seventh international conference — The tawhidi epistemology: Zakat and waqf economy. institutions. *Islamic Economic Studies*, *9*(2), 1–38.

Hydara, M. (2020). An integrative model of waqf, sadaqah and takaful for poverty alleviation through empowering women farmers in the rural Gambia. *Journal of Islamic Finance*, *9*(2), 1–12.

IFSB. (2020). *The COVID-19 Crisis and Islamic Finance.* Islamic Development Bank. Islamic Research and Training Institute, Jeddah, Kingdom of Saudi Arabia.

Kahf, M. (1989). Zakah: Unresolved issues in the contemporary Fiqh. *Journal of Islamic Economics*, *2*(1), 1–22.

Kahf, M. (2000). *Al Waqf al Islami, Tatawwuruh, Idaratuh, Tanmiyatuh (Islamic Waqf, Its Growth, Management and Development).* Damascus: Dar al Fikr.

Kahf, M. (2014). *Notes On Islamic Economics: The Charitable Sector.* Westminster: Monzer Kahf.

Khan, F. (2010). Waqf: An Islamic instrument of poverty alleviation — Bangladesh perspective. *Seventh Internation/Conference The Tawhidi Epistemology: Zakat and Waqf Economy.* Malaysia.

Kwon, H.-J. & Yi, I. (2009). Economic development and poverty reduction in Korea: Governing multifunctional institutions. *Development and Change*, *40*(4), 769–792.

Laughlin, R. (1995). Empirical research in accounting: Alternative Approaches and a case for "middle range" thinking. *Accounting, Auditing and Accountability Journal*, *8*(1), 63–87.

Miles, M. B. & Huberman, A. M. (1994). *Qualitative Data Analysis: An Expanded Sourcebook.* London: Sage Publications.

Mohammed, M. O., Pramanik, A. H., Haneef, M. A., Aliyu, M. D., & Amin, F. B. (2014). *Integration of Waqf and Islamic Microfinance for Poverty Reduction: The Case of Sudan.* https://pdfs.semanticscholar.org/4f71/fe7b324d7bbbc38d2cb8b6371563d93abe67.pdf.

Montagna, P. (1997). Modernism vs postmodernism in management accounting. *Critical Perspectives on Accounting*, *8*(1–2), 125–145.

Obaidullah, M. (2008). *Introduction to Islamic Microfinance.* IBF Net Limited. International Institute of Islamic Business and Finance, India.

Obaidullah, M. & Khan, T. (2008). Islamic microfinance development: Challenges and initiatives. *Islamic Research and Training Institute Policy*, (2).

OECD (2018). *Financing SMEs and Entrepreneurs 2016: An OECD Scoreboard.* Paris: OECD Publishing.

Pakistan, G. O. (2013–2014). *Pakistan Economic Survey.* Ministry of Finance, Government of Pakistan. https://www.finance.gov.pk.

Pakistan, G. O. (2014–2015). *Pakistan Economic Survey.* Ministry of Finance, Government of Pakistan. https://www.finance.gov.pk.

Pakistan, G. O. (2015–2016). *Pakistan Economic Survey.* Ministry of Finance, Government of Pakistan. https://www.finance.gov.pk.

Pakistan, G. O. (2016–2017). *Pakistan Economic Survey.* Ministry of Finance, Government of Pakistan. https://www.finance.gov.pk.

Pakistan, G. O. (2017–2018). *Pakistan Economic Survey.* Ministry of Finance, Government of Pakistan. https://www.finance.gov.pk.

Pakistan, G. O. (2018–2019). *Pakistan Economic Survey.* Ministry of Finance, Government of Pakistan. https://www.finance.gov.pk.

Pakistan, G. O. (2019–2020). *Pakistan Economic Survey.* Ministry of Finance, Government of Pakistan. https://www.finance.gov.pk.

Patton, M. Q. (1990). *Qualitative evaluation and research methods.* Newbury Park: Sage.

Qardhawi, Y. (2009). *Fiqh Al Zakat.* Translated by Monzer Kahf. (1st edn.). Jeddah, Kingdom of Saudi Arabia: Scientific Publishing Centre.

Rosmila, S. (2009). Understanding accounting research paradigms: Towards alternative methodologies. *Research Bulletin of the Faculty of Economics and Management, UPM*, (4), 5–8.

Ryan, B., Scapens, R. W., & Theobald, M. (2002). *Research Method and Methodology in Finance and Accounting.* London: Thomson.

Sadeq, A. M. (1995). *Awqaf, Perpetual Charity and Poverty Alleviation.* Dhaka. As cited in Hassan, M. K. (2010). An Integrated Poverty Alleviation Model Combining Zakat, Awqaf and Micro-Finance. Bangi: Seventh International Conference — The Tawhidi Epistemology: Zakat and Waqf Economy Institutions. *Islamic Economic Studies, 9*(2), 1–38.

Sekreter, A. (2017). Green finance and Islamic finance. *International Journal of Social Sciences & Educational Studies, 4*(3), 115–121.

Shahidah, H. (2011). *Case Study: Development of Waqf Property Using Musyarakah Bond in Singapore.* International Centre for Education in Islamic Finance, Inceif University, Kuala Lumpur, Malaysia.

Shirazi, N. S. & Yasin, H. M. (2010). Fiscal structure and social welfare program in the former state of Swat (Pakistan). A case study with implications for muslim countries. *Seventh International Conference The Tawhidi Epistemology: Zakat and Waqf Economy. Malaysia.*

United Nations (1995). *The Copenhagen Declaration and Programme of Action, World Summit for Social Development.* 6–12 March, 1995, United Nations, New York, USA.

United Nations (2015). We can end poverty: Millennium development goals and beyond 2015. Accessed 25 September, 2015. http://www.un.org/millenniumgoals/poverty.shtml.www.un.org.

Yumna, A. & Clarke, M. (2011). Integrating zakat and Islamic charities with microfinance.

https://doi.org/10.1142/9781800612426_0024

Chapter 24

Systematic and Unsystematic Determinants of Liquidity Risk of Islamic Banks

Ahmed Imran Hunjra, Murugesh Arunachalam, Rashid Mehmood, and Mahnoor Hanif

Abstract

We analyze the systematic (macroeconomic) and unsystematic (bank specific) determinants of liquidity risk in Islamic banks. We extract the data from DataStream of Islamic banks in Pakistan, Qatar, Malaysia, UAE, Bangladesh, Bahrain, and Saudi Arabia from 2011 to 2020. We collect macroeconomic variables data from World Development Indicator (WDI). We apply generalized method of moment (GMM) to analyze data. We find that non-performing loans, capital adequacy ratio, leverage ratio, bank size, return on equity, gross domestic product, and inflation have significant impact on liquidity risk. We recommend that Islamic banks should be strong enough to face the liquidity risk come from systematic and unsystematic ways.

Keywords: Systematic and Unsystematic Determinants, Liquidity Risk, Islamic Banks, Generalized Method of Moment (GMM).

24.1 Introduction

Islamic banking and financing have been formed as opposed to conventional banking system primarily to offer Sharia-compliant investment, financing, and opportunities for trade. There are three forms of Islamic banking, i.e., completely based on Sharia, conventional banks providing Islamic banking, Islamic subsidiaries of conventional banks (Khan, 2013). Islamic finance encourages ethical investments which are primarily asset-backed and focused on risk-sharing. Islamic banks make credit available to meet the needs of people. They do not invest in conventional derivatives such as hedging instruments, credit default swaps, futures or options nor involve in short selling (Pappas *et al.*, 2012). Islamic bank deposits are classified as remunerative and non-remunerative. Remunerative deposits consist of partnership contracts known as musharakah, while non-remunerative deposits consist of non-compensatory loan. For financing of these assets, there are few funding agreements such as diminishing musharakah, ijarah, salam, istisna, and murabahah. Further, another activity of Islamic banks is giving hibah (gift) to the depositors which is equal to the rate of return provided by conventional banks that also distorts the main Islamic banking structure (Dusuki, 2007). Income from these financing either relates to profit from credit sale or rent for using these assets. This income is distributed among shareholders and depositors of banks. To achieve better functioning of banks, profit is distributed between bank and depositors according to pre-decided proportion (Shaikh, 2015).

Conventional and Islamic banks face liquidity risk during their operations. Therefore, liquidity risk makes it difficult for bank to react quickly when they have to make payment. Further, this risk also makes bank to immediately sell its valuable financial asset with price which is low as compared to market price (Ruozi & Ferrari, 2013). This leads the bank to solvency issue. Due to lack of managing liquidity risk, there are chances of bank failure (Arena, 2008). Conventional banks operate with interest-based tools. However, Islamic banks cannot operate with this interest-based methods. Therefore, Islamic banks face problem of managing liquidity risk which is one of the major challenges for them.

Both Islamic and convention banks are dealing with illiquid assets and usually liquid liabilities. Otherwise, they face insolvency risk. Liquidity becomes a major risk in banking sector, and bank management may give preference to manage this issue. In the modern theory of financial intermediation, banks exit in economy because of the important role in creating liquidity and transform their risk. Managing liquidity risk ensures the ability of a bank to accommodate obligations regarding cash flow because they are influenced by the behavior of depositors and external environment (Mohamad *et al.*, 2013). As a result of low market depth, market interruption or the lack of ability of the bank to access markets, banks suffer liquidity risk. The liquidity problem can be because of ineffective management of funds or it can be because of sudden withdrawals by the depositors mainly during instable economic situation (Siddiqui, 2008). In response to prevailing risk, financial institutions to build liquidity management systems as to estimate needs for funds and also ensure the availability of funds at right time. These systems monitor and assess the funding needs of a firm.

It is important to understand how determinants of liquidity risk in order to make day-to-day decision-making. Matz and Neu (2006) identify liquidity risk as the basis of all consequences faced by banking institutions. Islamic banks find it hard to follow worldwide conventional standards completely because of their different approach from conventional banking. Islamic banks are also finding it difficult to deal with the developing global banking environment. Islamic banking industry realizes the problem, and some Islamic countries have stimulated the development of Islamic banking sector. Countries such as Qatar, Malaysia, Bahrain, and UAE have aimed to become the center of excellence, but these countries are separately addressing these issues rather than working collectively. Therefore, there is still no strategy and direction to manage the liquidity problem that will help the industry to attain its potential.

Literature suggests that various micro and macro factors affect the liquidity risk of Islamic banks. Bank size, non-performing loans, profitability, and capital requirement are internal factors which can be directly managed by banks. Macroeconomic factors, such as GDP, inflation, and interbank rate, cannot be directly managed, but banks must prepare to face the problem of liquidity caused by these factors. Our research incorporates the internal and external factors that influence liquidity risk of Islamic banks. Therefore, the aim of our study is to analyze the impact of unsystematic and systematic factors on liquidity risk of Islamic banks of Pakistan, Qatar, Malaysia, United Arab Emirates (UAE), Bahrain, Bangladesh, and Saudi Arabia.

We present literature in Section 24.2; methodology and data in Section 24.3. Section 24.4 describes the empirical outputs, whereas Section 24.5 concludes the study with insights for future work.

24.2 Literature Review

Liquidity risk for Islamic banks is more important for sustainability (Khan & Ahmed, 2001). Further, Ahmed (2010) and Mohamad *et al.* (2013) explain that Islamic banks face liquidity risks because of the following factors: First, there is lack of Islamic-based instruments in the money market. Second, there is limited number of Islamic financial instruments which are listed on secondary market. Sharia has defined several obligatory conditions for transactions related to financial obligation. Third, the liquidity management instruments, such as debt instruments and interbank market, have been established long ago.

There are many theories of liquidity management which defines how a firm performs, monitors, and measures liquidity as well as prevent shortage of liquidity. The first theory is financial intermediation theory that is Fisher's separation theorem. According to this theory, banks are important factors for economic development while providing liquidity through illiquid assets (Wang, 2002). As a liquidity provider, a bank can boost economy by providing cash and demand deposits. According to anticipated income theory of liquidity, term loans are more important where banks grant loans based on anticipated incomes of borrowers. In light of this, it is considered that the policies of bank loan play an important part in the process of credit (Wang, 2002). It is also discussed that Islamic financial products are not properly developed due to lack of capital and money market in Islamic financing industry (Hassan *et al.*, 2013).

Past studies found some major systematic and unsystematic determinants of liquidity risk. Non-performing loans (NPL) is one of them which is the ratio of defaulted financing of a bank to its total financing. Furthermore, a loan default may lead to increase in liquidity risk due to reduction in cash flow to a decrease in cash flow (Diamond & Rajan, 2001). Imbierowicz and Rauch (2014) document a positive relationship between credit risk and liquidity risk. Joseph *et al.* (2012) define NPLs as bad loans, defected loans, or the loans which are due for 90 days or more and are unable to generate income or accrue interest. Higher ratio shows banks face more loss (Iqbal, 2012). Non-performing loans have poor outcomes on banks; therefore, they have adverse impact on progress of an economy. Joseph *et al.* (2012) indicate that NPLs decrease the liquidity and banks' profit. NPLs affect the economy of a country and contribute toward low profits and minimal liquidity (Sharma, 2005).

According to Brigham and Ehrhardt (2005), the financial crisis of 2007–2008 was outcome of NPLs. Low ratio of non-performing loans shows less loss to the bank which means the banks should maintain the ratio of their NPLs minimum in order to avoid losses (Eakins, 2008). It is also considered that the lending policy of bank also influences NPLs. According to Mounira and Anas (2009), managers should properly measure the process of lending (deposits and loans). They argue that lending more loans increase the return of bank as well as liquidity risk. Less risk and less profit of a bank indicate high ratio of liquidity (Babihuga, 2007). If NPLs are not managed properly, they propose major risk for economy. NPLs lead to banking failure because they affect the growth and survival of banks. Auronen (2003) conducts a study and finds a significant influence of NPLs on liquidity risk. Khemraj (2009) shows significant outcome of NPLs on liquidity risk. Literature recommends that banks should adopt effective method for evaluating the borrowers. Zheng *et al.* (2020) argue that NPLs creates issue of loan loss which ultimately affects liquidity and insolvency. We develop the following hypothesis based on literature:

H1: Non-performing loans have significant impact on liquidity risk.

Capital adequacy ratio (CAR) plays an important part in determining the liquidity risk. Cantor (2001) defines that CAR absorbs losses to safeguard depositors, beneficiaries, and official institutions to maintain banking system stable by having sufficient funds. CAR also reveals the capability of bank to initiate additional business. When banks meet their capital requirements, it helps to overcome loan loss and decrease liquidity ratio (Ashraf *et al.*, 2016). For proper operation of financial sector in an economy, Basel II as well as Basel III functioning of the financial sector, Basel II and Basel III point out the reliability and solvency of banking industry and demand an improvement in quality and banks' capital level (Afzal, 2015). However, if a bank does not have adequate reserves, then it will face more leverage ratio, and ultimately, there will be credit and liquidity risk (Hunjra *et al.*, 2020). Ongore and Kasu (2013) argue that CAR represents the potential of the bank to meet the challenges at the time of crisis. CAR is usually expressed as percentage of risk under scope-weighted assets. Equity-to-debt ratio is determined by the capital requirement. Hunjra *et al.* (2017) prove that capital adequacy ratio plays a vital role in the liquidity risk of Islamic banks. According to Dang (2011), the strength of the bank to stand firm against crisis is shown by CAR. CAR reduces the possibility of insolvency (Caggiano & Calice, 2011). The above literature helps us to develop the following hypothesis:

H2: Capital adequacy ratio has significant impact on liquidity risk.

Leverage ratio also determines the liquidity behavior of banks. Koehn and Santomero (1980) explain that leverage increases risk of banks. However, it is argued that inappropriate selection of debt financing leads to financial distress, and as a result, there are chances of bankruptcy (Sheikh & Wang, 2011). Titman and Wessels (1998) explore negative influence of leverage on liquidity. Negative relation also increases risk of banks to meet their obligations. Luoma and Spiller (2002) conclude that an increase in leverage ratio leads to increase liquidity risk of a firm. Khanqah and Ahmadnia (2013) reveal significant impact of leverage on liquidity. Literature suggests that leverage can result in higher liquidity risk because of more reliance on liabilities by the banks. We develop following hypothesis:

H3: Leverage ratio has significant impact on liquidity risk.

Another determinant of liquidity risk is bank size, which includes physical assets, reserves, investment securities, and loans (Audretsch & Elston, 2002). Hackethal *et al.* (2010) define bank size as a total asset a bank owns. Ahmed *et al.* (2011) prove that bank size is directly related to liquidity risk. Shen *et al.* (2009) explain that bank size is one of the dominant determinants of liquidity risk in banks. They suggest that bank size contributes to its level of liquidity because it affects the ability of bank to generate funds as well. In emerging economies, bank size is an important determinant of liquidity risk (Bunda & Desquilbet, 2008). Their findings show that the bank size directly contributes to liquidity risk. Large banks find assistance from central bank (lender of last resort) in case of liquidity shortage. In such a way, large banks create high liquidity which results in sale of illiquid assets to fulfill the requirement of their customers. Furthermore, large banks face more risk, and therefore, they are not much stable as compared to small banks (De Haan & Poghosyan, 2012). Similarly, Galletta, and Mazzù (2019) also conclude that size of a bank increases liquidity risk. After critical review of bank size and liquidity risk, we present the following hypothesis:

H4: Bank size has significant impact on liquidity risk.

Profitability relates to non-systematic factor of liquidity risk. We use ROE and ROA as profitability measures. These measures justify the quality of banks to utilize their available resources to generate revenue. A study conducted by Iqbal (2012) examines liquidity risk of Islamic and conventional banks in Pakistan and finds better liquidity management in Islamic banks as opposed to conventional banks. Further, the study justifies a positive relationship between profitability and liquidity risk. Ghenimi and Omri (2015) find that ROE shows positive outcome, whereas ROA shows negative outcome on liquidity risk of banks operating in Gulf countries. In addition, Alzoubi (2017) concludes a significant and positive relationship between profitability and liquidity risk. Literature helps us to develop the following hypothesis:

H5: Profitability ratio has significant impact on liquidity risk.

The fluctuation in macroeconomic variables is important factor affecting banks' liquidity. Literature also suggests that systematic factors affect the liquidity risk, including gross domestic product (GDP), inflation, and output gap. Shen *et al.* (2009) argue that banks fail due to the intensity of macroeconomic shocks. Undoubtedly, GDP is a systematic factor that influences liquidity of bank. In recession, business activities increase non-performing loans in banks by reducing the capability of borrowers to meet obligations. As a result, banks become insolvent. Furthermore, empirical evidences reveal varying outputs. Dinger (2009) shows negative influence of GDP on liquidity of banks. Moussa (2015) and Bunda and Desquilbet (2008) show a positive influence of GDP on liquidity of banks. Trenca *et al.* (2015) find that GDP has positive impact on liquidity risk. We present following hypothesis based on the above literature:

H6: GDP has significant impact on liquidity risk.

Inflation affects decision-making of banks regarding liquidity management. Heffernan (2005) suggests that an increase in inflation significantly increases liquidity risk. Silveira and Wright (2010) explain that the proportion of liquidity constraint is dependent on the real value of money; furthermore, real value of money depends on rate of inflation. However, real value of money is reduced due to increase in inflation; therefore, it creates problem of liquidity risk. Trenca *et al.* (2015) reveal that inflation causes a decrease in banks' liquidity, which ultimately increases liquidity risk. Ghenimi and Omri (2015) show that inflation has positive impact and GDP shows adverse influence on liquidity risk of Islamic banks. They further find that inflation and GDP show positive impact on liquidity risk of conventional banks. Waemustafa and Sukri (2016) show positive significant impact of inflation on liquidity risk of Islamic banks. Singh and Sharma (2016) reveal a positive relationship between inflation and bank liquidity. We develop following hypothesis based on the above literature:

H7: Inflation has significant impact on liquidity risk.

An increase in economic activity leads to stimulated bank lending. Therefore, output gap also plays an important role in affecting liquidity risk of banks. De Mendonça *et al.* (2011) find a positive impact of output gap on bank risk, indicating that output gap helps banks to adopt riskier policies which increase profit of banks. Montes and Peixoto (2014) also conclude a positive influence of output gap on bank risk. Therefore, the above literature helps us to present following hypothesis:

H8: Output gap has significant impact on liquidity risk.

24.3 Methodology

We aim to investigate the determinants of liquidity risk in Islamic banks of Pakistan, UAE, Bangladesh, Bahrain, Qatar, Saudi Arabia, and Malaysia. We use panel data of 34 banks in our study. We extract data of bank-specific variables from DataStream for 2011 to 2020. We gather economic data from WDI. We apply descriptive statistics to summarize data. We use correlation matrix to explain the association among explanatory variables and multicollinearity problem. We apply generalized method of moments (GMM) for hypotheses testing. For this purpose, we apply two-step dynamic panel estimation, which is appropriate for the short period and long cross-sectional data. Arellano and Bond (1991) and Arellano and Bover (1995) introduce this method which handles the endogeneity problem. GMM deals with autoregressive properties of dependent variable and to overcome endogeneity issue prevailing in dependent variables along with unabsorbed characteristics relative to firms (González, 2013). Furthermore, we check the robustness of results to apply heteroskedasticity generalized least square, and panel ordinary least square on individual country sample.

24.3.1 *Statistics*

We use liquidity risk as dependent variable and systematic factors (GDP, inflation, and output gap) and unsystematic factors (NPLs, CAR, bank size, leverage, and profitability such as ROA and ROE) are used as independent variables. We describe measurements of each variable in Table 24.1.

We use the following model for the analysis of data:

$$\begin{aligned}(\mathrm{LQR})_{I,t} = {} & \beta_0 + \beta_1(\mathrm{NPL})_{i,t} + \beta_2(\mathrm{CAR})_{i,t} + \beta_3(\mathrm{LR})_{i,t} + \beta_4(\mathrm{BS})_{i,t} \\ & + \beta_5(\mathrm{ROA}_{i,t} + \beta_6(\mathrm{ROE})_{i,t} + \beta_7(\mathrm{GDP})_t \\ & + \beta_8(\mathrm{INF})_t + \beta_9(\mathrm{OG})_t + \varepsilon_{i,t}, \end{aligned} \tag{24.1}$$

where LQR (liquidity risk) is the dependent variable, β_o is a constant, NPL (non-performing loans), CAR (capital adequacy ratio), LV (leverage ratio), BS (bank size), ROA (return on assets), and ROE (return on equity) are the independent variables and are indicators of unsystematic risk while GDP (gross domestic product), INF (inflation), and OG (output gap) are indicators of systematic risk and used as independent variables, ε is the error term, i is the bank, and t is the year.

Table 24.2 explains summary of data and correlation analysis between explanatory variables of the study. Liquidity shows that banks hardly meet liquidity and minimum reserve ratio. Banks have to maintain certain portion of deposits as reserve to fulfill their financial liabilities. NPL shows that banks are better able to manage default risk in terms of receivables. A small portion of receivables

Table 24.1. Description of variables.

Variables	Abv.	Measurements/ explanations	References
Liquidity risk	LQR	Loans/Deposits	Matz and Neu (2006)
Bank size	BS	Log of total assets	Singh and Sharma (2016) and Mehmood *et al.* (2019)
Non-performing loans	NPL	Default loans/Gross loans	Lotto and Mwemezi (2015) and Lotto (2018)
Capital adequacy ratio	CAR	Capital/Assets	Rime (2001)
Leverage ratio	LR	Total debt/Total assets	Bhaduri (2002)
Return on equity	ROE	Net income/Equity	Mehmood *et al.* (2019)
Return on assets	ROA	Net income/Total assets	Singh and Sharma (2016) and Mehmood *et al.* (2019)
Gross domestic product	GDP	GDP growth rate	Singh and Sharma (2016)
Inflation	INF	The percentage increase in the price of goods and services	Singh and Sharma (2016)
Output gap	OG	The amount by which the actual output of an economy falls short of its potential output	Waemustafa and Sukri (2016)

represents NPLs which helps banks to manage business activities more efficiently. Results of capital adequacy ratio indicate that on average, banks in sample countries maintain minimum capital requirement which is 8% (Ashraf *et al.*, 2016). As per Basel II, minimum capital adequacy requirement is 8% (Chen & Hsu, 2014). Furthermore, the mean value of capital-to-assets ratio indicates that banks are maintaining better capital to finance their assets. Outputs also suggest that there is not much variation in the values of capital adequacy which means that banks maintain stability in this ratio.

Table 24.2. Descriptive statistics and correlation analysis.

Variables	Mean	SD	LQR	NPL	CAR	LR	BS	ROA	ROE	GDP	INF	OG
LQR	0.835	0.242	1.000									
NPL	0.038	0.033	−0.142	1.000								
CAR	0.176	0.065	0.005	0.074	1.000							
LR	0.746	0.256	−0.199	−0.070	−0.228	1.000						
BS	23.255	2.394	0.069	−0.119	−0.202	0.393	1.000					
ROA	0.013	0.040	−0.075	−0.156	−0.178	0.106	0.087	1.000				
ROE	0.211	0.403	0.052	−0.292	−0.175	0.245	0.352	0.187	1.000			
GDP	0.058	0.045	0.310	−0.107	−0.077	−0.085	0.260	0.104	0.229	1.000		
INF	0.049	0.058	−0.212	−0.020	0.066	0.100	0.048	0.022	−0.025	0.004	1.000	
OG	−0.016	0.032	−0.005	0.053	0.104	−0.034	−0.049	−0.043	−0.028	0.021	0.173	1.000

Note: NPL = Non-performing Loans, CAR = Capital Adequacy Ratio, LR = Leverage Ratio, BS = Bank Size, ROA = Return on Assets, ROE = Return on Equity, GDP = Gross Domestic Product, INF = Inflation, OG = Output Gap, SD = Standard Deviation.

Leverage ratio signifies that most of the investment in assets comes from debt financing. This also indicates that banks are able to manage NPLs while recovering receivables; therefore, they opt for debt financing. We measure bank size as natural log of total assets. The results suggest that although banks maintain their investment in total assets, but there is more fluctuation in the values due to different requirements in banking systems of respective countries. Therefore, standard deviation value is also high in case of bank size. Profitability measures of banks include ROA and ROE in our study. Mean values reveal that ROA is low as compared to ROE. Banks are maintaining investment in their total assets as compared to equity. Average value of GDP shows healthy and stable economies in selected countries with least variation in GDP values. Inflation rate also suggests that sample countries of our study maintain a reasonable level of prices of products. They focus to increase export of respective countries; therefore, they try to stabilize the prices and do not let inflation rate to rise. These results show economic stability in sample countries of our study country. Output gap is small which suggests that countries almost meet their potential economic output leaving very small portion short with small deviation in values of output gap.

Furthermore, correlation analysis reveals that highest value of correlation is 0.393, which is between leverage and bank size. Therefore, correlation analysis indicates that there is no multicollinearity issue in the data and all the variables can be included for the final estimation. We also apply the analysis, variance inflation factor (VIF), in Table 24.3 to verify multicollinearity problem among explanatory variables. Results indicate that the values of VIF do not exceed 3, which verify no multicollinearity issue in the model.

Table 24.4 estimates the systematic (macroeconomic) and unsystematic risk (bank specific) determinants of liquidity risk across Pakistan, Malaysia, UAE, Saudi Arabia, Bangladesh, Qatar, and Bahrain over the period of 2010–2018. The sample of present study is 34 banks from selected countries. We find that NPLs has significant positive relationship with liquidity risk. Findings signify that more proportion of NPLs lead to more loan loss, and as a result, it creates liquidity and solvency risk (Zheng *et al.*, 2020). In addition, banks capital is a considerable element to determine liquidity risk. CAR also affects liquidity risk significantly and negatively. This signifies that when banks meet their capital requirements, they are able to

Table 24.3. Test for multicollinearity.

Variables	**VIF**	**1/VIF**
BS	1.40	0.714
LR	1.32	0.755
ROE	1.31	0.763
GDP	1.17	0.852
CAR	1.12	0.892
NPL	1.11	0.900
ROA	1.08	0.926
INF	1.06	0.948
OG	1.05	0.955

Note: VIF = Variance Inflation Factor.

Table 24.4. Two-step system dynamic panel regression.

Variables	**Coef.**	**Std. err.**	***t*-values**	***p*-values**
L1.	0.635***	0.023	(27.360)	0.000
L2.	0.013	0.012	(1.100)	0.270
NPL	0.899***	0.173	(5.190)	0.000
CAR	−0.264***	0.101	(−3.600)	0.009
LR	0.156***	0.029	(5.350)	0.000
BS	0.003*	0.002	(1.830)	0.152
ROA	0.151	0.179	(0.840)	0.400
ROE	0.047***	0.005	(7.230)	0.000
GDP	0.303**	0.143	(2.120)	0.034
INF	0.500***	0.062	(8.020)	0.000
OG	−0.002	0.049	(−0.030)	0.974
C	0.502***	0.075	(6.660)	0.000
Sargan	9.471			
p-values	0.107			
AR1 (*p*-values)	0.038			
AR2 (*p*-values)	0.617			

Notes: L1 = First lagged value of Liquidity Risk, L2 = Second lagged value of Liquidity Risk, NPL = Non-performing Loans, CAR = Capital Adequacy Ratio, LR = Leverage Ratio, BS = Bank Size, ROA = Return on Assets, ROE = Return on Equity, GDP = Gross Domestic Product, INF = Inflation, OG = Output Gap, *, **, & *** represent the significance level at 10%, 5%, & 1%, respectively, Sargan = test showing overidentifying restrictions, AR1 = Arellano–Bond first-order autocorrelation, AR2 = Arellano–Bond second-order autocorrelation.

reduce their liquidity risk and get into better position to meet liquidity requirements. The result is similar to the outputs of Ashraf *et al.* (2016).

The findings reveal that leverage ratio has significant and positive impact on liquidity risk of banks which is similar to the outcomes of Titman and Wessels (1998) and Luoma and Spiller (2002). This means that when banks increase their leverage, there is chance of financial distress, and that may lead to bankruptcy (Sheikh & Wang, 2011). Liquidity risk of a bank increases with increase in leverage because cash flows of banks increase with more debts and banks rely more on liabilities. Furthermore, bank size has significant and positive effect on liquidity risk suggesting that large banks generate more funds and they are not much stable (De Haan & Poghosyan, 2012). The finding of bank size and liquidity risk is in line with the study of Galletta and Mazzù (2019). However, ROA does not have significant impact on liquidity risk implying that size of bank and ROA are not important while meeting business liabilities. However, ROE shows significant and positive influence on liquidity risk of banks, which is similar to the findings of Ghenimi and Omri (2015).

We also incorporate macroeconomic determinants of liquidity risk along with bank-specific determinants. Among macroeconomic determinants, GDP and inflation reveal significant positive relationship with liquidity risk implying that when there is increase in GDP, there is increase in liquidity risk of the banks. These findings are similar to the outputs of Trenca *et al.* (2015). Furthermore, the findings suggest that an increase in GDP also increases credit default risk and economic activity which results in decreasing liquidity of banks. As a result, liquidity risk of banks also increases. In addition, an increase in rate of inflation has an influence on the purchasing power of people, where the same product is purchased with more money. This leads to increase in lending of banks and liquidity is decreased which causes the liquidity risk. Therefore, this leads to increase in liquidity risk. Output gap reveals no significant relationship with liquidity risk of banks. Moreover, we use Sargan test to verify the validity of study instruments and find insignificant outcomes that are visible by probability values, which means that instruments used in our study are valid. We find significant results of AR1 and insignificant results of AR2, which verifies no autocorrelation problem.

In Table 24.5, we also analyze the country-wise results by applying heteroskedasticity generalized least square and panel ordinary least square to check the robustness of results. Table 24.5 shows that that non-performing loan has significant impact on liquidity risk in Bangladesh and Malaysia but not in other selected countries. Furthermore, bank size is sound determinants of liquidity risk in Bahrain, Bangladesh, Malaysia, and Saudi Arabia. Therefore, results show volume of bank size is considerable factors while determining the liquidity risk. However, it is not a significant determinant of liquidity risk in Pakistan, Qatar, and UAE. This is also consistent with Zolkifli *et al.* (2015) who conclude that non-performing loan and bank size have significant relationship with liquidity risk.

CAR does not have significant relationship with liquidity risk in all countries. These results are similar to the findings of Ghenimi and Omri (2015). Moreover, ROE reveals significant relationship with liquidity risk in Qatar and Saudi Arabia but not in other selected countries. Results also show that ROA is sound determinant of liquidity risk in Bangladesh, Malaysia, Qatar, and Saudi Arabia but not in Pakistan, Bahrain, and UAE. In this regard, banks should pay more attention toward assets utilization while managing liquidity risk in Bangladesh, Malaysia, Qatar, and Saudi Arabia as compared to Pakistan, Bahrain, and UAE. Leverage ratio is also important liquidity risk determinants in Qatar and Saudi Arabia but not in other selected countries. These results are consistent with Racic *et al.* (2016), and it is found that leverage increases the exposure to liquidity risk in banks, while larger banks tend to reduce the exposure of liquidity risk.

Furthermore, Ahmed and Naqvi (2011) confirm that leverage is an important variable to determine the liquidity risk as compared to profitability and size. These are bank-specific forces and have significant relationship with risk except CAR. GDP has significant relationship with risk in Bangladesh, Malaysia, Pakistan, and UAE but not in other selected countries. In this regard, we concluded that country-specific variables, such as GDP, inflation, and output gap, are also important determinants of liquidity risk. In fact, GDP, inflation, and output gap are market factors and liquidity is firm-specific feature, and it is affected by firms' internal factors more instead of country-level factors.

Table 24.5. Country-wise results of heteroskedasticity generalized least square and panel ordinary least square.

	Heteroskedasticity generalized least square							Ordinary least square						
Variables	BH	BD	MSIA	PK	QAT	SA	UAE	BH	BD	MSIA	PK	QAT	SA	UAE
NPL	0.462	−1.200*	−2.364**	−1.019	0.768	−0.027	−0.083	−0.195	−1.516**	−3.141*	−0.833	0.547	−0.209	0.048
	(0.598)	(0.032)	(0.004)	(0.118)	(0.378)	(0.975)	(0.833)	(0.855)	(0.010)	(0.013)	(0.310)	(0.677)	(0.945)	(0.939)
BS	0.205***	0.015***	0.054*	0.052	0.016	0.012**	0.005	0.243***	0.01	0.061	0.052	0.015	0.007	0.013
	(0.000)	(0.001)	(0.050)	(0.113)	(0.375)	(0.008)	(0.506)	(0.000)	(0.091)	(0.098)	(0.309)	(0.521)	(0.667)	(0.257)
CAR	1.002	0.083	1.125	0.429	0.81	0.614	1.512	1.05	0.031	0.119	0.408	0.451	1.23	0.611
	(0.092)	(0.833)	(0.172)	(0.080)	(0.179)	(0.395)	(0.109)	(0.152)	(0.946)	(0.940)	(0.145)	(0.581)	(0.483)	(0.637)
ROE	0.463	0.010	0.088	0.269	0.340**	0.404*	0.067	0.508	0.000	0.068	0.023	0.335***	−0.361	−0.052
	(0.094)	(0.431)	(0.071)	(0.187)	(0.001)	(0.038)	(0.618)	(0.157)	(0.994)	(0.141)	(0.951)	(0.001)	(0.372)	(0.785)
ROA	−4.159	5.919**	−12.139**	0.009	21.173***	14.758***	1.218	−4.136	4.320*	−9.164	−0.316	23.583***	8.960*	8.166
	(0.122)	(0.001)	(0.003)	(0.978)	(0.000	(0.000)	(0.709)	(0.229)	(0.020)	(0.100)	(0.548)	(0.000)	(0.035)	(0.070)
LR	−0.038	0.589	−1.362	−0.015	−0.408***	−0.332***	0.597	−0.186	−0.056	−1.789	−0.004	−0.334*	−0.26	−0.088
	(0.827)	(0.336)	(0.055)	(0.838)	(0.000)	(0.000)	(0.597)	(0.348)	(0.931)	(0.152)	(0.970)	(0.028)	(0.050)	(0.958)
GDP	−1.309	1.564	1.896*	2.161	−1.481	−0.343	−0.37	−1.107	1.083	1.01	4.166	−1.911	−1.222	0.349
	(0.591)	(0.147)	(0.041)	(0.360)	(0.346)	(0.645)	(0.497)	(0.706)	(0.502)	(0.486)	(0.307)	(0.362)	(0.578)	(0.694)
INF	0.936	0.045	1.243	−0.437	−3.91	−0.121	−0.132	1.448	−0.098	−1.465	−0.288	−6.241*	1.613	−0.233
	(0.826)	(0.883)	(0.688)	(0.542)	(0.081)	(0.908)	(0.448)	(0.781)	(0.837)	(0.762)	(0.824)	(0.029)	(0.613)	(0.367)
OG	−0.93	−0.013	−3.513	2.04	0.799	−0.144	4.528*	−0.869	0.135	−2.46	3.34	0.454	−1.164	−0.925
	(0.811)	(0.894)	(0.350)	(0.163)	(0.573)	(0.723)	(0.046)	(0.850)	(0.429)	(0.678)	(0.165)	(0.814)	(0.303)	(0.759)
C	−3.642**	0.602	3.060**	1.783*	1.045*	1.297***	0.005	−4.350**	1.125	3.908*	1.675	1.028	0.813*	0.413
	(0.004)	(0.308)	(0.001)	(0.017)	(0.048)	(0.000)	(0.996)	(0.003)	(0.069)	(0.013)	(0.157)	(0.161)	(0.018)	(0.797)

Notes: BH = Bahrain, BD = Bangladesh, MSIA = Malaysia, PK = Pakistan, QAT = Qatar, SA = Saudi Arabia, UAE = United Arab Emirates, NPL = Non-performing Loans, CAR = Capital Adequacy Ratio, LR = Leverage Ratio, BS = Bank Size, ROA = Return on Assets, ROE = Return on Equity, GDP = Gross Domestic Product, INF = Inflation, OG = Output Gap, *, **, & *** represent the significance level at 10%, 5%, & 1%, respectively.

24.4 Conclusion

We examine the systematic and unsystematic determinants of liquidity risk by applying GMM approach in Islamic banks of Pakistan, Malaysia, Bahrain, UAE, Bangladesh, Saudi Arabia, and Qatar. Major outcomes of our study explain that non-performing loan, CAR, leverage ratio, and ROE are key unsystematic drivers to determine liquidity risk. However, GDP and inflation are key systematic determinants of liquidity risk of banks. The results indicate that when the non-performing loans of a bank increases, then banks start raising their capital to meet the needs of liquidity, which results in minimizing liquidity risk. CAR shows a significant relationship with liquidity risk in the banks of selected countries, as CAR illustrates a bank's financial power to make payments to their depositors and still leave with funds for lending. It means that the higher the CAR, the higher the liquidity of a bank and the lower the liquidity risk. Furthermore, leverage ratio shows significant relationship with liquidity risk, which suggests that an increase in debt financing helps banks to have control over liquidity problems. Furthermore, it explains that their management of handling liquidity risk is good enough that their high leverage does not contribute to liquidity risk. Moreover, as the systematic factors, GDP and inflation show significant positive relationship with liquidity risk. The reason is that GDP and inflation increase lending of banks. As a result, liquidity risk of banks is also increased. The Islamic banking is gaining more attention as compared to the conventional banking because it is known as religious factor of the country. We recommend that Islamic banks should be strong enough to face the risks coming from systematic and unsystematic ways. Islamic banks face problems while managing liquidity risk due to the lack of interest-based instruments. Further, there is a lack of Sharia-compliant instruments to manage liquidity risk.

In order to avoid liquidity risk, banks should manage the low NPL ratio to lower the exposure of liquidity risk. The ratio of capital adequacy should be enough to meet the precaution. Leverage of banks explains the burden of debt which should be minimized. If banks control their unsystematic factors properly, they are able to face systematic shocks. There should be well-organized instruments in Islamic banking like conventional banking to manage the risks that will improve the confidence of the stakeholders and market participants, which will enhance their reputation, strengthen their ratings, and improve their profitability. The limitation of the study is that only three macroeconomic variables are used in this study, while there are a large number of macroeconomic factors that affect liquidity risk may be incorporated in future study.

References

Afzal, A. (2015). The impact of market discipline on banks' capital adequacy: Evidence from an emerging economy. *The Lahore Journal of Business*, *4*, 61–73.

Ahmed, A. M. E. T. (2010). *Islamic Banking: How to Manage Risk and Improve Profitability*. Vol. 640. Hoboken, New Jersey: John Wiley & Sons, Inc.

Ahmed, N., Akhtar, M. F., & Usman, M. (2011). Risk management practices and Islamic banks: An empirical investigation from Pakistan. *Interdisciplinary Journal of Research in Business*, *1*(6), 50–57.

Alzoubi, T. (2017). Determinants of liquidity risk in Islamic banks. *Banks and Bank Systems*, *12*(3), 142–148.

Arellano, M. & Bond, S. (1991). Some tests of specification for panel data: Monte Carlo evidence and an application to employment equations. *The Review of Economic Studies*, *58*(2), 277–297.

Arellano, M. & Bover, O. (1995). Another look at the instrumental variable estimation of error-components models. *Journal of econometrics*, *68*(1), 29–51.

Arena, M. (2008). Bank failures and bank fundamentals: A comparative analysis of Latin America and East Asia during the nineties using bank-level data. *Journal of Banking & Finance*, *32*(2), 299–310.

Ashraf, B. N., Arshad, S., & Hu, Y. (2016). Capital regulation and bank risk-taking behavior: Evidence from Pakistan. *International Journal of Financial Studies*, *4*(3), 01–20.

Audretsch, D. B. & Elston, J. A. (2002). Does firm size matter? Evidence on the impact of liquidity constraints on firm investment behavior in Germany. *International Journal of Industrial Organization*, *20*(1), 1–17.

Auronen, L. (2003). *Asymmetric Information.* (1st edn.). London, UK: Pitman Publication.

Babihuga, R. (2007). *Macroeconomic and Financial Soundness Indicators: An Empirical Investigation* (No. 7–115). International Monetary Fund, Washington.

Bhaduri, S. N. (2002). Determinants of corporate borrowing: Some evidence from the Indian corporate structure. *Journal of Economics and Finance, 26*(2). 200–215.

Brigham, E. F. & Ehrhardt, M. C. (2005). *Financial Management.* Thomson Publishers: Australia, Alice Springs.

Bunda, I. & Desquilbet, J. B. (2008). The bank liquidity smile across exchange rate regimes. *International Economic Journal, 22*(3), 361–386.

Caggiano, G. & Calice, P. (2011). *The Macroeconomic Impact of Higher Capital Ratios on African Economies.* Working Paper Series No. 139, African Development Bank Group, Tunis, Tunisia.

Cantor, R. (2001). Moody's investors service response to the consultative paper issued by the Basel committee on bank supervision "A new capital adequacy framework". *Journal of Banking & Finance, 25*(1), 171–185.

Chen, Y. K. & Hsu, C. L. (2014). Are bank capital buffers cyclical — Evidence for developed and developing countries. *Journal of Financial Studies, 22*(3), 27–56.

Dang, U. (2011). The CAMEL rating system in banking supervision. A case study. *Global Journal of Management and Business Research, 12*(15), 1–47.

De Haan, J. & Poghosyan, T. (2012). Bank size, market concentration, and bank earnings volatility in the US. *Journal of International Financial Markets, Institutions and Money, 22*(1), 35–54.

de Mendonça, H. F., Galvao, D. J. C., & Loures, R. F. V. (2011). *Economic Activity and Financial Institutional Risk: An Empirical Analysis for the Brazilian Banking Industry* (No. 243).

Diamond, D. W. & Rajan, R. G. (2001). Liquidity risk, liquidity creation, and financial fragility: A theory of banking. *The Journal of Political Economy, 109*, 287–327.

Dinger, V. (2009). Do foreign-owned banks affect banking system liquidity risk? *Journal of Comparative Economics, 37*(4), 647–657.

Dusuki, A. W. (2007). Commodity murabahah program (CMP): An innovative approach to liquidity management. *Journal of Islamic Economics, Banking and Finance, 3*(1), 1–23.

Eakins, G. S. (2008). *Financial Markets and Institutions.* (3rd edn.). U.S.A. Beverly Hills: Sage Publications.

Galletta, S. & Mazzù, S. (2019). Liquidity risk drivers and bank business models. *Risks, 7*(3), 89.

Ghenimi, A. & Omri, M. A. B. (2015). Liquidity risk management: A comparative study between Islamic and conventional banks. *Arabian Journal of Business and Management Review, 3*(6), 25–30.

González, V. M. (2013). Leverage and corporate performance: International evidence. *International Review of Economics & Finance*, *25*, 169–184.

Hackethal, A., Rauch, C., Steffen, S., & Tyrell, M. (2010). Determinants of bank liquidity creation. *Social Science Research Network*, 1–41.

Hassan, H. M. U., Razzaque, S., & Tahir, M. S. (2013). Comparison of financial instruments in Islamic versus conventional banking system and liquidity management. *African Journal of Business Management*, *7*(18), 1695–1700.

Heffernan, S. (2005). *Modern Banking*. New York, USA: John Wiley & Sons.

Hunjra, A. I, Faisal, F., Abdeen, Z., Kamal, A., Ghufran, M., & Bashir, A. (2017). The asset and liabilities gap management of conventional and Islamic banks: An empirical study of Pakistan, UAE, Malaysia, and Bahrain. *Journal of Islamic Business and Management*, *7*(2), 266–282.

Hunjra, A. I., Zureigat, Q., & Mehmood, R. (2020). Impact of capital regulation and market discipline on capital ratio selection: A cross country study. *International Journal of Financial Studies*, *8*(2), 21.

Iqbal, A. (2012). Liquidity risk management: A comparative study between conventional and Islamic banks of Pakistan. *Global Journal of Management and Business Research*, *12*(5), 55–64.

Imbierowicz, B. & Rauch, C. (2014). The relationship between liquidity risk and credit risk in banks. *Journal of Banking and Finance*, *40*, 242–256.

Joseph, M. T., Edson, G., Manuere, F., Clifford, M., & Michael, K. (2012). Non performing loans in commercial banks: A case of CBZ bank limited in Zimbabwe. *Interdisciplinary Journal of Contemporary Research in Business*, *4*(7), 467–488.

Khan, M. A. (2013). *What Is Wrong with Islamic Economics? Analyzing the Present State and Future Agenda*. UK: Edward Elgar Publishing.

Khan, T. & Ahmed, H. (2001). *Risk Management: An Analysis of Issues in Islamic Financial Industry*. Islamic Development Bank, Islamic Research and Training Institute.

Khanqah, V. T. & Ahmadnia, L. (2013). The impact of capital structure on liquidity and investment growth opportunity in tehran stock exchange. *Journal of Basic and Applied Scientific Research*, *3*(4), 463–470.

Khemraj, T. (2009). What does excess bank liquidity say about the loan market in less developed countries?. *Oxford Economic Papers*, *62*(1), 86–113.

Koehn, M. & Santomero, A. M. (1980). Regulation of bank capital and portfolio risk. *The Journal of Finance*, *35*(5), 1235–1244.

Lotto, J. (2018). The empirical analysis of the impact of bank capital regulations on operating efficiency. *International Journal of Financial Studies*, *6*(2), 34.

Lotto, J. & Mwemezi, J. (2015). Assessing the determinants of bank liquidity: Experience from tanzanian banks. *African Journal of Finance and Management*, *24*(1–2), 76–88.

Luoma, G. A. & Spiller, J. (2002). Financial accounting return on investment and financial leverage. *Journal of Accounting Education*, *20*(2), 131–138.

Matz, L. & Neu, P. (2006). *Liquidity Risk Measurement and Management: A Practitioner's Guide to Global Best Practices* (Vol. 408). Asia: John Wiley & Sons.

Mehmood, R., Hunjra, A. I., & Chani, M. I. (2019). The Impact of corporate diversification and financial structure on firm performance: Evidence from South Asian Countries. *Journal of Risk and Financial Management*, *12*(1), 1–16.

Mohamad, A. A. S., Mohamad, M. T., & Samsudin, M. L. (2013). How Islamic banks of Malaysia managing liquidity? An emphasis on confronting economic cycles. *International Journal of Business and Social Science*, *4*(7), 253–263.

Montes, G. C. & Peixoto, G. B. T. (2014). Risk-taking channel, bank lending channel and the "paradox of credibility": Evidence from Brazil. *Economic Modelling*, *39*, 82–94.

Mounira, B. A. & Anas, E. L. M. E. L. K. I. (2009). Managing risks and liquidity in an interest free banking framework: The case of the Islamic banks. *International Journal of Business and Management*, *3*(9), 80.

Moussa, M. A. B. (2015). The determinants of bank liquidity: Case of Tunisia. *International Journal of Economics and Financial Issues*, *5*(1), 249–259.

Ongore, V. O. & Kusa, G. B. (2013). Determinants of financial performance of commercial banks in Kenya. *International Journal of Economics and Financial Issues*, *3*(1), 237.

Pappas, V., Izzeldin, M., & Fuertes, A. (2012). Failure risk in Islamic and conventional banks. *Lancaster University and City University*, *1*(1), 1–38.

Racic, Z., Stanisic, N., & Stanic, N. (2016). A comparative analysis of the determinants of liquidity risk exposure in the banking sector of the republic of serbia and banking sectors of former socialist countries. *International Scientific Conference on ICT and e-business Related Research*, 424–434.

Raghavan, R. S. (2003). Risk management in banks. *Chartered Accountant-New*, *51*(8), 841–851.

Rime, B. (2001). Capital requirements and bank behavior: Empirical evidence for Switzerland. *Journal of Banking & Finance, 25*(4), 789–805.

Ruozi, R. & Ferrari, P. (2013). Liquidity risk management in banks: economic and regulatory issues. In *Liquidity Risk Management in Banks.* Berlin, Heidelberg: Springer.

Shaikh, S. A. (2015). Financing public infrastructure using sovereign Sukuk. *Journal of Islamic Banking and Finance, 32*(1), 11–22.

Sharma, M. (2005). Problem of NPAs and its impact on strategic banking variables. *Finance India, 19*(3), 953–967.

Sheikh, N. A. & Wang, Z. (2011). Determinants of capital structure: An empirical study of firms in manufacturing industry of Pakistan. *Managerial Finance, 37*(2), 117–133.

Shen, C. H., Chen, Y. K., Kao, L. F., & Yeh, C. Y. (2009). Bank liquidity risk and performance. In *17th Conference on the Theories and Practices of Securities and Financial Markets, Hsi-Tze Bay, Kaohsiung, Taiwan.*

Siddiqui, A. (2008). Financial contracts, risk and performance of Islamic banking. *Managerial Finance, 34*(10), 680–694.

Silveira, R. & Wright, R. (2010). Search and the market for ideas. *Journal of Economic Theory, 145*(4), 1550–1573.

Singh, A. & Sharma, A. K. (2016). An empirical analysis of macroeconomic and bank-specific factors affecting liquidity of Indian banks. *Future Business Journal, 2*(1), 40–53.

Titman, S. & Wessels, R. (1988). The determinant of capital structure choice. *The Journal of Finance, 43*(1), 1–19.

Trenca, I., Petria, N., & Corovei, E. A. (2015). Impact of macroeconomic variables upon the banking system liquidity. *Procedia Economics and Finance, 32*, 1170–1177.

Waemustafa, W. & Sukri, S. (2016). Systematic and unsystematic risk determinants of liquidity risk between Islamic and conventional banks. *International Journal of Economics and Financial Issues, 6*(4), 1321–1327.

Wang, Y. J. (2002). Liquidity management, operating performance, and corporate value: Evidence from Japan and Taiwan. *Journal of Multinational Financial Management, 12*(2), 159–169.

Zheng, C., Bhowmik, P. K., & Sarker, N. (2020). Industry-specific and macroeconomic determinants of non-performing loans: A comparative analysis of ARDL and VECM. *Sustainability, 12*(1), 325.

Zolkifli, N. A., Hamid, M. A., & Janor, H. (2015). Liquidity risk and performance: The case of Bahrain and Malaysian banks. *Global Economy and Finance Journal, 8*(2), 95–111.

https://doi.org/10.1142/9781800612426_0025

Chapter 25

Evaluating the Robustness of Basel Capital Accords to Combat the Effects of COVID-19 Pandemic in Islamic Banking

Monsurat Ayojimi Salami, Harun Tanrivermiş, Adel M. Sarea, and Yeşim Tanrivermiş

Abstract

The purpose of this chapter is to evaluate relationship between the capital adequacy ratio (CAR) and explanatory variables as well as the possibility that any of the three Basel Capital Accords adopted in Islamic banks is appropriate to combat the effect of COVID-19 pandemic. This study employed reverse regression estimation techniques, using random effect estimator and interaction modeling. Data were obtained from IFSB database. The findings of this study indicate that bank asset quality and ROE exhibit conditional negative relationship with CAR, while ROA and bank liquidity exhibit conditional positive relationship. Therefore, the relationship between CAR and bank asset quality, bank profitability, and bank liquidity fulfilled conditional hypothesis, that is, the relationship varies according to the Basel Capital Accords approach adopted by the Islamic banks. Among the three Basel Capital Accords, the capital requirement by Basel III could not be met, thereby made it inappropriate for adoption during the period of COVID-19 pandemic, while the capital requirement of Basel I exposes Islamic banks to serious challenges which support non-risk sensitivity framework in developing Basel I. This finding is novel, as previous studies on Basel Capital Accords neither simultaneously examined all the three Basel to make inferences nor explore the possibility of conditional relationship in their CAR studies. This is the first empirical study that establishes the existence of conditional hypothesis relationship between CAR and the explanatory variables using reverse regression.

Keywords: Basel Accords and CAR, Bank Asset Quality, Bank Profitability, Bank Liquidity, Conditional Hypothesis, Islamic Banks.

25.1 Introduction

Despite three different banks stringencies announced and implemented for decades to set minimum standard capital requirement for the banks for risk protection, the banking sector has not successfully fought financially related crisis. The establishment of Basel I standard was dated back to 1988 (Dermine, 2014; Zins & Weill, 2017) and regarded as cornerstone of bank regulation (Repullo *et al.*, 2010), which unsuccessfully protected the banks from Asian Financial Crisis in 1997 and other regional financial crises, such as in Russia and Brazil (Spring, 1998), Brazil devaluation (January, 1999) (Johnson *et al.*, 2000). Unfortunately, Basel I was unable to save banking industry from crashing at that period. This gave rise to Basel II regulatory framework to reform Basel I, and Basel II was adopted on risk sensitivity framework in 2004 and implemented in 2006 (Zins & Weill, 2017). As of then, experts such as Stefan Ingves and Nout Wellink doubted that there will be no new versions of Basel after Basel II.

Unfortunately, Basel II also failed in the face of 2008 global financial crisis because it was unable to mitigate the effect of global financial crisis in the banking sector. Basel II standards were extensively evaluated by several researchers (Demirgüc-Kunt & Detragiache, 2011; Zins & Weill, 2017) and faced a series of criticism. Researchers critically argued against Basel II that global financial crisis exposed significant weakness of Basel II (Demirgüc-Kunt & Detragiache, 2011; Dietrich *et al.*, 2014). In addition, some studies argued that Basel II allows the banking sector to reduce their capital buffers, which was considered to have contributed to destabilization of the sector, Hakenes and Schnabel (2011) argued that it led to competitive distortion in the banking sector because of the cost involved in adopting the policy. Either destabilization or competitiveness distortion, Basel II has been argued against as being incapable of mitigating risk associated with the banking sector.

As at the time of conducting this study, the most recent bank regulatory framework standard is Basel III that had been implemented in stages since 2010 and proposed to be implemented in 2027 but which also faced challenges as established by researchers. The argument that Basel III increased shareholders' risk exposure as well as equity states was raised in the study by Allen *et al.* (2012). With the evolvement of Basel III as the latest potent panacea at the time of COVID-19 pandemic, do Islamic banks need Basel that would use predictions from COVID-19 pandemic to suggest another capital adequacy ratio (CAR) to make banking sector more resilience to unpresidential shocks in the future? This question is necessary because the event of global financial crisis had triggered fresh widespread call for regulation and supervision reform (Demirgüc-Kunt & Detragiache, 2011) as both credit and liquidity risks had been alluded to as the main sources of banks failure during the crisis (Dermine, 2014). Unfortunately, in 2016, which was prior to COVID-19 pandemic, PricewaterhouseCoopers (PwC) proposed the need for Basel IV and the proposition has been gaining acceptance gradually and may be officially in use prior to full implementation of Basel III. Since proposition for Basel IV was much earlier than emergency of COVID-19 pandemic, will Basel IV risk sensitivity framework restructure to cater for severity of COVID-19 pandemic?

In addition, the above question is essential because the world has witnessed a series of pandemic and financial crises, but the novel COVID-19 seems to have assumed a new dimension that forces the global economy into recession as a result of bailout for some sectors during the lockdown. This has resulted in the loss of several billions of dollars as well as loss of job by millions of people. Malaysian authority reported that over RM 63 billion were lost during the movement restriction (MCO) period (www.thestar.com.my, May 2020) and over hundreds of thousands of job positions lost. In the recent MCO 3.0 lockdown in Malaysia, the authority has projected daily cost for the strategy to about RM 300 million (www.thesundaily.my, May 2021). In addition, over 30 million jobs lose were estimated in the US and many other countries. This implies that COVID-19 pandemic has created bad economic atmosphere for many business sectors, which forced them to seek bailout from concerned authorities. Bad economic conditions has tendency to worsen the quality of loan and adversely reduce bank profits (Albertazzi & Gambacorta, 2009).

Since government bailout is one reason for using extreme value model as internal model for Basel III (Rossignolo, Fethi, & Shaban, 2012), it is unimaginable that several governments embarked on another bailout during the current pandemic.

Obviously, bailout could not be made for all sectors as in the case of Malaysia. Some sectors that were unable to get bailout pleaded to the authority to come to their rescue by instructing financial sectors, most especially banking sector, to relieve them of their debt through allowing instalment payment leave of about three months. Among the most affected industries are hotels, airline, and automobiles because they rely heavily on banks for their huge investments without which they cannot function properly. With unexpected direct and indirect heavy financial burden on the banking sector, it is deemed fit that evaluation of the three Basel Capital Accords on Islamic banking risk mitigation is necessary at this point as this motive is in accordance with the core objective of Basel Accords which is to strengthen capital position as well as mitigating risks of banks (Majumder & Li, 2018).

Having reviewed earlier studies, this study takes the initiative of evaluating the three Basel Capital Accords introduced since 1988 until 2010 to assess risk mitigation of Islamic banks across several countries. Beck, Demirgüç-kunt, and Merrouche (2013) revealed that Islamic banks are less cost-effective and less likely to disintegrate during crisis due to better asset quality. In the same vein, Islamic banks are rich in product complexity and transaction mechanism, which constitute a buffer to the high risk-taking and better performance (Mollah *et al.*, 2016) but not equally open to external shocks as conventional banks due to *Sharia* supervision searchlight beam on risk-venturing.

Therefore, this study investigated relationship between CAR and explanatory variables as well as the possibility that any of the three Basel Capital Accords adopted in Islamic banks is appropriate to combat the effect of COVID-19 pandemic. Through that, the study arrived at some findings as follows. First, the finding shows that bank assets quality and ROE establish negative relationship with CAR, while ROA and liquidity establish positive relationship. Second, the finding shows that the relationship between the CAR and bank assets quality, bank profitability, and bank liquidity changes with respect to the type of the Basel adopted by the Islamic banks, which makes the finding fulfill conditional hypothesis. The finding of this study fulfilled both necessary conditions for conditional hypothesis; therefore, the result of this study is neither overstating nor understating. The finding also shows that only Islamic banks that adopt capital requirement of Basel III are more likely to have lesser impact of COVID-19 than the Islamic banks that still relies on Basel I. Furthermore, the finding indicates that neither Basel I nor Basel II is appropriate to be adopted by the Islamic banks, most especially at this period of COVID-19 pandemic. However, COVID-19 pandemic has marked final stage for the Basel III, while Basel IV is gaining acceptance by some bank authorities and to be officially in use prior to estimated period for full implementation of Basel III. Based on the library study conducted by Feridun and Ozun (2020), Basel IV was assumed to be officially in use as of January 2021. However, their prediction was not attained. It is obvious that Basel IV is on the way.

Therefore, this chapter contributes to the growing Islamic finance literature. Although, there are several articles on the Islamic finance, especially Islamic banking sector, the finding from this study is novel as it establishes conditional hypothesis in the relationship between CAR and bank asset quality, bank profitability, and bank liquidity. This indicates that the relationship between the CAR and the understudy explanatory variables of Islamic banks varies depending on the type of Basel employed. The study arrived at the conclusion that earlier Basel Accords prior to the COVID-19 pandemic are not resilient enough to mitigate uncertainty arising from global crises.

This chapter has six sections. The rest of this chapters are structured as follows: Section 25.2 focuses on IFSB as a Central Bank for Islamic banks. Section 25.3 presents the literature review, Section 25.4 presents data and methods of analysis adopted. Section 25.5 presents the empirical findings of this study, while Section 25.6 is the discussion and conclusion for the study.

25.2 Islamic Financial Services Board (IFSB)

IFSB is the international recognized central bank for Islamic banks. IFSB was established to develop and disseminate prudential standards regulation and supervision for the Islamic financial services industry (Islamic Finance and Global Financial Stability, 2010). Hence, IFSB provides jurisdictions on the issues relating to global Islamic banks prudential information and serves as database for the researchers to obtain data across 19 Islamic banks countries, both full-fledged and window Islamic banks. IFSB provides prudential standard and guiding principles for Islamic financial institutions (Chong & Liu, 2009; Rosman & Abdul Rahman, 2015). IFSB is responsible for designing transparency and disclosure to reflect the risk characteristics of institutions offering Islamic Financial Services (IFS). Part of achievement of IFSB is its successful abolishment of double stamp duty on Islamic home financing as being practiced in the UK and Singapore.

25.3 Theoretical Framework and Literature Review

The underpinning theory for this study is the extreme value theory (EVT). EVT focuses on the rare events and mostly used to explain risk cases (Ourir & Snoussi, 2012; Schaumburg, 2012). Basel III is the model suitable for capturing extreme risk as being argued in some studies. Rossignolo, Fethi, and Shaban (2012, 2013) argued that internal model for Basel III was based on value-at-risk, which is based on extreme value estimation. Similarly, capital requirement focuses on ensuring that financial institution have sufficient buffer to withstand unexpected losses on a going concern basis (Giustiniani & Thornton, 2011). Allen *et al.* (2013) further explain that EVT provides suitable method for capturing extreme tail risk. Usually, EVT is used to explain rare events (Ourir & Snoussi, 2012); therefore, EVT is more appropriate to explain the finding of this study.

Basel I is severely criticized as a result of being too crude and not providing enough buffer for risk protection (Decamps *et al.*, 2002). Similarly, King (2013) reports that during the global financial crisis between 2007 and 2009, several countries experienced liquidity shortages that led to many banks becoming insolvent. The author argued that Basel III liquidity requirements affect market liquidity indirectly through increasing cost of intermediary and changing specific characteristics of demand for asset.

Zins and Weill (2017) explored whether Basel II influenced the risk feature of Islamic banks for the period between 2007 and 2013 in 24 countries that comprises 411 convention banks and 147 Islamic banks using interaction modeling. The authors found positive coefficient of interaction term, which interpreted as Basel II expanding risk gap between convention and Islamic banks at the expense of Islamic banks. Beck, Demirgüç-kunt, and Merrouche (2013) compared business model, efficiency, and stability of Islamic banks with the conventional banks from 22 countries using interaction modeling with interaction terms variables for the Islamic bank and global financial crisis over the period 1995–2009. Their study revealed that Islamic banks are more stable and less likely to be disintegrated during crisis than conventional banks.

Demirgüc-Kunt and Detragiache (2011) explored whether Basel Core Principles (BCPs) for the Effective Bank Supervision compliance affect bank soundness using cross-sectional data of 3000 banks from 86 countries obtained from Bankscope. They expressed doubtfulness in continuous international efforts to improve financial regulation and supervision. Hakenes and Schnabel (2011) revealed that new bank regulation was criticized even prior to the inception of the Basel II because of sharp reduction in capital holdings by banks, especially for those who have competitive advantage of adopting an internal rating based (IRB). The authors further argued that Basel II led to asymmetric treatment between small and larger banks because of options to choose between standardization or IRB. Interestingly, in advanced economies, such as the US, the authority made it mandatory for the larger banks to use advanced IRB while small banks are still using Basel I with options to choose between advance IRB or US version of standardized approach (Hakenes & Schnabel, 2011).

Allen *et al.* (2012) revealed that profound structural changes were made in Basel III and that the adjustment would take place in stages to minimize adverse effects on output and employment, while upfront prediction of its optimal pace is impossible because it requires experience. It is argued that Basel III is likely to create less stress since its transmission takes longer period. It is being argued that CAR only reflects above 11% readiness of public banks in India to implement Basel III (Boora & Jangra, 2019).

Salike and Ao (2018) established negative significant relationship between poor asset quality and profitability after when examined 947 banks from 12 Asian countries from 2001 to 2015 taking Basel III into account.

Öhman and Yazdanfar (2018) revealed positive relationship between lagged profitability and capital adequacy among Swedish banks using panel data during 2005–2014. In the study conducted by Arif and Nauman Anees (2012) among Pakistani banks, profitability established negative relationship with the bank liquidity. Similarly, Adelopo *et al.* (2018) reported consistent significant relationship between profitability and liquidity for their event study on economic community of West African State banks for the data range 1999–2013.

Abbas *et al.* (2021) conducted study on banks of seven countries in Asia and revealed significant interdependence between bank capital and liquidity using yearly data ranges between 2011 and 2019 with two-stage least square (2SLS) technique. Mazioud Chaabouni *et al.* (2018) reveal negative relationship between bank capital and liquidity on studying French and UK banking industry.

Furthermore, Majumder and Li (2018) argued that bank liquidity may exert negative or positive impact on the relationship between bank liquidity and bank performance as higher volume loans tend to reduce performance of the bank especially if risk management system of the bank is weak. King (2013) also argued that findings on the relationship between liquidity and bank performance are mixed. Table 25.1 also presents mixed result on Basel II and Basel III.

However, Feridun, and Ozun (2020) used library-based approach and other secondary sources to reveal that Basel IV aims at providing an enhanced robustness through incorporation revised market risk standard that may be capable of withstanding credit and operational risks of the bank while legislative progress for implementation is slower than expected.

Connection between variables of the study is not clear as some of the studies found positive relationship while others found negative relationship. Similarly, Abbas *et al.* (2021) reported unclear relationship between bank capital and profitability during compilation of literature to draw hypothesis.

Therefore, this study developed the hypotheses as follows:

H1a: There is significant relationship between CAR and asset quality among Islamic banks.

H1b: There is significant relationship between CAR and profitability among Islamic banks.

H1: There is significant relationship between CAR and liquidity among Islamic banks.

Table 25.1. Summary of some previous findings on Basel Capital Accords: asset quality, profitability, and liquidity.

References	CAR	Data period	Methodology	Findings
Danìelsson *et al.* (2001)	Basel II	—	Value-at-Risk (VaR)	Argued against that VaR is insufficient to quantify the risk associated at banks because the approach treat risk as a fixed exogenous process while ignoring endogeneity which is essential especially at the time of crisis. Also argued that VaR provide spurious conclusion when return is not normally distributed
Repullo, Saurina, and Trucharte (2010)	Basel II	Spanish firm form 1987–2008	Logistic model	Found that Basel II is sensitive to risk and could amplify business cycle fluctuation by inducing severe contraction in the credit supply especially during recession
Zins and Weill (2017)	Basel II	2007–2013	Interaction model	Found that Basel II enlarge the risk gap between Islamic banks and conventional banks
Decamps, Rochet, and Robert (2002)	Basel II		Markov chain	Using static model alone failed to capture intertemporal effect
Yan, Hall, and Turner (2012)	Basel III	1997Q1–2010Q2	VECM	Reveal that Basel III still has room for more stringency on capital and liquidity requirements while providing positive effect
Dietrich, Hess, and Wanzenried (2014)	Basel III	1996–2010	GMM	Found negative relationship between higher capital ratio and bank liquidity

(Continued)

Table 25.1. (*Continued*)

References	CAR	Data period	Methodology	Findings
King (2013)	Basel III	Banks from 15 countries for the year 2009	Cross-sectional approach	Net stable funding ratio (NSFR) which is new liquidity requirement imbedded in Basel III is designed to address funding risk
Allen *et al.* (2012)	Basel II and Basel III	—	Leverage adjustment calculation	Suggest that if stringency process continue to the extent that it affects some small business to get access to finance, then adverse effect will be on economy growth. Propose that risk associated with Basel III cannot be precisely quantify but learning by doing may be appropriate approach
Hong, Huang, and Wu (2014)	Basel III	2001–2011	Scenario analysis	Argued that bank failure is due to systematic liquidity, which has not been addressed by both liquidity requirement of Basel III and NSFR
Feridun and Ozun (2020)	Basel IV	—	Library study and other secondary sources	Make inferences that purpose of Basel IV is to provide enhanced robustness that would be suitable to address risk sensitivity of the standard approaches for credit risk as well as operational risk

H2: Basel Accords prior to COVID-19 pandemic is not stringent enough to mitigate future global crisis that might be facing Islamic banks.

Note that several studies on Basel Accords are viewed from different dimension and can be observed that methodology adopted by the researchers varies. This indicates that there is no unique approach for modeling Basel Capital Accords.

25.4 Data and Methods

25.4.1 *Data*

Quarterly data of 19 Islamic banks from 17 countries were obtained from IFSB database from 2014Q1 to 2019Q3 and credibility of the data obtained is that the database was directly attained data from central bank of countries examined. Data selection for this study is based on three reasons. First, the data represents when global economic are relative stable. i.e., post-2008 global financial crisis and prior to the emergency of COVID-19 pandemic. Therefore, data do not have evidence of abnormal economic situation that may induce biasness in the findings. Second, the data range is also the maximum available data as at the time of conducting this study. Arif and Nauman Anees (2012) conducted their study using yearly data range from 2004 to 2009 and reported data constrain for their study. Third, even until present available data during global pandemic is not sufficient to conduct event study.

The three Basel Capital Accords were evaluated in the context of Islamic banks asset quality, profitability, and liquidity while leverage is used as control variable. Bhatt (2016) used bank leverage as control variables and reported several empirical studies that did the same. The essence of designing Basel III is to be globally applied across active intentionally banks (Feridun & Ozun, 2020), and being the most recent Basel in the banking sector, however, some banks are still using Basel I while some are using Basel II. The breakdown of the countries used in this study in relation to the Basel policy adopted are as follows: Islamic banks in Bahrain, Brunei, Indonesia, Jordan, Kazakhstan, Kuwait, Malaysia, Oman, Qatar, Saudi Arabia, Turkey, UAE, and Pakistan adopt Basel III. While Islamic banks in Egypt are using Basel II, Islamic banks from Iran, Nigeria, and Sudan are still using Basel I. This distribution provides opportunity for using Basel I, II, and III as indicators for Basel. The rest of the variables used in this study are CAR; banks asset quality which is ratio of gross non-performing financing on total financing; bank profitability as measured by ROA and ROE; bank liquidity as a ratio of liquid asset on total asset; and leverage as a ratio of Tier 1 capital on total asset.

25.4.2 *Methods*

This study also used reverse regression to evaluate strength of series of CAR policies and the marginal effect of CAR on Islamic banks risk mitigation techniques. Chenavaz and Schalck (2015) used reverse regression to examine the trends and challenges in commodity markets, and the authors claimed that the approach is helpful in predicting futures contract prices. Phiri (2014) used reverse regression on Okun's specification to evaluate nonlinear relationship between unemployment and economic growth in South Africa. Roll, Schwartz, and Subrahmanyam (2007) also reported using reverse regression in their study. To achieve this, we regress CAR on bank asset quality, bank profitability, bank liquidity, Basel-indicator, interaction term, and bank leverage. Thereby, CAR is a dependent variable and bank leverage is a control variable while other variables are explanatory variables. The regression equation is presented as follows:

$$\begin{aligned} \mathrm{CAR}_{it} = {} & \beta_0 + \beta_1 \mathrm{BAQ}_{it} + \beta_2 \mathrm{ROA}_{it} + \beta_3 \mathrm{ROE}_{it} + \beta_4 \mathrm{BL}_{it} \\ & + \beta_5 \mathrm{Basel\_Indicator}_{it} + \beta_6 \mathrm{Basel\_Indicator}_{it} * \mathrm{CAR}_{it} \\ & + \beta_7 \mathrm{BLV}_{it} + \varepsilon_{it}, \end{aligned} \tag{25.1}$$

where

$$\mathrm{Dummy}_{it} = \mathrm{BaselI}_{it}, \mathrm{BaselII}_{it}, \mathrm{BaselIII}_{it},$$

$$\mathrm{BaselI}_{it} = \begin{cases} 1 & \\ 0 & \text{otherwise,} \end{cases}$$

$$\mathrm{BaselII}_{it} = \begin{cases} 1 & \\ 0 & \text{otherwise,} \end{cases}$$

$$\mathrm{BaselIII}_{it} = \begin{cases} 1 & \\ 0 & \text{otherwise,} \end{cases}$$

$$\begin{aligned} \mathrm{Dummy}_{it} * \mathrm{CAR}_{it} = {} & \mathrm{BaselI}_{it} * \mathrm{CAR}_{it}, \mathrm{BaselII}_{it} * \mathrm{CAR}_{it}, \\ & \mathrm{BaselIII}_{it} * \mathrm{CAR}_{it}, \end{aligned}$$

where the subscript i represents cross-sectional dimension across banks and subscript t represents quarterly time frequency. CAR represents capital adequacy requirement; BAQ represents bank asset quality ratio; ROA and ROE measure bank profitability; Basel-indicators take dichotomous value of one or zero; interaction term otherwise known as moderator variables are the product of Basel-indicator and CAR policy adopted; BLV represents bank leverage which is a control variable in the regression; ε represents white-noise error term. β_0 and β_7 represent constant term and coefficient of control variable. $\beta_1, \beta_2, \beta_3, \beta_4, \beta_5, \beta_6$ in Equation (25.1) are the coefficient of interest for the present study; the sign of the coefficient represents the direction of the explanatory variable with the CAR, while the statistical coefficient value indicates magnitude of the relationship.

Since Equation (25.1) has interaction term, the interpretation of the findings follows conditional hypothesis if interaction term is true; therefore, the general form of interaction equation is expressed as in the study by Brambor, Clark, and Golder (2006) as follows:

$$\mathrm{CAR}_{it} = \beta_0 + \beta_1 X + \beta_2 Z + \beta_3 XZ + \epsilon. \tag{25.2}$$

If interactions exist $Z = 1$; otherwise, $Z = 0$.

If Z does not exist, i.e., $\left(\frac{dy}{dx} \text{ given } Z = 0 \text{ is } \beta_1\right)$, then the equation could be simplified as follows and interpretation could follow standard linear regression interpretation:

$$\mathrm{CAR}_{it} = \beta_0 + \beta_1 X + \epsilon. \tag{25.3}$$

However, if Z exists, i.e., $\left(\frac{dy}{dx} \text{ given } Z = 1\right)$, implies conditional Z is present $(\beta_1 + \beta_3)$, then equation would be as follows and interpretation follows condition hypothesis interpretation:

$$\mathrm{CAR}_{it} = (\beta_0 + \beta_2) + (\beta_1 + \beta_3)\,X + \epsilon. \tag{25.4}$$

This study adopted pooled OLS and RE estimator for Basel I, Basel II, and Basel III models to evaluate the effect of different bank stringiness policies for risk mitigation on Islamic banks and then conducted Breusch and Pagan Lagrangian multiplier test to select the best model. We also conducted diagnostic tests, such as heteroskedasticity, correlation matrix, variance inflation factor (VIF), and further run the interaction model to generate graphical illustration of the marginal effect of CAR on the Islamic banks risk mitigation approach. The adopted interaction model is also consistent with the argument by Decamps, Rochet, and Robert (2002) and Blum (1999) that static model alone could not provide sufficient justification for Basel Capital Accord predictions.

25.5 Empirical Findings

We explored information content of the dataset by conducting descriptive statistics on the data and examined degree of correlation among the explanatory variables for the three models, namely Basel I model, Basel II model, and Basel III model. VIF was also conducted to examine presence of multi-collinearity and J–B test used for normality. The test results are presented in subsequent tables. In summary, result of preliminary analysis do not violate the underlying assumptions for proceeding with analysis.

25.5.1 *Descriptive statistics*

Table 25.2 presents the descriptive summary of the variables used in this study. Among dependent variable, explanatory variables, and control variable, bank liquidity has the highest mean and standard deviation (mean = 0.2904, SD = 0.1619) followed by mean of CAR

Table 25.2. Descriptive summary of CAR and other Islamic banks risk mitigation indicators.

Variable	Mean	Min	Max	Std. dev.	Obs.
CAR	0.2533	0.0986	1.7052	0.2300	420
Bank Asset Quality	0.0369	−0.0016	0.1489	0.0317	414
Bank ROA	0.0136	−0.0478	0.0489	0.0108	420
Bank ROE	0.1434	−0.0720	0.9503	0.1173	420
Bank Liquidity	0.2904	−0.0001	0.7238	0.1619	416
Basel I	0.1095	0	1	0.3127	420
Basel II	0.1095	0	1	0.3127	420
Basel III	0.7810	0	1	0.4141	420
Interaction Basel I	0.0271	0	0.6467	0.0855	420
Interaction Basel II	0.0168	0	0.1901	0.0482	420
Interaction Basel III	0.2094	0	1.7052	0.2503	420
Bank Leverage	0.1319	0.0218	0.6924	0.0904	397

Note: Obs. represents observations.

(mean = 0.2533, SD = 0.2300), while the mean of ROE is the lowest (mean = 0.0136, SD = 0.0108). Positive mean signals good indication for the Islamic bank asset quality, Islamic bank profitability, and Islamic bank liquidity. Closeness in the mean of CAR and Islamic bank liquidity may support the finding by Abbas *et al.* (2021) that CAR and bank liquidity are determined simultaneously. In the category of Basel-indicator, Basel III has highest mean (mean = 0.7810, SD = 0.4141) and interaction III has the highest mean (mean = 0.2094, SD = 0.2503) among interaction terms. This implies that Basel III is widely employed relative to other types of Basel. In general, the means and standard deviations are closer to zero except for the mean of Basel III and the highest standard deviation is not greater than 0.4141, which implies that normality of the series is rejected. Therefore, residual distribution of the series would be better explained by non-parametric distribution test such as student t-test or generalized error distribution (GED).

25.5.2 *Correlation matrix*

Tables 25.3–25.5 present the result of correlation among the variables understudy. Table 25.3 presents mixed in direction of relationship among the variables under study and majority of the coefficient of relationship are within threshold range of less than 0.8 except for the relationship between Basel I and Interaction I (r = 0.9211). Such high correlation signals multi-collinearity. This supports that risk mitigation was not taking into consideration when Basel I was developed. Therefore, we further conducted VIF, although the VIF of individual variables are below 10 but the mean VIF (mean VIF = 3.34) exceeded threshold range of 2, which concluded that Basel I model has multi-collinearity issue. This implies that finding on Basel I is not supported by extreme value theory. This finding is not consistent with the findings by Anginer, Demirguc-Kunt, and Zhu (2014), who reported that the VIF of individual variables are below 10 and mean VIF is also less than 2. However, including all constituent variable irrespective of explanatory variables correlation coefficient increases fulfillment of the condition for modeling interaction model. Among the necessary condition to be observed in modeling interaction model is to include all constituent variables (Brambor *et al.*, 2006).

Table 25.3. Correlation matrix between independent explanatory variables of Basel I.

Basel I	**Asset quality**	**ROA**	**ROE**	**Leverage**	**Liquidity**	**Basel I**	**Interaction I**
Bank asset quality	1						
Bank ROA	0.0064[b]	1					
Bank ROE	−0.0006[b]	−0.5532[a]	1				
Bank leverage	0.2183[c]	0.2647	0.2444[a]	1			
Bank liquidity	−0.1704[b]	0.0917[c]	−0.5298[b]	−0.2138	1		
Basel I	−0.1097[b]	−0.0020[b]	−0.2305[b]	0.0486[c]	0.1168[b]	1	
Interaction I	−0.3684[b]	0.0069[c]	0.2248[c]	−0.0558[c]	−0.1169[c]	−0.9211[c]	1

Note: [a], [b], and [c]indicate 1%, 5%, and 10% significant level, respectively.

Table 25.4. Correlation matrix between independent explanatory variables of Basel II.

Basel II	**Asset quality**	**ROA**	**ROE**	**Leverage**	**Liquidity**	**Basel II**	**Interaction II**
Bank asset quality	1						
Bank ROA	−0.0447[a]	1					
Bank ROE	0.0720[b]	−0.6139[b]	1				
Bank leverage	0.2427[c]	0.2158[b]	0.2900[a]	1			
Bank liquidity	−0.1019[b]	0.0225[b]	−0.2818[b]	−0.1740[b]	1		
Basel II	−0.1110[a]	0.2159[b]	−0.3426[b]	−0.0802[b]	0.0258[b]	1	
Interaction II	0.0850[b]	−0.1792[c]	0.2667[b]	0.0616[a]	−0.0859[b]	−0.9847[b]	1

Note: [a], [b], and [c]indicate 1%, 5%, and 10% significant level, respectively.

Table 25.5. Correlation matrix between independent explanatory variables of Basel III.

Basel III	**Asset quality**	**ROA**	**ROE**	**Leverage**	**Liquidity**	**Basel III**	**Interaction III**
Bank asset quality	1						
Bank ROA	0.0195[a]	1					
Bank ROE	0.0756[b]	−0.6850[b]	1				
Bank leverage	0.2097[b]	0.4737[b]	−0.1074[a]	1			
Bank liquidity	−0.2054[b]	0.1418[c]	−0.2756[c]	−0.2212[b]	1		
Basel III	0.0698[a]	−0.0426[b]	0.1264[b]	0.0312[b]	0.2224[b]	1	
Interaction III	0.0234[b]	−0.0603[a]	0.0080[b]	−0.4424[b]	−0.1238[b]	−0.2598[a]	1

Note: [a], [b], and [c]indicate 1%, 5%, and 10% significant level, respectively.

Table 25.4 presents correlation matrix result for the Basel II regression. The correlation coefficient of Basel II and Interaction II ($r = -0.9847$) also shows the evidence of multi-collinearity since the mean of some individual variables have VIF greater than 10 and mean VIF (mean VIF = 21.23) exceeded the threshold range of 2. We further suspect that Basel II model for multi-collinearity issue. Similarly, extreme value as predicted by value-at-risk for risk mitigation was not the internal model for Basel II. Therefore, there is evidence that the findings on Basel II is not supported by extreme value theory. Sensarma and Jayadev (2009) also confirmed the presence of multi-collinearity in their study and follow the common approach of dropping some variables, but such treatment is not applicable to interaction model since all the interaction terms are to be in the model. Dropping of at least one of the variables in the case of occurrence of multi-collinearity violates one of the conditions for interaction modeling (Kingsley, Noordewier, & Bergh, 2017); therefore, none of the variables was dropped.

Table 25.5 presents correlation matrix for the Basel III model. Interestingly, the direction of the relationship among the variables under study for the Basel III model are indicated by the sign of the relationship and the magnitude of the coefficient of the correlations are within the threshold range since the highest correlation value in absolute term ($r = 0.6850$), which is below 0.8 threshold value for correlation (Gujarati, 2009). We further conducted VIF of individual variables, and the result shows that individual VIF is below 10 and mean VIF is 1.99, which also below threshold value for the mean VIF. This indicates that there is no evidence of multi-collinearity in Basel III model. The multi-collinearity issue is not assumed for the mean VIF lower than 2 (Abdullah *et al.*, 2015; Abu Hussain & Al-Ajmi, 2012; Khalid & Amjad, 2012). This may also indicate better hedge for Basel III over the lower versions of Basel (Basel 1 and Basel II). With no evidence of multi-correlation, this finding on Basel III supports that extreme value where taking into consideration and the only Basel Accord that supports extreme value theory.

We proceeded with interaction modeling for the three Basel Capital Accords because dropping Basel I and Basel II models due to presence of multi-collinearity as shown in the correlation matrix and VIF test result might lead into premature conclusion.

25.5.3 *Modeling results*

Table 25.5 presents findings for modeling the three Basel Capital Accords, namely Basel I, Basel II, and Basel III and the sign of relationship is consistent for all models. It is worth noting that despite the presence of multi-collinearity issues in Basel I and Basel II, we proceed with modeling based on the argument that interaction term has potentiality to increase the correlation of the variables (Burks *et al.*, 2019).

The findings show that the null hypothesis assumption that the variance of specific individual effect is zero as assumed by pooled OLS is rejected; therefore, pooled OLS is rejected. Alternatively, random effect (RE) estimator is accepted as the true model. We could not proceed with testing for the fixed effect (FE) estimator test because Basel indicators were used in the modeling and fixed effect will eliminate those Basel indicators. As noted before that Basel I, Basel II, and Basel III are Basel indicators adopted in different Islamic banks until present. Although majority of Islamic banks are using Basel III, still some Islamic banks stick to the lower Basel such as Basel II and even some Islamic banks are still using Basel I. We then conducted heteroskedasticity tests for Basel models, and we found that variance of the Basel I and Basel II are not constant while the variance of Basel III model is statistically insignificant. Therefore, Basel III model is the best model for this study, and the results are presented in Table 25.6.

According to the finding in Table 25.6, both bank asset quality and ROE exhibit negative relationship with CAR at 1% significant level, while ROA and liquidity exhibit positive relationship with CAR. Being an interaction model, the finding implies that negative relationship between CAR and Islamic banks asset quality, ROE varies according to type of Basel interaction employed. Similarly, the finding reveals that positive relationship between CAR and ROA, Islamic bank liquidity varies according to the type of Basel interaction adopted. The positive relationship between CAR and bank liquidity established in this study is similar to previous finding but not the same. Allen *et al.* (2012) that revealed that Basel III forces the banks to increase their liquid assets and restrict credit. The finding by Beck, Demirgüç-kunt, and Merrouche (2013) concluded that Islamic banks are better in asset quality relative to conventional banks.

Table 25.6. Capital adequacy ratio and other Islamic banks risk mitigation indicators.

	Basel I model		Basel II model		Basel III model	
Variables	**Pooled OLS**	**Random effect**	**Pooled OLS**	**Random effect**	**Pooled OLS**	**Random effect**
Constant	0.0686*	0.0519	0.0856**	0.0577	0.2852***	0.2398***
	(0.055)	(0.411)	(0.026)	(0.325)	(0.000)	(0.000)
Bank asset quality	−1.2961***	−0.5937**	−1.3738***	−0.8878**	−0.2538***	−0.7658***
	(0.000)	(0.047)	(0.000)	(0.001)	(0.000)	(0.000)
Bank ROA	7.4747***	1.5386*	7.9772***	2.2342**	0.8399**	1.5338***
	(0.000)	(0.080)	(0.000)	(0.013)	(0.001)	(0.000)
Bank ROE	−0.4433**	−0.1429*	−0.5634***	−0.2350**	−0.2833***	−0.2288***
	(0.004)	(0.095)	(0.000)	(0.007)	(0.000)	(0.000)
Bank leverage	1.3059***	1.0596***	1.2882***	1.1005***	0.0326	0.1878***
	(0.000)	(0.000)	(0.000)	(0.000)	(0.232)	(0.000)
Bank liquidity	0.0878	0.2737***	0.0777	0.3070***	−0.0109	0.0598**
	(0.255)	(0.000)	(0.340)	(0.000)	(0.401)	(0.003)
Basel I	−0.0163	−0.0506	—	—	—	—
	(0.837)	(0.777)				
Interaction I	0.1390	0.2675*	—	—	—	—
	(0.632)	(0.083)	—	—	—	—
Basel II	—	—	0.4150	0.0520	—	—
	—	—	(0.242)	(0.845)	—	—

(*Continued*)

Table 25.6. (*Continued*)

Variables	Basel I model		Basel II model		Basel III model	
	Pooled OLS	**Random effect**	**Pooled OLS**	**Random effect**	**Pooled OLS**	**Random effect**
Interaction II	—	—	−2.4987	−0.8797	—	—
	—	—	(0.291)	(0.267)	—	—
Basel III	—	—	—	—	−0.2484**	−0.2322**
	—	—	—	—	(0.000)	(0.000)
Interaction III	—	—	—	—	0.9716**	0.9373**
	—	—	—	—	(0.000)	(0.000)
R^2	0.2966	0.2263	0.2986	0.2484	0.9803	0.9712
F-Stat	22.83***	—	23.05***	—	2691.97***	—
	(0.000)	—	(0.000)	—	(0,000)	—
Wald test	—	330.68***	—	326.83***	—	7657.45***
	—	(0.000)	—	(0.000)	—	(0.000)
Breusch and Pagan Lagrangian multiplier test for random effects	—	3006.42***	—	2982.11***	—	498.31***
	—	(0.000)	—	(0.000)	—	(0.000)
	—	—	—	—	—	—
Heteroskedasticity	—	280.19***	—	307.79***	—	1.35
	—	(0.000)	—	(0.000)	—	(0.2456)
Obs.	387	—	—	387	—	387

Note: ***, **, and *represents 1%, 5%, and 10% significance level, respectively.

Finally, we plotted graph of interaction on the final model to show graphical illustration of the marginal effect of the Basel on risk mitigation approaches of Islamic banks to address second hypothesis of this study.

25.5.4 *Interaction model*

Table 25.7 presents the result of interaction model and graphical illustration is presented in Figure 25.1. Kingsley *et al.* (2017) review of 116 articles and Brambor, Clark, and Golder (2006) review 156 articles, both concluded that one of the challenges facing interaction modeling is that the result might be overstated or understated if excluding some of the constituent variables. Interaction modeling result is overstating when interaction coefficient is significant, but the marginal effect is not statistically significant while interaction result is understating when interaction coefficient is not significant but the marginal effect is statistically significant (Kingsley *et al.*, 2017). In the case of this study, Basel I interaction is not statistically significant and its interaction effect lies on the zero line of the x-axis which implies not statistically significant from zero. This is also supported that Basel I was not developed on risk sensitivity framework. Therefore, the extreme value theory is not supported for the findings on Basel I. The stakeholder in the bank using Basel I may often face challenges than stakeholders with the banks using Basel II and Basel III. However, the interaction coefficients of Basel II and Basel III model are statistically significant and their marginal effects are statistically significant and different from zero. This finding supports that Basel I and II were developed on risk-sensitivity framework. In addition, the

Table 25.7. Result of interaction model.

Variables	**Coefficient**
Basel III	−0.2322[a]
Interaction III	0.9373[b]
Variance of Basel III	0.0006
Variance of Interaction III	0.0026
Covariance of Basel III and Interaction III	0.0004

Note: [a]and [b]indicate 1% and 5% significant level, respectively.

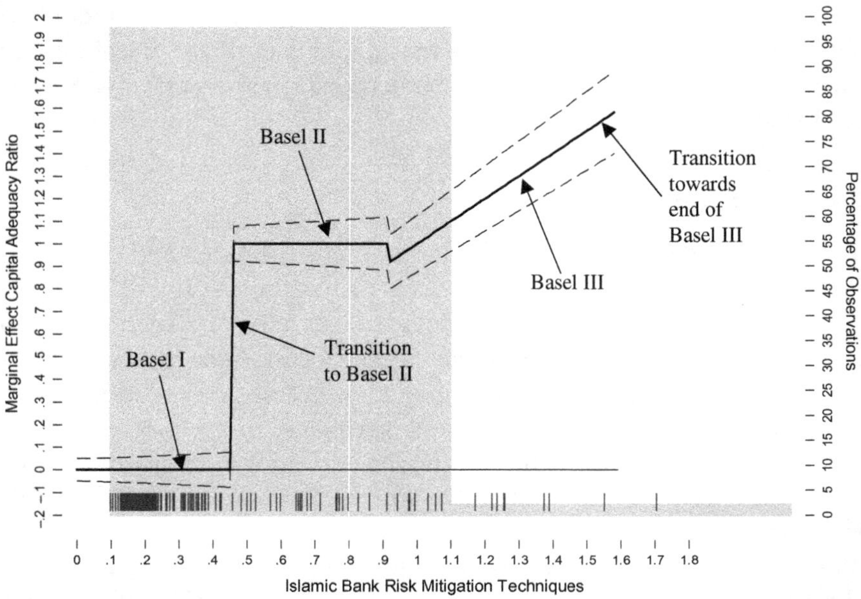

Figure 25.1. Marginal effect of Basel Accords on the relationship between CAR and explanatory variables.

finding implies that the result of this study is neither overstated nor understated.

The result of this study supports the theory that the relationship between the CAR and explanatory variables varies across implementing of different Basel. Dummy for Basel I relationship is not statistically significant, while the dummies for Basel II and Basel III are significant varies with the level of Basel adopted. This implies that the result of this study supports conditional hypothesis. This is because the result of this study satisfies the two necessary conditions for the conditional hypothesis.

The result of Basel I indicates that there is no statistics profitability and bank liquidity of those countries relying on Basel I as at the moment of this study. Therefore, relying on Basel I capital requirement at the current era of COVID-19 may be more challenging for those countries. Similarly, reduction in capital buffer as set in Basel II may pose challenges to the use of Basel II at the current era of COVID-19, as shown in the Figure 25.1. However, Basel III shows transition process since it has not been fully implemented.

With continuous series of COVID-19 waves, Basel IV may receive more attention as an alternative to provide direction for banking industry after global challenges as way forward.

Table 25.7 also presents more information about the interaction term. The coefficient of Basel III and interaction term are statistically significant as well as their variance. Coefficient of covariance of the Basel III and interaction term shows that understudy variables are moving in the same direction when the interaction term is present.

Figure 25.1 presents marginal interaction effect on the relationship between the CAR and different Basel Accords. The graph explicitly shows that Basel I only sustained for the period when economy was stable, i.e., prior to 1997 Asian financial crises and another regional financial crisis. It is obvious that Basel I was not developed on the risk sensitivity framework; however, uncertainty occurs spontaneously which made it clearly unfit to be resilient to the shocks. Therefore, several issues that were not considered when Basel I was developed were proposed to fix in advanced version of Basel. This means Basel Committees found it necessary to make changes to Basel I that led to Basel II. However, the changes made to Basel I was not sufficient enough compared to the changes arose during 2008 global financial crisis. Similarly, Basel III is in the transition its fully implementation stage by the time it was faced criticism of not able to meet the expected level of resilience and ability to withstand current shock from the recent novel COVID-19 pandemic. Despite that, King (2013) argued that series of reforms made to Basel III which increases resilience of banking sector. However, with the current pandemic keeps striking in waves multiple times within a year, it makes predicting severity of its uncertainty a paradox. It is unfortunate that Basel III failed on arrival because its full implementation stage has not attained when it faced unprecedented shocks. In the study conducted by Feridun and Ozun (2020), Basel III is considered its final stage and the beginning for Basel IV.

Therefore, graphical illustration consistently support that earlier Basel are less stringent and weak to combat the effect of earlier financial crisis (Demirgüc-Kunt & Detragiache, 2011; Hakenes & Schnabel, 2011). Thus, it is not different as in the case of Basel II and Basel III which are based on the risk sensitivity frameworks but still less stringent and weak to combat the shock from 2008 financial crisis and COVID-19 pandemic, respectively. In other words, this finding fails to support that series of reforms made to Basel III are stringent enough to increase resilience of banking sector. Therefore, the findings from this study do not support findings by King (2013). It might be due to the fact that predictions in the study by King (2013) was made prior the pandemic when the uncertainty was kept within a minimal range. It would amount to in appropriation of predicting severity of uncertainty led to failure in achieving underpinning objective of setting Basel standards, especially Basel II and Basel III, that were built on risk sensitivity framework. Therefore, implementations of Basel I, Basel II, and Basel III are less likely to be appropriate especially at this time that global economy is experiencing persistently high level of uncertainty. This is because banking crisis is more frequent and more vulnerable than expected (Yan *et al.*, 2012). Despite that Majumder and Li (2018) recommend implementation of Basel III as much as possible in the Bangladesh banks. Such recommendation may not be relevant once Basel IV is introduced.

25.6 Discussion and Conclusion

The findings from this study have revealed that capital buffers requirement may play significant role on the risk mitigation of the banking sector, but appropriate percentage has not been accurately predicted. This is because the most recent Basel is still considered inappropriate for bank risk mitigation especially at this era of COVID-19 pandemic. The stringency of the bank capital requirement with bank asset quality, bank profitability, and bank liquidity fulfilled conditional hypothesis, which implies that the relationship keeps changing based on the Basel adopted. The finding suggests Islamic banks, most especially those that are currently using the lower Basel such as Basel I and Basel II, to watch out for the impact of COVID-19 which may be severe if they are caught in the wind of the risk. Banks that rely on lower version of Basel need to upgrade to Basel IV once it is officially announced with hope to addressing credit risk and operational related risk. Despite underlining assumption, Basel III is designed to promote financial stability through stronger capital and liquidity requirements (Yan *et al.*, 2012), but the assumption tends to fail when level of uncertainty increase significantly even without Basel III fully implemented. Full implementation of Basel III is expected to be in 2027, while pandemic proposed end to the future implementation of Basel III since early 2020. This study suggests future research of evaluating resilience of Basel IV after COVID-19 pandemic and during the future global crisis. This is because despite that Basel III is considered to have been developed from complex risk sensitive framework. At the speech on Basel I, II, and III evolution of global banking regulation by Banks for International Settlements (BIS), in the presence of Sabine Lautenschlager, member of executive board, European Central Bank; Nout Wellink, former president Netherlands Bank; Stefan Ingves, Governor, Sveriges Riksbank; and Nor Shamsiah Mohd Yunus, Governor, Central Bank of Malaysia, Sabine informed the participants that architecture of Basel III is appropriate while arguing against capability of CAR in handling heterogenous banking system and complexity of financial institutions (Lautenschlager, Wellink, & Ingves, 2020). Therefore, it appears that introduction of new Basel Accords is a signal to the global business to be preparing for upcoming global crisis. Similarly, the experts revealed that world should be expecting series of Basel in the future especially since financial innovations are continuous and uncertainty is huge. Similarly, Basel IV may not mark the end of the introduction of new Basel Accord.

In summary, the finding of this study revealed that Basel Accords are still not perfected to mitigate the risk. The banking system keeps facing different challenges based on the intensity of the financially related crisis. It is also revealed that those banks that are using Basel III have lesser financial problem relative to those banks that are using Basel I. Furthermore, using Basel I and Basel II continuously do not provide justice for consistent effort in upgrading the Basel Accords. Similarly, several efforts were developed to further strengthen financial institutions after 2008 global financial (Nieto & Garcia, 2012).

This study contributes to the banking industry especially those banks that are still using Basel I to upgrade to Basel III and ready to implement Basel IV on arrival. This is because the consequence of not upgrading their Basel Accords is at the disadvantage of stakeholders of the bank. This is because shareholders net worth may be reducing, government may use tax payer money for bailout of some sectors.

The implication of this findings is that as time goes the banks that still operating with Basel I and Basel II may be easily affected by different types of bank risks, such as credit risk, liquidity risk, operational risk, and later end up with insolvency risk. Eventually, there may be increase in the unemployment level of the country. The findings from this study has several practical implications on the financial institutions most especially banking sector. The finding stresses that those Islamic banks that are currently using lower version of Basel may be more prone to challenges of COVID-19 pandemic than those Islamic banks that are using Basel III. Furthermore, caution may be required in using earlier version of Basel once Basel IV is officially available. Basel IV has been proposed to be officially in use even prior to fully implementation of Basel III (which proposed to be in 2027).

There are two noticeable limitations of this study. First, this study focused mainly on Islamic banks and data constrains due to different data frequency led to selection of some Islamic banks for this study. Second, as at the time of finalizing this study, there is no sufficient COVID-19 data that might enable us to conduct event study which may further enhance the findings. As a result of this, we suggest future research on this topic could be based on an event study that would take into account of before, during, and after COVID-19 pandemic prior to implementation of Basel IV.

References

Abbas, F., Ali, S., & Ahmad, M. (2021). Does economic growth affect the relationship between banks' capital, liquidity and profitability: Empirical evidence from emerging economies. *Journal of Economic and Administrative Sciences*, *1*(1), 1–16.

Abdullah, M., Abdul Shukor, Z., Mohamed, Z. M., & Ahmad, A. (2015). Risk management disclosure. *Journal of Applied Accounting Research*, *16*(3), 400–432.

Abu Hussain, H. & Al-Ajmi, J. (2012). Risk management practices of conventional and Islamic banks in Bahrain. *The Journal of Risk Finance*, *13*(3), 215–239.

Adelopo, I., Lloydking, R., & Tauringana, V. (2018). Determinants of bank profitability before, during, and after the financial crisis. *International Journal of Managerial Finance*, *14*(4), 378–398.

Albertazzi, U. & Gambacorta, L. (2009). Bank profitability and the business cycle. *Journal of Financial Stability Journal*, *5*, 393–409.

Allen, B., Chan, K. K., Milne, A., & Thomas, S. (2012). International review of financial analysis Basel III: Is the cure worse than the disease? *International Review of Financial Analysis*, *25*, 159–166.

Allen, D. E., Singh, A. K., & Powell, R. J. (2013). EVT and tail-risk modelling: Evidence from market indices and volatility series. *North American Journal of Economics and Finance*, *26*, 355–369.

Anginer, D., Demirguc-Kunt, A., & Zhu, M. (2014). How does competition affect bank systemic risk? *Journal of Financial Intermediation*, *23*(1), 1–17.

Arif, A. & Nauman Anees, A. (2012). Liquidity risk and performance of banking system. *Journal of Financial Regulation and Compliance*, *20*(2), 182–195.

Beck, T., Demirgüç-kunt, A., & Merrouche, O. (2013). Islamic vs. conventional banking: Business model, efficiency and stability. *Journal of Banking and Finance*, *37*(2), 433–447.

Bhatt, P. R. (2016). Corporate governance in Malaysia: Has MCCG made a difference. *International Journal of Law and Management*, *58*(4), 403–415.

Blum, J. (1999). Do capital adequacy requirements reduce risks in banking? *Journal of Banking and Finance*, *23*, 755–771.

Boora, K. & Jangra, K. (2019). Preparedness level of Indian public sector banks for implementation of Basel III: An empirical investigation. *Managerial Finance*, *45*(2), 172–189.

Brambor, T., Clark, W. R., & Golder, M. (2006). Understanding interaction models: Improving empirical analyses. *Political Analysis*, *14*, 63–82.

Burks, J. J., Randolph, D. W., & Seida, J. A. (2019). Modeling and interpreting regressions with interactions. *Journal of Accounting Literature*, *42*(December 2017), 61–79.

Chenavaz, R. & Schalck, C. (2015). Trends and challenges in commodity markets. *Research in International Business and Finance*, *33*, 287–289.

Chong, B. S. & Liu, M. H. (2009). Islamic banking: Interest-free or interest-based? *Pacific Basin Finance Journal*, *17*(1), 125–144.

Danìelsson, J., Embrechts, P., Goodhart, C., Keating, C., Muennich, F., Renault, O., & Shin, H. S. (2001). An academic response to Basel II. *LSE Financial Markets Group*, May, *1*, 1–17.

Decamps, J.-P., Rochet, J., & Robert, B. (2002). The three pillars of Basel II: Optimizing the mix in a continuous-time model. *In BIS Conference*, *2*(June), 1–25.

Demirgüc-Kunt, A. & Detragiache, E. (2011). Basel core principles and bank soundness: Does compliance matter? *Journal of Financial Stability Journal*, *7*, 179–190.

Dermine, J. (2014). Basel III leverage ratio requirement and the probability of bank runs. *Journal of Banking & Finance*, December, 1–38.

Dietrich, A., Hess, K., & Wanzenried, G. (2014). The good and bad news about the new liquidity rules of Basel III in western european countries. *Journal of Banking and Finance, 44*, 13–25.

Feridun, M. & Ozun, A. (2020). Basel IV implementation: A review of the case of the European Union. *Journal of Capital Markets Studies, 4*(1), 7–24.

Frank, A. C. R. (2010). *Unemployment and Economic Growth in Africa 1, 20*(2), 250–274.

Giustiniani, A. & Thornton, J. (2011). Post-crisis financial reform: Where do we stand. *Journal of Financial Regulation and Compliance, 19*(4), 323–336.

Gujarati, D. N. (2009). *Basic Econometrics.* Tata McGraw-Hill Education.

Hakenes, H. & Schnabel, I. (2011). Bank size and risk-taking under Basel II. *Journal of Banking and Finance, 35*(6), 1436–1449.

Hong, H., Huang, J., & Wu, D. (2014). The information content of Basel III liquidity risk measures. *Journal of Financial Stability, 15*, 91–111.

IFSB, IDB, & IRTI. (2010). *Islamic Finance and Global Finance Stability* (Issue April), Malaysia.

Johnson, S., Boone, P., Breach, A., & Friedman, E. (2000). Corporate governance in the asian financial crisis. *Journal of Financial Economics, 58*, 141–186.

Khalid, S. & Amjad, S. (2012). Risk management practices in Islamic banks of Pakistan. *The Journal of Risk Finance, 13*(2), 148–159.

King, M. R. (2013). The Basel III net stable funding ratio and bank net interest margins. *Journal of Banking and Finance, 37*(11), 4144–4156.

Kingsley, A. F., Noordewier, T. G., & Bergh, R. G. Vanden. (2017). Overstating and understating interaction results in international business research. *Journal of World Business, 52*(2), 286–295.

Lautenschlager, S., Wellink, N., & Ingves, S. (2020). At the speech delivered on Basel I, II, and III evolution of global banking regulation. *In Bank for International Settlements (BIS) Conference.*

Majumder, M. T. H. & Li, X. (2018). Bank risk and performance in an emerging market setting: The case of Bangladesh. *Journal of Economics, Finance and Administrative Science, 23*(46), 199–229.

Mazioud Chaabouni, M., Zouaoui, H., & Ellouz, N. Z. (2018). Bank capital and liquidity creation: New evidence from a quantile regression approach. *Managerial Finance, 44*(12), 1382–1400.

Mollah, S., Hassan, M. K., Farooque, O., Al, & Mobarek, A. (2016). The governance, risk-taking, and performance of Islamic banks. *Journal of Financial Services Research*, 1–25.

Nieto, M. J. & Garcia, G. G. (2012). The insufficiency of traditional safety nets: What bank resolution fund for Europe? *Journal of Financial Regulation and Compliance, 20*(2), 116–146.

Öhman, P. & Yazdanfar, D. (2018). Organizational-level profitability determinants in commercial banks: Swedish evidence. *Journal of Economic Studies*, *45*(6), 1175–1191.

Ourir, A. & Snoussi, W. (2012). Markets liquidity risk under extremal dependence: Analysis with VaRs methods. *Economic Modelling*, *29*(5), 1830–1836.

Repullo, R., Saurina, J., & Trucharte, C. (2010). Mitigating the procyclicality of Basel II. *Economic Policy*, 659–702.

Roll, R., Schwartz, E., & Subrahmanyam, A. (2007). Liquidity and the law of one price: The case of the futures-cash basis. *The Journal of Finance*, *62*(5), 2201–2234.

Rosman, R. & Abdul Rahman, A. R. (2015). The practice of IFSB guiding principles of risk management by Islamic banks. *Journal of Islamic Accounting and Business Research*, *6*(2), 150–172.

Rossignolo, A. F., Fethi, M. D., & Shaban, M. (2012). Value-at-risk models and Basel capital charges. evidence from emerging and frontier stock markets. *Journal of Financial Stability*, *8*(4), 303–319.

Rossignolo, A. F., Fethi, M. D., & Shaban, M. (2013). Market crises and Basel capital requirements: Could Basel III have been different? evidence from Portugal, Ireland, Greece and Spain (PIGS). *Journal of Banking and Finance*, *37*(5), 1323–1339.

Salike, N. & Ao, B. (2018). Determinants of bank's profitability: Role of poor asset quality in Asia. *China Finance Review International*, *8*(2), 216–231.

Schaumburg, J. (2012). Predicting extreme value at risk: Nonparametric quantile regression with refinements from extreme value theory. *Computational Statistics and Data Analysis*, *56*(12), 4081–4096.

Sensarma, R. & Jayadev, M. (2009). Are bank stocks sensitive to risk management? *The Journal of Risk Finance*, *10*(1), 7–22.

The Star, "Getting Malaysia bac to work", obtained on 7 May, 2020 from https://www.thestar.com.my/business/business-news/2020/05/02/geting-malaysia-back-to-work.

The Sun daily, "MCO 3.0 expected to cost Malaysia RM300 million daily PIVB", obtained on 11 May, 2021 from http://www.thesundaily.com/home/mco-30-expected-to-cost-malaysia-rm300-million-daily-pivb-AK7851244.

Yan, M., Hall, M. J. B., & Turner, P. (2012). A cost — Benefit analysis of Basel III: Some evidence from the UK. *International Review of Financial Analysis*, *25*, 73–82.

Zins, A. & Weill, L. (2017). Islamic banking and risk: The impact of Basel II. *Economic Modelling Journal*, *64*, 626–637.

https://doi.org/10.1142/9781800612426_0026

Chapter 26

Factors Influencing Interest of Indonesian Muslim Millennials in Waqf

Nashr Akbar and Nur Fikriani Fiqih Al Ihsan

Abstract

This chapter aims to identify factors that may influence the interest of Indonesian Muslim millennials in performing waqf. Five variables, namely waqf literacy, religiosity, trust in waqf institutions, religiosity, income, and social influence, were tested using SEM-PLS method. Data are obtained through online questionnaires with the number of sample is 321 Muslim millennials from the five major islands in Indonesia. The finding shows that four variables, literacy, religiosity, trust in waqf institutions, and social influence, have a significant impact on their interest in waqf donation. As a result, waqf institutions must nurture trust of prospective waqf through massive socialization such as social media which is widely accessed by millennials. This may attract their attention, leave a good impression, and create a supporting environment. In addition, waqf institutions need to instill trust by being more open, honest, and transparent about the programs they created through campaigns by bringing social and religious issues packed with excellent and exciting delivery that can help increase the interest of Muslim millennials in performing waqf. Furthermore, quality of nazhir should be improved, collaboration should be promoted, and the utilization of digital technology are highly recommended.

Keywords: Waqf, Millennials, SEM-PLS.

26.1 Introduction

26.1.1 *Background*

Waqf has an essential role in the economic development of the ummah. Cizakca (1998) explained that historical facts prove a significant role in reducing the burden of state spending and can even eliminate usury. During the Ottoman Dynasty, the waqf system, the imaret system, and other religious institutions had an essential role in the socio-economic development of cities in Ottoman Turkey. (Saduman & Aysun, 2009). Sadeq (1997) explains waqf's role in the developing society and economy by alleviating poverty.

The waqf institution in the early Islamic government has played a significant role in maintaining the social welfare of Muslims (Mahmud & Shah, 2010). Ahmad (2019) explained that waqf is a unique instrument connecting the three elements: government, religion, and social construction. Waqf is a religious instrument that is usually used for any religion-related activity. Waqf has a principle of conservation that makes it different from the foundations, charities, or regular donations that are widely done in Western countries (Oseni, 2012).

According to the Indonesian Waqf Agency, the potential of waqf assets reaches IDR 2,000 trillion per year, and the potential of cash waqf in Indonesia reaches IDR 188 trillion per year. Unfortunately, there has been a large gap between potential and realization. The total realization of cash waqf in Indonesia until 2020 only reached IDR 819.36 billion. The gap between potential and realization is a question mark as Indonesia is ranked in the top ten in the Charities Aid Foundation (CAF) report (2020). This report then made Indonesia the most generous country. The World Giving Index is measured by the percentage of people donating money to make donations, volunteer, and help strangers in a month. In terms of giving, Indonesian donations get points of 83%, according to the CAF (2020). Indonesia's population of more than 270.20 million (BPS, 2021) is undoubtedly a great potential, especially with the demographic bonus that Indonesia now earned.

Indonesia is currently entering a demographic bonus era where the productive age is greater than the non-productive age, where the productive age population reaches above two-thirds of the population. One generation in the productive age is the millennial generation, the most significant human resource in the demographic bonus era. According to UN World Population Prospects (2015), millennials are the backbone of the world, where the population is the largest compared to other generations. Based on IDN Research Institute (2019), many millennials today can be a challenge and an opportunity to encourage Indonesia to break the target of becoming a high-income country in 2045.

Currently, 69.38 million (25.87%) of the population in Indonesia, according to the Central Statistics Agency (2021), are millennials. A large number of millennials in Indonesia can be an excellent potential for waqf development. According to independent research conducted by Tirto.id and Jakpat (2018), of 1,012 respondents, of which 81.42% are Muslim, it was found that millennials make donations/alms/infaq at least once a month with an average amount of donations being 5% of their income. IDN Research Institute (2019) also found that millennials spend 5.3% per month on charity.

Koczanski and Rosen (2019), in their research, explained that millennials tend to donate for religious causes compared to donations that are not related to religion. Baranyi (2011) explains that millennials give and donate more often. The biggest motivation for volunteering contributions and donations is to help fellow human beings. Millennials also consider volunteerism and contributing very important.

In another study conducted by Gopay and Kopernik (2020), Millennials become the generation with the highest frequency of donating with an average of 1.5 times per month with the highest motivation to donate social values and followed religious values. It is also mentioned that the average amount of donations made by millennials increased by 19% during the pandemic.

The high spirit of millennials in donation needs to be directed to donations that provide longer-term benefits, one of which is waqf. Based on data owned by the Productive Waqf Forum, the profile of waqf donors among millennials dominates by 48%, although the number of donations is not significant because, at this time, millennials are not financially strong. The cultivation of solid literacy and supported by innovations that facilitate donation is expected to increase waqf in the future (Republika, 2021).

There are studies on factors that determine the participation of individuals in waqf, including Nizar (2014), Amin *et al.* (2014), and Hasan and Ahmad (2018), but there has been no research that focuses on examining the factors that influence millennials' interest in participating in waqf. An initial step has been conducted by Aldeen *et al.* (2021), Kasri and Chaerunnisa (2020), and Maivalinda (2021) that measures millennial's interest in a specific type of waqf, cash waqf. Millennials are often related to the cash waqf. In fact, there are many types of waqf where millennials are able to donate. Therefore, study on their perception about waqf in general is important.

This research is expected to be a reference in planning and strategies to develop and improve waqf in Indonesia. The systematic writing of this study begins with the background of the research, then continues with the theoretical foundations about waqf, factors that influence donation, the millennial generation, and previous research. The next part is an explanation of the research methods used. In Section 26.4, there are results and discussions. The final section contains the conclusions and recommendations of this study.

26.1.2 *Objective*

The main objective of this study is to identify factors influencing the interest of Muslim millennials in Indonesia to donate waqf. Furthermore, this study is expected to explore the behavior of Indonesian Muslim millennials in waqf literacy and performance.

26.2 Literature Review

26.2.1 *Legality of waqf*

Waqf comes from the Arabic "waqafa", which means holding (al-habs), stopping, staying in place, or remaining. Waqf has the plural forms awqaf and wuquf. Scholars agree that the word waqf is defined with another language term, al-habs, which means to hold (Cizakca, 1998).

According to Article 1 of Law No. 41 of 2004, waqf is defined by the act of wakif law to separate and/or hand over some of his property for use forever or a certain period following its interests for worship and/or general welfare according to Sharia.

In the Qur'an, there is nothing clearly explained about waqf, but there are several verses that can be used as the basis of waqf law.

Allah (SWT) commands Muslims to give up some of their sustenance for good:

> O you who believe (are âmenû)! Spend (for Allah) of that with which We have provided for you before a Day (Doomsday) comes in which there is no bargaining, neither friendship nor intercession and the unbelievers-they are the tyrants.
>
> (Q.S. Al-Baqarah — 254)

This verse is a command of Allah SWT to His servants regarding the factor of the sustenance that Allah gives to the way of virtue as a store of reward in the hereafter (Ibn Kathir, d. 774 H). Implicitly, the alms/infaq command also includes a command to act, which is one type of alms/infaq is waqf.

The legality of waqf from the positive legal side is based on Waqf Law No. 41 of 2004. In the law, it is stated that waqf is a legal act wakif to separate and/or hand over some of his property to be used forever or for a certain period following its interests for worship and/or general welfare.

26.2.2 *Motives for charity*

In general, a person's motive in charity is based on the benefits received by the donor, whether it is the benefits felt by the donor directly or felt by the donor indirectly (public benefit) through an affirmation of the value obtained. These benefits can be both materials (e.g., avoidance of taxes) or non-materials (e.g., confession and eliminating guilt). However, motives for personal benefit and motives for public benefits can coexist when a person decides to donate (Konrath & Handy, 2017).

Becker (1974) explained that altruism is a person's motivation to donate to improve the well-being of others, without expecting to receive from others. Meanwhile, Andreoni (1990) explained that some donors are often less concerned with the impact of donations. This suggests that his altruism is less pure. The existence of social pressure, feelings of guilt, sympathy, and the desire to get a "warm glow" (emotional warmth) makes altruism impure.

From different perspectives, a person's motivation for charity can be categorized into two main factors: intrinsic factor and extrinsic factor. Extrinsic factors include demographics and socioeconomic variables, such as age, gender, income level, and education level. These three variables (age, income level, and education level) positively affect the donation level. The higher the level of income and the level of education, the greater the level of donation. Similarly, age is also positively correlated to a person's retirement. Intrinsic factors include a sense of duty and responsibility to help people in need, a desire to change, religious factors, self-actualization, and social pressures. (Kasri, 2013).

26.2.3 *Hypothesis development: Factors that influence decisions in waqf*

One crucial factor that influences a person to perform certain behaviors is knowledge. Siswantoro and Dewi (2011) explained that one of the factors that make cash waqf ineffective in Indonesia is low literacy regarding waqf. Shukor *et al.* (2017), Nizar (2014), and Ahmad (2019), who proved the positive influence of knowledge on the participation of waqf, also conducted other studies. Nizar (2014) also explained that the low collection of waqf is due to people's understanding of cash waqf being very limited compared to other Islamic economic instruments and disagreements of scholars regarding cash waqf. Furthermore, Ahmad (2019) explained that the understanding of Indonesian people about waqf is still very minimum. Waqf is still always assumed limited to land, buildings, or other fixed assets.

H1: Waqf literacy positively affects the interest of millennials in performing waqf.

Another major factor is religiosity. Based on research conducted by Abreu *et al.* (2014), a religious person tends to contribute regularly to either religious organizations or secular organizations. In addition, they tend to make large donations. Therefore, religiosities can influence the behavior and practice of donations and the magnitude of donations.

Osman (2014), Amin *et al.* (2014), Mokthar (2016), and Shukor *et al.* (2017) also use religiosity as measurement variables in measuring people's intentions in performing waqf. The results showed that religiosity influenced participation in waqf. To measure the degree of religiosity, the researchers presented several dimensions. Nuradli *et al.* (2019) examined the measurements of religiosity that researchers often use. They concluded that only two dimensions are best suited to describe religiosity; they are the dimensions of trust and commitment/practice. In a study, Hasan and Ahmad (2018) also found that religiosity influences waqf' intention for higher education.

H2: Religiosity positively influences millennials' interest in performing waqf.

Many studies argued that social influences affect a person's behavior. Marimuthu *et al.* (2010) stated that social influence is one of the main factors determining the acceptance of Islamic banking in Klang Valley, Malaysia. Wahyuni (2012) also uses social influence as a variable in measuring decisions in using Islamic banks. Carman (2004), in his research, also stated that there is a positive and significant relationship between a person's decision to do charity. Furthermore, Sakti *et al.* (2016) found that social influence significantly affects a person's contribution to the waqf.

H3: Social influence positively affects the interest of millennials in performing waqf.

Trust is one of the factors used in measuring factors that affect waqf. According to Henslin (2002), trust itself is the expectation and trust of individuals in the reliability of others. Zaerofi (2020), in his research, sorted the definition of brand trust, which is found that the construction of brand trust is the belief or consumer perception of the reliability of a product. Therefore, the integrity of a person/engaged/brand that can meet expectations as promised will be responsible for problems that may arise. In this study, the trust was intended as a trust given by wakif to waqf institutions. In research conducted by Osman *et al.* (2016), trust has a significant favorable influence on the intention of giving waqf, which is said to be an essential element in the willingness of wakif in donation. Shukor *et al.* (2014, 2017) used waqf to precede their research.

H4: Trust positively influences millennials' interest in taking performing waqf.

Research conducted by Nizar (2014) stated that wakif in the Indonesian Waqf Agency is mostly a middle-income individual. Ahmad (2019) also found that income is one of significant factors to measure the intention of individual participation in waqf.

Other researchers, Ardianto (2011) and Vidiawan and Tisnawati (2015), also support the effect of income on the participation in waqf.

H5: Income positively affects millennials' interest in performing waqf.

26.2.4 *Previous research*

Research on the factors that affect millennials in waqf is still very little. Kasri and Chaerunnisa (2020) and Maivalinda (2021) related millennials to one type of waqf, cash waqf. In their research, Kasri and Chaerunnisa (2020) discussed the determinants of millennials in waqf decision by looking at the role of knowledge, trust, and religiosity using the theory of planned behavior. In this study, it was found that all the variables tested were significant. Among the recommendations given is the need to improve literacy about waqf and instill substantial Islamic value, mentions the benefits of cash waqf in every waqf product on social media or websites, and make waqf institutions more transparent and accountable will attract the interest of cash waqf online. Similarly, Aldeen *et al.* (2021) surveyed millennials' perspectives on waqf in Indonesia. They found that millennials have high awareness but lower willingness level to contribute to cash waqf. Waqf trustees are suggested to be more transparent

Meanwhile, Maivalinda *et al.* (2021) measured the interest in millennial cash waqf and its relationship to SDGs funding in West Sumatra. Millennials are used as research subjects and potential numbers, open to various views, also because millennials are considered concerned and sensitive to environmental issues. The study used attitudes, religiosity, and concern for the environment as measuring variables. Of the three variables used, only concern for the environment is not significant because many respondents think that waqf is only prioritized for religious activities.

Other previous studies have addressed the intentions but did not link them specifically to millennials. In terms of the scope of research, there is research on waqf in general, and there are also specifics discussing cash waqf and corporate waqf. In waqf, there is research by Hasan and Ahmad (2018) and Abd Mutalib *et al.* (2019). For corporate endowments, there is research by Hasbullah *et al.* (2015), while for cash waqf, there is research by Osman *et al.* (2014), Shukor *et al.* (2016, 2017) and Ahmad (2019).

Waqf, in general, Abd Mutalib (2019) found that social culture, promotion, and attitude as moderating variables affect waqf participation. In addition, it was found that there is a relationship between awareness of waqf participation directly. The authors also provide recommendations to include faith as an aspect directly related to waqf participation. Meanwhile, Hasan and Ahmad (2018) examined what factors determine the high literacy of waqf in Malaysia. Based on the results of the survey, it was found that personal characteristics, religious values, psychological benefits, social norms, and commitment influence the high understanding of waqf.

Hasbullah *et al.* (2016) discussed corporate waqf to look at factors that influence one's intentions in participating in corporate endowments whose results found that attitude, subjective norm, and perceived behavior are significantly related to the intention of contributing to corporate endowments.

As for the intention of waqf, Shukor *et al.* (2016) found that someone married, high income, has high knowledge, and ease of doing waqf have significant affects. Whereas, gender, age, education, trust in waqf institutions, and intentions are not significant in influencing contributions in the law. In a subsequent study, Shukor *et al.* (2017) found that religiosity, belief in waqf institutions, and ease of doing so affect attitudes in participating in cash waqf, where attitude also has a significant effect on the intention of money.

Ahmad (2019) revealed several significant factors of a person making cash waqf; knowledge, income, socio-cultural, and promotion also confirmed this finding. Research conducted by Osman *et al.* (2014) used the theory of planned behaviors (TPB) and added religiosity to identify factors that influence waqf participation. The results found that attitudes, subjective norms, religiosity, and perceived behavioral control were significant variables in the participation of cash waqf.

26.2.5 *Research framework*

This research framework was adopted based on theories in previous studies used to measure individual participation in waqf with variables used, namely waqf literacy (LW), religiosity (R), trust (T),

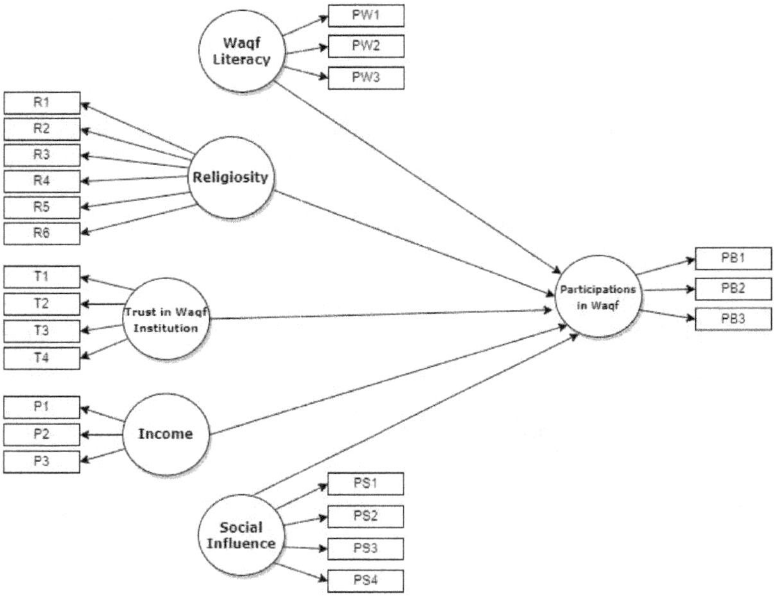

Figure 26.1. Research framework.

income (P), and social influence (PW) as a gauge of millennial participation in law (PB) (see Figure 26.1).

26.3 Methodology

This study employs a survey method with a random sampling scheme. The survey questionnaire is distributed through a google form, which is distributed through various social media. The survey was conducted for two weeks, from April 20, 2021 to May 4, 2021. This questionnaire consists of several parts as follows: (a) the identity/profile of the respondent, (b) waqf activities, (c) the waqf intention. Parts A and B, the form of questions there, are closed and some are open. Section C uses a Likert scale where respondents are given a choice of answers, which for positive questions are 1 (strongly disagree), 2 (disagree), 3 (disagree), 4 (agree), and 5 (strongly agree) while for negative questions rated the opposite.

26.3.1 *Data*

The population in this study is the millennial generation of individuals born in the period 1981–1996. According to the results of the Population Census of the Central Statistics Agency (2021), there are 69.38 million people or occupy 25.87% of the population in Indonesia. The Central Statistics Agency (2018) mentioned some differences in views between researchers related to the period of the millennial generation. For example, Tappscot (1998) defines millennials as those born from 1976 to 2000. Other researchers, Bencsik, Csikos, and Juhez (2016), define millennials as born between 1980 and 1995. In the 2020 census, the Indonesian Central Statistics Agency classified the population born between 1981 and 1996 as millennials.

26.3.2 *Model development*

In this study, questionnaires were adopted from several previous research questionnaires that include literacy (researcher), religiosity (researcher), trust (researcher), income (researcher), and social influence (researcher). Moreover, on the income variable and some of the religiosity variables, the question is self-made (see Table 26.1).

26.3.3 *Method: Structural equation models/ method–partial least squares*

Structural equation model–partial least square (SEM-PLS) is one of the methods based on variance. According to Henseler *et al.* (2016), PLS is suitable for explaining (explanative) or predicting research. Based on Vinzi *et al.* (2010), PLS is part of a regression method used to analyze high-dimensional data in a low-structure environment. Ghozali, Imam (2006) mentioned that PLS is an alternative approach to SEM based on variants from the previous covariance based.

According to Henseler *et al.* (2016), PLS agrees with abnormal data, small sample size, and measurement model (outer model) that determines the relationship between the construct and the observed indicator and the structural model (inner model) that determines the relationship between the construct. Ghozali and Imam (2008) also define PLS as a powerful analysis method because it does not require many assumptions, such as large samples, and data must be distributed normally.

Table 26.1. Research variables.

Variables	Code	Indicators	Reference
Waqf literacy	LW1	I know the difference between waqf and alms in general	Writer
	LW2	I know a lot about waqf (law, usability, waqf management form, etc.)	Shukor *et al.* (2016)
	LW3	Waqf is one of the best Islamic financial instruments	Sakti *et al.* (2016)
Religiosity	R1	I always carry out my duties as a Muslim (prayer five times, fasting during Ramadan, going to Hajj to Mecca) simply because of Allah SWT	Shukor *et al.* (2017)
	R2	I always stay away from non-halal income (usury, cheating, corruption, etc.)	Nuradli (2019)
	R3	My faith in my religion affects all my dealings with others	Shukor *et al.* (2017)
	R4	I need to do good deeds for others	Shukor *et al.* (2017)
	R5	Overall, I consider myself a devout Muslim	Shukor *et al.* (2017)
	R6	I often take the time to study religion either by attending studies/study groups or studying independently (reading)	Khraim (2010)
Trust in waqf institutions	T1	Waqf institutions in Indonesia can be trusted	Shukor *et al.* (2016)
	T2	I believe in waqf institutions	Shukor *et al.* (2016)
	T3	I believe in the information provided by the waqf institution	Shukor *et al.* (2016)
	T4	I am sure the waqf institution will distribute waqf funds to beneficiaries (mauquf 'alaihi) appropriately	Kasri and Chaerunnisa (2020)

Income	P1	I paid the waqf according to the level of income (the higher the income, the more waqf I spend)	Penulis
	P2	I perform waqf when I earn extra income	Penulis
	P3	I perform waqf when my needs are met	Penulis
Social influence	PS1	I collect information from friends or family before I participate in waqf	Shukor *et al.* (2017)
	PS2	People who mean to me assume that waqf is useful	Sakti *et al.* (2016)
	PS3	People who mean to me assume that waqf is beneficial	Sakti *et al.* (2016)
	PS4	I often consult other people to help me choose a waqf scheme	Shukor *et al.* (2017)
Participations in waqf	PB1	My intention to perform waqf is strong	Shukor *et al.* (2017)
	PB2	I will participate in waqf	Shukor *et al.* (2016), dan Shukor *et al.* (2017)
	PB3	I will make a recommendation for waqf	Hasbullah *et al.* (2015), dan Sakti *et al.* (2016)

26.4 Results and Analysis

26.4.1 *Profile of respondents*

In this study, the samples were obtained through questionnaires distributed online. There are 321 out of 337 respondents that meet the requirement. This study focused on Muslim millennials (24–41 years old) whose samples were based on five major islands in Indonesia. The data in this study was then processed with the SEM-PLS method using Smart-PLS software.

The profile of respondents who participated in this study is shown in Table 26.2.

Based on Table 26.2, the sample was dominated by women (54.5%). Majority are those aged 28–31 years (29.9%). They also have a good educational background that can represent knowledge about waqf. Most respondents work as private employees (39.3%), which is reasonable because millennials are in the productive age. Furthermore, 79 people or 24.6% respondents have income between IDR 2,500,000–5,000,000. Demographic variables for the origin of the most respondents are those on the island of Java of 180 people (56.1%) and followed by Sumatra (21.5%).

26.4.2 *Results & robustness test*

26.4.2.1 *Evaluation of measurement model (Outer model)*

Evaluation of measurement model aimed at evaluating the relationship between latent construct with its indicators obtained by conducting validity tests and reliability tests. The validity test is divided into convergent validity obtained by evaluating loading factors and average variance extracted (AVE) values, while discriminant validity is evaluated through Fornell–Larkker criterion/Root AVE. Then, reliability test is based on the value of composite reliability and Cronbach's alpha.

In the convergent validity test, loading factors are used to see the validity of an indicator in measuring its construct variables, while AVE is used to see the values that variables have. In the convergent validity test results, it can be concluded that all indicators and construct variables have excellent convergent validity (valid) as the value is more than 0.7 for loading factor testing and more than 0.5 on AVE testing (Tables 26.3 and 26.4).

Table 26.2. Respondents' profile.

Description	F	P(%)	Description	F	P(%)
Gender			**Income**		
Male	146	45.5	<IDR 2.500.000	54	16.8
Female	175	54.5	>IDR 10.000.000	50	15.6
Total	**321**	**100**	IDR 2.500.000–IDR 5.000.000	79	24.6
Age			IDR 5.000.001–IDR 7.500.000	62	19.3
24–27 Year	82	25.5	IDR 7.500.001–IDR 10.000.000	65	20.2
28–31 Year	96	29.9	IDR 6.500.000–IDR 7.500.000	6	1.9
32–35 Year	82	25.5	IDR 7.500.000–IDR 10.000.000	5	1.6
36–40 Year	61	19.0	**Total**	**321**	**100**
Total	**321**	**100**	**Region**		
Education			Sumatera	69	21.5
Master/Doctoral Degree (S2/S3)	78	24.3	Java	180	56.1
Bachelor Degree 1 (S1)/Diploma	196	61.1	Kalimantan/Borneo	20	6.2
Elementary School	1	0.3	Bali & Nusa Tenggara	18	5.6
High School/ Equivalent	42	13.1	Sulawesi/Celeber	24	7.5
Junior High School/ Equivalent	4	1.2	Maluku & Papua	10	3.1
Total	**321**	**100**	**Total**	**321**	**100**
Jobs					
Housewife	56	17.4			
Private Employee	126	39.3			
Civil Servants	48	15.0			
Students	23	7.2			
Self Employed	16	5.0			
Other	52	16.2			
Total	**321**	**100**			

Furthermore, discriminant validity testing is based on the value of cross loading, which is to see the correlation between the indicators and the constructed variables. The values on cross loading can be seen in Table 26.5.

Table 26.5 explains that the cross-loading value of each indicator that measures its construct variables has a higher correlation than other contract variables. Thus, it can be said that every indicator has a good discriminates validity.

The last tests on the evaluation of model were composite reliability and Cronbach's alpha. This test is conducted to see the reliability of the indicator in measuring its latent construct.

Table 26.3. Loading factors.

I	T	LW	P	PB	PS	R
L1		0.908				
L2		0.920				
P2			1.000			
PB1				0.886		
PB2				0.927		
PB3				0.841		
PS2					0.964	
PS3					0.966	
R6						1.000
T1	0.826					
T2	0.902					
T3	0.914					
T4	0.918					

Table 26.4. AVE 1.

Variable	Value
Trust in Zakat Institution (T)	0.793
Waqf Literacy (LW)	0.835
Income (P)	1.000
Waqf Influence (PB)	0.784
Social Influence (PS)	0.932
Religiosity (R)	1.000

Table 26.6 shows that the values of Cronbach's alpha and composite reliability are above 0.7. Thus, it can be said that construct variables have good reliability.

26.4.2.2 *Evaluation of structural model (Inner model)*

Structural model testing on PLS can be known by looking at the values of the R-square for its exogenous latent variables and the path coefficient to show the effect of exogenous variables on endogenous variables by looking at their t-statistical values.

Based on Table 26.7, the variables of waqf literacy, religiosity, trust, income, and social influence give a value of 0.350 or 35% to participation in waqf, while other variables beyond those studied

Table 26.5. Cross loading.

I	T	LW	P	PB	PS	R
LW1	0.040	0.908	0.063	0.376	0.292	0.415
LW2	0.035	0.920	0.105	0.401	0.360	0.540
P2	0.177	0.093	1.000	0.163	0.235	0.103
PB1	0.370	0.370	0.145	0.886	0.390	0.335
PB2	0.285	0.395	0.134	0.927	0.437	0.359
PB3	0.187	0.365	0.156	0.841	0.439	0.277
PS2	0.247	0.368	0.220	0.451	0.964	0.359
PS3	0.246	0.323	0.232	0.466	0.966	0.329
R6	0.063	0.524	0.103	0.367	0.356	1.000
T1	0.826	0.023	0.134	0.218	0.180	0.033
T2	0.902	0.049	0.182	0.301	0.235	0.061
T3	0.914	0.017	0.129	0.299	0.221	0.064
T4	0.918	0.052	0.180	0.309	0.264	0.060

Table 26.6. Cronbach's alpha and composite reliability.

Variables	Cronbach's alpha	Composite reliability
Kepercayaan/Trust	0.913	0.939
Literasi Wakaf	0.803	0.910
Pendapatan	1.000	1.000
Pengaruh Berwakaf	0.862	0.916
Pengaruh Sosial	0.927	0.965
Religiusitas	1.000	1.000

Table 26.7. R-square

	R-square	R-square adjusted
Participation in waqf	0.360	0.350

explain the remaining 65%. Thus, it can be categorized into moderate models because its value is between 0.33 and 0.66. Next, we test by bootstrapping to find path coefficients. Table 26.8 shows the significance of the influence of waqf literacy, income, social influence, religiosity, and trust on waqf institutions on waqf participation by looking at the t-statistics in Table 26.8.

Table 26.8. Path coefficient.

	Original sample	Sample mean	*T*-statistics (|O/STDEV|)	*P* values
LW -> PB	0.251	0.254	4.109	0.000
P -> PB	0.022	0.023	0.427	0.670
PS -> PB	0.280	0.279	4.269	0.000
R -> PB	0.119	0.115	1.982	0.048
T -> PB	0.227	0.230	4.299	0.000

There are five hypotheses developed in this study, based on Table 26.8 path coefficient results from the evaluation of structural models. Four of the five variables have significant influences. The trust variable has the highest significant influence on waqf participation among other variables ($t = 4{,}299$, p-value $= 0.000$). Furthermore, in the waqf literacy variable, we also obtained a significant positive result ($t = 4{,}109$, p-value $= 0.000$). Religiosity variables also have a significant positive results on the effect of waqf ($t = 1{,}982$, p-value $= 0.048$). Then, in the social influence variable also found a significant positive result ($t = 4{,}269$, p-value $= 0.000$). Lastly, there is one variable with insignificant result, namely the income variable ($t = 0.427$, p-value $= 0.670$).

Based on the above description, it can be concluded that Hypothesis 1 (H1) (waqf literacy on waqf participation), Hypothesis 3 (H3) (social influence on waqf participation), Hypothesis 4 (H4) (religiosity on waqf participation), and Hypothesis 5 (H5) (trust in waqf participation) are accepted. In contrast, Hypothesis 2 (H2) (income against waqf participation) is rejected.

26.4.3 *Analysis*

There are five hypotheses developed in this study, namely waqf literacy, income, social influence, religiosity, and belief. The research on waqf literacy found that high waqf literacy in each individual would increase waqf participation. Shukor *et al.* (2016) argued that understanding the concept and function of waqf is one crucial thing because it will affect waqf participation. These results are also in line with previous research conducted by Amin *et al.* (2014), Mokthar (2016),

Ahmad (2019), and Kasri and Chaerunnisa (2020). A good understanding of waqf can increase waqf participation. This is supported by another finding that 43% of respondents who consider themselves to be having sufficient knowledge about waqf have performed waqf.

In the second variable, religiosity has a significant effect (positive) on waqf participation of millennials. Kasri and Chaerunnisa (2020) found that religiosity is the strongest factor that influences behavior in donating cash waqf online. Usman *et al.* (2020) stated that religiosity has a more sensitive role when a Muslim deals with matters related to religion. The results are also supported by research conducted by Sakti *et al.* (2016), Shukor *et al.* (2017), Osman *et al.* (2014), Usman *et al.* (2020) and Hasan and Ismail (2018). This study also found that most respondents argued that they performed waqf for the sake of Allah SWT and they believe that their charity will contribute to the positive change of their community.

Furthermore, the social influence variable obtained a significant (positive) relationship in the intention of participation among millennials. In line with Carman (2004), there is a positive and significant relationship in the decision of someone to do charity. In their research, Sakti *et al.* (2016) also found that social influences significantly affect the contribution of waqf. This finding is in line with Shukor *et al.* (2017), Kasri and Chaerunnisa (2020), and Shukor *et al.* (2019). Wakif's trust in waqf institutions depends on the integrity and reputation of the waqf institution itself (Shukor *et al.*, 2019). Therefore, to attract millennials, waqf institutions must be more transparent to show integrity and get a good reputation in the waqf program they make. Shukor *et al.* (2015) explained that wakif in Malaysia often feels unsafe to contribute waqf due to lack of information from the waqf institution itself. Shukor *et al.* (2017) also stated that the trust developed in waqf institutions means wakif believes in the information provided and trusts the money to be given. Trusts will give them the "political license" they need to operate, which helps create moral space and lends credibility to the organizations' attitudes (Osman *et al.*, 2014).

On the other hand, relationship between income and millennial interest to donate is not significantly proven. This could be interpreted that millennials with lower income will still make waqf or other donations. The results of this study are contrary to the research conducted by Iskandar (2017) and Shukor *et al.* (2016). Shukor *et al.*

(2016), in their research, found that as individuals become more aware of the importance of giving back, they give to the needy. The more they can get, the more money they give for one good thing.

The high potential of waqf among millennials in Indonesia does not necessarily make waqf run optimally. There is still a long gap between the realization and potential of waqf. According to the Indonesian Waqf Agency, the potential of cash waqf nationally is IDR 180 trillion, but in fact, according to BWI data, the accumulation of cash waqf as of February 2021 has only reached IDR 830 billion. The realization of low waqf according to the Ministry of Finance's Financial Sector Policy Center, 2019 is due to the lack of socialization and education about waqf, institutional governance that is still below standard, limited waqf fundraiser, and still lack of promotion of programs/activities. Rusydiana *et al.* (2021) and Rusydiana (2018) also stated that low socialization and weak nazhir resources are the main weaknesses in the development of waqf. The problem of waqf in Indonesia itself because it is still considered waqf as a worship of the upper classes, is required by a significant amount, a stereotype that there is no need to be moved (waqf in old age), waqf is only limited to social-worship benefits and also the benefits of waqf only to be felt by among dhuafa.

26.4.4 *Millennial behavior in waqf*

Based on respondents in this study, as many as 90% know which waqf on average, information about waqf obtained from educational institutions (53%), religious leaders (16%), and also social media (13%). More than half of respondents (61%) claimed to have done waqf with at least one frequency with the value of donations made which is less than IDR 250,000 (63%), IDR 250,000–500,000 (21%), and the rest donated above IDR 500,000 (16%). As many as (12%) of them are routine wakif.

This study also found that millennial Muslims tend to distribute waqf through waqf institutions (35%), LKS-PWU (13%), Nazhir Masjid (21%), and both LKS-PWU and waqf institutions (11%). The types of waqf forms channeled are cash waqf and asset waqf (buildings, wells, Qur'an, and others) with the reason of waqf because it is recommended by religion (37%), a sense of duty and responsibility to help others (29%), satisfaction (9%), and want to give a change to society (9%). In addition, 39% have never done waqf on the grounds of preferring other forms of donation (44%), insufficient income (35%), and do not know waqf more deeply (18%).

BWI's move by creating a waqf goes to a campus program, and the waqf Philanthropic Institute introduces waqf through social media is undoubtedly an effective strategy because it is proven that millennials get much information about waqf from there. Planting an understanding of contemporary waqf must also be increasingly launched. There is still a stereotype that waqf requires a high cost and not yet understand about waqf proves that the understanding of waqf has not been evenly distributed.

26.5 Conclusions and Recommendation

26.5.1 *Conclusion*

This study was conducted to measure the interest of Muslim millennials in performing waqf. This study was conducted by testing five variables, namely waqf literacy, religiosity, trust in waqf institutions, income, and social influence. The study used the SEM-PLS method to test 321 Muslim millennials from five major islands in Indonesia. Among the five variables tested, four significant and positively influential factors are literacy, religiosity, trust in waqf institutions, and social influence.

26.5.2 *Recommendations*

Based on the results obtained, the important strategy to increase the interest of Muslim millennials in performing waqf is building the trust of prospective wakif through positive socialization to attract the attention of millennials and leave a new impression and create an environment that supports cash waqf through social media which is widely accessed by millennials. Waqf institutions need to instill trust by being more open, honest, and transparent about the programs they create through campaigns by bringing social and religious issues packed with excellent and exciting delivery that can help increase the interest of Muslim millennials in taking action. Furthermore, increasing trust also needs to improve the quality of nazhir so that waqf products are more developed and marketing strategies are more innovative. Collaborating will also help create something more innovative and more extensive in scope. In addition, digitizing waqf will also be highly recommended because it provides convenience to donate, especially if the target is millennials who use digital technology. The government contributes to effective laws and policies that facilitate the implementation of waqf.

References

Abdul Shukor, S., Johari, F., Abd Wahab, K., Kefeli Zulkefli, Z., Ahmad, N., Haji Alias, M., Abu-Hussin, M. F. (2019). Trust on awqaf institutions: Evidence from Malaysia. *Journal of Islamic Marketing, 10*(2), 511–524. Doi: 10.1108/JIMA-05-2017-0054.

Abreu, M., Laureano, R., Silva, R., & Dionisio, P. (2014). Drivers of donations: Does religiosity make a difference? *Social Science and Humanities Repository*, 1–27. Available at SSRN: https://ssrn.com/abstract=2380097.

Ahmad, H. (2019). Factors influencing willingness to contribute in cash waqf: Case of South Tangerang, Indonesia. *Islamiconomics: Jurnal Ekonomi Islam, 10*(1), 181–200.

Aldeen, K. N., Ratih, I. S., & Pertiwi, R. S. (2021). Cash waqf from the millennials' perspective: A case of Indonesia. *ISRA International Journal of Islamic Finance.* Doi: 10.1108/IJIF-10-2020-0223.

Amin, H., Abdul-Rahman, A. R., Ramayah, T., Supinah, R., & Mohd-Aris, M. (2014). Determinants of online waqf acceptance: An empirical investigation. *Electronic Journal of Information Systems in Developing Countries, 60*(8), 1–18. Doi: 0.1002/j.1681-4835.2014.tb00429.x.

Badan Pusat Statistik, (2018). *Profil Generasi Milenial Indonesia.* www.kemenpppa.go.id.

Baranyi, E. E. (2011). *Volunteerism and Charitable Giving Among the Millennial Generation: How to Attract and Retain Millennials.* Dissertations, Theses and Capstone Projects. Paper 451. Kennesaw State University.

Carman, K. (2004). Social influences and the designation of charitable contributions: Evidence from the workplace. In *NBER Working Paper.* http://www.rwj.harvard.edu/scholarsmaterials/carman/Social Influences Designation.pdf.

Charities Aid Foundation (CAF) (2020). CAF World Giving Index 2021: A Global Pandemic Special Report. https://www.cafonline.org/docs/default-source/about-us-research/cafworldgivingindex2021_report_web2_100621.pdf.

Çizakca, M. (1998). Awqaf in history and its implications for modern Islamic economies. *Islamic Economic Studies*, *6*(1), 43–70.

Gopay & Kopernik. (2020). *Gopay Digital Donation Outlook 2020.* http://ict4ngo.com/wp-content/uploads/GoPay-Digital-Donation-Outlook-2020.pdf.

Hasbullah, N. A., Khairi, K. F., & Ab Aziz, M. R. (2015). Intention to contribute in corporate waqf: Applying the theory of planned behaviour. *UMRAN — International Journal of Islamic and Civilizational Studies (EISSN: 2289-8204)*, *3*(1), 39–48. Doi: 10.11113/umran2016.3n1.39.

Hazriah, H. & Ahmad, I. (2018). Determinants od higher education islamic endowment (Waqf) attributes among muslims in Malaysia. *Journal of Islamic, Social, Economics and Development EISSN*, *3*(12), 1–9.

Hulland, J. (1999). Use of partial least squares (PLS) in strategic management research: A review of four recent studies. *Strategic Management Journal*, *20*(2), 195–204.

IDN Research Institute. (2019). *Indonesia Millenial Report 2019.* Jakarta: IDN Media.

Indonesia, B. W. (2015). *Himpunan Peraturan Perundang-Undangan Tentang Wakaf.* Jakarta: Badan Wakaf Indonesia.

Iskandar. (2017). Pengaruh pendapatan terhadap pola pengeluaran rumah tangga miskin di kota langsa. *Jurnal Samudra Ekonomika*, *1*(2), 127–134.

Kasri, R. A. & Chaerunnisa, S. R. (2020). The role of knowledge, trust, and religiosity in explaining the online cash waqf amongst Muslim millennials. *Journal of Islamic Marketing.* Doi: 10.1108/JIMA-04-2020-0101.

Mahmud, M. W. & Shah, S. S. (2010). Optimization of philanthropic waqf: The need for maqasid-based legislative strategies. *Shariah Law Reports*, *2*, 1–14.

Marimuthu, M., Jing, C. W., Gie, L. P., Mun, L. P., & Ping, T. Y. (2010). *Islamic Banking: Selection Criteria and Implications.* *10*(4), 52–62.

Mokthar, M. Z. (2016). Perceptions of universiti sains Malaysia muslim staff on factors influencing their intention to perform cash waqf. *Journal of Islamic Studies and Culture*, *4*(2), 101–109. Doi: 10.15640/jisc.v4n2a11.

Nation, U. (2015). *UN World Population Prospects: Key Findings & Advance Tables.* population.un.org.

Oseni, U. A. (2012). Towards the effective legal regulation of WAQF in Nigeria: Problems and prospects. *SSRN Electronic Journal.* In Rashid, S. K., and Hassan, A. (Eds.). Waqf laws and management with special reference to Malaysia. New Delhi: Institute of Objective Studies, pp. 339–354.

Osman, A. F., Mohammed, M. O., & Amin, H. (2014). *An Analysis of Cash Waqf Participation Among Young Intellectuals.* Paper Presented at Istanbul 9th International Academic Conference (IIES), Turkey.

Republika, (2021). Keren! jumlah wakif milenial lebih tinggi seniornya. Jakarta, DKI Jakarta, Indonesia.

Rizal, H. & Amin, H. (2017). Perceived ihsan, Islamic egalitarianism and Islamic religiosity towards charitable giving of cash waqf. *Journal of Islamic Marketing*, *8*(4), 669–685. Doi: 10.1108/JIMA-05-2015-0037.

Rusydiana, A. S. (2019). An analysis of cash waqf development in Indonesia using Interpretive Structural Modeling (ISM). *Journal of Islamic Economics Lariba*, *4*(1), 1–11.

Sadeq, A. M. (1997). Poverty alleviation: An Islamic perspective. *Humanomics*, *13*(3), 110–134. Doi: 10.1108/eb018797.

Saduman, S. & Aysun, E. E. (2009). The socio-economic role of waqf system in the muslim- Ottoman Cities ' formation and evolution. *Trakia Journal of Sciences*, *7*, 272–275.

Sakti, M. R. P., Thaker, H. bin M. T., Qoyum, A., & Qizam, I. (2016). Determinants of cash waqf contribution in klang valley and selangor: A Sem approach. *Journal of Islamic Monetary Economics and Finance*, *2*(1), 111–144.

Shukor, S. A., Anwar, I. F., & Sabri, H. (2015). Muslims participation in cash waqf: The case of Malaysia. *Paper Presented at International Conference of Management Sciences 2015* (IcoMS 2015), Yogyakarta, Indonesia.

Shukor, S. A., Anwar, I. F., Aziz, S. A., & Sabri, H. (2017). Muslim attitude towards participation in cash WAQF: Antecedents and consequences. *International Journal of Business and Society*, *18*(S1), 193–204.

Shukor, S. A., Anwar, I. F., Sabri, H., Aziz, S. A., & Ariffin, A. R. M. (2016). Giving behaviour: Who donates cash WAQF? *Malaysian Journal of Consumer and Family Economics*, *19*, 82–94.

Siswantoro, D. & Dewi, M. K. (2011). *The Effectiveness of Waqf Fund Raising through Mutual Fund in Indonesia.* In Kahf, M. and Mohamood, S. M. (Eds.). Essential Readings in Contemporary Waqf Issues. Kuala Lumpur: CERT, pp. 243–265.

Tirto.id & Jakpat. (2018). https://tirto.id/generasimilenial-suka-memberi-sumbangan-cLHu.

United Nations, Department of Economic and Social Affairs, Population Division (2015). World population prospects: The 2015 revision, key findings and advance tables. Working Paper No. ESA/P/WP.241.

Usman, H., Mulia, D., Chairy, C., & Widowati, N. (2022). Integrating trust, religiosity and image into technology acceptance model: The case of the Islamic philanthropy in Indonesia. *Journal of Islamic Marketing, 13*(2), 381–409.

Wahyuni, S. (2012). Moslem community behavior in the conduct of Islamic bank: The moderation role of knowledge and pricing. *Procedia –Social and Behavioral Sciences, 57*, 290–298. Doi: 10.1016/j.sbspro.2012.09.1188.

Appendix 1

Questionnaire

A. Respondent Identity

Gender:
- Male
- Female

Age:
- 25–30 Year
- 31–35 Year
- 36–40 Year

Education:
- Elementary School
- Junior High School/Equivalent
- High School/Equivalent
- Bachelor Degree (S1)/Diploma
- Master/Doctoral Degree (S2/S3)

Jobs:
- Student/College Student
- Private Sector Employee
- Civil Servant
- Housewife
- Others...

Income:
- < Rp. 2.500.000
- Rp. 2.500.000 – Rp. 5.000.000
- Rp. 5.000.001 – Rp. 7.500.000
- Rp. 7.500.001 – Rp. 10.000.000
- >Rp. 10.000.000

Region (Province): ________________________

B. Waqf Activity

1. Do you know waqf?

   a. Yes
   b. No

2. Where do you know about waqf?

   a. Friends
   b. Family Member
   c. Religious Leader
   d. Search Site (Google etc.)
   e. Social Media (Facebook, Twitter, WhatsApp, Instagram, Telegram etc.)
   f. Print Media (Newspaper, Magazine etc.)
   g. Other ...

3. Have you ever done waqf?

   a. Yes
   b. No

   (If you ever),

4. I have been performing waqf for ... times.

   a. 1
   b. 2
   c. 3
   d. Other

5. I have a waqf routine.

   a. Routine
   b. Not Really

6. (If it is a routine), I do waqf every ...

   a. Day
   b. Week
   c. Month
   d. Year
   e. Other ...

7. What is the average value of waqf donations distributed:

   a. <Rp 250
   b. Rp. 250–500
   c. 500.000–1 million
   d. >1 million

8. I used to channel my waqf through ...

   a. Nazhir Masjid
   b. LKS-PWU
   c. Waqf Institutions (TWI, Global Wakaf, Rumah Wakaf, etc.)
   d. Other

9. Form of waqf that you've done (can choose more than 1):

   a. Waqf of immovable objects (land/building)
   b. Cash waqf (waqf in the form of money. In this case, money is its object or a waqf treasure that will later be managed and developed so that its value continues to grow until it becomes a productive treasure
   c. Waqf through money (is a waqf of goods by wakif/someone who do waqf handing money to nazhir/money manager to buy goods desired by wakif/someone who do waqf or as a contribu-

tion to the waqf project program both social and productive offered by nazhir/waqf manager)

d. Other ...

10. Why I performed waqf?

    a. because of my sense of duty and responsibility to help people in need
    b. because I want to change society
    c. because there is a satisfaction of its own
    d. because it is strongly encouraged by religion

    (If you have never been a man)

11. I have not performed waqf yet because:

    a. I want to contribute in waqf, but at the moment the income is not enough
    b. I prefer waqf/donations to waqf
    c. I do not have an idea about waqf

12. **Waqf Intention**

    You can choose one of the answers to each question by selecting an answer in the provided column. Each question consists of five options:

    SA = Strongly Agree
    A = Agree
    NAD = Neither Agree nor Disagree
    D = Disagree
    SD = Strongly Disagree

No.	Questions	SA	A	NAD	D	SD
1	I know the difference between waqf and alms in general					
2	I know a lot about waqf (law, usability, waqf management form etc.)					
3	Waqf is one of the best Islamic financial instruments					
4	I always carry out my duties as a Muslim (prayer five times, fasting during Ramadan, going to Hajj to Mecca) simply because of Allah SWT					
5	I have always stayed away from non-halal income (usury, cheating, corruption, etc.)					
6	My faith in my religion affects all my dealings with others					
7	I need to do good deeds to others					
8	Overall, I consider myself a devout Muslim					
9	I often take the time to study religion either by attending studies/study groups or studying independently (reading)					
10	Waqf institutions in Indonesia can be trusted					
11	I believe in waqf institutions					
12	I believe in the information provided by the waqf institution					
13	I am sure the waqf institution will distribute waqf funds to beneficiaries (mauquf'alaihi) appropriately					

No.	Questions	SA	A	NAD	D	SD
14	I paid the waqf according to the level of income (the higher the income, the more waqf I spend)					
15	I perform waqf when I earn extra income					
16	I perform waqf when my needs are met					
17	I collect information from friends or family before I participate in waqf					
18	People who mean to me assume that waqf is useful					
19	People who mean to me assume that waqf is beneficial					
20	I often consult other people to help me choose a waqf scheme					
21	My intention to perform waqf is strong					
22	I will participate in waqf					
23	I will make a recommendation for waqf					

https://doi.org/10.1142/9781800612426_bmatter

Index

www.ingramcontent.com/pod-product-compliance
Lightning Source LLC
Chambersburg PA
CBHW070713080825
30593CB00092B/67
9781800612419